CIW E-Commerce Designer Certification Bible

CIW E-Commerce Designer Certification Bible

Chris Minnick and Margaret T. Minnick

Hungry Minds™

Best-Selling Books • Digital Downloads • e-Books • Answer Networks • e-Newsletters • Branded Web Sites • e-Learning

New York, NY ✦ Cleveland, OH ✦ Indianapolis, IN

CIW E-Commerce Designer Certification Bible

Published by
Hungry Minds, Inc.
909 Third Avenue
New York, NY 10022
www.hungryminds.com

Library of Congress Control Number: 2001092715

ISBN: 0-7645-4825-5

Printed in the United States of America

10 9 8 7 6 5 4 3 2 1

1P/SU/QX/QR/IN

Distributed in the United States by Hungry Minds, Inc.

Distributed by CDG Books Canada Inc. for Canada; by Transworld Publishers Limited in the United Kingdom; by IDG Norge Books for Norway; by IDG Sweden Books for Sweden; by IDG Books Australia Publishing Corporation Pty. Ltd. for Australia and New Zealand; by TransQuest Publishers Pte Ltd. for Singapore, Malaysia, Thailand, Indonesia, and Hong Kong; by Gotop Information Inc. for Taiwan; by ICG Muse, Inc. for Japan; by Intersoft for South Africa; by Eyrolles for France; by International Thomson Publishing for Germany, Austria, and Switzerland; by Distribuidora Cuspide for Argentina; by LR International for Brazil; by Galileo Libros for Chile; by Ediciones ZETA S.C.R. Ltda. for Peru; by WS Computer Publishing Corporation, Inc., for the Philippines; by Contemporanea de Ediciones for Venezuela; by Express Computer Distributors for the Caribbean and West Indies; by Micronesia Media Distributor, Inc. for Micronesia; by Chips Computadoras S.A. de C.V. for Mexico; by Editorial Norma de Panama S.A. for Panama; by American Bookshops for Finland.

For general information on Hungry Minds' products and services please contact our Customer Care department within the U.S. at 800-762-2974, outside the U.S. at 317-572-3993 or fax 317-572-4002.

For sales inquiries and reseller information, including discounts, premium and bulk quantity sales, and foreign-language translations, please contact our Customer Care department at 800-434-3422, fax 317-572-4002 or write to Hungry Minds, Inc., Attn: Customer Care Department, 10475 Crosspoint Boulevard, Indianapolis, IN 46256.

For information on licensing foreign or domestic rights, please contact our Sub-Rights Customer Care department at 212-884-5000.

For information on using Hungry Minds' products and services in the classroom or for ordering examination copies, please contact our Educational Sales department at 800-434-2086 or fax 317-572-4005.

For press review copies, author interviews, or other publicity information, please contact our Public Relations department at 317-572-3168 or fax 317-572-4168.

About the Authors

Chris Minnick is the founder, lead Web application developer, and business manager of Minnick Web Services (`www.minnickweb.com`). Chris has over 15 years of computer programming experience and has been developing Web sites since 1994. He has co-authored and contributed to several books on XML and e-commerce. He has also written numerous articles on Internet technologies that have been published in various paper and online magazines. Chris also occasionally teaches classes for Austin Community College's Webmaster Certificate Program. When he's not writing, programming, managing, or teaching, he trains in martial arts, plays video games, works on one of his "fun" Web sites, and juggles his variety of other interests, including fiction writing, film making, and media activism.

Margaret T. Minnick is Minnick Web Services' co-president, lead designer, and Web developer. Margaret has been designing and developing Web sites since 1997 and has extensive experience in the software industry and in client support. In addition to overseeing the creative side of site development, she is also involved in user interface design, content management, and application development at Minnick Web Services. Margaret has contributed to several books on Web-related topics. When she's not working, Margaret writes movie reviews, trains in martial arts, spends time trying to meet the challenge of Texas gardening, and ponders the origin of the universe.

Credits

Acquisitions Editor
Greg Croy

Development Editor
Alex Miloradovich

Project Editors
Marcia Brochin
Mary Burmeister

Technical Editor
Robert Shimonski

Copy Editor
Alex Miloradovich

Editorial Managers
Ami Frank Sullivan
Kyle Looper

Project Coordinators
Jennifer Bingham
Emily Wichlinski

Graphics and Production Specialists
Joyce Haughey
Adam Mancilla
Barry Offringa
Heather Pope
Betty Schulte
Brian Torwelle
Jeremey Unger

Quality Control Technicians
Andy Hollandbeck
Susan Moritz
Carl Pierce
Dwight Ramsey
Charles Spencer

Permissions Editor
Laura Moss

Media Development Specialist
Travis Silvers

Media Development Coordinator
Marisa Pearman

Proofreading and Indexing
TECHBOOKS Production Services

seventeen weekends

yes, the cat wrote the whole book.

we played games outside.

Preface

This book is designed to help you prepare for the CIW E-commerce Designer Exam (1D0-425). CIW certification is recognized as a leading industry standard for the Internet industry, accredited by the Association of Internet Professionals (AIP), and endorsed by the International Webmasters Association (IWA).

The exams are developed to certify an individual's expertise with Internet-related technologies and topics. CIW exams are currently offered at over 1,000 testing locations worldwide.

The CIW E-commerce Designer Exam tests the candidate on a broad base of general knowledge related to developing and managing an e-commerce Web site.

This book provides information on everything covered on the exam. In addition, we cover many topics more in-depth than the exam does, and have used our experiences in e-commerce to provide you with a practical guide to e-commerce in the real world. For this reason, this book is much more than a study guide for the CIW E-commerce Designer Exam. You'll also find that this book is useful as an introduction and guide to planning, building, and managing e-commerce businesses that you'll be able to refer to long after you've passed the E-commerce Designer Exam.

How This Book Is Organized

This book is divided into five parts. To get the maximum benefit, we recommend that you carefully study all of the material in each part and complete all of the exercises and sample exam questions.

The parts are roughly evenly divided in subject matter between teaching real world skills and diving into the legal, business, and theoretical aspects of e-commerce. The exam does a good job of measuring both types of skills, but, because of the ever-changing nature of the practical matters, it tends (correctly, we feel) to put greater emphasis on testing your knowledge of the big picture.

If you're short on time and you want to do the bare minimum amount of work to get the maximum amount of knowledge before taking the CIW E-commerce Designer exam, there are specific parts and chapters within those parts that you should be sure to study closely. We've noted those in this section. Of course, we hope that you'll come back to our book after you've successfully passed the exam to complete the exercises and get valuable hands-on experience with e-commerce tools.

Part I: E-Commerce in Context

This part begins by answering several fundamental questions, including:

- ✦ What is e-commerce?
- ✦ Why e-commerce?
- ✦ Where is e-commerce headed?

After defining the fundamental terms, laying out the case for e-commerce, and explaining the basic concepts, we discuss the ways that e-commerce is different from traditional commerce, and we discuss the fundamental legal, marketing, and promotion topics involved in doing business online.

Part II: Designing an Effective E-Commerce Presence

Part II begins the transition from mostly business-end topics to the technical end of e-commerce. This is the grey area between pure business and pure technical concerns. These are the topics that need to be understood by both the managers and the programmers.

We start out with a chapter on each of the two topics that must be at the foundation of any successful online business: usability and customer service. We then explain the factors that will influence which specific route you take to create your online storefront. In Chapters 8, 9, and 10, we'll also show you some of the storefront software options that are currently available. The exercises in these chapters will give you your first taste of the practical matters involved in e-commerce.

Finally, Chapter 11 looks at how to go about starting an e-commerce company, and analyzes some of the techniques of successful online ventures.

Part III: Building an E-Commerce Site Foundation

In Part III, we get technical. You'll learn about Web servers, database management systems, and the various other software components involved in creating the structure for an e-commerce Web site. In Chapter 13, we'll take an in-depth look at common configuration options and capabilities of Web servers — using Microsoft's Web server as an example. We'll also show you how to install and configure a Web server on your own computer.

In Chapter 14, you'll learn about one specific e-commerce development environment, Actinic Business. You'll see how to install and configure this storefront package, and you'll get hands-on experience with setting up an online storefront.

Part IV: Operating and Enhancing E-Commerce Sites

Part IV talks about how to populate your storefront with products and the very important topics of collecting payments, providing customer service, securing your site, and managing and using the various types of information that e-commerce sites collect to constantly improve your business.

Pay particular attention to Chapter 19. Of all of the chapters in this book, this one is perhaps the most important to fully understand before taking the exam. Security is vital to commerce of any type, and Chapter 19 shows you the tools and techniques that are used to secure e-commerce data and to keep it secure.

Part V: Appendixes

Part V, also known as the "Back Matter," contains several useful appendices that are designed to provide references to more in-depth information on topics covered in the book and to help you make the best use of this book.

Of particular interest is Appendix B, sample exam. We recommend that you don't look at this sample exam until you've read the entire book. If you can correctly answer at least 45 of the 60 questions in this sample exam, you're probably ready to take the real thing. If you need more help, the CD contains hundreds of sample exam questions that you can use to test and expand you knowledge of e-commerce.

After you're sure that you'll pass with flying colors, Appendix D will give you all the information you need to find a testing location, get signed up, and get certified.

How Each Chapter Is Structured

This book is designed to provide you with the best possible learning and exam preparation experience. The structure of each chapter, and the specific elements used, are designed to present the exam material in a clear and easy-to-learn way.

The elements that you'll find in each chapter are:

- A list of exam objectives covered in this chapter
- A chapter pre-test
- Clear, concise text on each topic
- Step-by-step instructions on how to perform specific tasks
- Screen shots and graphics to aid in your understanding
- A Key Point Summary

- A comprehensive Study Guide that contains:
  - Exam-style assessment questions
  - Scenario problems for you to solve
  - Lab exercises to perform on your computer
  - Answers to chapter pre-test questions, assessment questions, and scenarios
- A list of resources for more information on the topics discussed

How to Use This Book

This book can be used either by individuals working independently or by groups in a formal classroom setting.

We recommend reading this book sequentially. The chapters are designed to be studied in order, meaning that it's best to complete Chapter 1 before moving on to Chapter 2 (and so on). Some of the chapters can stand alone, but in many cases, the topics presented in a chapter are based on knowledge obtained in preceding chapters. Additionally, some Lab Exercises require completion of Lab Exercises in previous chapters to work properly. (In most cases, this is noted at the beginning of the Lab Exercise.)

When studying each chapter, we recommend the following approach: First, read the Chapter Pre-Test. Answer as many of the questions as you can. For those questions that you are unsure of, be on the lookout for the answers as you read the chapter. After you've read the chapter, use the Key Point Summary as a guide to what you have just learned. If any of the key points are unfamiliar to you, review that section of the chapter.

Next, complete the assessment questions. If you're unsure of an answer, make your best guess. When you're done, check your answers. For any incorrect answers, review the topic by re-reading the appropriate section of the chapter. Next, complete the Scenario(s) to test how you would apply the knowledge learned in the chapter to a real-world situation. Finally, get hands-on experience with the Lab Exercises.

After you've completed your study of the chapters and reviewed the Assessment Questions in the book, use the test engine on the CD included with this book to get some experience answering practice questions. The practice questions will help you assess how much you've learned from your study and will also familiarize you with the type of exam questions you'll face when you take the real exam. Once you identify a weak area, you can restudy the corresponding chapter(s) to improve your knowledge and skills in that area.

Prerequisites

This book assumes the same level of knowledge that the CIW E-commerce Designer Exam assumes — that is, a broad general knowledge of basic Web site development and management topics and technologies. Just as the CIW Foundations Exam (1D0-410) is a prerequisite to the CIW E-commerce Designer Exam, knowledge of the foundations of Web development are a prerequisite for readers of this book.

Necessary Hardware and Software

Although we've tried to keep requirements to a bare minimum, you will need access to various hardware and software to be able to do the Lab Exercises in this book.

Here are what we consider to be the minimum hardware requirements, although you may be able to get by with less if you're creative and patient:

- ✦ Intel-based computer with Pentium/133MHz processor, 64MB of RAM, and 2GB of hard disk space.
- ✦ CD-ROM drive
- ✦ Access to the Internet

Optional equipment that you might benefit from using includes:

- ✦ Network adapter card
- ✦ Printer

Here is the software you'll need:

- ✦ Windows 98, Windows 2000, or Windows NT is recommended, but many of the exercises in the book can be completed with other operating systems as well.

Conventions Used in This Book

This book uses a number of standards and conventions to help you process the material efficiently. It's helpful to familiarize yourself with the following items before reading the book.

New Terms

There are many terms unique to e-commerce. These terms can be confusing to e-commerce novices. New or potentially unfamiliar terms, such as *intellectual property*, are italicized in their first appearance in the book. In most cases, we define a new term right after its first mention. Unfamiliar words that are italicized but not followed by definitions can be looked up in the Glossary at the end of the book.

Code

All code listings in this book are presented in typewriter font, like this:

```
<time>6:00 A.M.</time>
```

This type of font is also used to identify names of files, folders, URLs, and code and words that you are to enter into a program in the Lab Exercises.

Icons

Several types of icons are used throughout this book to draw your attention to matters that deserve a closer look:

This icon is used to highlight a common mistake that could be made in working with the technology or topic being discussed. It represents our effort to steer you clear of potential problems.

This icon points you to another place in this book for more coverage of a particular topic. It may point you back to a previous chapter where important material has already been covered, or it may point you ahead to let you know that a topic will be covered in more detail later.

This icon points out important information or advice for those preparing to take the CIW E-commerce exam.

Sometimes things work differently in the real world than how they are described in books and on the CIW E-commerce exam. This icon draws your attention to our real-world experiences, which will hopefully help you on the job, if not on the exam.

This icon highlights a particular exam objective that's covered in the section where the icon appears. Use this visual clue to focus your study.

This icon is used to draw your attention to a little piece of friendly advice, a helpful fact, a shortcut, or a bit of personal experience that might be of use to you.

How to Contact Us

We've done our best to ensure that this book is technically accurate and free from errors. Our editors and technical reviewer have also worked their tails off to achieve this goal.

However, there will inevitably be some items that we have overlooked. So, if you find an error, or have a comment or insight you'd like to share, please send us an e-mail message at `CIWecomm@minnickweb.com`.

We promise to read all of our readers' e-mails and include corrections and ideas in subsequent editions, if possible. Due to the high volume of e-mail we receive, however, it may not be possible to respond to each e-mail. Please don't take it personally if you don't receive a response.

And one last request: For technical issues with the software used in this book, please contact the software vendor.

Good luck on the exam!

Acknowledgments

The authors would like to thank the following people for their help, encouragement, patience and support:

Our families; including Pat and Pat, Lujuana, Don, David, Kelly, Elizabeth, Paul, Carol, Kathy, Jay, Beth, Colin, Violet, Lydia, and Mr. Jones.

Our favorite editor, Mary Burmeister, and the whole crew at LANWrights, everyone at Hungry Minds (we hope we've given you something to eat!), and Prosoft Training for their assistance and guidance.

All of our clients, associates, co-workers, friends, and all of the people (too numerous to list here) who, by sharing their knowledge, insights and wisdom with us personally or in books, magazines and the Web, contributed to this book (sometimes without even knowing). We are thankful for the work of those who have come before us, and we hope that we've managed to contribute in some way to a future of well-trained and responsible e-commerce designers, architects, engineers, and managers.

Contents at a Glance

Contents

Part II: Designing an Effective E-Commerce Presence 137

Part IV: Operating and Enhancing E-Commerce Sites 407

E-Commerce in Context

PART

I

✦ ✦ ✦ ✦

In This Part

✦ ✦ ✦ ✦

E-Commerce Overview

EXAM OBJECTIVES

- Impetus for Web commerce
- Electronic commerce (e-commerce) definitions
- E-commerce predictions
- Types of e-commerce
- Electronic data interchange (EDI)
- Advantages of e-commerce
- Seven keys to success
- Issues in e-commerce
- Hardware and software
- The virtual enterprise

CHAPTER PRE-TEST

1. What are the two definitions of e-commerce?
2. What is the purpose of security in e-commerce?
3. How much time does the average Web user spend online per week?
4. What are the keys to e-commerce success?
5. What are four ways to build community on an e-commerce Web site?
6. What are the main advantages and disadvantages of hosting an e-commerce site in-house?

✦ Answers to these questions can be found at the end of the chapter. ✦

These days, it seems that *e-commerce* (electronic commerce) is the buzzword on everyone's lips. However, it's more than just a catchphrase—e-commerce is literally changing the way we live. This chapter examines why businesses are building Web storefronts, predictions for the future of e-commerce, potential pitfalls in e-commerce, and some of the practical matters of creating an e-commerce presence.

The Reasons for E-Commerce

In a very short time, the Web has grown from being an academic experiment in hypertext to an important part of thousands of businesses worldwide. Businesses and consumers are attracted to e-commerce for many reasons. Three of the most important reasons are:

- ✦ E-commerce opens new markets.
- ✦ E-commerce increases efficiency.
- ✦ E-commerce expands the capabilities of traditional commerce.

E-commerce opens markets

On the Internet, merchants are able to sell goods without the substantial overhead costs and geographical limitations of a physical store. Even merchants with existing real-world stores are able to sell *more* goods to *more* consumers, such as those living in remote areas or simply outside of the merchant's geographical coverage, if they have an e-commerce presence. With e-commerce, consumers can buy goods from a merchant without accessing the physical store.

E-commerce increases efficiency

Any barrier that stands between a business and its customers creates inefficiency. In the world of physical stores, some of the barriers include distance, business hours, and the need for distributors and middlemen. E-commerce appeals to businesses because it allows them to have a more direct relationship with customers.

The reasons that e-commerce appeals to shoppers vary. The reasons can range from a physical handicap, to limited free time, to an aversion to real-world shopping. E-commerce also gives shoppers the ability to easily compare prices and products. An additional bonus of online shopping is that purchases are often exempt from sales taxes. Any way you look at it, e-commerce is helping people introduce more efficiency into their lives.

E-commerce expands the capabilities of traditional commerce

One of the finest examples of e-commerce today is Amazon.com (`www.amazon.com`), the first major online bookstore. Amazon.com has been imitated and emulated repeatedly by other retail Web sites. Amazon.com provides something that real-world bookstores generally cannot: an extremely deep inventory. This means that Amazon.com stocks not only the most popular books on a given subject, but also pretty much everything else in print on that subject.

Whereas a good real-world bookstore has a fairly deep inventory and can order anything in print, access to this inventory and this service require physical proximity to a good bookstore — not something that we're all fortunate enough to have in our hometowns. Amazon.com solves this problem by bringing this capability to the Web. As a result of their success with book selling, Amazon.com has branched out, and now sells music, videos, electronics, and other products.

A less-proven business model is online grocery ordering, provided by Peapod (`www.peapod.com`), Webvan (`www.webvan.com`), Homegrocer (`www.homegrocer.com`), and others. These services work with local grocery stores to provide online shopping and delivery. One of the main concerns that potential customers have about this type of service is quality — many believe surrogate shoppers might select lower-quality meat and produce than they would. Actually, most surrogate shoppers do an excellent job selecting fresh items. As long as this continues to be true, online grocery services will continue to gain the trust of consumers, and may prove quite successful. This market has huge potential because grocery shopping is an unavoidable chore that few enjoy.

The History of E-Commerce

Contrary to popular belief, e-commerce has been around a lot longer than the World Wide Web (often called *the Web* for short).

The simplest definition of e-commerce is, "commerce conducted via any electronic medium." Using this definition, even the use of the telephone or fax machine to transact business is considered e-commerce. This means that every time you receive a catalog in the mail and pick up the phone or send in a fax to order an item, you are conducting an e-commerce transaction.

EDI and e-commerce before the Web

Electronic data interchange (EDI)

E-commerce through computer networks really started with the standard format for sharing business data that is known as Electronic Data Interchange (EDI). EDI is a method of transferring data between banks and other firms on a closed system. It's been used in ordering systems, credit card processing, direct deposit, and many other processes for the past three decades. Automatic teller machines (ATMs) and credit cards are excellent examples of the kind of e-commerce that's been around since before the Web.

E-commerce on the Web breaks down barriers

E-commerce has taken on new meaning, however, with the advent and rapid proliferation of its use on the Web. E-commerce Web sites are free of many of the constraints of previous types of e-commerce. For example, EDI has traditionally been very expensive to implement because of its need for dedicated networks. Phone ordering requires customers to wait for a customer service representative to pick up the phone. Many previous types of e-commerce had restrictions on the hours during which you could shop, and for those overseas (who have no access to toll-free numbers), an extremely expensive phone call was necessary to order products and services electronically.

The early days of the Web

The Internet was started as a way to exchange information, and was primarily used by researchers at academic institutions. With the introduction of Mosaic, the first graphical Web browser, in 1993, the possibilities of online e-commerce began to be seen by some very forward-thinking, entrepreneurial people. The Netscape browser (which eventually evolved into Netscape Navigator) was released in 1994, and by 1995, online retail sites, such as Amazon.com, were beginning to pop up. The rest, as they say, is history. Today, there are thousands of e-commerce Web sites, and more are launched each day.

Key Concepts for E-Commerce

Electronic commerce (e-commerce) definitions

Before you get into the details of e-commerce business and site development, it's important that you understand some of the lingo. The following terms and definitions are used throughout this book.

Commerce

Commerce is the exchange of goods and services for money. This definition of commerce holds true for any type of commerce as well as any type of money. The following three key capabilities need to be provided by a merchant in any type of commerce:

✦ **Communication.** This is the method of transferring information from the buyer to the seller. For example, when a shopper makes a purchase from a real-world bookstore, the shopper presents the books he or she wishes to buy and a method of payment, such as cash, check, or a credit card.

✦ **Data management.** This dictates the exchange format of the information. In the case of a check, your account number is preprinted on the check. When it's processed by the business' bank, the business uses the number to request the funds from your bank. With a credit card, the transaction is more immediate. Your credit card number is submitted for approval over a private digital network (PDN), and an (almost) instant response is received.

✦ **Security.** The private digital network provides the necessary security for the transaction. You're also given the customer copy of your receipt and any other duplicates, thus providing security for your credit card information. The cashier provides security for check purchases by storing the check in a secure area of the register until it's taken to the back office to be processed.

Electronic commerce

Electronic commerce is commerce conducted via any electronic medium, including commerce conducted via television and fax, as well as via the Internet and dedicated networks. This book focuses on electronic commerce as it applies to the Internet. This type of electronic commerce is often referred to as e-commerce.

A second definition of electronic commerce is more suitable to Internet commerce: In this case, *e-commerce* is an integration of communications, data management, and security capabilities that facilitate the exchange of information about the sale of goods and services.

The meaning of these three areas — communications, data management, and security — as they apply to the Internet is vital to understanding e-commerce. These terms are similar in meaning to those relating to traditional commerce, but on the Internet they take on some new dimensions, as follows:

✦ **Communication services.** This refers to the method of transferring information from the buyer to the seller. For example, when using a typical e-commerce Web site, the shopper uses a shopping cart function to sort which items he or she wants to buy, and then proceeds through the checkout process to submit the necessary information to the seller.

✦ **Data management.** This defines the exchange format of the information. When the customer's information is sent to the seller for transaction processing, it must be determined which format it will take when traveling over the Internet to its destination. On the Internet, payment information (for example, a credit card number) is transferred and managed using standard Internet protocols.

✦ **Security.** This is the method of securing information from potential hackers by authenticating the source of the information and guaranteeing its integrity and privacy. The most commonly used standard for transporting secure data over the Internet is Secure Sockets Layer (SSL). Browsers typically indicate that a connection is secure by displaying an icon (usually a padlock or a key) somewhere in the browser window. After the payment information reaches the server, it should be stored securely to prevent theft.

Forces Driving E-Commerce

Impetus for Web commerce

The speed at which the Web has brought e-commerce to the average person is astounding. In August 1995, there were 18 million Internet users in the U.S. and Canada. By April 1999, that number had skyrocketed to 92 million (statistics from CommerceNet 1999 U.S./Canada Demographic Survey, `www.commerce.net`). Of these, 60 percent were online shoppers.

Consequently, new e-commerce sites are being developed and launched very rapidly. Given the downturn in the stock market fortunes of many e-commerce companies in 2000, the casual observer might be prompted to wonder why businesses continue to feel that a Web presence is vital.

Despite the drop in stock prices of "dot-com" companies, e-commerce is rapidly becoming a staple of the business world. Indeed, this may be why the prices dropped — perhaps the "pie-in-the-sky" valuations of e-commerce ventures were a consequence of the hype surrounding the new industry. Now that this industry is more established, and traditional companies are also venturing into e-commerce, the stock prices are more commensurate with those of promising companies in other industries.

There are several forces that are driving the development of new e-commerce Web sites. As in the physical world of commerce, there are three key players:

✦ **Businesses.** Businesses want a piece of the pie. The number of people on the Web and their demographics are impressive. As you'll see in the following section of this chapter, the pie is still rapidly getting bigger. Also, online consumers are not the only market available to Web businesses. Increasingly, businesses are using the Web as a means to reduce the cost of conducting inter- and intra-company commerce. Inter-company e-commerce (also known as B2B e-commerce) reduces costs by avoiding middlemen. Intra-company e-commerce reduces costs by eliminating paperwork.

✦ **Customers**. There are many benefits of e-commerce for customers. At the simplest level, e-commerce makes the acquisition of goods and services much less burdensome in terms of time and effort. Customers also want privacy and security while benefiting from the advantages that the Web provides.

✦ **Government.** Government entities are still trying to figure out how or whether to take an active role in governing the Internet at all. One of the major issues with governance of the Internet is that it's a global entity, and, as such, has no clear boundaries of jurisdiction.

Issues of jurisdiction and other legal matters related to the Internet are explored in more detail in Chapter 2.

E-Commerce Trends and Forecasts

E-commerce predictions

Studies of Web usage and e-commerce growth show that the Web is a growing market. All indications are that the Web user population will continue to grow rapidly in the next 5 to 10 years. In addition, even though the Web population is currently dominated by English-speakers, the number of users in other parts of the world is growing. The Web has already become an important part of millions of people's lives.

The rapidly growing Web

Let's take a look at some of the statistics that illustrate the growth of the Web (all statistics from CommerceNet, `www.commerce.net`, which gathers information from a variety of freely available sources on the Web):

✦ In 1999, almost half of the Internet users worldwide were outside of the U.S. and Canada — the numbers for 2000 will probably push this over the 50 percent mark.

✦ Women are closing the gap in Internet shopping. In 1995, they represented about 36 percent of Internet shoppers; today, the number is 41 percent.

✦ In 1999, 40 percent of the adult population of the U.S. and Canada were using the Internet regularly. That number has been growing steadily since 1995.

✦ The average user spends 5 hours and 28 minutes per week on the Web.

Dominant trends in the evolution of e-commerce

As use of the Web for purchasing goods becomes more widespread and global, there are several dominant trends that will shape the evolution of e-commerce: internationalization, standardization, personalization, instant fulfillment, mobile Internet access, custom pricing, and intelligent agents. The following sections describe these trends in detail.

Internationalization

The expectation is that the user population of the Web will continue to grow very rapidly, and become more global. This internationalization of the Web means that businesses conducting e-commerce on the Web need to address the needs of non-English speakers if they want to access this global market. More information on the needs of non-English speakers can be found at the W3C's Internationalization site, `www.w3c.org/International`.

Standardization

The growing number of electronic transactions on the Web also requires the adoption of e-commerce standards by every company that wants to be a major player in the marketplace. These standards include data interchange and such user protections as meaningful privacy statements and trustworthy security systems.

See Chapter 7 for further information on data transfer standards.

Personalization

Personalization refers to the growing practice of gathering information about established customers and providing a personalized Web site for them when they return to your site. Information on products or topics in which users are interested can be presented as soon as they arrive at your site. This helps build loyalty. Amazon.com is a good example of a site that tailors information to the user.

Instant fulfillment

A trend in the purchase of digital products, such as software, is instant fulfillment. Instant fulfillment means that the user receives the product almost immediately after he or she purchases it — via download from the Web. Not only have online software vendors begun to offer this service, but e-book vendors such as Barnes & Noble (`www.bn.com/`) are also conducting order fulfillment via download.

The most recent trend in instant fulfillment is instant music delivery. This concept has proven to be so popular and difficult to control that it's meeting with resistance from the recording industry.

Mobile Internet access

Many people believe that wireless Internet access using handheld devices, such as personal digital assistants (PDAs) and mobile phones, will become more popular than using the Web through desktop computers.

Because of the limited graphical and processing capabilities of these devices, a special Internet protocol called the Wireless Application Protocol (WAP) has been developed to provide versions of Web sites that are suitable for these devices. To accommodate the growing number of users who will want to purchase products via their wireless devices, e-commerce businesses need to plan to implement WAP in the near future.

Some of the Internet businesses that are taking advantage of the wireless trend are providers of services that help Web sites make their content viewable on wireless devices. The leading such service is currently AvantGo (http://avantgo.com/frontdoor/index.html).

Custom pricing

Custom pricing is being pioneered by Priceline.com, an e-commerce site where a user can specify the price he or she wants to pay for a particular service. Currently, the site offers airline tickets, hotel rooms, new cars, home financing, rental cars, and long distance service. Service providers review each request and if one of the providers accepts, the user is usually bound to following through with the purchase. This is a novel business concept enabled by e-commerce on the Web.

Intelligent agents

Intelligent agents are software that acts autonomously on behalf of the user. These agents will eventually result in a vast improvement in Internet searching. Because of an intelligent agent's ability to understand concepts and search for related topics, this agent is better able to provide relevant search results for users. A good example of intelligent agent technology in use today is Apple Computer's Sherlock (www.apple.com/sherlock) functionality.

The Seven Keys to E-Commerce Success

Seven keys to success

Creating an e-commerce site can be very simple if you have the right elements in place. However, the process can also be extremely arduous if the project is not planned properly. A knowledgeable management staff with realistic expectations is key to e-commerce success.

A successful e-commerce management team must address all aspects of the project from start to completion. In this effort, there are seven key ingredients to e-commerce success:

1. Generating demand
2. Ordering
3. Fulfillment
4. Payment processing
5. Service and support
6. Security
7. Community

These elements are discussed in the following sections.

Know these seven key ingredients to e-commerce success like the back of your hand. We reference them throughout this book and they're important to passing the exam.

Generating demand

If you expect customers to visit your site, you'll need to create awareness of your products and services. There are several methods for generating awareness and demand, including Web advertising, traditional advertising, and direct e-mail.

See Chapters 3 and 4 for more information on methods of generating demand.

Ordering

After demand has been generated, the true test begins: Can you turn your visitors into buyers? The ordering process on your site must be as straightforward and efficient as possible. If it's too cumbersome, a potential buyer may abandon the process midstream. Keep the forms as short and simple as possible.

Fulfillment

After an order has been placed, stay in communication with the customer until it has been fulfilled. Immediately send an automatic e-mail to the customer verifying the order information. In addition, provide a phone number and e-mail address where the customer can reach a customer support representative to inquire about the status of the order. If applicable, provide a tracking number for the package, so the customer can check with the shipping company on the status of the shipment. Ensure that the package is shipped in a timely manner and that the packaging materials are sufficient to prevent damage.

Payment processing

Arguably, the most important part of the process is actually transferring funds from the buyer to your company. By far, the most common method is via credit card—but there are other options worth trying. The more options you give a customer, the more likely they are to purchase from your site.

The three models for payment processing in e-commerce on the Web are:

- **Credit card model.** The easiest and most common way of processing payment is via the buyer's credit card. Credit cards have been processed electronically for decades via private digital networks to which merchants are connected. Therefore, accepting a credit card via the Internet is not very different than it is in traditional commerce. After the credit card information has been received, it can be automatically routed to your company's merchant account or a third-party credit card processing service such as CyberCash or Verifone.
- **Cash model.** For customers who don't like the idea of giving their credit card number to online merchants, online *digital cash*, or *digital wallet*, services are available. Customers pay a chosen amount of money to a service, such as Flooz, via credit card. The buyer can then use this cash-equivalent at any e-commerce store that offers the service. For the broadest possible market base, offer this option as well.
- **Check model.** Some customers may prefer to pay via check. Checks can be processed over the Web, although this service is not frequently used today. Electronic check processing is offered by Electracash, Intellicheck, and other third-party vendors. An e-commerce site offering this service provides a form field for the customer to enter the transit numbers from the bottom of his or her check, similar to how the customer would enter his or her credit card number. Disadvantages for the merchant include slower processing time and increased risk of uncompleted transactions because of insufficient funds.

Detailed information on processing credit cards, digital cash, and paper checks can be found in Chapter 17.

Service and support

It's extremely important to provide excellent customer support, so you can generate trust and a loyal customer base. If a customer doesn't know how to contact your company after submitting an order, he or she will wonder whether the shipment will ever arrive. It's essential to have a clearly accessible help area on your site. Include instructions on how to use all of the features on your site — browsing products, changing account information, viewing order status, returning items, canceling an order, and so on — and provide contact e-mail and phone number information.

More advanced customer support software is also available. The Land's End (`www.landsend.com`) customer support area features an automatic call back request feature, a live chat feature, and co-browsing capabilities. These features are powered by Cisco Systems' Intelligent Contact Management Solutions. Table 1-1 defines some of the interactive customer support features.

Table 1-1
Interactive Customer Support Features

Term	*Definition*
Automatic callback	Customer submits a phone number for immediate callback from support staff (requires that the customer have a second phone line or dedicated Internet access).
Click-to-dial	Customer clicks a button on the Web site that initiates an automatic call to support staff (requires that the customer have a second phone line or dedicated Internet access).
Co-browsing	As the staff member browses, the customer's browser displays the same screen. This enables support staff to assist customer by leading the customer through the site.

Security

Security is a major concern for online shoppers, and it should be an e-commerce company's number one priority. Credit card numbers and home addresses are stolen from Web site databases with alarming frequency, so you must do everything possible to safeguard your data from unauthorized access. Use *certificates,* attachments that provide proof of identification, from a well-known vendor such as Verisign, and use SSL technology to encrypt the data sent across the Internet.

Chapter 19 discusses e-commerce transaction security in depth.

Community

One of the most important and least tangible aspects of e-commerce success is creating a sense of community at an online store. There are many books on this subject, and entire courses are available to study it — still, it remains an elusive goal for many sites. The most successful e-commerce sites, such as Barnes & Noble (`www.bn.com`), have made significant efforts in the area of community building via the use of message boards, notification e-mail, personal pages, and customer reviews.

See Chapter 3 for information on using community building in your marketing strategy.

Models for E-Commerce

Types of e-commerce

Two types of e-commerce make up nearly all the commerce activity on the Web: business-to-consumer (B2C) and business-to-business (B2B).

Although there are, naturally, many more users of the Web who would be primarily classified as consumers (at least by businesses), the B2B e-commerce market is currently larger in terms of dollars spent. The B2B market reached an estimated $137 billion in 2000, whereas B2C reached approximately $10 billion. Let's explore each of these two e-commerce business models in more detail.

Take note of the previously mentioned B2B and B2C statistics, as they will most likely be included in the exam.

Business-to-consumer

The B2C business model is commerce transacted between a business and a consumer. This model is characterized by high margins and low volume. This means that each individual shopper is not expected to buy more than one of any given item, and is further expected to make relatively modest purchases, generally under $100. As in a traditional retail store, the margin (price markup on products) is high.

The biggest difference between B2B and B2C e-commerce is the relationship between volume and margins. This will very likely be on the exam.

Business-to-business

B2B is commerce transacted between two separate businesses. It's similar to bulk rate buying in that it's characterized by high volume and low price margins. A business is likely to need large quantities of an item, such as a desk calendar for every employee or enough paper towels to stock six rest rooms for several months. Because such customers buy in bulk, and buy repeatedly, a B2B company is able to offer products at a lower margin.

Perhaps one of the best examples of a B2B Web site is the Federal Express Website (`www.fedex.com/us/`). Federal Express allows businesses to get shipping rates, print shipping labels, schedule pickups, and track packages.

E-Commerce Pros and Cons

One thing that you'll discover after working in e-commerce is that there are pluses and minuses to doing business on the Web. The second discovery you'll make is that there are e-commerce professionals (and hopefully, you'll be a certified one soon) and there are e-commerce con artists.

It can be said that the advantages (pros) to doing business on the Web are a result of the hard work of e-commerce professionals. Most of the disadvantages and hazards to doing business on the Web are caused and amplified by the people we're referring to as the e-commerce con artists.

Pros

Advantages of e-commerce

E-commerce trends and technologies are constantly changing. Staying up to speed on the latest e-commerce standards and techniques is a constant learning experience for e-commerce professionals. For those who are willing to do the work, the Web can offer the following benefits over traditional commerce:

- **Instant worldwide availability.** An e-commerce Web site is available globally, constantly. Only the largest businesses are able to achieve this with traditional commerce.
- **Easier entry into new markets.** You don't need to physically bring your company, and therefore your products, into new parts of the world. As more and more people join the Web community, they will bring your product to themselves by visiting your Web site.
- **Direct interaction between buyer and seller.** There's no need to contract a middleman, or find a reseller, to get your goods to your buyers. Buyers can access your business directly through your Web site.
- **Reduced overhead.** Opening a store in a new area can be a risky venture. This risk is minimized in an e-commerce business model, where overhead is limited to the Web site and fulfillment staff, and geographical coverage in a brick-and-mortar sense is not an issue.
- **Reduced paperwork.** Because transactions are conducted completely electronically, there's little or no need for paper.
- **New business opportunities.** As a new media for commerce and with its low start-up costs, e-commerce on the Internet has the potential to inspire many innovative business models.
- **Improved market analysis.** The community of Internet users can be surveyed to determine the probable success of a potential new product.
- **Improved product analysis.** The Internet can be used to locate extensive information about nearly any product or class of product. Sellers and buyers on the Internet have the ability to be much better informed than they are in traditional commerce.
- **Availability of vast stores of knowledge and expert (as well as not-so-expert) advice.** Many e-commerce sites offer reviews of products, sometimes from experts and sometimes from users, often both.

Cons

E-commerce con artists, on the other hand, approach commerce on the Web with a gold rush mentality. Rather than taking the time to research the unique culture, concerns and rules of the Internet, these get-rich-quick believers rush in — assuming that Internet business is the same as traditional business, only faster and with millions of dollars to be made overnight.

If you don't take the time to fully educate yourself about security issues (and even if you do, as shown by the much-publicized theft of data from Microsoft's internal network), it's possible that your e-commerce Web site will be hacked.

As an e-commerce professional, it's your responsibility to make sure that Web sites that you create are as secure as they can be, and that you (and as a result, your business) are a responsible Internet citizen. Online businesses have to work hard to earn the trust of customers so they can gain useful information about how to better serve them. The following section explores these important e-commerce concerns and issues in more detail.

See Chapter 19 for detailed coverage of security issues.

Open Issues for E-Commerce

Issues in e-commerce

Despite the progress that has been made in making e-commerce safe, secure, and user-friendly, there are still several legal and technical issues that are unresolved. E-commerce professionals need to be aware of these issues and stay informed of the latest developments in the following areas as they relate to the Web:

✦ **Intellectual property.** The protection of intellectual property rights is much more difficult in the e-commerce world than in traditional commerce. Any information presented over the Internet (images, text, sound files, and so on) can be easily duplicated.

✦ **Confidentiality.** The amazing abilities that we now have to track patterns of usage and to gather and analyze customer data are often misused by overeager Web merchants. For example, currently there is often no guarantee that merely visiting Web sites about vacationing in Las Vegas won't get you on the mailing list of hundreds of Internet casinos. (Trust us, we know this from experience!) After you've been added to any of the thousands of unscrupulous mailing lists that are out there, it's nearly impossible to be removed.

The issue of unsolicited e-mail and inappropriate targeted marketing is covered in Chapters 3 and 4.

- **Taxation.** Taxation of Web transactions is currently much debated. Many Internet technology experts and political leaders are proponents of a tax-free Internet, whereas many others see millions of dollars in potential tax revenue going down the drain.
- **Customs duties.** Taxation problems on the Internet extend beyond the boundaries of the U.S. (i.e., imports and exports, which are normally taxed when crossing international boundaries). Enforcement of international taxation on Internet transactions has been spotty at best. Many Internet retailers are not even aware of regulations on the goods they're shipping internationally.
- **International laws.** A related issue is the sale of goods that are illegal in some countries. It's currently nearly impossible to restrict products that are illegal in parts of the world from being sold to people in these countries.
- **Regulations.** Government regulation of the Internet is a contentious issue. Many users feel that too much regulation of the Internet will constitute an invasion of privacy. Security experts caution that regulation could make securing Web data even more difficult.
- **Credit card fraud.** As a merchant, it's your responsibility to verify credit card transactions. The U.S. Electronic Funds Transfer Act limits a consumer's liability in the case of fraud to $50. Fraudulent charges that are made on your Web site may result in charge backs. Charge backs occur when a customer disputes a charge made on his or her credit card and the charge is invalidated by the credit card company. The merchant could be charged as much as $25 in the event of a charge back. In addition, excessive charge backs on your merchant account can result in your account being jeopardized.

Cross-Reference

We'll take a closer look at ways to reduce fraud in Chapter 19.

- **Security.** It's often said that passing a credit card over the Web is more secure than handing it to a waiter or throwing those receipts in the trash. This may be true in some respects. It's much easier for a waiter to copy down your credit card number than it is for a hacker to intercept and decrypt packets of data containing credit card information on their way to a merchant.

Most theft on the Internet does not take place during the transmission of credit card data. A person who breaks into an e-commerce Web site's customer database can gain access to thousands of credit card numbers and post them on the Web within minutes. This has happened more times than you're likely to hear about. In addition, hundreds of con artists prey on unsuspecting Internet users daily by trying to trick them into handing over credit card numbers and passwords. Many small businesses that are new to the Internet assume that because they're relatively obscure players on the Web, they don't need to protect their site as much from outside attack as larger sites do. This is simply not true. Obscurity does not equal security.

- **Trust.** Many users are wary of shopping online because of the lack of a face-to-face transaction. In the real world, if something goes wrong with a purchase, the customer can walk into the store where the purchase was made and demand a refund. With online purchases, all a customer can do is e-mail or telephone customer support. Without a physical store, how can the customer be certain that an e-commerce retailer will even be there the next day? For this reason, you must work hard to develop your company's reputation of trustworthiness through availability and responsiveness to customer complaints and concerns.
- **Availability and risk of service disruption.** The Internet (and therefore most Web sites) is available 24 hours a day, seven days a week. With this advantage comes some risks. If your Web site goes down for any significant length of time, you face the prospect of not only lost sales, but also a diminished reputation. The extremely popular auction site eBay (`www.ebay.com`) experienced a series of crashes in 1999 that lasted several hours each. Auctioneers and their customers were left stranded, wondering when the site would return. eBay has been able to recover from the customer frustration and the bad press, but a newer, less popular site might not be able to bounce back from such an experience.

Types of E-Commerce Implementations

Today, there are many ways to get an e-commerce site up and running. Each of these methods offers different strengths and weaknesses. As an e-commerce professional, you have to evaluate the customer's needs and find the solution that best fits each site you create. With hundreds of different e-commerce services and software packages, this is not easy.

There are three levels of e-commerce stores: entry-level, mid-level, and high-level. Each of these categories contains several different methods of creating your online store.

The types of e-commerce implementations are described in greater detail in the next three sections as well as in Part II of this book.

Entry-level e-commerce outsourcing

In the early days of the Web, e-commerce was the exclusive domain of large companies. The development of any e-commerce Web site required extensive programming, database, and security knowledge—not to mention a large investment of money and time. Today, however, plenty of low cost and easy-to-use options are available for anyone who wants to do business on the Internet.

Affiliate programs and auction sites

Affiliate programs and auction sites give potential e-commerce entrepreneurs a way to harness the infrastructure of a more well-known and established e-commerce site to generate a profit for themselves. Let's take a closer look at these two options:

- **Affiliate programs** are programs that generate revenue for a small site, and increase customer traffic to a larger, more well-established site. For example, you can set up an affiliate relationship with the online bookseller Barnes & Noble (`www.bn.com`) by filling out an application on their Web site. After you're approved, you use special links on your site to send users from your site to theirs to buy a product. In exchange, you're given a percentage of the profit from the purchase.
- **Auction sites** allow you to post your products for auction. Popular auction sites, such as eBay, are visited by thousands of potential buyers each day, many more than a new Web site can hope to get. These sites also can provide secure transaction areas, saving you the need to have a bank merchant account, or accept payment via check.

Web-based e-commerce outsourcing

If you want to sell your own products, but you don't want to build your own store, many large sites allow you to easily and cheaply set up a store using standard templates and wizards.

For example, at Yahoo! Shopping (`http://shopping.yahoo.com`), you can sign up as a merchant and create a store that will be instantly available through the Yahoo! Shopping site. Nearly every aspect of running an e-commerce site is managed by Yahoo! in this case. The advantages to this type of outsourcing are:

- You don't need to worry about the technical details of running a Web storefront.
- The price to get into one of these Web malls is low.
- You can have your site listed among thousands of other sites at a very heavily trafficked location.

The disadvantages of selling your products through a Web mall such as Yahoo! Shopping are:

- You have very limited flexibility to determine how products are displayed; many small stores in these super-malls tend to look amateurish.
- Just because your products are on the same site as thousands of other companies (many of whom may be much bigger than you are) doesn't mean your products will ever be seen or purchased.

Mid-level storefront software

Many businesses start out selling products using entry-level storefronts and find that they either outgrow these services, or they require features and a level of customization that these services cannot provide. This is where the category of products we call *mid-level storefront software* comes in. Mid-level storefront software packages offer better customization features.

Mid-level storefront software costs more to get up and running, and will likely cost more to keep running. These packages typically require your Web site to be hosted somewhere that supports the particular software in question. The cost for setting up a store in this category can range from several hundred dollars to thousands of dollars.

High-level storefront software and custom development

At the upper end of electronic storefronts are custom-built stores and high-level storefront software. These solutions will typically provide the greatest level of flexibility, will be able to handle the greatest amount of traffic, and feature price tags that can range from on par with a mid-level storefront to millions of dollars.

Custom programming

Custom programming, done right, will result in a store that is exactly what the client wants. There are two primary problems with developing Web sites from the ground up:

- ✦ Custom development is the most expensive way to get a store up and running.
- ✦ The code that is written for the store is completely untested in a real-world environment until the day it goes live. The features that seemed so cool when you were testing them on your local network might bring down the entire site when it goes live.

In actual practice, there's really no such thing as a custom-developed site. Most sites use components, the software equivalent of interchangeable parts, to some degree or another (as described in the following section).

Component-based development

Component-based development combines the best aspects of custom programming with the best aspects of using pre-built Web storefront packages. For example, because credit card processing is such a common task in e-commerce, the necessary programs to accomplish this task have already been written and very highly refined. You can buy or outsource credit card processing relatively inexpensively (compared to creating your own program). It makes sense, then, to have your storefront simply pass off this part of the process to a component that is specifically designed for the purpose.

Other examples of specific parts of Web storefronts that can be implemented using standardized components include: shopping carts; shipping calculators; and customer service and support functions, such as knowledge bases and frequently asked questions (FAQ) lists. Component-based development generally results in nearly the same level of customization as custom development but at a lower cost.

High-level storefront software

At a level of complexity slightly above that of the mid-level storefront software, the high-level storefront software category requires anywhere from a little technical expertise to a moderate amount of Web programming savvy.

In addition, these types of stores usually give the store owner flexibility to modify the way the store works and to customize it as much as necessary. For medium to large businesses that are in a hurry to get a Web storefront up and running, this option generally provides the fastest time-to-market for the least cost. Because of the amount of customization that is typically done for a large e-commerce site, ease of maintenance and portability (the ability to move the site to different servers) are reduced.

Unlike entry-level and mid-level storefronts, high-level storefronts are often hosted in-house. This means that the business actually owns and maintains the software and hardware upon which the site resides. The advantage to this arrangement is that the site owner has complete control over the site. The disadvantage, once again, is that the business must hire enough staff and purchase enough equipment to properly run the business. The following section takes a closer look at the differences between in-house hosting and out-sourced hosting.

Considering Hosting Issues

The first and most basic decision that needs to be made before beginning construction of an e-commerce Web site is how you will host the site. In other words, you need to decide who will provide the Internet connection that allows your site to be accessed by anyone on the Internet. You have two basic choices:

- **In-house hosting** is a situation in which you own the computers that serve your site, and you lease the dedicated lines that connect your site to the Internet. In-house hosting can be a very costly operation, but it's a necessity for the largest Web storefronts.
- **Outsourced hosting** is much more common today, even among many large e-commerce Web sites. In an outsourced hosting relationship, access to the hardware on which your site resides is limited, which means you may have no access at all to the hosting facility, and you may not be able to physically interact with your Web server should it become necessary.

As you can see in Figure 1-1, the more customized and complex an e-commerce site is, the more likely it is to require the greater control that is provided by in-house hosting.

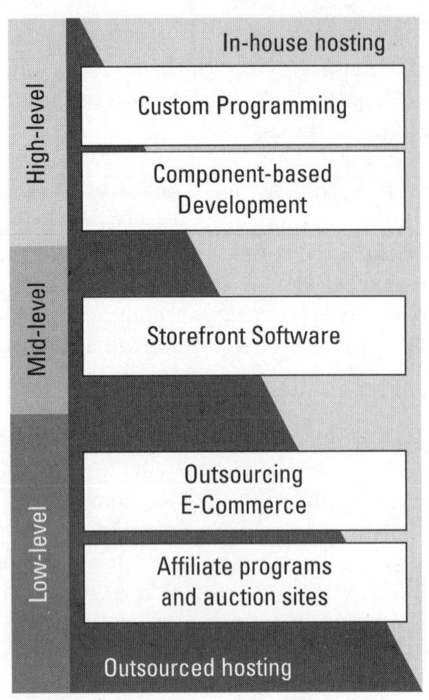

Figure 1-1: Types of e-commerce implementations

The following two sections of this chapter look at the hardware, software, and staffing requirements that need to be taken into account when building and running an e-commerce Web site. If you're outsourcing part, or all, of your e-commerce site, these requirements will be handled by someone else. If you're planning to run your Web site in-house, you'll need to be aware of the potential problems and costs. We'll also look at options for outsourcing these requirements.

Hardware requirements

Hardware and software

Most Web businesses require much less infrastructure than a traditional business. There is no need to provide shelf space, parking spaces, or rest rooms for your customers. The only real requirements are a Web server and a connection to the Internet.

If your Web server can't handle the traffic to your site, if your hard drive crashes and you don't make backups, or if your server's connection to the Internet goes down, you don't have a Web business. Although the up-front investment in good hardware may seem steep, hardware is the only part of your Web site that is guaranteed to break at some point. High quality hardware will make problems less frequent and less catastrophic when they do happen.

In-house hardware options

The minimum hardware required to build and operate a decent-sized Web storefront today includes the following:

- **A high-speed, dedicated Internet connection.** This generally means a leased line. A *leased line* is a direct wire between two points that is leased from a telecommunications carrier. The most popular leased-line option for businesses is a T-1 line, which supports data rates of 1.544 Mbits per second. T-1s are sometimes referred to as DS1 lines. If the cost of a T-1 is too expensive for your taste, or if a T-1 has more bandwidth than you require, most telephone companies also lease portions of T-1 lines, which are known as *fractional T-1s*. You should also have a backup plan for when the Internet connection goes down, such as a backup Internet connection or hosting arrangement.
- **A powerful computer for running server software.** Note that it's not always necessary to purchase the fastest computer available for serving your Web site. In late 2000 and early 2001, a typical computer for running a Web server has one or two 800 Mhz Processors, at least 264MBs of RAM (but more is always better), a 10-20GB hard drive, and a tape backup system.
- **At least one desktop computer for development and testing.** Many companies will configure their testing computer exactly the same as the Web server computer in order to provide a more accurate testing environment. Generally, however, a development machine does not need to be quite as powerful as a server, but it should be powerful enough to run the software you'll need to develop and test the site.
- **Uninterruptible power supply (UPS).** Web businesses are not only at the mercy of the telecommunications carriers, but they are also at the mercy of the electric company. Most power outages are very short, but a short outage is all it takes to bring down your site. Remember the e-commerce professional's motto (which also happens to be the Boy Scout's motto): "Be Prepared."

Outsourced hardware options

Many businesses opt to outsource the hardware and high speed Internet connection to a Web site hosting company, which charges a monthly fee for housing a server (or renting you space on a shared server) and keeping it connected to the Internet.

Outsourcing hosting can result in a much higher level of reliability and performance than an in-house solution can provide. Face it: Keeping someone on staff around the clock, 24 hours a day, 7 days a week, to watch your server probably isn't in the average company's budget. For a company that only does Web hosting, 24–7 staffing is practically standard practice.

If your business decides to outsource the hosting of its e-commerce Web site, be sure to do plenty of research first. Web hosting is a highly competitive business, and plenty of good deals can be found. When looking for Web hosting, a business should check for the following, in addition to a competitive price:

✦ **24–7 Customer Support.** Any good Web host will monitor your server around the clock and will not only have someone there to help you with any problem, but they'll also let you know if there's a problem as soon as it happens.

✦ **A low number of hops between the hosting facility and an Internet backbone.** The closer your Web site is to one of the Internet's major arteries, the faster your site will load for your users.

✦ **Multiple high-speed connections to the Internet.** The best Web hosting companies have connections to multiple Internet backbones.

✦ **Backup power generators.** If and when the power goes out, this will limit your down time.

Software requirements

Hardware and software

As discussed in the previous section, the hardware for e-commerce includes a dedicated Internet connection, a powerful computer to serve the site, and a desktop computer for development and testing (all depending on whether you choose to outsource or create and administer your site in-house). In a similar vein, software requirements are discussed in detail in the following sections.

In-house software options

Software requirements for in-house hosting include a Web server software package, File Transfer Protocol (FTP) and Telnet service, a payment component, and a database to manage your site's content. A detailed list of the software you'll need includes:

✦ **Web server software.** Web server software resides on a computer with a dedicated connection to the Internet, and accepts and handles requests using the Hypertext Transfer Protocol (HTTP).

The term *Web server* is commonly used to refer to both the computer (hardware) used to serve Web pages, and the software that accepts HTTP requests and serves documents to Web browsers. Either of these definitions is correct (although, technically, the software is the what does the serving). In this book, we use the term *Web server software* to describe programs such as Microsoft's Internet Information Services (IIS), the Apache Web Server, and Netscape's servers when the distinction between the hardware and software is important.

✦ **FTP and Telnet servers and clients.** FTP and Telnet servers installed on the same machine as the Web server allow people with the appropriate access to administer and modify a Web site.

✦ **Security certificate.** A security certificate is used to verify the authenticity of your Web site for security purposes.

For more information on e-commerce security and security certificates, see Chapter 19.

- **A directory server.** A directory server is used to securely manage user accounts and all of the information associated with user accounts (user profiles).
- **Payment infrastructure.** If you're going to ask for money in exchange for products or services, you need to have a method to get that money. A payment infrastructure can range from a secure form that e-mails payment information to someone for manual processing, to a real-time system for accepting and processing credit cards online.
- **A database.** Most Web storefronts store product and order information in a database to allow for easy management and reporting, as well as complex searching and dynamic page generation on the site.
- **A development environment.** The development and testing machine needs to have whatever software development tools are required for the type of storefront you've chosen to build. A development environment could be as simple as a text editor or as complex as a wizard-based tool that takes you through every step in building your store.
- **Testing and analysis software.** There are many good Web-site testing packages that can help you to determine if your site is ready for prime time. For example, stress-testing utilities, such as Microsoft's free InetLoad program, simulate thousands of users simultaneously hitting your site. This allows you to see where the weak links in your site are so you can fix them before letting the rest of the world find them.

Outsourced software options

If you choose to outsource the hardware end of your storefront, the hosting company will provide some of the software requirements. At the very least, the Web, FTP, and Telnet servers will be already installed on the computer you rent from the Web host. Some hosting companies will also provide the security certificates, directory servers, payment infrastructure, the database and testing and analysis tools for additional fees. Development software generally resides on your development computer, and is therefore not usually provided by a hosting company.

Staffing requirements

Although the number of employees required to support an e-commerce business is often less than the number of employees needed to support a traditional, or "bricks-and-mortar" business, the people you need to hire command much larger salaries than the average high school student working a register as a part time job.

In-house staffing options

A company that decides on a completely in-house solution for a medium- to large-sized Web storefront will find the following types of technical personnel essential. Note that this list does not cover the people who make the business run behind the scenes, including human resources, administrative staff, accounting, and management.

✦ **Programmers.** Programmers will make or break your site. The characteristics that managers should look for in programmers are experience, willingness and proven ability to learn new skills, and ability to communicate effectively in a language that is understood by management. Before you go looking for a programmer to work on your site, make sure you know what particular skills you're looking for.

Web programmer job listings often look like laundry lists of buzzwords with everything from graphic design to database administration to several programming and scripting languages thrown in. If you're having trouble finding programmers for your site, take a look at your job listing. Web programmers are savvy enough to know that if a job listing says "Photoshop and Illustrator skills, writing skills, C++, Java, Perl, XML, HTML, Visual Basic, and project management skills required," the company either doesn't know what it wants or is looking for a superman to do the work of four people and get the salary of one.

✦ **Database administrator (DBA).** DBAs generally specialize in one or two databases. Decide which database you're going to use before looking for a DBA. DBAs are notoriously expensive, and most e-commerce companies only bring in a DBA on an as-needed basis. Smaller sites may opt to simply have the programmers design the database. If you can afford it, a professionally designed database makes an enormous difference in the performance and reliability of your site.

We'll look at some of the most widely used databases in Chapter 12.

✦ **Graphic artists/Web designers.** Graphic artists create the look of your site. A successful Web designer has intimate knowledge of the limitations of various Web browsers and computer monitors, download times, Web file formats, and some knowledge of HTML. Web designers need to know how to work with programmers, as well as with user interface designers, to create a functional and flexible site design.

There's a big difference between print designers and Web designers. A good print designer may not be a good Web designer and vice-versa. Many companies choose graphic artists based on print work they've done in the past. This often doesn't work out well.

- **Customer support.** After people start visiting your site and buying your goods, they will have questions and they will send e-mail. It's a good idea to have someone on staff who is knowledgeable about your products or services and whose job it is to respond to customer questions in a timely manner. They can keep your customers happy and free up the rest of your staff to focus on improving and building the business.
- **Network administrators.** An e-commerce company relies heavily on various types of networks. The job of a network administrator is to keep the internal network working, to protect the company's internal network from unauthorized access, to maintain the Web, e-mail, FTP and other types of servers, and to monitor the Web site's vital statistics.
- **User interface designers.** Whereas creating a Web site's user interface used to be the job of the graphic designers, this is increasingly being done by specialists. User interface designers decide how the navigation of a site will be laid out and create logical paths through the site. User interface design becomes increasingly important as the variety of products a store sells increases.
- **Content engineers/HTML writers.** This is where the rubber meets the road. These are the folks who know browsers inside out and who take the work of the graphic designers and the output from the various programs and make them into Web pages.

It used to be that one person, who was given the title Webmaster, did all of the jobs in the previous list. With the increasing complexity of the Web, it's almost impossible for any one person to be able to perform all of the previous functions well.

Still, it's often the case that smaller sites will be able to find graphic artists who have user interface design skills, or programmers who can also fix server problems. If the business plan calls for growth (and it's the rare Internet business plan that doesn't), that business had better be prepared to pay a premium for high quality talent.

Outsourced staffing options

E-commerce businesses that are just getting started, or established businesses that just can't find enough employees, often supplement their staff with independent contractors. There is a huge demand for good Web contractors, but finding them isn't always easy.

Because most independent contractors doing Web-related work have more work than they can handle, most of them don't market themselves. The three ways that companies most frequently locate independent contractors are through staffing agencies, job boards, and word of mouth. Here's how they work:

- **Staffing agencies.** Web staffing agencies develop a pool of programmers, graphic artists, project managers, and other Web professionals from which companies can choose. Web staffing agencies eliminate the need for a company to recruit talent and screen applicants. The downside to staffing agencies, however, is that the agency marks up the worker's fee (often quite significantly) and the screening of applicants that goes on in staffing agencies may not be as rigorous as Web companies would do themselves.

✦ **Job boards.** Job boards are the Internet equivalent of classified employment ads. Every major high tech city has at least one widely used local job board Web site, and there are several very good national (and even international) job boards. Companies generally pay a fee to post job listings to these boards. People looking for jobs can then browse and search through listings to find jobs. Monster.com, one of the largest job boards, regularly has several hundred thousand job listings. Many industry associations also sponsor job boards and post resumes of members on their Web sites.

✦ **Word of mouth.** Even on the Internet, it's still true that the best way to find good people, or to land a good job, is to know people. Employers frequent message boards, mailing lists, and even real world high tech hangouts looking for potential employees. Being seen (or read) in places that potential employers or employees visit can be beneficial.

Moving Toward the Virtual Enterprise

The virtual enterprise

As a result of the extremely competitive nature of the business and the tight job market for Web-related jobs, many e-commerce companies are deciding that it's no longer in their best interests to expend their precious resources on additional office space and staff every time the business grows. Because the Internet has made it possible for many employees to work from home, or from anywhere that they want as long as they have Internet access, creative new ways to do business are being invented. One of these is the *virtual enterprise*.

A virtual enterprise is a decentralized, and typically short-lived, group of people working together through the Internet on a per-project basis.

For example, a certain Web development company may only consist of a project manager and one or two other key staff members. For each Web site that this company builds, though, they assemble a team of contractors who are well suited to the particular job. In this way, a company can remain small and flexible, while still being able to bid on and get large contracts.

Virtual enterprise pros and cons

The benefits of the virtual enterprise are:

✦ The development team can be hand picked from a large pool of independent contractors and companies for each job.

✦ A company with only a few permanent employees can weather slow periods much easier than one with a large staff.

- Overhead is significantly reduced by not having to provide office space, health insurance, and benefits for a large staff.
- Reduced overhead allows a virtual enterprise to be more flexible, as well as devote more money to paying contractors and vendors, which tends to build a loyal and happy pool of contractors.

There are, however, disadvantages to operating a company as a virtual enterprise, such as:

- Large companies are still hesitant to give contracts to companies that don't have large office buildings and hundreds of employees.
- Finding qualified contractors is often just as difficult as finding qualified employees.
- Personal interaction between people or companies who are brought in to work on a particular project is often minimal. If not managed correctly, and if an effort is not made to keep everyone involved informed, projects being worked on by a virtual enterprise can deteriorate into chaos.

Virtual enterprise technologies

Certain technologies make it possible for virtual enterprises to function securely over the public Internet. There are two ways to create secure networks between the different contributors in a virtual enterprise:

- **Value-Added Network (VAN).** This is a network that is used to facilitate EDI messaging. VANs are usually private, secure networks that provide services such as data routing and coordinating EDI transactions.
- **Virtual Private Network (VPN).** This is similar to a VAN, in that it facilitates secure communications between computers in different locations. However, a VPN uses encrypted data streams over the public networks rather than an actual private network—hence, the virtual part of the name. VPNs are cheaper to set up and maintain than VANs. A VPN can exist between two firewalls, between a client computer and a firewall, or between a standard client and a server.

Key Point Summary

This chapter presented a broad overview of e-commerce. You learned about the reasons for e-commerce, the definitions of e-commerce, the forces driving e-commerce, and e-commerce trends and statistics.

- E-commerce can be defined in two ways: commerce conducted over any electronic medium; and the integration of communication, data management, and security capabilities that allow organizations to exchange information about the sale of goods and services.

- E-commerce has been around for a while. One standard for e-commerce that has been around much longer than the Web is EDI.
- The introduction of the first Web browser, Mosaic, started the popularity of the Web, which led to the explosion of e-commerce we're experiencing today.
- The trends in e-commerce today include internationalization, standardization, personalization, mobile Internet access (anywhere, anytime access), instant fulfillment, custom pricing, and intelligent agents.

This chapter also covered information on e-commerce business models, evaluating potential, and the keys to success.

- The two e-commerce business models are B2B and B2C. B2B currently has a much larger market. B2B is characterized by high volume and low margins, whereas B2C typically has high margins and low volume.
- The seven keys to e-commerce success are generating demand, the ordering process, fulfillment, payment processing, customer service and support, security, and building community.

You also saw the two basic ways to run an e-commerce store: by outsourcing part or all of it and by doing everything in-house. We further divided these two broad categories into three levels of e-commerce, each with its own sub-divisions.

The hardware, software, and staffing requirements of e-commerce businesses were discussed in this chapter, as was the concept of the virtual enterprise.

- E-commerce hardware requirements include a dedicated Internet connection such as a T-1, a powerful computer to serve the site, and a desktop computer for development and testing.
- Software requirements include a Web server software package, FTP and Telnet service, a payment component, and a database to manage your site's content.

✦ ✦ ✦

STUDY GUIDE

This chapter covered quite a bit of material. Take a deep breath (maybe a break), and then apply what you've learned to do the exercises and answer the following questions about this chapter. The answers to these questions are revealed in the "Answers to Chapter Questions" section, later in this chapter.

Assessment Questions

1. Which of the following technologies cannot be used to conduct electronic commerce?

A. Telephone

B. Computer

C. Fax machine

D. Cash Register

2. Which of the following is the best definition of Internet e-commerce? (Choose the best answer.)

A. Commerce conducted via any electronic medium.

B. An integration of communications, data management, and security capabilities that facilitates the exchange of information about the sale of goods and services.

C. The sale of electronics on the Internet.

D. Commerce transacted between a business and a consumer on the Internet.

3. The owner of a successful chain of retail stores is skeptical about the merits of developing an e-commerce Web site. "After all, it is a lot of money to spend on an unproven idea," he says. Which of the following is not an example of the advantages of e-commerce over traditional commerce?

A. E-commerce provides potential customers with instant access to information about your products or services, 24 hours a day.

B. E-commerce will allow the company to enter new markets without needing a physical presence.

C. E-commerce is more secure than traditional commerce.

D. E-commerce will allow the company to take advantage of new and innovative business models.

4. Which of the following is an advantage of using a Web-based e-commerce outsourcing solution, or an online storefront, such as Yahoo! Stores?

A. Either can be maintained from any computer with a Web connection and a browser.

B. The vendor has control over the software.

C. Many customization options are available.

D. Software is maintained and upgraded by the merchant.

5. What are the characteristics of the B2B business model? (Choose the best answer.)

A. High margin and low volume.

B. High volume and low margin.

C. High volume and high margin.

D. Stable customer base and high margin.

6. Which of the following mechanisms helps provide security for e-commerce transactions?

A. Credit Cards

B. Secure Sockets Layer (SSL)

C. Virtual enterprise

D. Order numbers

7. What is a virtual enterprise?

A. A company that only exists in your imagination.

B. An e-commerce company that doesn't make money.

C. A decentralized, and typically short-lived, group of people working together through the Internet on a per-project basis.

D. A company with many different offices around the world.

Scenario

1. You're the Webmaster for a local bakery. The management of the company has asked for your input on whether anyone would buy items from an online bakery. The company is listed in the local phone book and already takes orders via phone and delivers within a ten-mile radius. Is an e-commerce site right for this company? If your answer is yes or maybe, what type of solution would you recommend to management?

Lab Exercise

Lab 1-1 First look at e-commerce sites

1. Go to a search engine and find e-commerce stores related to an interest of yours (for example, pets, cars, or food) that you've never visited before. Visit at least three different sites.
2. For each site, answer the following questions:
   a. Would I return to this site? If so, why? If not, why?
   b. Would I feel safe buying something from this store? If so, why? If not, why?
   c. Is it easy to find specific items in this store? If so, why? If not, why?

Answers to Chapter Questions

Chapter pre-test

1. E-commerce is defined as commerce conducted via any electronic medium; and an integration of communications, data management, and security capabilities that facilitates the exchange of information about the sale of goods and services.
2. Security authenticates the source of information, and guarantees the integrity and privacy of the information.
3. The average Web user spends 5 hours and 28 minutes on the Web per week.
4. The seven keys to e-commerce success are: generating demand, ordering, fulfillment, payment processing, service and support, security, and community.
5. Four ways to build community include e-mail notifications, customer reviews, personal pages, and message boards.
6. The advantage to hosting a Web site in-house is increased control over the server. The disadvantage is increased expense and staffing requirements.

Assessment questions

1. **D.** Although cash registers are an important part of traditional commerce, they are of little use conducting e-commerce as discussed in this book. This is covered in the section titled "The History of E-Commerce."
2. **B.** This is the best definition of e-commerce. This is covered in the "Key Concepts for E-Commerce" section.
3. **C.** C is correct because, although e-commerce may not be any less secure than traditional commerce, it's definitely not *more* secure. This is covered in the "E-Commerce Pros and Cons" section.
4. **A.** The main benefit of using a service such as Yahoo! Stores is that they can be built and maintained using only a Web browser. This is covered in the "Types of E-Commerce Implementations" section.
5. **B.** B2B e-commerce is characterized by high volume and low margins. This is covered in the "Models for E-Commerce" section.
6. **B.** Secure Sockets Layer is used in e-commerce to encrypt data in transmission between a server and a user's Web browser. This is covered in the "Key Concepts for E-Commerce" section.
7. **C.** A virtual enterprise is a loose-knit collection of people working on a common project. This is covered in the "Moving Toward the Virtual Enterprise" section.

Scenario

1. At this point in the book, we expect that your answer to this question is largely based on your gut feeling. Generally, any small business starting to do business on the Web should proceed with caution. E-commerce may not be right for every business. If you're unsure, a prudent course of action is to get your feet wet first with an entry-level outsourced solution. If this proves to be a success, you can think about moving up to a mid-level solution.

For More Information . . .

For more information on the topics covered in this chapter, please visit the following sites:

- ✦ **CommerceNet.** `www.commerce.net`. A non-profit organization promoting and advancing interoperable e-commerce. CommerceNet's Web site is an excellent source of information about e-commerce and companies doing business on the Web.
- ✦ **TheStandard.** `www.thestandard.com`. The Web site for the print publication "The Industry Standard." Here's where you'll find news about and insight into the Internet economy.

- **Monster.com.** www.monster.com. A large, international Web-based job board.
- **Internet and E-Commerce Statistics.** www.cnie.org/nle/st-36.html. A Congressional Research Service Issue brief from the National Council for Science and the Environment.
- **ZDNet's E-Commerce site.** www.zdnet.com/enterprise/e-business/. E-commerce news, directories, research links, and advice center.

Legal Issues and the Internet

EXAM OBJECTIVES

- Electronic publishing
- Intellectual property issues
- Areas of liability
- Privacy and confidentiality
- Jurisdiction

CHAPTER PRE-TEST

1. What is intellectual property?
2. What is a service mark?
3. How is software protected under intellectual property law?
4. What are customs and tariffs?
5. What were the results of the Internet Tax Freedom Act (ITFA) of 1998?
6. What are the key issues relating to taxation on the Internet?
7. What body oversees trademark disputes over domain names?
8. Why should a Web site that allows users to post comments and messages include a Terms of Use agreement?

✦ Answers to these questions can be found at the end of the chapter. ✦

The rise of the Internet has ushered in a new age of information access and data transfer. The laws currently in place to govern this new age, however, were largely enacted before the information era was more than a glimmer in anyone's eye. As a result, the early years of the Web and e-commerce have been fraught with legal problems and uncertainty—trying to make existing laws fit into the new framework and creating new laws specific to this new frontier.

In this chapter, we examine e-commerce legal issues in detail. We start with an introduction to the legal terms and concepts that are applicable to e-business. Next, you find out about intellectual property law and how it affects e-commerce and electronic publishing. Next, confidentiality matters, including privacy statements, are discussed. The difficult issue of legal jurisdiction follows, and we finish with two discussions of taxation on the Internet, both within the U.S. and in international transactions.

This chapter is intended to introduce you to the issues, not to give legal advice. As such, it should not be used as a substitute for sound legal counsel for your e-commerce business.

Understanding the Legal Side of Online Business

Online business ventures are subject to many legal concerns. The primary reason is that the laws of our country, and those of the rest of the world, were not made with Internet commerce in mind. Since the Internet became a venue for commerce in 1995, the justice system has been struggling to adapt yesterday's laws to today's e-commerce business issues. Here are some of the major issues:

- **Legal jurisdiction.** The Web is a global entity, and as such it's difficult to determine who governs the transactions that take place on it. Does the government of the purchaser have the final word or the government of the Web site's place of business? In the United States, the varied laws of the states have caused problems within our borders.
- **Intellectual property infringement.** This issue has also consumed much of the attention of lawyers and their clients. A fundamental question is whether information can legally be duplicated without the consent of the author. For logos, trademarks, books, and music, it's clear that excessive duplication and misuse are not legal. But how can this be enforced? And is it still okay to make a copy of a song for a friend, like you could with a cassette tape?
- **Privacy.** On the Web, public information is much more accessible than ever before. Even confidential information is more easily accessible because of the databases that e-commerce sites use to hold customer information. It's imperative that e-commerce companies use the best security available to protect this information.

Internet law is in its infancy. The rules are not yet in place and the issues are just starting to be addressed. In some cases, international bodies are emerging to regulate the Internet. In other cases, disputes are being resolved in local courts. Internet law is very much in a state of foundation building, and you should remember this as you read this chapter. Although we're presenting the issues and some possible protections for your company, we cannot begin to know where Internet law will be in the near future.

Basic Legal Concepts of E-Business

Before you get into the intricacies of legal issues and the Internet, you should familiarize yourself with some basic legal concepts that affect e-business: electronic publishing, intellectual property, and liability exposures. The following three sections explain each concept in detail.

Electronic publishing

Electronic publishing

Electronic publishing is defined as the use of computers — rather than traditional print mechanisms — to distribute information and data. In this book, electronic publishing is not limited to works that are typically produced on printed paper; it also includes works that can be transferred via digital means, such as software, music files, and digital images.

Be sure you know the correct definition of electronic publishing – it's probably a lot broader than you'd expect.

Part of the appeal of electronic publishing is that it's less expensive to produce than traditional media. For example, a CD-ROM that holds the equivalent of more than 150,000 printed pages of information can now be manufactured for less than a dollar. The cost of the paper alone to print this many pages of information would be much more than that. When printing costs are added to the cost of the paper, electronic publishing can be hundreds of times less expensive than traditional publishing. The reduced cost of manufacturing results in a lower cost for the consumer and also a higher profit margin for the producing company.

One of the main drawbacks of electronic publishing, given the ease of transferring digital files via the Internet, is the relative certainty that intellectual property laws will be violated, both intentionally and unintentionally.

Intellectual property

Intellectual property issues

The reason that electronic publishing has caused such concern to companies that produce digital products is the existence of intellectual property law. Intellectual property laws protect the rights of individual authors and corporations to profit from their creations, and require their permission for duplication.

Intellectual property issues are divided into two separate categories: industrial property and copyright law.

The differences between industrial property and properties covered by copyright law are important themes in the exam.

Industrial property

Industrial property encompasses industrial designs, inventions, and trademarks and service marks. These are the property of corporations and are used to maintain the individuality of processes and product identities. Patents are often issued to protect these properties.

Industrial property and the protections available for it include:

- **Industrial designs.** Refers to the shape or ornamentation given to a manufactured article to make it appealing or unique, such as the shape of a bottle or the colors and shapes used on a label. Industrial designs must be registered by a recognized government office, and be determined to be original or novel. This protection is intended to prevent a third party from using the design without consent.
- **Inventions.** An invention is a new process or practice that solves a specific problem, or represents a new way of doing business. The definition is usually limited to technological advancements. Patents on inventions are limited in time (the length of time varies), and require thorough documentation of the invention to be granted.
- **Trademarks and service marks.** A mark is something that a company uses to distinguish its products or services from those of competitors. It can include words, letters, numbers, drawings, pictures, or even containers. Trademarks are granted by the U.S. Patent and Trademark Office, and are intended to protect such marks from unauthorized use by third parties. Service marks serve the same purpose as trademarks, except they are granted for services rather than material goods.

International protection of patents and trademarks is not available in all countries, which is why you sometimes see imported fakes of popular products. Because industrial property protections are issued by individual countries, other countries are not required to recognize them. However, many countries are signatories on international treaties that provide reciprocal protection.

Copyright law

Copyright law protects original works that have traditionally been the product of an individual's effort, such as literary, musical, artistic, photographic, and audiovisual works. The Copyright Act of 1976 prevents the unauthorized copying of such a work. It applies only to the written work, however, not to the ideas or objects described within. For example, a technical description of a machine is protected, but not the machine itself (but it can be protected by a patent — see the previous section).

Copyrights can be registered in the Copyright Office in the Library of Congress. Newly created works do not need to be registered to be protected by copyright law, but registration can make it easier to defend yourself against infringement.

Liability exposures

Areas of liability

As more items are published electronically, more legal issues arise. Because the laws governing intellectual property were not crafted with the digital age in mind, interpretation of the laws on a case-by-case basis has become necessary. It's often difficult to determine liability for a given offense because of the new ways in which information is being used.

The possible areas of liability associated with electronic publishing are:

- Copyright, trademark, and patent issues
- Privacy and confidentiality issues
- Jurisdiction issues

Be sure that the three areas of liability are clear to you.

Consider the following examples and the difficulty of determining liability in each case.

Trading files

A Web site offers a forum for users to exchange digital music files. Is this copyright infringement? Is the act of swapping music files over the Internet inherently different from exchanging music on cassette tapes? If so, who's liable for copyright infringement — the users or the owner of the Web site?

Duplicating others' material

Your cousin sends you a photograph of the Super XtraSmall Stereo Deluxe, suggesting that you buy one for yourself because he likes his so much. It turns out that he downloaded this picture from a Web site that sells electronics and that the photograph is copyrighted by the stereo manufacturer. Did your cousin commit a copyright violation by downloading the picture, and/or by sending it to you? Are you participating in a copyright violation by receiving this picture?

Downloading data

A subscriber to a public bulletin board uploads a computer game for others to download. You download the game, play it, and like it so much that you send copies to your 10 closest friends. Is your distribution of the game an intellectual property violation? Or is the subscriber who originally uploaded the game liable? Or is the bulletin board liable for providing a forum in which this can happen?

Publishing defamatory information

An ISP is hosting a Web site that makes false claims about another person. Is the ISP responsible for the content hosted on its servers? Or is it simply the vehicle by which the defamatory information was spread? Is the ISP responsible for analyzing the content of the Web pages it hosts?

ISPs are limited from copyright infringement liability by the Digital Millennium Copyright Act, which was signed into law in October 1998. Among other provisions, the law protects ISPs from responsibility for the content of the Web sites that they host. See `www.gseis.ucla.edu/iclp/dmca1.htm` for more information on the Digital Millennium Copyright Act.

Exam Tip Be sure that you understand how the Digital Millennium Copyright Act limits ISP liability in intellectual property disputes.

These are just a few examples of how quickly the issue of liability can become muddled when it comes to electronic publishing and the distribution of data and information. The rest of this chapter explores these areas of liability and the implications of the Internet on the determination of each one.

Intellectual Property Law and the Internet

As we have seen, intellectual property law protects industrial designs, trademarks, inventions, and works of art from unauthorized duplication. However, the Internet has fundamentally changed the way in which these works are distributed.

For example, photographs can be scanned and published online. Any image on the Web can be downloaded by a user. If it's a crime every time a user downloads an image, we have a lot of criminals out there. On the other hand, the fact that images are easy to download does not make it legal for an e-commerce site to download the logo from another e-commerce site and use it as its own.

Copyright infringement

Copyright infringement, in its most basic form, is the act of profiting from someone else's creation without permission. In the case *Sega Enterprises, Ltd. v. MAPHIA*, Sega sued the online bulletin board operator MAPHIA for making a Sega game available for download. Users were charged for downloading the game. The case was decided in Sega's favor.

Unauthorized duplication of software

Copyright law can also be used to protect unauthorized duplication of software. The 1976 Copyright Act protects "original works of authorship," including "compilations," which are defined as works "formed by the collection and assembling of preexisting materials or of data that are selected, coordinated, or arranged in such a way that the resulting work as a whole constitutes an original work of art."

This definition of a compilation has led many to claim that software is protected under copyright law. Although many people may debate the artistry of software and the use of copyright law to protect the property of a corporation, this opinion has been upheld.

The fair use doctrine

When it comes to art, such as music, literature, and photography, the doctrine of fair use is often used to justify limited use of copyrighted material. The fair use statute is included in the Copyright Act, and it's designed to allow for limited use of artistic works in endeavors that are important to society, such as journalism, research, criticism, and teaching. Fair use was a murky issue before the Internet, and remains so, being decided on a case-by-case basis.

Terms of Use agreements

Many Web sites that allow users to post information, such as bulletin board messages and product reviews, protect themselves from possible copyright infringement suits by including a *Terms of Use* agreement to which users are required to agree before posting. These agreements require the author to relinquish rights to the message or review, or give permission for it to be circulated. Users must also accept responsibility for posting copyrighted materials to which they have no rights.

Trademark infringement

Read this section carefully. You need to understand the relationship between trademark law and domain name disputes.

Trademarks are words, letters, numbers, drawings, and pictures that a company uses to distinguish its products from those of competitors. In the world of Internet law, trademarks have been used to claim rightful ownership of domain names.

Domain name issues

A domain name is a company's sole identifier on the Internet, such as `www.cocacola.com`. Trademark law prohibits the use of a trademark by a third party. So what happens when a third party owns the domain name that a corporation claims is their trademark? Does this constitute trademark infringement?

Domain name disputes are one of the current hot topics in Internet law. The World Intellectual Property Organization's Domain Name Dispute Resolution Service (DNDRS) has emerged as the international body for resolving claims to domain names.

Domain name dispute resolution

The first case was decided by the DNDRS in January of 2000. It involved the World Wrestling Federation (WWF), which was suing the owner of `www.worldwrestlingfederation.com`. The DNDRS found that the owner was guilty of cybersquatting and awarded the domain name to the WWF.

The term *cybersquatter* is commonly used to refer to someone who has purchased a domain name in order to sell it later to a corporation or famous individual for a profit.

Sting lost his bid for ownership of `www.sting.com` on the grounds that "sting" is a common English word (which might make him regret taking *that* stage name). Madonna, on the other hand, has had a court rule in her favor regarding her claim to `www.madonna.com`, partly on the grounds that Madonna is her given first name.

Further information on the activities of the World Intellectual Property Organization's DNDRS can be found at `http://arbiter.wipo.int/domains`.

Patent infringement

Patents are awarded for new processes or practices that solve a specific problem, or represent a new way of doing business. Patent applications must be accompanied by documentation explaining the uniqueness of the invention. The patent gives the inventor the exclusive right to use a process or make and sell a specific product for a given length of time.

Patent law is used to protect software from duplication, as is copyright law. In the case of patent law, however, parts of a software program are protected rather than the whole program. Software patents do not generally cover the entire program—rather, they cover algorithms and techniques of programming. Problems arise when the algorithms and techniques specified in a patent application have been formulated and used independently by other software developers for other programs.

Many claim that the practice of patenting algorithms and techniques is fundamentally at odds with the nature of software development. Rarely in the process of developing a software application does a developer not use an algorithm or technique that has already been used in another program, either knowingly or unknowingly.

After all, present computer programs contain thousands of algorithms and techniques. In fact, the strength of today's software is based on the cumulative knowledge and reuse of code from decades of programming. Rendering code reuse illegal would hamper software developers' efforts significantly.

Nonetheless, the 1981 case of *Diamond v. Diehr* found that "a patent could be granted for an industrial process that was controlled by certain computer algorithms." This decision has been used as a precedent for allowing patents on algorithms and techniques.

For more information on patent law, visit the U.S. Patent and Trademark Office Web site at www.uspto.gov.

Confidentiality and Privacy Matters

Privacy and confidentiality

Easy access to information enabled by the Internet has another implication, one that everyone should be concerned about: easy access to personal information, whether it be addresses, shopping habits, or the names of your children. Should public information be available online? Do e-commerce companies have the right to collect data on what a customer buys? These questions have yet to be resolved. In this section, you take a closer look at the issues involved in privacy and confidentiality.

The Federal Trade Commission has issued guidelines for online privacy. See their Web site at www.ftc.gov for more information.

Public information

Not so long ago, the printed telephone directory was the only way for most people to look up public information, such as another person's phone number and address. Now, there are several Web sites that have compiled information from every telephone directory in the country into a searchable database.

The fact that this information is now available on the Internet makes it much easier to find someone else's public information. Before the Internet, physical access to a telephone directory was necessary. A complete collection of directories for the U.S. could be found in major libraries, but even that required a special effort to access.

Today, access to the Internet is all that is needed. Because information has become so much easier to find, many people claim that abuse of this information is more likely.

Public information access Web sites include:

- **Yahoo! People Search:** http://people.yahoo.com
- **Switchboard:** www.switchboard.com
- **WhitePages.com:** www.whitepages.com
- **Zip2:** www.zip2.com
- **Bigfoot:** www.bigfoot.com

Misuse of information

The ability of Web server software to collect information on the visitors to a Web site is impressive. The log files that are automatically created contain information on the type of browser used, the pages the user visited, how long the user stayed, and much more. Figure 2-1 shows a sample of this type of log file. With the use of *cookies*, the server can also detect when a user returns to the site. A cookie is a mechanism that allows a server-side program, such as a Common Gateway Interface (CGI) script, to store and retrieve information on the client-side of a Hypertext Transfer Protocol (HTTP) connection.

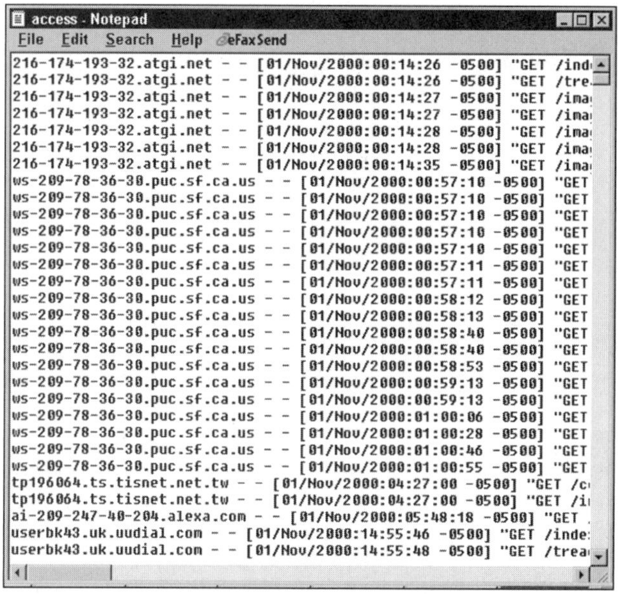

```
access - Notepad
File  Edit  Search  Help  eFaxSend
216-174-193-32.atgi.net - - [01/Nov/2000:00:14:26 -0500] "GET /ind
216-174-193-32.atgi.net - - [01/Nov/2000:00:14:26 -0500] "GET /tre
216-174-193-32.atgi.net - - [01/Nov/2000:00:14:27 -0500] "GET /ima
216-174-193-32.atgi.net - - [01/Nov/2000:00:14:27 -0500] "GET /ima
216-174-193-32.atgi.net - - [01/Nov/2000:00:14:28 -0500] "GET /ima
216-174-193-32.atgi.net - - [01/Nov/2000:00:14:28 -0500] "GET /ima
216-174-193-32.atgi.net - - [01/Nov/2000:00:14:35 -0500] "GET /ima
ws-209-78-36-30.puc.sf.ca.us - - [01/Nov/2000:00:57:10 -0500] "GET
ws-209-78-36-30.puc.sf.ca.us - - [01/Nov/2000:00:57:10 -0500] "GET
ws-209-78-36-30.puc.sf.ca.us - - [01/Nov/2000:00:57:10 -0500] "GET
ws-209-78-36-30.puc.sf.ca.us - - [01/Nov/2000:00:57:10 -0500] "GET
ws-209-78-36-30.puc.sf.ca.us - - [01/Nov/2000:00:57:10 -0500] "GET
ws-209-78-36-30.puc.sf.ca.us - - [01/Nov/2000:00:57:11 -0500] "GET
ws-209-78-36-30.puc.sf.ca.us - - [01/Nov/2000:00:57:11 -0500] "GET
ws-209-78-36-30.puc.sf.ca.us - - [01/Nov/2000:00:58:12 -0500] "GET
ws-209-78-36-30.puc.sf.ca.us - - [01/Nov/2000:00:58:13 -0500] "GET
ws-209-78-36-30.puc.sf.ca.us - - [01/Nov/2000:00:58:40 -0500] "GET
ws-209-78-36-30.puc.sf.ca.us - - [01/Nov/2000:00:58:40 -0500] "GET
ws-209-78-36-30.puc.sf.ca.us - - [01/Nov/2000:00:58:53 -0500] "GET
ws-209-78-36-30.puc.sf.ca.us - - [01/Nov/2000:00:59:13 -0500] "GET
ws-209-78-36-30.puc.sf.ca.us - - [01/Nov/2000:00:59:13 -0500] "GET
ws-209-78-36-30.puc.sf.ca.us - - [01/Nov/2000:01:00:06 -0500] "GET
ws-209-78-36-30.puc.sf.ca.us - - [01/Nov/2000:01:00:28 -0500] "GET
ws-209-78-36-30.puc.sf.ca.us - - [01/Nov/2000:01:00:46 -0500] "GET
ws-209-78-36-30.puc.sf.ca.us - - [01/Nov/2000:01:00:55 -0500] "GET
tp196064.ts.tisnet.net.tw - - [01/Nov/2000:04:27:00 -0500] "GET /c
tp196064.ts.tisnet.net.tw - - [01/Nov/2000:04:27:00 -0500] "GET /i
ai-209-247-40-204.alexa.com - - [01/Nov/2000:05:48:18 -0500] "GET
userbk43.uk.uudial.com - - [01/Nov/2000:14:55:46 -0500] "GET /inde
userbk43.uk.uudial.com - - [01/Nov/2000:14:55:48 -0500] "GET /trea
```

Figure 2-1: Automatically generated Web server log files collect a wealth of information on Web site visitors.

If you combine that information with the information that an e-commerce site can collect about a user — including what they like to buy, how they feel about certain products, the topics they're interested in, as well as their name and address — you have a powerful batch of information that many marketers would love to get their hands on. A responsible e-commerce company needs to inform its users of how this information will be used, and whether it will be sold.

Privacy statements

It's standard to include a privacy statement on every Web site. Privacy statements describe, in detail, how information is gathered and whether this information is ever transferred to third parties (and if so, how). Some key sections every privacy statement should include are:

✦ **Information gathering.** Describe how, technically, information about users is gathered at your site. Explain which information is required to create an account, and which is optional. List what information is linked to a specific user, and what information is gathered in aggregate.

✦ **Use of information.** Describe what purpose the information gathered serves in a user's interaction with your site. If the information is used to enhance a user's experience with personalized selections, or to send occasional e-mails on products that might be of interest, describe that here.

✦ **Transfer of information.** If your company ever sells or transfers this information to a third party, or ever intends to, be up front about that in this section. Describe what information is transferred and how.

It's better to be honest about the use of customer information than to try to conceal your practices. For example, Amazon.com recently got some flak from users because of a change in their privacy policy. The section added to the document was:

> "As we continue to develop our business, we might sell or buy stores or assets. In such transactions, customer information generally is one of the transferred business assets. Also, in the unlikely event that Amazon.com, Inc., or substantially all of its assets are acquired, customer information will of course be one of the transferred assets."

Although this received some media attention and caused some users to sit up and take notice, in the long run, this honesty should help rather than hinder the development of trust between Amazon and its customers. It's definitely better to let customers know beforehand if there is a possibility of their information being shared with another company. It's certainly better than selling the information without letting them know, and then having the media uncover it.

There are services available online that can automatically generate a privacy policy for your Web site. One of the best is offered by TRUSTe, a non-profit initiative for third-party Web site privacy oversight, and is available at `www.truste.org/wizard`.

Understanding Legal Jurisdiction

Jurisdiction

The Internet connects people and places, as well as commerce, in new ways — previously thought impossible. Because the Web is available anywhere in the world, e-commerce sites are also available anywhere in the world. This means your customers may live anywhere on Earth.

The jurisdiction quandary

This fact has massive implications for determining jurisdiction for any wrongdoing of which your site may be accused. If the products you're selling are illegal in some countries, you may be held responsible if you sell to customers in those countries. This can apply across U.S. state lines, as well.

An excellent example of such a quandary is the case of online gambling. Gambling is illegal in most U.S. states, except on lands owned by Native Americans and sometimes on riverboats. Yet, Web sites that offer gambling are plentiful. Gambling Web sites can and have been accused of illegal activity by allowing residents of states in which it's illegal to gamble to gamble online.

In the case *State of Minnesota v. Granite Gate Resorts*, the state attorney general of Minnesota successfully sued an online sports betting service, Granite Gate Resorts, for taking bets from residents of Minnesota, where gambling is illegal.

Protecting your site from lawsuits

If your site sells services or products that are illegal in some locations, there are some ways to protect yourself from lawsuits:

- **Restrict customers based on location.** If you sell an online service, post a notice on your site clearly telling residents of states or countries in which the service is illegal that they are not allowed to use the service. Make an attempt to exclude these residents. Such actions can help your company in a court of law.
- **Do not allow shipping to certain areas.** If your product needs to be shipped, do not ship it to any state or country where the product is illegal. Make sure that this policy is clearly stated on your Web site, at the beginning of the transaction process.
- **Limit interactivity.** If your site's products or services have a lot of potential jurisdictional problems, limit interactivity. Do not encourage customers to call your company. Some courts have found that when a site encourages out-of-state contact (such as by listing an 800 number), it's liable for illegal purchases made by customers.

Bringing crackers to justice

The global nature of the Web also means that it can be quite difficult to apprehend any crackers who may be guilty of breaking into your site with the intent of sabotaging the site or stealing customer information. For instance, if a user in Indonesia steals customer information, who do you turn to for help—your local police, the FBI? Neither organization has any authority in Indonesia.

Cracker is a term used to identify a user who breaks into sites for malicious purposes. The term was coined by hackers to differentiate themselves from such criminals.

In some high profile cases, U.S. authorities have worked with law enforcement agencies abroad to bring crackers to justice. However, in most cases, there is little that can be done, even if the perpetrator can be traced.

Taxing the Internet

The Web is a global medium and means of transacting commerce. As such, it defies and violates the constraints that are inherent to traditional commerce. In the realm of traditional commerce, it's easy to apply a sales tax based on locality, and levy charges for conducting commerce across borders. For those conducting e-commerce, however, it can be easier to ignore such taxes altogether.

The U.S. Constitution prevents states from taxing transactions beyond their borders. Therefore, states cannot require out-of-state companies to collect sales taxes for them. This means that if a resident of Montana buys a product from a company located in Colorado, no sales tax is paid (none is charged to the customer, and the company pays none). If, however, the company had a presence (such as an office, a warehouse, or a store) in Montana, sales tax would be charged and paid to the state of Montana.

The Internet Tax Freedom Act

As a result of the difficulties in determining the proper way to apply taxes to Web sales, U.S. Congress passed the Internet Tax Freedom Act (ITFA) in 1998. The ITFA imposed a three-year moratorium on new Internet taxes; it expires in October of 2001.

As a part of the ITFA, the Advisory Commission on Electronic Commerce (ACEC) was also established. The ACEC explored the issues related to Internet taxation, and submitted a report to Congress in April of 2000. The report failed to provide any substantial guidance, however, as to how the government should proceed with regard to Internet taxation. As it stands, the ITFA is scheduled to expire and it's unclear if another moratorium will replace it. You can read more about the ACEC at their official Web site, `www.ecommercecommission.org`.

To tax or not to tax?

Taxation of interstate e-commerce remains a very hot issue. Here's how the arguments, pro and con, break down:

- Advocates of a tax-free Internet claim that taxation of Internet transactions will place burdens on e-commerce and lessen its appeal to customers. They believe that prohibiting taxation encourages the growth of e-businesses.

- On the other hand, many state and local officials are concerned that they will lose out on millions of dollars in sales taxes if the Internet remains tax-free. These sales tax dollars are needed to provide local services. If a large amount of commerce shifts to the Internet, they claim, they may not be able to provide services in the future as they have in the past.

International Business Issues

As a part of the Internet Tax Freedom Act, U.S. Congress called upon the world to make the Internet free of foreign tariffs, trade barriers, and other restrictions. It has yet to be seen, however, whether this continues in the years to come.

If your e-commerce company intends to sell products to residents of foreign countries, it's very important for you to familiarize yourself with the legal issues associated with conducting international business over the Web.

Customs

When goods are imported to or exported from a country, customs are imposed. *Customs* are either taxes (commonly called *duties*, *tolls*, or *imposts*) or restrictions placed on items when crossing international borders. For example, an individual is generally not allowed to bring more than a certain dollar amount of alcohol into the U.S. from abroad.

The same rules are applied to corporations that ship products overseas. When the products leave the U.S., export taxes are imposed. When the products reach their destination, import taxes are imposed.

The impact of the Internet

E-commerce is having a major impact on customs regulation in the following two areas:

- E-commerce increases the number of individual transactions, because it's so much easier for an individual to buy goods from a foreign company over the Internet than it is in traditional commerce.
- E-commerce is a method for the international exchange of products and services.

Most customs regulations can easily be overlooked when conducting e-commerce, because products are shipped directly to customers on a one-to-one basis, instead of in large quantities to overseas middlemen. To avoid legal problems, your company should abide by customs laws if you're shipping to overseas addresses.

Meeting the challenges

Types of customs laws are quite varied and unique from country to country. For instance, technical books cannot be imported into Canada without special documentation and payment of extra taxes. The export rule that has had the biggest impact on the development of e-commerce is the U.S. Department of Commerce Bureau of Export Administration (BXA)'s regulation of the export of software containing strong encryption capabilities.

In October 2000, BXA updated its rules to allow easier export of strong encryption technology to the European Union, Australia, the Czech Republic, Hungary, Japan, New Zealand, Norway, Poland, and Switzerland. For the latest information on U.S. export policies, visit the BXA Web site at `www.bxa.doc.gov`.

E-commerce has created an enormous challenge for customs officials, which they have only just begun to contemplate, much less act upon. Customs agencies will need to be able to interact with e-commerce Web sites in order to implement a reliable method of collecting duties. Ideally, duties would be imposed automatically and recorded by both the e-commerce site and the regulating agencies. This is still a very long way from happening, and may become a moot point if the Internet becomes a duty-free zone as the U.S. government suggests.

If you plan to engage in international e-commerce, the following Web sites can help your company navigate the waters of customs regulations:

- **Imex Exchange.** `www.imex.com`
- **Federation of International Trade Associations.** `www.fita.org`
- **World Customs Organization.** `www.wcoomd.org`
- **United States Customs.** `www.customs.ustreas.gov`

Tariffs

Tariffs are the taxes that states and countries charge for goods brought across their borders. They can also be applied by a group of countries that have formed a customs union. Tariffs are usually assessed on imports, rather than exports.

A tariff can be assessed directly or indirectly. They are assessed directly when the goods are brought to the border. They are assessed indirectly by requiring the purchase of a license or permit to import given quantities of the product. The taxed products are usually items that are easily detected, classified, and measured or valued. Many types of services are not subject to tariffs.

Some of the terms and concepts used with tariff calculation are:

- **Harmonized System (HS) numbers.** An international standard for referencing products.

✦ **Most Favored Nation (MFN) treatment.** MFN status is applied to countries that have joined with the U.S. to agree on a common tax amount, adjusted for inflation, for certain products when trading with each other.

Tariffs are quite complex and can be very difficult to determine. For companies engaged in a lot of international sales, the assistance of a service such as Worldtariff (`www.worldtariff.com`) can be extremely helpful in determining tariffs.

Key Point Summary

This chapter explored the legal issues related to conducting e-commerce on the Internet. These issues are many and varied, and many of the answers have yet to be determined. The issues included the following:

✦ Electronic publishing has made duplication of intellectual property easier.

✦ Intellectual property laws protect the rights of individuals and corporations to profit from their creations.

✦ Intellectual property can be divided into two categories:

- Industrial property law, which protects industrial designs, inventions, trademarks, and service marks
- Copyright law, which protects literary, musical, artistic, photographic, and audiovisual works

✦ The areas of liability exposure for electronic publishing are:

- Copyright, trademark, and patent issues
- Privacy and confidentiality issues
- Jurisdiction issues

✦ Trademark law is used to dispute ownership of domain names.

✦ Patent law and copyright law are both used to protect software against unauthorized duplication.

✦ Ease of access to information via the Internet is cause for concern for many Internet users.

✦ Every responsible e-commerce company should include a privacy statement on their Web site. This statement should describe the ways that customer information is gathered, how the information is used, and whether it may be transferred to another company.

- If an e-commerce company sells a product or service that is illegal in another state or country, the company may be liable if they sell it to a resident of that location. Ways to prevent such lawsuits include:
  - Restricting customers by location
  - Prohibiting shipments to that location
  - Limiting site interactivity
- The taxes on e-commerce transactions can be difficult to determine because of the global nature of the Internet.
- The Internet Tax Freedom Act (ITFA) of 1998 imposed a three-year moratorium on new Internet taxes that is scheduled to expire in October 2001.
- The Digital Millennium Copyright Act of 1998 limits the liability exposure of Internet Service Providers (ISPs) in intellectual property infringement lawsuits involving content hosted on their servers.
- E-commerce companies conducting international business need to be sure to comply with all customs and tariffs.

✦ ✦ ✦

STUDY GUIDE

This chapter introduced you to the main areas of legal concern for e-commerce companies. This information can be a lot to swallow, especially all at once. Your goal here, however, is only to have a basic understanding of these concepts. Lawyers specializing in Internet law can help you fill in the particulars if necessary.

So, sit back, relax, and test how much you've absorbed with these assessment questions and exercises.

Assessment Questions

1. Which of the following is the best definition for electronic publishing?

   A. Distributing a software program on a CD-ROM

   B. Publishing a literary work as an electronic file rather than as a book

   C. Using computers to distribute information and data

   D. Downloading music files over the Internet

2. Your publishing company is considering publishing some materials electronically. What is an advantage of electronic publishing over traditional publishing? (Choose the best answer.)

   A. Lower production costs

   B. Improved intellectual property protections

   C. Ability to publish better materials

   D. Easy to make copies as needed

3. Your supervisor has asked you to give a presentation on intellectual property issues and the Internet. What are the two main branches of intellectual property law? (Choose the best answer.)

   A. Trademark law and copyright law

   B. Patent law and trademark law

   C. Copyright law and industrial property law

   D. Invention protection law and copyright law

4. What are the three areas covered by industrial property law? (Choose the best answer.)

   A. Product logos, package shapes, and company catchphrases

   B. Inventions, industrial designs, and trademarks and service marks

   C. Electronic publishing, trademarks, and industrial designs

   D. Trademarks and service marks, copyrighted materials, and music files

5. Your company decides to proceed with the electronic publishing project. Before you begin, the CEO needs to know to which liabilities this project might expose your company. What are the three areas of liability in electronic publishing? (Choose the best answer.)

   A. Unauthorized downloads, cracker attacks, and interstate commerce

   B. Trading of files, software duplication, and hosting Web sites

   C. Jurisdiction issues, privacy and confidentiality issues, as well as copyright, trademark, and patent issues

   D. Copyright, trademark, and patent issues

6. Hazel is dedicated to fostering trust between the company and its customers. She wants to make sure that customers' privacy is not violated. What are the two areas of privacy protection she should be concerned about? (Choose the best answer.)

   A. Access to personal information and misuse of information

   B. Intellectual property infringement and privacy statements

   C. Confidentiality and trust issues

   D. Areas of liability and security issues

7. You're drafting the privacy statement for a new e-commerce site. What three pieces of information should you be sure to include? (Choose the best answer.)

   A. Access to public information, security measures, and encryption techniques

   B. Transfer of information, information gathering, and use of information

   C. How information is gathered, stored, and protected

   D. Possible data sharing, partner Web sites, and data types gathered

8. If a copyrighted digital image is downloaded from a Web site message board, which of the following parties may be held liable? (Choose the best answer.)

   A. The user who downloaded the image

   B. The owners of the Web site

   C. The person who posted the image on the message board

   D. All of the above

9. Which law limits the liability of an ISP in an intellectual property lawsuit involving the content of a hosted site?

  A. Digital Millennium Copyright Act

  B. Internet Tax Freedom Act

  C. Electronic Publishing Copyright Act

  D. Electronic Commerce Act

10. What is the primary reason that jurisdictional issues are unclear for e-commerce transactions?

  A. Online gambling

  B. Outdated laws

  C. Crackers living overseas

  D. The global nature of the Internet

Scenarios

1. You're building a subscription-based online service for information on hog farming. The staff suggests the following ways of collecting information for the site:

  a. A page of links to hog farming information on the Web

  b. A page of pictures of hog farming techniques found on the Internet

  c. Text copied from a government report

  d. Text copied from a competitor's Web site

  e. Text copied from a magazine that you bought

Which of the previous options might expose your company to a copyright infringement lawsuit? Would the same concerns apply if the site weren't subscription-based, but instead were supported by advertising revenue?

Lab Exercises

Lab 2-1 Creating a privacy statement

In this exercise, you'll build a privacy statement for either your company or a fictitious company using TRUSTe's online privacy statement wizard. For each step, answer appropriately if you're creating a privacy statement for a real site. Otherwise, use our suggested answers.

1. Go to `www.truste.org/wizard` in your Web browser.
2. This is the first page of TRUSTe's privacy statement wizard. Read the introductory paragraph, and then enter the requested information into the form. Enter the following information into the appropriate fields if you're using our example:
   - Company name: SuperBig Bikes
   - Web site name: SuperBigBikes.com
   - Web site administrator: Sheila Jones
   - Mailing address: 555 Main Street, Anytown, MA
   - Phone number: (555) 555-8558
   - E-mail address: *leave blank*
3. Click the Continue button.
4. The next page of the form begins with a matrix covering information gathered at a Web site. Enter the following information:
   - In the row labeled Registration, check the box in the Contact Information column.
   - In the row labeled Order Forms, check the boxes in the Contact Information and Financial Information columns.
   - In the row labeled Surveys, check the box in the Demographic Information column.
   - In the row labeled Contests, check the boxes in the Contact Information and Demographic information columns.
5. The matrix is followed by five questions. Review these questions. Enter the following answers in this order: Yes, Yes, No, Yes, No.
6. The next section asks if your site uses public forums (chat, message boards, etc.). Answer Yes.
7. The next question asks if your site has security measures in place to protect customer information. Answer Yes.
8. The next question asks if your site is using information from a third party to supplement the information provided by users. Answer No.

9. The next two questions ask whether your site is targeted to children under 13 and whether the birth date of children is asked on your site. Answer No to both questions.

10. Click the Continue button.

11. The next page asks questions based on the answers given on the previous page. Read through each question, and select the answer(s) you think would be applicable to most e-commerce Web sites.

12. When you're finished with these questions, click the Continue button.

13. The next page displays your privacy statement. Read it through and answer the following questions:

    a. What do you think of this document? Is it understandable? Do you think that the average user would find it clear?

    b. Do you think that all major areas of concern are addressed? Are there components that you might add to the document?

    c. What are the benefits of such a privacy statement? Do you think that this document maximizes these benefits?

Lab 2-2 Examining legal issues of e-commerce sites

In this exercise, you'll take a look at some example e-commerce sites and consider what legal issues could affect them.

1. Using your Web browser, visit Barnes and Noble at `www.bn.com`.

2. Take a look through the Web site, thinking about what they are selling and to whom.

3. Answer the following questions:

    a. Is the Barnes and Noble Web site electronic publishing? Why or why not?

    b. Should Barnes and Noble be worried about copyright issues? Trademark issues? Patent issues? Privacy and confidentiality issues? Jurisdictional issues?

    c. If you answered Yes to any of the questions in b, explain why, and what can be done to limit legal problems for each area.

    d. For any questions in b that you answered No, explain why you think there is no legal risk for that area.

4. Repeat Steps 2 and 3 at `www.homegrocer.com` and `www.travelocity.com`.

Lab 2-3 Examining access to public information

How much public information can be found on the Internet? This exercise will help you find out.

1. Point your browser to `www.switchboard.com`.
2. Enter your name and city of residence in the Find a Person form, and click the Search button.
3. Did your name and address appear? How about your phone number?
4. Repeat this exercise for some other people you know. Was their information found?
5. Answer the following questions:
   a. Do you think it is appropriate to have this information available on a Web site?
   b. What implications do you think this service has on privacy?
6. Repeat this exercise on several other public information Web sites, such as `www.bigfoot.com`, `http://people.yahoo.com`, and `www.whitepages.com`.

Answers to Chapter Questions

Chapter pre-test

1. Intellectual property encompasses all original works of art and authorship, whether belonging to an individual or a corporation.
2. A service mark is a mark or device used to identify a service offered to customers.
3. Software can be protected by both copyrights and patents. Copyrights are issued for the entire program; patents are issued for individual algorithms and techniques used in the program.
4. Customs and tariffs are taxes assessed on imports and exports when crossing international borders.
5. The Internet Tax Freedom Act of 1998 established a three-year moratorium on new Internet taxes and created the Advisory Commission on Electronic Commerce (ACEC).
6. Issues surrounding taxation on the Internet include:
   - Increased volume of interstate and international shipments
   - Local sales taxes lost to interstate e-commerce
   - Challenges of levying tariffs on international e-commerce transactions
   - Lack of a clear mechanism for calculating taxes on e-commerce transactions

7. Domain name disputes can be tried in various courts, but the main international body for resolving these issues is the Domain Name Dispute Resolution Service of the World Intellectual Property Organization.

8. A Web site that allows user postings should require them to agree to a Terms of Use statement to protect the owners of the Web site from possible copyright infringement lawsuits resulting from the distribution of these postings.

Assessment questions

1. **C.** Although B and D are *examples* of electronic publishing, using computers to distribute information and data is the best and most complete *definition* of electronic publishing (see "Electronic publishing").

2. **A.** Electronic publishing has lower production costs than traditional publishing. C is incorrect because the quality of the published work is not affected. B is incorrect because electronic publishing actually makes intellectual property harder to protect (see "Electronic publishing").

3. **C.** Copyright law and industrial property law are the two branches of intellectual property law (see "Intellectual property").

4. **B.** Inventions, industrial designs, and trademarks and service marks are covered by industrial property law (see "Industrial property").

5. **C.** The three areas of liability in electronic publishing are jurisdictional issues, privacy and confidentiality issues, and copyright, trademark, and patent issues (see "Liability exposures").

6. **A.** The two key areas of privacy protection are access to personal information and misuse of information (see "Confidentiality and Privacy Matters").

7. **B.** The three main components of a privacy statement are information gathering, use of information, and transfer of information (see "Privacy statements").

8. **D.** All parties could be liable (see "Liability exposures").

9. **A.** The Digital Millennium Copyright Act of 1998 limits ISP liability in intellectual property cases (see "Publishing defamatory information").

10. **D.** Although the other answers are aspects of the jurisdictional muddle on the Internet, the key reason for that muddle is the global nature of the Internet (see "Understanding Legal Jurisdiction").

Scenarios

1. There are many concerns here. Let's go through them one by one:

   a. A page of links to hog farming information found on the Web sounds innocent enough, except that the subscription-based nature of your site means you're charging customers for the service. It's possible that the author of the information you've linked to would accuse your company of copyright infringement, because you're profiting from their copyrighted work. If the site were supported by advertising revenue alone, the chances of this happening would be considerably less.

   b. A page of pictures of hog farming that were found on the Internet is more clearly a case of copyright infringement. After all, you're using others' material and presenting it as your own. Being supported by advertising revenue alone would likely not help in this case. One way to solve the problem is to purchase rights to use the photos from their rightful owners.

   c. Text copied from a government report would be fairly risk-free, because the text is made available to the public for the good of the society. You would probably want to cite the source, however.

   d. Using text copied from a competitor's Web site is a big no-no. Your company will be setting itself up for a serious legal battle if it uses this material.

An alternative way to use the content could be to establish a relationship with the competitor's site. Perhaps your site could pay them a fee for each user who accesses the competitor's information. Also, your company could pay a monthly fee for using the content.

   e. Using text copied from a magazine you bought is another huge mistake. Just because you bought the magazine does not mean the content is yours to use. Once again, you could purchase rights to use the content from whoever holds the copyright, either the magazine or the author.

The best way of setting up this Web site is to hire experts to write information and reports on hog farming. Photographers could also be hired to provide photos. With this method, you would be certain you were not at risk of committing copyright infringement. Also, your site would be more valuable to users because it would be providing original content.

For More Information . . .

✦ **The Electronic Frontier Foundation.** `www.eff.org`. Covers current topics in Internet law and privacy.

✦ **The Internet Law and Policy Forum.** `www.ilpf.org`. An organization dedicated to "promoting global growth of e-commerce by contributing to a better understanding of the particular legal issues which arise from the cross-border nature of the electronic medium."

- **The Internet Law Journal.** www.tilj.com. Articles on Internet law issues.
- **Bitlaw.** www.bitlaw.com. Resource for technology law.
- **The World Intellectual Property Organization's Domain Name Dispute Resolution Service.** http://arbiter.wipo.int/domains/. The official Web site for the agency that decides many of today's domain name disputes.
- **TRUSTe.** www.truste.org. Non-profit initiative for third-party Web site privacy oversight. Web site includes information on privacy and tools for protecting customer information.
- **Electronic Commerce and Law Report.** http://web.bna.com/eplr.htm. Subscription-based Web site for e-commerce law information.
- **UCLA Online Institute for Cyberspace Law and Policy.** www.gseis.ucla.edu/iclp/hp.html. Provides articles on Internet law and case-by-case examinations of groundbreaking decisions.

CHAPTER 3

Marketing to the Web

EXAM OBJECTIVES

- ✦ Successful storefronts
- ✦ Web marketing vs. traditional marketing
- ✦ The goals that drive Web marketing
- ✦ New marketing possibilities in e-commerce
- ✦ Pricing your product
- ✦ Managing market niche
- ✦ Product delivery

✦ ✦ ✦ ✦

CHAPTER PRE-TEST

1. What interactive marketing capabilities are enabled by e-commerce?
2. What steps should be taken to attract a global audience?
3. What is the difference between hard goods and soft goods?
4. What are some of the issues associated with selling hard goods online?
5. What are some of the positive aspects of Web marketing compared to traditional marketing?
6. What are some of the negative aspects?

✦ Answers to these questions can be found at the end of the chapter. ✦

The advent of e-commerce on the Internet has opened new doors and created new challenges for businesses. It has done the same for marketing professionals — creating new capabilities, such as instant purchasing, enhanced product information, interactive features, and easier ways to gather information about your customers. With these new capabilities come new risks and responsibilities, however. Responsible e-commerce marketers need to use the data they have wisely, and not cross the boundaries of customer privacy.

Web marketing can generate a new level of loyalty among your customers. Community features can keep customers interested in your site, so they come back for more. If you treat your customers well, your efforts will likely be rewarded.

Understanding Web Marketing

Web marketing vs. traditional marketing

E-commerce offers marketing capabilities that weren't possible with traditional commerce. The following sections cover some of the marketing innovations made possible by e-commerce.

Immediate response

Web advertising offers the possibility of immediate customer response. The reaction of a prospective customer to your advertisement can be acted upon immediately. For example, if a prospective customer is browsing a site on which your company has an advertisement running, the customer can respond to the advertisement by clicking on it and be taken immediately to your online store. This action gets the customer "in the door," so to speak. Half of the battle for the customer's business has already been won.

By comparison, a billboard or television advertisement does not offer the possibility of an immediate response. A prospective customer may see the advertisement and be interested in learning more about your product, but before the customer has the chance to come to your store or visit your Web site, he or she may have forgotten about the advertisement and your products, all together.

Personal selection

Web advertising results in higher quality prospective customers because any customer who visits your site as a result of clicking on a Web advertisement or link has already expressed interest in your product. Another Web user might glance over your ad and not take notice at all. The advantage to the marketer is that if the user clicks the advertisement and visits your site, he or she can be considered a qualified prospect.

Interactivity

Once the prospective customer has arrived at your site, there are many options for interactive marketing. This is where Web marketing really shines. The following sections explore these options.

Product support

The possibilities for conveying information on the Web are much greater than they are in a 30-second radio or TV spot. The vast array of information on your company and its products that can be conveyed via a Web site is not only useful to customers who've already made a purchase, but also to prospective customers who may be researching an upcoming purchase. In the following sections, you take a closer look at the product support information that can, and should, be made available to visitors of any e-commerce site.

Product details

For all tangible products, your site should include information on the physical dimensions of the product, compatibility with other products, technical specifications, materials included, as well as a written product description.

Information on intangible products, such as software, should include all hardware requirements for running the software, compatibility with other software and operating systems, download size (if downloadable), new version features, and prerequisites for upgrades.

A quick visit to the Best Buy site at `www.bestbuy.com` shows how detailed product descriptions can get.

Upgrades and downloads

For some products, especially software, it's appropriate to offer upgrades and patches (software bug fixes) to customers who have purchased the software from your site. Buyers of a specific software title, for example, Software 2001, can be given access to a special area of your site specific to that software. This area can then provide these customers with current information on Software 2001, such as a list of recent patches and upgrades, and options to purchase (if applicable) and download these items. A message board area could even be offered for users to swap advice and opinions on Software 2001. An exclusive, tailored area gives past customers a reason to return to your site.

Troubleshooting

Many sites skimp on their troubleshooting areas, so developing a useful area for customers experiencing problems with your products is a good way to help your site stand out from the competition. Make sure that your site offers substantive suggestions for customers, and don't limit this area just to basic usability questions.

If your site sells hundreds or even thousands of products from a wide variety of manufacturers, building a comprehensive troubleshooting area could be a daunting task. One way to address this problem would be to create a database of links to troubleshooting information on the manufacturers' Web sites or to a third-party site that has such information. Then, customers could either navigate or search their way to the appropriate links for the product with which they're having trouble.

Customers who know they can return to your site to find information when they're having problems with a product are more likely to feel that your site is trustworthy, and, therefore, are more likely to buy from your company again.

Frequently asked questions

A frequently asked questions (FAQ) section is an important part of all e-commerce sites. Many Internet shoppers, and especially novices, need instructions on how to use your site as well as information on your company's business practices. Include everything from the most mundane details on your site's navigation design and searching functionality to the details of your return policy. Some items that should be included in any e-commerce Web site FAQ section are:

- A guide to the site's categorization scheme
- How to find a specific product
- Using the shopping cart functionality
- How to redeem a gift certificate
- Shipping rates
- Estimated delivery time
- Return policy
- How to edit information in the customer's account (name, address, credit card number, etc.)
- How to change or cancel an order

Online communities

Web sites offer the opportunity to create a community centered around your service or product that you can then monitor directly to assess market trends. Message boards and chat areas can be visited by your staff to find out what your customers think about your product and what other products and activities interest them.

The following sections give you a closer look at some common and innovative ways to build communities on e-commerce Web sites.

Customer reviews

Many e-commerce sites allow users to express their opinion of a particular product by rating and reviewing the product. These reviews are usually then read by Web site staff before being made available on site. Reviews are generally displayed via a link from the product detail page, or on the product detail page itself.

This is particularly widespread on book and music retailer sites, but is also used on sites selling other kinds of products. Many customers love to post their opinions, and other shoppers find the reviews helpful when making purchasing decisions, especially because they are viewed as relatively unbiased.

Check out www.amazon.com for a good example of the use of customer reviews.

Message boards

Another method for building a Web community is to use message boards, which are areas of the site where users post questions and responses to the questions of others. These are typically implemented with message board software installed on the Web server computer. For very specific needs, message boards can also be custom programmed.

Not every kind of online store can have a successful message board area, so keep your audience in mind. With the right audience, message boards can take on a life of their own. For example, PETsMART online, at www.petsmart.com, has a very active message-board community—after all, just about everybody loves to talk about their pets.

Allow users to log in to your message board as a guest. You're more likely to have an active message board if registration is not a prerequisite to using it.

Chat areas

Chat areas are similar to message boards. A chat area is a forum for users to exchange information with each another. In contrast to message boards, however, chat areas operate on real time, which means users can only hold conversations with one another when they are logged on at the same time. The benefit of this is that the conversation can proceed much more quickly than on a message board.

Chances are you won't need a custom-built chat area. Chat software components are readily available for implementation on your site.

Should you use a message board or a chat to allow customers to converse with one another? Well, why not both? Each has its strengths. Message boards offer the ability for lengthy, documented conversations on specific topics that take place over months or even years. Chats offer the advantage of immediacy, but lack the history of message boards. If budget dictates picking one option, go with the message board. The more formal nature of message boards encourages more substantive conversations than chat areas do.

Personal pages

Some e-commerce sites allow customers to create a customized Web page on their site. After a customer has written a review at Amazon.com, for example, a profile page is created about the customer, which lists his or her product reviews and other information. The customer then has the option of editing the information on this page. This practice is relatively new and not yet in common use.

E-mail newsletters

Opt-in e-mail newsletters and notification services help customers use your site more effectively. There are two main kinds of e-mail newsletters prevalent in e-commerce today: special offer notification and topic-centered news.

Special offer notification

Customers can request to be notified of discounts, special offers, and store-wide sales via e-mail. Include the option to receive such e-mails both during the transaction process and throughout the site.

If you give the customer the option to subscribe to an e-mail newsletter during the checkout process, make the default option on the form "no." That way, customers won't get unexpected e-mails from your company just because they failed to notice that question on the checkout form.

Topic-centered news

Shoppers who are interested in specific topics, for example, science fiction, jazz, or high-end stereo equipment, can sign up to receive periodic information on new releases, discounts, and highlighted products in that area of your site. Such newsletters can even include news items or interviews with influential figures in that topic or genre. Offer the opportunity to sign up for topic-centered e-mail newsletters in each section, or category, or your site.

E-mail newsletters are not the same thing as direct e-mail, or bulk e-mail. See Chapter 4 for information on responsible bulk e-mailing.

Personalization

Personalization techniques can be used to target individuals. By storing a *cookie* on a customer's computer, your server knows when that user has returned, and displays information specific to that user's needs. The user can choose some of the information shown, and some of the other information can be determined by your personalization software, based on the customer's past purchasing decisions and other information the customer may have submitted in surveys and questionnaires.

A frequent shopper at Amazon.com, for example, Margaret, is automatically presented with product suggestions based on past purchases when she logs into the site. However, if Margaret accesses Amazon.com from another computer, for example, John's computer, her recommendations won't be displayed until she logs into Amazon.com. In addition, if, for example, Mary uses Margaret's computer, she will be presented with Margaret's personalized recommendations (unless Margaret logged out of Amazon.com before she left).

Personalization is not the same as a personal page, one of the community-building techniques mentioned previously. Personalization is the technique of showing a customer information based on his or her past purchases or other information. A personal page is a special area of a Web site that shows information on a customer, generally someone who has posted reviews of products.

Online purchasing

The Web offers the capability for immediate purchase, which is an extremely powerful tool for converting a browsing customer into a buying customer. On each and every page of the site, it should be very clear to the user how to add a product to their shopping cart. This is true not only on the product detail pages, but also on category pages that feature lists of products, and even on the home page. Every highlighted product, every listed product — indeed, every product on every page — should have a link or button next to it reading something similar to "Add to Shopping Cart."

After a customer has set up an account, many e-commerce sites automatically offer an ordering option that enables the user to click one button on a product detail page to buy the product immediately, bypassing the usual checkout method. The customer's credit card is automatically charged and the product is shipped to the customer's default shipping address.

Amazon.com holds a patent on *one-click* ordering and has shown that they are willing to sue other online retailers to protect this patent. Being aware of possible patents on e-commerce techniques and technologies and making sure that you're on the right side of the law (no matter how controversial the patents may be) can save your company from potential legal nightmares.

Worldwide presence

No other medium has the capability of globally spreading your message like the Web. Marketing on television, radio, and in print publications is restricted by broadcast range and circulation. To achieve worldwide coverage using such traditional media, you would need the services of many advertising agencies and a very large marketing budget.

Your Web site and your online advertisements and sponsorships can be seen on any computer on the Internet. Web marketing allows your company to spread its message worldwide with much less effort and a much smaller budget.

Evaluating Market Potential

Despite all the press coverage that e-commerce receives, and despite the fortunes that have been made on the Internet, e-commerce is a risky undertaking. In fact, the vast majority of people who start e-commerce Web sites and plan to have an IPO and become fabulously wealthy end up seriously disappointed.

Although there's no e-commerce crystal ball, there are ways to evaluate the potential of an e-commerce venture and increase the chances of its success. Before you invest your time or money in building an e-commerce business, you would do well to consider the following guidelines.

✦ Creating a market for a new product or service is much more difficult than filling a need that already exists. If you're a fan of *The Partridge Family* and want to start a site to sell Partridge Family memorabilia, you should first make sure that there's an unmet demand for your goods before you quit your day job.

✦ Just as in the real world, starting a Web business has risks. Creating a new market for your existing company, on the other hand, is much less risky.

✦ Just putting up a Web site is not going to guarantee customers. Not only do you need to make sure you're listed in search engines, but you also need to advertise — both on the Web and in traditional media.

✦ An e-commerce Web site that sells products or services that are widely available in physical stores is only likely to succeed if making the purchase on the Web provides a significant benefit over traditional ways of accomplishing the same task. The purchase and printing of postage stamps over the Internet, for example, has not succeeded because buying stamps in the real world is easy, doesn't require any hardware or software, and the price is the same everywhere.

Definite Goals Drive Marketing

The most important step in determining your marketing strategy is defining the goals of your company. What is the purpose of your online presence? Are you bringing your established product to new audiences? Or, are you planning to use the Web to streamline customer service or business processes? Knowing the answers to these questions will help you define the key elements of your marketing strategy.

Developing new markets

New marketing possibilities in e-commerce

E-commerce on the Internet allows a company to expand its market base geographically without incurring the expense or risk associated with opening a new store in an untested area. An e-commerce site is typically less expensive to start than a physical store, and it establishes your market base in the realm of all Internet users. As the number of Internet users continues to grow, so does your market base — without an additional rollout effort on your part.

The number of Internet users in Europe is currently growing more quickly than in North America. Other parts of the world are also rapidly getting online. For example, in mid 2000, there were approximately 1.9 million users in the Middle East, and that number is expected to double every year. In addition, the population of Web users in Latin America is predicted to grow to as much as 38 million by 2004 (statistics from CommerceNet, at `www.commerce.net`).

Before Internet commerce, taking a business international was a daunting task, even for large companies. Establishing contacts and distribution networks overseas can be very difficult, and there are many legal and financial considerations. The Internet does not eliminate these issues, but it can make the challenge a bit more surmountable.

By establishing an Internet presence, your company has already made product information available worldwide, because of the global nature of the Web. In order to target the international audience and win their business, a few key measures should be taken, such as:

✦ Eliminating lingo

✦ Developing separate sites for targeted regions

✦ Complying with international commerce requirements

We discuss each of these in more detail in the following sections.

Eliminating lingo

Many people around the world speak English as a second language, and fairly well. Very few of them understand American lingo and colloquialisms, however. Even native English speakers from outside the U.S. sometimes have difficulty understanding tongue-in-cheek marketing catchphrases or humorous ad campaigns. If the international audience is important to your business, keep your message straightforward and factual.

Developing separate sites for targeted regions

If there are several specific countries or regions you'd like to target, consider developing separate Web sites for each of them. Establishing a second site altogether allows you to use the language and style of the target audience, creating a higher probability of success in winning their business.

There are several options when determining the URL of these sites and their relationship to your main Web site. Regional Web sites can be sub-sites of your main URL, for example `www.yourcompany.com/deutschland` or `deutschland.yourcompany.com`. You can also purchase a separate URL, such as `www.yourcompany-deutschland.com`, or use the target country's top-level domain, such as `www.yourcompany.de`. Figure 3-1 shows the IDG Swedish site.

A list of international top-level domains can be found at DomainGuideBook.com's International Domain page at `www.domainguidebook.com/international/`.

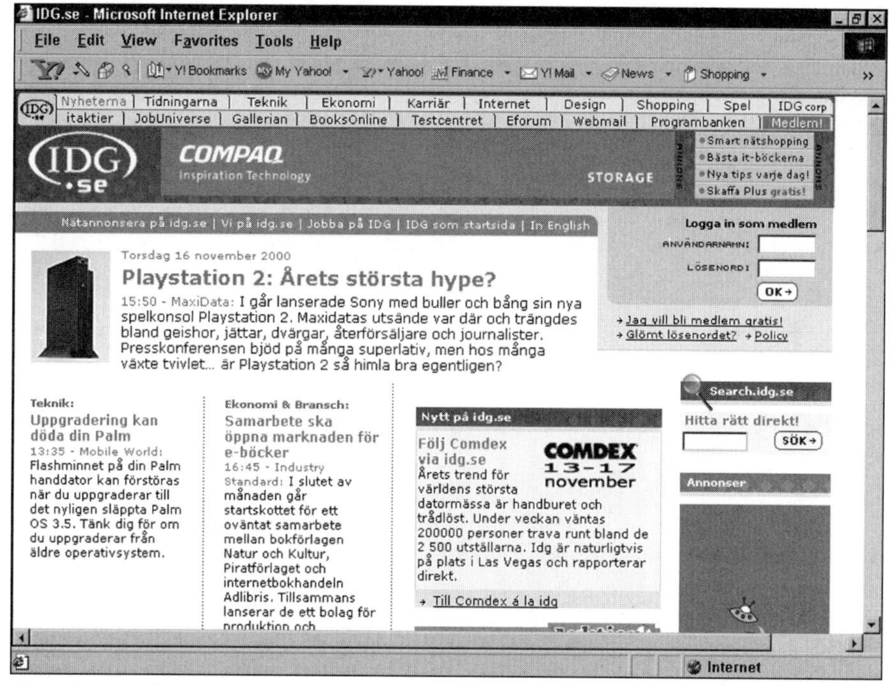

Figure 3-1: Creating a regional site, as shown on IDG's Swedish site

Complying with international commerce requirements

There are many legal issues associated with selling overseas. Make sure to devote staff to ensuring compliance.

For more information on the legal ramifications of doing business on the Internet, see Chapter 2.

Improving customer interaction

For many businesses, an e-commerce site is not primarily a way of generating new business, but rather a way of facilitating an established business process. This facilitation typically provides cost savings to the company, and it also gives customers a new way to interact with the company. Increased business volume is often a welcome by-product of such efforts to improve customer interaction through the Web.

For example, UPS and Federal Express offer automated package tracking information, drop box lookup, and pickup scheduling online. Prior to the Web, these functions were handled only by phone, which required a phone representative to enter the pertinent information into a computerized system. Now, customers can access the system directly via the Web.

Selling new products

In traditional commerce, it can be very difficult to introduce a new product to the market. Generating demand and product awareness through traditional channels is quite expensive, and probably not worth the investment for a product whose appeal won't be widespread.

The Web can give such niche products a chance, however, because Web marketing is much less expensive. Web marketing campaigns, therefore, involve less risk than traditional campaigns. An established company can offer a new product, promote it on their site alongside established products, and find the product's market niche. Many of these products would not be made if it weren't for Web marketing possibilities.

Computerizing business processes

The more your business processes are automated, the more efficient your business becomes. Ever-increasing efficiency is necessary for customer satisfaction and to stay competitive. Automation also enables information exchange with other automated systems, such as online partners, affiliates, and payment processing services.

One novel use of automation on the Web is in choosing custom features for a product. Sales people, either in person or on the phone, traditionally facilitate such choices. Some companies may never embrace this technique—jewelers, for example, might argue that it's highly unlikely that a couple would choose an engagement ring on the Web. For other products, such as computers, automated online features selection can be the perfect tool to streamline the process.

Strategies for Marketing Online

After your marketing goals have been defined, it's time to implement your marketing strategies. Focus on the areas discussed in the following sections when outlining your strategies.

Web site design

A key element in turning a visitor into a buyer is effective Web site design. Design not only refers to the color scheme and images, but also to the way in which information is presented on the page. A visitor to your site must be able to easily determine how to perform whatever function is their goal—whether it be searching for a product, finding contact information, or determining standard shipping charges.

The best way to ensure that customers can find what they're looking for is to provide as many ways as possible to reach the information. Therefore, you should include a navigation bar, searching capabilities, a site map, an FAQ section, and a home page with prominent links to the main sections of your site.

See Chapter 5 for more information on effective Web site design.

Online promotion

Online promotion is a delicate art that is still being perfected. Some Internet pundits have declared banner advertising to be ineffective and unsuccessful; however, banner advertising is still selling quite well. Other experts claim that although banner ads may not be clicked on very often, they do increase public awareness of products and services. Clearly, the jury is still out on this topic.

Promotion options other than banner advertising include sponsorship of a section of a site and cross-marketing agreements with other Web sites. Research has shown that some kinds of online advertisements are more effective than others. How online promotion is approached is largely determined by your company's marketing goals.

See Chapter 4 for an in-depth discussion of online promotion techniques.

Targeted marketing

Targeted marketing is the practice of determining where and by whom your online promotions are seen. After you've determined your target audience, you can decide where to promote your site. For example, a CD retailer would want to advertise on radio stations and in major music magazines.

Your target audience can be further segmented for specific marketing campaigns. For example, the same CD retailer could run a banner ad campaign promoting its Top 40 selection on a site catering to a teenage audience, and then target an entirely different audience by sponsoring a section of a classical music appreciation Web site.

Marketing on portal sites

Portal sites are Web sites intended as entry-points to the Web, or at least as central locations with links to many Web sites. Examples of portals are Yahoo! (`www.yahoo.com`) and Excite (`www.excite.com`). Both sites feature Web search engines and Web directories, as well as shopping areas with links to many e-commerce sites.

These shopping areas highlight stores and particular products. When shoppers search for a specific kind of product, they are shown a list of matching products available from a variety of vendors. When a product is chosen, the user is taken to the vendor's site to purchase it or to continue shopping.

The goal of a portal site is to deliver shorter marketing messages from a wide variety of companies.

Search engine placement

Despite the efforts marketing teams put into their advertising campaigns, many users ignore Web advertising altogether. Such people generally prefer to find online retailers through search engines. One of your marketing team's ongoing goals should be to make your site one of the top 10 to 15 search results for appropriate queries on popular search engines. Although there's no way to ensure such placement, certain practices can increase your chances of a high placement.

See Chapter 4 for more information on search engine promotion practices.

Understanding Growth

The goals that drive Web marketing

Just as in traditional commerce, there are numerous factors affecting growth in e-commerce. Many of these are unique to the Internet environment. To understand the forces at work in your e-commerce venture, you should be familiar with *growth drivers* and *growth barriers*.

Knowing the factors that help e-commerce and the factors that hinder e-commerce is important for the exam.

Growth drivers

Growth drivers are the positive aspects of conducting e-commerce on the Internet. Each driver increases profit potential and marketing options. The growth drivers are as follows:

- ✦ **Access.** The Web community is vast and grows every day. There are more potential customers on the Internet than any physical store could hope to have. As the number of Web users grows, the number of potential customers grows with it — which increases your market daily.
- ✦ **Constant availability.** The Web is open 24 hours a day, 7 days a week. As long as you keep your server up and running, your online store never closes. No matter what time your customers like to shop, your site is always there to serve them.
- ✦ **Electronic data interchange.** Allows e-commerce businesses to exchange data with shipping vendors, product suppliers, and other online partners automatically. This exchange allows for an unprecedented level of cooperation between e-commerce businesses, such as affiliate relationships and advertising partnerships.

- **Increasing bandwidth.** The increasing availability of high-speed Internet connections will allow more media-rich functions in the coming months and years. This will help alleviate one of the current problems in e-commerce: The fact that most users do not have the patience for media-rich interfaces. After the bandwidth hurdle has been jumped, Web marketing will start to be as visually compelling as most television advertisements.
- **Enabling technology.** There's a wide range of technologies available to automate the process of getting a business online. There are automated online storefront solutions on the low end, and software components on the high end. These technologies help keep the cost of developing an e-commerce site down by minimizing custom programming. For this reason, more businesses — and a greater variety of businesses — are able to enter e-commerce.
- **Cost.** The cost of entering the e-commerce marketplace varies widely. The options available to your company depend upon the goals of the site and the funds available for software and hardware purchases, as well as development. If necessary, the cost can be kept to little or nothing, allowing very small vendors onto the playing field.
- **Ease of access.** The Internet provides an easy way for shoppers to shop for your products — easier than in a physical store. Weather problems, time constraints, and lack of proximity are no longer deterrents for a potential buyer. Of course, this ease of access only applies to Internet users.
- **Critical mass.** The number of Internet users is growing rapidly every day. According to the CommerceNet 1999 U.S./Canada Internet Demographic Study, there were 92 million users in the U.S. and Canada alone in April 1999. There are enough users now to provide an excellent market base.
- **Physical locations.** Opening a new, physical store is full of weighty decisions with many potential pitfalls, such as choosing the proper location, rental pricing, buying fixtures and display areas, buying cash registers, choosing appropriate hours of business, and many more. The expense and risk of setting up a physical store is no longer necessary for selling products.
- **Diversification of offerings.** A physical store offers a finite area in which to display your products. You may be able to offer more products online than in a physical store, because there's no shelf space limit.
- **Centralization.** Geographical dispersion is not necessary with online stores but it is necessary with a network of physical stores. You can keep all your products and staff in one location if you like with an online store. Location is no longer centered around customers, but rather where you can find the best real estate price and the best pool of employees.
- **Information intensive.** Businesses are able to provide a wealth of product information online. This is especially useful when marketing products that require pre-purchase research. The product information at BestBuy.com, for example, fills three or more screens for each product. Such depth of information is generally unavailable in physical store displays or from the salespeople who work there.

Growth barriers

Growth barriers are unique challenges to marketing in the e-commerce industry. Familiarity with these barriers can keep your business from being blindsided by them, and increase your potential for success. The barriers to growth in e-commerce are:

- **Fragmented data and data formats.** Data can be exchanged with online partners, but only if the data is in the same format. The lack of data standardization can cause serious problems if a business is not prepared. Be sure to consult your partners well in advance before you launch any new functionality dependent upon data exchange. In addition, do a lot of testing and have knowledgeable developers on hand to smooth out any rough patches.
- **Large segmentation.** The Internet audience is larger and more diverse than the audience for any one conventional marketing campaign. Your Web marketing campaign has the potential to reach many more people than a radio ad in San Francisco or a television spot in Austin. Defining a target market is thereby made more difficult.
- **Rapid change.** Because it's a very new medium, Internet standards and the expectations of customers in terms of customer service, site design, and functionality are constantly changing and expanding. Work done today will need to be updated within the year. Be sure to visit your competitors' sites often to see whether they've introduced new functionalities. You need to keep up with or surpass them to ensure customer loyalty.
- **Increased competition.** The ease of entry into the e-commerce market has created a lot of competition for the attention of the Internet audience. Many sites are selling the same products. It remains to be seen just how much room there is on the Internet for redundancy. Be prepared to make your site stand out.
- **Lack of physical contact.** Many customers dislike being unable to handle a product before purchasing. This is especially true for expensive items. There is no easy way to overcome this, but you can start by offering extensive information on the product and a simple return policy.
- **Lack of support for complex processes.** Products and services that require physical interaction to set up or order are difficult to market online. For example, selling a housecleaning service online would be challenging, because purchasers need to provide your employees with a house key for access to the home to be cleaned and a house key can't be transferred over the Internet.
- **Saturation.** There are currently thousands of e-commerce businesses online, all of which can be accessed by anyone on the Internet. Is there already a business selling what you intend to sell? Developing a unique service or product can be difficult on the Internet, because there may be similar businesses already established. This is a case where the lack of geographic boundaries on the Internet can be a growth barrier.
- **Cost.** Although there are simple and inexpensive ways to get started in e-commerce, if you want to create a world-class Web site to compete with the big players, you'll need to make sizable up-front investments in hardware, software, warehouse space, and high-priced employees.

✦ **Restrictions.** Although, as of mid 2001, e-commerce is fairly free of restrictions, this could change very rapidly in the coming years. Be prepared to stay on top of changing regulatory requirements and to change your business processes to suit them.

✦ **Distribution.** The cost of shipping an item can outweigh the discounts a customer gets by shopping online. Some products sold on the Internet are quite difficult to ship, and shipping always creates a delay in the completion of the transaction — in other words, the customer receiving the product. Shipping large products, such as computer equipment, can also be expensive and take a long time.

Intangible versus Tangible Goods

Whether your site sells *soft (intangible) goods* (items, such as software, that you can't physically touch) or *hard (tangible) goods* (items you can physically touch) is a key aspect of determining your marketing strategy. Each presents its own challenges and possibilities, as discussed in the following sections.

Make sure that you understand the difference between intangible and tangible goods, as well as alternate terms for these, such as hard and soft goods.

Intangible goods

Intangible goods, also called soft goods, are seemingly perfect for Web marketing and sale. As intangible goods, they consist of information or digital data that is easily transmitted via the Internet. Software, music files, electronic books, news, and information are all examples of intangible products. The immediacy of online purchasing is taken to its full potential with intangible goods, because the product is on the buyer's computer within moments of purchasing it.

Music

The primary form of purchasing music today is on a CD from a music retailer. To play the music, you need a CD player and the CD itself; however, this is rapidly changing. The emergence of the MP3 compression format has enabled the swift transfer of music files over the Internet, and has the potential to change the way consumers purchase and acquire music.

Napster, the company that makes free software for trading music files among thousands of Internet users, was founded in May 1999 and immediately began challenging the music companies' distribution model. By late 2000, some music companies had begun to offer downloadable songs on their Web sites for a fee. With increasing numbers of Internet users burning their own CDs, the music distribution business may ultimately embrace the electronic transfer of music.

Software

After software is purchased, it can be transferred directly to the purchaser's computer via a secure download area, eliminating the need to send a CD-ROM to the customer via snail mail. The software is generally available for download only once within a certain time frame. Complications can arise if a download is interrupted in progress. If you offer software for download, make sure customer service is available 24 hours a day to address any download problems. As high-speed Internet connections become more prevalent, this will be less of a problem.

Electronic books

The two primary players in the electronic book market are the RCA eBook, a handheld device, and the MicrosoftReader, which is software for reading books on a Windows-based computer. Electronic books for both devices can be purchased and downloaded on the Internet. The eBook connects to the user's computer and the book files are transferred to it.

Electronic books are slowly gaining a following, but many potential buyers don't see the benefit of the technology yet. Some users find the resolution of the eBook insufficient for reading without eyestrain; others are simply very attached to paper books. It's possible that electronic books, in some handheld format, will eventually replace most paper books. The pace of this change is currently quite slow, however.

News and information

In the case of sites featuring news or advice, the intangible product is usually included on a Web page and is viewed in a Web browser. This product is either available for free or for a subscription fee.

Research reports can also be sold over the Web, usually in the Portable Document Format (PDF), which does not allow editing. These files are transferred via the Internet, just as all soft goods are, and read on the user's computer and printed as needed. One site selling research this way is Jupiter Research (`www.jup.com`).

Video on demand

A cutting-edge business model currently emerging is video on demand. Video on demand is a service that streams video files to the user's computer. These files are usually then played by software such as Real Player or Windows Media Player. *Streaming* means the video starts playing before it's completely downloaded, and then continues to download while it's being played. This service can be free or offered for a fee. To see video on demand in action, visit Ifilm (`www.ifilm.com`) or MovieFlix (`www.movieflix.com`).

Tangible goods

Tangible goods, also called hard goods, present more challenges for online marketing than soft goods. Because of their nature as physical objects, many customers want to examine the products in the real world before purchasing them.

Selling clothes online, for example, has proven quite challenging. Clothes shoppers generally want to try items on before purchasing. For those items where fit isn't an issue, the problem of accurately representing color on computer monitor displays may arise. Color varies from monitor to monitor, making it nearly impossible for online clothes retailers to display colors as they appear in real life.

Shipping charges are another issue with the sale of tangible goods. The delay in receiving shipped items can be a factor in a shopper's decision of whether to buy online. For many potential customers, the costs and delays of shipping outweigh the benefits of convenience and possible cost savings of purchasing online. See the section "Managing Product Delivery," later in this chapter, for ideas on how to address the challenges of shipping.

Pricing Products

Pricing your product

Online sales are the realm of moderately priced products. Very expensive and very cheap products are difficult to market online — expensive items, because shoppers generally want to examine them in person before buying them; and cheap items, because the cost of shipping can exceed the price of the product itself.

Nonetheless, very expensive and very cheap products can be marketed online for later sale in retail stores. BMW (`www.bmw.com`), a seller of expensive products, uses their online presence to provide users with information about options on their cars. Less expensive items, such as jackets and miniature cars, are available for purchase. At the other end of the spectrum, Kentucky Fried Chicken (`www.kfc.com`) offers product information, a store locator, and lighthearted advice features (such as "Create a Perfect Picnic").

Managing Market Niche: Global versus Micro

Managing market niche

Products with a *global market niche*, or mass appeal, are products that are needed or wanted around the world, without geographical constraints, such as computer software and hardware, music, books, and clothing. Products with global market niche are perfect matches for e-commerce. Web stores selling such items are among the most successful today (according to CommerceNet 1999 U.S./Canada Internet Demographic Survey at www.commerce.net).

Niche products are limited in appeal, and are much more difficult to market successfully online. For example, a store that sells paraphernalia for fans of Central Michigan University may enjoy a brisk business locally, but it's hard to imagine a wider demand for such products, especially on a global scale. Establishing an Internet commerce site in this case would probably be a waste of time and money.

On the other hand, some niche markets are constrained by interest rather than geography. A seller of decorative candles, for example, may not necessarily attract a large audience without a very highly targeted marketing campaign. One way to overcome this hurdle would be to use an outsourcing service, such as Amazon's zShops. Such a strategy would help the product find its market niche by taking advantage of the huge audience attracted by the mass appeal products of a site such as Amazon.com.

For more information on Amazon.com's zShops, see Chapter 8.

Managing Product Delivery

Product delivery

When selling online, product delivery becomes a major issue. All tangible products, and sometimes intangible products, need to be shipped. Shipping can be quite expensive, and the price tag can deter would-be buyers from your product, especially if your store has a lot of competition in the form of physical retail stores. Others may be deterred by the delay in fulfillment caused by shipping. There are ways to overcome these disadvantages, however, such as:

✦ **Discounted shipping.** Work out a deal for bulk shipping with UPS and/or Federal Express, and pass these savings on to customers.

✦ **Overnight shipping.** Overnight shipping almost eliminates the delay in online shopping. This can be especially effective for expensive items, such as computer hardware. A buyer is less likely to balk at expensive overnight shipping charges when purchasing an expensive item.

✦ **Special deals and discounts.** To compete with real-world stores, offer frequent specials, such as a free item with a purchase over a certain amount. These promotions keep your customers interested in shopping at your site.

✦ **Product reviews and research.** Offer shoppers a great deal of information on products. If customers come to your site to research their purchase, they are more likely to buy from you.

- **Complimentary return postage.** Cover the postage for any returned items, so customers don't incur additional costs if the product is defective or doesn't meet with their satisfaction. Customers feel more confident about their purchases if they don't have to pay postage for returned items.
- **Geographically dispersed warehouses.** It may be beneficial to operate several warehouses throughout the country to fulfill your orders and cut down on delivery time and cost. If you do substantial overseas business, you may want an overseas warehouse, a factor that may also ease international commerce restrictions.

Understanding Audiences

E-commerce on the Internet offers remarkable potential for collecting information about your potential customers — your *audience*. Information can be gathered about visitors to your Web site by inviting users to take a poll, or fill out a survey for a chance to win a prize. General Internet user data can also be gathered from secondary sources or from sites on which you are considering advertising. In the following sections, you take a closer look at some of the ways and means of gathering valuable audience information.

Log file analysis

Just about every kind of Web server software can keep log files, or records, of visitors to your site. These logs can then be run through log analyzer software, such as WebTrends or Accrue Insight. These products can provide valuable information, such as how long users typically spend at your site, which pages are most frequently visited, how many visitors are using overseas domains, and the most typical paths through your site.

This information can help you plan strategies to make your site more appealing. For example, when you know which pages are most frequently visited, you can emulate their style and content on other pages and advertise new products on them. In addition, if you find you have a large number of foreign visitors, you should tailor at least part of your site to their needs, if you haven't already. If customers don't spend a lot of time at your site, you likely need to work on developing some community areas, or enhancing those you already have.

Polls and surveys

The best way to accumulate data on your customers is to use polls and surveys. A *poll* typically consists of a small box on your site, usually on the home page, with a single question and several answer choices. When a user selects an answer, he or she is either taken to a subsequent page with a chart of results or the results are displayed on the home page itself. With polls, you can ask a wide variety of thought-provoking questions — visitors often respond just to see what others think.

Surveys are lengthier than polls, with typically five to ten questions. Surveys can be integrated into the home page or housed on their own page, with a teaser link on the home page. Survey content is generally a bit dryer than the tone of a one-question poll, which makes it less fun for respondents. Survey information, however, is potentially more useful for your marketing effort. To get visitors interested, it's wise to offer a chance to win a prize in exchange for filling out the survey. If the prize needs to be mailed, you also have a reason to ask for the respondents' addresses.

Community features

Establishing an online community can provide information about the opinions and hobbies of your users. Users are more likely to share their views with each other than with your company. As the sponsor of these community areas, however, you can monitor what your customers are saying to each other.

For example, message boards can be screened by your staff to determine the most popular topics. The subscription levels of e-mail newsletters should also be tracked for popularity. Customer reviews reveal users' feelings about your products. To gain a good understanding of your audience, your staff should regularly spend time observing community areas.

Transaction and inventory data

Transaction and inventory data should be analyzed to understand your customers' shopping habits. Inventory data reveals which products sell consistently and which are slow movers. Transaction data can be analyzed to find out which items are bought together more frequently.

After you start gathering this information, it can be used in your marketing effort in a variety of ways. Knowing what products are often purchased together allows you to provide suggestions to your customers based on what they are buying. Fast-selling items can be featured prominently on your site.

Web user population research

There are many Web sites that provide data on the Web user population. You should make a habit of visiting some of these sites on a regular basis to observe demographic shifts and usage patterns, and consider their implications for your marketing strategy. Some of these sites are:

- **CommerceNet.** `www.commerce.net`
- **Nua Internet Surveys.** `www.nua.ie/surveys/`

✦ **Jupiter Research.** www.jup.com

✦ **CyberAtlas.** http://cyberatlas.internet.com

✦ **eMarketer.** www.emarketer.com

Responsible Web Marketing

Marketing on the Web offers you many possibilities for gaining information about your customers — much more so than traditional marketing. Asking for too much information, however, can be harmful to your business. Customers may feel you're invading their privacy. Is it ethical, or even legal, to sell this information to other companies? Where do you draw the line? The following sections help you develop some guidelines.

Don't ask too much

Don't ask questions you, as a shopper, would feel uncomfortable answering. Using your own feelings as a gauge is not a foolproof method by any means, but it can help you draw the line. If you feel you must ask questions in such sensitive areas as age, education, and level of income, allow the user to opt-out, and don't make such questions a part of the checkout process (or a requirement).

Privacy statements

Every e-commerce Web site should have a privacy statement explaining what the operators of the site do with the information they collect from customers. This statement should be linked from every page of the site (usually along the bottom of the page, with the copyright information), and be written in plain English, not legalese or marketing-speak.

See Chapter 2 for information on the typical content of privacy statements.

It's extremely important to abide by the terms spelled out in your privacy statement. If you fail to do this, you risk the reputation of your company and the loyalty of your customers.

In June 2000, the Federal Trade Commission (FTC) filed suit against the failed e-commerce company Toysmart.com, which had offered its database of customer information for sale to other companies. This database included such sensitive information as children's names and birth dates. Toysmart.com's privacy policy had stated that this information would never be sold to a third party.

Drawing the line on data gathering and analysis

Just because it's possible to gather information about a user's shopping and browsing habits, doesn't mean you should. Gathering detailed information on purchases, paths through the site, searches performed, links clicked, and chat and message board conversations, can be interpreted as a way to determine interests and political leanings of the customer or as an invasion of privacy. These practices, when done without the customer's knowledge, may be illegal and are probably unethical.

Information about what products are most commonly bought together and the most common paths through your site can and should be collected, but without linking the information to a particular user.

Service should remain top priority

Customer service should always remain your top priority. Good customer service is one of the most powerful marketing tools available. It generates positive word of mouth about your site, which is more beneficial to your e-commerce sales than any advertising money can buy.

Good customer service takes many forms, not all of which we can discuss here. One excellent example, however, is the use of transaction data versus product information. For example, your transaction data research shows that customers who buy Acme Audio's Xtra Small Stereo are also likely to purchase the latest CD by the PopStarGirls. The product information for the Xtra Small Stereo states a requirement for six D-size batteries. Clearly, providing the option to buy six D batteries is more valuable and crucial to the happiness of the customer than providing the option to buy the PopStarGirls CD.

See Chapter 6 for more information on customer service on the Web.

Examples of Web Marketing Done Right

Successful storefronts

Now that you've explored a wide variety of Web marketing techniques, it's time to take a look at some e-commerce marketing successes — both business-to-business (B2B) and business-to-consumer (B2C). The following sections examine various businesses that have employed some of the techniques discussed in this chapter.

Dell

Computer manufacturer Dell (www.dell.com) has pioneered direct online computer shopping. The business operates on both a B2B and B2C model. Dell sells all its computers directly to the customer, without resellers or retailers, which allows Dell to take full advantage of one core possibility of e-commerce — the removal of distributors.

Automated business processes

Dell has automated its core business process, which is configuring computer systems. Customers can completely design their computer systems on the Dell Web site. Use of e-commerce has made this process independent of human interaction. However, there's still a phone number available if shoppers are wary of online purchases and prefer to order via the phone. This phone number is posted on almost every page of the Web site.

Improved customer interaction

For customers who are unsure of the precise features they need, the site offers an area where customers can fill out a short form that asks how they intend to use the computer. They are then presented with the system that best suits their needs. Just as the phone call option can help users who are unsure of online purchasing, this automated suggestion feature assists customers who are unsure of their ability to select their own computer hardware.

Product delivery

Dell has alleviated some of the problems of marketing such a large hard good (a computer) on the Web by offering free shipping on certain products. Dell also operates geographically dispersed manufacturing facilities, including several overseas.

Globalization

Dell is targeting the worldwide customer base with 80 different Web sites, each geared toward a different country. Every country from Anguilla to Vietnam is represented. In addition, Dell has sales offices throughout the world to handle the various regions. Check out www.euro.dell.com/countries/eu/enu/gen/ to see the various European countries Dell supports.

Personalization

For their B2B customers, Dell offers a personalized Web site service called Premier Dell.com. After logging in to this area, employees of the customer business can see available computer configurations and their contracted prices. The designated manager of this area (on the customer side) can control who has access to the site. The computer system options available to users from the customer company can also be changed by this manager as necessary.

Product support

After a computer has been ordered, the customer can follow the progress of his or her order from manufacture to shipping via an order status page. Dell.com also offers a personalized product support area. After customers log on, they can access information on the features of their specific Dell systems.

UPS

The primary goal of the United Parcel Service (UPS) online presence at `www.ups.com` is to improve customer interaction. To improve customer interaction, UPS offers all its common client-interaction processes on its Web site. These processes used to be handled exclusively via telephone or in person. By putting these processes online, UPS is better able to serve customers and alleviate some of the load on its telephone representatives. The client-interaction processes that UPS has brought online include:

✦ **Package tracking.** When customers ship packages with UPS, they are given tracking numbers. A customer can then enter this number into a form on the UPS Web site to get detailed information about the progress and current location of his or her package.

✦ **Scheduling shipping.** The Ship area of the site allows the user to schedule a shipment for pick-up or drop-off, and also pay for the shipping online. In addition, it allows users to maintain an address book and view their account information and past shipments — a service only available to customers with UPS accounts. The other services are for any anonymous user.

✦ **Cost calculator.** This feature allows a visitor to enter the origin and destination for their package, and then it returns the total costs for all shipping options. Note that this form does not ask for more information than necessary — it doesn't ask for the street address, just the postal code and country.

✦ **Delivery time.** The Transit Time feature is very similar to the Cost Calculation feature in that the user enters the origin and destination for the package. This area, however, tells the user how long the package will take to reach its destination.

✦ **Schedule pickup.** This area allows the visitor to schedule a pick-up time for a package.

✦ **Order supplies.** Users with a UPS account can order UPS packaging supplies to be delivered to their home or place of business.

✦ **Drop-off locator.** This feature searches for the nearest package drop-off location based on the address entered by the user. The user can specify a search for self-service or staffed drop-off locations, or both. The locations are then shown on a map, with address information, hours of operation, and a phone number for each location. Visit `www.ups.com/using/services/locate/locate.html` to see the locator in action.

Amazon

Amazon.com is the Web's ultimate B2C e-commerce site. Started in 1995 as an online book retailer, the site has expanded its inventory exponentially over the last few years and now sells CDs, DVDs and videos, electronics, hardware, toys, software, health and beauty products, and much more. The site also hosts auctions and storefronts for small merchants called zShops. With all of this expansion, Amazon has had to remain focused on top-notch customer service to establish itself as one of the top Web superstores.

Customer service

Amazon offers excellent customer service via its account management page. This page provides customers with one central location to find information on everything from order status to their gift certificate balance. It also allows users to change their default shipping addresses, manage their e-mail newsletter subscriptions, and manage any auctions they might be running.

Introducing new products

Amazon.com has opened many new sections of its site over the last few years. Every time it introduces a new area, such as Camera & Photo or Health & Beauty, Amazon.com promotes the new area but doesn't let it dominate their home page. This key concept is based on Amazon.com's desire to generate interest in its new product offerings while not alienating its core customers — those who primarily think of Amazon as a bookstore.

Community building

Amazon.com has made extraordinary efforts to build its community of customers, and has been very successful in this effort. Its customer review system, for example, is very elaborate. Not only can customers review products, but other customers can also evaluate these reviews, and mark them as helpful or not helpful. Each day, two reviews for each product are highlighted.

Each customer who has written a review has his or her own Web page, which highlights his or her reviews and favorite sections of the site. Customers can designate certain reviewers as "favorite people" and any new reviews by one of these people are then highlighted on the customer's personalized home page.

Key Point Summary

In this chapter, we've taken a close look at Web marketing and the possibilities it offers for e-commerce companies. The key points covered were:

- ✦ Web marketing offers techniques not possible in traditional marketing, such as immediate response, personal selection, and interactivity.

- Interactive marketing tactics include product support, online communities, e-mail newsletters, personalization, online purchasing, and worldwide presence.
- The potential market for your product must be proven before going forward.
- The goals of your marketing effort determine the key elements of your marketing strategy. Some possible goals include developing new markets, improving customer interaction, selling new products, and automating business processes.
- The areas to focus on when developing your marketing strategy are Web site design, online promotion, targeted marketing, portal sites, and search engine placement.
- Growth drivers are the e-commerce factors that encourage growth; growth barriers limit growth.
- Intangible products, or soft goods, include music files, software, electronic books, video-on demand, news, and research. These products can be transferred to the user via the Internet.
- Tangible products, or hard goods, are any actual, three-dimensional items that need to be shipped. Examples are clothes, CDs, electronics, books, and toys.
- Moderately priced products are easy to market online, whereas very expensive and very cheap products present more challenges.
- Micro niche markets are more difficult to market online than markets with a global niche, or mass appeal.
- Product delivery is one of the most challenging aspects of marketing hard goods online. Some ways to meet this challenge are discounted and overnight shipping, special deals and discounts, product research information, and complimentary return postage.
- Log file analysis, polls and surveys, community features, transaction and inventory data, and Web population research are excellent ways to get to know your audience.
- When gathering information on your audience, remember to not ask questions that may constitute an invasion of privacy. Never violate your privacy statement and remember to keep customer service your top priority.

✦ ✦ ✦

STUDY GUIDE

Now that you've studied the key aspects of Web marketing in detail, it's time to test that knowledge. The following questions and exercises will help you gauge your grasp of Web marketing. Good luck!

Assessment Questions

1. Which of the following is *not* an example of an interactive element that can be used to market your products or services on the Web? (Choose the best answer.)

A. Survey

B. FAQ

C. Payment gateway

D. Message board

2. You're in charge of writing the FAQ for your company's Web site. Which of the following questions might be included? (Choose the best answer.)

A. How long does shipping take?

B. What is your return policy?

C. Do your products have a warranty?

D. All of the above.

3. Which of the following is a characteristic of growth drivers? (Choose the best answer.)

A. Increase profit potential and marketing options

B. Increase bandwidth

C. Improve usability

D. Can be downloaded from the hardware manufacturer's Web site.

4. To sell products and services to foreign countries via the Web, which of the following should you do? (Choose the best answer.)

A. Eliminate lingo from your Web site and comply with international commerce requirements.

B. Develop a highly interactive Web site.

C. Obtain a permit.

D. Establish a server in the target country.

5. Management has asked you to explain targeted marketing. Which of the following is the best description of targeted marketing?

A. Targeted marketing uses cookies to find potential customers.

B. Targeted marketing is the practice of determining where and by whom your online promotions will be seen.

C. Targeted marketing selects people randomly.

D. Targeted marketing is like bulk mail.

6. Which of the following is *not* an example of intangible, or soft, goods? (Choose the best answer.)

A. Digital music files

B. Software

C. Information

D. Pillows

7. You're asked by the marketing department to use data that customers originally entered for shipping purposes to find out additional information about them— such as criminal records, birth date, phone numbers, and lawsuits they've been involved in. Which of the following answers best describes the reason why you should not do this?

A. Customers originally gave this information for shipping purposes. Using it for additional purposes without their knowledge could be considered invasion of privacy.

B. It would take a long time to search all of these different databases.

C. There is no guarantee that the information found on the Web about the customers would be correct.

D. It would be too expensive to find this information, because the sites that sell this information charge a fee.

8. Which of the following accurately describes a product with a global market niche? (Choose the best answer.)

A. It comes in many different languages.

B. It's found in stores around the world.

C. It appeals to people regardless of geographic boundaries.

D. It can be taken anywhere.

9. Which of the following is not a goal of online marketing? (Choose the best answer.)

A. Opens new markets

B. Improves customer interaction

C. Analyzing Web data

D. Computerizes business processes

10. Which of the following is a barrier to e-commerce growth? (Choose the best answer.)
    - A. Increased competition
    - B. Multimedia
    - C. The global nature of the Internet
    - D. Increased bandwidth

Scenarios

1. You're considering starting a Web storefront to sell bubble gum. What steps would you take to determine whether there's a market for this product on the Web?
2. Your newly launched site, e-bubblegum-zone.com, is not doing very well in certain parts of the world. After an in-depth study, you determine that the $50 + shipping charge to many parts of the world is one of the biggest barriers to the growth of your international bubble gum business. What are some possible solutions to this problem?
3. From surveys that you've done of the customers of your online bubble gum store, you discover that people who purchase from your site are no more likely to buy from you than from similar e-commerce sites. You would like to try to build a community of loyal customers for your site. How might you accomplish this?

Lab Exercises

Lab 3-1 Evaluating community building

1. Direct your Web browser to Amazon (`www.amazon.com`).
2. Choose Friends & Favorites from the navigation bar across the top of the screen.
3. After you're in the Friends & Favorites section, select Top Reviewers from the left-hand navigation area, which is titled Explore.
4. The Top Reviewers section is a list of Amazon's most prolific and popular customer reviewers. Choose one of the top 10 reviewers from the list and click on his or her name.
5. Review the page about the customer reviewer you've selected.
6. Repeat steps 4 and 5, looking at a different reviewer's page each time, carefully looking over the information presented. Take notes on information of interest to you.

7. Consider the following questions about the customer reviewer's pages:
   - Does Amazon.com provide too much information about its customers to the public?
   - These pages are created automatically when a customer writes a review of an Amazon product. Do you think this is an appropriate way to build an online community?
   - How effective do you think this community-building technique is? Would customers be more likely to make purchases from Amazon.com as a result of the Top Reviewers section?

Lab 3-2 Evaluating product support

1. Point your browser to the Lands' End Web site (`www.landsend.com`).
2. Look for information on shipping options on the Web site — phone numbers or e-mail addresses to contact for shipping information do not count.
3. Answer the following questions about your search for shipping information:
   - How easy was it to find this information?
   - Do you think this site does a good job of presenting shipping information to potential customers?
   - What improvements do you think could be made to make this information easier to find?
4. Try this exercise with several more prominent e-commerce sites.

Lab 3-3 Marketing hard goods

1. Go to the clothes retailer J. Crew's Web site at `www.jcrew.com`.
2. Navigate your way to the page featuring men's ties.
3. Review the page displaying men's ties and answer the following questions:
   - Do you think the products are displayed well?
   - How effective do you find the photographs of the ties?
   - Are the colors and patterns of the ties clear? Why or why not?
4. Now, navigate your way to the women's sweaters section of the site and answer the following questions:
   - Are the products displayed well?
   - Are the products displayed more effectively than in the men's ties section? Why or why not?
5. Now, navigate your way to Eddie Bauer's online store at `www.eddiebauer.com`.

6. Go to the section for women's sweaters and answer the following questions:
   - Does this site display its sweaters more or less effectively than jcrew.com? Why or why not?
   - If you based your purchase solely on the level of product detail presented, from which site would you be more likely to buy? Why?

Lab 3-4 Marketing via portal sites

1. Point your browser to Yahoo! Shopping at `http://shopping.yahoo.com`.
2. Look over the site, and click on products that interest you. Do a search for a kind of product — for instance, search for toaster.
3. Answer the following questions about your experience browsing Yahoo! Shopping:
   - How effective do you find the most prominent product advertisements on the home page of Yahoo! Shopping?
   - If your company had a prominent placement on this site, what kind of picture and ad copy would you use to attract shoppers?
   - How effective is the search function?
   - Do the smaller vendors' products look as appealing as the big-name vendors' products? Why or why not?

Answers to Chapter Questions

Chapter pre-test

1. E-commerce enables the following interactive marketing capabilities: online communities, enhanced product support, e-mail newsletters, personalization, online purchasing, and a worldwide virtual presence.
2. To attract a global audience, an e-commerce site should eliminate American lingo and colloquialisms, develop separate Web sites for targeted regions, and comply with international commerce rules.
3. Soft goods consist of information or digital data that is easily transmitted through the Internet. Hard goods are tangible products that exist in three dimensions and always need to be shipped to the buyer.
4. Issues associated with selling hard goods online include the cost of shipping, the fact that users cannot examine the product themselves, and the difficulties of presenting such items on a Web site.
5. Positive aspects of Web marketing compared to traditional marketing include immediate customer response capabilities, personalization, and interactivity.

6. Negative aspects of Web marketing include the difficulty of fostering trust and an image of dependability without a visible staff and "real-world" presence, as well as the difficulty of segmenting the large market of Web users.

Assessment questions

1. **C.** A payment gateway processes credit cards; it's not an example of an interactive element that can be used to market your products or services on the Web. However, surveys, FAQ, message boards, and customer reviews (answers A, B, D, and E) are all interactive elements that can be used to market your products or services on the Web (as discussed in the "Interactivity" section).
2. **D.** All of these questions would be appropriate for an FAQ (as discussed in the "Interactivity" section).
3. **A.** Growth drivers increase profit potential and marketing options (covered in the "Growth drivers" section).
4. **A.** To sell products and services to foreign countries via the Web, you should eliminate lingo from your Web site and comply with international commerce requirements. Answers C and D are not necessary for you to sell products and services to foreign countries via the Web (covered in the "Understanding Audiences" section).
5. **B.** Targeted marketing is the practice of determining where and by whom your online promotions will be seen (covered in the "Targeted marketing" section). All other answers are incorrect descriptions of targeted marketing.
6. **D.** Soft goods are products that can be delivered electronically. Pillows are hard goods that must be shipped to the customer (covered in the "Intangible versus Tangible Goods" section).
7. **A.** Customers originally gave this information for shipping purposes. Using it for additional purposes without their knowledge could be considered invasion of privacy (covered in the "Responsible Web Marketing" section). All other answers are incorrect.
8. **C.** A product with a global market niche appeals to people regardless of geographic boundaries (covered in the "Understanding Growth" section). All other answers are incorrect.
9. **C.** Analyzing Web data is not a goal of online marketing. Online marketing should open new markets, improve customer interaction, sell new products, and computerize business processes. See the "Understanding Web Marketing" section.
10. **A.** As covered in the "Understanding Growth" section, barriers to e-commerce growth include increased competition, cost, and restrictions.

Scenarios

1. Possible steps that can be taken to determine if there's a market for a product include the following: conducting surveys, analyzing Web demographic data, and analyzing the real-world competition (if there is any), and establishing what benefit your company can provide to consumers that businesses with physical locations cannot.

2. Some solutions to this particular problem might include the following: not targeting foreign markets, selling only to distributors who buy large quantities and for whom the savings of ordering online outweigh the cost of shipping, and building warehouses in the countries where you would like to sell products in order to reduce shipping charges.

3. To generate more interest in your Web site and to stay ahead of the competition, you might try adding some online community building. Building community on a Web site requires you to allow visitors to express themselves and to communicate with other visitors. To accomplish this, you might use customer reviews, chat, message boards, polls, surveys, or other interactive features.

For More Information . . .

- **Jupiter Research.** `www.jup.com`. This site features demographic and behavior data on the Web community.
- **eMarketer.** `www.emarketer.com`. The world's leading provider of Internet statistics.
- **Market It Right.com.** `www.marketitright.com`. Here's where to find advice and contacts for Web marketing professionals.
- **Promotion 101 – Web Marketing Info Center.** `www.promotion101.com`. A site providing Internet promotion services and advice.
- **Webreview.com's E-Commerce area.** `http://webreview.com/pub/v/ecommerce`. The place to find articles on e-commerce marketing.

CHAPTER 4

Online Promotion Techniques

✦ ✦ ✦ ✦

EXAM OBJECTIVES

- Banner advertisements
- Advertising revenue
- Documenting traffic for advertisers

CHAPTER PRE-TEST

1. What is the standard size for a banner ad?
2. What is the most common format of a banner ad?
3. What is the `meta` element?
4. What is the advantage of buying ad space at the top of a Web page? What is the disadvantage?
5. What kinds of Web sites are supported only by advertising revenue?
6. What is a banner referral program?
7. Is it a good idea to buy e-mail addresses from another company for an e-mail promotion campaign?
8. What tools can be used for documenting advertising traffic?
9. What is the difference between opt-in and opt-out e-mailing lists?

✦ Answers to these questions can be found at the end of the chapter. ✦

You may be asking yourself: How is online promotion different from Web marketing? Well, the two go hand in hand, but they are different. Marketing is the message; promotion is the vehicle. In this chapter, we discuss the vehicles you can use to deliver your message to potential customers.

Understanding Online Promotion

Online promotion offers new vehicles that provide a closer, more individual interaction with potential customers than traditional promotion can provide. Although this may be exciting to you when you're planning your online promotion campaign, it also means that you have to be very careful in how you use these possibilities.

E-mail promotion, for example, can allow you to send your message directly to the audience of your choice. However, sending e-mail to those who have not requested it, or sending too much e-mail to those who have requested it, can be the death knell for your company's reputation.

Your customer's trust in you is the most important asset any e-commerce company possesses. Use the powers of online promotion wisely.

Categorizing Web Sites

When discussing online promotion and advertising campaigns, it's useful to divide Web sites into two categories: those that sell advertising and those that buy advertising. Although these two categories include some overlap in actual practice, they're generally separate and provide useful ways to assign roles to Web sites.

Exam Tip

Be sure you understand the definitions of publisher and marketer sites.

Publisher sites

Sites that sell advertising can be called *publisher sites*. Publisher sites depend on advertisers for revenue. Although these ads contain advertisers' marketing messages, they do not make up the bulk of the site. Some attract advertisers because of their large volume of traffic; others appeal to a highly specialized audience and are able to sell targeted advertising. Some examples of publisher sites are:

✦ **Portals.** Portals are entryways into the Internet for the average user (hence the term portal). Essentially, these sites function as a central location for Web browsing by providing services such as current news, weather information, and, most importantly, a Web site directory or search engine. Successful portals such as Yahoo! and Excite boast some of the highest traffic numbers on the Web. They offer top-level advertising that is seen by everyone that visits the site, and also targeted advertising in the topical categories of their Web directories.

✦ **Content-driven sites.** Content-driven sites come in varying gradations of targeting. Although they cannot boast the traffic volume of a portal site, some online magazines, such as `www.salon.com`, have a fairly broad readership. Highly targeted, content-driven sites include technical magazines such as Webmonkey (`http://hotwired.lycos.com/webmonkey`) and Internet World (`www.internetworld.com`). These sites attract advertising from companies targeting Internet professionals.

Marketer sites

Marketer sites are not dependent upon advertising for revenue — rather, they are trying to sell a product. In fact, it may not be in the best interest of a marketer site to carry any advertising at all. By definition, they are marketing their own products, and have very little or no interest in marketing the products of others. Most e-commerce retailers fall into this category.

Where the categories overlap

These definitions overlap when a marketer site decides to sell advertising in a limited way. For example, when a marketer site with a small marketing budget decides to join a banner-trading network. The marketer site is then obligated to show banner ads on its site for other members of the network. In return, their banner ads are shown on the other members' sites.

Another instance of the categories overlapping is when a content-driven site advertises on a portal or other high-traffic site. Although content-driven sites depend on advertising for their revenue, they also need to engage in some advertising of their own to expand their readership.

In both cases, the primary goal of each site remains the same: advertising. The e-commerce site that engages in banner trading is still primarily a marketer site that is dabbling in a little publishing. The content-driven site, on the other hand, is still a publisher site, and is just doing a little bit of marketing.

All About Banner Ads

Banner advertisements

Banner advertisements are the most ubiquitous form of Web advertising today — that is to say: Web users see them everywhere. Some use the term *banner ad* only to refer to the wide, horizontal advertisements typically seen at the top and bottom of Web pages. Others use the phrase as a catchall for visual Web advertisements of every shape and size.

At any rate, banner advertisements are the number one method of online promotion, despite the ongoing debate over their effectiveness. Some Web experts claim that banner ads are ineffective and a waste of time for marketing campaigns. They point out that banner ads have average clickthrough rates of two to three percent and that they have become so common that users have stopped noticing them.

Banner ad proponents point out that clickthrough rates for banner ads are no less impressive than the average rate of customer response to print or television advertising. They also cite studies indicating that banner ads increase product awareness and are therefore extremely valuable in any online promotion campaign.

The final word on banner ads is still up in the air. Nonetheless, banner ads are very common and continue to sell very well. For that reason, it's important that every e-commerce professional is familiar with the technology and terminology of banner advertisements.

Banner ad concepts and terms

To gain a clear understanding of banner ads and the issues associated with them, you need to be familiar with the following banner ad concepts and terms:

✦ **Ad click.** The act of a user clicking on a banner ad. This is one of the units of measurement used by Web advertising professionals to measure the effectiveness of a campaign. Ad click is synonymous with *clickthrough* (defined later in this list).

✦ **Banner.** A banner, also called a banner ad, is an image advertisement on a Web page that links to a page on the advertiser's Web site. Banner ads are generally 468 pixels wide by 60 pixels tall, although they do vary in size. Small banners are sometimes referred to as *tiles*.

✦ **CASIE.** The Coalition for Advertising Supported Information and Entertainment (CASIE) was founded in 1994 by the Association of National Advertisers (ANA) and the American Association of Advertising Agencies (AAAA) with the stated purpose of guiding "the development of interactive advertising and marketing." The organization offers guidelines for Web advertising at its Web site, `www.casie.org`.

✦ **Click rate.** A measurement of the number of clicks on a banner ad per number of *impressions* (defined later in this list). This number is typically given as a percentage.

✦ **Clickthrough.** The act of a user clicking on a banner ad. Clickthrough is synonymous with *ad click*.

✦ **CPC.** This stands for *cost-per-click* and is an Internet marketing formula used to price banner ads. Internet publishers are often paid by advertisers based on the number of clicks a specific banner ad gets. The CPC usually ranges from 10 to 20 cents.

✦ **CPM.** This stands for *cost-per-thousand* (M being the roman numeral for 1,000), and is also used by Internet marketers to price ad banners. Publisher sites that use the CPM pricing model guarantee an advertiser a certain number of impressions, and then set a rate based on that guarantee times the CPM rate. For example, a Web site that has a CPM rate of $30 and guarantees advertisers 900,000 impressions will charge $27,000 ($30 x 900) to run ad banners on their site.

✦ **Hit.** A *hit* is logged for a Web site each and every time a file is sent to a user's Web browser. Every image, object, and Web page is recorded as a hit. This means that when a user loads a Web page with 11 static graphics, and one Shockwave animation, 13 hits are logged (11 for the graphics, and 1 each for the Shockwave animation and the Web page itself).

Hit counts should be used to measure server workload, and not as an indication of site traffic. All too often, they are used as a measure of site traffic because the numbers are usually so much higher than the number of actual visitors logged. To get an accurate idea of the traffic your site is getting, however, you should refer to the number of *visitors* (defined later in this list).

✦ **Impression.** An instance in which a particular advertisement is downloaded to a user's computer and displayed in the user's browser. It's assumed that the user saw the advertisement, but this is not always true. The ad may have been displayed further down the page than the user scrolled, for instance. Impressions are often used in the equation for pricing Web advertising.

✦ **Log file.** Log files are maintained by the Web server, and record use of the Web site, such as hits, visitors, and click patterns (paths through the site). Log analysis software is then used to determine such information as where visitors came from (i.e., the site where they clicked on a link to your site) and how long they stayed.

✦ **Page view.** A page view is each time a page is accessed by a user. It's similar to a hit, except images and objects are not counted — just Web pages. Page views are a more accurate gauge of site traffic than hits.

✦ **Tile.** A term often used by Web advertising professionals to refer to banner ads that are narrower and smaller than traditional banner ads. Tiles are generally 120 by 60 pixels, or 125 by 125 pixels.

✦ **Unique user.** Refers to each individual computer (and, by association, each person) that accesses a Web site. The number of unique users in a given time period is recorded in the log file.

✦ **Visit.** A visit is each series of requests made by a unique user, usually during a 30-minute time frame. Visits are also recorded in the log file, and can be used to analyze how users move through your site.

Exam Tip Banner ads are the most common type of online promotion. Be sure you're familiar with the most common banner dimensions and ad terms.

Standard banner sizes

The size of a banner ad is measured in pixels. The term *pixel* is short for picture element, and is a single point in a graphic image. As mentioned in the previous bulleted list, the standard size for a banner ad is 468 by 60 pixels. There are a variety of other sizes often seen, however. Web sites that offer advertising space generally have a variety of spaces available, and provide potential advertisers with a list of appropriate sizes and shapes. Here's a list of common shapes and sizes of banner ads (all sizes in pixels):

- **468 by 60.** The traditional shape and size of banner ads that are displayed across the top and bottom of Web pages. Arguably, the most common banner ad shape currently used.
- **120 by 60.** The second most common shape of banner ad, these are also called *tiles* and can be placed alongside 468 by 60 banners or in the left- or right-hand column of a Web site (as shown in Figure 4-1).

Figure 4-1: A 468 by 60 banner ad is flanked by two 120 by 60 tiles across the top of a Web page.

- **234 by 60.** Sometimes called a half-banner, this size is the same height but half the width of a traditional banner ad. Two of these can be placed side by side at the top or bottom of a Web page. One can also be placed next to a 468 by 60 banner ad if the site design is wide enough.
- **125 by 125.** These square banner ads are becoming more common, and are often seen in the top right corner of Web pages, or in the left or right column.
- **120 by 90.** These are 30 pixels taller than the more common 120 by 60 tiles; these tiles are also often seen in the left- or right-hand column of a Web page.
- **125 by 400.** This vertical banner ad size is striking because users are so used to banner ads being horizontal. These can take up a large proportion of a column on a Web site. See Figure 4-2 for an example.

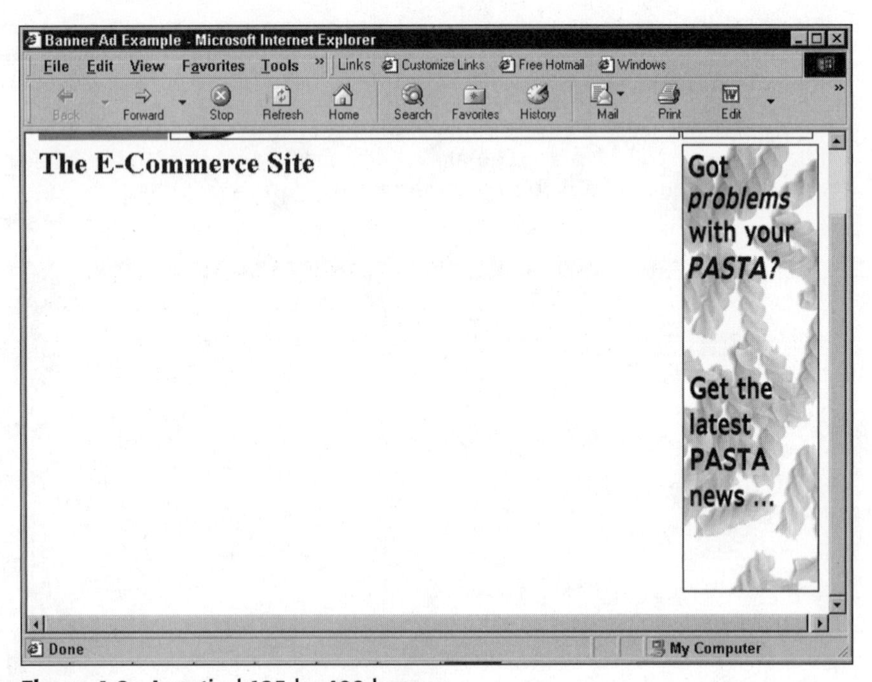

Figure 4-2: A vertical 125 by 400 banner

There are many more banner ad sizes and shapes being used on Web sites today. For the most part, the shape of your banners is determined by the sites on which you're advertising. The 468 by 60 and 120 by 60 sizes are the most common and you should always have some ads in these shapes available for an active online promotion campaign.

Types of banners

Until recently, all banner ads were formatted as Graphic Interchange Format (GIF) files. GIF, along with the JPEG (Joint Photographic Experts Group) format, is one of the most prevalent image file types used on the Web today. Rich media is now also making inroads into banner ad technology. In the following sections, you take a closer look at the GIF and rich media formats.

Static and animated GIFs

Banner ads in the GIF format can be either static or animated. A static GIF is a single image that does not change. As such, static GIFs have much smaller file sizes than animated GIFs. Static GIF banner ads were not popular for several years, but they're being used more lately because recent research shows that static ads are no less effective than animated ads, and that some users prefer them.

Animated GIFs are created from a series of static GIFs, strung together by a program such as GIF Builder or Ulead GIF Animator to create a moving image. Figure 4-3 shows an example of an animated GIF, frame by frame.

Figure 4-3: An animated GIF frame by frame

Although they have larger file sizes, animated banner ads have several advantages over static banners. The following list explains these advantages:

✦ **Complex marketing message.** Animated GIFs can display a more complex marketing message than static GIFs. Whereas static GIFs can only show a single set of stationary text and images in the available space, animated GIFs can display multiple images and text elements within the same available space over a period of time.

✦ **Visually interesting.** Because they're moving and changing images, animated GIFs stand out from the (usually) static content of the Web site. Not only does this movement make the banner more clearly identifiable as an advertisement, but it also draws the viewer's attention.

✦ **Create suspense.** A well-conceived and well-executed animated GIF can create suspense for the viewer. For example, the first frame can ask a question, such as "Where can you find the hottest Christmas toys at a fraction of the cost?" After letting this question hang for a few moments, the answer can be revealed: "At Super Toy Land, of course!"

Rich media

Rich media is an exciting way to enliven a banner ad campaign and add some interactivity. Two common formats in which these banners are made are Shockwave and interactive CGI (Common Gateway Interface).

✦ **Macromedia Shockwave.** This is an animation format that allows for much smoother and more complex animation than is possible with animated GIFs. Shockwave banners can also be used to create interactive experiences, such as games, that can generate interest in an advertisement and product.

One drawback of using Shockwave banners is that Shockwave files require the user to install a plug-in so the file can be viewed. If the user doesn't have the Shockwave plug-in installed, he or she sees an empty shape with an icon indicating that the content cannot be viewed.

✦ **Interactive CGI.** This type of programming enables banners to display small forms. For example, a banner could present a viewer with four choices (each with a radio button) and a Submit button. When the user makes a choice and submits the form, the user is taken to the advertiser's site. The results of the form are then recorded and can be used to tailor the visitor's experience.

There are some general drawbacks to using rich media banner ads. First, the file sizes for such banners are much larger than those of GIFs. The download time can be long for users without high-speed connections to the Internet—which currently includes most Internet users. Second, some Web sites won't accept rich media advertisements because of the bandwidth requirements. Therefore, if you plan on using rich media banners in your advertising campaign, be sure to have plenty of GIFs available as well.

Building Effective Banner Ads

There are several ways to get your audience interested in your banner ad. Banners are most effective when they observe the following techniques and guidelines:

Exam Tip

Make a note of the following banner ad techniques. They are covered on the test.

- **Pose questions.** Use your banner ad to pose a question. Many users feel compelled to answer, especially if their opinion is asked. For example, if you're advertising a store with both electronic and regular books, you can ask, "Are electronic books the wave of the future?" Because people tend to have strong feelings about electronic books (both positive and negative), this question would interest many viewers.
- **Call to action.** Get bossy with your banner ads — that is, tell the viewers what to do. This can range from a simple "Click Here!" to something more specific such as "Get off that chair and get moving with an XtraFast Bike 3000!"
- **Refresh often.** Replace your banner ads frequently. According to Yahoo!, viewers tire of a banner ad within about two weeks, which means you should be prepared to switch to a new ad every few weeks. If you have a limited number of banner ads and are advertising on several sites, you can rotate your banners among the sites.
- **Standard sizing.** If you're making a batch of banner ads, have them made to standard sizes — 468 by 60 for horizontal banners, and 120 by 60 and 125 by 125 for tiles. Most sites adhere to these standards. Some sites may deviate, however, so be prepared to have a banner made in a less-common size when necessary.
- **Small file.** Make sure the file size of the banner is as small as possible. Most sites have a size limit. Good Web designers know how to optimize colors and animation techniques to make files as small as possible.
- **Animation.** Clever animation can create interest and help your banner stand out from the rest of the page.

Tip

Complex animations create bulky files. Isolating the animation in one section of the banner—for example, one half or two-thirds of the banner never changes—can help keep the file size down.

- **Avoid false claims.** Be sure the banner accurately describes what the viewer will find at your site. If you're advertising an online brokerage, for example, it wouldn't be wise to use a banner slogan such as "Want riches beyond your wildest dreams? Click here!" Such *trick* banners used to be common; however, it quickly became clear that they only increased the number of clickthroughs, not the number of visitors who were actually interested in what the site had to offer.

✦ **Visually attractive.** A banner ad should be appealing. Have your banner ads made by a professional Web designer. Poor design and poor use of Web technologies reflect badly on your company. Poor use of color can look amateurish. A good Web designer is able to work with limited colors and creative animation to create a visually pleasing banner while maintaining a small file size.

✦ **Obvious hyperlinks.** Make it obvious that your advertisement is a hyperlink. There are new Internet users every day, and this might not be clear to everyone. A non-animated advertisement can blend into the design of a Web site if you don't make an attempt to highlight the fact that it's hyperlinked. It can be as simple as putting a blue border around the image, or making particular words blue and underlined (which is the common format for HTML hyperlinks).

Banner page positions

The position of your advertisement on a Web page can be as important as your message. Be sure to evaluate the available placements on the site where you're advertising, and choose the position that makes the most sense for your campaign. The design of your banner can even be tailored to the position.

Many banner ads are placed at the top of the Web page. This can be a good location, because it means your banner is the first item that loads, and may be the only thing the user sees for a few moments while the rest of the page downloads — especially if the user has a slow Internet connection.

On the other hand, placement at the top of the page can be a drawback, because it's the most typical placement. Banner ads have appeared at the top of Web pages as long as they have existed. This means that users are accustomed to seeing banner ads in that location, and may ignore your ad simply because it appears at the top of the page.

Some advertisements get better clickthrough rates if they are placed lower on the page. A location being used with more frequency is the right-hand column, employing 120 by 60 and 125 by 125 tiles as well as custom-sized vertical banners. Banners in this location tend to be viewed more as a part of the site's content, rather than exclusively as banner ads.

Tracking ad effectiveness

Documenting traffic for advertisers

To evaluate the effectiveness of your banner ad promotion campaign, you need to be able to answer certain questions, such as:

- ✦ How many people clicked on the ad?
- ✦ Did they stay at my site?
- ✦ Did they make a purchase?

The site on which you advertise can tell you how many impressions your banner got during a given time period. However, to gather meaningful information on a banner's effectiveness, you also need to have statistics on clickthroughs and the behavior of the visitors who chose to do so.

There are two primary tools for tracking the effectiveness of banner advertising: log analysis and tracking services. In the following sections, you take a look at each of these methods in more detail.

Log analysis

Analysis of the log files created by your Web server software can reveal plenty of information on the effectiveness of a banner ad. For example, you can set up a special page to which each particular banner ad links. This page could, in turn, redirect the user to your site's home page. By calculating the number of visits to the redirecting page, your log analysis tool would reveal how many users entered your site by clicking on a particular advertisement.

You don't have to use a redirecting page, but in many ways it's the simplest method to track hits. Another possible method is to pass a unique value in the URL associated with each banner. That value could then be recorded in a database or in your log files and checked for frequency as well as a total count of clickthroughs for each banner. This method accommodates users whose browsers do not support Web page redirects.

Log analysis tools, such as WebTrends (`www.webtrends.com`), also tell you where your visitors come from — that is, the top referring URLs for your site. This information can be used to decide whether to continue advertising on a given site. For example, you advertise both on Web Site One and Web Site Two, and pay the same amount for each. Your log file analysis reveals that Web Site Two sends more traffic to your site than any other referring URL. On the other hand, Web Site One barely makes a blip on the screen — it ranks 21st of all referring URLs. It might be time to stop advertising on Web Site One, and spend your advertising dollars on a different site.

For more information on log file analysis tools and techniques, see Chapter 3 and Chapter 21.

Tracking services

Log file analysis can also be provided by third-party companies rather than software. The way these services generally work is that specific HTML code is included in each of your Web site pages, which then sends information to a third-party server that records traffic data. You can then view the data in a secure area on the tracking service's Web site.

Tip

Two popular tracking services are WebSTAT (www.webstat.com), and eXTReMe Tracking (www.extreme-dm.com/tracking).

This method has the following drawbacks:

- ✦ It can be quite an undertaking for your staff to go through your entire Web site to add the required HTML code to each page. If your site uses a database for content management, these services may not be able to provide impression information for each product on your site.
- ✦ Because your Web server software automatically generates log files, it makes sense to use these. You do need software to analyze these log files in-house, but this software is affordable unless you have an extremely tight budget.
- ✦ This method means that a third party, the tracking service, also knows how much traffic your site is getting. Some companies may see this as privileged information and may not want a third party to have access to it.

Buying and selling banner ads

Objective

Advertising revenue

Your company needs to decide if it just wants to buy advertising, or if it also wants to sell advertising as a part of its revenue model. If you're just buying advertising on other sites but not displaying advertising on your own site, you may be missing out on potential profits. However, it may be better for your e-commerce site if you don't accept advertising. After all, you want to use your screen space to promote your own products, not somebody else's.

If you do accept advertising, it's clearly a better idea to offer such advertising to sites selling *complimentary* products and services, rather than *competing* products and services. For example, an online music store could carry advertisements for a site where concert tickets can be bought, but not advertisements for other music stores. Offering advertising can give your site another revenue stream, as long as you don't let it drain customers away from your site.

Targeting banner ads

Deciding on which Web site to advertise is a very important and often challenging part of online promotion. On the one hand, there are high-traffic portal Web sites such as Yahoo! and Excite that can charge a premium for ad space. However, do such sites provide the kind of targeting you'd like?

A more targeted campaign might not be seen by as many people, but it will be seen by more of the *right* people. For example, if you run an online baseball supply store, it might make more sense to advertise on `http://majorleaguebaseball.com` than on Yahoo!, even though Yahoo! is visited by more people than `http://majorleaguebaseball.com`.

Working with ad reps

To negotiate the complexities of targeted online promotion, it may be in your best interest to use the services of a Web advertising representative. These professionals have many contacts and will likely have access to more Web sites that accept advertising than you possibly could.

Web advertising firms can help you gain access to high-profile sites, help your site with tracking banner ad performance, and may even be able to help you find a Web graphic designer. Developing alternatives to banners, such as sponsorship promotions, may also be easier when working with ad reps because of their established network of contacts.

To get a better idea of what services are available, check out two Web advertising firms. Visit 24/7 Media (`www.247media.com`) and choose Advertisers on the left. You can also visit DoubleClick (`www.doubleclick.com`) and click on Advertisers at the top to view their offerings.

Banner ad networks

An efficient way to target your message is through the use of a banner ad network. These networks are created by collecting a large pool of Web sites that offer advertising and then dividing these sites into categories. Impressions and clickthroughs are then sold to advertisers for placement on a group of Web sites, not on an individual Web site.

Instead of choosing a specific site on which to place your ad, you can use a banner ad network to simply choose a category in which you want your ad displayed. This service increases your banner ad impressions for any given time period. It also means that you won't need to maintain individual relationships with each of the sites on which your ads are running.

For example, your site sells computer hardware. A banner ad network could advertise your site on a pool of sites containing content about computers for a variety of audiences — from corporate IT department managers to home users and hobbyists.

Bartering for banners

If your advertising dollars are limited, the previously discussed banner ad promotion avenues may be out of your reach. However, you can still conduct an online promotion campaign without using cash — that is, you can barter, or trade, ad space with other sites. Such a relationship can be set up on a one-to-one basis, but it's generally more efficient and more successful if you use a banner-trading network.

Members of a banner-trading network must include code on their Web site that shows other members' banner ads. Some networks require these banner ads to be shown at the top of your Web pages.

Although your site shows banner ads of other members, your ads are also shown on your fellow members' sites. Your banners are allocated a certain number of impressions on other members' Web sites. The more impressions your site records for network banners, the more impressions your banners are allocated.

You can also target your campaign with banner-trading networks, much like you can with paid banner ad networks such as DoubleClick. The performance of your ads can also be tracked online.

Two of the largest banner-trading networks are SmartAge's SmartClicks program (`www.smartage.com`) and Microsoft bCentral's LinkExchange (`http://adnetwork.bcentral.com`).

Banner referrals

Another way to direct traffic to your site is through the use of a referral program, also called an affiliate program. Such programs do not require your site to show banner ads, and don't involve the large cash outlays that banner networks or advertising agencies require.

Referral programs get other companies' sites to show your banner ad, and you pay them a commission for new traffic. Payment can be based on clickthroughs, new visitors, or purchases — per-purchase or a percentage of the purchase total.

Don't assume referral programs are cheap advertising for your company. If you fail to accurately estimate the number of companies that will enroll in your program, or the amount of traffic that your program will generate, you may end up paying a lot more to the program's members than you originally estimated. Plan your commission payment structure appropriately.

All About Search Engine Promotion

Despite your best efforts at creating visually pleasing, informative, and well-placed banner advertisements, the truth is that many Web users will overlook your banners altogether. When visiting a Web site, most users are only interested in the content found there, and many have learned to ignore visuals in favor of text.

When they're planning to make a purchase online, however, such users often turn to a search engine to find an appropriate vendor. Therefore, to attract the full spectrum of online shoppers, it's important to make sure that your site is properly represented on the major search engines.

Web directories

There are two ways that portal sites present their links to other sites. One is by using a search engine; the other is by creating a Web directory. A Web directory is a database of URLs sorted into a hierarchical category structure. Excellent examples of Web directories are Yahoo!, Excite, and LookSmart.

When a user enters keywords into the search form on any one of these sites, the results returned are actually based only on the Web sites in the portal site's database. This collection of URLs is not based on an automated indexing of the Web, but rather by manual addition of Web sites to the directory database. The editors of Excite, for instance, look for appropriate Web sites to add to their directory. They also depend on the owners of the Web sites to enter their information into a form on their site, and then decide how to categorize it.

Some directories, such as Yahoo!, will list your Web site for free upon request. Yahoo! also offers an enhanced directory listing for a fee. By contrast, search engines do not charge a fee.

How search engines index sites

Search engines are automated, whereas Web directories are not. Search engines gather information about the content of the Web through software programs called *spiders*, or *crawlers*. These programs search the Web every day, finding new Web sites and indexing each of their pages. This information is then included in the search engine's database.

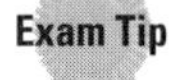

Exam Tip Be sure to study this section carefully before the exam.

The result of the search engine information-gathering method would then seem to be that search engines are more thorough than Web directories. The truth, however, is that the number of Web pages in existence is far greater than the ability of a spider to index. Therefore, it's possible your Web site would never be indexed without some action on your part.

Luckily, there are ways to intervene in this process on behalf of your site. Most search engine sites have a form for submitting a URL for indexing. The URL is then queued for indexing by the spider. It can take several weeks for the spider to get to your request, however.

Registration

Registering with search engines and Web directories is an essential part of any e-commerce business and cannot be overlooked. If your site is not among the results for appropriate queries on major portal sites, you're missing out on a lot of potential business.

Registering with search engines

Registering with search engines is a fairly painless process. Generally, all you need to do is enter your site's URL in a form field and hit the submit button. Search engine registration forms generally do not request any other information about your site, because the spider collects that information from the Web pages themselves.

See "Tips and tricks for improved visibility," later in this chapter, for more information on how a spider determines the topic of a Web page.

Although registering with each individual search engine site is relatively unchallenging, it can be fairly time-consuming because of the sheer number of existing search engines. See the "Automating registration" section, later in this chapter, to learn about speeding up the process.

If you must do your registration by hand, there are Web sites that provide comprehensive lists of the search engines in use. Examples of such sites are Search Engine Watch (`www.searchenginewatch.com`) and AllSearchEngines.com (`www.allsearchengines.com`). Visiting these sites, and working through their lists, can help make your registration effort more thorough.

Registering with Web directories

In contrast to search engines, Web directories tend to ask for more information about your site when you register. Common requests are a short description, keywords, and a category in their categorization hierarchy. The Web directory's editors, however, always make the final category determination.

Although many Web directories list your site for free, many charge a fee. In addition, free directories often offer you a better placement on the category page (an "enhanced listing") for a fee. It's also possible to purchase small advertisements on the category pages of many Web directories.

It can take as long as six months after submission for your site to be listed on a Web directory. Fee-based listings tend to be much faster and offer guaranteed results.

Your site should be re-submitted to the top Web directories and search engines once every two or three months so the information the Web directories have on your site remains current. Do not submit your site more than once every two or three months, however—multiple registrations within a short time frame can be considered spamming, and your site may be permanently removed from the search engine's database.

Automating registration

Because registering your site with all the major search engines and Web directories one by one is an extremely cumbersome and time-consuming task, there are many services and products available to automate the process. These registration automators come in the form of software or Web-based services. In the following sections, you take a closer look at each of these options.

Web-based registration services

Automated registration services are available on a variety of Web sites. Web-based registration services publish a list of all Web directories and search engines to which sites are submitted. Make sure the service you use covers the majority of the most popular search and directory sites. Two of the most popular Web-based registration services are SubmitIt.com (`www.submitit.com`) and !Register-It! (`http://register-it.netscape.com`).

These services charge a fee that is generally less than you might pay individual Web directories if you were to register with each of them separately. The process works by collecting information from you in a series of forms. Your site's URL, description, and keywords are submitted to Web directories. For search engines, just the URL is submitted.

Many registration services also provide their subscribers with reports on their success with the search engines and directories to which the service has submitted information. This can be a helpful tool in assessing the success of your online promotion campaign. Although this information would be very difficult for a person to compile on a site-by-site basis, these services can access it automatically and display it in your browser immediately.

Registration software

Registration software is run on your computer, and provides services similar to Web-based registration services. The advantages of using software are that it keeps the registration process in-house, and you gain more detailed and customized services than are often offered by Web-based services. Two of the most popular registration software packages are AddWeb by CyberSpace HQ (`www.cyberspacehq.com`) and WebPositionGOLD (`www.webpositiongold.com`).

Registration software packages come with a database of search engine and directory Web sites. These databases are usually maintained and updated by the staff of the software company, and you can download upgrades over the Web. These packages can be better integrated into your site's development, because they have features that modify the code on your Web pages to improve your search engine's performance. They can also be programmed to re-submit your site information to specific Web sites according to a schedule. Many even include HTML editors as part of the package.

Some Web-based registration services and registration software packages offer trial versions for prospective customers. If you're not sure which method is best for your company, you can give them both a try on a temporary basis.

Tips and tricks for improved visibility

Of course, all your site registration efforts may be for naught if they don't result in your site being among the top 10 or 15 listings returned for appropriate queries. In the following sections, you learn how to increase the chances of your site being among the first listed.

Web directory visibility

When it comes to Web directories, you get what you pay for. Site owners who have paid the most for a listing in any given category are going to be listed first, often with their link highlighted in some way.

When browsing LookSmart's directory, for example, you may notice the first few listings on each category page are not in alphabetical order. About halfway down the page, however, the list continues with sites beginning with "A" and proceeds through the alphabet. The first sites listed paid more, so they get top billing.

You can also buy ads on certain category pages on Web directory sites. The Literature section of a Web directory may have a banner ad across the top or tile ads down the right side advertising online booksellers. These placements can be purchased in much the same way that regular banner advertising is purchased. Visit the advertising information areas of Web directory sites to explore the available options.

Search engine visibility

Improving your search engine placement takes skillful HTML coding rather than money. The techniques described in the following sections should be used when developing your site to optimize search engine placement.

Use HTML rather than images

Spiders index the text on each page of your Web site to determine the topic. The main content of your Web page (that is, the text that describes what the page is about, or contains the information for which search engine users may be looking) should be displayed in HTML text rather than as an image. A spider cannot index the text in an image. If the key content of your site is presented in an image, the search engine software cannot correctly evaluate how relevant the page is to a query.

Include HTML links

If your site relies on an *image map* for navigation, be sure to also include HTML links to all of the sections of your site. These links can be listed along the bottom of each page — a common practice today.

Search engine spiders follow the links on your Web site to index each page. Spiders cannot follow image map links, however, so make sure to include HTML links. These links are helpful to your human visitors, as well, especially those with slow Internet connections that may not have images automatically loading in their browsers.

Tell the spider where to go: site maps and robots exclusion files

You can provide both the spiders and your human visitors with a site map, which is a Web page containing a hierarchical list of links to all of the major sections of your site. Site maps help users who may have difficulty understanding your site's navigation scheme. It also provides spiders a central location from which to start the indexing process. In fact, you can submit the URL of your site map to each search engine, rather than your home page URL to make the indexing process more efficient and accurate.

To keep certain directories private, include a *robots exclusion file*, which tells spiders which directories not to index. A robots exclusion file is a text file kept in the root directory of your Web site. This file must be named *robots.txt* for it to be used properly. It essentially consists of a list of directories or files to be excluded from indexing by spiders.

The following is an example of the code found in a robots exclusion file. It allows every spider to index every directory of the Web site except for the `admin` directory and the `software` subdirectory of the `downloads` directory:

```
User-agent: *
Disallow: /admin/
Disallow: /downloads/software/
```

You can also tell certain spiders to ignore folders, but let other spiders have access to them. For example, the following code excludes the fictitious spider `BadSpider` from the `admin`, `database`, `photos`, and `privatestuff` folders, but excludes other spiders from the `admin` folder only:

```
User-agent: BadSpider
Disallow: /admin/
Disallow: /database/
```

```
Disallow: /photos/
Disallow: /privatestuff/

User-agent: *
Disallow: /admin/
```

There are other, more complex exclusions you can code into your robots exclusion file, but most sites use one list of excluded files for all spiders, much like the previous code sample.

Use meta elements

When a search engine returns a list of results, they are generally listed with a title, in bold, that links to the Web page, plus a description paragraph below the title. Sometimes these descriptions make sense, but sometimes they don't. You can improve the way your site appears in results listings through the proper use of `meta` elements.

The *`meta` element* is an HTML element that contains information about the document, or Web page. The two most important parts of a `meta` element to use for search engine display are keywords and descriptions (inserted using the `name` and `content` attributes). The `meta` element is included in the `head` element of a Web page, for example:

```
<head>
<title>Joe's Stereo Shop</title>
<meta name="description" content="The place to research and
purchase your next stereo system. Joe's has it all!" />
<meta name="keywords" content="stereos, purchase, shop,
research, radios, cassette decks, CD players, home theater" />
</head>
```

When displayed in a list of search engine results, this page appears something like this:

```
Joe's Stereo Shop
The place to research and purchase your next stereo system.
Joe's has it all!
```

The keywords in the `meta` element help ensure that your site is displayed among appropriate results. It's especially important to include any words or phrases that describe your site but are not included anywhere in the text of the page.

E-mail as a Promotion Tool

E-mail promotion is very appealing to many e-commerce companies simply because of the sheer number of e-mail addresses in the world and the number of e-mails sent every day. Using e-mail to promote your e-commerce company is a delicate art, however. Because users are wary of receiving excessive e-mails, you must step carefully through the process of e-mail promotion to avoid its many pitfalls.

E-mail advertising

One excellent way to get your message to many thousands of potential customers is by advertising on someone else's e-mail newsletter. Content-oriented sites, such as online magazines, often have an e-mail newsletter that goes out every time new content is added to the site (the online equivalent of a new issue being published). Topic-oriented e-mails may also be sent periodically.

The e-mail addresses to which these mailings are sent belong to people who are loyal readers of the Web site, and who have requested that the mailing be sent to them. These readers recognize the necessity of having two or three advertisements included in each mailing, because content-oriented Web sites rely solely on advertising for income.

Advertising on someone else's e-mail is also risk-free: You're not held accountable if the e-mail is sent to people who did not request it or have unsubscribed. You're also not blamed if those on the mailing list feel they are being sent too much e-mail.

Responsible bulk e-mailing

If you decide to develop your own bulk e-mailing campaign, be very careful about how you build your mailing list and how you treat your subscribers. If you do not treat your customers with the utmost care, your reputation can be quickly sullied. The following sections describe how to become a responsible bulk e-mailer.

Collecting e-mail addresses: opt-in versus opt-out

The only legitimate way to create an e-mail list is by giving users the opportunity to subscribe via a form on your Web site. This method of collecting e-mail addresses is called *opt-in*.

The most straightforward technique for opt-in e-mail address collection is a small form on your home page (and other areas of your site as appropriate) for users to submit their e-mail addresses for inclusion on your mailing list. You may want to ask for other information as well, but try to keep the form as short as possible. Do not ask for addresses or phone numbers.

Exam Tip Be sure you understand the difference between opt-in and opt-out mailing lists.

Opt-out e-mail address collection is the method of sending bulk e-mail to a list of people who have not specifically requested to receive the e-mail. People on this list are then expected to unsubscribe themselves (i.e., opt-out) if they don't want to receive any more e-mails from the source.

Opt-out mailing lists are not a good idea if you want customers to have positive feelings about your company. For example, you could decide to add the e-mail addresses of every person who has ever purchased anything from your site to a mailing list, and then send them e-mail every two weeks detailing the new products on your site. Some people may not mind receiving your e-mail; many others may find it highly irritating and will not shop at your site again.

What is spam?

Spam is Web-speak for unsolicited e-mail. There are probably millions of spam e-mails sent every day. We personally each receive more than 20 per day. Most of these messages come from casino Web sites, get rich quick schemes, and weight loss scams. Spam is the electronic equivalent of junk mail — except the content is sometimes much more offensive than anything we've ever received in the U.S. mail.

Exam Tip

The definition of spam is covered on the test, so be sure to study this section.

Companies that send spam buy mailing lists from other companies that compile lists of e-mail addresses, loosely categorized by interests. These companies, in turn, sell their lists to other companies, and so on. The net result is a whole lot of unsolicited e-mails sent to people who have no interest in the products being promoted.

If you want to run a respected and legitimate e-commerce business, do not send spam. Not only is it not very well targeted, but it will also give your company a bad reputation so fast it will make your head spin. Nothing moves faster than word of mouth on the Internet.

Many ISPs do not allow e-mails from companies that engage in spamming to enter their servers. There's also a very active online movement to report and sue spammers. See EmailAbuse.org (`www.emailabuse.org`) for the latest information on this campaign.

Targeting e-mail delivery

If you'd like to send e-mail to your subscribers more than approximately once a month, it's a good idea to break your mailing lists down by topic — that is, create multiple mailing lists with different themes.

An online music retailer, for example, could create a separate mailing list for each genre of music available at their site — classical, pop, rock, hip-hop, and so on. An e-mail could then be sent to each mailing list once a month listing new releases for the genre, editor's picks, and maybe an artist interview. This allows aficionados of rock to avoid classical listings. It also makes it more likely that people will subscribe, because they know the e-mails will only be about products in which they might be interested.

Another option is to create separate mailing lists for certain promotions, such as a discounted items newsletter, a weekly specials newsletter, a new release listening area promotion, or whatever is appropriate for your site.

By targeting your e-mails and creating separate mailing lists, you can increase the total number of subscribers and the number of e-mails being sent without overwhelming your recipients' in-boxes. This allows you to generate interest in more products than one e-mail could, while keeping your customers happy.

Managing mailing lists

One of the most important responsibilities for a site engaging in e-mail promotion is to keep its mailing lists well maintained. This means removing duplicate e-mail addresses, including clear instructions on how to unsubscribe on every e-mail, and making sure these unsubscribe requests are promptly executed.

Mailing list management software

Mailing list maintenance is easily automated with the use of bulk e-mail management software. Majordomo (`www.greatcircle.com/majordomo`) and ListMate (`www.listmate.com`) are two examples of software packages that can manage your database of subscriber information. They include duplicate removal, automated unsubscribing, and feedback on how well your newsletter is doing. E-mails can also be sent directly from your server computer.

Outsourced bulk e-mailing

Third-party companies also offer mailing list management and bulk e-mailing services. This is a very good option for companies who do not have the resources or do not want to maintain bulk e-mailing management software in-house. Some of these outsourcing services offer Web-based interfaces similar to the software packages previously mentioned.

Promotion through Listservs, Newsgroups, and Chat

Listservs, newsgroups, and chat areas are potential vehicles for online promotion — just as tempting as e-mail but requiring even more careful handling. Listservs and newsgroups are topic oriented, non-commercial mailing lists that allow recipients to post e-mails to a group, which is usually moderated by one member. Chats are areas of Web sites where users can converse in real time in a text-based format.

Listservs and newsgroups are intended for people who are serious about a particular topic, and are interested in sharing knowledge and learning from one another. There is very little place for promotions on such lists. If a member joins and posts some blatant marketing materials, such as a press release, for no purpose other than promoting a product, they will most likely be shunned by the community and possibly deleted from the group by the moderator. The only legitimate way to promote your company in a listserv or newsgroup is to provide unbiased, helpful information when appropriate, and assume your good behavior and advice will reflect well on your company.

Chats are somewhat more informal than listservs and newsgroups, but blatant marketers are not welcome here either. Operating on the same philosophy of helpfulness without promoting your product will serve you well in chat areas, too.

Key Point Summary

This chapter covered all the main points of online promotion, its techniques, and vehicles. The main points are:

- Publisher sites earn revenue from advertising.
- Marketer sites buy advertising on publisher sites.
- Banner advertisements are the most common form of online promotion today.
- The standard size for a banner ad is 468 by 60 pixels.
- Static and animated GIFs are the most common format for banner ads.
- Rich media banner ads offer more interactivity than GIFs but use more bandwidth. Some publisher sites do not accept them.
- The proven techniques for creating effective banner ads are to pose questions or call the viewer to action; frequently refresh your ads; use standard sizing, small file sizes, and animation; avoid false claims; create visual appeal; and make hyperlinks obvious.
- The position of your banner ad on the publisher's site can be as important as the message in your banner.
- Ad effectiveness is tracked by log analysis tools and tracking services.
- It may not be in the best interest of an e-commerce site to accept advertising, despite the potential for additional revenue.
- Banner ad networks, banner-trading networks, and referral programs are all good avenues for spreading your message.
- Building search engine and Web directory visibility is an essential part of online promotion, because many users ignore banner ads altogether.

- ✦ Search engines index sites with a software program called a spider or a crawler.
- ✦ Registration with search engines and Web directories can be automated by using registration software or a third-party service.
- ✦ Advertising on somebody else's e-mail newsletter is a good way to reach a targeted audience without the risks of conducting your own e-mail campaign.
- ✦ Spam is unsolicited e-mail.
- ✦ The only legitimate way to assemble a mailing list is to allow members to opt in.
- ✦ Listservs, newsgroups, and chat areas are potential vehicles for online promotion but require even more careful handling than e-mail.

✦ ✦ ✦

STUDY GUIDE

Now is the time to assess how well you've absorbed the main concepts and techniques of online promotion. Use the following questions, scenarios, and exercises to see how well you understand this material. Return to any chapter topics that are not quite clear for you.

Assessment Questions

1. Which of the following best describes the function of a search engine spider, or crawler?

A. To make a critical judgment on the relevance of a Web site to a given query

B. To index the content of a Web site's pages and return that information to the search engine

C. To find the title and description of a Web page

D. To attach a Web site to the World Wide Web

2. What is the most common form of online promotion? (Choose the best answer.)

A. Special cross-promotions

B. Tile ads

C. Banner advertisements

D. Link-trading

3. Which of the following is an example of a publisher site? (Choose the best answer.)

A. The Hungry Minds Web site

B. A portal site, such as Excite

C. The New York Public Library site

D. An online store, such as Amazon

4. Which of the following is the best definition for click rate?

A. The act of a user clicking on a banner ad

B. The number of times an image is downloaded

C. An instance in which a banner ad is displayed in a user's computer

D. The number of clicks on a banner ad per number of impressions

5. What are the two primary methods of documenting advertising traffic?

   A. Redirecting pages and log analysis

   B. Impression numbers gathered from the publisher site and log analysis

   C. Tracking services and log analysis

   D. WebSTAT and eXTReMe tracking

6. What is a drawback of using an advertising traffic tracking service? (Choose the best answer.)

   A. The tracking service has access to privileged information.

   B. It keeps the process in-house.

   C. It's more expensive than log analysis software.

   D. High bandwidth requirements.

7. Your online electronics store decides to offer advertising to select advertisers. Which of the following businesses should you approve as an advertiser? (Choose the best answer.)

   A. An online CD retailer

   B. A Web site that sells high-end audio equipment

   C. A discount stereo outlet

   D. A Web site that sells cables for audio equipment

8. Why might an e-commerce site decide not to accept advertising? (Choose the best answer.)

   A. Advertising is not e-commerce.

   B. A marketer site cannot also be a publisher site.

   C. An e-commerce site does not offer targeted marketing.

   D. It can drive traffic away from your site.

Scenarios

1. The marketing manager at your company is trying to decide whether to join a banner ad network or to set up individual relationships with publisher sites. What are some aspects of a banner ad network important to making this decision?

2. You're explaining the differences between search engines and Web directories to your CEO. What are the key differences you should point out?

3. You're testing a search engine to see whether your site is listed in appropriate queries. You're pleased with the results, but not with the way the search engine displays your site's listing:

```
Amy's Pet Shop
Kitty toys on sale for 20% off! Get 'em while supplies last.
Need a squeaky bone for Rover? Well, we've got . . .
```

This text refers to a sale you had several months ago. What can you do to make sure that this outdated information is not stored in the search engine again?

Lab Exercises

Lab 4-1 Register your site with a Web directory

1. Point your browser to Yahoo! at `www.yahoo.com`.
2. Navigate through this Web directory's hierarchy to the category in which you'd like your Web site listed. If you don't have a Web site, use the following links to reach the pet store area:
   a. Click the Business & Economy section.
   b. Choose Shopping and Services and then choose Animals.
   c. Choose Supplies, Equipment, and Gifts. This is where your pet store should be listed.
3. After you're in the proper section, scroll to the very bottom of the page and click the Suggest a Site link.
4. Read the information presented, and click the Proceed to Step One button.
5. The next page tries to sell you an enhanced listing for $199. Ignore this, and click the link underneath this advertisement to suggest a site using Yahoo!'s standard site suggestion process.
6. Go through the steps to enter your site into Yahoo!'s directory. If you don't have a real site, do not complete the process, just familiarize yourself with the kind of information requested.

Lab 4-2 Register your site with a search engine

1. Point your browser to AltaVista's search engine at `www.altavista.com`.
2. Scroll to the bottom of the home page, and click on the Submit A Site link.
3. Choose the option to submit your site to the AltaVista Search Index only (the free option).

4. Scroll to find the blue box with one form field titled AltaVista Search Index: Add or Remove a Page. Enter the URL of your site in this form field. Click the submit button. (Again, if you don't have a real site, do not complete the process; just familiarize yourself with the kind of information requested.)

Answers to Chapter Questions

Chapter pre-test

1. The standard size for a banner ad is 468 pixels wide by 60 pixels tall.
2. The most common format for a banner ad is a GIF, animated or static.
3. The `meta` element is an HTML element that contains information about a Web page.
4. The advantage of buying ad space at the top of a Web page is that the advertisement is the first image on the page that loads, and therefore the first image that the viewer sees. The disadvantage is that this is the most common ad placement and therefore ads in this location are often ignored.
5. Publisher sites, such as portals and content-driven sites, are supported only by advertising revenue.
6. A banner referral program pays referring Web sites a commission for traffic or purchases made on the sponsoring Web site.
7. Buying a list of e-mail addresses from another company and using the list as a mailing list for unsolicited e-mails is called spamming and is a very bad idea.
8. Advertising traffic can be documented by log analysis tools and tracking services.
9. Opt-in e-mailing lists are lists on which every e-mail address belongs to a person who specifically requested that e-mail be sent to them. Opt-out e-mailing lists are made up of e-mail addresses obtained from another company or from your own customer database. The owners of these e-mail addresses have not requested that e-mail be sent to them and need to opt-out in order to be removed from the list.

Assessment questions

1. **B.** The function of a search engine spider, or crawler, is to index the content of a Web site's pages and return that information to the search engine. All other answers are incorrect (see "How search engines index sites").
2. **C.** Banner ads are the most common form of online promotion (see "All About Banner Ads").

3. **B.** A portal site, such as Excite is the best example of a publisher site because publisher sites rely on advertising for revenue (see "Categorizing Web Sites").
4. **D.** Click rate is best defined as the number of clicks on a banner ad per number of impressions (see "Banner ad concepts and terms").
5. **C.** Tracking services and log analysis are the two primary methods of documenting advertising traffic (see "Tracking ad effectiveness").
6. **A.** The drawback of using an advertising traffic tracking service is giving the tracking service access to privileged information (see "Tracking ad effectiveness").
7. **A.** E-commerce sites that offer advertising should only allow companies whose products are complimentary to their own to advertise (see "Buying and selling banner ads").
8. **D.** The reason an e-commerce site may decide to not accept advertising is to avoid a practice that can drive away traffic (see "Buying and selling banner ads").

Scenarios

1. There are several advantages to banner ad networks. First, they provide you with the opportunity to purchase advertising on many Web sites at once without having to negotiate terms with each site individually. This provides your ads with more impressions with less effort on your part. Banner ad networks are not for the budget-constrained, however. If your marketing manager is looking for deals, he or she might have better luck negotiating contracts with each publisher site.
2. The essential difference between Web directories and search engines is that Web directories are assembled manually — by editors and by Web site owners who submit URLs for inclusion. Web directories are hierarchical databases of Web links organized by topic. Their content can be searched, but it's restricted by editors. Search engines use an automated program to index the Web systematically, and they return lists of links in response to queries. They are not organized hierarchically, but use the content and `meta` elements in Web pages to determine relevance.
3. The best way to ensure that a search engine displays the appropriate description for your site is to include a description in the `meta` element on your Web pages. That way, search engine spiders use the description portion of the `meta` element as the description for your Web site, rather than the first few lines of text content on your site. In this case, including something similar to the following code on your home page should solve the problem:

```
<meta name="description" content="We offer the best prices
and selection on the Web. Our pet supplies are guaranteed to
make your pets happy!" />
```

For More Information . . .

- **Coalition for Advertising Supported Information and Entertainment (CASIE).** www.casie.org. Offers guidelines for Web advertising.
- **Millward Brown Interactive.** www.mbinteractive.com. Conducts research on online promotion effectiveness. Results of selected studies are available online.
- **Banner Ad Placement Effectiveness Study from Webreference.com.** www.webreference.com/dev/banners/. Discusses the effectiveness of banner ad placement on Web sites.
- **Search Engine World.** www.searchengineworld.com. Search engine promotion and optimization site.
- **EmailAbuse.org.** www.emailabuse.org/. Dedicated to informing users of potential e-mail abuse and providing them with the tools to avoid becoming a victim.
- **Search Engine Watch.** www.searchenginewatch.com. Provides optimization tips and resources, plus submission information.

Designing an Effective E-Commerce Presence

P A R T

✦ ✦ ✦ ✦

In This Part

✦ ✦ ✦ ✦

CHAPTER 5

Building Usable Web Sites

EXAM OBJECTIVES

- The importance of usability
- Factors affecting usability
- Screen flow
- Analyzing usability
- Click patterns

CHAPTER PRE-TEST

1. What are the four goals of e-commerce?
2. What are a user's purchasing requirements?
3. Name the four steps involved in information architecture?
4. What is a click pattern?
5. What can a merchant do to streamline the ordering process?

✦ Answers to these questions can be found at the end of the chapter. ✦

Web design at its best puts usability first — not coolness or gee-whiz features. Many new Web site designers assume that multimedia and cutting-edge design will attract users and ensure frequent returns. Although this may be the case for entertainment-oriented Web sites, it's not true for business and e-commerce sites.

Although attractive design is important, users of business and e-commerce sites are extremely goal-oriented. Because bandwidth and screen space are limited, flashy graphics and complex site structures often end up taxing the limits of the average user's patience.

This chapter examines the Web from the user's point of view, and provides you with techniques for increasing the usability of an e-commerce Web site.

Understanding Web Usability

The importance of usability

The idea behind Web usability is that Web sites should be as efficient and easy to use as possible. The less a user has to think about how to work the various functions of a site, the more useful the site is. Because there are few or no design standards on the Web, every time a user visits a new site he or she has to learn a completely different user interface.

Imagine what it would be like if every time you switched the channel on your television, there were different buttons on your remote control or all the buttons rearranged themselves. Unless there was an overwhelming reason for you to switch channels often, you'd just stick to familiar ways of watching TV and familiar channels.

Getting a grip on the Web

Unfortunately, the problem of usability on the Web is not as simple as television difficulties. The primary reason for Web usability problems is that there is so much more you can do on the Web than you can do with a television. The Web's flexible and multipurpose nature is most like that of traditional software applications, where the tools and controls that are available depend on the task that the particular application is designed to perform.

Traditional software applications (such as word processors and spreadsheet applications), however, always have at least a few familiar features for users to grasp onto. For example, most programs developed for the Microsoft Windows operating systems have menus named File, Edit, and View in the upper left-hand corner. In addition, nearly every traditional software application has a Help menu that users can go to when they're confused.

In stark contrast to software applications, however, most Web sites don't have standard menus (outside of those provided by the browser), nor do they provide help features.

Building basic interface standards

Factors affecting usability

Fortunately, there are some user interface elements that have become standard safety nets for users who are trying to learn new Web sites. The following elements can have a direct impact on the usability of your site:

- **Search features.** Usually located near the top of each page, the search feature often serves as a new user's first and last option.
- **Logo to home page links.** A second feature that is starting to become standard practice in Web design is to link the company's logo back to the site's home page.
- **Back buttons.** Perhaps the most commonly used Web user interface standard is the Web browser's Back button. When users are attempting to locate information on a Web site, they either use the search feature, or try to find a site map. If following a hyperlink doesn't immediately provide them with the information they need, or if it appears to be useless information (such as a mission statement), they use the browser's back button rather than clicking deeper into the site's hierarchy.
- **Other standard elements.** Many design elements are also quickly becoming standard in certain types of online stores. These include tabbed menus across the top of the screen, left-hand navigation, and *breadcrumb* navigation, which shows all levels of hierarchy, from the highest level (parent) to the lowest level (child), as shown in Figure 5-1.

Figure 5-1: Breadcrumb navigation is a useful navigation aid that is rapidly becoming standard for certain types of sites.

Many people feel that it's only a matter of time before more user interface standards are adopted for the Web. Although many designers may see standardized user interface elements as creative limitations on Web design, most users would welcome some level of standardization. The evidence shows this is already happening.

Despite the movement towards standard design elements, the Web is still far behind traditional software user interface design (which, itself, still has quite a ways to go). To get a feeling for just how different Web user interface design is from software user interface design, just visit some different online shopping areas. For example, `www.walmart.com` and `www.target.com` are similar retailers yet their sites have very different navigational controls and the look and feel is very different. However, look at the software applications shown in Figures 5-2 and 5-3. They have very different functions, but similar user interfaces.

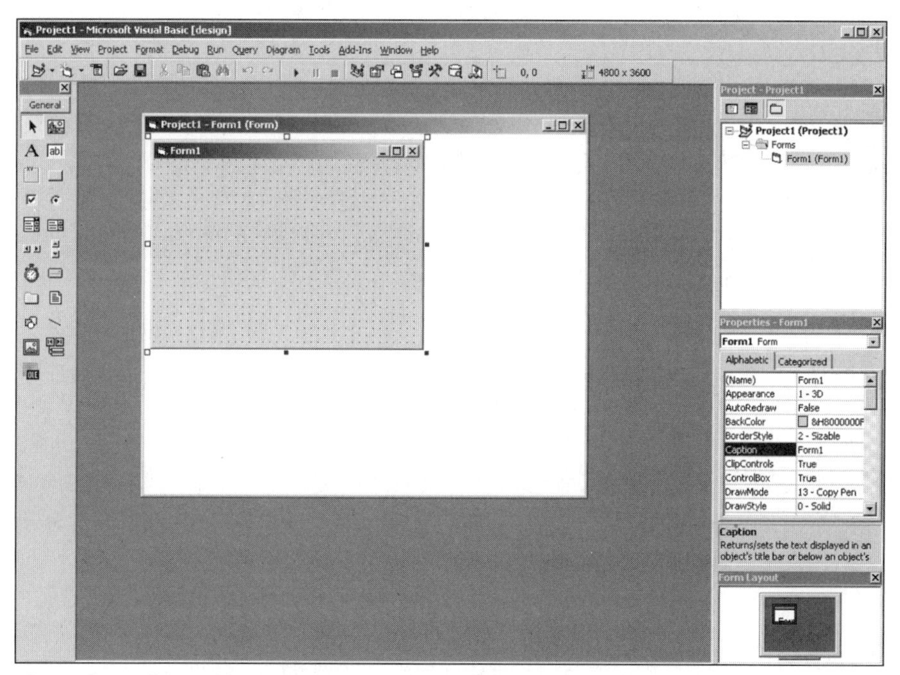

Figure 5-2: This software application has a different function, but its user interface is similar to the application shown in Figure 5-3.

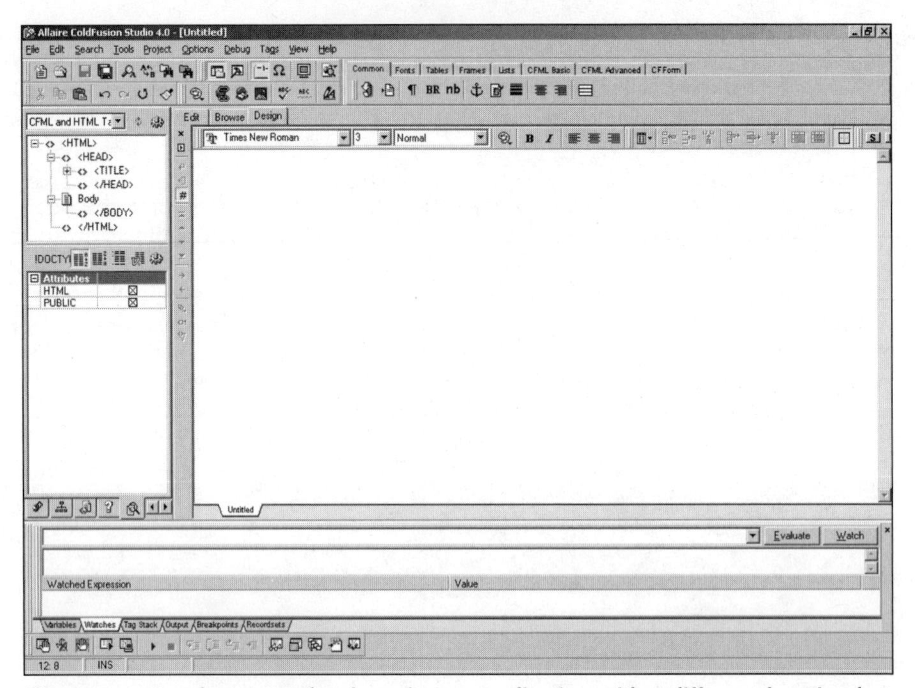

Figure 5-3: Another example of a software application with a different function but a similar user interface

Goals of E-Commerce

A usable Web site makes it possible for users (and hopefully, customers) to accomplish the following four e-commerce goals:

1. Getting to the site
2. Locating a product or service
3. Researching a product or service
4. Purchasing a product

Exam Tip Be sure that you understand why usability is important for e-commerce sites.

Getting to the site

Web usability begins before the user even loads your site's home page. Getting people to type your company's URL into their browser, or click on a link to your site is, of course, the first step in getting them to make a purchase on your site. Beyond promoting your site, here are some other ways you can make it easy for people to get there:

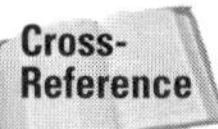

See Chapter 4 for some of the best techniques and tricks available to promote your Web site.

✦ **Choose a short domain name.** The domain name for your site should be short and easy to remember (and preferably easy to spell).

✦ **Test the load time.** To make your site usable by the greatest number of people, you need to test it using the lowest common denominator computer, browser, and Internet connection. The good news is that the lowest common denominator keeps getting higher!

Currently, you can safely assume that most users on the Web have at least a 33.6K modem, are using version 4.0 or higher of one of the major browsers, and have their monitors set at 800x600 pixel resolution. Even with these assumptions, there's plenty of room for incompatibility.

✦ **Test your site.** If your brand new site goes live before you've thoroughly tested it, and users see broken links, missing images, and error messages, chances are they may not return.

Locating a product or service

To improve the ability of users to locate information on your site, it's helpful to know how people typically use the Web. Usability analysis is the study of how easy it is for people to make sense of and successfully navigate Web sites.

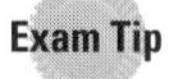

Usability analysis is an important concept in Web development, and will very likely be on the exam.

Studies of how people use the Web consistently discover and confirm the following facts:

✦ People typically scan Web pages for specific information, rather than analyze pages in detail.

✦ Users pay more attention to a site's content than to its design.

✦ Web users are very goal-driven. By the time they enter your e-commerce site, the chances are very high that they already know why they're there. No matter how badly you want to sidetrack a user who's shopping for envelopes into the higher-margin maps and art area of your site, it's very unlikely that you'll succeed — especially during a user's first visit to your site.

✦ Most visitors to Web sites don't look at the navigation (especially when the navigation is complex), they don't care about spinning logos and high-concept design, and they ignore advertising.

The purpose of Web site navigation and information architecture is to assist users in finding their way around your site. It's becoming clearer these days, however, that most people don't actually use a Web site's navigation. According to Jakob Nielsen, one of the Web's leading experts on Web usability, most Web users rely very heavily on search features rather than the site's navigation buttons.

Whether this is because so many Web sites are so difficult to navigate, or because users simply don't have the patience for learning a new user interface for every site, the message is clear: A usable Web design keeps the number of navigation elements on any one page to a minimum and provides a functional and centrally located search feature.

Some experts have recently even gone so far as to say that you should relegate your site's global navigation (navigation that's on every page of the site) to just a few very important text links in an inconspicuous location on every page and a prominently positioned search function. Our opinion is that this is too extreme for most sites.

Analyzing and designing usable navigation schemes are covered later in this chapter.

Researching a product or service

The conventional wisdom on the Web is that more information is better, but users shouldn't be shown more information than they request. A user's first view should generally show a list of products, with a brief description of each, and links to further information. At this level, it's vital that there's enough information shown about each product to uniquely identify it, but not so much that a user is overwhelmed.

Users should be able to dig through several layers of details to find as much information about a product as possible. Some companies worry that they will bore or alienate people if they put too much highly technical data on their site. This attitude, however, is inappropriate when it comes to the Web.

There can be such a thing as too much information in space and time-limited media such as television, radio, and print. On the Web, there's no minimum or maximum amount of time that someone can look at your product. It doesn't cost much to electronically publish large amounts of data, and hyperlinks make it possible for you to organize data so people interested in in-depth information can access it.

If you have long, dry white papers about your product and you're not sure whether they should be included on the Web site, make them available to customers anyway. Be sure, however, to separate these white papers from the main product page.

That way, you can not only convey a clear and simple message about your product for people who may be just starting to learn about it, but you can also provide in-depth information for those who are already familiar with the basics.

Purchasing a product

The end goal of a user's visit to an e-commerce Web site is usually to make a purchase (and this is certainly your goal for the user). This final step occurs provided the following purchasing requirements are met:

- Product availability
- Sufficient information
- Acceptable pricing
- Delivery terms

The usability of a site is very often the key factor that determines whether a shopper becomes a buyer.

Once a user decides to make a purchase on a Web site, however, there's still a very good chance that they won't follow through with the purchase. For example, a new user to an e-commerce site may have to enter billing information, shipping information, information about the specific products he or she is buying (such as size or quantity), and then confirm the purchase. This process can involve filling out forms on four or more separate Web pages. The longer the purchasing process takes, the more likely it is that the shopper will take their business elsewhere.

One technique for gathering the necessary purchase information is to ask for it all on the same page. The rationale for doing this is that users will have to click fewer times in order to purchase a product. Studies have found, however, that people are less likely to finish completing a single, lengthy form than several short forms.

Streamlining the purchase process

To minimize the number of aborted transactions, e-commerce site designers need to streamline the purchasing process as much as possible. Both users and owners of the Web sites can make improvements in this area.

User-side solutions

The AutoComplete and Autofill features in Microsoft Internet Explorer are two ways to speed up the process of gathering purchasing information. Here's how they work:

- **AutoComplete.** This feature stores information entered into previous forms and makes suggestions a user can choose or ignore when encountering forms asking for similar information. Figure 5-4 shows the AutoComplete feature in action.

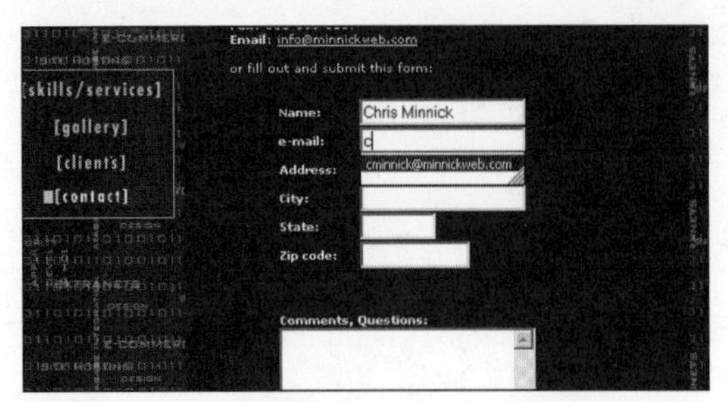

Figure 5-4: Microsoft Internet Explorer's AutoComplete feature

✦ **Autofill.** The Form Autofill feature, which was introduced with the Macintosh version of Internet Explorer 4.5, allows you to store specific personal information in your browser and use it to fill in forms when you encounter them.

The problem with AutoComplete and Autofill (from a merchant's point of view) is that they rely on the user to actually use them. Many users do not enable these types of features because of security concerns.

Server-side solutions

Browser-based solutions for simplifying the purchase process can only go so far. The following issues are those that need to be addressed by Web site owners and designers:

✦ **Creating a usable site.** The most important improvements are those designed and programmed into the site itself.

✦ **Storing user information and preferences.** The best way for an e-commerce site to simplify the purchasing process is to store user preferences and information on the server. Although there are many variations in the way this is accomplished, a user who has allowed a site to store his or her name, address, and possibly credit card information, can complete the ordering process with a minimal amount of effort.

✦ **Eliminating unnecessary forms.** To make this all function, however, new users still need to enter their personal information. Especially for first time users, forms must be simple and not ask for information beyond what is needed for payment processing and delivery of purchased goods.

Don't ask demographic questions during the ordering process – it may turn some potential buyers off. You can get that information later, after the buyer becomes a loyal customer.

Page Usage and Access Behavior

Web users have come to accept a certain amount of wait, confusion, and useless information from any site they visit. As a result, it's easy to impress users if an effort is made to reduce all three of these factors. If you're successful, your reward is customers who enjoy returning to your site.

Click patterns

Click patterns

A *click pattern* is the route a single user takes through your site. Web server log file analysis tools, such as WebTrends, can assist a site owner by identifying frequently used click patterns. The results can be used to improve the navigation and structure of a site. Click patterns are sometimes referred to as *paths*.

Understand the usefulness of click path analysis for identifying possible usability issues.

Listing 5-1 shows a click pattern through a typical store that allows you to purchase and download software.

Listing 5-1: Example of a click pattern

```
1.  http://www.fictitioussoftware.com/
2.  http://www.fictitioussoftware.com/products/
3.  http://www.fictitioussoftware.com/products/supersoft/
4.  https://www.fictitioussoftware.com/order/
5.  https://www.fictitioussoftware.com/order/
    paymentinformation.asp
6.  https://www.fictitiousoftware.com/downloads/supersoft/
```

The complete process of entering the site, finding a product, getting information about the product, ordering the product, and acquiring the product takes only six clicks in this example. This is an efficient click pattern, which either indicates that the site is extraordinarily usable, or the user is extraordinarily familiar with the site.

Listing 5-2 shows a click pattern that is much less efficient, and clearly indicates that the user is not having an easy time finding what he or she wants. In many cases, a visit that is going this poorly ends with the user hitting the back button until he or she is out of your site. If click patterns such as this one show up repeatedly in the Web logs, a good look should be taken at the site's usability.

Listing 5-2: An inefficient click pattern

```
1.  http://www.fictitioussoftware.com/
2.  http://www.fictitioussoftware.com/search/
3.  http://www.fictitioussoftware.com/products/hardware/
4.  http://www.fictitioussoftware.com/search/
5.  http://www.fictitioussoftware.com/support/faq/
6.  http://www.fictitioussoftware.com/search/
7.  http://www.fictitioussoftware.com/products/
8.  http://www.fictitioussoftware.com/about_us/
9.  http://www.fictitioussoftware.com/products/supersoft
10. https://www.fictitioussoftware.com/order/
```

Multiple paths

Providing multiple ways for users to locate the same information is a common technique for increasing their chances of having a successful and happy visit to your site. Typically, a Web site provides a search form, an advanced search form, and a means to get to anything on the site through hyperlinks.

In the following section, you examine Web site structure, information architecture, and screen flow. These three factors determine how easy it is for users to use a site's navigation features to locate information.

Web Site Structure and Screen Flow

Usability should be an important consideration from the very beginning, and one of the first steps in planning a Web site is to determine the organization of its content. This process is called *information architecture*.

Information architecture

Information architecture on the Web is about creating a consistent and logical structure of links. When the Web first began, people would refer to their presence on the Web as their *home page*. For many businesses, a home page was all that they had. These pages were typically long rambling documents with links to outside resources.

Creating a Web site architecture

Eventually, Web developers moved from creating independent pages to creating collections of linked pages, or Web sites. At first, Web developers simply gave the same level of importance to every page. As Web sites became larger and more complex, it became clear some information was just not as important as other types of information, and it's not possible to give every element on the home page equal weight.

Information architecture on the Web combines knowledge of user interface design with library sciences to find ways to logically organize and link Web pages. *Architecture* is the difference between a Web page and a Web site.

Here are the four steps to effective information architecture on the Web:

1. **Establish goals.** The goals and mission of the site should be agreed upon and clearly understood by everyone involved in creating the site. It seems rather simple, but all too often, the goals and mission of a Web site are not clearly understood before the design process begins. Taking the extra time to build consensus and understanding between everyone involved pays off in the long run.
2. **Understand the users.** When designing a usable site, it's vital to understand certain things about your users such as their ages, genders, income levels, education, and geographical locations. In addition, you should take into account factors such as the Internet connections and computers they're likely to have.

It's helpful at this stage to work with various departments in the company to get a clear picture of who the customers are and how various people in the company envision the user's experience of the site.

3. **Create a content inventory.** At this stage, you need to make decisions about the information you want on the site, and about the site's functionality. These determinations make up the *content inventory,* which is the basis for the final phase in the process.
4. **Organize the content.** Web sites generally use what is called an *organizational metaphor* for organizing content. For example, a Web site about animals could use an organizational metaphor based on how animals are classified in a zoo (reptiles, farm animals, felines, etc.). Other organizational metaphors might use alphabetical or numerical orders, or sorting by type, manufacturer, or color. If users understand how items are organized in other settings (such as physical stores), they shouldn't have a problem understanding the organization on a Web site. Because users are different, however, it's important to build as much redundancy into your organization as possible. For example, a shopper at a car-buying site should be able to locate the same car by clicking on the manufacturer as by clicking on the model year or color.

Creating a hierarchical organization

Most Web sites are organized as inverted trees. A user can locate any information on the site by following increasingly specific links. This type of structure is called a *hierarchical organization of information*. A Web directory such as Yahoo! is a classical example of hierarchical arrangement of Web data.

Here are three keys to creating a usable hierarchical Web site structure:

- **The fewer clicks the better.** Specific information should always be as few clicks away from the home page as possible. For someone designing a site's information architecture, this means eliminating unnecessary levels in a hierarchy. It also means hierarchically organized Web sites may have a large number of links on any one page. For example, one way to navigate to a garden hose in a home improvement catalog might be (with clicks shown as arrows): *Home ⇨ Outdoor Items ⇨ Water-related Items ⇨ Items for Moving Water ⇨ Flexible Items for Moving Water ⇨ Hoses.* A more intuitive path to the hoses might be: *Home ⇨ Yard & Garden ⇨ Hoses.* The second path to the hoses is much shorter than the first. This is possible because it makes one pretty big, but also pretty safe, assumption — namely, that people associate hoses with yards and gardens.
- **Intuitive categories.** It must be obvious to the user which link to click, from any level of a hierarchy, to get to the information he or she requires. As shown in the previous garden hose example, people have different experiences and ideas about how things should be organized. Your job is to find the most commonly used categories for items. This is not easy, as evidenced by the difficulties that most people have navigating the categorization scheme in a commercial phone book or the Yellow Pages. On the Web, fortunately, it's much easier to have cross-references and multiple names for the same information.
- **Redundancy.** Build in redundant links whenever possible. If there's only one link to every document on your site, it's very difficult for users to get around. If you include cross-references and multiple ways to get to documents (especially popular ones), users are less likely to feel lost.

By keeping these three rules of creating hierarchical navigation for the Web in mind (the fewer clicks the better, intuitive categories, and redundancy), it's possible to organize large amounts of data in a structure that can function without a search engine.

Screen flow

Screen flow

Less is more when it comes to Web page design. Users generally do not read entire Web pages but quickly scan the page looking for relevant information. By keeping the information on your pages concise and easy to access, you increase its impact and readability.

Many Web sites use the newspaper model to organize information. In fact, Web sites are very similar to newspapers in many respects. Newspapers generally have a main, or lead, story featured above the fold with an eye-catching photograph. Less important features are placed in the left column, with references to the full story inside. If a reader finds one of the short descriptions or titles interesting, he or she goes to that page.

The newspaper model is familiar and comfortable for readers. It allows them to see a large number of choices, but provides the opportunity to easily skip content of little interest.

Exam Tip: Be sure to remember that the newspaper model is a widely used way to organize content on the Web.

Analyzing Web Site Usability

Objective: Analyzing usability

After you've created a site that you believe is intuitive and user-friendly, you need to take one last step before launching it: usability testing. Usability testing can be as simple as just getting a couple friends who've never seen the site to try their hand at specific tasks. It can also be as involved as inviting strangers to pound on the site and give feedback in exchange for some sort of payment.

Watching people who are not familiar with a site attempt to navigate it can be a painful experience for the average Web site developer. The natural desire is to point to the screen and say, "Click here;" however, to get the most from the testing process and not contaminate results, you must refrain.

Some of the common usability problems that occur during testing include:

- ✦ **Overlooked links.** It's common for users to completely miss the most prominent link on a page, because it doesn't fit in with the way they think the site should work or their previous experience with the Web.
- ✦ **Broken links.** No matter how careful you are, there may be places where you misspelled a Web address, or where you renamed or moved a page and forgot to change a link. The result is broken links.
- ✦ **Unclear navigation labels.** Stick with commonly used labels, such as About Us or Contact Us, rather than trying to be clever or original and using a label such as Flying Pigs Here.
- ✦ **Poorly identified links.** Although it's currently fashionable to require users to roll their mouse pointer over items before its revealed that some parts of a page are links, this is not usable design. People expect links to be easily identifiable as such, either because they are colored differently and are underlined, or because there are other visual clues an action will occur when an item is selected.

Key Point Summary

The key points you learned in this chapter were:

- Usability is the primary factor in e-commerce Web design.
- There are four goals that people have in e-commerce: get to a site, locate a product or service, research the product or service, and purchase the product or service.
- Most users are more concerned with the content of a site than they are with its design or navigation.
- Information architecture is the process of organizing data.
- Both the user and the merchant can help streamline the purchase process.
- A click pattern is the route a user takes through a site.
- Click patterns can be studied to determine the usability of a site.
- Usability testing is the process of allowing people who are unfamiliar with a site to test it and provide feedback.

✦ ✦ ✦

STUDY GUIDE

Now it's time, once again, to get out your pencil and see what you've learned. When answering questions about usability, your best guide (besides this chapter, of course) is your own experience as a Web user.

Assessment Questions

1. Which of the following is not a characteristic of a usable Web site? (Choose the best answer.)

A. Fast download times

B. Uncluttered design

C. A search feature

D. Audio and video presentations

2. You're in charge of creating an e-commerce store for your company, Big Time Electric Devices. From your conversations with the company's marketing manager, you learn that a large percentage of the company's current customers are electrical engineers. Knowing this, which of the following items from your content list should be most prominently featured on the site? (Choose the best answer.)

A. Multimedia dinosaur-robot game

B. Technical specifications

C. Management biographies

D. Stock market quotes

3. What two items make up a content inventory?

A. Functionality and usability

B. Functionality and structure

C. Functionality and information

D. Information and structure

4. What is the difference between a Web page and a Web site? (Choose the best answer.)
   - **A.** Web sites have their own URL.
   - **B.** Web sites can have many different types of elements.
   - **C.** Information architecture.
   - **D.** Web pages don't have search buttons.

Scenarios

You're the information architect for a site that sells pet supplies. You're given an unorganized list of the products the company sells. Use the partial list shown in Table 5-1 to accomplish the following:

1. Think about how the items in Table 5-1 might be reorganized to accommodate future additions to the catalog and make it easy for shoppers to find products for their pet.
2. Using the knowledge gained from the previous exercise, make a list of the navigation elements that should be on this Web site's home page. (Any product can be placed in more than one category.)
3. Using the List of home page navigation elements you created in Step 2, create a list of second-level navigation items underneath each home page item.
4. Using the second-level navigation scheme you created in Step 3, fit each of the items into one of the categories from Step 2.

Table 5-1
List of Pet Supply Products

Item	*Item #*
chewy bones for dogs	dog100
fake mice for cats	cat101
rubber squeaky toys for cats and dogs	squ212
collars for cats and dogs	col001
cat food	cat002
cat litter	cat001
pet doors for cats, dogs, and ferrets	pet503
The Pet Handbook	book01

Lab Exercises

Lab 5-1 Comparing standard elements

As a result of the Web super-stores, standard categorizations and navigation elements are catching on quickly for sites that sell certain types of goods, including books, music, and software. Find eight Web sites that sell the same products or the same category of products and make a list of the similarities between them.

Lab 5-2 Finding your dream cruise

For this exercise, you're shopping for a Caribbean cruise leaving from anywhere but Miami, Florida. You would be happiest with a cruise that departs from Houston for a seven-day cruise and stops in Aruba. Visit several travel sites and compare how easy (or difficult) it is to find your dream cruise on each — without using the search feature.

Answers to Chapter Questions

Chapter pre-test

1. The four goals of e-commerce are: getting to the site, locating a product or service, researching a product or service, and purchasing a product or service.
2. A user's purchasing requirements are product availability, sufficient information, acceptable pricing, and delivery terms.
3. The four steps in information architecture are to establish goals, understand the users, create a content inventory, and organize the content.
4. A click pattern is the route a user takes through a Web site.
5. A merchant can streamline the ordering process by creating a usable site, eliminating unnecessary forms (especially during the order process), and providing a way to store user information and preferences securely on the site.

Assessment questions

1. **D.** As mentioned in the earlier sections of this chapter, "Understanding Web Usability" and "Goals of E-Commerce," users are goal oriented. To maximize the chances of them attaining their goals and being happy customers, you need to do everything possible to reduce impediments to them making a purchase. Although multimedia can be useful on a Web site, it usually does not add to a site's usability.

2. **B.** B is correct because this group of users will read as much information about your product as you provide (see the "Locating a product or service" section). A is incorrect because users are goal oriented. Don't sidetrack them, or you may lose them. C and D are incorrect because this information is not central to the goals of the users.
3. **C.** Web sites contain functionality and information. It's the job of the information architect to organize the functionality and information to create a usable structure. This is covered in the "Information architecture" section of this chapter.
4. **C.** Organized data and structure are necessary for a group of Web pages to be considered a Web site. Although some of the other choices may be true in many instances, these are only characteristics of Web pages and Web sites, not the fundamental difference between them. This is covered in the "Information architecture" section of this chapter.

Scenarios

In response to Steps 1 and 2, here's one possible way to list the home page navigation elements:

- Cats
- Dogs
- Other Pets

Another way to organize the information might be:

- Food
- Toys
- Books
- Other Supplies

Neither of these ways is perfect, of course. The final architecture should be based on usability testing and knowledge of the merchant's and the users' goals.

In response to Steps 3 and 4—for the first list displayed previously—the first- and second-level navigation might look similar to the following:

- **Cats**
  - Food
  - Toys
  - Books
  - Other Supplies

✦ **Dogs**
  - Food
  - Toys
  - Books
  - Other Supplies

✦ **Other Pets**
  - Food
  - Toys
  - Books
  - Other Supplies

For More Information . . .

For more information about Web usability and effective Web site design, please visit the following sites:

✦ **The Alertbox: Current Issues in Web Usability.** `www.useit.com/alertbox/`. This is Dr. Jakob Neilson's bi-monthly column.

✦ **Usable Web.** `www.usableweb.com`. This site contains links about Web usability.

✦ **WebWord.com.** `www.webword.com`. This site contains links to usability resources and an e-mail newsletter.

CHAPTER 6

E-Service for E-Customers

EXAM OBJECTIVES

- Define e-service
- Define synchronous, asynchronous, and self-service customer service methods
- Formulate an e-service action plan

CHAPTER PRE-TEST

1. What is e-service?
2. What are three examples of synchronous e-service?
3. What are two examples of asynchronous e-service?
4. Why are asynchronous service and self-service more commonly used than synchronous service?
5. What are the eleven keys to developing an effective e-service plan?

✦ Answers to these questions can be found at the end of the chapter. ✦

The Internet today is a buyer's market. For any product or service a person wants to buy, there are generally several (if not dozens) of merchants from which to choose. Many companies selling their products exclusively through real-world stores also use the Internet to increase the level of customer support, as well as reduce costs in this area.

In this highly competitive environment, if the quality of the products and the usability of the site are equal, the difference is determined by which merchant treats their customers better. This chapter looks at the pros and cons of the various methods available for providing the high level of customer service required in today's Internet market place.

Defining E-Service

Define e-service

Online customer service, or *e-service*, is changing the way merchants and customers think of customer service. In the past, the only way to increase the level of customer service was to increase costs. In a traditional business environment, adding a technical support department also means adding staff and equipment. E-service, on the other hand, can usually be implemented with less up-front costs than traditional customer service and far less on-going costs. For example, a list of frequently asked questions (FAQ) may take some time to compile, but once the FAQ is established, it can significantly reduce the number of technical support calls.

Be sure you can accurately define e-service.

The Internet economy has raised the bar for the level of service customers expect. Here's how:

- ✦ At the very least, customers expect to use the Web to locate a phone number or e-mail address for a company.
- ✦ Major shipping companies that have made commitments to e-service provide customers with the ability to at least track packages online, and in some cases, to actually get rates and print labels. This type of totally automated process is a win-win situation. The process costs the company very little, and it increases convenience for the customer.
- ✦ The Web is doing for many businesses what the ATM machine did for banking. Some analysts suggest that increasing the quality and capabilities of e-service are the next major transition on the Web.

In the business world, customer service is often referred to as *Customer Relationship Management* (CRM). CRM using the Internet is sometimes called *electronic CRM* (eCRM). According to forecasts by InfoTech Trends (`www.infotechtrends.com`), the business of providing CRM services is expected to grow to $23 billion dollars by the end of 2004.

✦ E-service also provides companies with an opportunity to get to know customers and personalize customer service. For example, a computer manufacturer's Web site might ask a user to rate his or her level of computer expertise. This data could then be used to display information that has a greater chance of being appropriate for the particular user. The ultimate goal of e-service is to create loyal customers for your product or service.

Providing E-Service

Define synchronous, asynchronous, and self-service customer service methods

All of the available e-service support options can be put into the following categories:

✦ Synchronous

✦ Asynchronous

✦ Self-service

These categories are discussed in the following sections.

Make sure that you understand the differences between asynchronous, synchronous, and self service, and that you can define and give examples of each of them.

Synchronous e-service

Synchronous e-service is service that is delivered personally and in real time. The advantage of synchronous service is that it's highly personalized. The disadvantages of synchronous service are: It's often more expensive for the company; it may have a higher learning curve than other methods; and it can be limited by hardware and software incompatibilities. Examples of synchronous e-service include:

✦ Chat services

✦ Voice connections

✦ Co-browsing

Chat services

Chat services allow specific and immediate exchange of information between the customer and the company in real time. This method generally requires the customer to use chat software such as an Internet Relay Chat (IRC) client or another stand-alone chat application. Some Web sites provide chat service through Java applets or ActiveX components, which load in the user's browser when the chat service is requested.

Some disadvantages of chat services are:

- ✦ They can be expensive to implement, and they have to be staffed. In addition, customers expect a level of service with live chat that is at least equal to what they would get in person or on the phone.
- ✦ Companies often use chat services to reduce the number of phone calls. However, if there aren't enough people responding to chat requests online, a chat service can be even more frustrating for a user than being on hold on the phone.

Companies providing software for online chat include:

- ✦ **Live Assistant.** www.liveassistant.com
- ✦ **Live Person.** www.liveperson.com
- ✦ **Brightware.** www.brightware.com
- ✦ **Kana Communications.** www.kana.com

It may not be long before chat support is commonly provided by artificial intelligence software, called chat robots, which can be "taught" to answer questions about a company and its products. For more information about artificial intelligence and e-service and to talk to a few chat robots, visit www.alicebot.org.

Voice connections

Products that allow people to speak to each other over the Internet have been around for several years now. Live voice over the Internet (called *telephony*) is still not fully ready for prime time — mostly due to bandwidth constraints. However, telephony is expected to become a viable option for many people in the not-too-distant future.

The advantages of telephony are that customers can place calls anywhere in the world without incurring long distance charges, and merchants can provide toll-free telephone support without having a toll-free phone number.

Other audio and voice connection options allow customers to enter phone numbers to place calls to merchants. A central calling hub then makes a standard telephone connection between the customer and the merchant. The advantage to customers is they are not billed, because it's actually the call center that places the calls. The disadvantage to customers is they need to have the ability to be on the phone and the Internet at the same time. This is not usually a problem for businesses, but it still is for many home users.

Co-browsing

Co-browsing (also known as *remote control*) is a concept that allows a customer support representative to control the customer's browser. Recent studies estimate more than 60 percent of all shopping transactions end before anything is actually purchased, and one of the reasons for this high number is that customers don't know what to do. Rather than attempting to figure out where on the site a customer is when they call in to customer support, co-browsing allows representatives to actually see and control what customers see on their screens.

Several vendors offer co-browsing tools, and several Internet conferencing or chat applications also have co-browsing or remote control functionality. Some of the companies that offer co-browsing software include:

- **Cisco Systems.** `www.cisco.com`
- **Microsoft.** `www.microsoft.com`
- **ICQ.** `www.icq.com`
- **n2g.** `www.net2gether.com/`
- **NetDive.** `www.netdive.com`

Asynchronous e-service

Asynchronous e-service is a concept that includes interactions between a customer and a live merchant representative, but not in real-time. Whereas a telephone call (or a face-to-face meeting) is an example of synchronous customer service, the physical world equivalent of asynchronous service is letter-writing or faxing. On the Web, however, the lag between the question and reply is often significantly less than in the real world. Instead of customer service requests taking several days to a week to be answered (as happens with written or faxed requests), many Web merchants answer e-mails within 24 hours.

Because it's very easy for a merchant to simply put a customer support e-mail address or a Web form on a site, asynchronous service on the Internet is the easiest and most common type of customer support.

E-mail

It's a fairly standard practice for companies to put general e-mail addresses at the bottom of Web pages so visitors to a site can contact the company. For example, a company might list the following e-mail addresses at the bottom of every page: `information@companyname.com`, `sales@companyname.com`, and techsupport@companyname.com. These e-mail addresses are generally links, that when clicked, open an e-mail message addressed to the company.

E-mail customer service is not suited for urgent or time-sensitive communications. If a customer has a question about a specific feature on your Web site or simply needs another bit of information before purchasing an item, e-mail is probably not the best way for the customers to get their questions answered quickly, or immediately.

Our experience is that e-mail is best suited for long explanations or requests for a merchant to fix something. Examples of when an e-mail is a better option than making a phone call or using another real-time service include:

- Filing complaints
- Requests requiring document or file attachments
- Letters telling of particularly good experiences
- Reports detailing technical problems with a site

Although it's simple to give customers the option to send you e-mail, failing to respond to e-mail in a timely and professional manner often results in the loss of customer trust and good will.

In dealing with a high volume of e-mails, it's common for large merchants to outsource at least part of the process of responding to customer e-mails.

Web forms

Web forms are similar to e-mail. Generally, the customer submits a form and the results go to someone who responds to the customer via e-mail. Forms have the following advantages:

- **Enhanced customer service.** Forms allow you to ask for specific information to help you to better serve the customer. Some examples of information that you might ask for on a Web form include:
  - Operating system
  - Type of browser
  - Phone number
  - User name
  - Preferred contact method
- **More specific information gathering.** Forms give you the opportunity to request information that a customer might not think to include in an e-mail, but that is important for solving the problem. The structure and specific questions of a form give customers a format for asking questions or making comments, which is often a more comfortable way for customers to provide

feedback. Many forms also have drop-down lists that allow customers to select one of several choices or choose Other and enter their specific questions. A well-designed form helps customers express themselves and helps merchants gather all the information necessary to provide good service.

✦ **Easier processing.** Forms can be processed more efficiently than e-mail. For example, the results of a form can get sent to different people or departments, depending on the choices the customer makes. If the customer indicates there's a problem with the shipment of his or her order, the message can be routed to shipping. If the customer indicates that his or her credit card was charged the wrong amount, the message can be automatically routed to billing.

✦ **Better data storage.** The results of form submissions can easily be stored in databases. These questions and the answers can then be used to create an area of the site where customers can look at the answers given to similar requests by other customers — similar to a FAQ.

Self-service

Self-service customer support options are often faster than either synchronous or asynchronous service, and are the least expensive service a merchant can provide. Self-service support options are often created as a result of synchronous or asynchronous support options.

For example, if most of the customer e-mails you get ask for the same information, you can dramatically reduce the number of calls, as well as make life easier for your customers, by simply making this information available on the Web site. The following sections detail some of the self-service methods that you may choose to use.

Client accounts and profiles

Giving customers the ability to view and alter account information is one of the best and most basic ways to improve customer service. Some examples include:

✦ Submit a change of address

✦ Check account balance

✦ Track shipments

✦ View order history

Banks and financial institutions are on the leading edge of customer self-service. Many banks now give customers the ability to check their balances, transfer funds, pay bills, apply for loans or lines of credit, trade stocks, and much more.

FAQ access

FAQ lists are often compiled from questions asked via e-mail or phone support and the answers that are commonly given. The idea behind a FAQ is to serve as the first place that a customer looks for answers to their questions. A FAQ is the most cost-effective form of online customer service, because it simply reuses answers already given to customer questions using some other form of service.

Knowledge databases

Knowledge databases (also called knowledge bases) can be thought of as better-organized FAQ lists. A knowledge database allows customers to select products or services, or search for particular keywords to gain access to lists of articles or a specific FAQ related to their query.

In Chapter 18, we walk through the process of creating a knowledge database for our fictitious e-commerce store.

Web-based/HTML help systems

Web-based help systems are similar to the systems included in traditional software applications. Using Dynamic HTML or Java applets, this type of online help offers a robust interface that customers can use to search through documentation, FAQ lists, and other support options.

These days, most developers of software applications provide at least some documentation for their products using Web-based HTML help. There are several vendors that offer products to automate the process of creating easy-to-use Web-based help interfaces and for populating them with information.

Bulletin boards and newsgroups

Bulletin boards and newsgroups are public areas where customers can post messages and get responses — either someone at the company or from other customers. When customers are gathering information from one another, these services fall into the self-service category. If the company monitors the bulletin board and responds to questions, these services fall into the asynchronous service category.

Whether you consider them self service or asynchronous service, or a combination of the two, bulletin boards and newsgroups can be effective ways to provide customer service, as well to encourage the growth of a community around your Web site.

If you're using an online community as a type of asynchronous service, make sure you do your best to quickly respond to every comment.

Enacting E-Service

Formulate an e-service action plan

Building a plan for providing e-service requires the involvement of several departments of a company. To develop the best plan, every department that interacts with customers should be involved (for example, marketing, communications, technical support, and sales).

Although it takes time and experience to create the best possible customer service plan, you should take the following steps (discussed in more detail in the following sections) to build a solid foundation for your plan:

1. Identify the customer.
2. Examine current Web traffic patterns.
3. Use suppliers when appropriate.
4. Use existing information.
5. Analyze potential tools.
6. Create a close relationship with the customer.
7. Gather information to be used for future planning.
8. Remove the fear of online purchasing.
9. Ensure privacy.
10. Provide transaction incentives.
11. Conduct service metrics.

Identify the customer

Finding out who your customers are is one of the basic marketing principles. When applied to customer service, knowing your customer greatly influences how you decide to provide service.

For example, your marketing staff may know the level of technical expertise of the average visitor to your site. This knowledge may influence your decision of whether to focus your efforts more heavily on synchronous, asynchronous, or self-service options.

Examine current Web traffic patterns

Click patterns can give you valuable insights into where visitors to your site are running into problems and the types of problems they're having. If an analysis of click patterns finds that a large number of users turn away from your ordering process at a certain point, it may be worthwhile to look at your ordering process and determine if additional help or customer service options at that point might keep users from abandoning the site.

For more information on click patterns and usability analysis, see Chapter 5.

Use suppliers when appropriate

If your online business depends on suppliers or outside companies — such as Web contractors, shipping companies, or fulfillment centers — these suppliers can often help identify ways to improve customer service.

For example, most paper magazines outsource shipping and management of their subscriptions lists to fulfillment centers. These centers often receive and process address changes primarily through paper forms and letters sent in by subscribers. However, the fulfillment centers can easily implement the capability to accept address changes via the Web or e-mail, which can dramatically speed up the process.

Outside suppliers may also be valuable in giving you insight into what other companies are doing to improve customer service. Your suppliers have an interest in your success and are often happy to share their specialized knowledge with you.

Use existing information

If you have an existing business that is branching out to the Internet, you probably already have a significant amount of information about your clients and customers, as well as the questions they may have. This information can be used to give you an advantage over newer businesses.

For example, a business can probably assume that some of the questions that visitors to a Web site may have are going to be similar to the questions received by its telephone support centers. If you already have a standard list of questions and answers, you may decide to use those answers as a FAQ list on the Web site.

Analyze potential tools

After you've collected as much information as possible about your customers and the types of questions they have, and after you've gotten input from all of the stake holders in your business, it's time to decide on specific tools.

There's certainly no lack of tools available for providing and managing e-service. A company creating a support system can spend anything from a few hours of an HTML writer's time to hundreds of thousands of dollars on software, ongoing support, and staffing costs, depending on their budget and needs.

Chapter 18 takes a look at some of the tools available for supporting e-service.

Take your time when deciding how to provide support. Inadequate options for customer support, or the wrong options, can be devastating to your business. After a customer leaves your site out of frustration, it's very difficult to get him or her to return.

Create a close relationship with the customer

Your Web site gives you the opportunity to create a one-on-one relationship with your customers. If you take advantage of this opportunity to make customers feel like a part of your site and the member of a community, you build loyalty. If you're only concerned with attracting new customers, the well eventually dries up. Repeat business is much more cost-effective than first time business.

Gather information to be used for future planning

After you have a system in place, you need to take full advantage of it to continuously improve the level of support you provide. If a user asks a question, add the question (or a generic version of the question) and its answer to a knowledge database or FAQ list so other visitors with similar questions can benefit.

Remove the fear of online purchasing

People's fears about e-commerce, whether justified or not, are a major barrier to the growth of business on the Web. As an online merchant, you need to make sure that your customers trust and respect your business. Providing professional and prompt customer service is key to this effort. If you ignore customer concerns, you can seriously damage your reputation and risk losing customers. Some of the ways that you and your business can remove the fear of online purchasing include:

- ✦ Create relationships with better known or more established e-commerce stores.
- ✦ Establish and enforce a privacy policy.
- ✦ Have your site's privacy policy certified by a trusted third party. For example, TRUSTe certifies privacy statements and allows sites that measure up to display a logo saying so.
- ✦ Provide a high level of security for purchasing.

For more information on building a firm foundation for e-commerce and overcoming customer fears, see Chapter 1.

Ensure privacy

Part of what customers are afraid of on the Web is that personal information about them can be stolen, sold, or traded without their knowledge. As a business, you need to be very up-front about your privacy policy, making sure that customers know what every bit of information you request is used for.

Your site's privacy policy should be easy to read and rigidly enforced.

Privacy policies, as well as other legal issues on the Internet, are discussed in more detail in Chapter 2.

Provide transaction incentives

Providing incentives to new customers and to regular and valued customers builds loyalty and repeat business. Some possible incentives include:

- Free shipping
- Discounts
- Free items
- Membership/frequent customer clubs

Conduct service metrics

Metrics are a way of objectively measuring a customer's experience on a site. Some of the factors to look at include download times, site availability, consistency of service, order turnaround time, shipping time, and the number of mistakes made or complaints received.

Although you may have a good feeling about the success of your e-service action plan, the only way to determine whether it's actually successful is to test it. A company can either devise tests of their level of service themselves or use one of the various third-party tools and services available for conducting service metrics.

Key Point Summary

Customer service is perhaps the most important part of running a successful Web storefront. Here's an overview of the main points in this chapter:

- Providing good service on the Internet can be much less expensive than providing traditional customer service.
- The three methods of providing e-service are synchronous, asynchronous, and self-service.

- Synchronous service involves a representative from the merchant providing support to the customer in real time. Examples of synchronous service include chat, telephony, and co-browsing.
- Asynchronous service involves a time delay in the communication between the customer and the merchant. Examples of asynchronous service include e-mail and Web forms.
- Self-service options provide ways for customers can get information on their own. Examples of self-service include profile/account access, online communities (such as message boards), FAQ lists, knowledge databases, and HTML help.
- Creating an e-service action plan should not only involve the information systems staff, but also marketing, communications, and other departments that interact with customers and suppliers.

✦ ✦ ✦

STUDY GUIDE

Once again, it's time to quiz yourself on the contents of this chapter and hopefully pass a real-world test of your grasp of the concepts of e-service. As always, the answers to all the questions in the study guide are at the end of the chapter in the "Answers to Chapter Questions" section.

Assessment Questions

1. Which of the following is the best definition of e-service?

A. E-service is online customer service.

B. E-service allows the customer to have real-time communication with the merchant.

C. E-service is limited by bandwidth.

D. E-service gives you insights into who your customers are.

2. Your company doesn't sell products or services over the Internet, but you're considering offering customer support options through your Web site. Which of the following is not a reason to implement e-service?

A. E-service is more cost effective than traditional customer service.

B. Customers expect a high level of customer service, and this increasingly includes e-service options.

C. Providing good e-service requires no effort.

D. E-service can reduce the load on your traditional customer service.

3. Which of the following is not an example of synchronous service?

A. Telephone or telephony support

B. Chat

C. Message board

D. Co-browsing

4. Your company has decided to sell products over the Web. To make the customer's experience as pleasant and easy as possible, you're considering various types of synchronous service, asynchronous service, and self-service support options. Which of the following is an advantage to using synchronous support options?

   A. Low cost

   B. Highly personalized service

   C. Creates community

   D. Synchronous service options are searchable

5. How can analysis of click patterns be useful for developing your e-service action plan? (Choose the best answer.)

   A. Click pattern analysis can tell you what customers think of your site.

   B. Click pattern analysis can give you insight into problems customers are having on your site.

   C. Click pattern analysis provides highly personalized service.

   D. Click pattern analysis creates community.

6. Which of the following is not a way you can build customer trust and goodwill in order to remove the fear of online purchasing?

   A. Establish a privacy policy and make sure it's strictly enforced.

   B. Create relationships with other trusted e-commerce businesses.

   C. Provide a high level of security for purchases.

   D. Lend information about your customers to other companies so they may tell your customers about other products they might be interested in purchasing.

Scenarios

As the customer support manager for a shoe manufacturer planning to offer e-service through its Web site, you have been asked to come up with an action plan. A study of the types of information people most often request about your products reveals the following list of top ten reasons people contact your company's customer support department. How do you think each of these requests could best be handled through the Web?

Top ten reasons people contact CyberShoes:

1. Questions about where they can purchase the shoes.
2. Questions about availability of sizes.

3. Questions about availability of colors.
4. Questions about prices.
5. Defective shoe complaints.
6. Wish to express satisfaction with shoes.
7. Special requests, such as the possibility of buying two left shoes or pair of differently sized shoes.
8. Catalog requests.
9. Change of address for catalog mailings.
10. Suggestions for improving current products or developing new products.

Lab Exercises

Lab 6-1 Working with a Web knowledge database

Enter `http://kb.indiana.edu` in your browser to see the Indiana University Knowledge Base screen. This is a good example of self-service knowledge base. The questions and answers in this knowledge base were probably compiled from a variety of sources, including e-mail support and standard answers to telephone or live support questions. Try a few searches and view the questions and answers that result.

Lab 6-2 Viewing examples of self-service, synchronous, and asynchronous e-service

Enter `http://www.expedia.com/daily/service/` into your browser. This page contains links and information about many of the types of e-service mentioned in this chapter. See how many different service options you can find and identify.

Answers to Chapter Questions

Chapter pre-test

1. E-service is customer service that is provided online.
2. Three examples of synchronous service include chat, voice connection, and co-browsing.
3. Two examples of asynchronous service include e-mail and Web forms.
4. Asynchronous service and self-service are more common because they're easier to implement.

5. The eleven keys to creating an e-service plan are: identify the customer, examine current Web traffic patterns, use suppliers when appropriate, use existing information, analyze potential tools, create a close relationship with the customer, gather information to be used for future planning, remove the fear of online purchasing, ensure privacy, provide transaction incentives, and conduct service metrics.

Assessment questions

1. **A.** This is the simplest definition of e-service. Some of the other options may be benefits of e-service, characteristics of some types of e-service, or predictions about e-service, but only A is actually a definition of e-service (see the "Defining E-Service" section).
2. **C.** Although e-service provides benefits, it's important that it's done correctly, and that takes some effort (see "Defining E-Service").
3. **C.** Message boards can be either asynchronous or self-service (see the "Bulletin boards and newsgroups" section).
4. **B.** Synchronous service allows you to have personal interactions with customers and provide highly personalized support (see the "Synchronous e-service" section).
5. **B.** By analyzing click patterns, you can often discover areas of your site where customers have problems or where they abandon the purchase process (see the "Enacting E-Service" section).
6. **D.** The key to becoming a trusted e-commerce merchant is to conduct your business in a professional manner and be respectful of your customers. Because of the horror stories we've all heard, the bad experiences some of us have had, and the lack of physical contact with merchants on the Web, establishing trust and goodwill for your e-commerce Web site is often an uphill battle (see the "Enacting E-Service" section).

Scenarios

There are no absolutely correct answers for this scenario, but reasonable solutions for providing e-service options for each of the top 10 reasons people contact customer support might be as follows:

- ✦ Reasons 1 through 4 — questions about where shoes can be purchased, sizes, colors, and prices — can all best be handled by a FAQ or simple product information pages on the Web site.
- ✦ Reason 5 — defective shoe complaints — should either continue to be handled over the phone or should be handled using a Web form that asks customers for specific information about the nature of the defect.

- Reason 6 — people who wish to express their satisfaction with any product or service — is best handled by always welcoming contact with the merchant in any way they please.
- Reason 7 — special requests — are best handled using asynchronous service. This gives customers time to explain their needs, and it gives the merchant time to research the possibility of filling the request.
- Reasons 8 and 9 — catalog requests and address changes — are perfect for self-service customer support or simple Web forms.
- Reason 10 — suggestions for improving current products or developing new products — are rarely time-sensitive and can therefore be done using either e-mail or Web forms.

For More Information . . .

To find out more about providing customer service on the Internet, please visit the following Web sites.

- **Internet.com's CRM Library.** `http://ecommerce.internet.com/resources/library/crm`
- **eHelp Corporation.** `www.ehelp.com`
- **Customer service resources at the Open Directory project.** `www.dmoz.org/Business/Customer_Service/Resources`
- **Customer Service Review.** `www.csr.co.za`

Supporting Business-to-Business Activities Online

✦ ✦ ✦ ✦

EXAM OBJECTIVES

- B2C and B2B business models
- Electronic Data Interchange (EDI)
- Open Buying on the Internet (OBI)
- Open Trading Protocol (OTP)
- Business-to-business networks

CHAPTER PRE-TEST

1. What are the goals of EDI?

2. How is the Internet changing EDI?

3. How do businesses of different sizes benefit from Internet EDI?

4. What is XML?

5. What are the four components of OBI?

6. What are the three key features of OTP?

7. What is a business-to-business network?

✦ Answers to these questions can be found at the end of the chapter. ✦

In Chapter 1, commerce was defined as the exchange of goods and services for money. Commerce is made up of three components: communication, data management, and security. The idea behind business-to-business (B2B) e-commerce is to automate each of these processes in inter-company commerce.

Building and working with B2B applications requires an understanding of existing infrastructure and integration issues. This chapter briefly revisits the differences between B2B and B2C e-commerce. You then take a look at some B2B e-commerce-specific issues and a few of the standards and frameworks used to conduct B2B e-commerce over the Internet.

Understanding Online Business Models

B2C and B2B business models

The two most widely used models for conducting online business are B2B and B2C (also sometimes abbreviated as B-B and B-C, respectively). The fundamental difference between these two models, of course, is that in B2B, the purchaser is another business and in B2C, the purchaser is an individual. As a result of this difference, B2B e-commerce is conducted differently than B2C e-commerce. B2B e-commerce is more complex than B2C e-commerce because of the unique needs and requirements for business purchases and the higher costs involved in B2B transactions.

Two other online business models, consumer-to-consumer (C2C) and consumer-to-business (C2B), are sometimes talked about among e-commerce businesses. C2C e-commerce usually refers to online trading activities between consumers, and C2B refers to customers sending purchase requests to businesses. In our opinion, these two possible combinations are simply unnecessary buzzwords for types of business that are already covered by B2B and B2C. C2C and C2B are not covered on the exam.

Business-to-consumer

Although the business-to-consumer (B2C) model has many variables, it's essentially less complex than the business-to-business (B2B) model. B2C relies on many individuals making individual purchases. The margins for B2C are large because of the low volume of the purchases. For example, an individual is unlikely to buy more than one computer during a single purchase. The company selling the single computer to an individual charges a higher price, because the company selling the computer pays a higher wholesale price than if it bought ten computers at the same time.

The small purchases that are typical of B2C require companies in this market to have a broad enough market niche to attract a large number of customers.

Chapters 3 and 4 deal with the issues involved in determining your market niche and promotion of goods and services online.

Business-to-business

The B2B market is driven by high-volume transactions between businesses. The commonly used metaphor in B2C of a shopping cart and a checkout process doesn't fit very well with the nature of B2B business. Businesses commonly buy commodity goods and services in bulk and expect a different level of service than consumers.

For example, businesses making large purchases may expect discounts or have specific shipping or processing needs. Companies selling commodity items can increase their profit margins in B2B commerce by improving the process and reducing the cost of selling goods and services to other businesses. The Internet is becoming a major factor in B2B commerce because of the potential it holds to reduce costs and streamline the process of conducting transactions.

As a result of the specific needs of suppliers and buyers of commodity items, standard methods and protocols have been developed over the years for conducting these transactions. The most common standard for conducting B2B e-commerce is Electronic Data Interchange (EDI). EDI is not a new standard. It is, however, getting a major makeover as a result of Internet technology. The next generation of EDI is rapidly emerging. It's known as Internet EDI.

For more information on the genesis of the EDI standard and how it has evolved, see Chapter 1.

All About Electronic Data Interchange

Electronic Data Interchange (EDI)

EDI is a standard for inter-organizational exchange of documents in standardized electronic form directly between participating computers. EDI is often used as a replacement for paper-based transaction infrastructures; such as purchase orders, invoices, bills of material, and material releases.

The purpose of EDI and the goals of EDI are the foundation for several questions on the exam.

EDI explored and explained

The goals of EDI are as follows:

- To make communication of structured information easy and inexpensive throughout an entire transaction
- To reduce the number of errors and the time spent handling errors in transactions
- To speed up the process of handling transactions to increase cash flow

Organizations that exchange EDI transmissions are called *trading partners*. EDI has been widely adopted by large companies in many industries, including automotive, retail, chemical, electronics, electrical, petroleum, metals, paper, and office products.

Limiting factors

More widespread adoption of EDI has been hampered by several factors, including the following:

- **High cost of entry.** Traditionally, smaller organizations have only adopted EDI if they have been forced to in order to do business with large organizations.
- **Lack of clear standards.** Because of the unique nature of transactions between different businesses and different industries, many industries and businesses created their own flavors of EDI. Lack of standardization in message formats slows down the process because trading partners have to agree on whose standard to use before they can conduct business using EDI.

In recent years, both of these concerns have been largely addressed, and the result has been a new and improved EDI. Combined with Internet technologies, such as the Extensible Markup Language (XML) and Virtual Private Networks (VPNs), EDI is finally starting to deliver on its goals for more than just the largest organizations.

The X12 standard

One of the most important steps in making EDI more accessible was the creation of standard formats. In North America, the standard for EDI messages is the X12 standard. The X12 standard was developed and maintained by the Transportation Data Coordinating Committee (TDCC) from the early 1970s until the early 1990s, when it was adopted by the American National Standards Institute (ANSI).

The X12 standard for EDI is modeled on the structure of a relational database. Here are some key terms related to EDI messages with which you should become familiar:

- **Data element.** Exactly what it sounds like: a single discrete piece of information, such as a price or a date. Data elements are similar to fields in a database record.

✦ **Segment.** A collection of related data elements. For example, a segment might identify one of the organizations involved in a transaction using the company name, address, and other contact information. A segment is similar to a record in a database table.

✦ **Transaction set.** The basic unit of EDI business. Transaction sets are the EDI equivalent of paper invoices or forms. They describe the order and format of the data to be exchanged.

✦ **EDI messages.** The container in which transaction sets are exchanged.

A typical EDI transaction

So you can get a clearer picture of the process that takes place in EDI transactions, Figure 7-1 illustrates a transaction between a buying organization and a selling organization.

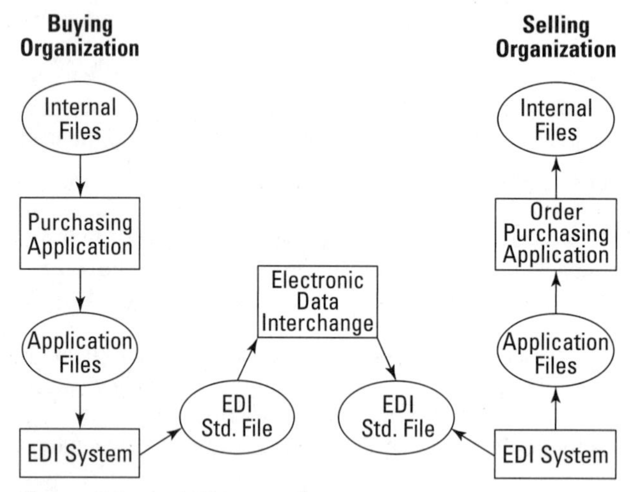

Figure 7-1: An EDI transaction

Here's a detailed description of the step-by-step process illustrated in this graphic:

1. A buying organization enters purchase information into purchasing software.
2. The files created using the purchasing files are then sent to an EDI system.
3. The EDI system creates standard EDI files using the format described previously.
4. These EDI files are routed over a network, which may be either a Value Added Network (VAN) or a VPN, to the selling organization.
5. At the selling organization, the EDI message is read and converted into a format that can be read by the order processing system and an order is generated. It's that easy.

Who should use EDI?

Exam Tip — For the exam, you should have a good idea of what sort of company can use EDI.

Although progress has been made in making EDI accessible to a broader range of companies, EDI still doesn't make sense for everyone. The following is a list of the characteristics of a company or industry that should consider a conversion to EDI:

- Handles a large volume of repetitive, standard transactions
- Operates on a very tight margin
- Faces strong competition, requiring significant productivity improvements
- Operates in a time-sensitive environment
- Has received requests from partner companies to convert to EDI

EDI on the Internet

Although there are newer ways to conduct B2B e-commerce, EDI should be around, in one form or another, for quite some time. EDI has been the established format for about 30 years, and people are rightly reluctant to throw out that much experience.

EDI that is conducted using the Internet is called, appropriately enough, *Internet EDI*. Traditional EDI, with its rigid transaction sets and high cost of entry, is going to be largely transformed in the coming years as a result of two factors:

- Inexpensive networking between any two companies using the Internet
- Flexible new data description languages

Inexpensive networking

The biggest change taking place in EDI is that the Internet is making it possible and cost-effective for small- to medium-sized businesses to participate in an arena that has, until recently, been dominated by large companies. Internet EDI is much less expensive than traditional EDI, mostly because it eliminates the need for private networks.

Traditionally, private VANs have been used to insure the delivery and the security of EDI messages. Today, encryption and authentication technologies make it possible for EDI to be conducted over the public Internet, as you find out in the "Security issues for EDI" section later in this chapter.

Flexible data description

The second factor transforming EDI into Internet EDI is the growth of new and more flexible ways to describe data. The technology that is making this possible is the Extensible Markup Language (XML).

XML is a trimmed-down and simplified version of Standard Generalized Markup Language (SGML), which has been used to describe data for many years. In much the same way that Internet EDI is a more accessible version of traditional EDI, XML is a much more accessible version of SGML.

SGML and XML are languages for creating languages, or *metalanguages*. In much the same way that grammar defines a language, XML is used to define new markup languages for very specific computing needs.

For example, you could create an XML language to use to exchange information about pie selling between restaurants and their pie suppliers. A typical message in this new pie ordering markup language might look like this:

```
<pie_order>
    <filling_type>Apple</filling_type>
    <quantity>40</quantity>
    <price_per_pie>$5.99</price_per_pie>
    <delivery>
        <method>Express</method>
        <time>6:00A.M.</time>
    </delivery>
</pie_order>
```

Whereas traditional EDI message formats use one very large, standard language with specific business rules embedded in it, XML's generalized nature allows many different languages to be created for exchanging different types of information.

The benefit of using XML is that very specific languages can easily be created to meet the particular needs of a business or industry. The potential danger of XML is that businesses and industries need to decide on standard XML vocabularies in order to communicate with each other effectively.

Benefits of Internet EDI

Benefits for both large and small businesses are expected to result from the growth of EDI among smaller businesses. These benefits are:

- Established EDI users will have new trading partners with access to EDI. This is significant, because the cost of doing business with non-EDI vendors is estimated to be about 25 times higher than with EDI vendors. As a result, some large organizations have decided to only conduct business with other organizations that use EDI.
- Small to medium-sized businesses will be able to compete with large organizations that they couldn't compete with in the past.

Make sure you know the benefits of Internet EDI over traditional EDI.

Security issues for EDI

Traditional EDI is conducted via messaging over secure frame relay or leased lines. Messages sent this way are fairly well insulated from the outside world. On the Internet, however, EDI messages travel over the same lines and through the same computers as the rest of the Internet's traffic. This increases security risks.

One of the ways security risks are reduced in Internet EDI is by using secure e-mail. Secure Multipurpose Internet Mail Extensions (S/MIME) is a standard that was endorsed in 1995 by a group of leading networking and messaging vendors in collaboration with cryptography developer Rivist-Shamir-Adelman (RSA) Data Security. Here's how S/MIME works:

Pay close attention to S/MIME and all other security-related issues, standards, and terminology.

- S/MIME allows encrypted e-mail messages to be exchanged among different e-mail programs. In other words, an S/MIME message that was composed using one operating system (Windows, for example) and using one vendor's e-mail application (Microsoft Outlook, for example) can be decoded and read by any S/MIME-capable e-mail program on any other operating system.
- S/MIME is based on the Multipurpose Internet Mail Extensions (MIME) protocol. MIME is the standard that provides a general structure to the content of Internet mail and allows files to be associated with different applications (such as security applications). Chances are you've encountered MIME types frequently while trying to open files on your computer for which you don't have the right program.
- S/MIME describes how encryption information (which provides privacy) and a digital certificate (which provides authentication) can be included as part of the message body of e-mails. S/MIME uses RSA's public key encryption system.

If you just glanced over the previous bullet point, go back now and read it again. Don't worry if you don't understand it yet. Encryption and digital certificates are covered in great detail later in the book in Chapter 19.

Open Buying on the Internet

Open Buying on the Internet (OBI)

Open Buying on the Internet (OBI) is a freely available Internet e-commerce standard for B2B transactions. The OBI standard was created in 1996 and 1997 by the Internet Purchasing Roundtable. OBI is developed and improved by the OBI Consortium (`www.openbuy.org`), a non-profit group that is managed by CommerceNet, and is underwritten by corporate sponsors including American Express, Visa, Netscape, Microsoft, and Dell.

OBI explored and explained

OBI is intended for use in high-volume, low-dollar transactions, which are estimated to make up 80 percent of the purchasing activity of most organizations. Because OBI is an open standard, it's not subject to many of the incompatibility problems that are associated with EDI. OBI supports the open technologies listed in Table 7-1.

Table 7-1
Open Technologies Supported by OBI

Purpose	*Technology*
Content Display	W3C Hypertext Markup Language (HTML)
Order Request	X12 850 EDI Standards
Order Transmission	Hypertext Transfer Protocol (HTTP) 1.0
Transmission Security	Secure Sockets Layer (SSL)
Cryptography	SSL
Public Key Certificates	X.509, Version 3

Don't worry if you don't know what all of the technologies listed in Table 7-1 are just yet. You'll know by the time you're done with this book.

OBI allows for any approved person in an organization to buy needed products or services. By automating the process of purchasing non-production supplies, such as office supplies, cleaning products, and so forth, the processing costs associated with these necessary tasks are dramatically reduced. The following section takes a look at the components and steps involved in OBI transactions.

OBI transactions

OBI transactions consist of four components:

- **Requisitioner.** The person or software initiating a purchase transaction.
- **Buying organization.** The organization to which the requisitioner and the OBI server being used by the requisitioner belongs.
- **Selling organization.** The company with an OBI server and that offers the product or service for sale.
- **Payment authority.** An organization that acts as a neutral third party to settle the financial component of the transaction.

An OBI transaction consists of the following four steps:

1. Order placement using an OBI server at either the buying organization or the selling organization.
2. Approval by the buying organization.
3. Transfer to the selling organization for fulfillment.
4. Money transfer by the payment authority.

The OBI transaction process involves several safeguards against fraud and unauthorized purchases, as the following hypothetical OBI transaction demonstrates.

- **Step 1.** Sam, the mailroom manager at Big City Industries, needs to order envelopes. He accesses the online catalog at Major Office Supplies. This catalog is hosted on the OBI server at Major Office Supplies.
    - In this situation, Sam is the requisitioner, Big City Industries is the buying organization, and Major Office Supplies is the selling organization.
    - The Major Office Supplies catalog has prices that are specific to Big City Industries. For example, because Big City Industries purchases far more envelopes than Small Town Industries (who also happens to be a customer of Major Office Supplies), Big City Industries gets envelopes cheaper.
    - Sam (the requisitioner) locates the products he requires and adds them to a shopping cart and places an order with Major Office Supplies.
- **Step 2.** Sam's order is sent back to Big City Industry's OBI server for approval. The order is checked to insure it was actually placed by Sam and that he has proper spending authority. This process can be completely automated, or it may require intervention by management.
- **Step 3.** The order is approved and sent to Major Office Supplies' OBI server for fulfillment.
- **Step 4.** The payment authority, a bank, handles the billing and money transfer.

OBI and EDI compatibility

OBI messages are formatted using the North American standard for EDI messaging, ANSI EDI X12 850. This makes it easier for companies who have already invested in EDI to transition to OBI.

OBI solutions

To locate some of the applications that support OBI, check the following sites:

- **Netscape CommerceXpert.** http://home.netscape.com/commapps/products/index.html
- **Epic Systems' B2B Toolkit.** www.epic-systems.com
- **IBM's WebSphere Commerce Suite (formerly Net.Commerce).** www.ibm.com/websphere

The future of OBI in e-commerce

As OBI moves forward and becomes more widely used, the next steps in its development are support for XML technologies and internationalization. To learn more about the latest developments with OBI, visit the OBI Consortium at www.openbuy.org.

Open Trading Protocol

Open Trading Protocol (OTP)

The Open Trading Protocol (OTP) is an open protocol for B2B transactions that has been promoted by a group of corporations, including AT&T, CyberCash, DigiCash, Hewlett-Packard, Oracle Corporation, Sun Microsystems, Wells Fargo Bank, and the Royal Bank of Canada.

Open Trading Protocol (OTP) is currently being developed by the Internet Engineering Task Force (IETF) and is now known as Internet Open Trading Protocol (IOTP). Find out more at www.ietf.org/html.charters/trade-charter.html.

OTP explored and explained

According to the OTP Web site, OTP is a protocol for the development of software products that allows product interoperability for the electronic purchase independent of the chosen payment mechanism. This means that e-commerce software that supports OTP can work with different types of hardware and software, as well as different payment methods. The idea behind OTP is to provide a consistent and easy-to-use online experience for customers, merchants, and banks.

OTP uses XML to describe transactions, and it supports EDI. Here are three key items you need to know about OTP:

- It provides Trading Protocol Options, which control how the trade occurs.
- It manages the process of providing a record of a trade for consumers as well as merchants. This record can be used for tax purposes, making expense claims, for importation into financial management software, and so on.
- It supports both real and virtual delivery of goods and services. For example, a merchant could manage the trade of downloadable files over the Internet, as well as the sale and shipment of books or computers.

OTP spans the entire life cycle of a business transaction and is optimized for transactions in which the buyer and the seller do not have a prior acquaintance.

OTP standards

To learn more about OTP (or IOTP), visit the Internet Engineering Task Force at `http://www.ietf.org`.

Business-to-Business Networks

Business-to-business networks

Some businesses are using B2B Web sites that focus on bringing buyers and sellers together. The benefit to using these networks is that participants don't need to make a large investment in infrastructure in order to get the benefits of B2B e-commerce.

Some of these networks use an auction format where anyone can be a seller, and others have affiliations with established suppliers. These e-commerce sites are different from typical e-commerce merchant sites because they provide support for the distinct needs of business customers. Many are also targeted to specific vertical industries.

Examples of some B2B networks are as follows:

- `www.supplyworks.com`. Manufacturing procurement site
- `www.works.com`. An online purchasing management application for medium-sized businesses
- `www.tradeout.com`. For buying and selling surplus business goods
- `www.purchasingcenter.com`. For purchasing on the maintenance, repair, and operating (MRO) market
- `www.liquidation.com`. For buying and selling surplus business equipment

Key Point Summary

In this chapter, you learned B2B e-commerce is more complex than B2C e-commerce as a result of the unique needs and requirements for business purchases and the greater amounts of money that are involved in B2B transactions. Some of the other concepts involved in supporting B2B activities online are:

- The purpose of EDI is to serve as a standard for inter-organizational exchange of documents in standardized electronic form directly between participating computers.
- Two organizations exchanging EDI transmissions are called trading partners.
- The standard for EDI messaging in North America is ANSI X12.
- EDI messages are made up of transaction sets.
- Internet EDI is making EDI more accessible to small to medium-sized businesses.
- XML is a metalanguage for markup languages.
- S/MIME uses RSA public key encryption and digital certificates to provide security for e-mail over the Internet.
- Open Buying on the Internet (OBI) is designed for high-volume, low-dollar transactions.
- OBI uses standard protocols to eliminate compatibility problems that may occur in B2B e-commerce.
- The Open Trading Protocol (OTP) is a protocol for the development of software products that permits product interoperability for electronic purchases, independent of the chosen payment mechanism.

✦ ✦ ✦

STUDY GUIDE

Several important topics were covered in this chapter. Now it's time to test your knowledge of the main points of the various B2B e-commerce standards before you move on to the next chapter.

Assessment Questions

1. Which of the following is not a goal of EDI?

A. To make communication of structured information easy and inexpensive throughout an entire transaction

B. To reduce the number of errors and the time spent handling errors in transactions

C. To enable small businesses to compete with large businesses

D. To speed up the process of handling transactions to increase cash flow

2. Which of the following is not a characteristic of a company that is a good candidate for EDI?

A. Operates on a very tight margin

B. Has received requests from partner companies to convert to EDI

C. Operates in a time-sensitive environment

D. Sells highly customized, high dollar items

3. Your company is considering adopting Internet EDI to be competitive with large organizations. Your manager is concerned about the security of sending transaction information over the Internet. Which answer explains the security measures used in Internet EDI?

A. They are sent over private networks.

B. They are sent using S/MIME, which provides security using encryption and digital certificates.

C. They are sent using S/MIME, which provides security using public key authentication and VPNs.

D. They are encrypted using public key encryption, which cannot be broken.

4. Which of the following standards is not supported by OBI?

A. HTML

B. ANSI X12 850 EDI

C. HTTP 1.0

D. OTP

5. What is the correct order of the four steps involved in an OBI transaction?

A. Order placement, money transfer, approval by buying organization, transfer to the selling organization for fulfillment

B. Approval by buying organization, order placement, money transfer, transfer to the selling organization for fulfillment

C. Order placement, approval by the requisitioner, transfer to the selling organization for fulfillment, money transfer

D. Order placement, approval by the buying organization, transfer to the selling organization for fulfillment, money transfer

6. Which of the following is an advantage of using OTP?

A. It provides a standard way to conduct e-commerce regardless of the payment infrastructure, hardware, or software used.

B. It allows a merchant to sell to other businesses as well as to consumers.

C. It simplifies e-commerce by making businesses use the same payment software.

D. It's highly specialized, which results in much greater efficiency.

Scenarios

1. Your company, Midstate Office Supplies, is considering creating an e-commerce Web site. The company's physical stores currently serve business customers as well as individual customers. Eventually, you'll be building two separate sites: one for B2B e-commerce and one for B2C e-commerce. Given only what you know about the differences between B2B and B2C, which site do you think should be built first? What are the benefits and drawbacks of each choice?

2. While building your B2B Web site, you decide to create a custom language for exchanging purchase information about your products. What are the advantages and drawbacks of doing this?

Lab Exercises

Lab 7-1 Viewing EDI messages

1. Go to `http://www.perwill.com/Product/productdemo/html/demo-01.htm`.
2. Either read through the informational pages about EDI, or click on the View Demo Files link to go directly to a page of demonstration EDI files.
3. Click on the links on this page to view examples of different types of EDI messages.

Lab 7-2 Researching B2B e-commerce standards

EDI, OBI, and OTP are not the only standard protocols available for B2B e-commerce. To find out about other up-and-coming standards, enter the keywords "B2B e-commerce standards" in your favorite search engine and visit the sites that are shown as results. Some of the things that you should look for include: UDDI, PIPs, cXML, FpML, BizTalk, and ebXML. See if you can find out what purpose each of these standards or proposed standards is meant to serve.

Answers to Chapter Questions

Chapter pre-test

1. The goals of EDI are:
    - To make communication of structured information easy and inexpensive throughout an entire transaction
    - To reduce the number of errors and the time spent handling errors in transactions
    - To speed up the process of handling transactions to increase cash flow
2. The Internet is changing EDI by making it more cost-effective and more flexible.
3. Small to medium-sized businesses benefit from EDI by being able to compete and do business with large organizations. Large organizations benefit from having more potential trading partners.
4. XML is a subset of SGML. XML is a metalanguage for markup languages.

5. The four components of OBI are:
    - Requisitioner
    - Buying organization
    - Selling organization
    - Payment authority

6. The three key features of OTP are:
    - Trading Protocol Options
    - Record of trade
    - Supports physical and electronic delivery of goods and services

7. A B2B network is a Web site that brings buyers and sellers together without requiring each business to invest in traditional B2B infrastructure.

Assessment questions

1. **C.** To enable small business to compete with large business is not a goal of EDI (see "EDI explored and explained").
2. **D.** EDI is most useful for the purchase and sale of commodity items, not highly customized items (see "Who should use EDI?").
3. **B.** Secure Multipurpose Internet Mail Extensions (S/MIME) provides authentication using digital certificates and privacy using encryption (see "Security issues for EDI").
4. **D.** OTP, of course, is a separate protocol (see Table 7-1 for a list of the standards supported by OBI).
5. **D.** Order placement, approval by the buying organization, transfer to the selling organization for fulfillment, and money transfer are the correct order of the steps involved in an OBI transaction (see "OBI transactions").
6. **A.** An advantage of OTP is that it provides a standard way to conduct e-commerce regardless of the payment infrastructure, hardware, or software used (see "OTP explored and explained").

Scenarios

1. This question really has no right answer. Knowing only that there is much more money to be made in B2B e-commerce may lean a company in favor of building the B2B site first. However, B2B is much more complex than B2C. A B2B site takes longer to build, may be more expensive to build, and requires you to deal with issues such as how to set pricing for different trading partners.

2. The benefit of creating a language specifically designed for exchanging information about your products is that you will have something suited to your product line when the process is complete. One drawback is that your trading partners need to be able to understand this language. One of the biggest benefits of XML is that it makes it possible for industries to create and adopt standard data interchange languages. This gives companies the benefit of a language suited to their specific needs, while allowing them to easily conduct B2B e-commerce using a standardized language.

For More Information . . .

For more information about the topics covered in this chapter, visit the following sites:

- **World Wide Web Consortium.** `www.w3.org`
- **The OBI Consortium.** `www.openbuy.org/`
- **The Data Interchange Standards Association (DISA).** `www.disa.org`
- **Advanced Data Exchange (ADX).** `www.adx.com/index.htm`
- **B2BExplorer.** `www.b2bexplorer.com`. An online B2B community

Entry-Level E-Commerce Outsourcing

✦ ✦ ✦ ✦

EXAM OBJECTIVES

- Online outsourcing solutions
- Evaluating online storefront solutions
- Auctions
- Affiliate programs

CHAPTER PRE-TEST

1. What is a shopping portal site?
2. What are the advantages of using an entry-level e-commerce outsourcing solution?
3. If you're planning a large-scale marketing effort for your online store, should you develop an independent storefront or a portal storefront?
4. What is an affiliate program?
5. What are the benefits of participating in an affiliate program?
6. What are the benefits of selling your products in an online auction?
7. What kind of product line is best suited to an entry-level e-commerce outsourcing service?

✦ Answers to these questions can be found at the end of the chapter. ✦

Many new e-commerce companies want to make a big splash on the Internet by custom developing an online store and marketing it widely, which is appropriate for some business models. For others, however, entry into e-commerce should be undertaken in a cautious, incremental way. This is especially true for small companies with limited cash flow. For small businesses just starting out in e-commerce, an entry-level e-commerce package may be the answer.

There's a fairly wide variety of options among entry-level solutions. In this chapter, you take a close look at independent storefront, portal storefront, auction, and affiliate program entry-level e-commerce solutions. After you've examined the available service options, you look at how to decide which product to use.

Understanding Entry-Level E-Commerce Outsourcing

Online outsourcing solutions

E-commerce development doesn't have to be a huge project — in fact, it can be quite simple. Outsourcing your store is a viable alternative for small businesses, and should be seriously considered. Entry-level e-commerce outsourcing solutions can make developing and administering your store just about as easy as using a Web site. This is because all the tools you need are accessible using a Web browser.

When choosing an entry-level solution, one of the most important decisions you'll make is whether your store should operate independently, or as a part of a larger, more well known, Web site. Independent stores maintain their individual identity, but necessitate more effort in generating demand — that is, they require more promotion. If you decide to become a part of a larger Web site, there's a choice between becoming a portal storefront, or an affiliate of a larger site, or even selling products at auction.

The exam refers to entry-level e-commerce solutions as *online storefronts*, because they are created and configured using Web sites – in other words, created "online." Other solutions (mid-level and high-level) are typically created using software that is kept in-house – in other words, created "offline" – and then taken live on the Web server. This book uses the term "online" to refer to anything that happens on the Internet (online business or online payment processing, for example). The term *offline* is used for anything that happens without the aid of the Internet (offline payment processing, or offline business, for example).

The appeal of entry-level e-commerce outsourcing

The reasons that e-commerce companies turn to entry-level e-commerce packages are many and varied, but they usually involve limitations, such as a restricted budget or lack of programmers. Some factors that commonly steer a business to an entry-level e-commerce solution are:

- **Small inventory.** If you're only selling a few items, it may be simpler and easier to use an entry-level package. You won't have many customization options, but you also won't need to develop your own product database to house just those few items.
- **Small staff.** It can often be difficult to find and hire competent Web programmers. If your company has a limited programming staff, entry-level packages can help ease the burden on your employees by taking care of much of the work involved in setting up a storefront.
- **E-commerce not the primary goal.** A non-profit organization, or a business, may have a Web site that is not primarily an e-commerce site. The site may consist mostly of information, and have a small area for selling a few products, such as reports or self-published books. In such a case, an entry-level e-commerce package can do the trick quite nicely, without the organization having to put together a full-blown e-commerce department.
- **Limited budget.** Entry-level e-commerce packages are much cheaper than mid- and high-level packages. This is primarily because the e-commerce company has less control over their site. For a company just starting out, an entry-level package can help lessen the monetary commitment of starting an e-commerce venture.
- **Niche products.** Specialty products that cater to a niche market are best suited to entry-level e-commerce solutions. This is because merchants selling such items are not likely to receive a large volume of orders, and entry-level solutions can help save money. Also, niche products can benefit from the large audiences of shopping portal sites.

The factors that lead your company to select an entry-level package can also help determine what kind of package you choose. In the following sections, you take a closer look at the options available: independent storefronts, portal and community storefronts, auctions, and affiliate programs. You examine the pros and cons of each type of entry-level storefront, and several example services for each type are outlined.

Independent storefronts

Independent entry-level storefronts are services that provide their clients with a pre-defined structure in which to put their online store. The structure of each store created by such a service is identical, but the structure is populated with data from each individual store owner. The service also hosts the database, or catalog, of products for each store, processes transactions, and usually hosts the Web site as well. There's generally a fee for these services — some charge on a per month basis, others per transaction.

Independent storefront services provide a foundation upon which you can build your store. Your store remains independent, however — hence, the name *independent* storefront service — because your site has its own domain name. The fact that you outsource the functionality of your store is usually transparent to your users. Some services require you to pay an extra fee for maintaining your own domain name.

The advantages and disadvantages of using independent storefront services, include:

- **Maintains individuality.** (Advantage) Your site has its own domain name, and is not obviously associated with the independent storefront service provider.
- **Easy administration.** (Advantage) You can make changes to your site using only your Web browser — no programming knowledge is required.
- **Need to generate demand.** (Disadvantage) Independent storefront solutions do not help with generating demand — you still need to promote your site because the service does not direct traffic to you.

To get an idea of the variety of independent storefront packages available, let's take a look at some sample services.

MerchandiZer

MerchandiZer (`www.merchandizer.com`), from HipHip Software, provides a solution for developing online stores. MerchandiZer offers the following features, some of which are enhanced features:

- **Browser-based setup.** Like all entry-level solutions, users of the MerchandiZer Web Store service use a Web browser to access the software that sets up their store. Products are entered one by one in your site administration area. MerchandiZer offers a variety of design templates to choose from and allows for limited customization of design.
- **Automated merchandising.** The MerchandiZer Web Store offers merchandising capabilities such as sales, featured items, cross-selling, and up-selling. Individual products can be designated for such merchandising efforts within the site administration area. After a product has been selected, the promotion is automatically handled by the underlying storefront software.
- **Order notification.** Orders placed on the site are sent to the merchant via e-mail. The merchant is then responsible for processing payment and fulfilling the order.
- **Site management.** Using the site administration area, you can view orders and their status, as well as maintain your product catalog and customer database.

- **Customer and sales reports.** A variety of reports about your store can automatically be generated, such as a customer information list or a report of best-selling products.
- **Demand generation.** MerchandiZer offers promotion opportunities such as listings on well-known sites, search engine registration, and statistics on search engine rankings. Some of these services cost extra.
- **Domain name.** With MerchandiZer, you can have a top-level domain for your site (for example, `www.yourcompany.com`).
- **Hosting.** MerchandiZer hosts your Web site on their servers and provides 24/7 customer service and monitoring.
- **Credit card and check processing.** MerchandiZer processes payment for the merchant, completing the transaction before the order information is sent to the merchant for fulfillment.
- **Internationalization.** MerchandiZer supports multilingual versions of your site, and can perform currency conversion.
- **Accounting system integration.** Account information can be downloaded into popular accounting software such as QuickBooks and Peachtree.
- **Customization.** Merchants can upload their own HTML pages for use with the MerchandiZer service.
- **Merchandising and marketing.** Advanced merchandising and marketing features are included, such as support for gift certificates, coupons, downloadable products, buyer's club discounts, graduated discounts, and more.
- **Domain name.** All MerchandiZer stores have their own top-level domain names.
- **Various levels of service.** MerchandiZer offers four levels of service: Standard, Plus, Gold, and Premium, ranging in cost from $80 to $500 per month.

Other options

Some other independent storefronts you can choose from include:

- **Complete Merchant.** `www.completemerchant.com`. Offers an independent storefront service with a shopping cart, online payment processing, Web-based maintenance, site hosting, and optional marketing services. Prices start at $99 per month.
- **Bigstep.** `www.bigstep.com`. Provides an independent storefront with 12MB of Web server space and a Web-based site building interface for free. Fees are required for credit card processing and your own domain name.

Portal storefronts

Portal storefronts, which are also commonly called *community storefronts*, are entry-level solutions that allow you to create a store within a pre-existing Web site. They allow small e-commerce companies to benefit from the large amount of traffic well-known sites enjoy.

Shopping portals are Web sites that aggregate Web merchants in one central location, allowing shoppers to browse products from a wide variety of stores on one site. As a client of a portal storefront service, your products and store are listed in a directory at the portal site, and are listed in search results.

The advantages and disadvantages of joining a shopping portal or community site, include:

- **Demand generation provided.** (Advantage) Most shopping portals are run by well-known Web sites with large user bases. Therefore, it's not necessary to engage in a full-scale promotion campaign to get users to your store.
- **Trust.** (Advantage) Well-known shopping portals already have a reputation for trustworthiness as well as data and transaction security. By selling your products at such a site, you benefit from that perception.
- **Lack of individuality.** (Disadvantage) In a shopping portal, your products are listed alongside those of many other merchants, which makes it difficult to maintain your distinct identity and harder to develop brand awareness.
- **Competition.** (Disadvantage) If you offer the same products as other merchants at the shopping portal, your products are listed side by side. If you charge more than your competition, you may lose potential customers.
- **Ease of administration.** (Advantage) All storefront set-up and maintenance tasks are done through a Web interface, which is accessible from any computer.
- **Low cost.** (Advantage) Many of these services are free, or very inexpensive, with additional small charges for enhanced services such as payment processing.

Most shopping portals offer essentially the same services — such as transaction processing, optional credit card processing, order tracking, and Web-based store set-up. Let's take a look at the services offered by three leading shopping portals to help you make more informed decisions about this option.

Amazon.com's zShops

Amazon.com introduced zShops to give smaller merchants the ability to sell products through the trusted Amazon.com Web site. zShops are stores within Amazon.com's site. Products from zShops are listed in search and browsing results, along with Amazon.com's own inventory. Take a look at the main characteristics of zShops by examining the following parameters:

✦ **Storefront design.** zShop merchants have limited flexibility with the design of their stores. The color scheme can be changed, and a store logo can be added, but that's about it. zShop storefronts are very integrated with the Amazon.com look and feel.

✦ **Promotion.** Amazon.com does an excellent job of promoting zShop products alongside their own. Just about every time a customer looks at a product list or conducts a search, zShop items are displayed as well. Featured placement is available for a fee.

✦ **Trust.** Amazon.com has a very good reputation in terms of data and transaction security. A forum for customer feedback is also provided, so unreliable merchants are forced to improve their practices or close shop. Customers are more likely to buy from a small merchant in such an environment.

✦ **Payment processing.** zShop merchants can decide how to process payments — either themselves or through the Amazon.com Payments service for a small fee.

✦ **Traffic volume.** Amazon.com has 20 million customers, which means that their site gets a lot of traffic every day. zShops merchants benefit from this built-in audience.

✦ **Low cost.** A zShop *subscription* — i.e., a storefront — costs $39.99 per month for up to 5,000 items. Closing fees (for completed transactions) are calculated on a commission structure based on the total purchase cost.

Yahoo! Stores

Yahoo! Shopping is a part of the extremely popular Yahoo! portal site. The main shopping page is dominated by big-name retailers such as Barnes & Noble, Banana Republic, and Eddie Bauer. Yahoo! also caters to smaller retailers, however, and allows them to create their own stores, which are hosted on Yahoo!'s servers for free through the Yahoo! Stores service.

Here's how Yahoo! Stores compare to zShops:

✦ **Storefront design.** Yahoo! Stores are more visually unique than zShops. Merchants are offered a wider variety of design templates and are allowed to add more custom graphics to their site than zShops merchants.

✦ **Promotion.** Yahoo! Stores are listed on the Yahoo! Shopping site, but they are more difficult to find than Amazon.com's zShops. This is because Yahoo! Shopping also works with large online retailers, who dominate the prime promotion spots on their site.

✦ **Trust.** Yahoo! is a big player in the Internet, and potential customers are more likely to feel safe purchasing through Yahoo! than directly from a less well-known merchant. The Customer Rating System offers customers the ability to rate their experience with merchants. However, negative feedback is not visible to other customers, as it is at Amazon.com zShops.

✦ **Payment processing.** Online credit card processing is available on Yahoo! for a fee. Otherwise, merchants collect order information via the Web, e-mail, or fax. Order data can also be downloaded into QuickBooks.

✦ **Traffic volume.** The Yahoo! portal site is one of the most visited Web sites on the Internet, so your potential audience is huge.

✦ **Low cost.** The Yahoo! Stores service is free, with fees for enhanced services such as credit card processing.

Auctions

Auctions

Many small businesses choose to sell their products at online auctions. When using an auction site, a merchant does not have its own storefront. Rather, its products are listed in the auction site's directory, which allows the merchant to conduct e-commerce without the need for an in-house or outsourced e-commerce package of any kind.

The advantage of using an auction site is that you may receive more money for your product than you would normally sell it for. It also removes the need for Web site development altogether. However, it's more difficult to sell many copies of the same product simultaneously at online auctions. Therefore, auctions are best suited to specialty, or niche, products that are not sold in great volume.

eBay

eBay is the most well-known and popular auction site on the Internet today. Over 12 million auctions have been conducted and completed on eBay since its founding in 1995.

To conduct an auction on eBay, a small fee is charged to the seller. This fee is paid by credit card. The information on each item to be auctioned is entered into the site using forms. Merchants should supply one or more photos and a detailed description for each item to be auctioned.

If there's a minimum price that you would like for your item, you can set a reserve price. If no bid exceeds the reserve price, the item is not sold. A reserve price auction protects you from having to sell an item for less than you think it's worth.

Other auction sites

Due to the popularity of eBay, other sites have jumped into the online auction hosting business. These sites include:

- ✦ Amazon.com Auctions (`www.amazon.com`)
- ✦ Excite Auctions (`http://auctions.excite.com`)
- ✦ CNET Auctions (`http://auctions.cnet.com`)
- ✦ CityAuction (`www.cityauction.com`)

Affiliate programs

Affiliate programs

Affiliate programs allow Web site owners to earn money on purchases made at an e-commerce site. When using such programs, merchants do not actually sell any items themselves. They simply refer customers to an online retailer.

For example, a company whose employees are frequent contributors to technical books can set up an area of its site that lists books its employees have written. It can then link each listing to a Web site selling the book. The company earns commissions based on users who buy the book from the retailer, and often, for any other items the user buys, as well.

Amazon.com Associates program

To become a member of the Amazon.com Associates program, you submit your Web site's URL to Amazon.com for approval—which you do in the Associates area of Amazon.com's Web site.

After your site is approved, you can use the Associates area to create the correct HTML code for links from your Web site to Amazon. You can link to Amazon.com's home page or to specific products. You can also place an Amazon.com search box on your site.

Amazon.com pays commissions of up to 15 percent on items bought by customers who enter the site through your links. Associates are paid by check on a quarterly basis—but only if their total referral fees are $100 or more. Otherwise, the total is rolled into the next quarter.

Other affiliate programs

Many other online retailers also feature affiliate programs. Two of the most well known are:

- ✦ **CDNow's C2 Program.** `www.cdnow.com`. Affiliated sites earn between 7 percent and 12 percent in commissions on sales completed through their links.

✦ **Barnes & Noble's Affiliate Network.** www.barnesandnoble.com/affiliate/. Offers up to 7 percent commissions on purchases made by customers who enter the site through an affiliated site.

Selecting an Entry-Level E-Commerce Solution

Evaluating online storefront solutions

Entry-level e-commerce solutions are intended for businesses that do not want to be responsible for choosing and maintaining hardware and software, hiring programmers and support staff, and developing a custom user interface. The tradeoff, however, is that such entry-level packages relinquish much control to the service provider, rather than the merchant company.

It's important to study what factors drive a business to choose a particular entry-level solution. You should also know how to choose the appropriate e-commerce solution for a given situation.

When choosing an entry-level solution, you need to carefully consider your company's e-commerce needs. If you want to create a strong brand identity, you should choose an independent storefront solution rather than a portal storefront. If you have only a few items to sell, which are targeted to a very specific niche market, you may want to take advantage of the large audience that a portal site or auction site provides.

Table 8-1 presents the types of solutions that are best suited to each of the major reasons for using an entry-level solution, as outlined at the beginning of this chapter.

Table 8-1
Solutions for Specific Situations

Limited budget	*E-commerce not primary goal*	*Small staff*	*Small inventory*	*Niche products*
Independent storefront or portal storefront	Independent storefront or affiliate program	Independent storefront or portal storefront	Independent storefront, portal storefront, or auctions	Portal storefront or auctions

Some services allow you to make a trial run, giving you 30 days of free service or a free test site. Use this time to assess whether the service is for you. Does the service provide the capabilities your e-commerce company needs? Consider whether the design templates are adequate. Do they allow you to create a store that fulfills your company's visual branding needs?

To evaluate the features of different types of entry-level storefront packages, you should use the following seven keys to success (first introduced in Chapter 1) as your guide:

1. Generating demand
2. Ordering
3. Fulfillment
4. Payment processing
5. Service and support
6. Security
7. Community

Let's take a look at how the various entry-level storefront packages can help an e-commerce business address each key to success.

In Chapters 9 and 10, we also apply the seven keys to success to mid-level and high-level packages.

Generating demand

Entry-level e-commerce solutions vary in their support of demand generation. On one hand, shopping portals and auction sites provide a built-in audience because they're usually well known to Internet users. For this reason, use of a portal storefront or an auction site does not require much effort from the merchant in terms of promotion and brand awareness.

On the other hand, independent storefronts and affiliate programs do not provide demand generation. These services do not steer any traffic to their clients' sites, so the merchant company remains entirely dependent on its own promotion and brand awareness to get users to visit its site.

Ordering

One of the main requirements of e-commerce that is filled well by all entry-level services is the ordering process. With some services, that's about all they do. All entry-level services take care of the ordering process, by providing product information, a shopping cart, and order forms. The order information is then sent to the merchant, usually via e-mail or fax.

Fulfillment

With entry-level solutions, fulfillment is generally left up to the merchant. After the order information arrives, it's up to the merchant to get the product shipped to the buyer in a reasonable time frame.

Some services assist in this effort by providing order data in a format that can be imported into accounting software, which may help speed up the process for the merchant. Some services also offer support for downloadable soft goods, such as software.

Affiliate programs, by their nature, take care of fulfillment, because the product is, in fact, being purchased from another merchant. For sites selling their own products, however, entry-level solutions generally leave fulfillment to the merchant.

Payment processing

The most basic entry-level e-commerce packages provide the merchant with order information (including payment information) from the purchaser, and then the merchant is responsible for processing the payment. With many services, it's now possible to upgrade to online credit card processing — and sometimes check processing — for a small per-transaction fee.

Service and support

Customer service is not well addressed by entry-level e-commerce packages. For the most part, it's up to the merchant to develop these areas of the Web site. Some services provide built-in pages for FAQ lists, but it's up to the merchant to populate these pages with information. Many services also provide a customer feedback form that sends information to the merchant's e-mail address.

The notable exception to this rule is affiliate programs. Because the products are being purchased from another merchant's site, customer service is taken care of by that merchant.

Security

Security is addressed very well by entry-level e-commerce solutions. All stores created with such services are housed on the servers of the service provider, who supplies security software and (usually) constant monitoring of the Web sites housed there.

Community

Community building is a challenge with entry-level solutions. Because they're essentially cookie-cutter Web sites on the back end, owners of entry-level Web sites must make do with what the service offers. There's little to no room for implementing community-building features on your own.

Most independent storefront packages provide no support for personalization and do not offer a message board or chat area. With portal storefronts and auctions, personalization is out of the question. If such features are important to your business, you'll be hard-pressed to find an entry-level solution to suit your company.

One notable exception is MerchandiZer, which offers support for *buyer's club* capabilities, where customers can be specified for special discounts.

Key Point Summary

For small businesses making their debut in the e-commerce arena, an entry-level e-commerce package may be the best solution. Here are the key points covered in this chapter:

✦ Entry-level e-commerce outsourcing solutions are appropriate for small businesses when they have:

- Small inventory
- Small staff
- E-commerce not the primary goal
- Limited budget
- Niche products

✦ The four main kinds of entry-level solutions are:

- Independent storefronts (provide easy administration while maintaining the site's individuality, but require more promotion and marketing than portal storefronts)
- Portal storefronts (also called community storefronts, provide easy administration and trust with less individuality, and typically cost less than independent storefronts)
- Auctions (an alternative for very small businesses)
- Affiliate programs (allow Web sites to earn commissions on sales at another e-commerce Web site)

✦ The needs of your company's e-commerce project determine which entry-level product is right for you, if any.

✦ ✦ ✦

STUDY GUIDE

This chapter introduced the main kinds of entry-level e-commerce outsourcing solutions. Now that you've read the chapter, test your knowledge with the following assessment questions, scenarios, and lab exercises.

Assessment Questions

1. Nelda is an avid knitter and wants to sell her sweaters online. She wants to avoid paying for promotion for her site, and is not looking to do huge volume on her products. Which kind of e-commerce solution would work best for her?

A. Affiliate program

B. Independent storefront

C. Portal storefront

D. Mid-level solution

2. What kind of e-commerce solution is best suited to a small business?

A. Offline solution

B. Small businesses should not conduct e-commerce

C. Affiliate program

D. Online solution

3. Which of the following is not a characteristic of entry-level auction selling? (Choose the best answer.)

A. Seller has own storefront

B. Can set minimum selling price

C. May receive more money than expected

D. Provides large traffic volume

4. Why might a portal storefront elicit more trust from potential customers than an independent storefront? (Choose the best answer.)

A. Established shopping portal sites are well known to consumers and have reputations for security.

B. The ability to shop with a digital wallet

C. The large number of well-known brands featured on shopping portal sites indicates the site is trustworthy.

D. The fact that credit card processing is done by a well-known company

5. Harry Whyn is the director of a drug rehabilitation center. One of the center's staff members has written a book about drug rehabilitation. How can the center use their existing informational Web site to share in the profits from the sale of the staff member's book? (Choose the best answer.)

A. Purchase books from the publisher in bulk for resale on the Web site

B. Develop an independent storefront

C. Join an affiliate program

D. Use a portal storefront service

6. Which two entry-level e-commerce solutions provide the most demand generation?

A. Affiliate programs and auctions

B. Independent storefronts and auctions

C. Auctions and portal storefronts

D. Affiliate programs and independent storefronts

Scenarios

Kim Soo is the owner of Simple Toys, a small business that sells hand-crafted wooden toys. Kim Soo's business functions as follows:

- She operates three stores in the Baltimore area.
- Her staff consists of 3 store managers, 18 part-time clerks, and 5 part-time stock boys.
- Simple Toys publishes a catalog four times a year, and orders from the catalog are processed by phone at the three retail stores.
- Store clerks are accustomed to taking phone orders and processing credit cards without the customer actually being present in the store.
- They are also equipped to handle shipping to phone customers.

Kim is interested in taking her business online. Her primary goal is getting new customers from outside of the Baltimore area who don't already know about Simple Toys. Her limitations and assets for accomplishing this are:

- She doesn't have a lot of money to spend.
- She has doesn't have any programmers on her staff.

✦ She has limited desktop publishing experience (she designs the catalog herself).

✦ She has digital files of product pictures.

If Kim asked you for advice on how to build her online store, what would you recommend?

Lab Exercises

Lab 8-1 Evaluating independent storefronts

In this lab, you take a look at sample storefronts created using MerchandiZer.

1. Point your browser to `http:// www.merchandizer.com`.
2. On the MerchandiZer's home page, under Resources, choose Featured Stores (as shown in Figure 8-1).

Figure 8-1: Locating the Featured Stores link on the MerchandiZer home page (Images provided courtesy of HipHip Software)

3. Now you should see MerchandiZer's Featured sites page. There are many Web sites pictured. Select one that interests you.
4. Spend some time in the site you've chosen. Evaluate the graphic design, navigation, and product presentation.
5. Return to the MerchandiZer Featured sites page. Select another site, and repeat Step 4.
6. Return to the MerchandiZer Featured sites page, and look at one more site, repeating Step 4.
7. Answer the following questions about the three sites you visited:
   a. Was the navigation structured the same way on each site?
   b. Did the graphic design on any of the sites look like it was created using a template? Why or why not?
   c. How much effort do you think was put into customizing the look and feel of each site? Why?

Lab 8-2 Creating a portal storefront

In this exercise, you create your own portal storefront at Yahoo! Stores.

1. Point your browser to `http://store.yahoo.com`.
2. On the Yahoo! Stores introduction page, choose Get Started Now.

Note: This site changes quite frequently so you may not see the exact phrase "Get Started Now." You may see something like "Create a New Store" or "Set up Store."

3. If you already have a Yahoo! account, sign in. If not, create one by providing some information about yourself.
4. Now you should be at the Yahoo! Stores Create a Store page. Enter an ID for your store and the full name of your store, and then click Create.
5. The next page confirms the creation of your trial store. Click the I Accept button after reading the information.
6. Return to `http://store.yahoo.com`, and select the link to your store under the Manage My Store header on the left-hand side of the page.
7. The next screen presents the management options for your store. From the first column, Edit, choose the link Simple.
8. This page shows the layout of your store with options for editing. Choose Edit.
9. On the edit page, you can enter a message for your site. Enter the Welcome to my store! area and click Update.
10. Your edited store is now on screen, with the editing options listed. Choose Look.

11. Choose Lab from the Look choices. Your site should change colors and fonts. Choose the look that you prefer, and then proceed to Step 12.
12. Choose New Section from the editing options.
13. On the next page, you can enter information for a new page on your site. Enter a title for the page, and a description. Click Update.
14. You're now on the new page that you just created. Notice that the navigation features on the left have been automatically modified to include a link to the new page.
15. Click New Item to add an item to this page.
16. Enter a name, SKU (which is a Stock-Keeping Unit and is the equivalent of an inventory number), price, and description for a fictitious product. Click Update.
17. Continue adding products to this page. Return to the home page (using the left navigation buttons) and add another section, and some products there. Try out some of the other editing tools that interest you.
18. Answer the following questions:
    - **a.** Do you find the user interface of the Yahoo! Stores maintenance area to be intuitive?
    - **b.** Would you find it simple to create a store using this service?
    - **c.** What do you think would be the benefit of customizing the navigation images or adding a company logo to the site?

Answers to Chapter Questions

Chapter pre-test

1. A shopping portal is a Web site that aggregates merchants in one central location.
2. The advantages of using an entry-level e-commerce outsourcing solution include:
    - Low cost
    - No need for programming skills
    - No need for a large staff
3. An independent storefront is a better choice for those companies planning a large-scale marketing and promotion effort.
4. An affiliate program is a system whereby an online retailer offers other Web sites a commission for referring customers to them through hyperlinks.

5. The benefits of participating in an affiliate program include:
   - No need to develop an e-commerce site of your own
   - Fulfillment provided by the online retailer
   - Customer service provided by the online retailer
6. The benefits of selling products at an online auction include:
   - No need to develop your own e-commerce site
   - May receive more money for a product than expected
   - Large audience provided by auction hosting site
7. Specialty products, or niche products, are best suited to entry-level e-commerce outsourcing services.

Assessment questions

1. **C.** A portal storefront is the best solution for Nelda's hand-knit sweater business. Independent storefronts require promotion, and an affiliate program doesn't work for selling your own products. Mid-level products would be too expensive (see "Selecting an Entry-Level E-Commerce Solution").
2. **D.** Remember that an entry-level e-commerce outsourcing solution (which is typical for small businesses) is also called an online solution, because all development is done online — that is, on the service provider's Web site. Although mid-level and high-level storefronts are also online (meaning on the Internet), there's a distinction between online and offline on the basis of where they are generally created (see "Understanding Entry-Level E-Commerce Outsourcing").
3. **A.** When selling products at auction, the seller does not have an e-commerce storefront. Rather, the seller's products are listed along with others in the auction site's directory (see "Auctions").
4. **A.** Established shopping portal sites are well known to consumers and have reputations for security (see "Portal storefronts").
5. **C.** The simplest way for the center to make money on the sale of the staff member's book is by joining an affiliate program with an online bookseller and linking directly to the book. The center earns commissions on sales of the book made by using their link, and they do not need to launch an e-commerce project, as they would with the other three options (see "Affiliate programs" and "Selecting an Entry-Level E-Commerce Solution").
6. **C.** Auctions and portal storefronts provide the most demand generation (see "Selecting an Entry-Level E-Commerce Solution").

Scenarios

Simple Toys could probably do modestly good business if taken online. If initial cash investment is kept to a minimum, the return on investment could be quite good. Here are the issues you should consider before making a recommendation:

- The first things to consider are Kim's limited staff resources and budget. This automatically puts her project into the category of entry-level e-commerce solutions. Because she only wants to augment her current business, not create an entirely new business, this should work fine.
- Because Kim publishes her own catalog using desktop publishing software, she is proficient enough with computers to be able to create a store herself using an entry-level solution's Web-based set-up and maintenance interface. Her existing product pictures can speed up the process of building her online catalog.
- Her employees are already used to conducting electronic commerce through the phone and sending products through the mail. It will not be too much of a leap, then, for them to begin processing e-commerce orders as well. If the employees receive orders through a central e-mail address, for example, they can process the orders in the store during slow times or after the store is closed. Therefore, it's not necessary for Simple Toys to pay for online payment processing.

The best solution for Simple Toys' online store is probably going to be a portal storefront without online payment processing. The reasons for this are:

- Simple Toys does not have a lot of money for promotion, and portal sites have a built-in, worldwide audience.
- Payment processing and fulfillment can be done by current employees.
- Hand crafted wooden toys are a niche product. Simple Toys is more likely to find an audience through a site with a large number of potential customers, like a shopping portal.

A portal storefront will get Simple Toys on the Web, and help Kim get a feel for e-commerce. Eventually, if the volume of orders exceeds her employees' abilities to process them, she may want to switch to online payment processing. If the e-commerce side of her business really takes off, she'll eventually want to upgrade to a mid-level solution or even a high-level solution someday. Still, an entry-level solution is a great way for the seller of such a specialty product to dabble in e-commerce.

For More Information . . .

- **MerchandiZer.** www.merchandizer.com. Detailed information on the MerchandiZer product
- **Complete Merchant.** www.completemerchant.com. Contains information on the Complete Merchant program
- **Bigstep.** www.bigstep.com. For complete information on the Bigstep service
- **Amazon.com.** www.amazon.com. Look for information on the Associates Program and zShops
- **Yahoo! Stores.** http://store.yahoo.com. Complete information on the Yahoo! Stores program
- **eBay's How to Sell page.** http://pages.ebay.com/help/basics/n-selling.html. Overview of the selling procedure at eBay's auction site

CHAPTER 9

Mid-Level Online Storefront Packages

✦ ✦ ✦ ✦

EXAM OBJECTIVES

- Mid-level online storefront solutions
- Evaluating online storefront solutions

CHAPTER PRE-TEST

1. What is a CSP?
2. What are six ways that mid-level outsourcing options are different from entry-level options?
3. What factors, besides the seven keys to e-commerce success, should merchants look at when evaluating mid-level outsourcing options?
4. What features do mid-level online storefront packages typically provide for generating demand for the products or services an e-commerce storefront is selling?

✦ Answers to these questions can be found at the end of the chapter. ✦

In this chapter, you find out how mid-level outsourced storefronts differ from entry-level storefronts. You examine several different products in the mid-level category and investigate their various customization, security, payment processing, ordering, marketing, service and support, and community-building options.

Understanding Mid-Level Online Storefront Packages

There's no absolute way of determining the type of storefront your store should use. This section examines the most common issues merchants evaluate when they're considering upgrading from an entry-level to a mid-level product. Basically, mid-level e-commerce outsourcing solutions provide experienced e-commerce merchants or established companies with a greater level of customization and store growth options than entry-level products. Similar to entry-level products, mid-level storefronts are generally designed for business-to-consumer (B2C) commerce.

In this chapter, we sometimes refer to mid-level online storefronts as *mid-level instant storefronts* or *mid-level outsourced storefronts*. These are simply different names for the same class of e-commerce storefront packages. Perhaps the most accurate name for the type of products we discuss in this chapter is *mid-level online outsourced instant storefront software.*

Mid-level storefront outsourcing options are different from entry-level storefronts in the following ways:

✦ **Customization.** Mid-level storefronts provide more customization options.

✦ **Cost.** Mid-level storefronts typically cost more to set up and operate.

✦ **Security.** Mid-level storefronts have greater security options.

✦ **Independence.** Mid-level storefronts generally can stand-alone. That is, your store does not need to be part of a larger portal or collection of stores, and you have a wider variety of hosting options.

✦ **Administration, reporting, and set-up tools.** Although many mid-level stores feature Web-based administration and set up (a requirement with entry-level solutions), mid-level products may also feature ways to edit the catalog or store offline. Some products allow you to modify the functionality of the storefront programmatically.

✦ **Variety of e-commerce functions and tasks supported.** Mid-level products may allow you to manage more of the functions involved in e-commerce—including banner ads, bulk e-mailing, calculating shipping, and creating relationships with other stores.

Each of these differences between entry-level and mid-level outsourcing options is discussed in greater detail in the following sections. Figure 9-1 shows a graphical comparison between entry-level and mid-level instant storefronts.

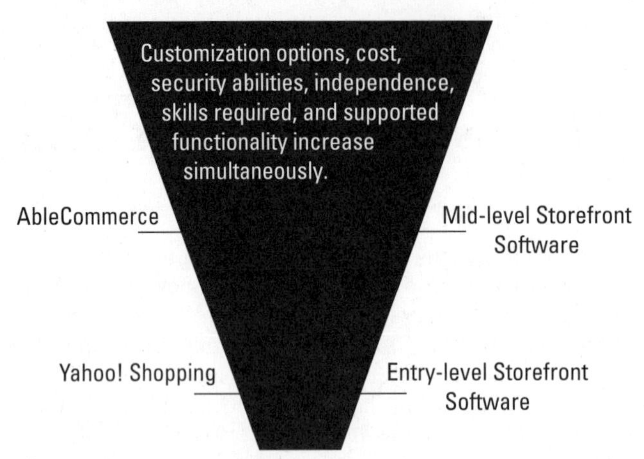

Figure 9-1: Comparison between entry-level and mid-level instant storefronts

Customization

In Chapter 8, you examined Web sites that allow you to create a complete store using only a Web browser. This interface hides the many complexities of e-commerce from the merchant. For merchants who are just getting their feet wet with e-commerce, this is an ideal arrangement. Entry-level stores make setting up shop on the Internet simple, but this same simplicity limits the amount of control merchants have over the store.

Mid-level outsourcing options give you more control over how a site works as well as the user experience. Some of the customization options provided by mid-level instant storefronts include:

✦ Customizable templates, or ability to create new design templates.

✦ Control over certain parts of the user's purchasing experience. For example, a mid-level store may allow you choose whether a final invoice is shown to the customer or whether the customer gets a confirmation e-mail.

✦ Greater ability to customize payment and shipping options.

✦ Some mid-level storefronts allow programmers to modify the product to create custom functionality.

Cost

In many entry-level products, the merchant simply pays a monthly fee to the company hosting the site, or pays a certain percentage of each sale. This model is based on the idea that you're simply renting the hosting company's software, hardware, and bandwidth to sell your own products or services.

With the mid-level products, the merchant generally provides the Web server and purchases a license for the software. The cost of setting up a mid-level store is usually greater than the cost of setting up an entry-level store. In addition, running a mid-level store may require you to pay several different vendors, including the company that created the storefront software that you use, a hosting company, and the payment gateway.

If you decide to host your mid-level store at an ISP, a good Web hosting company integrates the various fees and software into one package and charges you an initial set-up fee plus a monthly maintenance fee.

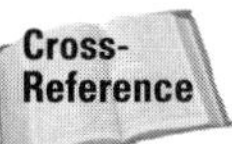

For more information about Web server software, see Chapter 12.

Many mid-level outsourcing solutions can be hosted at a new type of Web hosting company, called a *Commerce Service Provider* (CSP). CSPs often handle the day-to-day operation of your site, including setting up payment processing, backing up your site regularly, providing a secure environment, and hosting the software that runs your store. Although hosting a site with a full-fledged CSP may cost more per month, it relieves you of many of the most frustrating parts of setting up and maintaining a storefront.

Security

Entry-level online storefronts generally provide standard security options for merchants. Someone setting up one of these stores doesn't have to worry about obtaining a digital certificate or storing payment information securely. This is one of the largest benefits of using an entry-level store.

Mid-level storefront packages, on the other hand, often assist in setting up security on a site, but they do require the merchant to have a slightly better knowledge of how Web site security works. Some hosting companies take care of all the security issues for the particular types of storefront packages they support. Other hosting companies, particularly those that provide dedicated hosting or co-location, leave it up to you.

Chapter 19 discusses the various security issues and technologies that are available to secure an e-commerce site. Chapter 13 shows you how to configure various security options in Internet Information Server (IIS).

Independence

Independence is one of the main reasons people choose mid-level solutions or upgrade to a mid-level solution. Many entry-level packages don't allow stores to have their own domain names (`www.yourcompany.com`, for example). This is a major issue for a merchant who is trying to become known on the Web.

Mid-level storefronts are more likely to be hosted in-house or on a dedicated server than entry-level storefronts, although most merchants still outsource the hosting of their mid-level storefronts.

Administration, reporting, and set-up tools

The tools that are available for administering, reporting, and setting up mid-level stores may be more robust than those provided for entry-level online storefronts. These features include:

- User account management
- Product catalog importing and exporting
- Ability to set up several stores on the same server
- Order tracking and site statistics reporting
- Inventory management

With mid-level products, the merchant is better able to keep track of customers, orders, and products. At this level, you're no longer selling your products to Yahoo!'s customers or Amazon.com's customers; you're selling to your own customers.

Variety of e-commerce functions and tasks supported

The biggest differences between entry-level, mid-level, and high-level stores are how well they handle increases in traffic, and the number of features that can be added later on. Mid-level storefront packages support more e-commerce functions, including:

- Banner ad management
- Integration with different payment gateways
- Bulk e-mailing
- Shipping calculators or integration with third-party shipping calculation services
- Integration with existing systems and software
- Integration with financial planning and management software

Many features that were once found only in mid-level or high-level outsourced storefronts are steadily becoming common in entry-level products. In the same way, mid-level stores are rapidly encroaching upon territory that once was the sole domain of high-level products. The limits of this movement up the food chain are dictated by performance and catalog-size issues. In other words, an entry-level product may contain features similar to those of a mid-level or high-level product, but the entry-level product does not use the high-performance databases and other infrastructure of higher-level options.

Mid-Level Storefront Options

Mid-level online storefront solutions

To better understand the implications of mid-level options for e-commerce merchants or developers, the following sections explore some examples of existing mid-level e-commerce outsourcing solutions.

The exam doesn't contain any questions about specific product features; so don't worry about memorizing them because they're likely to change, anyway.

iHTML Merchant

The iHTML Merchant (iHTML stands for Inline Hypertext Markup Language) is included with O'Reilly's WebSite Professional server. It's also available as a separate product from Inline Internet Systems at `www.ihtmlmerchant.com`.

As with most mid-level e-commerce products, merchants can either leave the server setup and hosting to an ISP that offers iHTML Merchant hosting, or buy their own copy of the software and set it up on their dedicated server.

The price of software for hosting iHTML Merchant ranges from $90 per month for hosting a small store on one of Inline Internet Systems' iHTML servers, to $4090 for the iHTML Merchant Mall software, which allows you to host numerous iHTML sites yourself. The typical cost for the software needed to set up a single store on an in-house or dedicated server is currently about $1000.

Here's how it works, along with its advantages and disadvantages:

- ✦ iHTML Merchant requires that you have O'Reilly's iHTML server scripting language installed on your server. iHTML, an extension of HTML, allows non-programmers to add interactivity and dynamic content to HTML pages.
- ✦ The iHTML interpreter on the server interprets iHTML markup in your Web site's HTML pages and follows the instructions they provide.

  The benefit of working with iHTML is the ability to use familiar HTML-like elements to program tasks that would normally require more complicated scripts and code. For example, using iHTML, you can insert the date anywhere in an HTML page by simply using the `<iDate>` element, or you can insert the results from a database query by using the `<iSQL>` element.

✦ Perhaps the greatest benefit of using a storefront package based on a simplified programming language, such as iHTML, is that all of the store's functionality can be modified by anyone who knows any iHTML. This provides a level of customization that most other storefront packages cannot provide.

✦ A potential disadvantage to using a language such as iHTML is that the extra steps that the server goes through to interpret and execute the instructions contained in iHTML elements may slow down your Web server's performance. Unless you're operating a very large store with heavy traffic, you and your visitors will not notice the difference. We have personally developed e-commerce sites with several thousand products that use storefronts based on this type of simplified programming language.

✦ iHTML Merchant can be almost completely administered using a browser-based interface. The administration control panel includes the following areas:

- Site setup
- Products
- Customers
- Sales

Each of these areas is described briefly in the following sections.

Site setup

The site setup area of the iHTML Merchant store administrator allows you to set store-wide settings. The options provided in the site setup area are:

✦ General setup

✦ Custom site properties

✦ Shipping setup

✦ Tax configuration

✦ E-commerce setup

✦ Banner ad maintenance

✦ Editable pages

✦ Templates

General setup

The general setup area, shown in Figure 9-2, allows you to configure site-wide information such as the name, address, phone, fax, and e-mail address of the store. You can also set other options such as font colors and how products are ordered and displayed on the site.

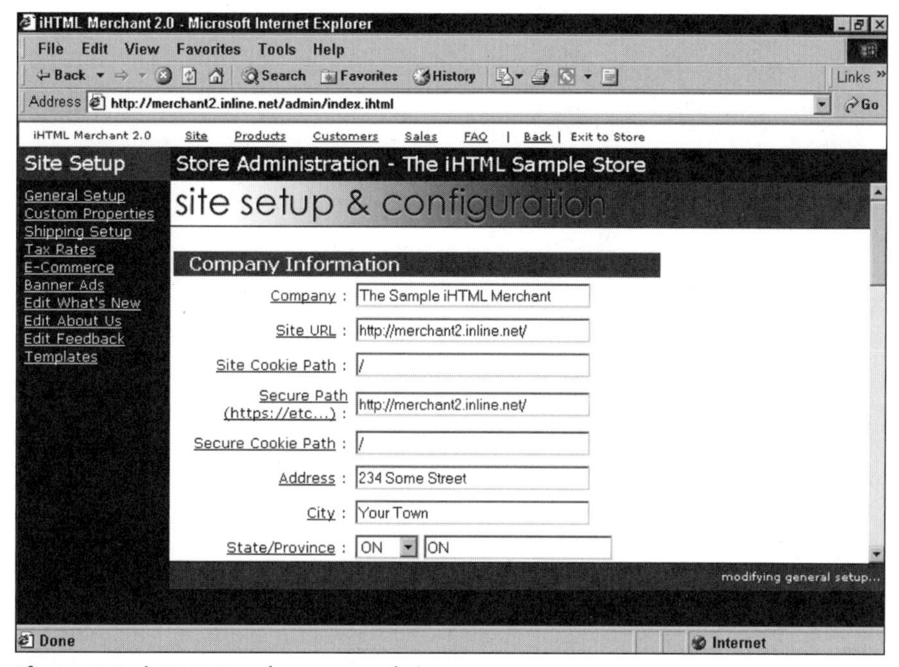

Figure 9-2: iHTML Merchant general site setup

Custom site properties

The custom site properties page allows you to specify your own site-specific settings for use throughout the site. Custom site properties can be useful for adding features to the store.

Shipping setup

The shipping setup interface allows you to set the shipping methods that your store uses. Most mid-level storefronts—iHTML Merchant included—calculate shipping charges based on simple formulas, rather than using rates that come directly from shipping companies.

Although calculating shipping in this manner is not as accurate as getting rates directly from various shippers, merchants benefit from not having to look up the exact shipping charge for each order, which outweighs the occasional undercharge for shipping. Generally, the undercharges are more than balanced out by the overcharges.

Some of the formulas used to calculate shipping charges are:

✦ **Base shipping charge plus a weight rate.** For example, assume that two items are ordered, with a total weight of two pounds. If the base rate is $3.00 and the weight rate is $1.00 per pound, the total shipping charge for this order would be $3.00 + ($1.00 x 2), or $5.00.

✦ **Base shipping charge plus count rate.** This method multiplies the number of products by the count rate, and then adds the base charge. This method is useful if all of the products you ship have similar weights (greeting cards or Compact Disks, for example).

✦ **Base plus product charge.** In this case, the base shipping charge is added to a shipping cost that is associated with each item being shipped. This method requires that you specify a shipping charge for each product.

✦ **Base plus range.** This method adds the base charge to a shipping charge that is based on the price of each product. For example, if a product costs between $2.00 and $5.00, you might have a different shipping charge than if the product's price is between $50.00 and $100.00. This calculation method and the next method require you to create a table of prices and associated shipping charges.

✦ **Base plus order.** This is similar to the base plus range method, except the shipping cost is based on the total price of the order, rather than each individual item.

Tax configuration

Figure 9-3 shows iHTML Merchant's tax configuration administration screen. In much the same way that the shipping calculation methods are not 100 percent accurate, taxes are also simplified in e-commerce — especially among mid-level merchants.

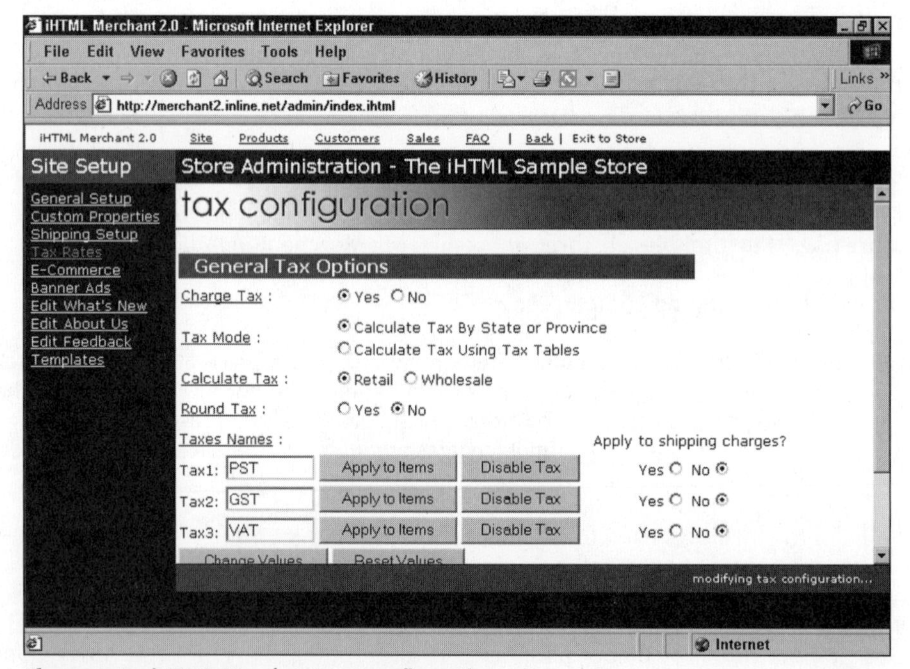

Figure 9-3: iHTML Merchant tax configuration

As you saw in Chapter 2, it's generally agreed that e-commerce merchants need to charge sales tax in states where they have a physical presence. Unfortunately, different counties or localities within a state often have different tax rates. A merchant could take the time to set up tax rates to be calculated by zip code, but this is generally not done. Most merchants simply calculate taxes based on state or province, which is the most common way entry- and mid-level stores configure taxes.

E-commerce setup

The e-commerce setup screen allows you to set the currency that your site uses and easily configure your site to work with any one of over twenty different payment-processing methods. This screen is shown in Figure 9-4.

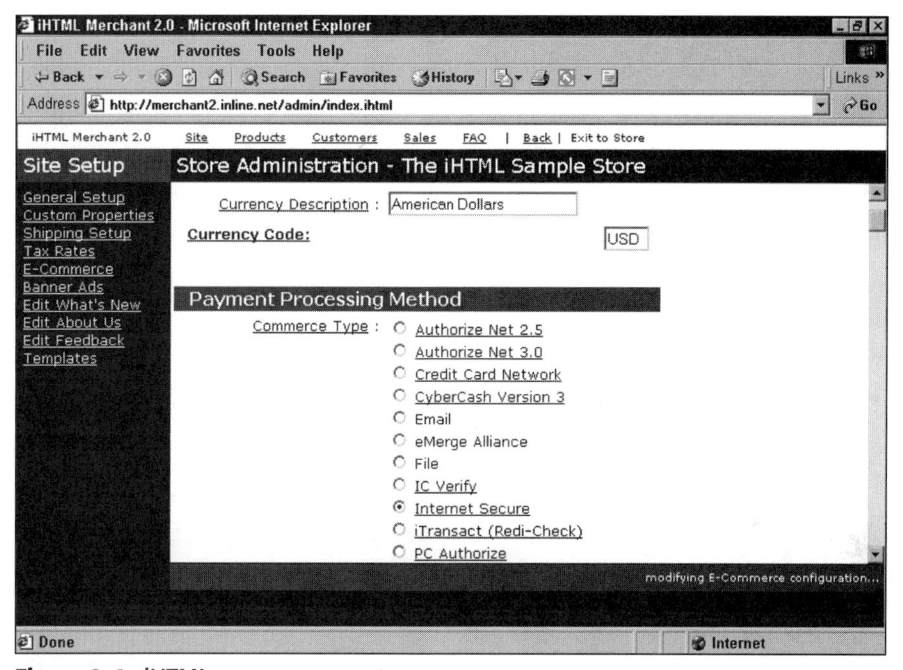

Figure 9-4: iHTML e-commerce setup

Chapter 17 discusses the various ways you can automatically process payments.

Banner ad maintenance

If you decide to run banner ads on your e-commerce site, iHTML Merchant provides a good ad management tool. As shown in Figure 9-5, the banner ad maintenance tool allows you to specify the length of a banner run using several different methods.

Using the banner ad maintenance administration area, you can set a particular ad to run for one month or until it has gotten a certain number of impressions or click-throughs (the act of a user clicking on a banner ad). You can also associate banners with products, categories, and keywords. This feature allows a merchant to sell very specific ad runs. For example, if your store sells books, a certain advertiser that sells sporting goods may choose only to advertise in the sports books section of your site or when certain keywords are used in site searches.

The ad maintenance screen also has a simple interface that allows you to quickly see how many impressions, clickthroughs, or days an advertiser has left in their banner run.

In general, iHTML Merchant has much better banner ad management tools than most mid-level storefronts. Banner ad management, a feature generally left to standalone tools for higher-level stores, is increasingly being included as part of complete entry-level or mid-level storefronts.

Editable pages

Several standard pages are included with iHTML Merchant, including a "What's New" page, a "Feedback" page, and a "About Us" page. The content for these pages is stored in the site database, and is editable through the administration area using the iHTML Merchant Page Editor, which has a menu of styles you can apply to the text you enter.

The Page Editor also has options for inserting data into these pages — such as fax number, company address, and so forth — from the site database. In essence, the Page Editor allows people with no knowledge of HTML or programming to modify the content of their site's pages.

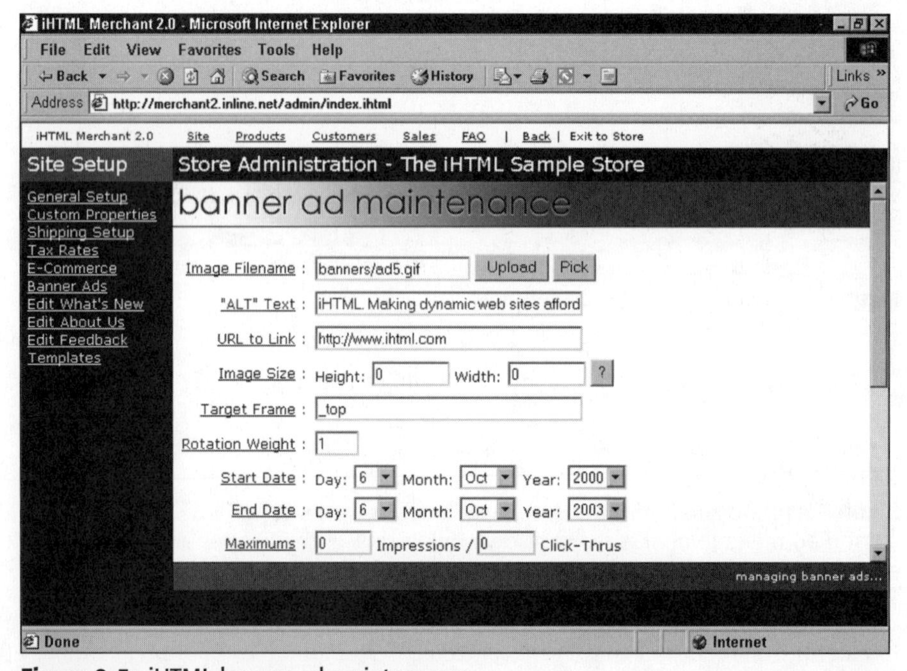

Figure 9-5: iHTML banner ad maintenance

Templates

iHTML Merchant provides several pre-designed templates you can use for your site. The template configuration screen is shown in Figure 9-6.

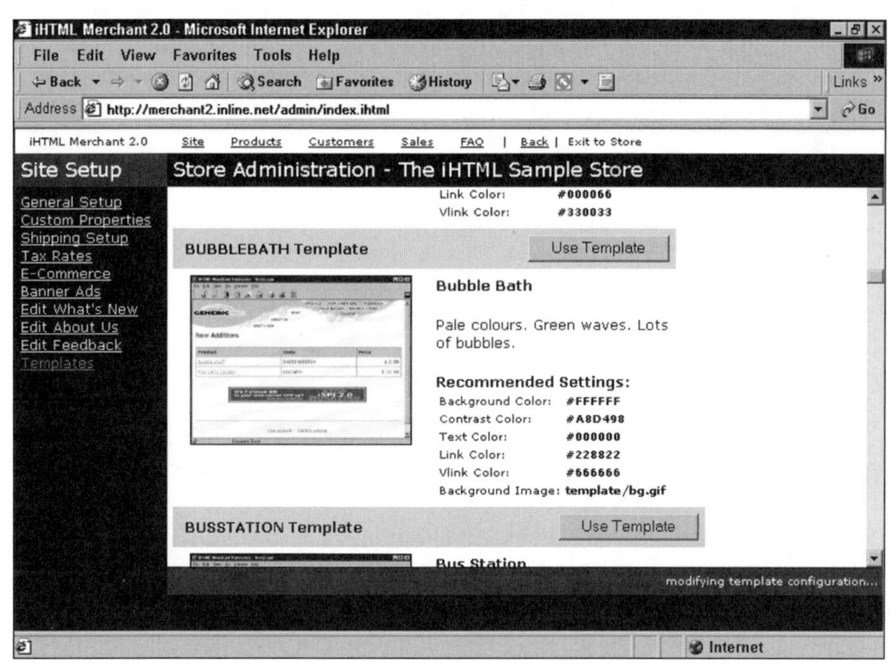

Figure 9-6: iHTML Merchant templates

Adding categories and products

Most outsourced storefront packages give you the option of dividing your product catalog into categories. iHTML Merchant's product administration section allows you to create categories and products using a scheme that looks and works very much like a file system browser, such as Windows Explorer.

To add a new product using iHTML Merchant, you simply navigate to the appropriate product category and click on the Add New Item icon. The product editor screen (see Figure 9-7) allows you to enter product information, such as name, description, member/non-member price differences, and shipping charges.

Customer administration

The customer administration area in iHTML Merchant allows you to search for and edit customer records. Administrators can use this area to add new customers and set variables, such as whether a customer is a member or should be included in the bulk e-mail list.

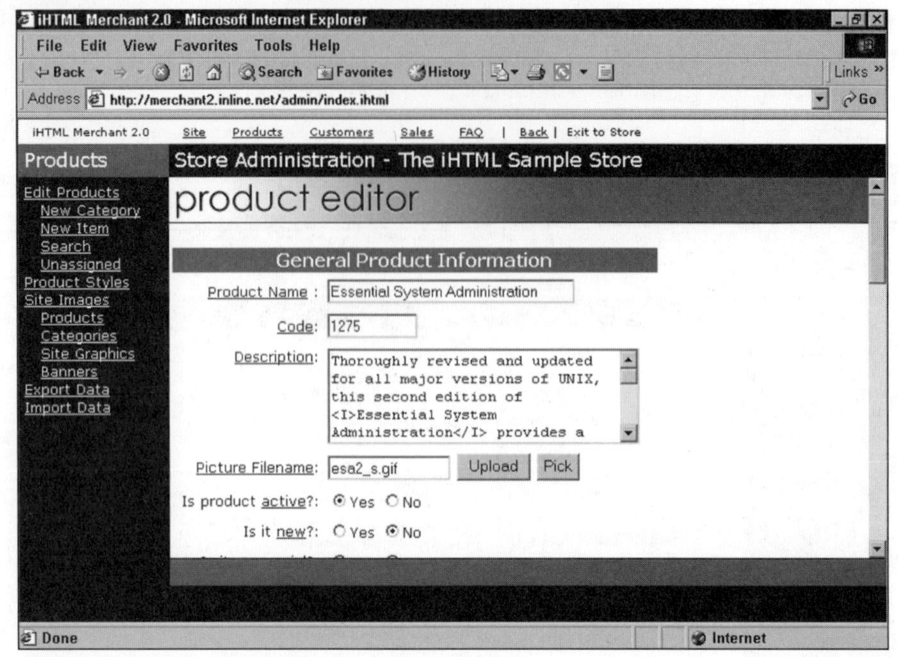

Figure 9-7: Adding a product in iHTML Merchant

The customer administration area also allows you to compose and send e-mail to everyone on the customer list who allows you to send them mail. Customer lists can also be imported and exported in this area.

Sales administration

The sales administration area of iHTML Merchant includes several features that control the customer-purchasing process and provide tools for viewing information about individual sales or aggregate sales. Here's how it works:

✦ **The Sales Options screen.** This allows you to create the message that is displayed at the end of the purchase process and compose the text for the customer's confirmation e-mail.

✦ **The Manage Orders screen.** Here's where you can view new orders, as well as orders already processed and shipped.

✦ **The Sales Graph screen.** The features on this screen allow you to display a sales graph for your site.

AbleCommerce

AbleCommerce from Able Solutions Corporation is another popular instant mid-level storefront solution. The setup, administration, and day-to-day maintenance of AbleCommerce are done using a Web-based interface.

AbleCommerce uses Allaire's Cold Fusion server. Cold Fusion is an application server, similar to the iHTML server, that interprets Allaire's simplified programming language, called Cold Fusion Markup Language (CFML). Similar to iHTML Merchant, a version of AbleCommerce is available that allows merchants to modify the actual program. Experienced Cold Fusion programmers can add almost any feature to a storefront created with AbleCommerce. In addition, the functionality of AbleCommerce can be expanded using add-ons, such as AbleCommerce's AbleShipper application and third-party plug-ins.

The standard features of AbleCommerce include:

- Pages can be customized using styles and custom HTML.
- Multiple levels of product detail.
- Support for multiple currencies. For example, a merchant could define a store's primary monetary unit as the U.S. dollar, and the secondary monetary unit as the Euro.
- Products can be associated with each other as *options*, which allow merchants to create bundles of products or cross-sell items.

iCommerce ShopZone

ShopZone from iCommerce (formerly Breakthrough Software) comes in ISP and CSP versions, as well as a version that you can install on your own server. ISPs that currently offer ShopZone site hosting include Earthlink, Sprint, and Interland. Version 2.0 of ShopZone uses a desktop-based application for creating stores that run on Windows.

iCommerce has developed a new e-business solution called inSite. Some people still use ShopZone but you may want to check out the inSite StoreBuilder instead (`www.icommerce.com/cgi-bin/shopzone30/main/ic_solution_storebuilder.html`).

The steps in establishing a ShopZone store include:

1. You first create a project directory for your site, which ShopZone calls "creating a new Web." This forms the basic structure of a ShopZone site.
2. After the new Web has been created, you're prompted to choose a style from a menu of pre-designed templates.
3. You can create stores within that workspace by using the Online Store Data Definition dialog box, shown in Figure 9-8.
4. After you've created a new store, categories and products can be added to it. Figure 9-9 shows the Online Store Products dialog box.

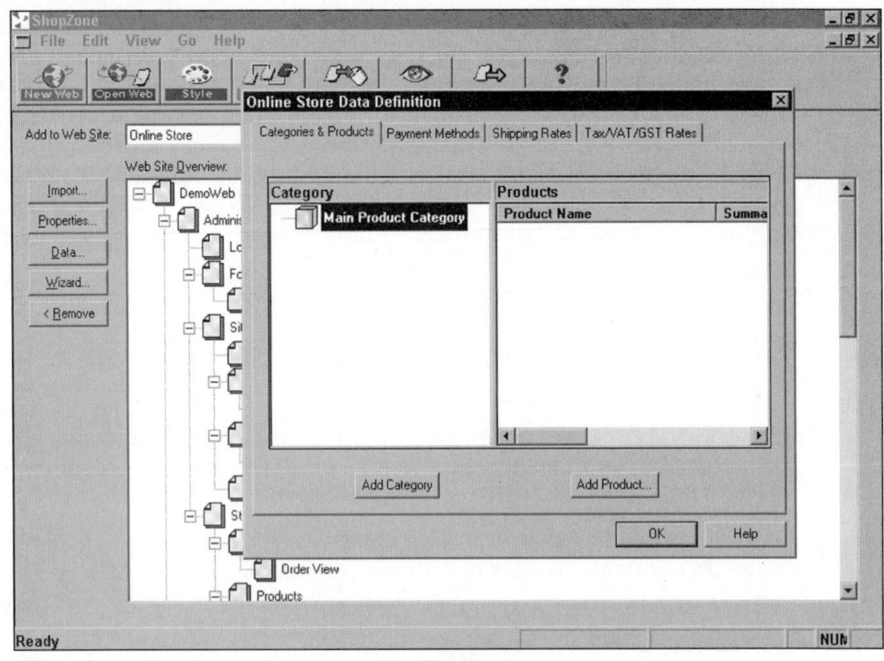

Figure 9-8: Creating a new store with ShopZone

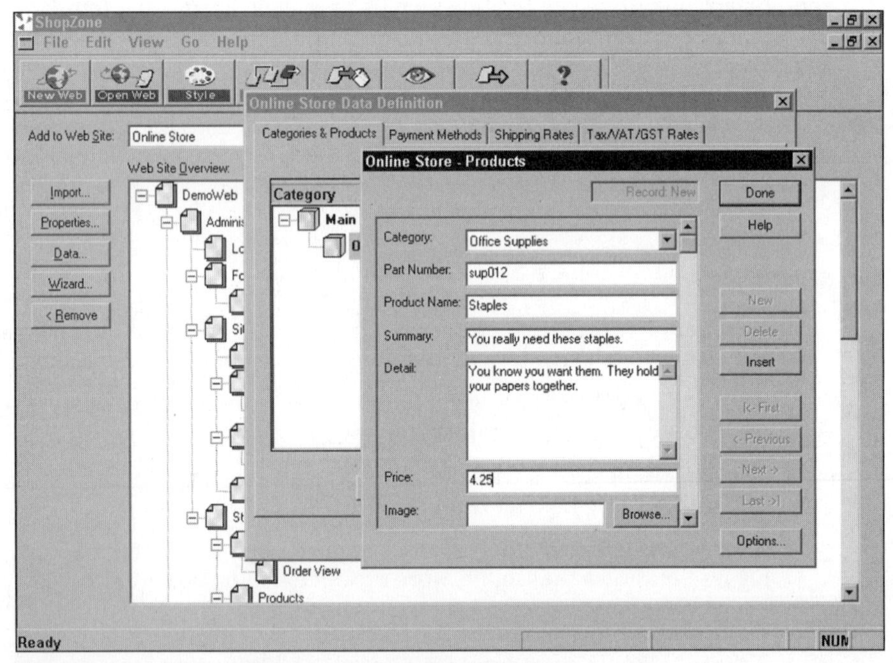

Figure 9-9: Adding products to a catalog in ShopZone

ShopZone has the ability to track inventory and notify the site administrator when the reorder level is reached. The ShopZone application also allows you to configure features such as taxes, shipping options, and so forth. Tax rates can be set by state, province, or country. Shipping rates can be set using a unit rate.

More mid-level options

Several other mid-level instant storefront tools are available through CSPs or as standalone tools.

The URLs for each of these products can be found in the "For More Information . . ." section at the end of this chapter.

Mercantec SoftCart

The features supported by Mercantec SoftCart include:

- Secure Sockets Layer (SSL) and public key security
- The capability to create custom site templates using third-party HTML development tools
- Administration via the Store Manager software
- Order routing to up to 15 destinations
- Electronic Data Interchange (EDI) support (SoftCart can send EDI X.12 850 purchase orders)
- Integrates with CyberCash and American Express's ExpressCommerce for payment processing

WebCatalog 4.0

The key features of WebCatalog 4.0 are:

- Allows you to build an unlimited number of stores
- Uses an internal database to speed data access time, but can also query standard databases
- Stores built using WebCatalog's StoreBuilder are Wireless Application Protocol (WAP) enabled, which makes them usable with certain wireless devices, such as Internet-enabled mobile phones
- Includes a site search engine
- Supports major payment gateways

Actinic Catalog

Actinic Catalog has all of the features that you would expect from a good mid-level instant storefront. Some of its features include:

- Manual product entry or importation from a database
- Product search engine
- SSL support as well as built-in 128-bit encryption
- Inventory management
- Shipping charges can be configured based on quantity, price, or weight
- Taxes can be set based on geography

Selecting a Mid-Level Online Storefront Package

Evaluating online storefront solutions

After a merchant has upgraded to a mid-level outsourced storefront, the e-commerce hardware and software requirements from Chapter 1 become more important. A merchant using one of these stores may need to make some choices regarding operating system, hardware, and server hosting. At the mid-sized storefront level, the merchant may also need to start thinking about whether additional staff or independent contractors are needed to support the server and software.

For more information on the hardware and software requirements for e-commerce, see Chapter 1.

When evaluating the features of different mid-level storefront packages, you should consider the seven keys to success, first introduced in Chapter 1. Once again, these are:

1. Generating demand
2. Ordering
3. Fulfillment
4. Payment processing
5. Service and support
6. Security
7. Community

As we did for entry-level storefronts in Chapter 8, let's take a look at how a typical mid-level package can help an e-commerce business address each key to success.

Generating demand

As you saw with iHTML Merchant, mid-level instant storefronts often give you the ability to maintain lists of customers and give certain members discounts. Other tools give you the ability to use customer lists to generate personalized bulk e-mails. When used correctly, these tools can be a part of your promotion strategy.

Ordering

As with entry-level storefronts, the order process in mid-level stores is fairly rigid. The customer browses products by category. If the customer is interested in a particular product, he or she can go to a screen containing more detailed information about the product. Products can be added to a shopping cart and there's generally a three- or four-step checkout process.

You won't find simplified quick checkout options in the mid-level range of storefronts, but the user experience should be easy and polished enough to give a customer confidence in placing an order.

Fulfillment

The merchant generally configures shipping options based on factors such as product weight rates or piece rates. Depending on your needs, some products may give you more options for calculating shipping. Other instant storefronts have electronic fulfillment options for downloadable products. These options may work as follows:

- ✦ Although any instant storefront option you select is likely to send you a notification when a product is purchased, it is, of course, up to you to handle any shipping that may be involved. Some products generate a shipping label that you can print and use for shipping.
- ✦ If the product you're selling can be delivered electronically, some instant storefronts simply send the user to a URL where he or she can download the product. Other storefronts generate a "key" for the user to use to access a secure download area or to unlock downloaded software.

Payment processing

Most mid-level storefronts provide several payment processing options. The most basic payment processing option is offline processing. In this case, the merchant is simply notified that an order has been placed. The merchant can then go to the site to pick up the order information, including the payment information. The software generally verifies that an actual credit card number and expiration date were entered, but it won't actually verify whether the credit card is valid.

Some storefront packages offer numerous options for electronic credit card processing. Other packages require the use of one of the most common payment processing vendors, such as CyberCash.

Additional payment options that may be supported include purchase orders, checks, faxed payment information, and digital wallets.

Service and support

Service and support options, because they're so particular to the products being sold, are generally minimal for any instant storefront solution. Mid-level stores generally provide a form customers can use to contact the merchant and a page that you can use for general information about the company and products. Some stores may also provide an area for you to create an FAQ or knowledge base using the administration area.

Instant storefronts are geared towards reducing the amount of work involved for the merchant. Many service and support options are labor intensive, however, and you may need to look for third-party add-ons to a mid-level store in order to provide more advanced types of support.

Security

Security options for mid-level storefronts are fairly standard. Most rely on Secure Sockets Layer (SSL) security on the server to provide secure transmission of payment information. Measures are also taken in these storefronts to protect credit card information once it's on the server — although you should certainly research the particulars of any instant storefront's security mechanisms before you decide on one.

Community

The community-building options supported by instant storefronts are generally limited or non-existent. Again, this is because of the generalized nature of instant storefronts. If your store sells music, the options you have for community building are different from those for a pet supply store.

Several common community building features may be provided by some mid-level storefronts, however. These include bulletin boards, some level of personalization, and e-mail newsletter functionality.

Key Point Summary

This chapter compared mid-level outsourced storefronts to entry-level storefronts and examined several different products that fall into the mid-level category. You also investigated customization issues and the seven keys to success — generating demand, ordering, fulfillment, payment processing, service and support, security, and community-building — relative to the options various mid-level products allow. In the process, you discovered how:

✦ Mid-level e-commerce outsourcing solutions provide experienced e-commerce merchants or established companies with a greater level of customization and store growth options than entry-level products.

✦ Mid-level outsourced storefronts generally cost more and require more effort to set up and maintain.

✦ Customization options include a variety of site design templates or ability to create new ones, greater control over the ordering process, and more flexibility in creating specialized payment and shipping plans.

✦ Some mid-level outsourced storefronts, such as iHTML Merchant or AbleCommerce, allow you to modify the program code using simple programming languages such as iHTML or CFML (Cold Fusion Markup Language).

✦ A CSP (Commerce Service Provider) is an ISP that handles many of the setup and technical tasks involved in operating an e-commerce storefront.

✦ ✦ ✦

STUDY GUIDE

At this point in the book, you should have a good idea of all of components involved in creating and running an entry- or mid-level e-commerce site. Now it's time to test your knowledge of the exam topics covered in this chapter, before we move on to high-level online storefront packages, which are the topic of the next chapter. The lab exercises are designed to give you a practical look at the types of tools covered in this chapter and at some of the sites created using these tools.

Assessment Questions

1. Which of the following is not a reason to upgrade to a mid-level instant storefront?

A. More customization options

B. Increased cost

C. Increased growth potential

D. Increased independence

2. Which of the following usually describes the trade-off between entry-level and mid-level storefront outsourcing? (Choose the best answer.)

A. Mid-level storefronts provide greater simplicity at more cost.

B. Mid-level storefronts provide greater security at less cost.

C. Mid-level storefronts provide greater customization ability at more cost.

D. Mid-level storefronts provide more features for less cost.

3. Your company has been doing quite well selling products using an entry-level storefront. If you want to improve your storefront, you should do which of the following? (Choose the best answer.)

A. Immediately upgrade to a mid-level storefront.

B. Base any changes that you make to your storefront software on the needs of your store.

C. Hire a consultant to install a high-performance database.

D. Outsource your customer support.

4. In deciding how to host your mid-level storefront, your company is considering using a CSP. Which of the following is an advantage of using a CSP? (Choose the best answer.)

   A. A CSP simplifies the process of setting up and operating your storefront.

   B. CSPs guarantee that your store will make money.

   C. CSPs cost less than ordinary hosting solutions.

   D. CSPs are more secure than other hosting solutions.

5. Which of the following is not an important factor in evaluating the features of mid-level instant storefronts?

   A. Fulfillment

   B. Security

   C. Price

   D. Payment processing

6. Which of the following fulfillment-related services are generally not provided by mid-level instant storefronts? (Choose the best answer.)

   A. Shipping calculation

   B. Shipping label creation

   C. Shipment tracking

   D. Support for download of intangible goods

Scenarios

A merchant who has been selling products to consumers using an entry-level online mall asks your opinion on whether he should upgrade to a mid-level instant storefront. What questions could you ask the merchant to help him make a decision?

Lab Exercises

Lab 9-1 Working with iHTML Merchant

1. Go to `http://www.ihtmlmerchant.com`.
2. Click on the Demo link.
3. Choose the Merchant2 Professional demo.

4. Click the demo store link of your choice. A new browser window opens with that store. Go back to the menu listing the stores and admin area and click on the link for the Store Administration of the demo store you chose. You should then see a screen similar to Figure 9-10.

Figure 9-10: The iHTML Merchant Store Administration home page

5. Click on the link titled Site (on the left in the horizontal bar just below the Address box) to go to the site administration area. The first link on the left should then be General Setup. Choose that option. You should then see the site setup & configuration screen (refer to Figure 9-2).

6. Scroll down the page to the Site Information section. Try changing the values of the colors and font face input fields. If you're not familiar with the hexadecimal notation used to specify colors in HTML, try changing the values to the ones shown in Figure 9-11.

7. Scroll to the bottom of the screen and click the Change Values button. Don't worry about messing anything up. These are not live sites and Inline Internet Systems regularly resets these demo sites.

8. Switch to the browser window containing the demo store, and click the Reload button to view the changes you just made.

9. Go back to the store administration area and try changing other parameters on the Site Information screen.

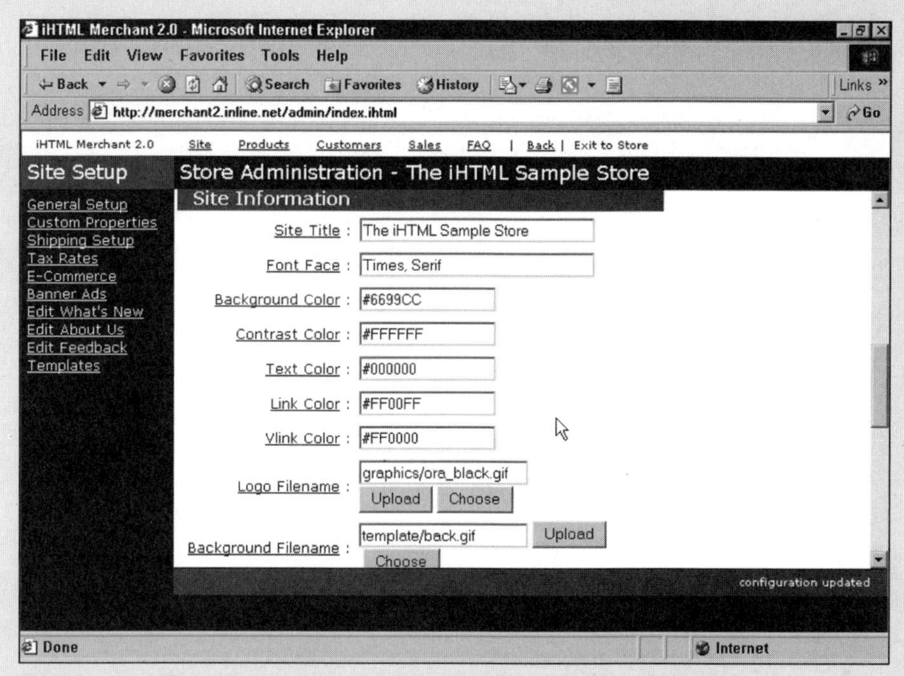

Figure 9-11: The iHTML Merchant Site Information screen

Lab 9-2 Evaluating a mid-level storefront solution

1. Open `http://www.mercantec.com/demo/index.html` in your browser.
2. View the demonstrations of Mercantec's SoftCart on this page.
3. Answer the following questions for this instant storefront software:
   a. Does it provide features for generating demand?
   b. Is the product browsing and ordering process consistent and user-friendly?
   c. Does the product provide assistance with fulfillment? What specific features support order fulfillment?
   d. Does the product provide service and support options?
   e. What sort of security does this product use?
   f. Does the product have features for building community?

Lab 9-3 Legal issues in mid-level instant storefronts

1. Visit a demo store or a live store created using one of the mid-level instant storefront packages mentioned in this chapter. You can usually find these by going to the maker of the software's site. The addresses for each of these products are listed at the end of this chapter, in the "For More Information . . ." section.
2. What, if anything, does this store do to avoid each of the following legal pitfalls?
   - **a.** Copyright issues
   - **b.** Trademark issues
   - **c.** Patent issues
   - **d.** Intellectual property issues
   - **e.** Privacy and confidentiality issues
   - **f.** Jurisdictional issues
   - **g.** International trade issues
   - **h.** Tax issues
   - **i.** Shipping issues
   - **j.** Currency conversion issues

Lab 9-4 Installing AbleCommerce

This, and the rest of the labs in this chapter, involves working with AbleCommerce. To try this at home, follow these steps:

1. Install a Web server on your local computer. If you're using Windows 9x or Windows NT Workstation, you can download and install the Windows NT Option pack from Microsoft, which installs Microsoft's Personal Web Server. If you're using Windows NT Server, Internet Information Server should be installed. If you're using Windows 2000, you can install a Web server from the Windows 2000 installation CD, if it's not already installed.
2. Install the Cold Fusion Application Server. A free 30-day evaluation version is available from `www.allaire.com`. This software is also available on the CD-ROM that comes with this book.
3. Install AbleCommerce. A free 30-day evaluation version is available from `www.ablecommerce.com`. This software is also available on the CD-ROM that comes with this book.

After you've successfully installed these three components, you can proceed to the next lab exercise.

Lab 9-5 Creating a new store with AbleCommerce

1. Open your Web browser and go to the AbleCommerce Administrator Login page at `http://127.0.0.1/acb/dsmaster/index.cfm?DS_ID=1` or by double-clicking on the Administrator menu in your windows Start menu. The administrator login screen is shown in Figure 9-12.

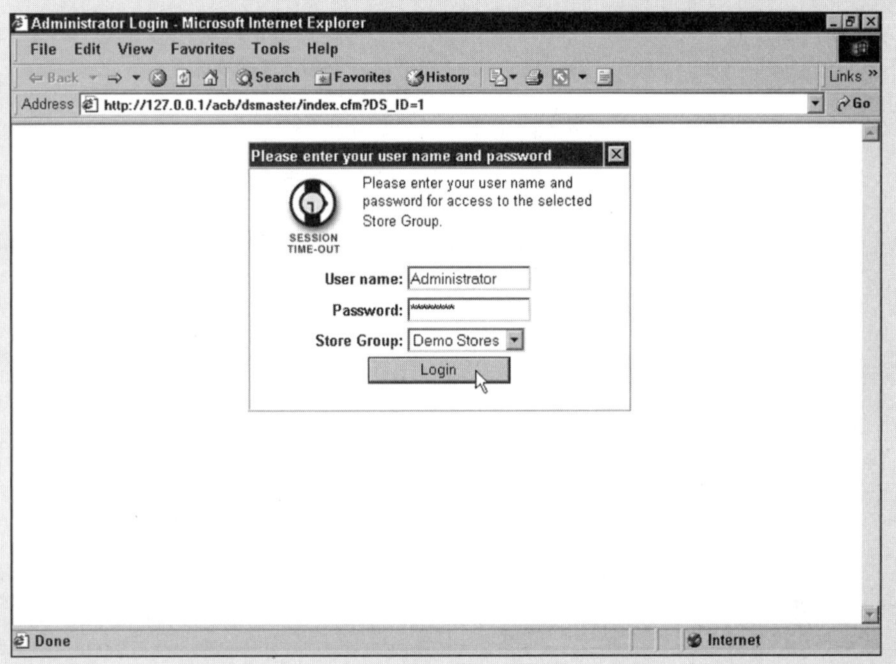

Figure 9-12: The AbleCommerce administrator login screen

2. Enter the default user name (Administrator) and the default password (password) to login to the demo stores.
3. After you successfully login, you see the Administrator menu. At this point, you should follow the instructions in the Able Commerce Readme file to change the default password. After you've changed the administrator password, return to the demo stores Administrator Menu.

4. To create a new store, click on the Add/Remove Stores icon, and then click Add a Store, which displays the screen shown in Figure 9-13.

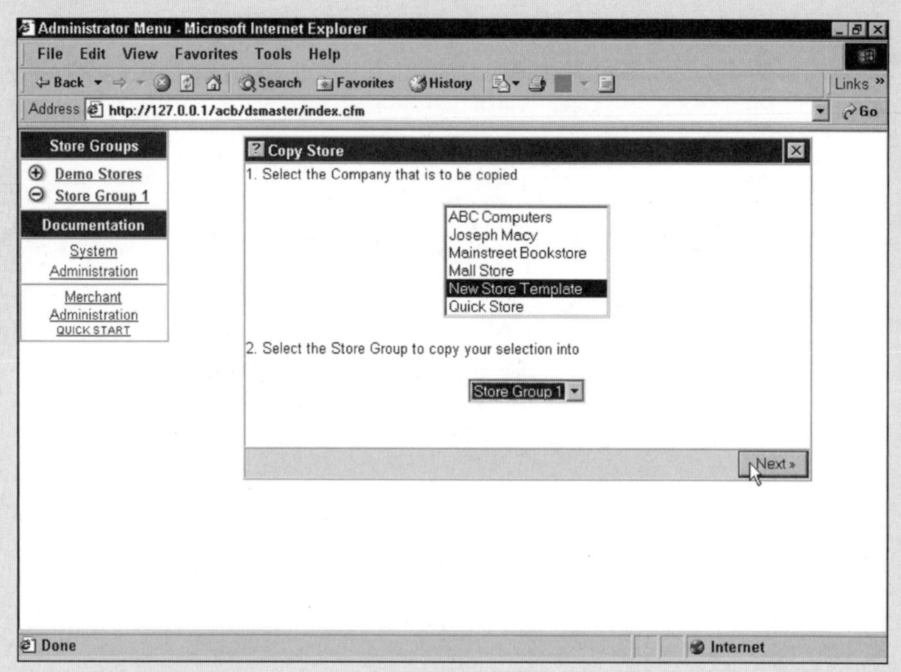

Figure 9-13: The Copy Store administration area

5. Highlight the choice called New Store Template, make sure that you're copying to Store Group 1, and then click Next.

6. The next screen allows you to give your new store a name (say FancyStore) and name the directory on your server. Leave all check boxes on this page checked. AbleCommerce then makes a copy of the new store template. This may take a few moments. When the copying is complete, you're returned to the main administration page.

7. Click on Store Group 1 to switch to the group containing your new store. You may need to log in. Click on the plus sign next to Store Group 1 to see a link to your new store, as shown in Figure 9-14 (noting that the plus changes to a minus sign next to Store Group 1, as the FancyStore link is displayed).

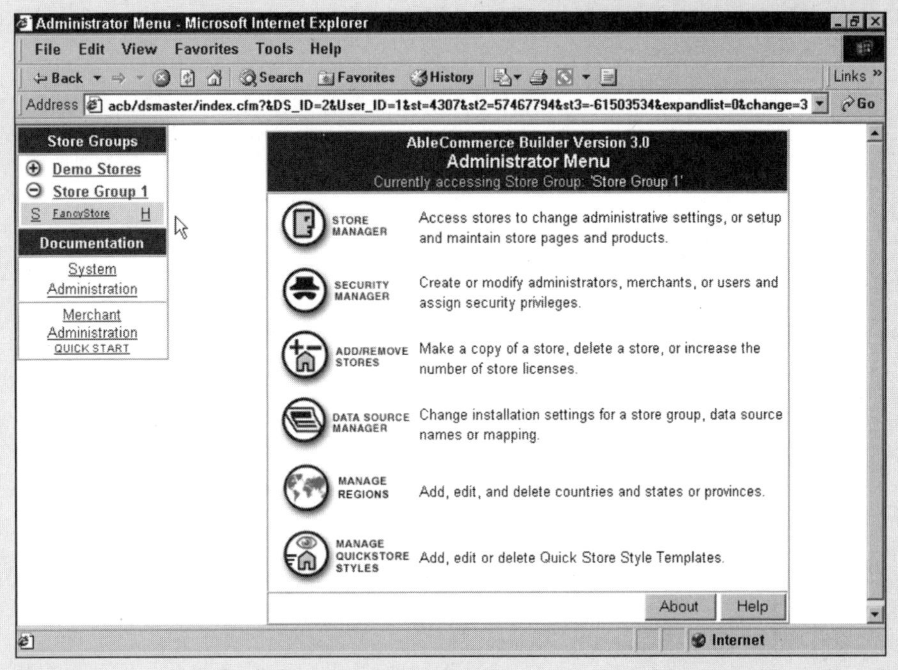

Figure 9-14: View the link to your new store

Lab 9-6 Adding products to a store in AbleCommerce

1. Click on the name of your new store to go to the Merchant Menu, as shown in Figure 9-15.
2. Click on the inventory link to go to the Category page. AbleCommerce organizes products using categories and groups. Select one of the pre-defined categories and then click next to select a group within that category.
3. After you've selected a group, click Next to go to the Products screen, as shown in Figure 9-16.
4. Using the Products screen, you can add, edit, view, delete, and move products. Select one of the products, and then click the Add button. A copy of that product is created.
5. Highlight the new product, and then click Edit. You then see the Editing Product screen.
6. Change the information on this page as much as you like. To see and change more detailed information about the product, click on the More Detail link. Before moving to the next step, make sure you check the check box in the upper right hand corner called Activate for Viewing.
7. When you've finished editing your new product, click the Finish button to return to the Products page.

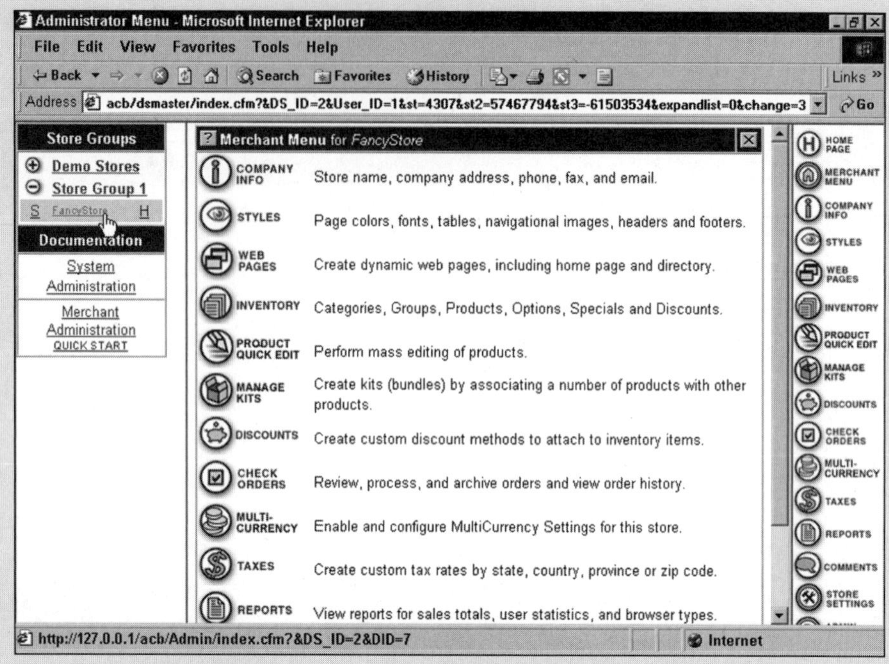

Figure 9-15: The AbleCommerce Merchant Menu

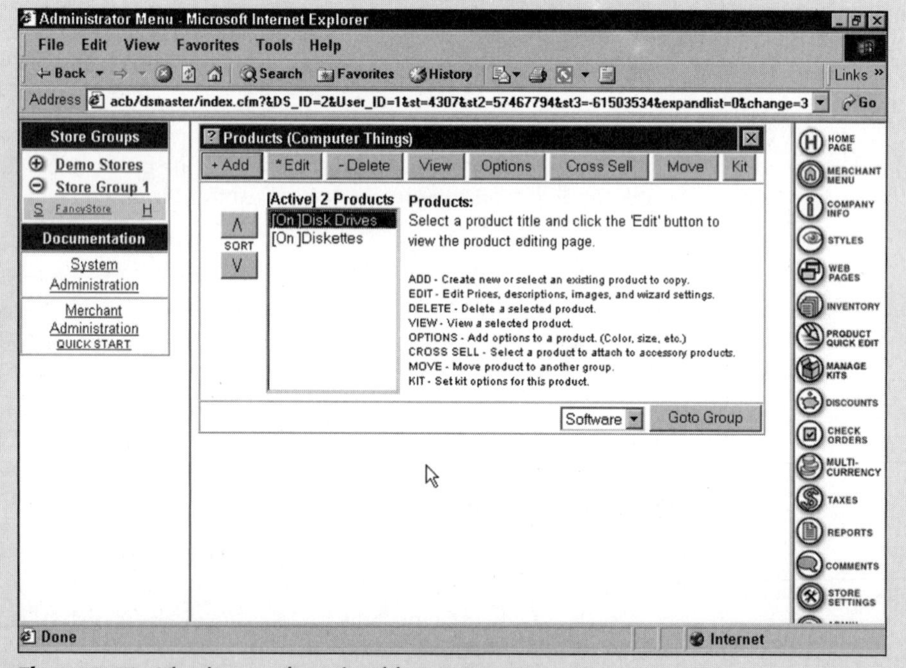

Figure 9-16: Viewing products in AbleCommerce

8. To preview your new store, click the Home Page button on the right side of the browser window. You should then see the demo store previewed in the middle frame of the browser window.

9. Navigate through your store to find the product you just created. Try adding additional products, and maybe even new categories and groups to your store, before moving on to the next section.

Lab 9-7 Publishing a site with AbleCommerce

1. Click the Store Settings icon on the right-hand menu of the AbleCommerce administration interface.

2. The first choice on the store settings menu is Activate Store. Because you're creating this site on your local computer, and not on a server with dedicated Internet access, this option won't let you begin selling on the Internet. You do, however, have access to your store using a Web browser on your local computer or your local network.

Caution

Although it's not likely to happen, it's possible that someone who knows the IP address of your computer could view your store on your local computer while you're connected to the Internet. Never use a Web server directory to store sensitive information.

3. Activate your store for viewing by clicking the Activate Store icon, and then selecting Yes (as shown in Figure 9-17).

4. Click the Next button to view additional store settings that you can configure in AbleCommerce.

5. View your store by going to `http://127.0.0.1/acb/webpage.cfm?&DID=7&WebPage_ID=2`. The address you use to connect to your local server (127.0.0.1) may be different for you, depending on how your server is configured.

Tip

If you've created more than one custom store, the URL shown in Step 5 may not be right. The DID variable in the URL stands for dealer ID. Try changing the 7 to a 6 or a 5 to visit the demo stores. Or, go to `http://127.0.0.1/acb/index.cfm` to view a menu of all the demo stores.

6. The next step is to make the URL of your store more attractive. From the Administration menu, go back to the administration area for your store.

7. Go to the Store Manager and click the Store Settings image for the store.

8. Click the Wizard Settings image to access the Wizard Settings page (shown in Figure 9-18).

9. At the bottom of the page there are radio-button selections. Select Custom Wizards and click Update. Be patient. This may take a few moments.

10. Go to `http://127.0.0.1/`*`yourstore`*`/index.cfm` in your Web browser (where *`yourstore`* is the actual name of the directory you created for your store, and 127.0.0.1 is the address or name of your local Web server).

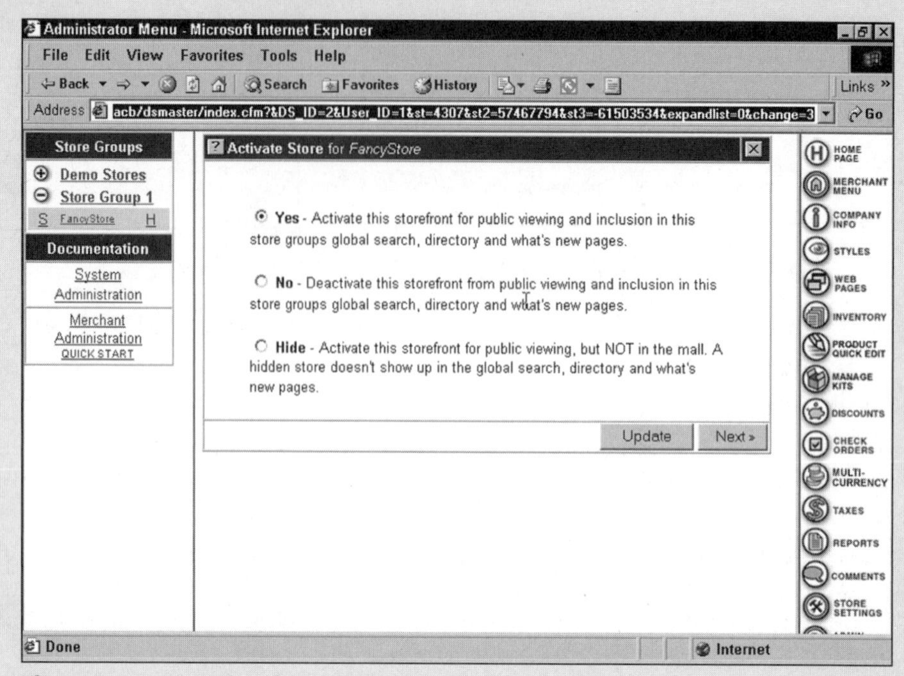

Figure 9-17: Activating the store

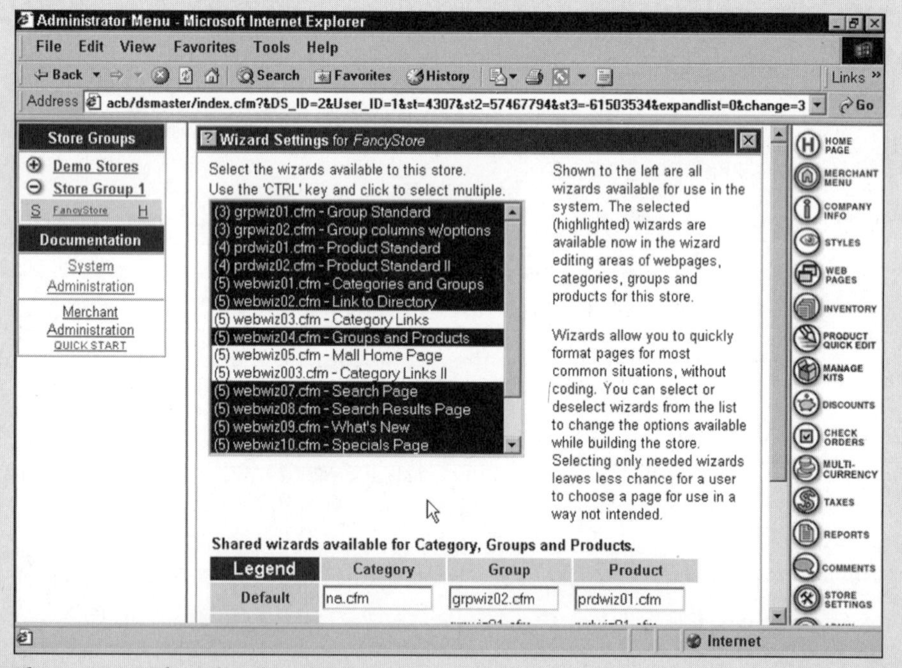

Figure 9-18: The Wizard Settings page

Answers to Chapter Questions

Chapter pre-test

1. A CSP, or Commerce Service Provider, is an e-commerce hosting service that includes everything needed to run an e-commerce site — including security, backups, and commerce software.
2. Mid-level solutions are different from entry-level solutions in the following six ways:
   - Customization
   - Cost
   - Security
   - Independence
   - Administration, reporting, and setup tools
   - Variety of e-commerce functions supported
3. Beginning with mid-level outsourcing solutions, merchants need to start being concerned with the hardware, software, and staffing requirements of the storefront package they choose.
4. Mid-level online storefront packages typically provide the ability to send e-mails to customers and to give discounts to members.

Assessment questions

1. **B.** Any storefront solution you choose has tradeoffs. Mid-level storefronts provide greater customization ability, growth potential, and independence (among other benefits) than entry-level products. The downside is that mid-level solutions are more complex than entry-level products and generally cost more (see "Understanding Mid-Level Online Storefront Packages").
2. **C.** This is essentially the same question as the previous one. To determine what type of storefront you require, it's important to have a good understanding of the tradeoffs involved (see "Understanding Mid-Level Online Storefront Packages").
3. **B.** There are no hard rules about when you should upgrade to a mid-level storefront (see "Understanding Mid-Level Online Storefront Packages").
4. **A.** A CSP handles many of the basic server setup and maintenance tasks involved in running an e-commerce site. Hosting your site with a CSP may cost more than with other solutions, but can save you time and effort (see "Understanding Mid-Level Online Storefront Packages").

5. **C.** This is a trick question. Although cost is an important factor when evaluating a storefront, it's not a feature or capability of the storefront (see "Selecting a Mid-Level Online Storefront Package").

6. **C.** Mid-level instant storefronts generally provide basic features for supporting fulfillment. More advanced features, such as shipment tracking, are generally not provided (see "Selecting a Mid-Level Online Storefront Package").

Scenarios

Some of the questions you might ask to determine whether a merchant should use a mid-level storefront over an entry-level storefront are:

- Does the store need its own domain name?
- How many products are in the store catalog?
- What is the merchant's budget for storefront software and hosting?
- How does the merchant currently process credit cards?
- Does the merchant want to be able to use a custom site design?

For More Information . . .

For more information about the topics, products, and companies covered in this chapter, please visit the following sites:

- **O'Reilly WebSite Professional.** `http://website.oreilly.com`
- **iHTML.** `www.ihtml.com/`
- **AbleCommerce.** `www.ablecommerce.com`
- **Maestro Software.** `www.maestrocommerce.com`
- **iCommerce.** `www.icommerce.com`. Makers of ShopZone and inSite.
- **Mercantec, Inc.** `www.mercantec.com`. Makers of Mercantec SoftCart
- **Smith Micro Software.** `www.smithmicro.com`. Makers of WebCatalog 4.0
- **Actinic Software.** `www.actinic.com`. Makers of Actinic Catalog

CHAPTER 10

High-Level Online Storefront Packages

EXAM OBJECTIVES

- High-level online storefront solutions
- Evaluating online storefront solutions
- Auction software

CHAPTER PRE-TEST

1. How are high-level storefront packages different from mid-level storefronts?
2. What two features of high-level storefronts enable their high level of customization ability?
3. Why are B2B e-commerce storefronts more likely to use high-level storefront software?
4. What types of products are ideal for selling through auctions?

✦ Answers to these questions can be found at the end of the chapter. ✦

In this chapter, you first find out how high-level outsourcing options differ from the entry-level and mid-level products. You then look at the product features suitable for medium-to-large sized online storefronts and examine a few of the products that meet those needs. Next, you get some tips for choosing a high-level online storefront, and finally, you explore some tools for conducting business-to-business (B2B) or business-to-consumer (B2C) online auctions.

Understanding High-Level Online Storefront Packages

High-level online storefront solutions

High-level online storefront software packages are more likely to be used for B2B e-commerce than low-level or mid-level storefront packages. High-level packages are also used for high-volume B2C e-commerce, because they're able to handle much more traffic than mid-level storefronts.

B2B e-commerce and high-volume B2C e-commerce require more stability, more security, and better performance than entry- or mid-level storefronts can provide. High-level online storefront packages are designed to meet these requirements, while providing greater functionality than other instant storefront software and easier setup than custom-built software.

Figure 10-1 shows the relationship between the storefront software packages covered in this chapter and other storefront software.

The particular features that differentiate high-level online storefront software from other storefront options are:

- ✦ Customization
- ✦ Cost
- ✦ Security
- ✦ Administration, reporting, and installation
- ✦ Stability and performance
- ✦ Functionality

Be familiar with the main differences between entry-level, mid-level, and high-level outsourcing solutions.

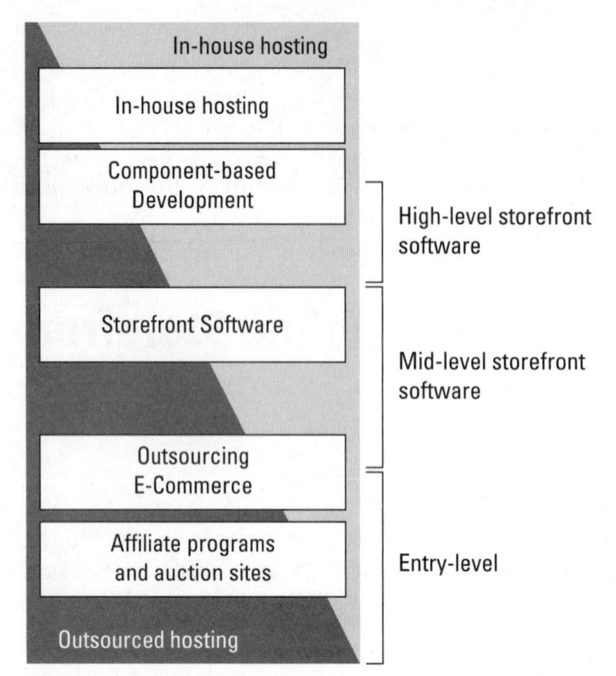

Figure 10-1: High-level online storefronts in context

Customization

High-level storefront packages give the merchant more control over the customer's shopping experience than either low-level or mid-level storefronts. Whereas mid-level stores generally allow the merchant to use custom site designs and, sometimes, custom functionality, high-level stores *always* allow the merchant to use custom site designs and custom functionality.

High-level storefront software also allows merchants to change a site's design and functionality based on factors such as seasonal issues, evolving marketing goals, or the user's preferences or past purchases. Two intertwined features of these stores — componentization and personalization — provide high levels of customization and control over the user's experience.

Componentization

Component-based Web site development breaks up each piece, or function, of a Web site into independent parts, each of which can be customized separately and arranged in different ways. Components can be parts of a Web site that the user sees, such as design elements or forms, or they can be back-end parts, such as a database table or a program for managing user information. This method of creating Web sites provides much greater flexibility than stores with fixed structures. Figure 10-2 shows a simple example of some of these components.

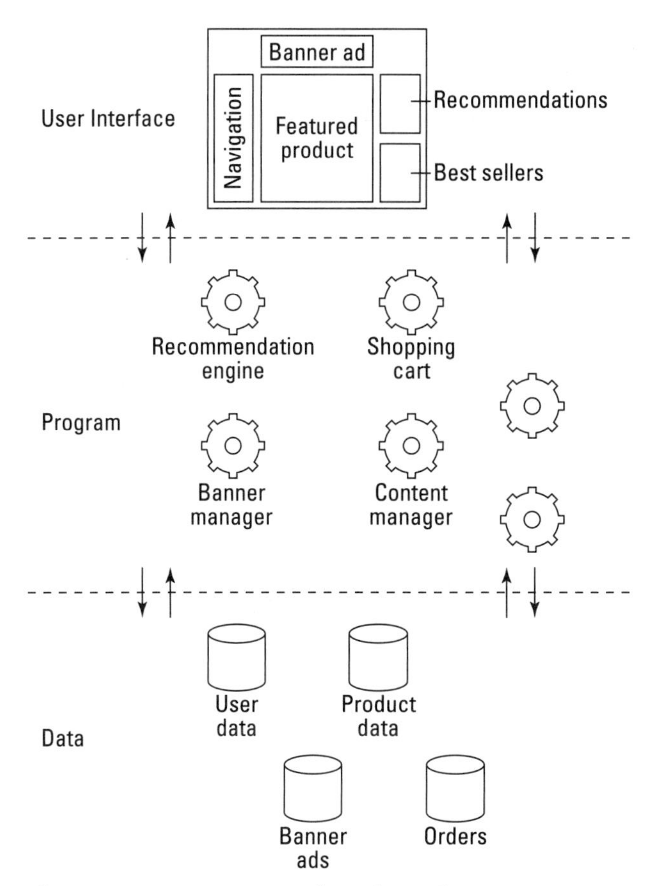

Figure 10-2: A component-based storefront

Besides illustrating component-based development, Figure 10-2 also portrays the *three-tier computing model.* Three-tier computing separates the software into three tiers (or layers): the user interface (also known as the *client tier*), the program (also known as the *business logic* or *application tier*), and the data (or *data-storage tier*).

A merchant can use a component-based storefront package to decide which components to use and how those components fit together. This works as follows:

✦ **User interface.** The user interface in a component-based system can be made up of several different dynamically generated pieces that are assembled as the user requests pages. The merchant can decide how and where each of these components appears.

✦ **Program.** In this part of the site, also known as the business logic tier, a merchant may choose whether to include a banner ad system, or decide to purchase or create a new component for functions specific to his or her business.

✦ **Data.** The different components of the data storage part of the site depend upon what functionality the site contains. If the site needs to calculate shipping, there needs to be some kind of shipping information database or a connection to an external source of shipping information.

Figure 10-3 shows a Web page that's made up of individual components. Figure 10-4 shows an alternate way to arrange the same components.

Figure 10-3: A component-based site design

A component-based design allows merchants to test various configurations to see which layout is most effective. It also allows users to arrange a site's components to suit themselves.

Personalization

Personalization is the practice of customizing a Web site for an individual user, or allowing users to customize how they view the site. Personalization is made possible by componentization. For example, the banner ad component of a site and the user management component can work together to show banner ads to users based on past purchases. Or, the product catalog component can work with the user management component to show a customer products that he or she is more likely to purchase.

Figure 10-4: A component-based site design, rearranged

Done correctly, personalization can be a valuable service. However, personalization also presents many potential hazards for the over-eager marketer. If personalization is done wrong, customers get a creepy "Big Brother" feeling when they visit your site. Refer to Chapter 2 for tips on protecting and respecting the privacy of your customers.

Cost

The price of purchasing, installing, and maintaining high-level storefront packages can be much higher than other outsourcing solutions. On the other hand, purchasing a high-level storefront package and paying consultants or hiring staff to set it up and maintain it is much less expensive than custom building a comparable storefront.

Merchants can expect to pay tens or hundreds of thousands of dollars for high-level storefront packages. The producers of many high-level storefront software packages require you to hire their consultants to install the software and that you attend training courses.

Security

Security is important for e-commerce storefronts of all sizes, but those with the most to lose are more concerned with guarding against fraud and theft. A merchant that is doing or expects to be doing enough business over the Web to justify high-level storefront software needs to invest heavily in security, with features such as:

- **Roles-based security.** Roles-based security allows merchants to create multiple levels of users. The most basic type of user is, of course, a customer. Other groups of users might include customer service representatives, content developers, and managers. A roles-based security system gives administrators the ability to limit what capabilities other users have. For example, a customer service representative shouldn't be able to change product pricing, and a content developer shouldn't be able to set shipping rates.
- **Secure storage of customer data.** Customer data is encrypted and stored behind a firewall. Some packages use multiple layers of encryption or firewalls.

A firewall is a device (usually software) that blocks computers outside a private network from accessing files inside the network.

- **Secure Sockets Layer (SSL) encryption.** Digital certificates and encryption are used to provide authentication and encryption of transmitted data.

Administration, reporting, and installation

Installing a high-level storefront package is much more involved than installing other storefronts. Software developers, database administrators, designers, and system administrators are all involved in the process.

After the store is up and running, administrators should be able to monitor traffic on any product or site component, rearrange components, post new content, adjust pricing, send targeted e-mails, and much more.

Administration of a high-level storefront package is generally not a simple task. The high level of customization and the high volume of traffic involved require administrators to go through training to be able to run one of these stores.

Stability and performance

High traffic B2C and B2B Web sites can generate millions of dollars in sales every day. As a result, every second that a Web server is down or slow to respond can result in lost sales. The systems running these sites must provide ways to protect the site from outages. The following technologies are generally used to provide the high-level availability that these storefronts require:

- **Clustering.** A way to group multiple Web servers so they can serve higher traffic volume than one server.

✦ **Failover.** Allows a server in a cluster to take over for another server in the event of a failure.

✦ **Load balancing.** This technology routes traffic between the different servers in a cluster so they share an equal amount of the work.

The hardware and software that supports high-level storefronts also needs to be more robust than for other storefronts. These sites are served using multiple high performance computers connected to high-speed redundant Internet connections. To optimize performance, high-level storefront packages integrate with high-performance database servers and application servers. These storefronts are also more likely than low- or mid-level storefronts to use and require knowledge of traditional programming languages such as Java, C, or C++.

See Chapter 12 for more information about server and database technologies.

Functionality

High-level storefronts often have built-in support for all of the features supported by low-level or mid-level stores. In addition, high-level stores give merchants the ability to add custom functionality by building or purchasing add-on components.

Some of the advanced e-commerce features that may be supported by high-level storefront packages include:

✦ Affiliate programs

✦ Order and shipment tracking

✦ Support for gift certificates

✦ Personalization

✦ Support for alternate browsing and shopping methods, such as wireless devices

✦ Electroni Data Interchange (EDI) support

✦ Syndication

✦ Workflow and process automation

✦ Integration with existing business systems and databases

As you'll see in the following two sections of this chapter, high-level storefronts have the most complete support for the seven keys to e-commerce success of any storefront packages.

See Chapter 1 for a refresher on the seven keys to e-commerce success.

High-Level Storefront Options

In the following sections, you examine the features and the structures of two high-level storefront software packages. Although these products can be used for B2B e-commerce, for simplicity's sake, we focus mainly on their B2C capabilities.

Open Market e-Business Suite

Open Market e-Business Suite is an integrated suite of content and commerce management applications. The e-Business Suite consists of the following eight products, which are explained in detail in the following sections:

- Content Server
- ShopSite
- Transact
- Marketing Studio
- Personalization Centre
- Content Centre
- Catalog Centre
- Syndication Centre

Content Server

The Content Server is the foundation upon which the rest of Open Market's e-Business Suite's components are built. In other words, the other components of the e-Business Suite get and also store the data they use in the Content Server. Content management systems, such as the Open Market Content Server, allow organizations to:

- Store and manage different kinds of information, such as text, graphics, audio, PDFs, and so forth
- Greatly increase the flexibility of using stored data, by organizing it in searchable databases that can be accessed programmatically and updated easily
- Use the information stored in these flexible databases to dynamically generate Web pages, reports, Extensible Markup Language (XML) data, documents for wireless devices, and more — a process known as *multi-target delivery*
- Manage changes to documents with revision tracking (sometimes known as *version control*), which prevents multiple people from simultaneously making changes to the same files by locking out all other users except the one who has checked it out for revision
- Provide security services and other features such as load balancing and caching, which reduce the amount of work the servers need to do by storing the results of frequently used database queries

ShopSite

ShopSite is the store-building component of Open Market's e-business suite. ShopSite can be used by small to medium-sized businesses to generate online storefronts through a Commerce Service Provider (CSP).

Open Market has several demo ShopSite stores available on their Web site at www.openmarket.com.

Transact

Transact provides transaction processing, subscription administration, order management, and customer service capabilities to storefronts. The features supported by Transact include:

- Secure capturing of customer and order information
- Analysis and reporting of customer and order information
- Multiple language support
- Multiple currency support
- Use of a universal shopping cart, which allows customers to purchase items from different stores, and use one form for checkout
- Encryption of customer payment information
- Fulfillment through the delivery of intangible goods to customers upon payment, or by sending notification to the correct department in the company for shipment of hard goods
- Customer self-service options that allow customers to view order, payment and shipping details, as well as tracking information from third-party shippers

Marketing Studio

Marketing Studio is an environment used to manage marketing campaigns. Some of the features of marketing studio are:

- An interface for non-technical users
- The ability to specify customer segments based on factors such as purchase history, activities while on the site, and more
- The creation of promotions such as free shipping, percentage or value off products or groups of products, and others
- Cross-selling (in which customers are shown similar products to the ones they select or are currently viewing) and up-selling (in which customers are shown upgrades to the products they select)

Personalization Centre

Personalization Centre allows users to create rules for site personalization. Using Personalization Centre, business managers can specify related products using a method called *concept mapping*. After content maps are created, a user who views computer products may be shown lists of related products, or lists of related news articles. Users can also use personalization to indicate which types of content they are interested in viewing.

Content Centre

Content Centre allows non-technical members of the site staff to create and publish content to multiple targets. Content Centre is basically a Web interface to the Open Market content server.

Catalog Centre

Catalog Centre provides an interface for creating and maintaining a store's catalog. Catalogs created using Catalog Centre can be searched and browsed using hierarchical navigation.

Syndication Centre

Syndication Centre allows data to be automatically exchanged between organizations. Syndication Centre can be used to create partner Web sites and to share data with other Web sites.

Allaire Spectra

Allaire Spectra is a packaged system for content management, e-commerce, and personalization. Built on Allaire's Cold Fusion Application Server, Spectra consists of these three parts, which are examined in detail in the following sections:

- COAPI
- Services
- WebTop

For more information on Allaire's Cold Fusion Application Server, see Chapter 9. A free thirty-day evaluation version of Cold Fusion Application Server can also be found on the CD-ROM that comes with this book.

COAPI

The ContentObject Application Programming Interface (COAPI) is the foundation of an application created using Spectra. ContentObjects in Spectra are site content components, such as navigation elements, news articles, and products. The COAPI allows the rest of the Spectra system to use these components.

Services

Services are program components that provide specific functionality to a larger program. Spectra has six services that manage the functionality of a Spectra storefront. These services are:

- **Content Management.** Provides users with a Web-based interface for creating, updating, and editing content.
- **Workflow and Process Automation.** Allows users to specify rules for how tasks are done in the business. For example, new content can be routed to managers for approval before it's posted on the site, or new orders can be automatically routed to all of the people or departments that need to perform an action as a result of the order.
- **Roles-Based Security.** Allows an existing company directory to be used to create different levels of access to the site.
- **Personalization.** Uses rules to determine how to personalize the site for users. For example, the site could suggest products from the same category as products that the user may have previously purchased.
- **Business Intelligence.** Gives the merchant details on how different parts of the site are doing, common click patterns, which products or types of products are most popular, and so forth.
- **Syndication.** Allows you to extend your business to outside sites. You can use syndication to create an affiliate program, to allow other sites to use content from your site, and to allow partner sites to provide your site with content.

WebTop

WebTop is the user interface component of the Spectra system. Depending on their role in the organization (as specified by the Roles-Based Security service), different users see different components and have access to different functionality on the site.

For example, site designers have access to the site layout tools, security administrators have access to security administration tools, and business managers have access to site reporting features. The most basic type of user, of course, is a customer. The customer sees only the public part of the storefront.

About other options

Other options for creating and maintaining high-level e-commerce storefronts using packaged applications include:

- **Broadvision Business Commerce.** `www.broadvision.com`
- **Ariba.** `www.ariba.com` or `www.ibm-i2-ariba.com/us1/`
- **Intershop Enfinity.** `www.intershop.com`
- **Interworld Commerce Exchange.** `www.interworld.com`
- **Microsoft BizTalk Server.** `www.microsoft.com/biztalk/default.asp`
- **WebSphere.** `www-4.ibm.com/software/webservers/`

Selecting a High-Level Storefront Package

Evaluating online storefront solutions

High-level storefront packages should assist merchants with every aspect of running an e-commerce storefront — from marketing, to promotion, to fulfillment. In the following sections, you take another look at the seven keys to e-commerce success and how a high-level storefront package meets these goals.

Generating demand

High-level storefront packages provide sophisticated control and management of user data, purchase history, and click patterns. When used correctly, this data can be extremely valuable in generating repeat business and creating a loyal customer base.

For example, high-level storefronts may provide marketers with the ability to run targeted campaigns in which certain types of users receive special offers or discounts. Tools may also be provided for cross-selling or up-selling products based on user profiles.

Ordering

The order process in high-level stores is highly customizable. Some of the ways that high-level stores give merchants greater control over the ordering process are:

✦ Enabling simplified purchasing for members

✦ Providing order and order history tracking

✦ Offering discounts, promotions, and additional items during the ordering and checkout process

Fulfillment

After an order has been received using a high-level storefront and payment has been received and verified, the order can be automatically fulfilled (in the case of intangible goods), or automatically routed to a fulfillment or shipping department.

Payment processing

Payment options in this type of store are unlimited. It's common for high-level merchants to accept multiple forms of payment, multiple currencies, and gift certificates.

Service and support

Along with the ability to store and manage detailed information about customer purchases comes the ability to provide helpful self-service options to customers, such as order and shipment tracking, account management, and personalization management.

Just because high-level storefronts provide more help with customer service and support, don't think you have to worry about them less. The service and support capabilities provided by any high-level storefront still need to be managed and backed up by a staff of customer support representatives who can handle phone and e-mail support issues.

Security

Everything possible should be done to provide the maximum amount of security in high-level storefronts. This generally includes hosting the site in-house, providing physical security to the servers, encrypting customer information, and hiding customer information behind multiple firewalls.

Community

Personalization and user management services give merchants an opportunity to create a sense of community. A high-level storefront should be able to use personalization not only to present ads for more products, but also to present users with information and content designed to keep them returning to your site. This content can include product reviews, customer reviews, discussion areas, and the ability to rate products.

Auctions for E-Commerce

Auction software

Auction site software enables a business to become an auctioneer — creating an environment in which products are priced dynamically, based on supply and demand. As a result, auctions are ideal for B2B e-commerce or for high-volume B2C e-commerce. Some examples of businesses that could benefit from having their own auction site include sellers of the following:

- ✦ Commodity items
- ✦ Rare items
- ✦ Collectable items
- ✦ Surplus items

For more information on how to sell products through third-party auction sites, see Chapter 8.

The following sections explore some auction site options.

Be sure that you understand what kinds of products are suited for auctions, and how selling products at auction can be beneficial.

FairMarket

FairMarket provides auction software, software hosting, and commerce services to portals and Web-based communities. Using FairMarket's AuctionPlace software, companies can put their products up for auction on their own sites. In addition, items can also be listed on other sites that are part of the FairMarket Network. Web portals that use FairMarket's software include Excite, Lycos, and MSN.

FairMarket AuctionPlace software works as follows:

- ✦ Sellers can manage all of the features that are commonly provided in online auctions — post listings, list auctions, provide descriptions of products, control auction start and end times, set prices, and notify successful bidders via e-mail.
- ✦ Site owners can customize the site's design and content, create categories of products, and set pricing options and fees.
- ✦ Shipping, billing, and security options are similar to those of other high-level storefronts.

About other options

Other options for creating your own auction site are:

- ✦ **Auction Broker.** `www.auctionbroker.com`
- ✦ **Strictly Exchange.** `www.expressbid.com`
- ✦ **AuctionBuilder.** `www.ablecommerce.com`
- ✦ **AuctionWorks.** `www.auctionworks.com`
- ✦ **Commerce One Auction Services.** `www.commerceone.com`
- ✦ **LiveExchange.** `www.moai.com/solutions/le.htm`
- ✦ **Visual Auction.** `www.beyondsolutions.com`

Selecting an auction environment

As with other types of e-commerce, it's important to understand your business's needs and your target audience when selecting auction software. After you've fully analyzed your business needs, apply the same seven factors we've used to evaluate other storefront software.

Other key factors to consider in auction software are:

- ✦ How well it integrates with your existing systems
- ✦ Whether it supports the type of auctions you want to operate
- ✦ The number of bids processed in a given time period (per minute or per second, for example)
- ✦ Whether you're hosting the software in-house or outsourcing
- ✦ Security features
- ✦ Ease of use

Key Point Summary

This chapter discussed and evaluated high-level online storefront solutions, and explored some auction software options.

- ✦ High-level storefront software is more likely to be used for B2B e-commerce or high-volume B2C e-commerce.
- ✦ B2B and high-volume B2C e-commerce require more stability, security, and performance than entry-level or mid-level storefronts can provide.
- ✦ High-level storefront packages supply advanced functionality at lower prices than custom-built software.
- ✦ High-level storefronts are usually component-based and have a high level of customization capabilities as a result.
- ✦ Many high-level storefronts allow personalization.
- ✦ Roles-based security allows different types of users to have different types of access to the site.
- ✦ Clustering, failover, and load balancing make high-level solutions more stable than other storefronts.
- ✦ High-level storefronts provide more assistance with the entire process of running an e-commerce storefront.
- ✦ Auctions are ideal for selling commodity, rare, collectable, and surplus items.
- ✦ Important factors to consider when selecting auction software include integration with existing systems, types of auctions supported, number of bids processed per second, whether the hosting is outsourced, security, and ease of use.

✦ ✦ ✦

STUDY GUIDE

This chapter covered high-level storefront software. You looked at several products for creating enterprise-strength e-commerce storefronts, and got some tips for selecting this type of product. Let's see what you remember from this chapter.

Assessment Questions

1. Which types of Internet businesses are most likely to use high-level storefronts?

A. B2C and C2C

B. B2B and high-volume B2C

C. B2B and extranets

D. B2C

2. Which of the following is not a way in which high-level storefronts are different from mid-level storefronts?

A. High-level storefronts are more stable.

B. High-level storefronts cost more.

C. Mid-level storefronts don't provide security for transactions.

D. Mid-level storefronts are less customizable.

3. Which of the following is an example of a user interface component?

A. Product database

B. Product navigation

C. Content map

D. Personalization service

4. What is clustering?

A. Grouping of users for personalization

B. Automatic data exchange between organizations

C. The ability for other servers to take over in the event of a server failure

D. Grouping servers to provide better performance

5. Pablo wants to sell his paintings on the Internet. He wants to use flexible, demand-based pricing. Which of the following solutions would be the best way for him to get started?

   A. He should use an entry-level auction site, such as eBay.

   B. He should use an entry-level outsourced storefront, such as Yahoo! Stores.

   C. He should use auction software, such as FairMarket.

   D. He should use a high-level storefront software package, such as Open Market e-Business Suite.

6. Drawing on what you've learned about high-level storefront software in this chapter, which of the following businesses would be most likely to benefit from using high-level storefront software?

   A. A provider of Web site design services

   B. A home-based business

   C. A large, multinational reseller of office supplies

   D. The law school at a large university

Scenarios

You've been asked to evaluate possible components for inclusion in a high-traffic B2B storefront for selling paper to printers of computer books. The vendor from whom you decide to purchase the software gives you a list of standard and optional storefront components. Knowing only the type of product and the type of customer, which of the optional features from the following list might need to be included in your storefront?

✦ EDI support

✦ Gift certificate management

✦ Integration with existing business systems

✦ Affiliate program support

✦ Order and shipment tracking

✦ Personalization

✦ E-mail marketing

✦ Clustering support

✦ Shipment management

✦ Inventory management

Lab Exercises

Lab 10-1 Exploring the features of a high-level storefront

1. Open your browser and go to `http://www.commerceone.net/buyers/`.
2. Read the description of the services CommerceOne provides for buyers.
3. Click on the Trade Directory link to go to the Buyer and Supplier search screen.
4. Enter **electronics** into the search box, and submit the form to search for buyers and suppliers of electronic equipment.
5. View the profiles and storefronts for several of the buyers and sellers.
6. Keep the following questions in mind as you read about and explore CommerceOne:
   a. Who or what is the target for this service?
   b. How is purchasing through this system different from purchasing through a B2C store?
   c. What are the advantages to using CommerceOne.net for the target audience?

Answers to Chapter Questions

Chapter pre-test

1. High-level storefronts are different from other types of storefronts in the following ways:
   - Customization
   - Cost
   - Security
   - Administration, reporting, and installation capabilities
   - Stability and performance
   - Functionality
2. The high level of customization that is possible with high-level storefronts is largely due to componentization and personalization.
3. B2B storefronts are more likely to use high-level storefront software because of the volume of transactions they handle.

4. Products that are ideal for selling through auctions are:
   - Commodity items
   - Rare items
   - Collectable items
   - Surplus items

Assessment questions

1. **B.** B2B and high-volume B2C both require the types of features that are provided by high-level storefront software (see "Understanding High-Level Online Storefront Packages").
2. **C.** All storefront software provides some type of security, although high-level packages generally provide a higher level of security (see "Understanding High-Level Online Storefront Packages").
3. **B.** User interface components are the parts of the site that the user sees; therefore, product navigation is the correct answer to this question (see Figure 10-2).
4. **D.** Clustering is grouping servers to provide better performance. It also creates failover possibilities, which are described in answer C (see "Stability and performance").
5. **A.** Because he is just getting started, and because he probably won't be doing a high volume of business, he should use an entry-level auction site (see "Auctions for E-Commerce" in this chapter and also see the information on auction sites in Chapter 8).
6. **C.** A large office supply reseller is more likely to sell a large number of products, and is also likely to have the resources necessary to invest in a high-level storefront package (see "Understanding High-Level Online Storefront Packages").

Scenarios

Given only the information that was provided in this scenario, you can establish the following facts about this proposed storefront:

- ✦ It will be used for high-traffic B2B e-commerce.
- ✦ Buyers purchase large amounts of product.
- ✦ The item being sold is a commodity.

Given a little more information about the computer book publishing industry, you might further surmise:

- Timeliness of shipments is extremely important.
- Paper suppliers are very interested in reducing transaction costs.

It's fairly safe to assume that all of components that are focused on the needs of B2C e-commerce do not need to be included in this storefront. The remaining components that should be included are:

- EDI support
- Integration with existing business systems
- Order and shipment tracking
- Clustering support
- Shipment management
- Inventory management

For More Information . . .

- **Open Market, Inc.** www.openmarket.com
- **E-Commerce Times Store Software Guide.** www.ecommercetimes.com/product_guide/store_software
- **CommerceOne.net.** www.commerceone.net
- **Internet.com's E-commerce Product Guide.** http://products.ecommerce-guide.com

CHAPTER 11

Case Studies: Creating an E-Commerce Company

✦ ✦ ✦ ✦

EXAM OBJECTIVES

- E-commerce planning
- Creating a company
- Phased approach
- Case studies

CHAPTER PRE-TEST

1. What benefit does a phased approach to e-commerce implementation offer?
2. Why might a new e-commerce company decide against a phased approach?
3. Why do sellers of services — as opposed to products — sometimes find it more difficult to take their businesses online?
4. What kinds of skills might telephone customer service representatives need to acquire before providing customer service for an e-commerce site?
5. How and why are "limited-transaction Web sites" limited?

✦ Answers to these questions can be found at the end of the chapter. ✦

E-commerce development and implementation is not the same for every company. New businesses, based solely upon an Internet presence, want to ramp up quickly. Existing companies, however, need to accommodate established business practices and systems when transitioning to e-commerce.

This chapter discusses not only new online businesses, but also the potential pitfalls and the complexities encountered by established businesses when integrating their existing systems and processes into an e-commerce presence.

Understanding the Role of E-Commerce in Business

E-commerce planning

It's extremely important for every company entering e-commerce to carefully analyze and plan their approach. For new companies, the very survival of the business depends on this approach. For existing companies, the company's reputation is at stake. If an e-commerce effort is to succeed, the e-commerce process must be carefully planned from start to finish.

These days, it's imperative for virtually every company to maintain a Web site. Here's why:

- ✦ Current and potential customers expect to be able to use the Web to find your company's contact information, at the very least. Most Web users also expect to find information on your products and services, real-world locations, and a form to request a paper catalog, if your company publishes one.
- ✦ If it's possible to sell your products online, but your company does not, many potential customers become frustrated when they find out they're unable to purchase your products over the Web. It's wise to evaluate the potential of your business to go online — and if it can go online, take it there.

Evaluating the potential of your product or service to be sold online is key to a successful e-commerce implementation. As a starting point for such an analysis, the following points (each of which is detailed in the following sections) should be considered:

- ✦ Accessibility
- ✦ Method
- ✦ Adaptability
- ✦ Business model

Exam Tip Be sure you're familiar with each of these topics.

Accessibility

Consider whether it's possible to take your business online. This is a relatively simple question for sellers of tangible products, for whom the answer is most often "yes." A company that sells services rather than products, however, may find this question much more complicated to answer. How, for instance, does one provide psychoanalysis or music instruction over the Web?

Most accessibility barriers are temporary. In the near future, high bandwidth may make video conferencing a commonality, in which case, psychoanalysis and music instruction (but probably not daycare services) over the Web may indeed be possible. If your company's answer to the accessibility question is "no" today, it should be revisited every six months or so.

If your company's staff is unable to determine whether your product or service is suitable for e-commerce, it's in your best interest to conduct extensive research, and perhaps hire a consultant to evaluate your company's e-commerce potential.

Caution If you do hire an Internet business consultant, be sure to check his or her references and track record. As with all new industries, there are many untrustworthy and unqualified "Internet consultants" out there who are trying to make money off of other people's ignorance.

Method

After you've established that your business can be taken online, you need to consider how your business can be conducted via e-commerce. At this stage, it's not necessary to consider actual applications and technologies to be employed. Instead, you need to consider broad themes of functionality. For example, you should decide whether all or just some of your products will be available online, whether you will offer online credit card payment processing, and how your company's existing Web site (if you have one) will relate to the online store.

Adaptability

Consider how your e-commerce business can interact with your traditional business and staff. Current employees who are a part of your traditional commerce model can be integrated into the e-commerce model, or kept separate (at least for the time being).

For example, you must decide whether existing telephone customer service representatives can be trained to handle calls relating to e-commerce transactions. Will all telephone customer service representatives handle e-commerce calls, or just a select group? Who will handle customer service related e-mail?

Business model

Consider whether you can use your online store to sell to other businesses (a B2B business model) or to consumers (B2C), or both. Of course, your company's current customer base and business model has a major impact on this decision. If you're selling to both businesses and consumers, do you need two separate stores to service each kind of customer?

See Chapter 7 for more information on the B2B and B2C business models.

Creating a Company Presence Online

Creating a company

For new e-commerce based companies, creating a company presence online is essentially the same thing as opening a store. The company may go through months of planning, but business does not begin until the Web site goes live and you start taking orders.

Establishing a company presence online is a somewhat different task for existing companies. It's important that the Web site is in harmony with the company's existing promotional materials, both visually and in terms of quality of content and presentation. For example, a company known for publishing catalogs on high-quality paper with professional photographs and thoughtful graphic design should make sure that its Web site is also high quality. This requires skilled, artistic Web designers and practical, efficient Web programmers.

Choosing and registering a domain name

One of the first steps in establishing an online presence is choosing and registering a domain name. New companies should not make a final decision on the name of their company until their domain name has been registered. Naming a new e-commerce company can be a creative process because unusual names are less likely to already be registered.

For existing companies, this step is a little tougher, especially if the company does not already own its logical domain name. For instance, if a well-known company named Super Dirt Bikes doesn't already own `superdirtbikes.com`, it's likely that this domain name has already been purchased, perhaps by someone who is willing to sell it to Super Dirt Bikes, but certainly for a higher cost than a domain registration. If, on the other hand, `superdirtbikes.com` is already registered and being used as an information site on dirt bikes, Super Dirt Bikes may never be able to purchase it.

See Chapter 2 for information on how trademark law is being used to assert ownership of domain names.

To find out whether your company's choice of domain name is already taken, visit Network Solutions at www.networksolutions.com. At the top of the home page is a form to search for available domain names. If your company's number one choice is already taken, get creative. You could add the word "store" or "shop" to the name of your company, for instance. Super Dirt Bikes could hypothetically register *dirtbikeshop.com* or *superdirtbikestore.com*.

In addition, you can research available domain names at Whois.Net (www.whois.net).

Your company may also be using a domain name for an informational Web site. If you don't want to replace the informational Web site with an online store, you should create a new URL for your e-commerce site. In this case, you could add "store" or "shop" to your domain name, as discussed previously, or set up a separate Web server called *store.companyname.com*.

Network Solutions was the first company to provide domain name registration services. These days, Web hosting and development companies are also offering this service, sometimes at a reduced rate. However, some problems with these services have been reported. If you choose to register your domain name with a company other than Network Solutions, make sure it's an accredited Internet Corporation for Assigned Names and Numbers (ICANN) registrar. You can check this at www.internic.net/regist.html. Discount registrations may also have strings attached — such as requiring a Web hosting contract of several years.

Determining the scope of your project

When establishing an online company presence, you need to decide whether your Web site will be informational only, or whether you will offer e-commerce capabilities. If you do offer e-commerce, you may want to start with a limited catalog in order to test the waters. This makes it easier to implement changes based on customer feedback and your initial e-commerce experience before launching a complete e-commerce site.

Establishing a Presence in Phases

Phased approach

It's advisable for established companies to implement an e-commerce presence using a gradual, phased approach. At each step, successes and failures can be evaluated along with customer feedback. Improvements to site architecture, functionality, and customer support can then be implemented in the next phase.

You should be familiar with the four stages of the phased approach, and the order in which they're completed.

The phased approach (discussed in detail in the following sections) typically consists of these steps:

1. Creation of an information-only Web site
2. Creation and implementation of a limited-transaction Web site
3. Creation and implementation of a full-transaction Web site
4. Integration of legacy systems (if applicable)

Legacy system is an industry euphemism for existing computerized processes and databases, such as inventory systems, accounting systems, or fulfillment systems.

New businesses with few customers can likely afford to take more risks than the phased approach allows. This may involve moving through all the phases in a matter of months or even weeks, or going straight to full transactions upon the launch of their Web sites. New businesses also do not have any legacy systems to worry about.

Information-only Web sites

An information-only Web site is used to test whether an online store is appropriate for your business. Such sites are very common today and typically contain information on a company's products and services, telephone and e-mail contact information, and are also used to solicit feedback from customers.

The 7-Eleven Web site, `www.7eleven.com`, is an excellent example of an information-only site. Because it's highly unlikely that anyone would purchase convenience store products online, the site is geared toward providing information to customers and potential franchise owners. This site provides an example of how an information-only site can generate demand without actually selling anything. It features the following functionality, and can be used as a template for a successful information-only site:

✦ **Products.** Provides an overview of 7-Eleven specialty items, and offers timely information on discounted items. There is, however, no way to *purchase* items online.

✦ **Franchises.** Provides information on how to start a 7-Eleven franchise.

✦ **Careers.** Lists job openings by location and offers general employment information.

✦ **Investor relations.** Gives the latest financial information, as well as information on how to invest in the company.

✦ **About us.** Provides general information and the history of the company.

✦ **Store locator.** Provides location information for every 7-Eleven store in the United States and Canada. Users can search for the closest location to a given address.

Limited-transaction Web sites

After establishing an information-only Web site, the next logical step is to implement some sort of limited e-commerce. At this stage, the goal is not to implement a full-scale online store but rather to experiment with e-commerce in a limited fashion, to get acquainted with your potential online customers, and to identify potential problems.

Limited-transaction Web sites can either be limited in terms of the number of products available for purchase or the means by which a transaction is completed, or both. For example, a limited selection of products from your company's catalog can be offered for purchase online. Or, you could choose to accept payment only over the phone or through the mail — not online. Eliminating online payment processing helps lessen the need for site security.

Some possible ways that an informational site could implement limited transactions are:

✦ **Printable order form.** A shopping cart application could be implemented to select items from the store catalog for purchase. The site could then generate a printable order form listing the items the customer has chosen. The customer could then fax the form to a customer service representative, or send it through the mail with a check.

✦ **Automatic call back.** Using the same shopping cart application, a customer could select items to purchase. When the customer is ready to make a purchase, the site could forward his or her phone number to the company's customer service department for immediate call back. The transaction could then be completed over the phone.

✦ **Limited catalog.** To limit the quantity of orders coming through the Web site, a limited product catalog could be offered. The choice of which products to offer could be based on price or ease of shipment.

A limited-transaction Web site should only be used as a testing phase for your e-commerce implementation, for only a limited amount of time, and not as the end goal. This is because your customer base will always be limited to those who accept the inconveniences of limited transactions. After the difficulties of integrating e-commerce into your business have been identified and addressed, it's time to move on to a full-transaction Web site.

Full-transaction Web sites

A full-transaction Web site is what most people think of when they hear "e-commerce Web site." This type of Web site has a full product catalog and a full range of payment options. There are many examples of such sites today. For the purpose of this discussion, the PETsMART Web site at `www.petsmart.com`, provides an excellent example.

PETsMART is a pet supply store that was started in 1987 in Phoenix, Arizona. They now operate retail stores across the United States, and went online in 1999. Petsmart.com offers a full range of products and information. It features the following functionality, and can be used as a template for a successful full-transaction Web site:

- **Online payment processing.** Accepts Visa, MasterCard, Discover, and American Express.
- **Large catalog.** Features a wide variety of items.
- **Site security and guarantee.** Covers the liabilities of customers whose credit card numbers have been used fraudulently, backing up the claim of a secure shopping environment, and is certified as a secure site by several third-party agencies.
- **Customer support.** Provides an informative help section and an FAQ list, along with customer service e-mail addresses and telephone numbers, which demonstrate the extensive customer support required on full-scale e-commerce sites.
- **Privacy statement.** Features a well-written and easy-to-find privacy statement.

See Chapter 2 for more information on privacy statements.

- **Community.** Includes community-building features, such as message boards, to cultivate repeat business and a core pool of regular visitors.

See Chapter 3 for more information on techniques for building a Web site community.

Integrating legacy systems

For existing companies with established practices and computerized business processes, one of the most challenging aspects of developing an e-commerce presence is the integration of their legacy systems, including billing and inventory tracking systems. The older such legacy systems are, the more difficult the challenge.

It's possible, at least temporarily, to run an e-commerce business in parallel with traditional business systems, by handling e-commerce orders via a separate system. Although this can work well on a temporary basis, it hampers efficiency and should not be seen as a complete solution to the problem of integrating legacy systems.

Over the past few years, many companies have put incredible effort into integrating their legacy systems into their e-commerce functionality. A good example of a successful effort is Dell Computer's e-commerce system. Dell was founded in 1984 with the novel concept of bypassing the middleman by selling computers directly to end-users. When the company launched its e-commerce Web site in 1996, it faced the challenge of integrating existing billing, inventory, and manufacturing data systems into the Web presence.

Today, these systems are fully integrated, providing Web customers with up-to-the-minute information on the status of their orders, including the status as the product's being assembled. This integration of business systems with e-commerce systems provides a very high level of customer service.

E-Commerce Case Studies

Case studies

When preparing for a transition to e-commerce, it's helpful for traditional companies to look at the transitions others have already made. Their successes and failures illustrate the key strategies and potential pitfalls of companies transitioning to e-commerce.

Barnes & Noble

Traditional bookseller Barnes & Noble has been around for almost 100 years. The first Barnes & Noble bookstore was opened in 1917 in New York. The company currently operates over 940 stores under the names Barnes & Noble and B. Dalton. In 1997, the emerging success of the online bookseller Amazon.com caused Barnes & Noble to sit up and take notice — and launch its own e-commerce Web site. Since then, barnesandnoble.com has become one of the world's largest Web sites and the second-largest online distributor of books, after Amazon.com.

Barnes & Noble has employed several clever strategies on its e-commerce presence, including:

- **Using aspects of its retail marketing on its Web site.** It offers the same extensive selection of discounted books online as it offers in its real-world stores. In fact, the online selection is much deeper, because it's not limited by shelf space.
- **Trying out niche products.** For instance, it offers Rocket eBooks for sale, which only a few other online booksellers — and no other large online booksellers — are currently offering.
- **Fostering community.** Its college textbook store offers used books to help students save money. Free online courses are also available to all users.

Carfax

Carfax started in 1986, providing used car dealers with title information on used cars. The company initially served only Missouri; however, by the end of 1993, the Carfax database contained information from across the country and began offering the service nationally. Today, the Carfax database contains information compiled from over 100 separate sources, such as motor vehicle departments, inspection stations, auto auctions, insurance companies, and police departments. This information is now available to both dealers and consumers via Carfax's e-commerce presence at www.carfax.com.

Carfax has founded its success story on:

- ✦ Integrating a legacy database with an e-commerce front-end, which allows Carfax to provide customers with on-screen information based on a car's Vehicle Identification Number (VIN) immediately after purchase. Carfax thereby avoids the complexities of fulfillment by providing the product as a soft good (digital data presented on screen) rather than a hard good (report printed on paper and mailed to the customer).
- ✦ Providing limited information for free, which encourages customers to purchase the full report. For example, we entered the VIN of one of our old cars, and were told there were seven records available for that VIN. We were very curious about what those records were, but needed to pay 15 dollars to find out. This feature also helps protect customers from spending their money needlessly, because it tells the user whether the database has any information on a given VIN before the transaction takes place.

Understanding the Implications of E-Commerce Activity

In the transition to e-commerce, it's wise for traditional companies to keep in mind that moving to e-commerce affects every aspect of the company. In this section, you find out how various aspects of business are affected by e-commerce, and discover some tips for a smooth transition.

Effect on the seven keys to e-commerce success

The seven keys to e-commerce success provide a useful basis for evaluating the effect of e-commerce on a traditional business. Once again, those keys are:

1. Generating demand
2. Ordering
3. Fulfillment
4. Payment processing
5. Service and support
6. Security
7. Community

In the following sections, we go through each key and consider how it's changed by e-commerce.

Generating demand

The move to e-commerce does not require a complete change in a company's marketing and promotion strategies. After all, an established company most likely has a well-developed promotion campaign for its traditional business. There's no need to change that campaign, except in terms of adding the e-commerce URL to print and audiovisual advertisements.

A traditional marketing campaign should, however, be extended and built upon to promote the new e-commerce site. Specifically, you should add traditional advertisements promoting your e-commerce site, as well as online promotions at carefully chosen Web sites. Any special features that e-commerce adds to your business should be highlighted in these new promotions.

Ordering

The primary aspect of the ordering process that e-commerce affects is the involvement of your customer service representatives. In traditional commerce, orders are placed in person or over the phone, requiring your staff to enter order information into your fulfillment system themselves. Orders placed on your Web site, however, do not require human interaction. Customers place orders and enter information into your system themselves. That information can then be automatically routed into your fulfillment department.

Fulfillment

Fulfillment is where traditional companies tend to have problems in their transition to e-commerce. If your legacy system is not fully integrated into the e-commerce system, fulfillment staff may not have access to complete order information, or may be receiving orders from two separate sources. In such cases, it's very important to implement a workable system to make sure that neither order stream is neglected.

Even if your systems are fully integrated, your fulfillment staff may be overwhelmed by the quantity of orders placed on your e-commerce site. Be prepared to hire extra staff quickly if necessary. Make sure that you have enough inventory to cover demand and that your suppliers are ready to quickly provide your company with more products as needed.

Payment processing

In traditional commerce, staff members generally process credit card payments manually—that is, by sliding the credit card through a processing device, which then automatically processes the transaction. Payment processing on the Internet requires implementation of new technologies, but also removes the human element. By entering in their own credit card numbers, customers essentially take over the role of the staff member.

Companies with existing merchant accounts should be able to use these accounts for online transactions. Check with your bank to find out what options they provide for e-commerce merchant accounts.

See Chapter 17 for more information on payment processing.

Service and support

E-commerce requires your company to support customers in new and innovative ways. The 800 number and banks of customer support representatives, typical in traditional companies, need to be augmented by e-mail customer support. Chat and other interactive methods of customer service can also be implemented, but only if the company has the necessary staff to support them.

E-commerce customer support representatives should be trained to:

- ✦ Browse the Internet
- ✦ Know the site's architecture and user interface
- ✦ Answer e-mail
- ✦ Access data on e-commerce transactions

E-commerce also makes it possible for customers to support themselves more successfully, and your site should provide a well thought-out and comprehensive help area. Be sure to provide ample resources for this effort.

See Chapter 6 for more information on customer service.

Security

If it isn't already, the security of your customer's sensitive information will become your company's number one priority with the implementation of e-commerce. The security of the credit card information provided for online transactions is vital to the success of your online store.

Security in e-commerce is more complex than in the real world of security guards and safes. Your company should hire or contract proven Web security experts to make sure that any holes in your digital security system are identified and closed.

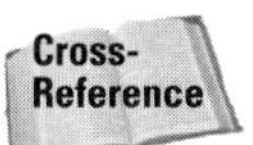

See Chapter 19 for more information on online transaction security.

Community

E-commerce offers companies new and exciting ways to foster community among their customers and within the company itself. In order to build a core group of loyal customers, it's important to provide forums for information exchange, such as product reviews, message boards, personal pages, and e-mail newsletters.

Companies operating in traditional lines of commerce often have difficulty fostering community among their customers — especially a community in which they can monitor and host themselves. Real-world bookstores host author events and book groups, for example, but the amount of customer feedback garnered from such events pales in comparison to the kind of feedback an active message board or customer review system provides.

Tips for a smoother transition

By keeping the following tips in mind, the potential pitfalls of taking your company into e-commerce can be largely avoided.

- **Keep traditional business channels open.** Keep your traditional ways of doing business intact to avoid alienating loyal customers who are not comfortable with e-commerce.
- **Know your customers.** Get to know your customer's concerns and tastes, and tailor your site to them. The most successful e-commerce companies have used this information to their advantage.
- **Be ready for change.** Prepare to evolve — quickly — along with the Web. Be ready to change technologies as standards are established. Expect to be in an almost constant state of development.
- **Be flexible.** Prepare to bend the rules on returns and refunds to ensure complete customer satisfaction.
- **Create an e-commerce business framework.** Define processes and build relationships with your customers and vendors.
- **Anticipate hurdles when possible.** Assume that expansion, new technologies, and customer expectations will continue to challenge your e-commerce team in the future.
- **In-house programmers vs. outsourcing.** Decide whether to hire programmers or outsource the project to consultants for each piece of your e-commerce development. In-house programmers are preferable in terms of control over the project; however, they are generally more expensive and sometimes very hard to find.

Key Point Summary

This chapter presented tips for e-commerce planning, creating a company or transitioning to e-commerce from traditional commerce, different approaches to e-commerce, and case studies. The key points covered in this chapter include:

- Planning your e-commerce strategy is key to the success of your online store.
- Analyzing the potential of your product or service to be successfully sold online should center on the following key points:
  - Accessibility
  - Method
  - Adaptability
  - Business model
- Registering domain names can be done with Network Solutions (`www.networksolutions.com`) or any other ICANN accredited registrar.
- Establishing an e-commerce presence using the phased approach consists of the following stages:
  1. Information-only Web site
  2. Limited-transaction Web site
  3. Full-transaction Web site
  4. Integrating legacy systems
- When launching a full-transaction Web site, security becomes an extremely important aspect of e-commerce.

✦ ✦ ✦

STUDY GUIDE

In this chapter, you learned about the implications of taking an existing business into the e-commerce world. Now, put that knowledge to the test with these assessment questions, scenarios, and lab exercises.

Assessment Questions

1. Which of the following business types is likely to find e-commerce the most challenging? The seller of:

   A. Classic films on VHS and DVD

   B. Hand-crafted rugs

   C. Marriage counseling services

   D. Glass figurines

2. What was the first company to provide domain name registration services?

   A. Network Solutions

   B. InterNIC

   C. ICANN

   D. Netscape

3. What is usually the first stage in a phased approach to bringing a traditional business online?

   A. Limited transactions

   B. Legacy system integration

   C. Full transactions

   D. Information-only Web site

4. What is the major difference between in-house and outsourced programmers?

   A. In-house programmers are less expensive and offer more control.

   B. Outsourced programmers are less expensive and offer less control.

   C. In-house programmers are less expensive and offer less control.

   D. Outsourced programmers are less expensive and offer more control.

5. What is the primary purpose of a limited-transaction Web site?

A. To assess the demand for your products and identify potential e-commerce problems

B. To integrate existing systems with your Web-based storefront

C. To offer a full product catalog and a range of payment options

D. To test whether an online store is appropriate for your business

6. Why does an e-commerce company need to be flexible and ready to evolve? (Choose the best answer.)

A. Because the kinds of customers that your site attracts will change rapidly.

B. Because Internet commerce standards and customer expectations will change rapidly.

C. Because customer service skills and programmer skills will change rapidly.

D. There is no need to be flexible — too many changes will alienate your customers.

Scenarios

The Web site for Super Dirt Bikes has been live for about a year. It contains the following information and functionality:

- Address and contact information
- Company history
- Current job openings
- Help and FAQ areas
- Technical information on the dirt bikes sold by the company
- Partial listing of products, with option to purchase
- Shopping cart application
- Checkout function with printable order forms that can be faxed to the company

What phase of development is this e-commerce site currently in? What features could be implemented to take it to the next phase?

Lab Exercises

Lab 11-1 Choosing and registering a domain name

1. In your Web browser, go to `http://www.networksolutions.com`.
2. At the Network Solutions home page, look in the yellow area near the top of the screen to find the domain name search form.
3. Enter a hypothetical domain name, either for your company or a hypothetical company. Click the "Go!" button to start the search.
4. If the domain name you entered is unavailable, the site may offer some suggestions for alternatives. At the bottom of the screen is another search box for trying another domain name. You can also try the NameFetcher tool or search for domain names for sale at GreatDomains.com via the links at the bottom of your search results. (If the domain name is available, the site may suggest other domain names you might also want to purchase.)
5. Select the domain names you want to purchase, and click "Continue."
6. Stop here, unless you actually would like to purchase the domain name. In that case, proceed through the steps to purchase the domain name online.

Lab 11-2 Evaluating e-commerce potential

1. Decide on a company for this exercise — either your own company or a hypothetical company.
2. Evaluate the accessibility of your product or service. Can your product or service become accessible via the Internet? Why or why not? If you answered no, do you anticipate your product or service becoming accessible via the Internet in the near future?
3. Evaluate the method of taking your business online. Will you offer all of your products for sale, or just a few? How will payments be processed — online or offline?
4. Evaluate the adaptability of the existing business to e-commerce. What staff members need to be added, and which need to be retrained? What business processes need to be changed?
5. Determine the business model of the e-commerce arm of the company. Is your current business B2B or B2C? Will it be the same for your e-commerce business? Why or why not?

Answers to Chapter Questions

Chapter pre-test

1. A phased approach to e-commerce implementation offers the benefit of evaluating your successes and failures at each stage, and correcting them in subsequent stages.
2. A new company whose business is dependent upon e-commerce is likely to skip the phased approach and launch a full-transaction Web site immediately, because the Web site is its only line of commerce.
3. Service providers can find e-commerce challenging because many services require human interaction.
4. Telephone customer service representatives need to have the following skills before they engage in e-commerce customer support:
    - Internet browsing
    - Knowledge of site architecture and user interface
    - E-mail
    - Ability to access data on e-commerce transactions
5. Limited-transaction Web sites are limited either by types of transactions available or by the number of products offered. They are used to assess the potential of an e-commerce store.

Assessment questions

1. **C.** It's currently not possible to offer services that require human interaction via the Internet (see "Understanding the Role of E-Commerce in Business").
2. **A.** The first company to provide domain name registration services was Network Solutions (see "Choosing and registering a domain name").
3. **D.** An information-only Web site is usually the first stage in a phased approach to bringing a traditional business online (see "Establishing a Presence in Phases").
4. **B.** Outsourced programmers are less expensive and offer less control (see "Tips for a smoother transition").
5. **A.** The primary purpose behind a limited-transaction Web site is to assess the demand for your products and identify potential e-commerce problems (see "Establishing a Presence in Phases").
6. **B.** Rapidly changing Internet commerce standards and customer expectations require companies engaged in e-commerce to be flexible and have the ability to evolve (see "Tips for a smoother transition").

Scenarios

The Super Dirt Bikes Web site is in the *limited-transaction* phase because customers have to print an order form and fax it to the company instead of completing their transaction completely online. To bring the site to the next phase—*full transactions*—the development staff of Super Dirt Bikes should implement the following items:

- ✦ Secure online payment processing
- ✦ Privacy statement
- ✦ Community-building features
- ✦ Full catalog of products
- ✦ Third-party security verification

For More Information . . .

- ✦ **ZDNet's E-commerce Case Studies.** www.zdnet.com/ecommerce/. Click on "Learn About E-commerce" for case studies.
- ✦ **CIO magazine's E-commerce Case Studies.** www.cio.com/forums/ec/ec_case.html. Articles from *CIO*, *CIO WebBusiness*, and *Darwin*
- ✦ **Microsoft's E-Commerce Case Studies by Implementation Goals.** www.microsoft.com/business/ecommerce/casestudies/. Choose from a number of business case studies.

P A R T

Building an E-Commerce Site Foundation

✦ ✦ ✦ ✦

In This Part

✦ ✦ ✦ ✦

CHAPTER 12

Going Behind the Scenes

✦ ✦ ✦ ✦

EXAM OBJECTIVES

- Web server software overview
- Choosing Web site development software

CHAPTER PRE-TEST

1. What six factors should you look at when evaluating a Web server platform?
2. What are the steps involved in an HTTP transaction?
3. What is the purpose of CGI?
4. What are several programming languages that are commonly used for CGI programs?
5. What is a relational database management system (RDBMS)?

✦ Answers to these questions can be found at the end of the chapter. ✦

In Chapters 8, 9, and 10, you explored the different types of online storefront packages and some tips for evaluating them. In this chapter, you examine the choices a merchant needs to make about server software and storefront software when setting up mid- to high-level storefronts.

First, you compare the features of several operating systems commonly used for hosting Web sites. You then look at exactly what a Web server does and explore some of the more common Web server software options. Next, you find out about databases, and then you take a brief look at choosing e-commerce software.

Exploring Server Software Options

Web server software overview

Making informed decisions about the server environment in which your e-commerce site runs is one of the most important aspects of the site development planning stage. The server environment consists of the hardware and software that run your Web site. In this book, you look mostly at server software. Although hardware is an important consideration when deciding where to host your Web site, it's easier than choosing software.

Knowing the following six factors to consider when choosing a server environment may help you on the exam.

Despite the claims of companies and enthusiasts on every side, there really is *not* one best server solution. The six variables that you should consider when choosing a server environment are:

- **Cost.** Cost is one of the more complicated factors involved in selecting a server environment. With server software, especially, low cost is not always an indication of low quality.
- **Performance.** How quickly a server can do its job is determined by a wide range of factors, including the operating system and its configuration, the computer itself, the Web server, and the actual Web site being served.
- **Stability.** Stability is usually measured in terms of how long a server can run without needing to be restarted. A server's *uptime* is the length of time it has been running since it was last rebooted. This figure may be anywhere from several days to hundreds of days. Some operating systems are known for having longer uptimes than others.
- **Software options.** The variety of software that is supported by your server platform is an important consideration.

✦ **Ease of use.** If you plan to host your site on a dedicated server, or if you're going to host your site in-house, ease of use is an important factor to consider. If you're simply hosting your site on a shared server, the relative ease of use of your server operating system is not important.

✦ **Support options.** Different types of server environments provide different technical support options. In the case of many types of freely available UNIX operating systems, technical support is easily available, although you may need to look for it. With many commercial operating systems, you're charged each time you call technical support.

The three most important types of software that reside on the computer where your Web site lives are the operating system, the Web server, and the database server. In the following sections, you take a look at each of these types of server software, while keeping the six factors previously listed in mind.

Platform options

The operating system you choose to host your Web site will likely be limited to one of these options: UNIX, Windows, or possibly Macintosh.

UNIX

In this book, we use the term *UNIX* to refer to all of the different types, or *flavors*, of UNIX, or UNIX-like operating systems. Some of the more popular operating systems that fall into this category are:

✦ **Linux.** Linux (most often pronounced LIH-nucks) is one of the most popular UNIX-like operating system on the Internet. Although the core Linux operating system is freely available, companies and individuals are also free to add to Linux and sell their own versions, or distributions. The biggest benefit that you get from purchasing a commercial distribution of Linux is technical support and greater ease of installation. Linux is given away under the GNU (`www.gnu.org`) Public License, which gives developers permission to change the source code as long as they offer the changes they make back to the developer community (except when they make changes solely for their own uses). Some of the more popular Linux distributions are:

- Red Hat Linux
- Slackware
- Corel Linux
- S.u.S.E. Linux
- Caldera OpenLinux
- Debian GNU/Linux

✦ **BSD (including BSDi, OpenBSD, FreeBSD, and NetBSD).** The Berkeley Software Distribution (BSD) flavor of UNIX was originally created at the University of California in the 1970s. The following list explains the fundamental differences between the various distributions of BSD that are currently available.

- **BSD/OS.** The commercially available distribution of BSD, which is sold by BSD, Inc. (also known as BSDi). It's sold under the Berkeley software license, which allows developers to modify the source code without offering the changes back to the developer community.
- **OpenBSD.** A freely downloadable open source code version of BSD that focuses on cryptography and security.

Tip

The term *open source code* simply means that developers have access to the instructions, or source code, of the software. It usually also implies that the software is freely available, although this is not always true.

- **NetBSD.** A multi-platform version of BSD. It's also freely available and open source.
- **FreeBSD.** A freely downloadable, open source version of BSD that is end-user oriented and easier to install than NetBSD. It's currently distributed by BSDi.

✦ **Solaris.** A version of UNIX sold by Sun Microsystems.

✦ **HP-UX.** Hewlett-Packard's version of UNIX.

✦ **AIX.** IBM's version of UNIX.

✦ **Tru64.** Compaq's version of UNIX.

✦ **IRIX.** SGI's version of UNIX.

UNIX has many advantages over other operating systems. Because UNIX operating systems have been around so long, many of the bugs have been worked out. Therefore, UNIX operating systems tend to crash less frequently than newer operating systems, and after they are set up, they are easier to maintain than newer operating systems. As other operating systems mature (or, more often, adopt UNIX technologies), however, the difference is shrinking. Another potential benefit is that some versions of UNIX are free.

Because UNIX is more stable and freely available, purchasing Web hosting on a computer running UNIX is usually less expensive than similar hosting on other operating systems.

The biggest perceived negative to Web hosting on a UNIX server is that it is more difficult to use than a graphical user interface, such as Windows or the Macintosh operating system (Mac OS). For people who are accustomed to using graphical user interfaces, this is true. However, the increasing popularity of Linux and the user friendliness of several Linux distributions are beginning to change this.

Windows

Currently, there are two server operating systems from Microsoft: Windows NT Server 4 and Windows 2000 Server. They are popular because they allow organizations to standardize on a single platform for development and deployment. For businesses, this means that files created on desktop computers running Windows also work on a Windows server.

Using the same operating system (or family of operating systems) on desktop computers as on the Web server also simplifies the problem of integrating the Web site into the company's workflow. As the vendor of the operating system, the Web server, and the development and administration tools, Microsoft is able to provide a very high level of integration between the various components involved in e-business.

It's not impossible to integrate Windows desktop computers with a UNIX server; this has been done very successfully many times, using third-party software, such as NFS and Services for UNIX. .

According to several reports, including ones done by the GartnerGroup (`www.gartnerweb.com`), the drawbacks to using Windows NT Server or Windows 2000 Server include:

- ✦ Windows servers are more expensive to set up than many UNIX operating system choices. This is mainly because of the cost of the Windows license.
- ✦ Windows servers are often less stable (must be restarted more often) than UNIX (according to statistics from `www.netcraft.com`).
- ✦ Windows servers are more expensive to maintain than UNIX servers.
- ✦ Windows uses proprietary languages, protocols, and file formats that make integration with other platforms difficult.

Thus far, ISPs have been slow to upgrade from Windows NT Server to Windows 2000 Server. As they do, however, many of the disadvantages that have been associated with hosting on Windows servers will be reduced.

Windows NT Server 4

Windows NT Server 4 is currently the most widely used Windows server operating system. The features of Windows NT Server include:

- ✦ **Internet Information Server 4.0 (IIS 4.0).** Included with the operating system

More information about Internet Information Server can be found in the section "Microsoft IIS" later in this chapter and in Chapter 13.

- ✦ **Crash Protection.** Allows applications on the server to keep running even if other applications crash

✦ **A wide variety of software.** Is available for developing and deploying Web sites

✦ **Load balancing.** Supported by the enterprise edition of Windows NT

✦ **Digital certificates and 128-bit encryption.** Are supported

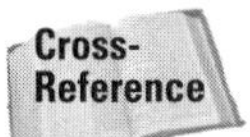

Digital certificates and encryption are covered in detail in Chapter 19.

Windows NT 4, although still very widely used, is now an old version of Windows. In the future, Windows NT will increasingly be replaced by Windows 2000 Server, which was originally known as Windows NT Server 5.0.

Windows 2000 Server

Windows 2000 Server is a big improvement over Windows NT Server 4. Besides some cosmetic changes, and general improved stability, Windows 2000 also includes a host of new features. Some of these features are:

✦ Improved Security

✦ Internet Information Services 5.0 (IIS 5.0)

✦ Improved administration facilities

In this book, we refer to Microsoft's server operating system as Windows or Windows NT/2000 in most cases, and UNIX-like operating systems as UNIX, unless the context makes differences important.

There are actually three different versions of Windows 2000 Server: Windows 2000 Server, Windows 2000 Advanced Server, and Windows 2000 Datacenter Server. Advanced Server and Datacenter Server are designed for applications requiring high performance and high availability, such as large-scale e-commerce.

See Chapter 13 for more information on Internet Information Services and the improved administration facilities in Microsoft.

Macintosh

Although not traditionally thought of as a Web server platform, Apple's Macintosh OS has gone through a major makeover in the last couple of years. As a result, Apple now has a user-friendly, BSD-based server operating system, called MacOS X Server.

Because MacOS X Server is based on UNIX, and fully supports a wide range of UNIX technologies, it can take advantage of many of the same technologies as other UNIX operating systems. In addition, it features the same benefits, such as speed and reliability, as other UNIX platforms.

MacOS X also features the Macintosh operating system's legendary user-friendliness. Any task that most users will ever need to perform can be done using the graphical user interface. For power users, MacOS X Server features access to a standard UNIX command-line interface.

Although Macintosh currently only has a small share of the server market, MacOS X has the potential to become a good alternative to other server operating systems.

Understanding the Web server's role

By this point in this chapter, you probably have a good idea of the Web server's role. In this section, you find out exactly what happens behind the scenes, and then explore the features of several popular Web servers.

In this section, when we refer to a Web server, we're referring to the software.

HTTP requests and responses

Another name for a Web server is *HTTP server*. HTTP, or Hypertext Transfer Protocol, is the protocol used to transmit data between Web servers and Web clients (browsers). To accurately understand the role of HTTP and how it's used to transmit data, it helps if you understand the process involved. The following steps take place when a user clicks on a link, submits a form, or enters an address into a Web browser:

1. The client contacts the server at a designated port number. By default, the port number is 80. For example, if you type `http://www.lanw.com` into your Web browser, it interprets this as: "Use the HTTP protocol to locate a computer over the Internet at `www.lanw.com`. Connect to this computer at port 80."

2. After contacting the server computer, the client sends a request for a document using an HTTP command, called a *method*. The method is followed by the address of a document and an HTTP version number. The following sample line tells the server to get the document at the server root (/), which is translated by the server to mean the default document—usually `index.html` or `default.htm`. HTTP/1.1 is the version of HTTP that the browser uses.

   ```
   GET / HTTP/1.1
   ```

3. The client sends optional header information informing the server of types of documents it can accept. This part of the HTTP request might look like this:

   ```
   Accept: image/gif, image/x-xbitmap, image/
       jpeg, image/pjpeg, */*
   Accept-Language: en-us
   Accept-Encoding: gzip, deflate
   User-Agent: Mozilla/4.0 (compatible; MSIE
       5.01; Windows NT)
   Host: www.lanwrights.com
   Connection: Keep-Alive
   ```

4. The client can then send additional data, such as data submitted through forms. This may be any type of data, as long as the client and server agree on the format. For example, form submissions take the following format:

```
firstname=Chris&lastname=Minnick
```

5. The server responds with a status message. This status message tells the browser the version number of HTTP that it's using, a three-digit number (the status code), and a human-readable version of the status code. A typical status message is: `HTTP/1.0 200 OK`. HTTP status codes are broken into five categories by the first number of the three-digit code, as follows (with the most common codes that may result from an HTTP request described in Table 12-1):
   - `1xx` — informational
   - `2xx` — successful
   - `3xx` — redirection
   - `4xx` — client error
   - `5xx` — server error

Table 12-1
Common HTTP Status Codes

Status code	*Human-readable form*	*Description*
200	OK	The request was successful and the server's response contains the requested document.
400	Bad Request	The server detected a syntax error in the client's request.
401	Unauthorized	The client's request lacked proper authorization.
404	Not Found	The document specified in the client's request does not exist.
425	Unable to connect with remote host	The client cannot connect with the requested server.
500	Internal Server Error	This code indicates that part of the server (such as a CGI program) has crashed or has encountered a configuration error.

6. The server sends header information to the client. The header indicates the date, the type of server, the type of content that it's about to send to the client, and the file size, among other information; for example:

```
HTTP/1.1 200 OK
Server: Microsoft-IIS/4.0
```

```
Content-Location: http://www.lanwrights.com/Default.htm
Date: Fri, 08 Dec 2000 18:07:27 GMT
Content-Type: text/html
Accept-Ranges: bytes
Last-Modified: Sat, 11 Nov 2000 14:24:11 GMT
ETag: "744778feb4bc01:4dd2"
Content-Length: 5143
```

7. If the request that the client sent is valid, the server sends the requested data. If the request cannot be filled, a human-readable error message is sent back to the client. Figure 12-1 shows a complete HTTP request and response.

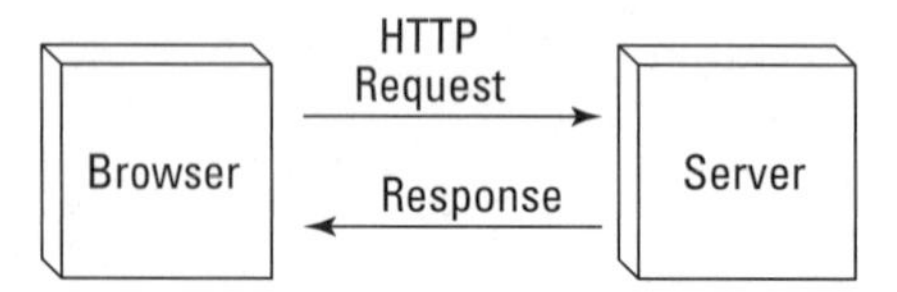

Figure 12-1: An HTTP request and response

CGI

A Web server basically has a very simple job: to listen for HTTP requests and to return appropriate responses. In the very early days of the Web, this was plenty. As people began to desire more interactivity, Common Gateway Interface (CGI) was created to allow developers to extend the capabilities of a Web server.

Exam Tip It's important to know the purposes and roles of HTTP and CGI. Specifically, you should know that HTTP is used for communications between a Web client and a Web server, and CGI is used to extend the capabilities of a Web server.

CGI allows a Web server to communicate with other programs. Using programs through CGI, Web pages can be dynamically generated. This makes interactive applications, such as quizzes, forms, and shopping carts possible on the Web. The process of requesting and running a CGI script works as follows:

1. To call a program via CGI, a client sends a standard request to the server for a program.
2. The server recognizes a request for a program by its content type.
3. The server sends any data sent by the client to the program. For example, the results of a form submitted by the client may be sent to the program.
4. The program then executes its instructions and returns a response to the server, which is then returned to the client. Figure 12-2 shows a typical HTTP request and response involving a program called using CGI.

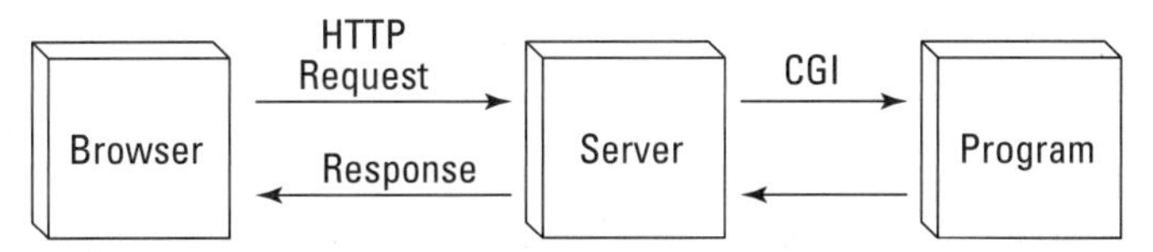

Figure 12-2: An HTTP request and response with a call to a CGI program

CGI programs can be written in any programming or scripting language supported by the server operating system. Some of the popular scripting languages commonly used are:

- Perl
- Java
- C/C++
- PHP Hypertext Preprocessor (PHP)
- Python
- awk
- Visual Basic

Web server options

According to `www.netcraft.com`, there are over 100 different types of Web servers in use on the Web. Some of these are freely available, and others cost thousands of dollars; some are optimized for very specific types of hardware, and others are more generalized. Out of all the available types, over 85 percent of the millions of Web servers in use today fall into one of the following three types:

- Microsoft IIS
- Apache Web Server
- Sun-Netscape iPlanet Web Server

We cover the features of each of these types of servers in the following sections, followed by a list of alternative servers.

Microsoft IIS

Internet Information Server (IIS) is the default Web server for use with Microsoft's Server Operating systems. Internet Information Server 4.0 is included with Windows NT 4.0 Server. Internet Information Services 5.0 is included with Windows 2000. Microsoft's Web servers are currently used by approximately 20 percent of the servers on the Web. (Note that in Windows NT, IIS stands for "Internet Information Server," and in Windows 2000, it stands for "Internet Information Services.")

IIS is tightly integrated with Windows NT and 2000. This provides two advantages:

✦ IIS uses the Windows NT or 2000 security structure. As a result, administration of security on Windows servers is simplified.

✦ Setup and administration of IIS can be done using familiar Windows-style tools.

The following sections summarize the features of IIS.

Security

IIS 4.0 and 5.0 have built-in capabilities for secure communications. Security certificates obtained from a certificate authority (CA) can be used to conduct transactions securely. In addition, the Microsoft Key Manager allows you to generate and manage your own certificates. IIS 4.0 and 5.0 also support SSL for encryption of data. The features unique to IIS 5.0 are:

✦ Management of security in IIS 5.0 is greatly simplified because of its integration with Windows 2000. The Windows 2000 Active Directory provides administrators with very specific control over security and server resources.

✦ The IIS 5.0 Permissions Wizard simplifies the process of setting permissions on a Web server. Using either the Public Web Site Wizard or the Secure Web Site Wizard helps to ensure that sites are correctly configured for maximum security.

Active Server Pages

Active Server Pages, or ASP, is a collection of Microsoft technologies that allows developers to create Web applications using client-side and server-side code. ASP code, which is usually written in VBScript or JScript, can be embedded directly in HTML pages. When a Web server encounters an ASP page, it runs the code embedded in the page. ASP is a competitor to Netscape's Server-side JavaScript, Allaire Cold Fusion, iHTML, and PHP.

VBScript is a scripting language based on Microsoft's Visual Basic programming language. JScript is a Microsoft scripting language that is similar to Netscape's JavaScript language.

Integrated services

IIS is not simply a Web server. In addition to its HTTP serving capabilities, IIS also includes:

✦ A File Transfer Protocol (FTP) server

✦ A Simple Mail Transfer Protocol (SMTP) server

✦ Built-in indexing and searching capabilities

✦ Remote administration capabilities

✦ Distributed Authoring and Versioning (WebDAV), which allows users to share documents over the Internet or intranet, while controlling access to the documents using Windows' built-in security

✦ A Network News Transfer Protocol (NNTP) server

Integration with other Microsoft products

IIS is designed to work well with other Microsoft products to make development of sophisticated Web sites as easy as possible.

Microsoft's Web server has been a big beneficiary of Microsoft's status as a monopoly. Lately, Microsoft has been making a very big push to adopt and even lead the way in the adoption and promotion of industry standard technologies such as XML. As a result, non-Microsoft software will be able to better integrate with Microsoft products in the future.

Microsoft has a complete set of development and server tools for creating e-commerce sites. These tools are, of course, optimized to work with each other as well as with IIS and Windows 2000. Some of Microsoft's other server products include:

✦ Commerce Server

✦ SQL Server

✦ Exchange Server

✦ BizTalk Server

Virtual directories and virtual servers

Virtual directories are ways to map Web server directories to different physical locations on the server's hard drive. Virtual servers allow you to run multiple Web sites on the same server.

The IIS administrative tools make it easy to create both of these, as you will see in Chapter 13.

Apache Web Server

The Apache Web server is an open source Web server maintained by The Apache Group. The software is continuously being improved by a central group of volunteers (The Apache Group) along with input from hundreds of developers worldwide.

The Apache Web server project originally started in 1995 as an attempt to combine the efforts of various developers who had written improvements to the leading UNIX HTTP server daemon at the time, which was called httpd. This base Web server was created at the National Center for Supercomputing Applications at the University of Illinois, Urbana-Champaign and was in the public domain (which means anyone was free to use it).

A *daemon* is a process, or a program, (usually on a UNIX server) that runs in the background and performs a specific task at a specific time, or in response to specific events. In the case of an HTTP server daemon, its job is to respond in the event of an HTTP request.

Today, versions of Apache are available for every major computing platform, and Apache is the most widely used Web server — making up 60 percent of all the public Web sites on the Internet.

As a result of being so widely used and open source, Apache has been highly refined over the last few years. Bugs, security holes, or places where the server can be tweaked are discovered quickly and reported back to the Apache group. As a result, Apache is on par (or better) than many commercially available Web servers in terms of performance, stability, and security.

To maximize performance and stability, Apache is a fairly bare-bones HTTP server. You won't find a lot of the extra features, such as those provided by other Web servers, included in Apache. Some of the features Apache includes are:

- ✦ The use of the latest protocols, including HTTP 1.1
- ✦ Support for password protection of pages using databases of authenticated users
- ✦ Support for virtual hosting, which is the same as the IIS virtual servers; it allows one machine to serve multiple Web sites as if each Web site were on its own server
- ✦ The capability of configuring server logging

Apache has a modular structure that makes it possible for third-party developers to add features using add-ons, or modules. A third-party module can be found for nearly any capability you might need. For example, Microsoft's ASP and WebDAV technologies can both be used on Apache through server modules. Other modules include:

- ✦ A graphical user interface
- ✦ SSL support
- ✦ Support for various scripting languages
- ✦ Database connectivity

Apache is more difficult to configure than other Web servers, including IIS. The default method to configure Apache is to manually edit a text file containing the various settings of the server. Increasingly, though, commercial versions of Linux (which usually include the Apache server) focus more on creating user-friendly interfaces and administration tools.

Sun-Netscape iPlanet Web Server

After AOL's acquisition of Netscape, Sun Microsystems acquired Netscape's server tools. The result was the Sun-Netscape alliance, and the iPlanet Web Server, which is currently used by about seven percent of the Web sites on the Internet. There are currently two versions of the iPlanet Web Server: the free FastTrack Edition and the Enterprise Edition.

✦ **iPlanet FastTrack Edition.** This version focuses on making it possible to develop and deploy high-performance Web sites using Sun's Java technology. The server runs on most major server operating systems, including Sun Solaris, Windows NT, Linux, Novell Netware, HPUX, Compaq Tru64 UNIX, and IBM AIX. Other features include:

- An easy-to-use graphical user interface for management and configuration
- Built-in 56-bit SSL support
- Lightweight Directory Access Protocol (LDAP) directory support
- Support for server-side JavaScript

✦ **iPlanet Enterprise Edition.** This version of the iPlanet Web Server has the same features as the FastTrack Edition, plus:

- Load balancing
- Integration with the iPlanet Directory Server for managing users
- Native connectivity to databases including Oracle, IBM DB2, Sybase, and Informix

Other options

Besides these three market leaders, there are many other Web servers available. Some of them are based on the Apache server; others are designed for specialized purposes. Some of the most popular are:

✦ **Stronghold.** A secure server, based on Apache

✦ **HTTPd.** A Web server that was originally developed at the National Center for Supercomputer Applications (NCSA) but that is no longer actively supported

✦ **Jigsaw.** The W3C's Java Web server

✦ **WebSTAR.** One of the leading Web servers for the Macintosh operating system

✦ **AOLserver.** The server used by AOL to host its Web sites (also available for download)

✦ **WebSite Professional.** O'Reilly Software's Web server

✦ **Zeus.** A highly scalable, high performance Web server

Database options

Earlier in this chapter, you saw how browsers and Web servers communicate using HTTP (shown in Figure 12-1). You then saw how Web servers communicate with other programs using CGI (shown in Figure 12-2). This part of the chapter looks at the third server component of an e-commerce Web site, the database.

The role of the database

The purpose of a database is to store information for retrieval. Databases are used in e-commerce for storing every type of data used by the site, including:

- ✦ Product data
- ✦ Customer data
- ✦ Order data
- ✦ Tax and shipping data

E-commerce site databases are accessed using CGI programs that are called by the Web server in response to a client request. This relationship is shown in Figure 12-3.

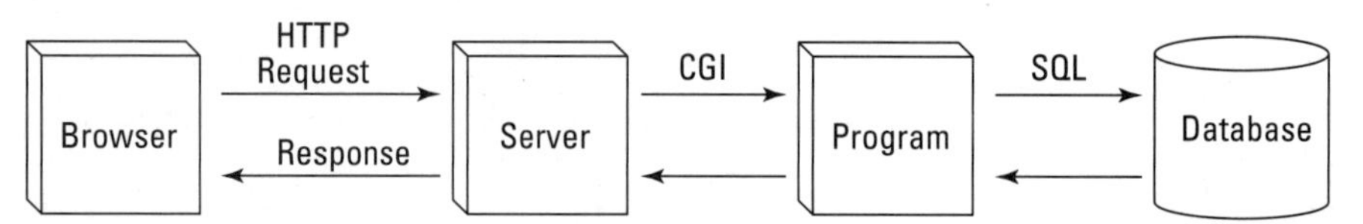

Figure 12-3: The relationship between a browser, a Web server, a CGI program, and a database

Flat file databases

Many people who are new to data storage and retrieval often start out by creating a spreadsheet. A spreadsheet is an example of a flat file database. All of the data is contained in a single table containing rows and columns, and each piece of information is stored as a record. However, this type of data storage is difficult to maintain, and wastes storage space.

To store this information in a single flat file would require a repeat of the customer information for each item in each order. Table 12-2 shows how part of this hypothetical flat file database might look.

Table 12-2
A Flat File Storefront Database

Customer #	*Customer name*	*Order number*	*Item #*	*Quantity*	*Item price*
23	Albert Jones	0002	34	1	$5.00
23	Albert Jones	0002	98	1	$4.95
78	Paul Jackson	0003	22	2	$1.99
78	Paul Jackson	0003	33	10	$4.95
78	Paul Jackson	0003	44	1	$44.50

Notice how much data must be repeated in this file for each item. In addition, a change to a piece of data in a flat file, such as a customer's address or the price of an item, requires you to update every record in which that piece of data appears.

Relational databases

A relational database management system (RDBMS) is software that manages related records using multiple tables. This is a much more efficient way to store many types of data. For example, a typical storefront application that allows customers to order multiple items and place multiple orders must have customer, order, and product data. The following is a simplification of the data involved in this application:

- ✦ Customer information
  - Customer number
  - Customer name and address
- ✦ Order information
  - Order number
  - Order date
- ✦ Ordered items
  - Item number
  - Description
  - Quantity
  - Price

In the relational model, as opposed to the flat file model, the three groups of related items are broken out into three tables: Customers, Orders, and Items. Relationships can then be defined between the three tables using unique identifying information in each table to eliminate unnecessary repetition of data.

A relational database can also be used to provide certain safety measures for your data. For example, imagine that your store stops selling a certain product and you want to remove it from the database. The product record, however, is part of several order records. If you remove the product, you create the database equivalent of broken links in the order table. The solution is for the database to either not allow the deletion of this product (perhaps you could have a check box indicating that it's no longer active) or cascade any changes to the product database through to the rest of the order table. This "link-checking" is called enforcing *referential integrity*.

Most e-commerce sites use a relational database management system for storing information. Some of the other benefits of using a full relational database management system, rather than flat files or the server's file system, include:

- Useful database administration tools
- Indexing and searching capabilities
- Security
- Increased performance
- Improved manageability and flexibility

SQL

The language most often used by programs to access databases is the Structured Query Language (SQL), which is an American National Standards Institute (ANSI) and International Organization of Standardization (ISO) standard. SQL has the following two functions:

- **Data manipulation.** This part of SQL has four statements:
  - `SELECT`—Used to retrieve information from a database
  - `UPDATE`—Used to modify existing database records
  - `DELETE`—Used to delete existing database records
  - `INSERT`—Used to create new database records
- **Data definition.** This part of SQL defines the statements that are used to work with database tables.

Most databases have their own language that can be used internally to work with data. SQL's purpose is to work as a common language between them.

Two of the most popular commercial databases are Oracle8i and Microsoft's SQL Server. You take a brief look at each of these in the following sections.

Oracle8

Oracle8, from the Oracle Corporation, is an object-relational database. Object-relational databases are designed to store information in a wide variety of formats including images, sound, video, and other forms of multimedia, in addition to the text-based data that is stored in traditional relational databases. Object-relational databases allow you to specify your own types of data "objects" to represent real-world structures.

Oracle8 overview

Oracle8's features include:

- **Multi-threaded architecture.** To improve performance, Oracle8, like many databases and servers, can perform multiple tasks simultaneously.
- **Platform independence.** Oracle 8 can be used with a wide variety of operating systems including Windows NT/2000, Linux, Solaris, OS/2, HP-UX, and others.
- **Partitioning.** Partitioning improves manageability and scalability of large databases.
- **Transaction processing support.** Transactions are ways to link events into a single unit, or an atomic execution unit. Transaction processing ensures that all of the steps in a transaction will be completed, or none of them will be completed. For example, there are several steps involved in an e-commerce purchase transaction. The product must be taken out of inventory, the buyer's credit card must be debited, and the merchant's account must be credited. Transaction processing links these events, so if, for example, the customer's credit card cannot be processed, the credit won't be applied to the merchant's account.
- **Advanced security and networking features.** Oracle security features include encryption and authentication using digital certificates for internal data storage as well as for server-to-server and client-server communications.

Oracle8i and Internet capabilities

Oracle8i is a version of the Oracle8 database management system (DBMS) specifically designed for development, deployment, and management of Internet applications. A few of Oracle8i's Internet-savvy features include:

- Multimedia support
- Management using a Web browser
- Support for the latest Java technologies
- XML support

Microsoft SQL Server

SQL Server is Microsoft's high-end relational database management system. SQL Server shares most of the same features as other major database management systems. Some of the notable features of SQL Server include:

- Ease of installation and use
- Integration with Windows and other Microsoft server and development products

- E-mail, Internet, and Web publishing features
- Graphical administration interface
- Natural language querying

SQL Server only runs on Windows server platforms.

Other DBMS options

The area of database management systems and database servers is extremely competitive, and rapidly changing. Still, there are several products besides SQL Server and Oracle8 that are consistently popular and frequently used on the Web. Some of these products are:

- **MySQL.** A popular option because it's free, although it lacks the high-end features of other database management systems.
- **DB2.** IBM's database management system.
- **UniVerse.** Informix's Web database management system.
- **Adaptive Server.** Sybase's database server for the Web.
- **FileMaker Pro.** An easy-to-use, and inexpensive, DBMS for sites that don't require the high-end features or performance of some of the databases previously listed. FileMaker Pro is from FileMaker Software (a subsidiary of Apple Computers).
- **Microsoft Access.** One of the most commonly used databases on the Web. Because Access databases are easy and inexpensive to create, they can be used with very little trouble on Windows servers. Similar to FileMaker Pro, Access databases are not designed for the same situations as Oracle, Microsoft SQL Server, Informix, Sybase, and IBM's products.

Choosing an E-Commerce Site Development Environment

Choosing Web site development software

Previous chapters in this book explored the various types of online e-commerce software available for getting a site up and running. So far in this chapter, you've examined the different operating systems, servers, and database management systems available for creating in-house e-commerce Web sites. Now that you have a broad picture of the e-commerce landscape, it's time to get specific — choosing a platform, e-commerce development software, as well as a database, so you can get to work configuring and building an e-commerce site. The remainder of this chapter gets you started in that direction, by giving you an overview of the selection process for the tutorials in the remainder of this book.

One of the goals of the e-commerce designer exam (as opposed to the CIW curriculum, where choices necessary for effective demonstration and teaching purposes need to be made) is to take a vendor-neutral approach to the concept of e-commerce. The exam does this very well, and doesn't contain questions about vendors or specific products.

The official CIW curriculum uses Microsoft's e-commerce solutions, specifically Microsoft Site Server Commerce Edition, to demonstrate the process of building an e-commerce site in-house. Because of the hardware and software requirements for using Microsoft Site Server Commerce Edition, or the more recent version, Commerce Server 2000, we chose an e-commerce package that can be used with a greater variety of hardware and software configurations.

The products that we considered for building the store for this book included the mid-level storefronts that we talked about in Chapter 9, as well as the following storefront software packages:

- **FishCartSQL.** (`www.fishcart.org`) An open source shopping cart and catalog management system. It's written in the PHP scripting language and uses mySQL for data storage. Although it's designed to run on UNIX servers, it's possible to install FishCartSQL on a Windows platform as well.
- **Zelerate AllCommerce.** (`www.zelerate.org`) An open-source shopping cart and catalog management system. It's written in Perl and is fairly easy to install on either a UNIX server or a Windows server. It can use a variety of different databases for data storage.
- **Actinic Business.** (`www.actinic.com`) A complete B2C or B2B e-commerce software package. It allows you to build a storefront using a user-friendly Windows application, and then upload it to either a Windows or UNIX server.

The specific e-commerce software you use in developing an e-commerce site should be determined by your specific needs. Our choice of e-commerce software for demonstration purposes in this book should not be seen as an endorsement or a recommendation.

After considering each of the available options, we decided on Actinic Business for this store. Our reasons for choosing this package were:

- The installation process is simple.
- A demonstration version is available.
- The demonstration version doesn't require developers to have their own servers.
- Sites created using Actinic Business can run on Windows or UNIX.
- The development interface is easy to use and understand.
- No additional software is required.

- Actinic Business supports all of the essential components of electronic commerce, including product catalog browsing and searching, security, payment processing, inventory monitoring, customer account management, and more.
- Actinic Business supports the pricing structures that are required in B2B e-commerce, such as tiered pricing and quantity-based pricing.
- Data from third-party databases can be imported into the Actinic Business database.

Before you move on to the specifics of building an e-commerce site in the following chapters, test your knowledge, and take a closer look at the specific features of Web servers, by working through the lab exercises in this chapter. They show you how to download, install, and configure the Apache Web server as well as how to create your own intranet.

Chapter 13 deals with setting up and configuring the Microsoft Internet Information Server. Chapter 14 takes you to the next step in the site building business with Actinic Business, and Chapter 15 deals with customizing your e-commerce site.

Key Point Summary

This chapter presented differences between several operating systems commonly used for hosting Web sites. You also learned exactly what a Web server does and explored Web server, software, and database options. The main points of this chapter are:

- The majority of Web servers run on either UNIX or Windows operating systems.
- HTTP is the protocol used to transmit data between Web servers and Web clients.
- Web servers are also known as HTTP servers.
- CGI allows a Web server to communicate with other programs.
- The three most commonly used Web servers are Apache, Microsoft IIS, and iPlanet.
- The purpose of a database is to store information for retrieval.
- The advantage of using relational databases over flat file databases is that flat file databases waste storage space and are difficult to maintain.
- Structured Query Language (SQL) is a standard language for working with databases.

✦ ✦ ✦

STUDY GUIDE

In this chapter, you saw the pros and cons of several server platform options. You also learned about the relationship between a Web server, CGI programs, and databases. This chapter also marks the point at which we shift gears temporarily and begin the process of developing an e-commerce site. Before we move forward, take a moment to test your knowledge.

Assessment Questions

1. How is a server environment's stability usually measured?

A. Kilobytes per second

B. Using uptime or period of time between restarts

C. Cycles per second

D. Megabytes per second

2. Which of the following best describes HTTP?

A. A protocol for creating links on Web pages

B. A protocol for communicating with other e-commerce Web sites

C. A protocol used to transmit data between Web servers and Web clients

D. A protocol for ensuring privacy on the Internet

3. Which of the following is the best definition of *open source* software?

A. Software that doesn't come from any one company

B. Software that is free to use, but has some features disabled

C. Software that is free to use for a limited period of time

D. Software that is distributed with an agreement that allows the user to modify the program's source code

4. What is the purpose of CGI?

A. CGI, or Computer Graphic Interface, allows a monitor to understand commands from a Web browser.

B. CGI, or Cryptographic Initiative, is a program for securing e-commerce transactions.

C. CGI, or Common Gateway Interface, is a way for Web servers to communicate with other programs.

D. CGI, or Common Gigabyte Instruction, is a high-speed networking protocol.

5. What is a virtual server?

A. A way to host multiple Web sites on one Web server

B. A way to host a Web site without having a Web server

C. An outsourced Web server

D. A poorly functioning Web server that may as well not even exist

6. Which of the following is least like Microsoft's ASP technology?

A. Cold Fusion

B. PHP

C. SQL

D. iHTML

Scenario

Your company sells products to customers who use every kind of computer imaginable. As the person in charge of developing an online storefront for the company, you want to make sure your site is usable by anyone likely to visit. What specific choices regarding server hardware, HTTP server software, and database management systems can you make to provide maximum compatibility?

Lab Exercises

Lab 12-1 Downloading and installing the Apache Web Server for Windows

Apache HTTP Server for Windows is also included on the CD-ROM that comes with this book.

1. Open your Web browser and go to `www.apache.org`. Click on the Apache Server link on the left side.

2. You should see the Welcome to the Apache HTTP Server Project screen. Click on the Download! link.

3. Scroll down the download page until you find the folder called binaries. Click on that link to enter the folder.

4. On the next screen, find the link titled Win32, and click on that (as shown in Figure 12-4). You can also find versions of the Apache server for other operating systems here.

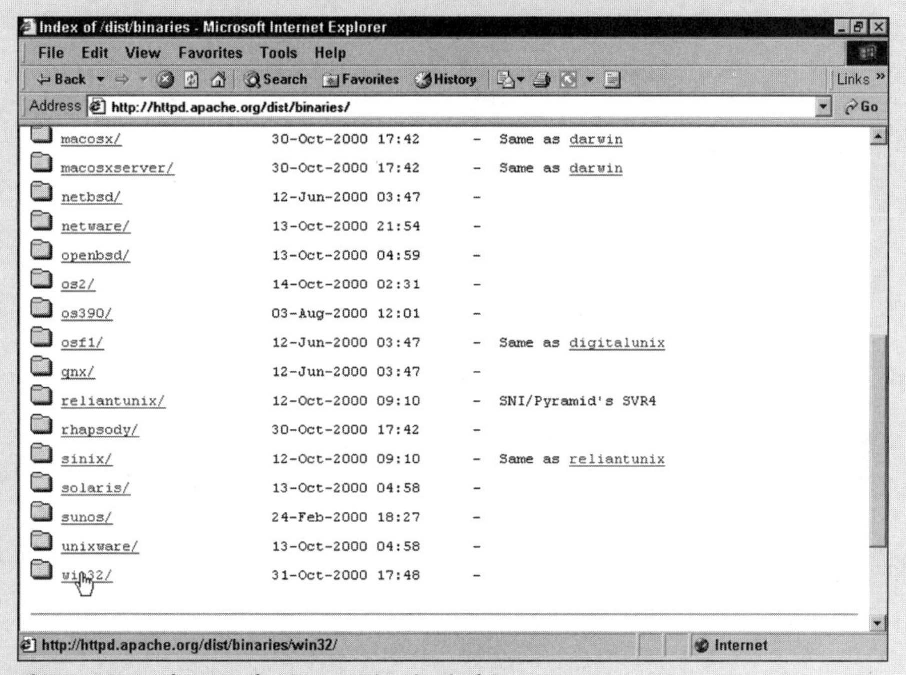

Figure 12-4: The Apache Server Binaries index

5. Find the link to the file that is the current release of Apache for Windows, and click on that. Select save to disk when prompted, and save the installer to your computer.

6. Open the folder on your computer where you saved the Apache installer, and double-click the file to start the installation of the server.

7. Click through the screens in the Apache installer. If you aren't sure how to answer a question, choose the default option (just click Next). When installation is complete, click Finish.

8. After viewing the README file, find the Apache Web Server program group in your start menu and navigate to Management, Start Apache. A command-line window should appear. It indicates the name of the server and its address, as shown in Figure 12-5. Write down the address (usually 127.0.0.1, but your site is also be accessible at `http://localhost`).

Apache may also run as a service under Windows NT or Windows 2000. A service is the Windows equivalent of a UNIX daemon.

Figure 12-5: Starting the Apache server

9. Open a Web browser and go to the address you wrote down in the last step. If installation was successful, you see the page shown in Figure 12-6. Spend some time reading the Apache documentation linked to this page.

If you don't see this page, it may be because you have another Web server running on your computer (such as IIS or Personal Web Server). Stop this server and try again.

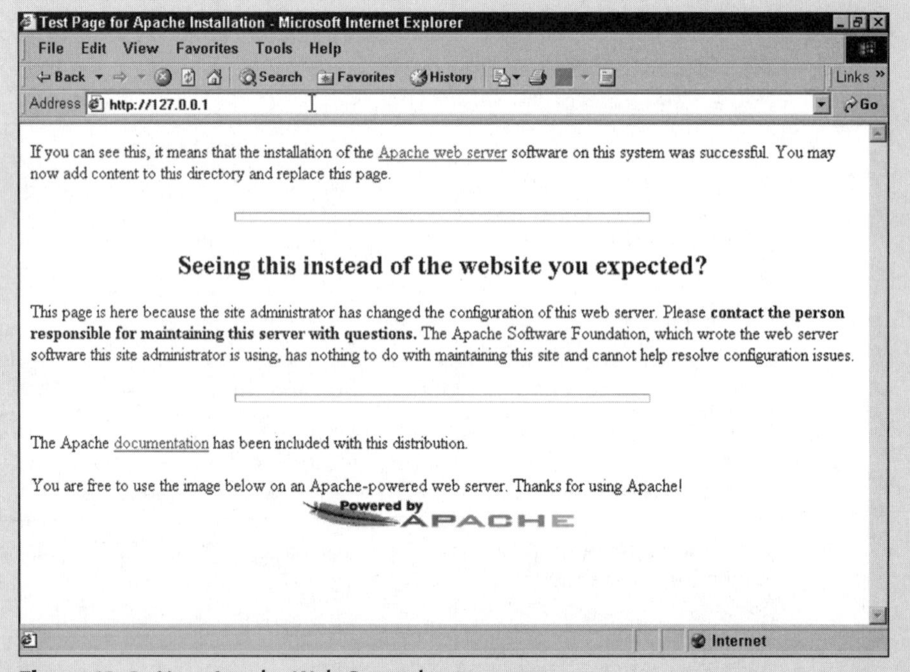

Figure 12-6: Your Apache Web Server home page

Lab 12-2 Viewing and changing the Apache configuration file

1. Stop the Apache server using the Stop Apache link in the Windows Start Menu or by pressing Ctrl+C.
2. Open `httpd.conf` in a text editor (such as Notepad). If you installed Apache in the default location, `httpd.conf` can be found at `c:\Program Files\Apache Group\Apache\conf\httpd.conf`. You can also use the Edit Configuration link in the Start Menu to open `httpd.conf` in a text editor.
3. Begin reading through `httpd.conf`. Note that most of the lines begin with a hash mark (#). This mark tells the Apache server to ignore everything on that line. The information provided on a line starting with # is for your benefit. Every line that doesn't begin with # configures a setting in the server.
4. Find Section 2 in the configuration file. You should see text similar to what is shown in Figure 12-7.

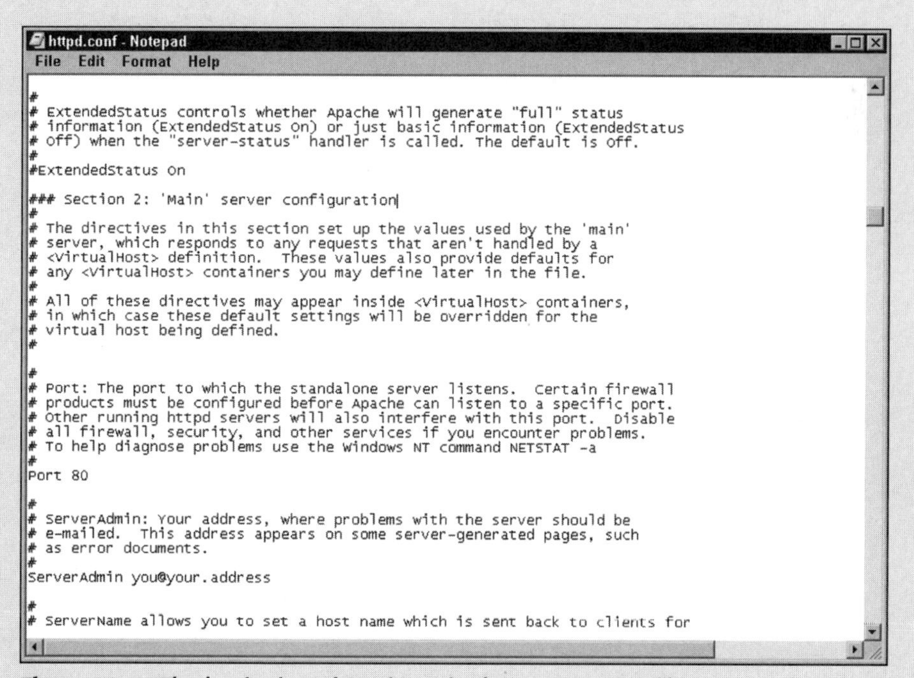


```
#
# ExtendedStatus controls whether Apache will generate "full" status
# information (ExtendedStatus On) or just basic information (ExtendedStatus
# Off) when the "server-status" handler is called. The default is Off.
#
#ExtendedStatus On

### Section 2: 'Main' server configuration
#
# The directives in this section set up the values used by the 'main'
# server, which responds to any requests that aren't handled by a
# <VirtualHost> definition.  These values also provide defaults for
# any <VirtualHost> containers you may define later in the file.
#
# All of these directives may appear inside <VirtualHost> containers,
# in which case these default settings will be overridden for the
# virtual host being defined.
#


#
# Port: The port to which the standalone server listens.  Certain firewall
# products must be configured before Apache can listen to a specific port.
# Other running httpd servers will also interfere with this port.  Disable
# all firewall, security, and other services if you encounter problems.
# To help diagnose problems use the Windows NT command NETSTAT -a
#
Port 80

#
# ServerAdmin: Your address, where problems with the server should be
# e-mailed.  This address appears on some server-generated pages, such
# as error documents.
#
ServerAdmin you@your.address

#
# ServerName allows you to set a host name which is sent back to clients for
```

Figure 12-7: The beginning of Section 2 in the `httpd.conf` file

5. Find the line that begins with ServerAdmin and enter your e-mail address in place of the default value.
6. Find the line that begins with DocumentRoot. Write down this address. This is the directory on your computer from which your Web server gets files to serve to Web clients.

7. Find the line that begins with ServerSignature and change the value from On to Email.
8. Save `httpd.conf` and start Apache Server.
9. Open your Web browser and type in the server address (`http://127.0.0.1`, for example) followed by a slash and the name of a Web page that generates an error message (for example, `nothing.html`).

Tip: If you're using Internet Explorer, you need to turn off the friendly HTTP error messages. Go to Tools, Internet Options and select Advanced. Uncheck the box next to Show Friendly HTTP Error Messages. Click OK or Apply to save your changes.

10. You should see an error message similar to the one shown in Figure 12-8. The server address should be a `mailto:` link to the e-mail address you entered in Step 5.

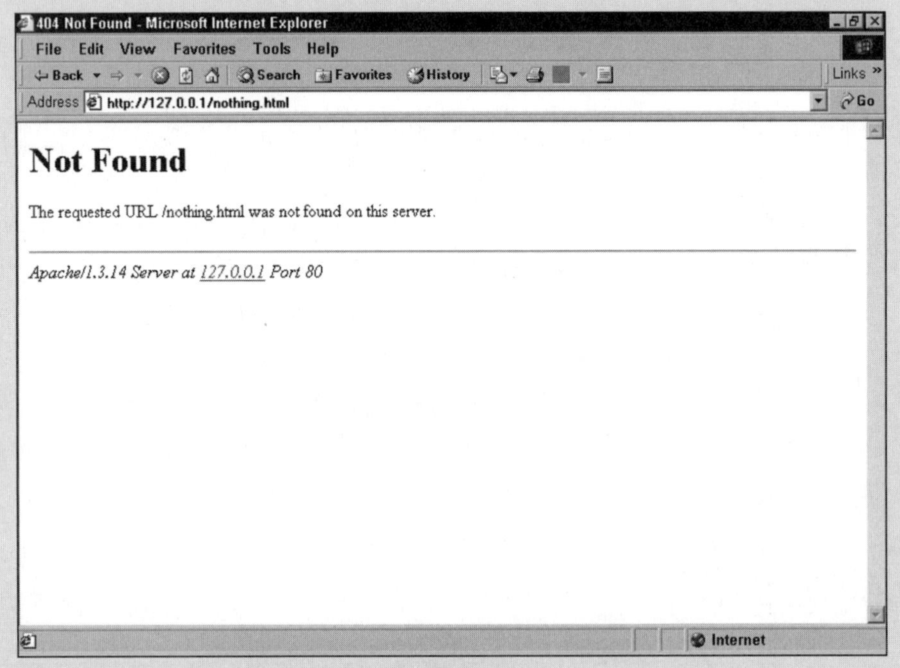

Figure 12-8: The Apache 404 error message

11. Stop the server. Open `httpd.conf` and find the section starting with the following:

```
# Customizable error response (Apache style)
```

12. Use this section to create a custom file not found (404) message using either a text message or an HTML file. Figure 12-9 shows an arrow pointing to an example of a custom text error message.

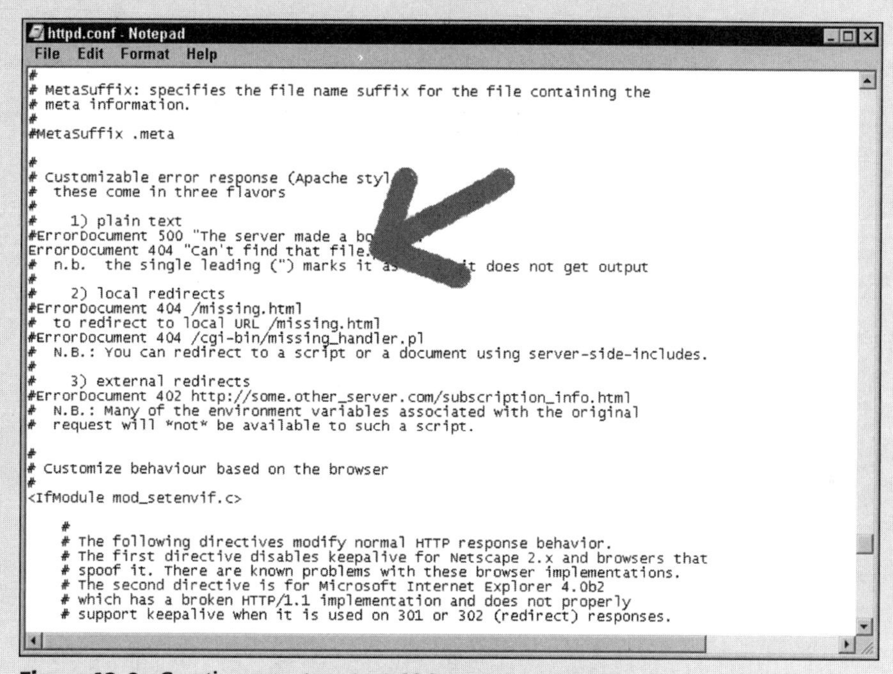

Figure 12-9: Creating a custom text 404 error message

13. To test your custom message, start the Apache server, and attempt to access a page that doesn't exist on your server (like you did in Step 9).

Lab 12-3 Creating your own intranet

1. Create a new HTML file to be your intranet home page. We've included a sample, called `intranet_home.html`, on the CD-ROM that comes with this book.

2. Save the new HTML to your Web server document directory. This is `C:\Program Files\Apache Group\Apache\htdocs` by default. Rename the file to `index.html`.

3. Start Apache server (if it isn't already running). Go to the server in your Web browser to view your new default home page on your Apache server.

Answers to Chapter Questions

Chapter pre-test

1. The six factors that you should use to evaluate a Web server platform are: cost, performance, stability, software options, ease of use, and support options.
2. The steps involved in an HTTP transaction are:
   a. The client contacts the server.
   b. The client sends a request for a document.
   c. The client sends optional header information.
   d. The client sends any additional information, such as data submitted through a form.
   e. The server sends a status message.
   f. The server sends header information to the client.
   g. The server returns the requested document or an error message to the client.
3. CGI allows a Web server to communicate with other programs.
4. Some of the programming languages that are commonly used to create CGI programs are: Perl, Java, Visual Basic, C, C++, Python, awk, and PHP.
5. A relational database management system (RDBMS) is software that stores data using related tables.

Assessment questions

1. **B.** Uptime is usually used to measure a server's stability (see "Exploring Server Software Options").
2. **C.** HTTP is the protocol used for communication between Web servers and Web clients, or browsers, (see "Understanding the Web server's role").
3. **D.** Open source software is distributed in source code form and can be modified by the user, sometimes with certain conditions attached (see "Platform options").
4. **C.** CGI, or Common Gateway Interface, allows Web servers to communicate with other programs (see "Understanding the Web server's role").
5. **A.** A virtual server is a way to host multiple Web sites on a single Web server (see "Web server options").
6. **C.** SQL, or Structured Query Language, is a database querying language. The other choices are languages for embedding program instructions in HTML pages (see "Database options").

Scenario

This is a trick question. The hardware you use, which HTTP server you choose, and which database system you decide on don't matter in terms of compatibility. The end result of the work of hardware, the database, and the Web server is to send data to a client. If the data being sent is in a standard format (such as HTML), it's readable by anyone with the proper software on his or her computer (such as a Web browser). In other words, what matters is what you send to the client, not what you use to send it (as long as you use HTTP).

For More Information . . .

For more information on the topics covered in this chapter, visit the following sites:

- **Netcraft Web site finder and survey.** `www.netcraft.com`
- **Microsoft IIS.** `www.microsoft.com/iis`
- **Linux Online.** `www.linux.com`
- **The Apache Group.** `www.apache.org`
- **The Open Source Page.** `www.opensource.org`
- **Internet.com's Web Server Compare site.** `http://webcompare.internet.com`

CHAPTER 13

Working with Internet Information Server

EXAM OBJECTIVES

- Internet Information Services (IIS)
- Preparing and examining IIS

CHAPTER PRE-TEST

1. What security features does IIS 5.0 provide?
2. What is the purpose of ISAPI?
3. What is a virtual directory?
4. Why is a new user account created on a Windows server when IIS is installed?
5. What is the purpose of Index Server?

✦ Answers to these questions can be found at the end of the chapter. ✦

Internet Information Services (IIS) is Microsoft's Windows 2000 Web server software. Although there are currently several different and widely used versions of IIS, this chapter mainly focuses on the features, installation, and management of IIS 5.0 on Windows 2000 Professional. The version of IIS that you use and the features to which you have access depend on the version of Windows you're using. If you're using a different operating system, some of the features discussed in this chapter might not be available to you. The major differences between operating systems and server versions, however, are carefully pointed out.

Understanding Microsoft's IIS

Internet Information Services (IIS)

Table 13-1 shows the different versions of IIS, on which version of Windows they run, and what software you must download to install the Web server.

Remember that in Windows NT, IIS is expanded as Internet Information *Server*, and in Windows 2000, it's expanded as Internet Information *Services*.

Table 13-1
Microsoft's Web Servers

Web server	*Operating system*	*How to install*
Personal Web Server (PWS)	Windows 95, Windows 98, Windows NT Workstation 4.0	Install Windows NT 4.0 Option Pack
Internet Information Server 4.0	Windows NT Server 4.0	Install Windows NT 4.0 Option Pack
Internet Information Services 5.0	Windows 2000	Use Add/Remove Windows Components in the Add/Remove Software Control Panel

In understanding the Web server software information in Table 13-1, it's important to note the following:

- ✦ **PWS.** Personal Web Server (PWS) is compatible with IIS in many ways. However, it's designed to be used for serving one small Web site, a small intranet, or for testing purposes, and doesn't contain many of the advanced features of IIS.

It may also be possible to install PWS on Windows Me. See www.overclocktips.com/asp/downloadasp.asp for more information.

✦ **IIS 5.0.** The version of IIS (5.0) that's included with Windows 2000 Professional is similarly disabled, but it has more features than PWS.

Now that you've gained a very basic understanding of Microsoft's Web servers, and two versions of IIS in particular, it's time to move on to an exploration of specific features, and the tasks of installation and management — subjects to which the remainder of this chapter is devoted.

IIS Features and Functions

Preparing and examining IIS

You touched briefly upon the features of IIS 5.0 in Chapter 12. In this chapter, you focus on how to accomplish various tasks by looking at step-by-step examples. The following sections begin by examining some of the features of IIS.

Remember that the exam does not contain product-specific questions. Knowledge of how a specific Web server functions will help you answer general questions about Web server software on the exam.

Security

Two of the most important keys to securing a Web server are authentication and encryption. IIS was designed to provide both of these. IIS 5.0 expands upon and strengthens the security foundation of IIS 4.0 using the Kerberos v5 authentication protocol, which is an integral part of Windows 2000.

Kerberos authentication allows a Windows 2000 Server to pass user authentication information to connected computers, so users only need to log on once to a Windows 2000 Server domain.

IIS (through Windows 2000 Server) also supports the following security technologies:

✦ **Digest Authentication.** Is the W3C's authentication standard.

✦ **Server-Gated Cryptography (SGC).** Transmits documents across the Internet; used by financial institutions.

✦ **Fortezza.** Is the U.S. Government security standard.

✦ **Digital Certificates.** Provides server authentication information to clients as well as authenticates clients. Administrators can create Certificate Trust Lists (CTLs) to specify lists of trusted certifying authorities for different directories.

✦ **IP and Domain Restrictions.** Allows an administrator to allow or disallow access to certain domains or certain computers.

✦ **Secure Sockets Layer 3.0 (SSL).** Enables secure communications between the Web server and the browser. IIS allows you to use up to 128-bit encryption.

Active Server Pages (ASP)

As you found out in Chapter 12, Active Server Pages (ASP) is a collection of Microsoft technologies that can be used together to allow Web developers to create dynamic Web sites. All of the Microsoft Web servers listed in the previous section support ASP.

ISAPI

Internet Server Application Programming Interface (ISAPI) is Microsoft's high-performance replacement for Common Gateway Interface (CGI).

As you may remember from Chapter 12, CGI is a way to extend a server's capabilities by using other programs. The disadvantage of using CGI is that each time a CGI program needs to be used, it must be started up. This can slow down the performance of Web sites that rely on these programs.

ISAPI, on the other hand, extends the server's capabilities using Dynamic-Link Libraries (DLLs) rather than executable programs. Dynamic linking provides a way for programs in Microsoft's operating systems to call external functions. After the Web server has loaded a DLL, it remains in memory and is available for the next time it's needed. Executable files called using CGI, on the other hand, are shut down after each use and must be restarted the next time they're needed.

Web file formats supported

Using ISAPI and CGI, IIS can serve and work with almost any type of file in use on the Internet — including many scripting languages, multimedia formats, images, streaming video and audio, and more.

In the Lab Exercise later in this chapter, we show you how to install a DLL that interprets and runs programs written in the Perl language.

Content management

Web sites that have a large amount of content, as well as multiple publishers of content, require systems and procedures for controlling how content is published to the Web. IIS can be integrated with Microsoft Site Server to provide content management functionality. The features of Microsoft's content management tools include:

- Multiple people can publish content to the Web site.
- A content approval process can be implemented.
- Content is organized in the server using content stores, which can group content according to function (for example, sales, marketing, and so forth).
- Approved content can be posted to a staging server where it can be tested before it's copied to the live, public Web site.

Site analysis

IIS can create log files in several formats. You can use these log files with a site analysis tool, such as Site Server's Express Analysis tool or a third-party tool such as WebTrends.

The Web file formats supported by IIS are Microsoft's Log File format, the National Center for Supercomputer Applications (NCSA) Common Log File format, and the W3C Extended Log File format. The format you choose is determined by the log file analysis software you use and the amount of information you require.

IIS allows you to use a properties sheet to specify exactly what information you need logged. When used correctly, this capability can save hard drive space and reduce the workload on your server.

Analysis of log files is covered in detail in Chapter 21.

ASP script debugging

If you've ever worked with ASP, you know that the error messages produced by ASP scripts are notoriously unhelpful. Fortunately, the Microsoft Script Debugger can help you interactively test your Web applications and quickly locate problems in the scripts.

The Microsoft Script Debugger can be installed during the IIS installation process by choosing the Custom installation option and then selecting the Microsoft Script Debugger option.

Some of the important capabilities Microsoft Script Debugger provides developers are:

- It runs server-side scripts one line at a time.
- It allows you to view the values of your variables, properties, or array elements while your ASP script runs.

✦ It allows you to set pauses with either the debugger or by inserting a statement into your scripts to suspend execution of your server-side scripts at a particular line.

✦ It allows you to trace procedures and functions while running the ASP script.

Index Server

Index Server is an add-on to Microsoft's Web servers. The purpose of Index Server is to index Web content and provide full-text searching capabilities. Unlike many Web content-indexing systems, Index Server can index formatted documents as well as HTML and plain-text files. Index Server has built-in support for indexing and searching Microsoft Word, Microsoft Excel, Microsoft PowerPoint, and, as mentioned, HTML and plain-text files. Additional file types can be added using content filters. A *content filter* simply tells Index Server how to extract the textual information from proprietary document formats. Index Server can be queried using Web forms, and results are returned in HTML format.

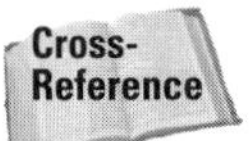

You learn how to install, start, and use Index Server later in this chapter. See the sections titled "IIS Installation" and "Starting and testing Index Server."

IIS Installation

In Chapter 14, you begin developing an e-commerce site using Actinic Business. To prepare your computer to serve as a test server for the e-commerce site, you need to have a Web server installed. This section steps you through the process of installing IIS on Windows 2000 Professional. If you're using Windows NT, Windows 95, or Windows 98, you need to download and install the Windows NT 4.0 Option Pack.

See the "For More Information . . ." section at the end of this chapter to find the URL where the Windows NT 4.0 Option Pack can be downloaded. The Windows NT 4.0 Option Pack (including the Microsoft Personal Web Server, also known as Peer Web Services, for Windows 9x or Windows NT) can also be found on the CD-ROM at the back of this book.

To install IIS 5.0 on Windows 2000 Professional, follow these steps:

You must be an administrator on the computer you're using to install IIS and to perform many of the exercises in the rest of this book. If you're using your home computer, you probably have administrative access. If you're using a computer at an office, you may not be an administrator. In that case, you should ask someone who is an administrator to assist you.

1. Close any open windows and applications.
2. Open the Control Panel by clicking Start, Settings, Control Panel.

3. Double-click on Add/Remove Programs.
4. In the Add/Remove Programs window, click Add/Remove Windows Components. The Windows Components Wizard appears, as shown in Figure 13-1.

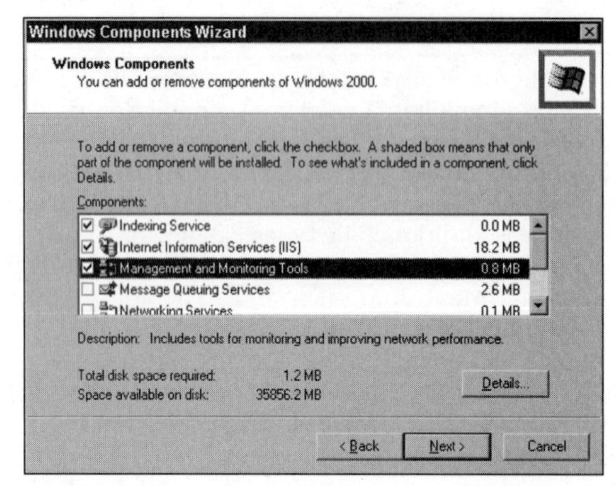

Figure 13-1: The Windows Components Wizard

5. In the Windows Components Wizard, check at least the following boxes:
   - Indexing Service
   - Internet Information Services (IIS)
6. If you would like more information about any of the optional components listed, click the Details button. This shows you the sub-components of each option.
7. Click Next.
8. You may be asked to insert your Windows 2000 CD. Insert the CD if you're asked to do so. When installation is finished, click Finish to close the Components Wizard.

Anonymous logins account

When IIS or PWS is installed, a new user account is created on your computer. To view this account, open the Control Panel, and then double-click on Users and Passwords. If the installation of the Web server was successful, you see a new user whose name is IUSR_ followed by the name of your computer. This is the user name for anonymous visitors to your Web site.

To view the details of this user and confirm Guest access to your computer, highlight the user in the Users and Passwords window and click Properties. Guest access allows Web visitors to see pages in your Web directory without having to log on.

In the "Directory Security properties" section of this chapter, you find out how to restrict access to certain directories on your IIS server.

You learn more about the Users and Passwords windows later in this chapter and in this book, but for now, it's only important to know that there's a special account for guest Web users.

Do not modify or delete this guest Web user; if you do, your Web server will not work correctly.

Starting and testing Index Server

Although you installed the Index Server in the last step, it's not automatically started. To start and test Index Server in Windows 2000, follow these steps:

1. From the Start menu, choose Programs, Administrative Tools, Computer Management.
2. Expand Services and Applications by clicking on the plus sign next to it.
3. Highlight Indexing Service, and then right-click on it and choose Start.
4. You're asked if you want Index Server to start automatically. If you intend to use Index Server regularly, click Yes. Otherwise, click No.

Index Server then populates the two default catalogs: System and Web. You can add new catalogs or edit these two catalogs using this interface. To query a catalog, follow these steps:

1. Expand Indexing Service in the Services and Applications node in the Computer Management window.
2. Expand one of the catalog nodes, as shown in Figure 13-2.
3. Click Query the Catalog. You'll see an HTML form in the right-hand pane of the window.
4. Use the form to query the catalog.

This query page uses Dynamic HTML to generate the query form. If you'd like to look at the source code for this HTML document, you can find it on your Windows 2000 or Windows NT computer at `c:\Windows\Help\ciquery.htm` or `c:\WINNT\Help\ciquery.htm`.

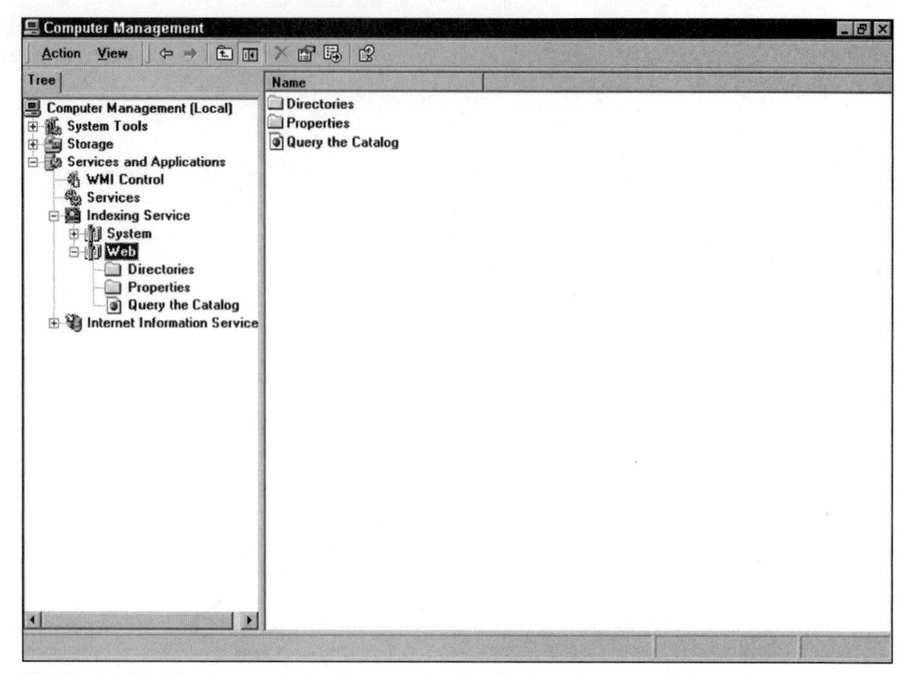

Figure 13-2: Viewing an Index Server catalog in the Computer Management window

Managing IIS

The Internet Services Manager is the Microsoft Management Console snap-in used to configure and administer IIS. To access the Internet Information Services Manager in Windows 2000:

1. Select Start.
2. Select Programs.
3. Select Administrative Tools.
4. Choose the Internet Services Manager icon.

In the following sections, you learn how to configure several parts of IIS to get ready to create an e-commerce site.

Internet Services Manager

The Internet Services Manager appears, at first glance, to be a simple tool. After you start to use it, however, you'll discover its complexity and usefulness. Figure 13-3 shows what the Internet Services Manager looks like when it's first started.

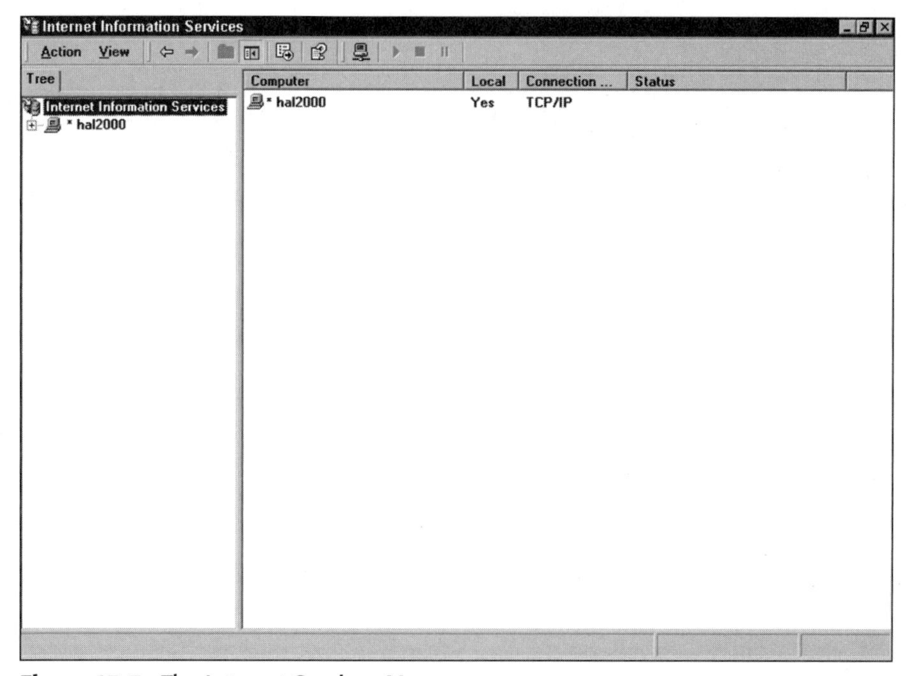

Figure 13-3: The Internet Services Manager

Your Internet Services Manager, of course, displays the name of your computer.

Virtual directories

Virtual directories are a way to map computer directories to Web server directories. This is done by creating an alias in the Web site directory that points to another directory on the server (or even another computer that your server has access to). For example, you may want to make a directory containing letters accessible through your intranet at `http://yourserver/letters`. There are two ways to do this. The first is to move this directory of letters to `c:\inetpub\wwwroot\letters\`. The other method is to create a virtual Web directory that points to the computer directory. For example, you could specify that `http://yourserver/letters` actually points to `c:\documents\letters`.

Virtual directories provide additional security for your site because visitors don't know where your files are physically located on your server and cannot use that information in an attempt to modify them. Table 13-2 demonstrates the relationships between physical directories and virtual directories for a sample intranet server named yeOldeIntranet.

Table 13-2
Relationship Between Physical Directories and Virtual Directories

Physical Directory	*Virtual Directory*	*URL*
c:\inetpub\wwwroot	(home directory)	http://yeOldeIntranet/
d:\docs\letters\from_customers	letters	http://yeOldeIntranet/letters/
c:\inetpub\wwwroot\Scripts	Scripts	http://yeOldeIntranet/Scripts/
d:\catalog	products	http://yeOldeIntranet/products/

Setting up a virtual directory for IIS

This section shows you how to set up a virtual directory for IIS, using the following steps:

1. Using Windows Explorer, find your IIS home directory. By default, this is `c:\inetpub\wwwroot\`.
2. Create a new folder inside of the `wwwroot` directory. The name of this directory doesn't matter. For demonstration purposes, call it `ecomm`.
3. For the site you create in Chapter 14, you need a directory for running scripts. Create a directory named `cgi-bin` inside of the `ecomm` directory.

Tip

If you're using PWS (on Windows 95, Windows 98, or Windows ME) skip to the next set of steps in the section entitled "Creating a virtual directory in PWS."

4. Open the Internet Services Manager in Windows NT or Windows 2000 as follows:
   - In Windows NT (assuming you have the latest service pack installed), this is probably located in Start, Program Files, Windows NT 4.0 Option Pack, Microsoft IIS, Internet Service Manager.
   - In Windows 2000, select Start, Programs, Administrative Tools, and then choose the Internet Services Manager icon.
5. Expand the tree menu in the left pane of the Internet Services Manager and highlight the Default Web Site.
6. Right-click on the Default Web Site node, highlight New, and then select Virtual Directory.

7. In Windows NT, you're asked to specify an alias. In Windows 2000, you need to click Next in the Virtual Directory Wizard to get to the Virtual Directory Alias screen.

8. Type a virtual directory alias. This should be a name that is legal in a Web URL. This means that it must be made up of letters and numbers only, and not contain spaces. For demonstration purposes, enter `ecomm` as the virtual directory alias, and then click Next.

9. Browse to the directory you created in the `wwwroot` directory. Select it, and then click Next.

10. The next screen asks you to specify permissions for this new virtual directory. Make sure Read and Scripts are checked, and then click Next and Finish (on Windows 2000) or just Finish (on Windows NT).

11. Expand your new virtual directory, right-click on the `cgi-bin` directory, and then select Properties.

12. In the Properties window for the `cgi-bin` directory, turn on Execute access as well as Read access, and then click OK.

Creating a virtual directory in PWS

The following steps show you how to create a virtual directory in PWS:

1. Open the Personal Web Manager (shown in Figure 13-4) by double clicking the PWS icon on your Windows taskbar.

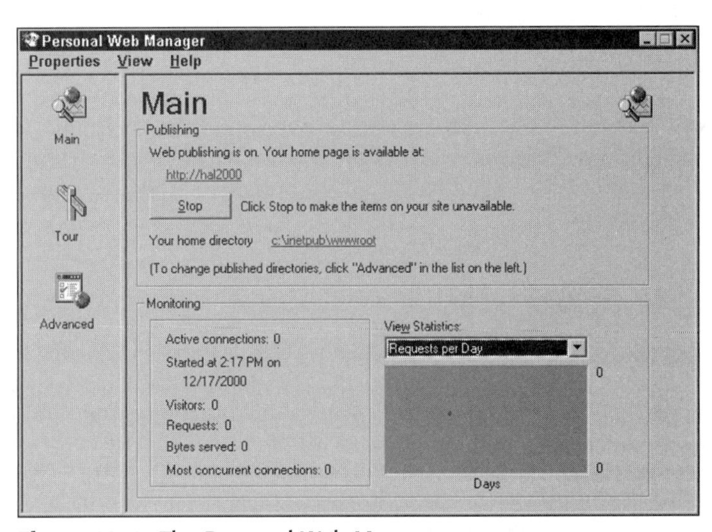

Figure 13-4: The Personal Web Manager

2. Click the Advanced button on the left side of the Window.
3. Click the Add button; the Add Directory window appears.
4. Enter the path to the directory on your computer that you want to be accessible through your Web server. This directory can be anywhere on your computer. For example, `c:\Documents\MyHomePage\`. You can also use the browse feature to locate this directory.
5. Enter an alias for this directory. For example, if you enter **myweb** as the alias, this directory will be accessible at `http://`*`yourservername`*`/myweb`.
6. Select the appropriate access and application permissions for this virtual directory. The default permissions are fine in most cases.
7. Click OK to finish. Your new virtual directory is listed in the virtual directory listing.
8. Expand your new virtual directory, and right-click on the `cgi-bin` directory. Select Properties.
9. In the Properties window for the `cgi-bin` directory, turn on Execute access as well as Read access, and then click OK.

Virtual servers

As you saw in Chapter 12, virtual servers are a way to host more than one Web site on a Web server. Virtual servers are an important feature in full-scale Web server software, because they allow a single computer to serve tens or hundreds of Web sites. If it weren't for virtual servers, Web site hosting would be far beyond the budget of many small businesses, and free personal Web site hosting would be nonexistent.

The versions of IIS included with Microsoft's server operating systems (Windows NT Server and Windows 2000 Server) include the ability to create virtual servers. PWS and the version of IIS 5.0 on Windows 2000 Professional do not have the ability to create virtual servers.

IIS Web site properties

The behavior of the Web server can be set using the properties window for each Web directory in the Internet Services Manager. By default, the directory settings you define using the properties window cascade down through that directory's subdirectories. Therefore, to change the settings for all of the Web directories on your server, you can simply edit the settings on the highest-level directory (also known as the root or home directory). In the following sections, you look at and configure some of the global settings for your Web server.

To open the Web Site Properties window, right-click on the Default Web Site node in the Internet Services Manager to access the window shown in Figure 13-5).

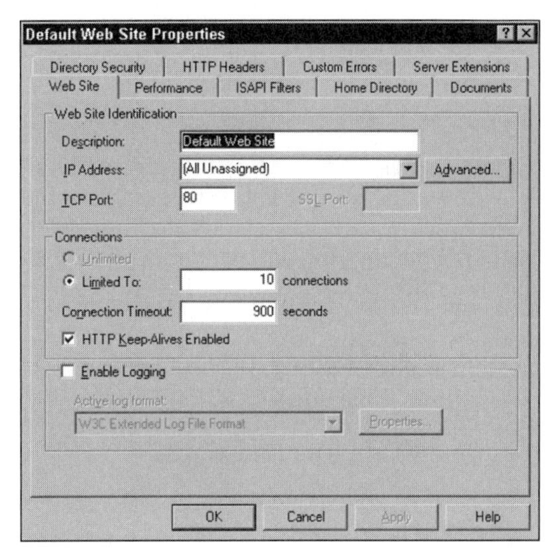

Figure 13-5: The Default Web Site Properties window

Using the Web Site properties sheet

The first tab in Default Web Site Properties window is the Web Site properties sheet (refer to Figure 13-5). This properties sheet allows you to configure several general settings for your Web site as follows:

✦ **Web Site Identification.** This section allows you specify the following:

- The name of the server and the IP address (if your computer has more than one) where you would like users to be able to access this site.
- The site's port number, which by default for public Web sites is 80, can also be changed to any other valid port number. If your Web site is at a port other than 80, users must include the port number in the URL when they want to go to your site.

Tip

Using port numbers other than 80 is one way to have multiple Web sites in a single domain. For example, you could have one Web site at `http://www.yourdomain.com/` (port 80 is implied) and another site at `http://www.yourdomain.com:8080` (8080 is the port number).

- The option to specify the SSL port, unless you have a server certificate installed, is inactive. If you do have a server certificate installed, the default SSL port is 443.

Exam Tip

Make sure that you know the most common default port numbers, such as SSL (port 443), HTTP (port 80), and FTP (port 21).

Learn how to obtain and install a server certificate in Chapter 19.

- ✦ **Connections.** This is mostly useful for tweaking performance for larger Web sites. It allows you to specify how many users can be connected to the site at any one time and how long the server tries to return a requested document before timing out. HTTP Keep-Alives allow a client to maintain an open connection with the Web server, rather than creating a new connection for every HTTP request. This can improve Web site performance and is enabled by default.
- ✦ **Enable Logging.** This part of the sheet allows you to turn server logging on and off and to choose the log file format. If it's not already turned on, check the box next to Enable Logging, and then click the Properties button to view the Extended Logging Properties window, shown in Figure 13-6.

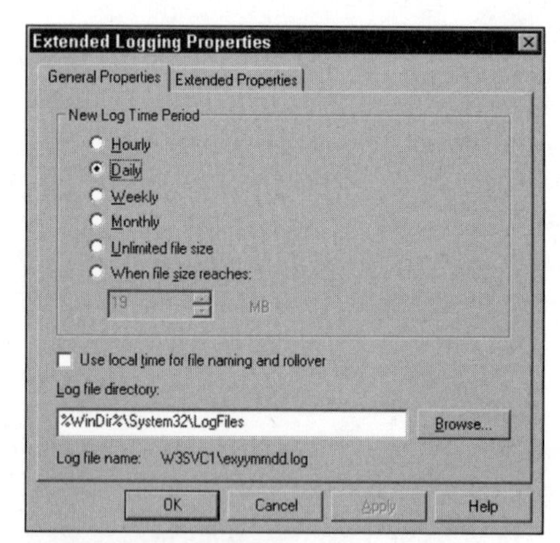

Figure 13-6: The Extended Logging Properties window

Using the Performance properties sheet

The Performance properties sheet, shown in Figure 13-7, allows you to tune your site for the amount of traffic you expect.

In Windows 2000 Professional, many of the options in this window are not available or needed. The performance tuning slider should be set slightly higher than the number of hits your site gets each day. Setting the slider much higher than the actual number of hits will waste memory.

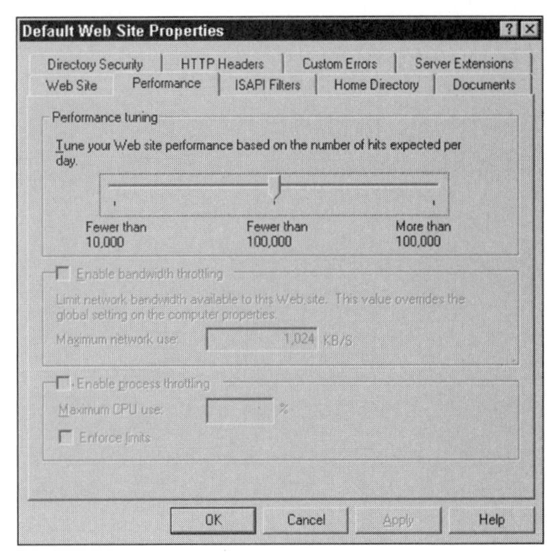

Figure 13-7: The Performance properties sheet

Using the Home Directory properties sheet

The Home Directory properties sheet, shown in Figure 13-8, is where you can set the Web site's default directory, and the default permissions and settings for files and directories in the Web site, which work as follows:

✦ **Directory browsing.** This option determines whether visitors to your site can see a listing of the files and subfolders in a directory if no default document (such as `index.html`) is specified. Being able to see a directory listing is useful for testing purposes, but this feature should be turned off on live sites.

✦ **Application Settings.** This section of the Home Directory properties sheet is particularly important. You can set up properties regarding how programs run on the server. Some of these function as follows:

- The permissions that you set in the Execute Permissions box are for the entire Web site, so they should be as restrictive as possible. Generally, you want to specify just Read access if you're creating a static Web site. If you're using ASP scripts, you need to also allow Script access. (This is turned on by default.) Execute access allows any application to run in this directory.

Be careful when giving directories Execute access. If a directory has both Write access and Execute access, harmful scripts could be uploaded to the directory and executed.

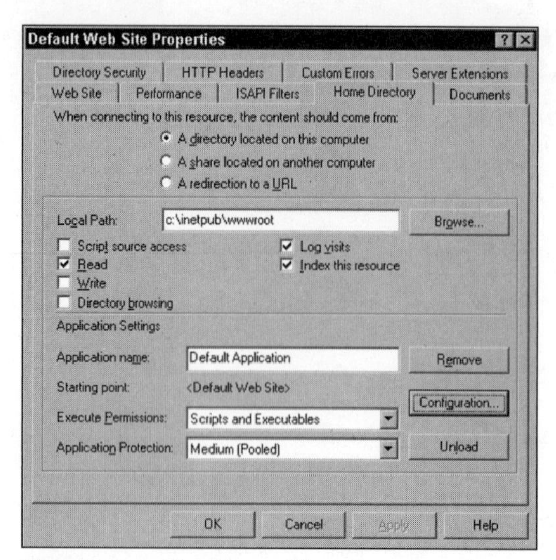

Figure 13-8: The Home Directory properties sheet

- This properties sheet also contains important functionality that is used to associate file extensions with ISAPI DLLs or CGI programs. You can access this functionality by clicking the Configuration button in the applications section to bring up the Application Configuration window, shown in Figure 13-9. The App Options tab allows you to set several options related to how server applications run. In most circumstances, you don't need to worry about these. If you're an ASP programmer, you can use the options under the App Debugging tab to turn on ASP debugging. If you're not an ASP programmer, you may want to turn off ASP error messages (especially on a live Web server), so visitors to your site see a more user-friendly error message when ASP scripts don't work correctly.

The Lab Exercise for this chapter show you how the Application Configuration window can be used to allow your server to execute scripts written in the Perl language.

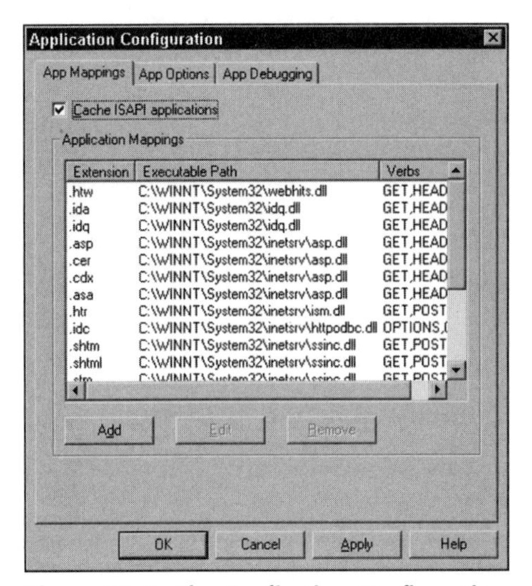

Figure 13-9: The Application Configuration window

Using the Documents properties sheet

The Documents properties sheet, shown in Figure 13-10, is where you can set the default document.

A default document is a document that a Web server sends to a Web client when a directory name is specified without a file name. Common default document names include:

- `index.html`
- `default.html`
- `index.htm`
- `default.htm`

The options on this properties sheet are:

- **Enable Default Document.** You can have as many default document names as you like, and they can be called anything that you like. Microsoft predefines three default documents: `default.htm`, `index.htm`, and `iisstart.asp`. You should add `index.html` to this list because it's the most common name for default documents on UNIX servers. When a directory is requested without a filename, IIS looks for each default document listed in this properties window until it finds one. If the directory doesn't contain a default document, either an error message or a directory listing displays, depending on the setting of the directory browsing permission for the directory.

✦ **Enable Document Footer.** This option allows you to specify a file that should be included at the bottom of every Web page this Web server serves. A common use for the document footer is to put a copyright notice on every page.

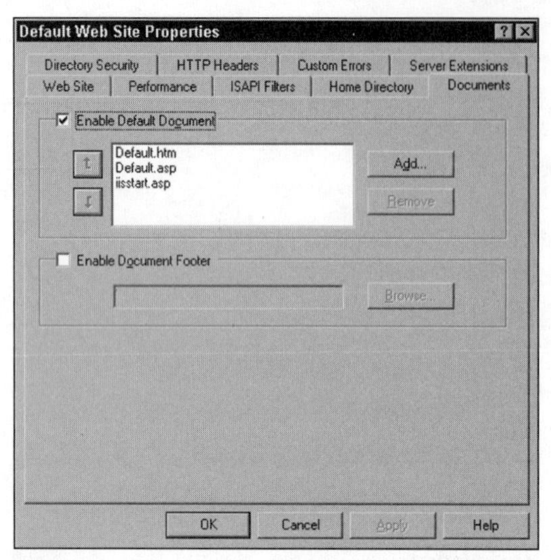

Figure 13-10: The Documents properties sheet

Using the Directory Security properties sheet

The Directory Security properties sheet, shown in Figure 13-11, allows you to configure several Web site security settings:

✦ **Anonymous access and authentication control.** For users to be able to view your Web site, they have to have access permissions. By default, Web sites grant the ability for anyone to read documents. As we mentioned earlier, IIS uses a default user account, which is named `IUSR_yourcomputername` to provide Anonymous access. For public Web sites, it's usually not necessary or desirable to restrict access to files. However, if you want to secure a directory or a server, you can disable Anonymous access and authentication control, and users will be prompted to log in to access the site.

✦ **Editing directory access.** Because you're currently working with global Web site properties, if you want to restrict access to just one directory (and the directories below it), you need to edit that directory's properties. For example, to restrict access to the IIS documentation, follow these steps:

1. Right-click on the IISHelp virtual directory in the Internet Services Manager and select Properties.
2. Open the Directory Security properties sheet.

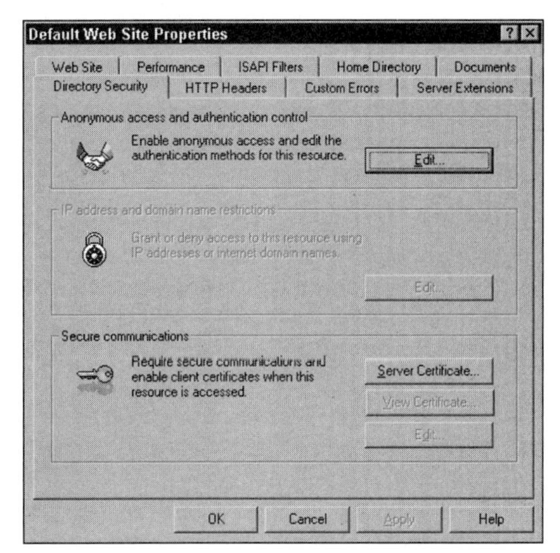

Figure 13-11: The Directory Security properties sheet

3. Click the Edit button in the Anonymous Access and authentication control part of the window.
4. Uncheck the Anonymous Access check box.
5. Click OK to exit the Properties window.
6. Enter `http://127.0.0.1/IISHelp` in your Web browser.
7. Type the user name, password, and domain of any user account on your computer that has access to the physical directory where this content is located (for example, `c:\winnt\help\iishelp`).

✦ **IP address and domain name restrictions.** This section of the Directory Security properties sheet lets you, for example, disallow access to your site to anyone who tries to use your site from `aol.com`.

✦ **Secure communications.** This part of the Directory Security properties sheet allows you to work with server certificates. If you don't currently have a certificate installed, you can click the Server Certificate button to obtain and install one using the Certificate Wizard.

You'll work through the process of installing and working with server certificates in Chapter 19.

Using the Custom Errors properties sheet

The Custom Errors properties sheet is where you can specify which pages are shown when various HTTP errors occur. Different custom error messages can be defined for every directory or virtual directory on a server.

FTP settings

The IIS File Transfer Protocol (FTP) server properties can also be configured using the Internet Services Manager. In this section, you learn how to configure an FTP server to work with the Actinic Business e-commerce software. Because PWS does not include an FTP server, these instructions are for Windows NT or Windows 2000 only.

To configure your FTP server, follow these steps:

1. Open the Internet Services Manager and locate the Default FTP Site node.
2. Highlight the FTP Site node, right-click on it, and select Properties.
3. Go to the Home Directory properties sheet.
4. Enter the path to your Web site root as the home directory. (This is probably `c:\inetpub\wwwroot`.)
5. Check the appropriate boxes to allow both Read and Write access.
6. Switch to the Security Accounts properties sheet and uncheck the appropriate check box to disallow anonymous access.
7. Make sure that a group of users to which you belong (Administrators, for example) is listed in the box called FTP Site Operators.
8. Click OK to exit the FTP site properties.
9. Using an FTP client (WSFTP, for example), attempt to connect to your local FTP server using the following settings:
   - Host Name: 127.0.0.1
   - User ID: *your administrator ID*
   - Password: *your password*

If these settings don't allow you to successfully connect, make sure everything is configured correctly, your FTP server is running, and the user name and password you used have access to the FTP site.

Key Point Summary

After reading this chapter, you should have a better understanding of Microsoft's IIS, as well as of Web servers in general. IIS is much more than a simple HTTP server; therefore, you also learned about FTP, Indexing, and security. The major points of this chapter are:

✦ IIS is included with Windows NT and Windows 2000.

✦ ISAPI is a high-performance replacement for CGI.

✦ Index Server provides content indexing and full-text searching capabilities for Microsoft servers.

✦ PWS can be installed on some of Microsoft's desktop operating systems, including Windows 95 and Windows 98, using the Windows NT 4.0 Option Pack.

✦ The Internet Services Manager provides a single, easy-to-use interface for configuring IIS.

✦ Default documents are documents that are displayed when a directory is requested without a file name.

✦ ✦ ✦

STUDY GUIDE

In this chapter, you learned about many of the features of Microsoft's IIS. After a couple of questions to test your understanding of the topics covered in this chapter, this chapter's lab exercise takes you through the process of installing an ASAPI module for running Perl programs on IIS.

Assessment Questions

1. Which of the following operating systems should not be used to host a public Web site? (Choose the best answer.)

A. Windows NT 4.0 Server

B. Windows 2000 Advanced Server

C. Windows 2000 Server

D. Windows 98

2. What is the default SSL Web server port?

A. 80

B. 8080

C. 443

D. 21

3. Which of the following combinations of Web site permissions should not be used on public IIS Web sites? (Choose the best answer.)

A. Read and Script access

B. Read and directory browsing

C. Write and Execute access

D. Read and Execute access

4. What is a virtual server? (Choose the best answer.)

A. A server that doesn't really exist

B. A server that shares physical hardware with other virtual servers

C. A Web server directory that points to a directory outside of the server home directory

D. A server mostly used for testing

Scenario

As the person in charge of setting up an e-commerce site for your company, you must evaluate possible Web server software. The two Web servers you're considering are Apache and IIS. Based on this chapter and Chapter 12, as well as the particulars of your situation (which, admittedly, you don't know from this scenario), what might the advantages of using IIS rather than Apache be? What might the advantages of using Apache rather than IIS be?

Lab Exercise

Lab 13-1 Installing support for Perl on IIS using ActiveState's ActivePerl

1. Go to `http://www.activestate.com/Products/ActivePerl/index.html`.
2. Locate a link to the download page for the Windows binary version of ActivePerl.

A version of ActivePerl for Windows is included on the CD-ROM that comes with this book.

3. Download the installer for the version of Windows you're using.
4. Extract the installation program and run it to install ActivePerl on your computer. Remember where you installed it — you'll need this information shortly.
5. Open the Internet Services Manager and highlight the Default Web Site node.
6. Right-click on the Default Web Site and select Properties.
7. Go to the Home Directory properties sheet.
8. Click on the Configuration button in the Application Settings. You should see the Application Configuration window.
9. Click Add to open the Add/Edit Application Extension Mapping dialog box.
10. Locate the file called `PerlIS.dll` using the browse button. If you installed ActivePerl in the default location, it should be at `c:\Perl\bin\PerlIS.dll`.
11. Enter **.pl** in the extension field.
12. Leave the other settings as they are and click OK to exit the Application Configuration window and the Web Site properties window.
13. Test your Perl configuration by placing a Perl script in the Scripts in your `Inetpub` directory. We've provided a sample Perl script, called `hello.pl`, on the CD. After copying it to your Scripts directory, you should be able to run this script by going to `http://127.0.0.1/Scripts/hello.pl` in your Web browser.

Answers to Chapter Questions

Chapter pre-test

1. The security features of IIS 5.0 include SSL, Kerberos authentication, Digest authentication, Server-Gated Cryptography, Fortezza, IP and domain restrictions, and digital certificates.
2. ISAPI is a high-performance replacement for CGI.
3. A virtual directory is an alias in the Web site directory that points to another directory on the server.
4. An anonymous user account, named `IUSR_`*`yourcomputername`* is created when IIS is installed, so people can access your Web server without logging in.
5. Index Server creates searchable indexes of the contents and properties of documents.

Assessment questions

1. **D.** Windows 98 is not intended for use as a Web server operating system. However, it does support PWS for serving Web sites to your local network or for testing Web sites (see "Understanding Microsoft's IIS").
2. **C.** Port 443 is the default SSL Web server port. Port 80 is the default public HTTP server port, and Port 21 is the default FTP server port (see "IIS Web site properties").
3. **C.** By giving both Write and Execute permissions, you're giving anonymous users the ability to upload and run any program on your server, including programs that may harm your server or files (see "IIS Web site properties").
4. **B.** Virtual servers make it possible for multiple sites to be on one computer while each appears to have its own computer (see "Virtual servers").

Scenario

This scenario is wide open, but there are different situations that would create distinct advantages to using one server over the other. For example, if you want to host your site on a UNIX server, IIS is not an option. If you have little experience with non-GUI environments, IIS running on a Windows server may be better for your needs. If you want the best possible performance and security, Apache on UNIX may be better. But, if you want a complete Web server system you can easily integrate with your Windows network and applications, IIS may be the best choice. To make an informed decision, you must be aware of all of your options. Don't fall into the trap of thinking one platform or piece of software is always the answer.

For More Information . . .

- **ServerWatch's Review of PWS.** http://serverwatch.internet.com/reviews/web-mspws.html
- **Microsoft Windows NT 4.0 Option Pack (including PWS).** http://microsoft.com/ntserver/nts/downloads/recommended/NT4OptPk/default.asp
- **ServerWatch's Review of IIS 5.0.** http://serverwatch.internet.com/reviews/web-msiisv5.html
- **Microsoft Server Information.** www.microsoft.com/iis

CHAPTER 14

Working with E-Commerce Software: Actinic Business

EXAM OBJECTIVES

- E-commerce software
- Store administration
- Creating products and items
- Store categories

CHAPTER PRE-TEST

1. What is the purpose of e-commerce software?
2. What is a catalog tree?
3. Why are product catalogs divided into categories?

✦ Answers to these questions can be found at the end of the chapter. ✦

In this chapter, you begin developing and maintaining a prototype online store using Actinic Business e-commerce software. A trial version of Actinic Business for Windows is included on the CD-ROM that comes with this book. The software can also be downloaded from `www.actinic.com` and can be used on a trial basis for 30 days.

Although all e-commerce sites are not developed and maintained with the same e-commerce software, working with Actinic provides you with excellent experience in using e-commerce software. This experience can then be applied to developing your own e-commerce site using Actinic or another software solution.

Understanding Actinic Business

E-commerce software

Actinic Software specializes in e-commerce solutions for small and medium-sized businesses. Actinic offers e-commerce software and hosting and works with other ISPs to provide e-commerce hosting for users of their software. They have over 8,000 customers around the world.

Beginning in this chapter, you use the Actinic Business e-commerce package to develop a prototype e-commerce site. You can host this site on a trial basis with Actinic Hosting, or, if you prefer, with your own ISP or on your local computer.

Actinic Business provides an easy-to-use solution for building a sophisticated online store. Its features include:

- ✦ Shopping cart
- ✦ Ability to import a product catalog or enter products manually
- ✦ Customizable search engine
- ✦ Secure transactions
- ✦ Inventory management
- ✦ Complex shipping calculations
- ✦ Complex sales tax calculations
- ✦ Ability to use external data sources
- ✦ Multiple pricing schedules (for conducting B2C and B2B commerce concurrently, for instance)
- ✦ Customizable design templates
- ✦ Printable packing lists and invoices
- ✦ Payment gateway integration

By using Actinic business, you'll get a feel for how an e-commerce site is set up. In the next few chapters, you learn how to use Actinic's store development and administration features, how to customize the look and feel of the site, set tax and shipping rates, and much more. This experience will not only reinforce the principles learned in previous chapters, but will also provide hands-on experience developing an e-commerce store.

Although the exam does not cover Actinic Business specifically, a general knowledge of how e-commerce software works will help you on the exam.

Installing Actinic Business

This section takes you through the process of installing Actinic Business, step by step. Please follow along to install the software on your system.

To work with the practice site used in the book, you need to install Actinic on your computer.

Planning for setup

Before beginning the Actinic Business installation program, you should do the following:

✦ Close all programs

✦ Close any programs or processes that may be using Data Access Objects (DAO)

You also need to make sure that your computer is capable of running Actinic Business. The requirements for installing Actinic are:

✦ Windows 95, 98, NT 4, or 2000

✦ 16MB of memory or more

✦ 50MB or more free on the hard disk

Installation

Follow these steps to install Actinic Business on your computer:

1. Locate the file called `BusinessTrial.exe` on the CD-ROM included with this book. It's in the Actinic folder. Double-click on this file to run it.
2. In the WinZip Self-Extractor dialog box, choose the folder to which you would like the Actinic files extracted. Click Unzip to extract the files.
3. Use Windows Explorer to navigate to the folder to which the files were extracted. Find the file `setup.exe` and double-click it.

4. If your system does not already have the Microsoft Data Access Components (MDAC) installed, the Actinic Business installation program can install this for you. You may need to restart your computer after installing MDAC.
5. After restarting, your computer automatically returns to the Actinic Business installation program. You're prompted to read and agree to the software license. Click Yes to agree and proceed.
6. The next dialog box presents information on the four stages of the Actinic installation. These four stages are:
   - Install system files
   - Install Actinic Business
   - Install payment service providers
   - Install database drivers
7. Click Next to proceed with the first stage: installing system files.
8. The next dialog box describes the purpose of installing system files. If you're using Windows 2000, you may skip this installation by clicking Skip. Otherwise, click Next.
9. You may be prompted to restart your computer after installing the system files. If so, restart the computer. Your computer returns to the installation program automatically once it's restarted.
10. The next stage of the installation is installing the actual Actinic Business software. Click Next to continue.
11. The next dialog box asks you to choose a version. In all likelihood, Install New v4 is the only option available to you, unless you've used Actinic on your computer before. Choose this option and click Next.
12. Next, you're prompted to choose a destination folder for your installation. Either select the default or click Browse to choose another folder. Click Next when you're done.
13. In the subsequent dialog box, enter your name and company and click Next.
14. You're asked whether you want backups made of files replaced during installation. Select Yes and click Next.
15. The following dialog box is used to select the folder in which these backups will be stored. Either select the default or click Browse to choose another folder. Click Next when you're done.
16. In the next dialog box, you select startup options for Actinic. You can have an Actinic icon added to your desktop and have Actinic automatically start up when your computer is turned on. For now, let's just have the desktop icon. Check the checkbox for Add A Desktop Icon and leave the other option blank. Click Next.
17. The following dialog box reviews your installation information. Make sure it's correct. Go back to correct any information by using the Back button. When everything is correct, click Install Now.

18. Wait while the program is installed.

19. The next dialog box prompts you for domain information, and should already be populated with URLs for an Actinic trial site. Because this information can be changed after installation, there's no need to change it now. Click Next to continue.

20. The basic installation of Actinic Business is complete. Click Finish.

21. The installation now walks you through installing payment service providers. Stores created using Actinic Business can work with a variety of online payment processing providers, and this part of the installation program adds such providers to Actinic. Click Next to proceed.

22. The following screen welcomes you to this stage of the installation process. Click Next to continue.

23. This dialog box asks whether you would like to create backup copies of any files changed by the installation process. Select Yes and click Next.

24. Specify where the backup files will be saved. Either select the default or click Browse to choose another folder. Click Next when you're done.

25. Now you're ready to install payment service providers. Click Install Now to proceed.

26. Wait while the installation is performed.

27. The following dialog box informs you when the installation is completed. Click Finish to go to the last stage.

28. The fourth, and last, stage of the installation program is installing database drivers. If you do not have Data Access Objects (DAO) on your system, you need to perform this installation to use a spreadsheet or database file for your product catalog.

29. You're now finished with the installation. Click Finish to exit the installation program.

Working with Actinic Business

Now that you've installed the Actinic Business software, it's time to get acquainted with its functions and get started developing your store.

Starting Actinic Business

Start Actinic Business using the following steps:

1. Double-click on the Actinic e-commerce v4 icon on your desktop. The Actinic Business program will be launched.

2. You're prompted for a Software Authorization Key. Click Bypass to start your 30-day trial period for using Actinic Business.

3. You may be presented with a dialog box prompting you for a user name and password. These are required to use a trial site hosted on the Actinic servers. If you've registered for a trial site with Actinic, enter your user name and password. If not, click Cancel to bypass this dialog box and enter the main Actinic interface.
4. The Actinic Business interface, shown in Figure 14-1, should be displayed on your screen.

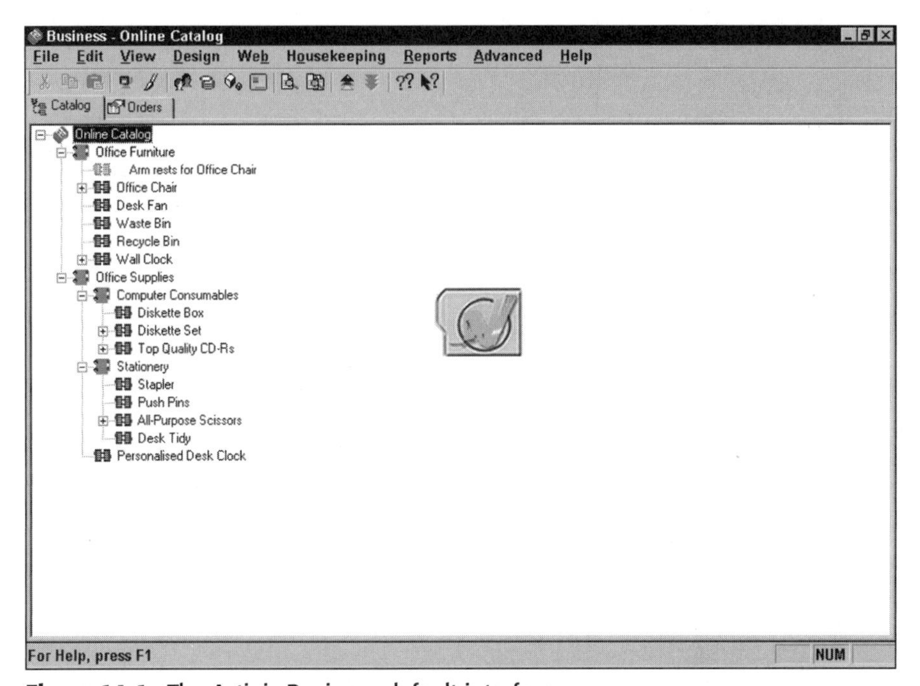

Figure 14-1: The Actinic Business default interface

Exploring the Actinic interface

Take a look at the Actinic interface and the options available. The two items in the main white part of the screen are the catalog tree and the Actinic Navigator. The next two sections take a closer look at these tools.

Catalog tree

Store categories

Actinic comes with a pre-installed demo product catalog, which you will replace with your own catalog. The structure of this catalog is presented vertically along the left side of the screen (see Figure 14-2). It's very similar in design to the

Windows Explorer interface. Subfolders can be viewed by clicking on the plus (+) signs in front of folders.

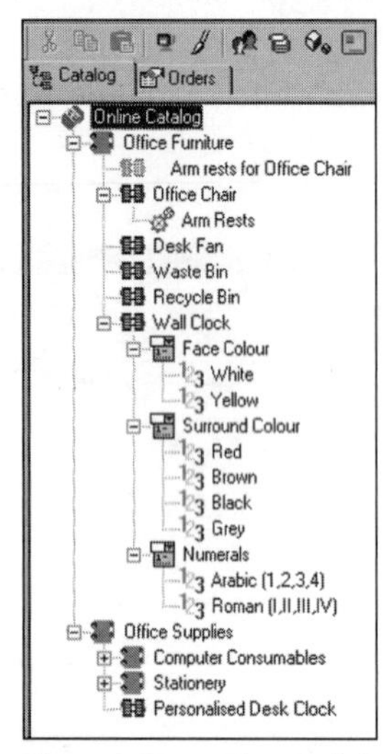

Figure 14-2: The Actinic catalog tree

Although Actinic's Catalog Tree isn't specifically covered on the exam, the concept of a hierarchically structured catalog *is* covered.

To get an idea of how Actinic structures product information, take a look at the demo catalog. The top level of the hierarchy is Online Catalog, which is the name of the demo catalog. The catalog is divided into two main categories: Office Furniture and Office Supplies. Office Supplies has two subcategories: Computer Consumables and Stationery.

You can make your online store more easily browsable by dividing your catalog into logical categories and subcategories. For example, imagine that you're a customer visiting an online tool shop, and you want to buy a socket wrench. There are many, many kinds of tools for sale. Imagine that you have to scroll through a list of hundreds of sanders, saws, and nail guns to find what you're looking for. It would be much easier to find a socket wrench if the site provided a Hand Tools section rather than just a list of products with no categorizations. A large store should also break the Hand Tools category into subcategories, such as Wrenches, Hammers, Drills, and so on.

Most online stores have several layers of categorization that make up their product catalog hierarchy. Only stores with a very small number of products should work with a flat catalog (that is, a catalog with no hierarchy).

Each category in the tree is populated by individual products. For instance, the Office Furniture category features the following items:

- ✦ Office chair
- ✦ Desk fan
- ✦ Waste bin
- ✦ Recycle bin
- ✦ Wall clock

Individual products, or items, contain sub-items, which are called attributes, choices, and components. These are visible by clicking on the plus (+) sign in front of the item name. For example, in Figure 14-2, you can see that the Office Chair item has a sub-item called Arm Rests, which is represented by two small gears. If you double-click on the words Arm Rests, the Component detail view appears, as shown in Figure 14-3.

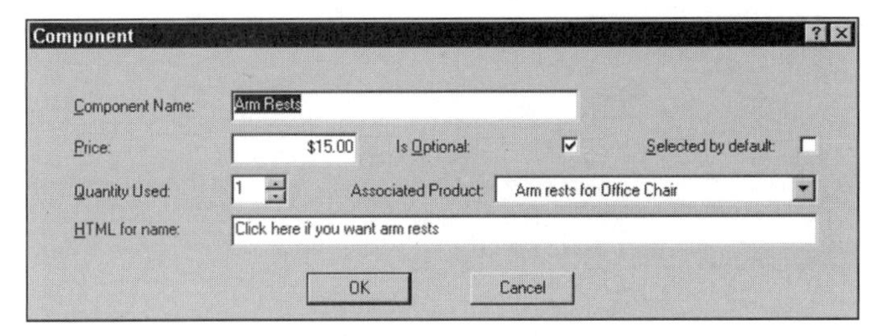

Figure 14-3: Component detail view

The Arm Rests are a component of the item Office Chair, which means Arm Rests are an optional part of the Office Chair. An option to purchase armrests is presented when a user purchases the Office Chair. Other sub-items of products are attributes and choices. You will take a closer look at these in the Lab Exercises portion of this chapter.

To learn more about building effective product catalogs, see Chapter 16. The Actinic User Guide and Chapter 16 also provide more detailed information on using catalogs in Actinic.

The Actinic Navigator

Store administration

The Navigator is a handy tool with shortcuts to the main functions of the program. It's the gray file folder icon with a brown checkmark on it in the middle of the Actinic interface (see Figure 14-4). You can drag it around the screen by clicking and holding while you move your mouse.

If the Navigator is not visible on your screen, choose Navigator from the View menu or press Ctrl+N to activate it.

Figure 14-4: The Actinic Navigator icon

The Navigator can be expanded to show links to the main functions of the software. By clicking on the center of the Navigator, you can expand it to look like Figure 14-5.

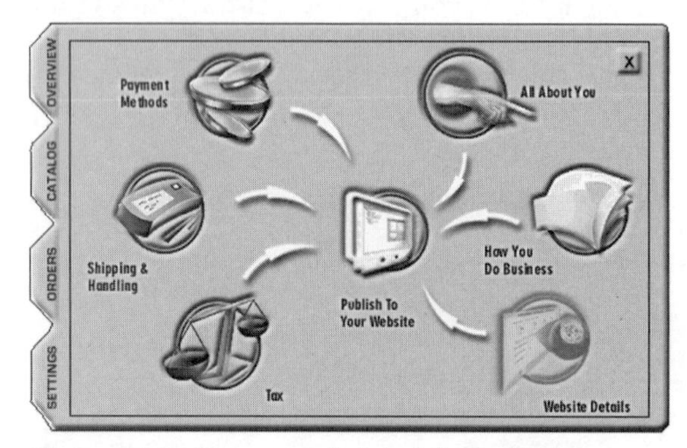

Figure 14-5: The expanded Actinic Navigator

The expanded navigator has four tabs along the left side. Each contains a variety of functions. The following sections describe how these work.

Overview

On the Overview tab, you can access the following functions:

✦ **Set up your product catalog.** Link to the Catalog tab, which is described in the following section.

✦ **How you do business.** Link to the Settings tab, described in a later section.

✦ **Publish to your Web site.** Upload the store's files to your Web server.

✦ **Collect new orders from the site.** Retrieve any orders that have been placed at your site since the last time you downloaded orders.

✦ **Process orders.** Link to the Orders tab, described in the "Settings" section later.

Catalog

On the Catalog tab, you can modify the following areas:

✦ **Stock levels.** Manage inventory and issue warnings when stock is low.

✦ **Setup search.** Set up the parameters for searching your product catalog.

- **Products.** View and change product details.
- **Sections.** View and change sections in the catalog hierarchy.
- **Themes and colors.** Choose from design themes and color templates.
- **Import catalog.** Launch wizard for importing an existing product catalog.
- **Design options.** View and change the way your catalog and individual items in your store are presented, as well as navigation element labels, the way pricing is displayed, and more.
- **Publish to your Web site.** Upload the store's files to your Web server.
- **Catalog reports and stock level reports.** Generate reports based on your store data.

Orders

On the Orders tab, you can choose from the following functions:

- **Collect new orders from the site.** Retrieve any orders placed on your site since the last time you downloaded orders.
- **Order details.** View and search the database of orders placed.
- **Print invoices.** Print any outstanding invoices.
- **Warehouse packing lists.** Print outstanding packing lists.
- **Order reports.** Generate reports on order data.

Settings

On the Settings tab, you can work with the following:

- **Tax.** View and change sales tax information for your store.
- **Shipping and handling.** View and change shipping and handling charges.
- **Payment methods.** View and change approved payment options and the transaction security method.
- **All about you.** View and change company contact information.
- **How you do business.** Set up information on company policies, such as returns and money back guarantees.
- **Web site details.** Set up technical details of your site, such as the URL, user name, and password.
- **Publish to your Web site.** Upload the store's files to your Web server.

Toolbar and menus

The toolbar across the top of the Actinic window consists of icons that allow you to access some of the same functions as the Navigator, as well as more advanced functions. The menus (File, Edit, View, etc.) do the same as the toolbar. Take a moment to explore these. You'll use them as necessary in the Lab Exercises portion of this chapter.

For complete information on the toolbar and menus, please refer to Actinic's Advanced User Guide, which you can download from `www.actinic.com/techsupport/index.html`.

Entering your company's information

One of the first things you should do when setting up your store is to enter your company's information. Actinic comes with the Actinic corporate information as a default. You need to replace it with your own before configuring the server and uploading the site.

Follow these directions to enter your company information:

1. From the Actinic Navigator, select the Overview tab.
2. Click the icon labeled All About You.
3. You see the Company/Contact tab of the Business Settings window, as shown in Figure 14-6. The form is currently populated with information from Actinic. Replace it with your own information.

Figure 14-6: Entering your company information

4. When you're finished, click OK.

Tip

The Actinic Server software must be properly configured, as specified thus far in this chapter, for you to set up and use the site as described in the remainder of this chapter and in the later chapters in this book.

Configuring the Actinic Server

In this section, you configure Actinic to work with your Web server software or hosting company. You can choose to use Actinic Hosting on a trial basis, upload the store to your own ISP, or host the site locally. If you have limited technical skills, we recommend that you use Actinic Hosting.

Actinic Host mode

If you're not comfortable with entering technical details about your site into the software, you can use Actinic Hosting on a trial basis. Your test site will be hosted at Actinic's Web servers for a limited time. Use the following steps to activate this option:

1. Go to `http://www.actinic.com/about/register.htm` in your Web browser to register with Actinic. After you've registered, you're given information on your trial site with Actinic Hosting. This information includes a CGI-BIN URL and a Codebase URL.
2. In Actinic, choose Advanced, Network Setup from the menu bar to view the Advanced Network Setup window shown in Figure 14-7.

Figure 14-7: Advanced Network Setup window

3. All of the fields in this window should be inactivated (gray) except for: Web Site URL, Catalog URL, CGI-BIN URL, and Codebase. If the other fields are active, click the Convert button on the right to switch to Actinic Host mode.
4. Enter the CGI-BIN URL and Codebase information you received from Actinic into the appropriate fields.
5. Click Test. If everything checks out, click OK.

Using your own ISP

If you already have server space at an ISP and feel comfortable about setting up Actinic to work with that ISP, use the following steps to set up the software to host the site remotely, at a specified location:

Tip You must have the ability to run CGI scripts in your server directory.

1. In Actinic, choose Advanced, Network Setup from the menu bar.
2. If you're in Actinic Host mode (which is indicated by inactive fields), you need to convert to Standard mode. Click the Convert button on the right to convert from Actinic Host mode (where published sites are hosted by Actinic) to Standard mode (where you can determine where the site is hosted).
3. Click Yes when the program asks you if you're sure about this.
4. Fill out the requested information. You may need to ask your ISP for some of this information if you're uncertain. See Figure 14-8 and Table 14-1 for prototypical entries for such a set-up.
5. Click Test. If everything checks out, click OK.

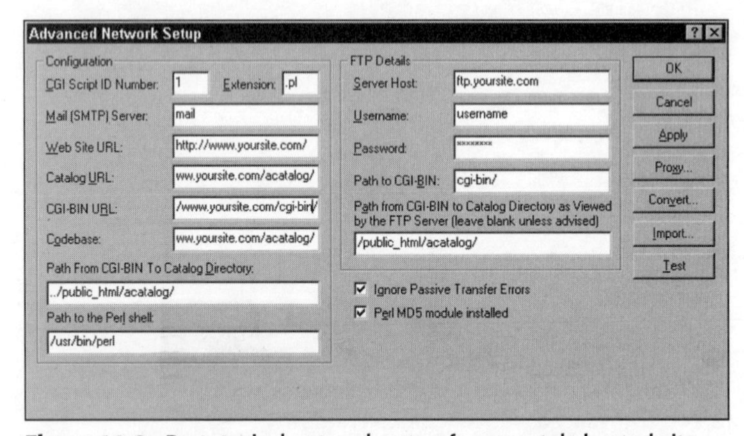

Figure 14-8: Prototypical network setup for remotely hosted site

Table 14-1
Prototypical Entries When Using Standard Mode

Field	*Hosted at ISP*	*Locally hosted*
Configuration		
CGI Script ID Number	1	1
Extension	.pl	.pl
Mail (SMTP) server	as specified by your ISP	mail
Web Site URL	`http://www.yoursite.com`	`http://127.0.0.1/ecomm`
Catalog URL	`http://www.yoursite.com/acatalog/`	`http://127.0.0.1/ecomm/acatalog/`
CGI-BIN URL	`http://www.yoursite.com/cgi-bin/`	`http://127.0.0.1/ecomm/cgi-bin/`
Codebase	`http://www.yoursite.com/acatalog/`	`http://127.0.0.1/ecomm/acatalog/`
Path from CGI-BIN to Catalog Directory	`../public_html/acatalog/`	`../acatalog/`
Path to the Perl shell	`/usr/bin/perl`	`c:\perl`
FTP Details		
Server host	`ftp.yoursite.com`	127.0.0.1
Username	your user name	your user name
Password	your password	your password
Path to CGI-BIN	`cgi-bin/`	`/ecomm/cgi-bin/`
Path from CGI-BIN to Catalog Directory as Viewed by the FTP Server	`../acatalog/`	`../acatalog/`

Hosting the site locally

If you would like to set up the practice site on your local machine, and feel comfortable working with IIS, this is the option for you. You need to have your FTP server configured as explained in Chapter 13. You also need to be able to run Perl scripts on your local machine. See the Lab Exercise in Chapter 13 for instructions on how to configure this. After creating a virtual directory as specified in Chapter 13, do the following:

1. In Actinic, choose Advanced, Network Setup from the menu bar.

2. If you're in Actinic Host mode (which is indicated by inactive fields), you need to convert to Standard mode. Click the Convert button on the right to convert from Actinic Host mode to Standard mode.
3. Click Yes when the program asks you if you're sure about this.
4. Fill out the requested information. See Table 14-1 for prototypical entries for such a set-up.
5. Click Test. If everything checks out, click OK.

Publishing a Web Site with Actinic

To verify that everything is working as it should, you should publish the demonstration Web Site to your Web Server. To do so, follow these steps:

1. From the Actinic Navigator, select the Overview tab.
2. Click the icon labeled Publish to your Web site.
3. The publishing wizard publishes the site as specified by your configuration. Wait until it's finished.
4. Click OK.
5. To verify that the site is working, go to your store's URL.

If it's not working correctly, try reconfiguring Actinic's Network Setup features, as described earlier in this chapter.

Key Point Summary

In this chapter, you gained practical experience in using e-commerce software—specifically Actinic software. The key points from this chapter are:

✦ E-commerce software provides a development environment for an online store. The features of such packages vary by vendor.

✦ Product catalogs are divided into categories for easier browsing. The hierarchy of a product catalog can be represented in a catalog tree.

✦ Actinic, like most e-commerce software packages, requires little programming knowledge.

✦ ✦ ✦

STUDY GUIDE

In this chapter, you had hands-on experience with e-commerce software. Now, it's up to you to answer a few questions based on that experience and do some more hands on projects in the Lab Exercises section.

Assessment Questions

1. What is the primary purpose of e-commerce software? (Choose the best answer.)

A. To create the look and feel of your online store

B. To automate credit card payments

C. To develop an e-commerce site with little programming knowledge

D. To save money

2. A product catalog hierarchy is made up of what elements?

A. Products

B. Categories and products

C. Pricing schedules and inventory data

D. Categories

3. Which tab in the Actinic Navigator contains links to inventory management controls?

A. Catalog tab

B. Overview tab

C. Settings tab

D. Orders tab

4. In which of the following cases would you *not* use Actinic's Standard mode for network settings?

A. Hosting site locally

B. Hosting site at an ISP

C. Using Actinic Hosting

D. Using remote host

Scenarios

1. Take a look at the Actinic catalog tree in Figure 14-9. List the subcategories of the Office Supplies category.

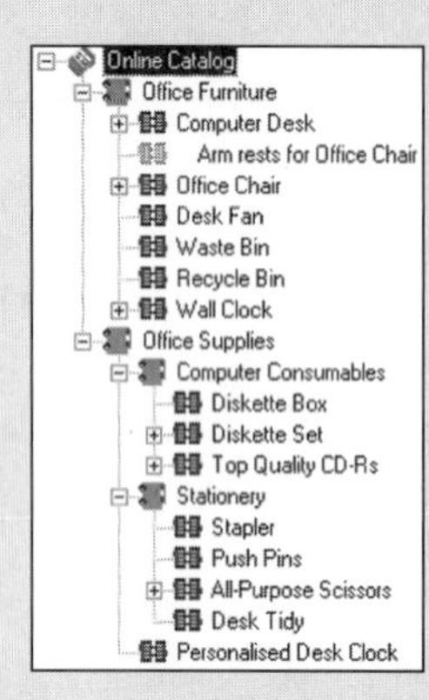

Figure 14-9: An Actinic catalog tree

2. Take a look at the catalog tree in Figure 14-10. What choices do customers who buy the Wall Clock need to make?

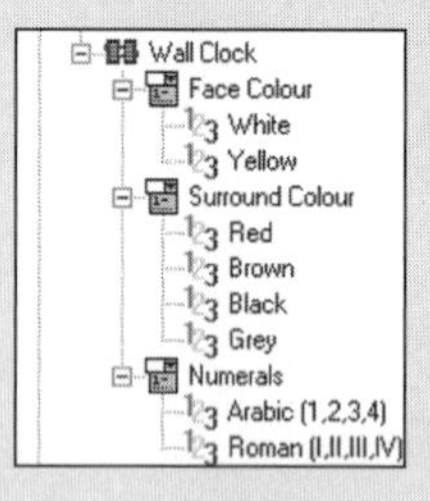

Figure 14-10: An Actinic category tree showing choices for a Wall Clock item

Lab Exercises

Lab 14-1 Add a product to the catalog

Creating products and items

In this exercise, you add a product to the catalog.

1. In the Actinic catalog tree, highlight the category Office Furniture by clicking on it once.

2. From the Edit menu, select New Product. This adds a new product to the Office Furniture category and displays the Product Details window, as shown in Figure 14-11.

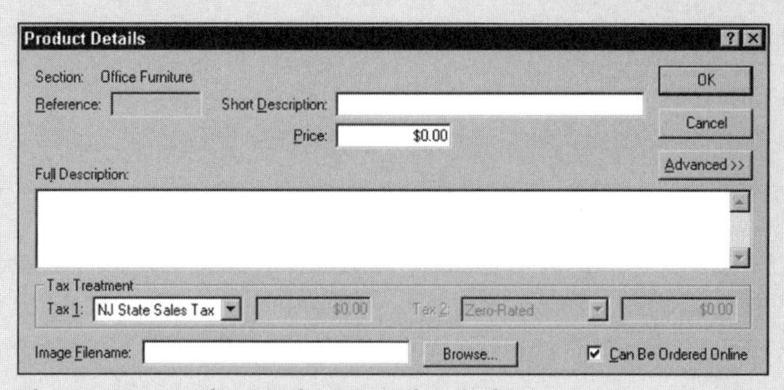

Figure 14-11: The Product Details window

3. In the Short Description field, enter the following: **Computer Desk**.
4. In the Price field, enter: **$250.00**.
5. In the Full Description field, enter: **This computer desk can be adjusted for any user's ergonomic needs. Accommodates a standard computer tower and large monitor. Optional wheels are included. Requires assembly.**
6. Click OK. Note that the Computer Desk has been added to the catalog tree. You're done!

Lab 14-2 Add an attribute to your product

In this exercise, you add an attribute to the product you created in Lab 14-1.

1. In the Actinic catalog tree, highlight the Computer Desk product (which you created in the previous lab) by clicking on it once.
2. From the Edit menu, select New Attribute.
3. An Attribute icon, with an empty box for a name, is added below the Computer Desk item (see Figure 14-12). Enter **Finish** into this box, and press the Enter (or Return) key on your keyboard.

Figure 14-12: Adding an attribute

4. Computer Desk now has an attribute called Finish. Highlight the word Finish (if it isn't already highlighted) by clicking on it once.
5. From the Edit menu, select New Choice.
6. A Choice icon, with an empty box for a name, is added below the Finish item (see Figure 14-13). Enter **Cherry** into this box, and press the Enter (or Return) key on your keyboard.

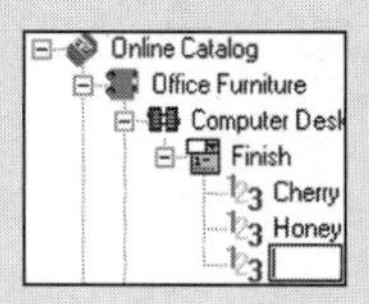

Figure 14-13: Adding choices

7. Highlight Finish and select New Choice again. This time, enter **Honey** as the Choice name.
8. Repeat Step 7, adding the choices **Walnut** and **Black**.
9. Buyers of the Computer Desk item now have to choose a finish for the desk: cherry, honey, walnut, or black. To see a preview of how this is presented on the Web site, choose Offline Preview from the Web menu.
10. A preview of your store automatically opens in your default navigator. Navigate to the Office Furniture section. The Computer Desk item should be listed there, and the screen should look similar to Figure 14-14.

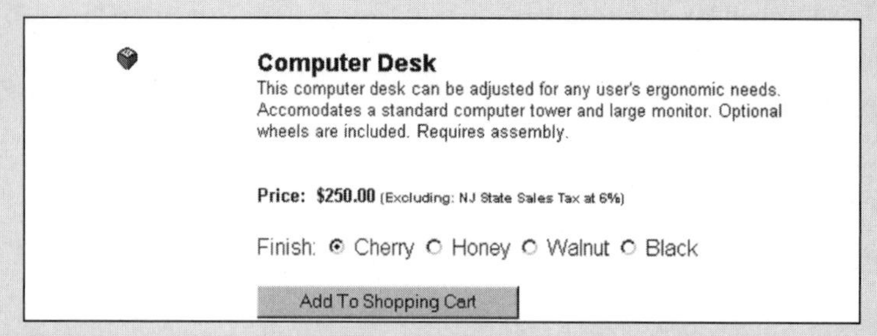

Figure 14-14: The new computer desk product as presented on the Web site

Answers to Chapter Questions

Chapter pre-test

1. E-commerce software provides an automated way of developing an e-commerce store. The software generates the necessary code for the Web site. E-commerce software packages generally include support for product catalogs and shopping carts. More advanced functionality is available, depending upon the vendor.
2. A catalog tree is a hierarchical view of the product catalog. Products are shown as sub-items of categories.

3. Product catalogs are divided into logical categories and sub-categories in order to help site visitors find the correct product. For example, if you're looking for a stuffed bear, it's easier to find a bear in a list of 10 stuffed animals than in a list of 100 toys. By making Stuffed Animals a sub-category of Toys, you can help your shoppers find the stuffed bear more easily.

Assessment questions

1. **C.** The primary purpose of e-commerce software is to develop an e-commerce site with little or no programming knowledge required. Many e-commerce software packages also offer the features listed in the other three answers, but they are not the primary purposes (see "Understanding Actinic Business").

2. **B.** The product catalog hierarchy is made up of both categories and products. Categories are the highest level of the catalog. Sub-categories and products break out below the top-level categories in one or more levels (see "Catalog tree").

3. **A.** Actinic's inventory management controls can be found in the Catalog tab (see "Working with Actinic Business").

4. **C.** Standard mode is used for every case *except* when you're using Actinic Hosting (see "Configuring the Actinic Server").

Scenarios

1. The subcategories of Office Supplies are Computer Consumables and Stationery.

2. Purchasers of the Wall Clock need to decide on a face color and surround color, and the type of numbers they'd like on their clocks.

For More Information . . .

✦ **Actinic Software.** `www.actinic.com`. Full product information, downloads, and registration.

CHAPTER 15

Customizing an E-Commerce Site

✦ ✦ ✦ ✦

EXAM OBJECTIVES

- ✦ Design goals
- ✦ Design templates
- ✦ Custom graphics

CHAPTER PRE-TEST

1. What are the key components of Web design?
2. Why is Web site customization important?
3. Why should Web site navigation behave consistently?
4. Should Web site navigation be placed along the right side of the page?
5. What are design templates?

✦ Answers to these questions can be found at the end of the chapter. ✦

In the previous chapter, you set up an e-commerce Web site using Actinic Business. Now, it's time to make that Web site unique by determining the layout and graphics, and customizing its look and feel by altering the navigation and text.

This chapter introduces a real case study site — a fictitious company called Texas-Shaped.com, an exclusive purveyor of Texas-shaped products — for which you'll be creating a custom look and feel. In Chapter 16, you'll learn how to create and implement a catalog of products for the store.

Understanding Web Site Customization

Customization is an essential step in the development of your e-commerce Web site. There are two main components of Web site customization:

✦ Design

✦ Business practices

Be sure that you know the main components of Web site customization, and the purpose of each.

It's extremely important to customize an e-commerce Web site to handle your business's transactions. Sales tax, for example, depends on the location of your business and needs to be set up correctly. Formulas for calculating shipping and handling charges also need to be programmed into your site.

See Chapter 17 for information on setting up sales tax and shipping charges in Actinic.

Although it's essential to alter the site to accommodate your business practices, customizing the site's design is not absolutely necessary. A small business with a small e-commerce budget may find that a template design suits its needs and budget.

In this chapter, you'll find out how to customize the design (look and feel) of a site using Actinic Business, both using design templates and custom graphics. You'll also make some small changes to the text on the site. The Lab Exercises at the end of the chapter introduce you to more advanced customization techniques. In Chapters 16 and 17, you'll learn about customizing the site for business practices.

Web design fundamentals

It's natural to want a custom look for your Web site. In the physical world, stores use architecture and signs to promote their identities. An e-commerce Web site uses graphics and layout to emphasize its unique identity and distinguish itself from competitors. In fact, a unique look can be vital to a store's success. There are several key components of Web site design:

- ✦ Colors
- ✦ Logo
- ✦ Layout
- ✦ Navigation scheme

You take a quick look at each component in the following sections.

Colors

The colors used on a Web site are key determinants of a design's success. These are often determined by the colors used on the company's logo or the theme of the Web site. For instance, Texas-Shaped.com uses the colors of the Texas state flag: red, white, and blue. A Web site with a Brazilian theme might use green and yellow instead.

The tenets of color theory can be very helpful in determining a color scheme. Color theory is centered on the color wheel.

Tip

For an example of a color wheel and for more information about color theory, see `www.webdesignclinic.com/ezine/v1i1/color/`.

Color theory is too complex to cover fully in this book, but the basic idea is that the following combinations of colors are most pleasing to the eye. Here's how it works:

- ✦ **Complementary colors.** Colors that are opposite one another on the color wheel
- ✦ **Double-complementary colors.** Three colors equidistant from one another on the color wheel
- ✦ **Analogous colors.** Colors side by side on the color wheel
- ✦ **Monochromatic (one-color) schemes.** A variety of shades and tones of one color along with white, gray, and black

Another important aspect of using color is to familiarize yourself with those color combinations that are indistinguishable to colorblind people – approximately five percent of men.

Logo

Most existing companies already have a corporate logo that has been used on paper marketing materials, letterhead, and the like. This logo should be incorporated into the Web design.

In some cases, the logo is ill suited for use on a Web page. For example, the logo may be too wide for display on a screen or have a catchphrase in small text that is unreadable at screen resolution. In such cases, the original logo designer or another professional graphic designer should be hired to create a Web-ready version of the logo for use on the e-commerce site.

Layout

Layout is the term that describes the placement of images and text on a screen. A good rule when it comes to developing the layout of your Web site design is to be consistent throughout the site. For example, navigation should be located on the same part of the screen on every page of your site. This consistency helps users find what they're looking for more quickly — no matter where they are in your site. Every page doesn't need to look exactly the same, but they should all clearly look like part of the same site.

For example, consider a hypothetical Web site with a company logo in the upper left corner of the home page and a navigation column beneath it. To the right of the navigation column, a static space for a large photo with descriptive text is provided. The photo, along with a brief story about the latest goings-on at the company, changes every week. The placement of the logo and navigation column should be considered fixed and unchangeable parts of the design — consistent through every page of the site. The area occupied by the photo and story on the site's home page is available for displaying different information on each of the other pages of the site.

Navigation scheme

The site's navigation area should be a fixed part of your Web site's layout on every page. It should be well placed and easily recognized as such, and, although its content may vary from page to page, it should behave consistently throughout (when clicked on, for example).

Consistent behavior

Web site navigation consists of a list of links to the main areas of the Web site (or, for very small sites, links to every page of the site). These links are rendered either as HTML text or as images. The following are among the more prevalent navigation styles being used today:

- **Rollovers (or mouseovers).** The image or text changes when the mouse cursor is over the link.
- **Drill down.** When a navigation item is clicked on, a list of links to sub-sections appears below the item and the user chooses from one of these links
- **Drop-down menus.** Links are listed in a drop-down menu from which the user selects a section of the site.

No matter which style of navigation a site uses, it's important to be consistent from each navigation item to the next. For instance, if clicking on one navigation item opens a list of sub-sections to choose from, all navigation items should do so. If some navigation items open a sub-list, and others link the user directly to another page on the site, the user won't know what to expect and may become confused.

Placement

It's vital to place site navigation elements where every visitor to your site can see them. Almost every Web site designed within the last four years has navigation placed either horizontally across the top of the page or vertically along the left side of the page. There is one simple reason for this: Many users will not scroll to find the navigation.

If your navigation is along the bottom of the page, users may need to scroll to see it. If the navigation is in a column on the right side of the page, users with monitors set to a low resolution may need to scroll to see it as well. Even if you can see the navigation on your computer screen, this is no guarantee that other users are able to see it. This is a result of the variety of default text sizes, resolutions, and monitor sizes.

Because the majority of sites are using either top or left-side placement, users expect navigation to be in one of these two locations. It improves the usability of your site to stick with one of these placements.

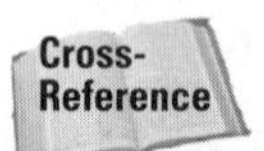

See Chapter 5 for more information on Web usability.

Audience drives design goals

Design goals

A key aspect of determining the design of any Web site is an analysis of the expected audience for the site; for instance:

- ✦ A Web site geared toward children should be very colorful and use clear images — in addition to simple words — for navigation and other key functions. Sound effects, such as squeaks and beeps when the mouse cursor is over an image, can also help keep children engaged.
- ✦ A Web site catering to senior citizens should have larger text than the average site, because older people often have trouble reading small text on a computer screen. The navigation should be kept simple, straightforward, and standard (either across the top or down the left side of the screen), because some senior citizens may not be as Web-savvy as other adults.

In the case of Texas-Shaped.com, the clientele are expected to be a general cross-section of the online buying population — who are typically neither children nor senior citizens. Still, it's important to make sure that the site's purpose and navigation scheme are clear to potential customers.

A satisfying user experience can be accomplished by using the following the guidelines (which were presented in the previous sections):

- ✦ Consistency of behavior and placement of navigation
- ✦ Consistency of layout throughout the site
- ✦ A pleasing color scheme

Customizing Look and Feel

Actinic Business provides a library of design templates and color schemes to create a custom look for your site. This satisfies the needs of many businesses, especially when they do not have the resources for custom graphics. The program can also be directed to use graphics you've created, which provides an alternative to the pre-loaded design templates.

In the following sections, you learn how to use Actinic's design templates and how to replace their default images with your own graphics.

Using design templates

Design templates

Design templates are pre-designed Web pages included with an e-commerce or Web site development package. You enter your own information into the template, but the images and layout remain the same.

The exam does not specifically cover Actinic design templates. However, you should be familiar with the concept and purpose of design templates.

To access the Actinic design templates, choose Themes & Colors from the Design menu. The Themes & Colors interface is shown in Figure 15-1.

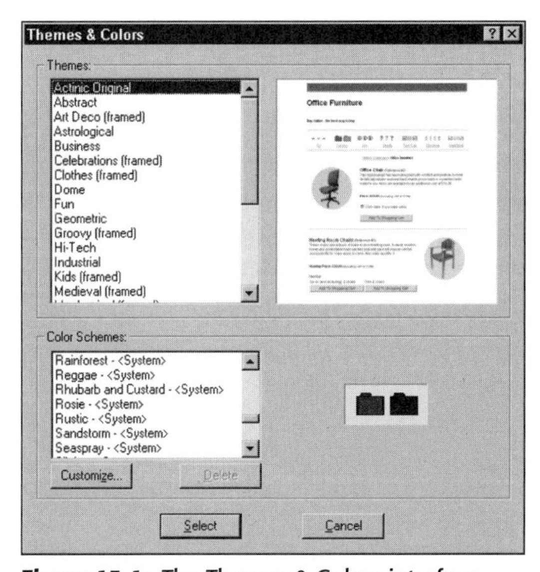

Figure 15-1: The Themes & Colors interface

The Themes & Colors interface works as follows:

- **Themes.** The top half of this interface is for selecting the site design theme. On the left, there's a scrolling list of available themes. To the right of the scrolling list is a small preview image of the theme. This image changes when you highlight a new theme in the selection field, which allows you to preview the theme before selecting it.
- **Color Schemes.** On the bottom half of this interface is the area for selecting a color scheme. As in the theme selection area, a list of options is provided in a scrolling list. A preview of how the color scheme looks when used with the selected design theme is presented in an image on the right. In addition, you can create a custom color scheme by clicking the Customize button beneath the scrolling list.

To select a pre-programmed design template using Actinic (including a design theme and color scheme to determine your design template), follow these steps:

1. If Actinic is not already open on your computer, start it.
2. Choose Themes & Colors from the Design menu.
3. The Themes & Colors window shown in Figure 15-1 appears.
4. In the top half of the window, use the scrolling list selection box to view the choices available for a design theme. Click on some of them that sound appealing to you and notice how the image to the right changes to show a preview of the selected theme. Choose Time as a theme.
5. In the Color Schemes area of the Themes & Colors dialog box, scroll through the color scheme choices, selecting some of them to see how the image to the right changes. Highlight Metallic Blues when you're done looking.
6. Click the Select button at the bottom of the window.
7. Actinic presents you with a warning to verify that you want to change your templates. Click OK.
8. Back in the main Actinic window, select Offline Preview from the Web menu to see a preview of the new theme and color scheme design in your default browser. Notice that the site contains the same information as it did previously, but the design has changed. The images associated with products and categories are the same as well — if you were to use this template for your real site, you might want to change those images to suit the new color scheme.
9. Because our site is Texas-themed, let's go back and choose another, more appropriate, template by returning to the main Actinic window, and choosing Themes & Colors from the Design menu.

10. Choose Wild West from the Themes, and Rustic from the Color Schemes areas of the Themes & Colors dialog box.
11. Click Select.
12. Choose Offline Preview from the Web menu to see a preview of the new design in your default browser.

Now, that's more like it. With some new product images, this display could be almost perfect for our site. Still, a company logo and customized navigation would be nice. For that, you have to delve into the world of custom graphics, which are described in the following section.

Using custom graphics

Custom graphics

There are many cases in which an e-commerce site should use its own graphics rather than a template. Using custom graphics virtually eliminates any risk of your Web site looking just like somebody else's. Actinic has built-in mechanisms for using your own graphics. Here's where you learn how to take advantage of that capability.

Be sure that you understand the key differences between design templates and custom graphics, as well as the benefits of each.

Adding a company logo

The first, and most important, part of using custom graphics is to put your company logo on the Web site. In this case, you need to add the Texas-Shaped.com logo, which is provided on the CD-ROM included with this book. To do so, follow these steps:

1. Insert the CD-ROM into your computer's CD-ROM drive.
2. Using Windows Explorer, copy the files in the `Texas-Shaped.com\misc_images\` folder of the CD-ROM to the to appropriate folder on your hard drive. In most cases this will be `C:\Program Files\Actinic ecommerce v4\Sites\Site 1\`. By copying these files, you make them available to Actinic for uploading to the server.
3. Return to the Actinic program window.
4. Choose Options from the Design menu to bring up the Design Options window.
5. In the Design Options window, select the Defaults tab, if it's not already in front. The window should look similar to Figure 15-2.

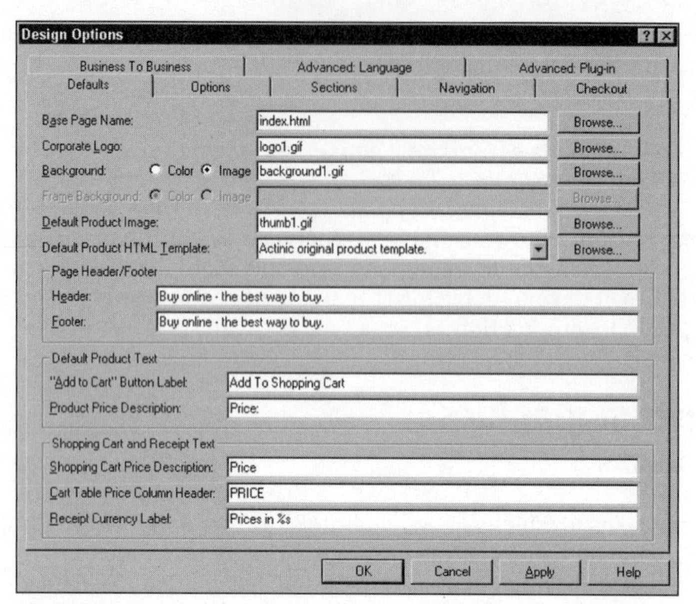

Figure 15-2: The Design Options window with the Defaults tab selected

6. Although there is quite a lot that can be done in this window, in this exercise, you just replace the logo image and the first line of text on the site. The Corporate Logo field has a default value of `logo1.gif`. To change this to the Texas-Shaped.com logo, click the Browse button to the right of the field and choose the file called `txshaped_logo_horiz.gif` from the folder you copied the images into.
7. Click Open. Now, the Corporate Logo field should have a value of `txshaped_logo_horiz.gif`.
8. Next, jump about halfway down the window to the section labeled Page Header/Footer. Replace the default text in the Header field with **Welcome to our store. Please take a look around!** and delete the text in the Footer field.
9. Click OK to make the changes.
10. Choose Offline Preview from the Web menu to see a preview of the site in your browser. It should look similar to Figure 15-3.

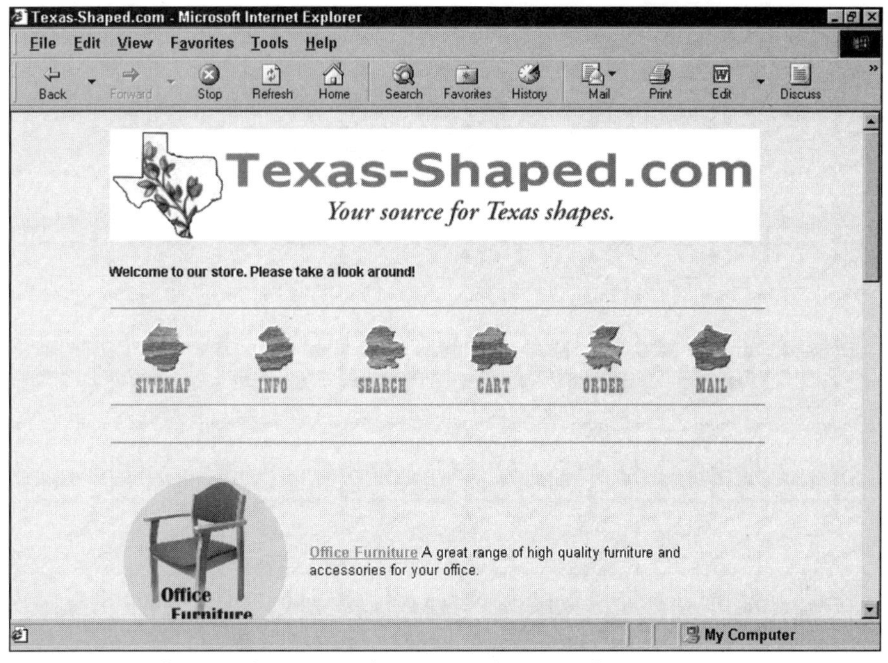

Figure 15-3: The template site with a custom logo graphic

Custom navigation and background

Now that the site has a custom logo, use the following steps to add custom navigation buttons and change the background color to match the new logo image:

1. To change to background color, select Options from the Design menu once again.
2. In the Design Options window, select the Defaults tab.
3. The third field on this screen is labeled Background (see Figure 15-3). There are two radio buttons labeled Color and Image. Select Color.
4. Click the Navigation tab, shown in Figure 15-4. This window can be used to change the images and labels associated with the items in your site's navigation. Each navigation item has two images: The first field is the default image shown, and the second field is the image shown when the user has his or her cursor over the image (also known as a *rollover*).

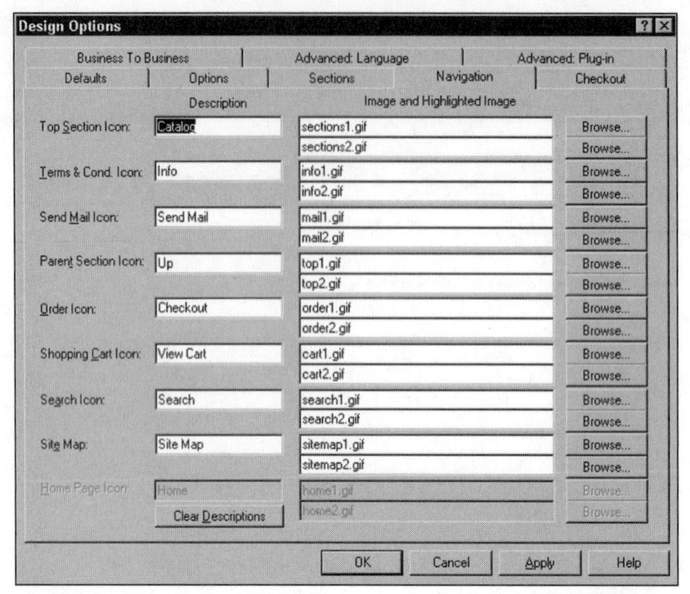

Figure 15-4: The Design Options window with the Navigation tab selected

5. Before you can change the navigation images, you must copy the custom navigation image files to the `Site 1` folder. These images are located in the `Texas-Shaped.com\nav_images\` folder of the CD-ROM.

6. Using the Browse button to the right of each field, replace each image name with the following, putting the first image listed into the top field, and the second image listed into the bottom field:

   - **Top Section Icon.** `tx_sections1.gif`, `tx_sections2.gif`
   - **Terms & Cond. Icon.** `tx_info1`.gif, `tx_info2.gif`
   - **Send Mail Icon.** `tx_mail1.gif`, `tx_mail2.gif`
   - **Parent Section Icon.** `tx_top1.gif`, `tx_top2.gif`
   - **Order Icon.** `tx_order1.gif`, `tx_order2.gif`
   - **Shopping Cart Icon.** `tx_cart1.gif`, `tx_cart2.gif`
   - **Search Icon.** `tx_search1.gif`, `tx_search2.gif`
   - **Site Map.** `tx_sitemap1.gif`, `tx_sitemap2.gif`

7. Click OK to make the changes.

8. Choose Offline Preview from Web menu to see a preview of the site with the new background color and navigation images in your browser. It should look like Figure 15-5.

Figure 15-5: The Texas-Shaped.com Web site with custom navigation graphics

In Chapter 16, you'll learn how to change category and product images.

Customizing the User Interface

Web site customization is more than just graphics; you also need to specify how the site works and designate the appropriate text for your business. Actinic interfaces allow you to make many changes to how the site is presented and how transactions are processed. In this section, you start making those changes.

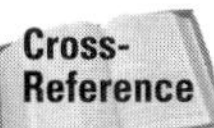

In Chapter 17, you'll configure Actinic to handle your store's online transactions.

One of the most important steps in site customization is to make sure the text describing your company and its policies is present and accurate. To take a look at how the information is currently displayed, and then modify it so it's more appropriate for your own site, follow these steps:

1. Open Actinic and select Offline Preview from the Web menu.
2. A preview of the site opens in your default browser (see Figure 15-5).
3. Scroll to the bottom of this page to see the Information section — a lot of text describing the site and its policies. Although this is the default setting, for most sites, it's preferable to house this information on a separate page.

4. Choose Options from the Design menu to open the Design Options window.
5. In the Design Options window, select the Options tab to bring it to the front. The bottom section of the Options window is labeled Information Link. In this area, there are four radio buttons to choose from:
   - None
   - Terms and Conditions on Separate Catalog Page
   - Terms and Conditions on Catalog Front Page (selected by default)
   - URL (a custom URL can be entered if this radio button is selected)
6. Select the radio button labeled Terms and Conditions on Separate Catalog Page.
7. Click the OK button to close the Design Options window.
8. Select Offline Preview from the Web menu to preview the change you've just made.
9. Click the About Us navigation item to see the new page. It should look similar to Figure 15-6.

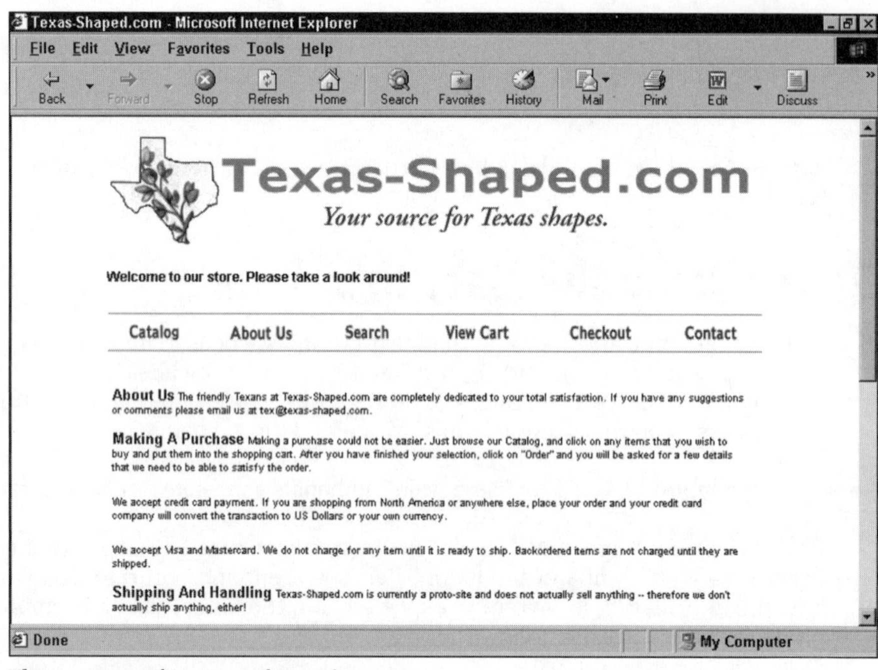

Figure 15-6: The new Information page

10. To populate the page with correct information about this Web site, choose Business Settings from the View menu to open the Business Settings window.

11. Select the Terms and Conditions tab, shown in Figure 15-7.

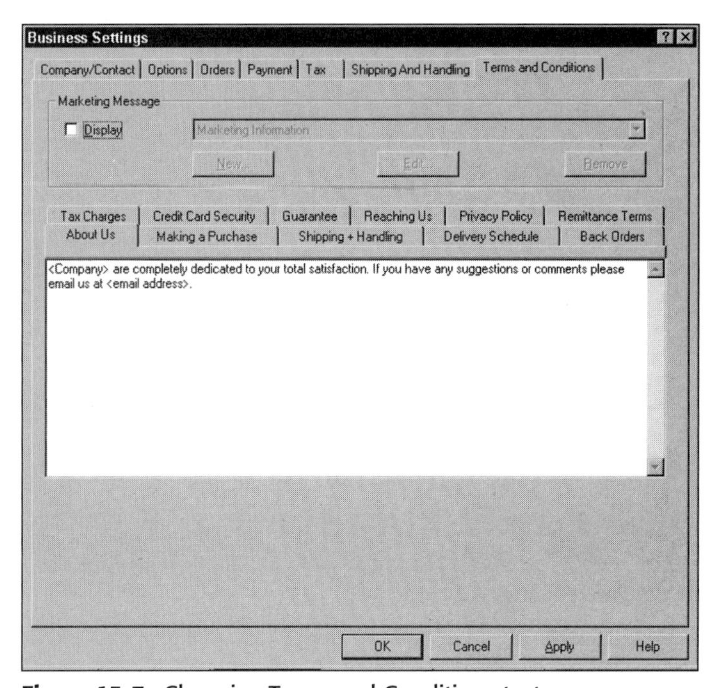

Figure 15-7: Changing Terms and Conditions text

12. The lower half of the window consists of eleven tabs, each corresponding to a section of the Information page. Go through each tab one by one, editing the text. Your edits do not need to be extensive, but at the very least replace the text in brackets (such as <Company>) with the appropriate information (in this case, **Texas-Shaped.com**).

13. After you're done, click OK and select Offline Preview from the Web menu to look at your changes. The text in the About Us page should have changed according to your edits.

Key Point Summary

This chapter covered the purpose of Web site customization, basic Web design issues, and started the process of customizing a site using Actinic Business. The key points in this chapter are:

- ✦ The two main components of Web site customization are:
  - Design
  - Business practices
- ✦ A Web site's graphics and layout are used to promote its identity and distinguish it from competitors.
- ✦ The key components of Web site design are:
  - Colors
  - Logo
  - Layout
  - Navigation scheme
- ✦ The two most common placements for Web site navigation are the top of the page and the left side of the page.
- ✦ Design templates are pre-designed Web pages provided by an e-commerce or Web site development software package.
- ✦ For most businesses, custom graphics are preferable to design templates because they virtually eliminate the risk of the site being confused with another site.

✦ ✦ ✦

STUDY GUIDE

In this chapter, you learned the importance of Web site customization and started customizing the Texas-Shaped.com case study site. Before moving on to Chapter 16, take a moment to assess your knowledge and complete an advanced customization exercise.

Assessment Questions

1. Which of the following is *not* an advantage of using Web design templates, as opposed to custom graphics? (Choose the best answer.)

A. Less expensive

B. Less time-consuming

C. More unique

D. More expensive

2. Which of the following businesses is most likely to use a design template?

A. Large clothes maker

B. Book distributor

C. Grocery store chain

D. Small bookstore

3. Which of the following is *not* recommended on a site geared toward senior citizens?

A. Large blocks of small print

B. Standard navigation design

C. Pleasing color scheme

D. Standard banner ad placement

4. Which of the following is *not* a key component of a Web site design? (Choose the best answer.)

A. Navigation scheme

B. Banner ad placement

C. Colors

D. Layout

Scenarios

1. Take a look at the Texas-Shaped.com Web site as it currently looks in your offline preview (select Web, Offline Preview from the Actinic menu) and determine how you would change its design for the following audiences:
   - Children
   - Seniors
2. In the next chapter, you'll add the product catalog and product images to the Texas-Shaped.com site. How do you think the products should be presented? Do you think the current layout of the product list is good?

Lab Exercises

Lab 15-1 Advanced customization: Using Template Manager

Actinic uses a series of HTML templates to generate Web pages for your site. In this exercise, you become familiar with Actinic's Template Manager, and make changes to some of the templates' code.

1. In the main Actinic window, choose Web, Offline Preview from the menu to open the main page of the Texas-Shaped.com Web catalog in your browser (see Figure 15-5). Notice how there's a horizontal line between the line directly beneath the navigation items and above the catalog section listing. That line isn't very aesthetically pleasing, is it? Let's use the Template Manager to get rid of it.
2. In the main Actinic window, choose Advanced, Template Manager from the menu. The Template Manager window will open (Figure 15-8).

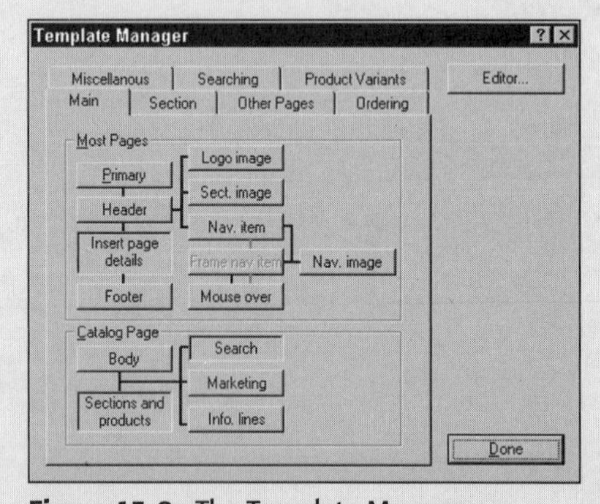

Figure 15-8: The Template Manager

3. In the Template Manager Window, the Main tab should be selected. If it isn't, click it to bring it to the front. This window shows a breakdown of the templates that make up the different parts of the Web site. Each button corresponds to a different template, and clicking on a button opens that template in a text editor, usually Notepad.

4. To delete the extra line in the catalog page of your site, go to the bottom area of the window (labeled Catalog Page) and click the Body button.

5. The code for the template `Act_CatalogBody.html` opens in Notepad (see Figure 15-9). We're looking for the following code, which that makes the horizontal line above the list of categories:

   ```
   <HR SIZE="1" ALIGN="CENTER" WIDTH="600">
   ```

   Delete that code and save the document by selecting File, Save from the Notepad menu.

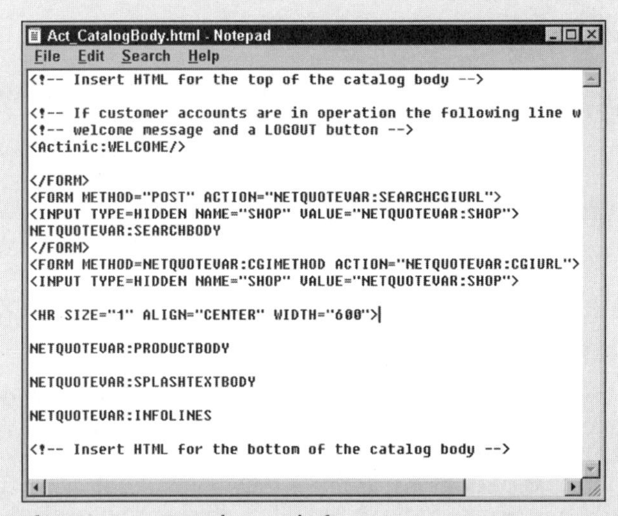

```
<!-- Insert HTML for the top of the catalog body -->

<!-- If customer accounts are in operation the following line w
<!-- welcome message and a LOGOUT button -->
<Actinic:WELCOME/>

</FORM>
<FORM METHOD="POST" ACTION="NETQUOTEVAR:SEARCHCGIURL">
<INPUT TYPE=HIDDEN NAME="SHOP" VALUE="NETQUOTEVAR:SHOP">
NETQUOTEVAR:SEARCHBODY
</FORM>
<FORM METHOD=NETQUOTEVAR:CGIMETHOD ACTION="NETQUOTEVAR:CGIURL">
<INPUT TYPE=HIDDEN NAME="SHOP" VALUE="NETQUOTEVAR:SHOP">

<HR SIZE="1" ALIGN="CENTER" WIDTH="600">

NETQUOTEVAR:PRODUCTBODY

NETQUOTEVAR:SPLASHTEXTBODY

NETQUOTEVAR:INFOLINES

<!-- Insert HTML for the bottom of the catalog body -->
```

Figure 15-9: Template code for `Act_CatalogBody.html` in Notepad

6. Return to the main Actinic window, and close the Template Manager by clicking Done.

7. Choose Offline Preview from the Web menu to take a look at this change. It should look like Figure 15-10.

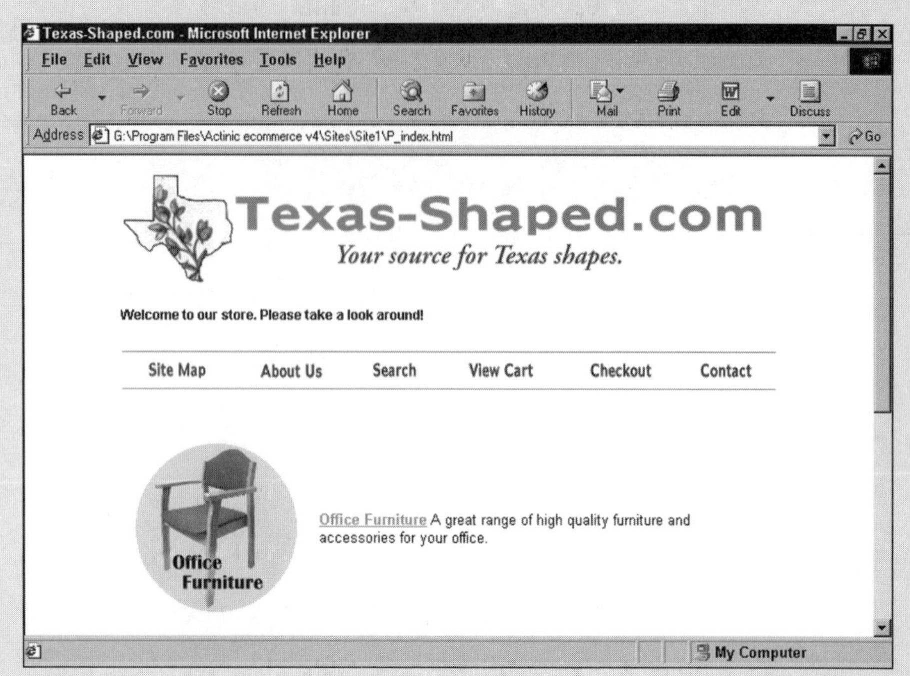

Figure 15-10: The results of using Template Manager: Look, no line!

Lab 15-2 More advanced customization: using an image as the Add to Cart button

In this exercise, you learn another advanced Actinic customization technique that allows you to specify an image to replace the default Add to Shopping Cart button.

1. Return to the Offline Preview of Texas-Shaped.com in your browser. Click on Office Furniture from the categories listed. The Office Furniture section opens with a list of products. Notice how each product has an Add to Shopping Cart button (see Figure 15-11).

2. If you didn't do it in an earlier exercise, copy the `addcart.gif` image file from the `Texas-Shaped.com\misc_images\` folder to the `C:\Program Files\Actinic ecommerce v4\Sites\Site 1\` folder.

3. In the Actinic main window, choose Template Manager from the Advanced menu to open the Template Manager window (see Figure 15-8).

4. Click the Section tab to bring it to the front. See Figure 15-12 for how this should look.

5. In second column is a button labeled Cart. Click it to open the template in Notepad.

Figure 15-11: The Add to Shopping Cart button

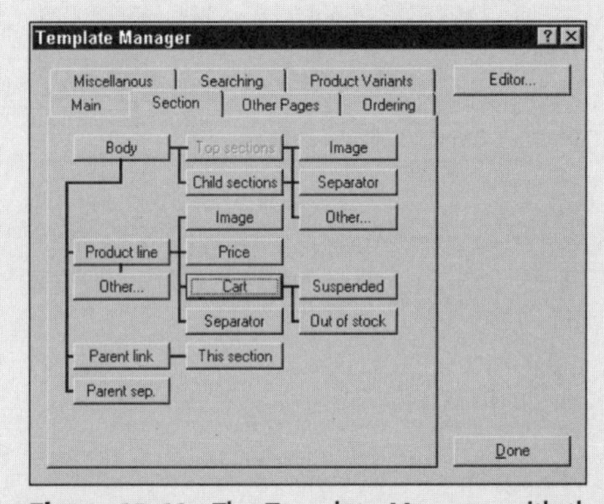

Figure 15-12: The Template Manager with the Section tab selected

6. Replace the code:

```
<P><INPUT TYPE=SUBMIT VALUE="NETQUOTEVAR:BUTTONLABEL"
NAME="NETQUOTEVAR:BUTTONNAME">
```

with:

```
<P><INPUT TYPE="IMAGE" BORDER="0"
SRC="NETQUOTEVAR:BUTTONLABEL.gif"
NAME="NETQUOTEVAR:BUTTONNAME">
```

7. Select File, Save in the Notepad menu to save this change.
8. Return to the Actinic main window and close the Template Manger by clicking Done.
9. Now, you need to specify a value for BUTTONLABEL. Start by opening the Design Options window (choose Options from the Design menu).
10. In the Design Options window, select the Defaults tab to bring it to the front.
11. In the section labeled Default Product Text, locate the field labeled Add to Cart Button Label. Here, enter the name of our new image (`addcart.gif`) but without the file extension — in other words, enter **addcart**.
12. Click OK to make this change and close the window.
13. Select Advanced, Additional Files. Click Add in this window, and then find and select the graphic called `addcart.gif` in the directory where you copied the image in Step 2 (`C:\Program Files\Actinic ecommerce v4\Sites\Site 1\`, assuming that Actinic is installed at this location on your computer). You may need to change the file type in the browse window to be able to locate the image file. Adding a file in the Additional Files window simply tells Actinic to include this file when it is uploading the site to your server.
14. Select Offline Preview from the Web menu to refresh the preview in your browser. Now, the Add to Shopping Cart buttons should be replaced with our `addcart.gif` image, as shown in Figure 15-13.

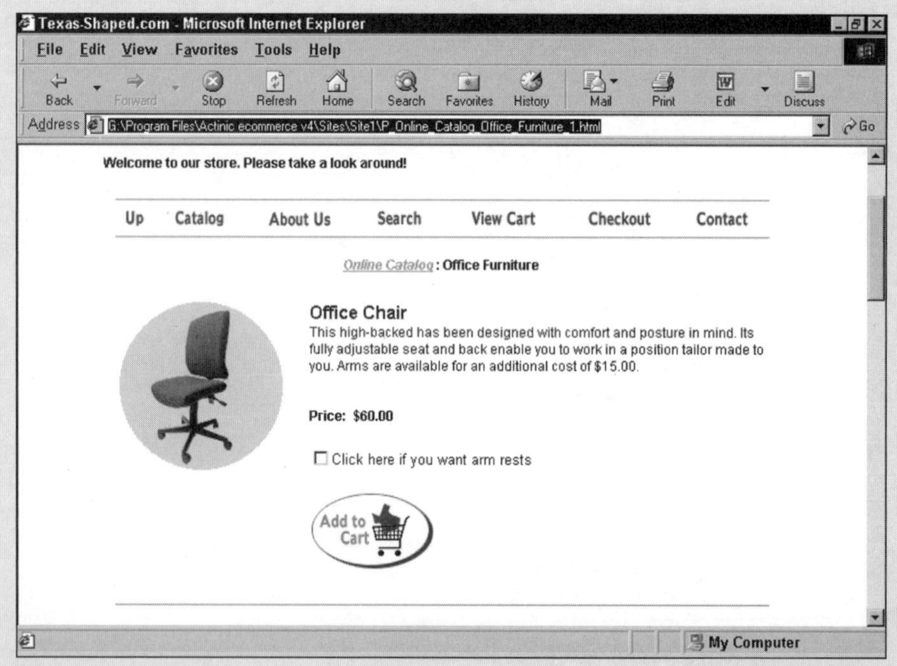

Figure 15-13: The `addcart.gif` image has replaced the Add to Shopping Cart button.

Answers to Chapter Questions

Chapter pre-test

1. The key components of Web design are:
   - Colors
   - Logo
   - Layout
   - Navigation scheme
2. Web site customization is important for two reasons:
   - To program your company's business practices (such as sales tax and shipping charges) into the e-commerce ordering system
   - To uniquely identify your site
3. Web site navigation should behave consistently so the user does not become confused. For example, if a user comes to expect a certain result when he or she clicks on a navigation item, the user may be confused if this is not the result of clicking on another navigation item.
4. In most cases, Web site navigation should not be placed along the right side of a page because some users — particularly those with monitors set to low resolutions — may not be able to see the navigation without scrolling.
5. Design templates are pre-designed Web pages provided by an e-commerce or Web site development software package.

Assessment questions

1. **C.** Design templates actually create pages that are less unique (see "Understanding Web Site Customization").
2. **D.** Small businesses with limited budgets are most likely to use design templates (see "Understanding Web Site Customization").
3. **A.** Small text can be very hard for seniors to read, especially on a computer screen (see "Audience drives design goals").
4. **B.** This is a bit of a trick question. Banner ad placement is not a *key* component of a Web site design — rather, it's a subcategory of the layout component (see "Web design fundamentals").

Scenarios

1. You can improve this design for the specific audiences mentioned as follows:
   - **Children.** You might want to add images to the navigation items, so children who cannot read can still navigate the site. Also, the site could be made more colorful and you could add some audio for feedback.
   - **Seniors.** The site is fairly well suited to seniors. The images are large and clear, and the text sizes are, for the most part, adequately sized. You might want to increase the default text size for the product names and descriptions.
2. This answer is largely subjective — there really is no "correct" answer. Some possible ways to redesign the product listings are:
   - Smaller product images would allow more products to be presented on the screen before the user needs to scroll. On the other hand, smaller images make the products harder to see.
   - Put all product images on the left or right. Currently, the product images alternate between being to the left and the right of the product description. For many designs, it may be preferable to consistently have the images on one side or the other.
   - Bring text closer together. Currently, the price and attributes for each product are a few lines below the end of the product description. The Add to Cart button is even lower. One way to keep the product images large but still tighten the layout might be to bring the prices and attributes up closer to the bottom of the description, and perhaps put the Add to Cart button to the right of the price.

For More Information . . .

✦ **Colour Blind Design Hints and Tips.** www.cimmerii.demon.co.uk/colourblind/design.html

✦ **Lynda.com (Lynda Weinman's Web design site).** www.lynda.com

✦ **WebVoodoo's WebDesignClinic, Introduction to Color.** www.webdesignclinic.com/ezine/v1i1/color/

Operating and Enhancing E-Commerce Sites

P A R T

IV

✦ ✦ ✦ ✦

In This Part

✦ ✦ ✦ ✦

CHAPTER 16

Creating Online Catalogs

✦ ✦ ✦ ✦

EXAM OBJECTIVES

- Online catalog components
- Store categories
- Building an Internet catalog
- Creating products and items

CHAPTER PRE-TEST

1. Why should products in a catalog be divided into categories?
2. What are product attributes?
3. What is the role of a shopping cart in an e-commerce Web site?

✦ Answers to these questions can be found at the end of the chapter. ✦

In Chapter 15, you found out how to customize the look and feel of an e-commerce site. In this chapter, you examine the concepts, issues, and techniques involved in creating a catalog for an e-commerce site. You then discover how to create a catalog that enhances the user's experience and, hopefully, increases the number of sales on your site.

Understanding Online Catalog Functions and Components

Online catalog components

A *catalog* is a group of products or services that can be browsed by customers. Creation of your product catalog is where the abstract usability concepts we discussed in Chapter 5 get put into practice. At this point, it's useful to recall the four goals customers have in e-commerce:

1. Getting to the site.
2. Locating a product or service.
3. Researching a product or service.
4. Purchasing a product.

How successful customers are in achieving Steps 2 and 3 in this list is directly dependent upon how usable the catalog is. The usability of your catalog is determined by how easy it is for customers to locate items. As we discussed Chapter 5, most e-commerce Web sites provide two ways for customers to locate products:

- ✦ Through searching
- ✦ By navigating a hierarchical structure (browsing)

Catalog searching

Searching capabilities are usually provided in one of two ways — either by searching a database (querying) or by searching the site's HTML and text files.

Database searching (querying)

The first method of searching is the more flexible. For example, Table 16-1 shows a portion of a product catalog as it may appear in a simple, flat file (not relational) database.

Table 16-1
A Sample Table of Products

Product	*Description*	*Color*	*Size*	*Price*	*In Stock?*
Tennis Shoes	Good shoes for tennis.	White	10	$48.99	Yes
Running Shoes	Run faster with these shoes.	Black	13	$78.99	Yes
Golf Shoes	Improve your game by wearing these shoes.	Brown	14	$89.99	Yes
Gardening Shoes	A little dirt won't hurt these shoes.	Green	9	$34.95	No

With the products stored in a database table, complex searches can be performed to locate the exact desired item. For example, a customer could search for products that cost less than $50.00 and are white and larger than size 9. The database table provides structure to the information and thereby enables this type of querying.

There are great benefits to searching site databases directly. In some instances, however, it's not ideal. For example, it doesn't make sense to store some parts of an e-commerce site in a database. If a page of information about a product changes very infrequently, storing that information as an HTML file rather than in the database can reduce the load on the server and increase performance.

For this reason, some e-commerce packages, including Actinic Business, store products in a database until you publish them to the live site. During the publishing process, the products in the database are turned into static HTML pages that can then be used on the site without the overhead of querying the database whenever a product listing is requested.

Full-text searching

In contrast to a database table, an index of text and HTML documents has very little structure. Consider the following excerpt (see Listing 16-1) from a static HTML page that might contain one of the products listed in Table 16-1.

Listing 16-1: Excerpt from an HTML product page

```
. . .
<h1>Golf Shoes</h1>
<p>Improve your game by wearing shoes. These shoes should not
be used for playing basketball or tennis.</p>
<p><b>Price:</b> <i>only</i> $89.99<br />
<b>Color:</b> Brown<br />
```

```
<b>Size:</b> 14<br />
</p>
...
```

HTML pages usually have very little useful structure for searching. Most HTML search engines allow you to perform only a full-text search on this document. Full-text searches generally rank search results by the number of times search words appear in a document and where they appear in a document. However, because a full-text search doesn't have any way of knowing what the text means, full-text searching is much less exact than querying a database. For example, because the words *basketball* and *tennis* appear in the document in Listing 16-1, it's highly likely that this page about golf shoes would also appear in the search results for either of these search terms.

The `meta` element is often used to add structured information to HTML documents. The `meta` element is explained in Chapter 4.

XML to the rescue

One solution to the problems of database queries and full-text searches is provided by the Extensible Markup Language (XML). XML, as you saw in Chapter 7, is a metalanguage. Like a database, documents marked up using XML can contain detailed information about what the data is. Like plain text and HTML documents, XML is simple to use and can be served very quickly by a Web server.

Pure XML, however, does not (by itself) contain any information about how data should be displayed in a Web browser, and there is no simple and widely used and agreed upon replacement for HTML's formatting capabilities. As a result, it's difficult to use on Web sites. As a temporary solution, the Extensible Hypertext Markup Language (XHTML) has been created. XHTML is a cross between HTML and XML. It allows you to use (with some restrictions) familiar HTML elements (such as `p`, `img`, and so forth), but it also allows you to take advantage of the data structuring capabilities of XML.

Exam Tip You should know that XHTML is a reformulation of HTML using XML.

Listing 16-2 shows an example of how the HTML excerpt from Listing 16-1 might look in XHTML with XML markup used to describe the data.

Listing 16-2: Excerpt from an XHTML product page

```
...
<product>
<h1><product_name>Golf Shoes</product_name></h1>
<p><product_description>Improve your game by wearing shoes.
These shoes should not be used for playing basketball or
tennis.</product_description></p>
<p><b>Price:</b> <i>only</i>
<price>$89.99</price><br />
<b>Color:</b>
<color>Brown</color><br />
<b>Size:</b>
<size>14</size><br />
</p>
</product>
...
```

XHTML documents can combine the descriptive capabilities of XML with the browser compatibility of HTML to create Web sites that can be easily and accurately searched.

As you saw in Chapter 7, XML is most widely used in e-commerce as a standard language for transferring data between computers or computer programs.

Structuring a hierarchical catalog

Although many of the users of an e-commerce site simply search for the items they need, others want to browse the site using a more traditional method. The structure of the catalog makes this possible.

The three major components of an online catalog are:

✦ Categories

✦ Products

✦ Attributes

We look closer at each of these in the following sections of this chapter.

Categories and sub-categories

Store categories

Most catalogs divide a store's products or services into groups. Other names for these groups include: categories, departments, or divisions. The catalog's categories generally determine how the site can be navigated. Although this may seem, at first glance, to be intuitive, creating an effective hierarchical catalog structure is one of the most difficult parts of creating an e-commerce site.

To understand why creating a hierarchical structure is difficult, consider the example of shoes from Table 16-1. We only know a few pieces of information about each shoe, but there are already several ways this information could be divided into categories. It appears that sports could be used as the top-level categories for these products. The gardening shoes don't fit easily into this scheme, however.

Another way to organize the products is by size. The home page of the site could ask for your shoe size, and then display all of the shoes available in your size. A potential problem with this way of organizing the products is that it may result in a large number of products being displayed in which the customer has no interest. For example, a gardener with size 10 feet would be shown all of the size 10 basketball shoes along with the gardening shoes.

The third way these products might be organized at the top level is by gender. Although this is rather broad, it's likely to be the best way to categorize these products at the top level. At the very least, it makes a user's first choice in navigating your site obvious. Of course, once this first choice is made, the user still requires sub-categories in order to navigate to the products he or she wants to view.

As this example demonstrates, it's important to plan ahead when deciding on a catalog structure. Later in this chapter, in the "Establishing business objectives" section, you find out more about planning ahead. For now, we go back to our demonstration store, Texas-Shaped.com, and explain the types of products in the catalog and how they should be organized.

Products and services

Products and services, naturally, are the actual things your store exists to sell. One of the most time-consuming aspects of making the transition to e-commerce is entering data about these products and services into the catalog.

Some of the types of information that may be included in a typical product listing include:

- Product number, or Stock Keeping Unit (SKU)
- Product name
- Description (and perhaps even multiple levels of descriptions, or several different kinds of descriptive information, such as technical specifications)
- Price
- Discount price
- Product images
- Inventory information

✦ On sale date

✦ Product categorization information

Options and attributes

The lowest levels in a hierarchical catalog are product options and attributes. Options and attributes are choices the user needs to make after he or she has chosen a particular product.

To better understand options and attributes in a catalog, consider the example of buying a vehicle. The first decision you must make is the type of vehicle you want. You can choose from motorcycles, trucks, bicycles, cars, and so forth. If you choose to buy a car, there are additional choices you need to make, such as whether you want a sports car or a station wagon. These choices are all considered category-level choices.

After numerous category choices, you eventually decide to purchase a particular product, the Gutwagen Extranto 500BLT. The Gutwagen Extranto 500BLT comes in several colors. You can also get leather seats, power steering, and a CB radio if you like. None of these attributes or options changes the fact that you're purchasing a Gutwagen Extranto 500BLT.

Although options and attributes are both lower in the catalog hierarchy than products, there are differences between options and attributes, as follows:

✦ **Attributes.** These are usually variable properties of a product (such as color or size) that must be chosen and do not have additional costs associated with them.

✦ **Options.** These are generally add-on products or features that have additional costs associated with them. Options can often be products that are available for purchase by themselves elsewhere in a store. Products can be associated with each other to enable cross-selling or up-selling. For example, a customer purchasing a stapler might also be interested in other related office supplies, such as staples.

There are clearly many decisions that need to be made when creating an online storefront. In the following section, you find out how catalog and categorization decisions should be made.

Building Internet Catalogs

Building an Internet catalog

At this point, you may feel like we're spending an exorbitant amount of time explaining a simple concept. You would be surprised, however, at how often there's confusion or debate on the issue of whether similar items are different products or the same product with different attributes. Unfortunately, there's no good rule for making this decision.

As we mentioned earlier, a good catalog design should, at the very least, make it easy for customers to locate specific products. If a customer wants a toothbrush, he or she should be able to locate it with a minimal number of clicks.

For many types of stores, however, giving customers the ability to easily browse or explore the catalog without a specific goal in mind is just as important. For this type of user, flexibility is important. The site shouldn't contain dead-end links, and different sections (if not all of the sections) of the site should be easily accessible from anywhere else on the site.

Establishing business objectives

The first step in deciding how to categorize your products is to establish or analyze your business objectives for the site. The more clearly the objectives of your store are defined, the more effective your store will be.

Planning is important in e-commerce, and this is emphasized on the exam. Establishing goals and objectives is usually the first step in any e-commerce venture or activity.

Some typical business objectives for an e-commerce catalog might include:

- Attract new customers to the company's products
- Reduce the cost of selling to existing customers
- Reach a broader audience
- Sell new products
- Provide better service to customers
- Sell surplus items
- Sell products to businesses

Chapter 3 covers establishing business goals and objectives in more detail.

Starting an online catalog

After you've examined your e-commerce objectives, the next step in building an online catalog is to gather vital data about the products or services you'll be selling. A good starting point for this step is to simply make a list of the products you intend to sell.

If you're transitioning an existing paper catalog to the Web, you have a head start, but as you'll find as you read on, what works well for paper catalogs may not necessarily work well for online catalogs.

Remember that Web users are goal-oriented. This doesn't mean that Web users don't "browse the aisles," however. It simply means they shouldn't have to browse if they don't want to.

Categorizing catalog data

Many print catalogs simply arrange products on pages without any sort of apparent categorization scheme. Perhaps the best examples of this type of print catalog are the major computer catalogs that arrive in our mailboxes by the dozens. Although it may not be obvious at first, these catalogs probably do have some sort of organization scheme. It's usually not based on maximum usability, though. Organization in print catalogs may be based on who paid the most for the ad or which products are on sale. This is fine (and often desired) when users can flip through the catalog, browsing the pages for whatever catches their eye.

Although we do not pretend to understand what goes on in the minds of Web surfers, we suspect that people are much more reluctant to click a link than they are to flip a page or move to the next aisle—simply because of the delays and the uncertainty involved in clicking.

In online catalogs, however, lack of logical organization tends to turn visitors off. If you look at a typical Web site for a mail order computer catalog, you'll notice that logical organization of the products is obviously important. For the most part, these sites do an admirable job at organizing the vast number of products they must contain. The navigation generally allows visitors to search, as well as to navigate to specific products using a variety of different paths.

For example, check out `www.warehouse.com`. To locate a toner cartridge for a laser printer using this site, you can click first on Printers and then on Supplies. Or, you could click first on Supplies and then on Printer Supplies. Another way to locate the toner cartridge for your specific printer is to first locate your printer, and the toner cartridges are often listed as add-on products.

After you've analyzed your business objectives and you have a list of the products and services you intend to sell, you can start creating categories and fitting the products into these categories.

Case Study Catalog

Texas-Shaped.com is a fictitious (for now) store that sells products shaped like the state of Texas. Our extensive market research has shown that the shape of Texas is very popular in, as well as outside of, Texas. Inside the state, Texas-shaped items are not difficult to locate. Outside of Texas, however, these items can be more difficult to find.

As a new online-only store, Texas-Shaped.com doesn't have an existing product list to work from to develop the catalog. The number of Texas-shaped items that can be acquired is truly mind-boggling, though. Everything from blocks of cheese to T-shirts, to stained glass windows, to swimming pools is available in the shape of Texas.

Refining the product list

In planning our store, we decided that the Texas-shaped items best suited for sale through the Web all have the following characteristics:

- They are non-perishable.
- They can be easily shipped.
- There are no restrictions on their sale or shipment.
- They are priced for sale to a large audience.

This list of characteristics eliminates products such as swimming pools, weapons, perishable food items, and buildings from our catalog, and leaves us with a long list of novelty and gift items. To simplify the process of starting up the site (as well as to reduce the need for inventory storage), the limited list of products (shown in Table 16-2) has been established.

Table 16-2
Texas-Shaped.com Products

Product name	***Price***
Gift Basket	$45.00
Key Chain	$3.00
Refrigerator Magnet	$4.50
Texas Recipe Book	$15.00
Notepad	$5.00
Dallas Playing Cards	$10.00
Austin Playing Cards	$10.00
Houston Playing Cards	$10.00
San Antonio Playing Cards	$10.00
Texas Puzzle	$15.00
Guide to Not Messing with Texas	$12.00
Map of Texas	$6.00

Continued

Table 16-2 *(continued)*

Product name	***Price***
Framed Map of Texas	$30.00
Laminated Map of Texas	$12.00
Sounds of Texas	$20.00
Texas-Shaped CD Player	$219.00
Clock Radio	$25.00
Wall Clock	$15.00
History of Texas	$45.00
Pictures of Texas	$55.00
Texas Truckin' Songs	$22.00
Texas Sing-Along	$18.00
"I'm not from Texas" Coffee Mug	$7.00
Texas Sunglasses	$14.00

Developing a hierarchical outline

An analysis of our products and our business objectives leads us to a hierarchical list of categories for our e-commerce site. These categories and subcategories are shown in a hierarchical outline in Listing 16-3.

Listing 16-3: **Hierarchical outline of the Texas-Shaped.com catalog categories**

```
A. Novelty Items
B. Electronics
C. Music
D. Books
   1. Children's Books
   2. Coffee table Books
   3. History and Culture
E. Games and Puzzles
   1. Playing Cards
   2. Puzzles
   3. Games
F. Maps
```

Adding categories to an online catalog

Now that we have a list of products and a list of categories, we can begin adding these to the catalog in Actinic Business. The first step in creating the catalog is to rename the catalog and to delete the demonstration products and categories.

Renaming the catalog

To rename the catalog in Actinic Business, follow these steps:

1. If Actinic is not already open on your computer, start it.
2. Right-click on the name of the catalog (currently Online Catalog) and select the Edit option from the pop-up menu.
3. You should see a window containing the words Online Catalog. Replace this with **Texas-Shaped.com**.

Deleting the demonstration products

To delete the demonstration products and categories in Actinic, follow these steps:

1. Right-click on the Office Furniture category and select Delete from the pop-up menu.
2. After you delete the category, the icon next to the category name, and the icons of all the sub-categories and products in that category are crossed out with red Xs.
3. Repeat Step 1 to delete the other top-level category, Office Supplies, and its sub-categories, so all of the demonstration products have Xs over them, as shown in Figure 16-1.
4. Products marked for deletion (with the red Xs) are still in the database and are still recoverable. To complete the deletion of these demonstration products, choose Purge, Purge Catalog from the Housekeeping menu, as shown in Figure 16-2.

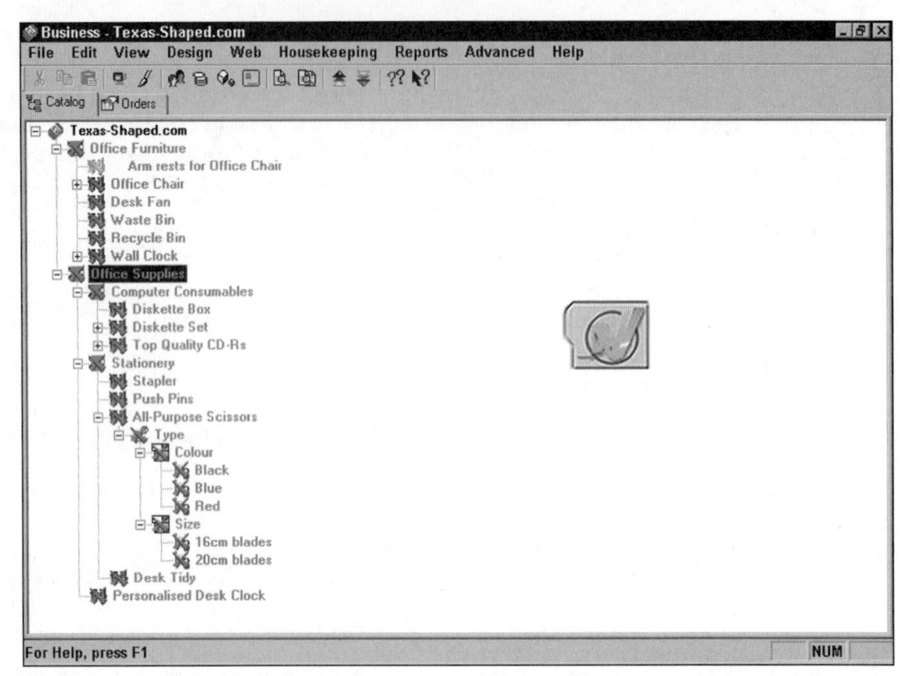

Figure 16-1: Actinic Business with all of the demo products marked for deletion

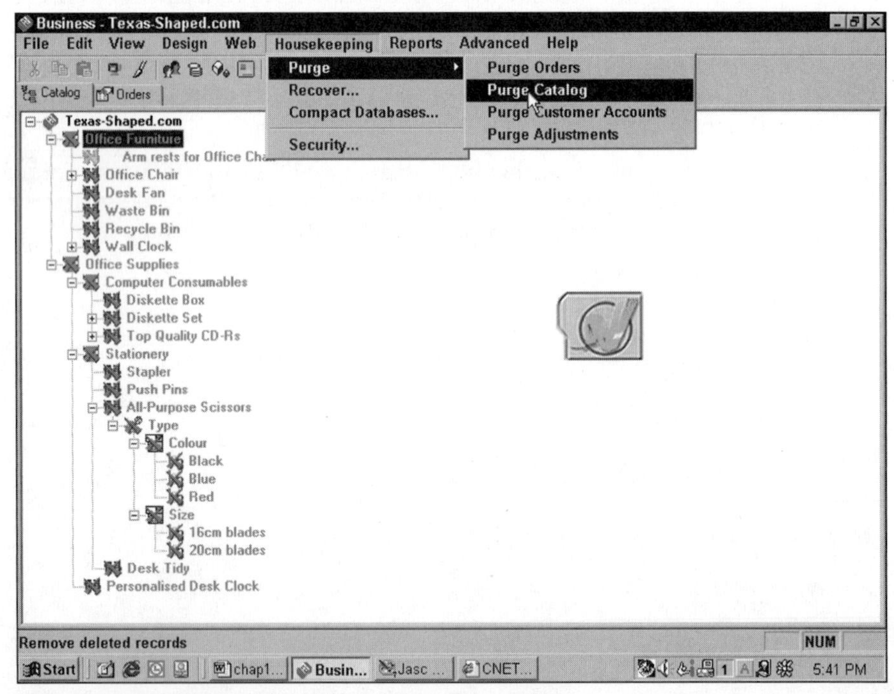

Figure 16-2: Purging deleted items from the catalog

Adding categories

You should now have a clean slate from which to begin building the Texas-Shaped.com catalog. To add categories to the catalog, follow these steps:

1. Right-click the name of the catalog (Texas-Shaped.com) and select New Section from the pop-up menu.

Tip

Actinic Business refers to categories in your catalog as *sections*.

2. When you're prompted for the name of the new section, enter the name of the first catalog category (section) **Novelty Items** (refer to Listing 16-3), and then click OK. The new category is added as the first branch, or *node*, under the name of the catalog, as shown in Figure 16-3.

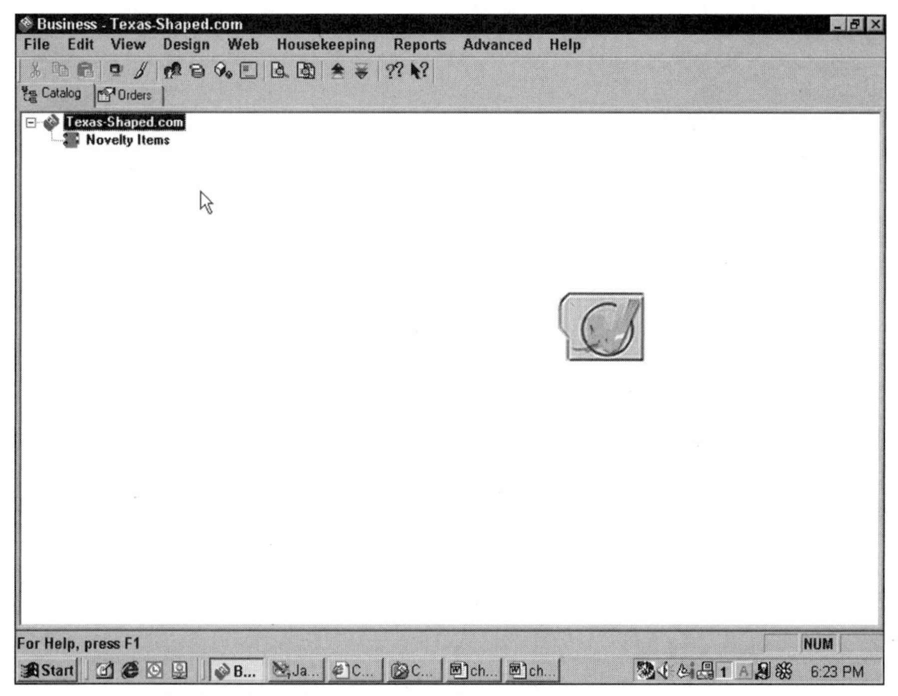

Figure 16-3: The first branch, or node, in the catalog tree

3. After you've added the Novelty Items category, repeat the previous steps to create the other five top-level categories, which are:
   - Electronics
   - Music
   - Books

- Games and Puzzles
- Maps

4. According to our hierarchical categorization from Listing 16-3, two of the top-level categories have sub-categories. To add these, highlight the Books category. Right-click it and select the New Sub-Section option from the pop-up menu.
5. Enter the name of the first sub-section (**Children's Books**), and then click OK.
6. Repeat this process for each of the sub-sections of the Books category and then for the sub-sections of the Games and Puzzles category (see Listing 16-3).
7. The resulting catalog tree is shown in Figure 16-4.

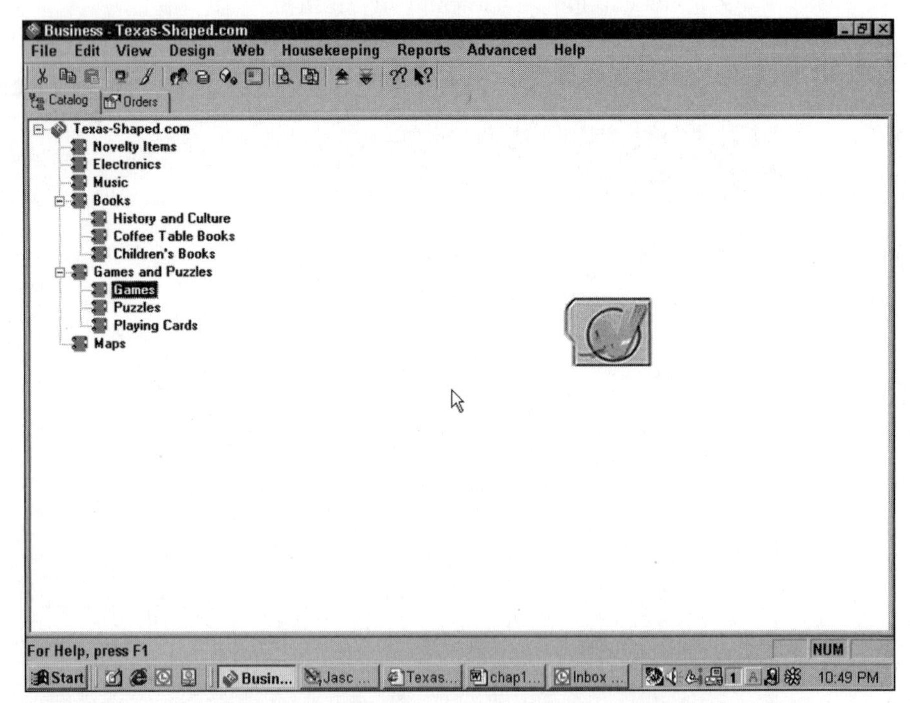

Figure 16-4: The completed tree of categories and sub-categories for Texas-Shaped.com

Adding custom category images

If you preview the site using Actinic's Offline Preview feature, you notice the Catalog image is used as the default image for each of the categories. To use a custom image for each of the sections, follow these steps:

1. Right-click the name of a section and select Edit from the pop-up menu.
2. Click the Advanced button in the pop-up window to view the advanced configuration options (the Section dialog box), as shown in Figure 16-5.

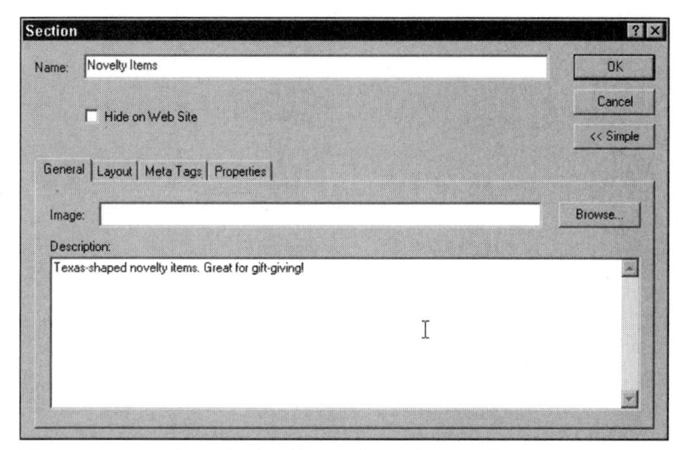

Figure 16-5: The advanced configuration options

Note that descriptions you enter into the Description text box appear next to the name of the category on the site.

3. Click the Browse button to the right of the Image text box to locate an image to use as the category image. You can find the category images for Texas-Shaped.com in the folder called `category_images` in the Texas-Shaped.com folder on the CD-ROM that comes with this book.
4. For each category and sub-category, locate the corresponding image in the `category_images` folder and select it.
5. Click OK to close the Category editing window when you're finished.
6. Preview the site. The home page should look similar to the page shown in Figure 16-6.

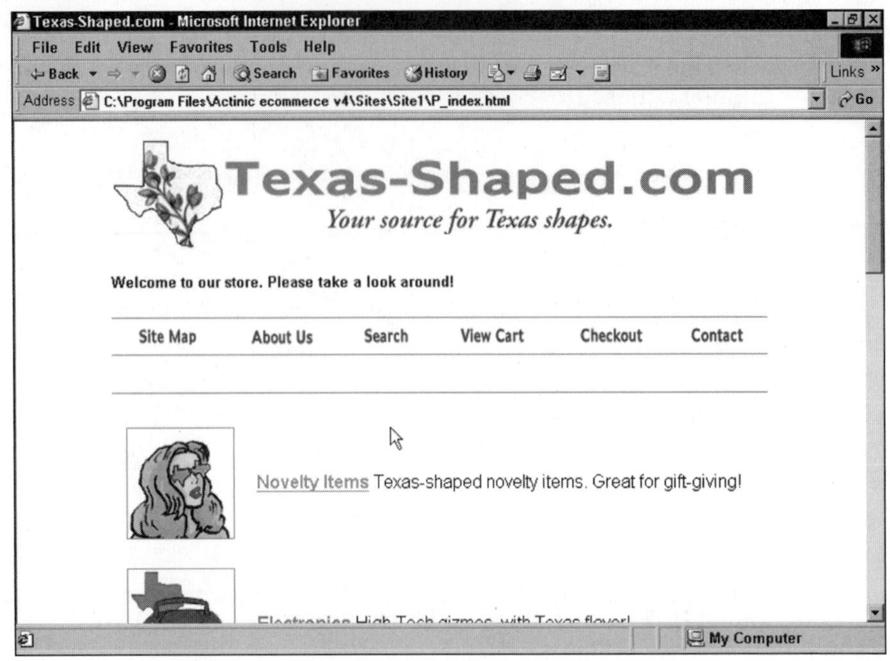

Figure 16-6: Texas-Shaped.com with categories and category images

After all of the categories have been added to the catalog, you're ready to start adding products.

Adding products to a catalog

Creating products and items

As we mentioned earlier, populating a catalog with products is often the most time-consuming part of building an online storefront. Actinic provides two ways to enter product data into a storefront. The first is to manually enter each piece of information directly into the Actinic business program. If you're creating a catalog specifically for your Web site, this is probably the fastest way to get started with Actinic.

The second way to populate a catalog using Actinic Business is to import records from an external database into Actinic. If you have an existing catalog of products stored in a database, this can save you quite a bit of time and typing.

Although knowing how to create products in Actinic Business isn't covered on the exam, knowing how to create products in an e-commerce program will help you on the exam.

Manually entering product information

To create a new product in Actinic business, follow these steps:

1. Right-click on the category in which you want to create the product. For this example, add a product to the Novelty Items category.
2. Select New Product from the pop-up menu. The Product Details shown in Figure 16-7 appears. Click the Advanced button to view all of the properties that you can specify for a product.

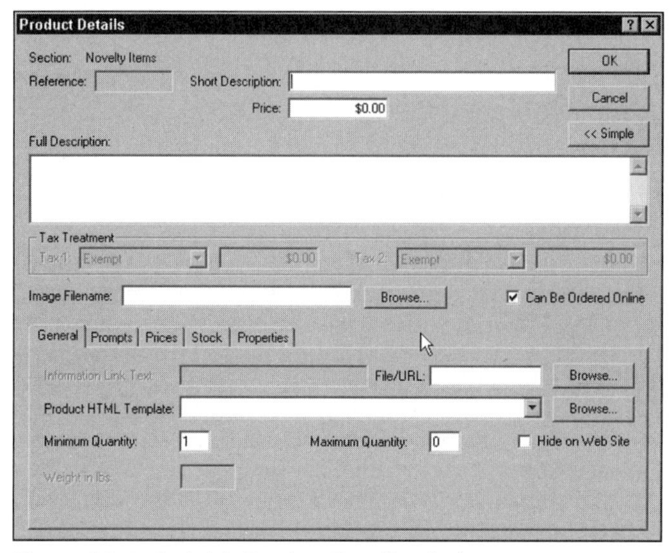

Figure 16-7: Actinic's Product Details window

3. Enter the name of the first product, **Gift Basket**, into the Short Description text box.
4. Enter the price (**$45.00**) and a description for the product. (You can find descriptions of the products in the product spreadsheet on this book's CD, called `texproducts.xls`.)
5. Enter the path to the product image into the Image Filename text box or use the Browse button to locate the image. If you haven't already done so, you can find the product images in the Texas-Shaped.com folder on the CD that comes with this book. Copy them to the `Site 1` folder in the Actinic folder on your hard drive.

Tip

You don't need to fill in every text box in the Product Details window. In fact, all you really need to enter is a name for the product and a price. If you want people to be able to purchase the item, you must also make sure that the box labeled Can Be Ordered Online is checked and the Hide on Web Site box is unchecked.

Changing product property default values

Many of the product properties use default values if you leave them blank. For example, a default image is shown for products that don't have pictures. To change default values, including default product images, follow these steps.

1. Pull down the Design menu from the top of the Actinic window, and choose Options.
2. In the Design Options window, click the Defaults tab to bring it to the front.
3. Find the text field labeled Default Product Image and replace its value with the name of the Texas-Shaped.com default product image, **tx_default.gif**. (In other words, type **tx_default.gif** in the Default Product Image field.)

Importing products from an external data source

One way to import products into Actinic Business is to use the External Links feature. If you already have a large catalog from a physical store or another e-commerce software package, this function can save you considerable time and effort.

The External Links feature uses the Open Database Connectivity (ODBC) protocol to connect to a database or spreadsheet that contains product records. Using ODBC, Actinic can import data into its database from a wide variety of sources, including Microsoft Access databases, Excel spreadsheets, any database with an ODBC driver, and delimited text files.

The ODBC drivers needed to import data into the Actinic database were installed as part of the Actinic Business installation process.

To use the External Links feature, you must first turn off the automatic product reference numbering feature. To do this, follow these steps:

1. Open the View menu and select Business Settings.
2. On the Options tab, uncheck the Auto Generate Product References checkbox.
3. Change the value in the Product References Character Count text box to **4**. This allows you to create your own product identification numbers or import them from a database, as in this case.
4. Edit the Gift Basket product — which you entered earlier, in the "Manually entering product information" section — by changing the Product Reference number to NV01 to match the numbering system the Excel product spreadsheet uses. This record will automatically be updated when the spreadsheet is imported.

To import the rest of the products for Texas-Shaped.com, follow these steps:

1. From the File menu, select External Links. You will see the Product Links window shown in Figure 16-8.

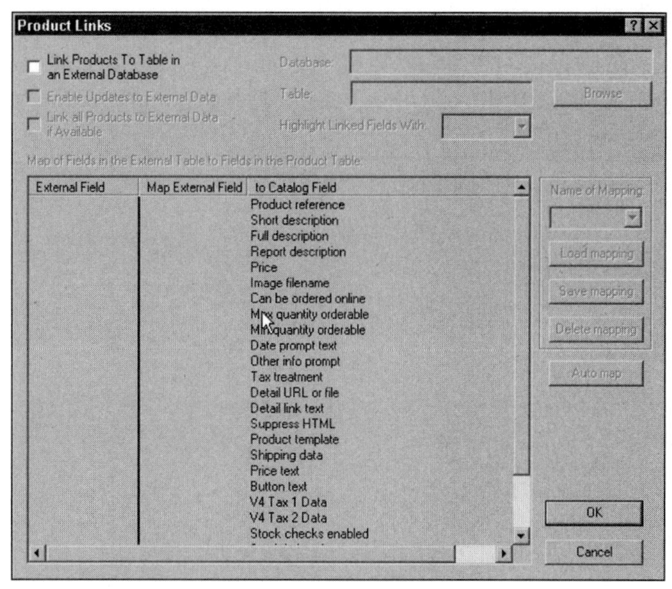

Figure 16-8: The Product Links window

2. Check the checkbox labeled Link Products To Table in an External Database.
3. Click the Browse button to see a list of types of data you can import. Select Excel 2000 Workbook from this list.
4. A new window appears asking you for the path to the spreadsheet and the name of the workbook. Use the Browse feature to locate the spreadsheet on this book's CD, and then enter **products** into the Workbook Name field. Check the box labeled First Line is Field Names, and then click OK.
5. The fields from the Excel workbook are listed in the Product Links window with red question marks next to them. These fields need to be associated with fields in the Actinic database before the products can be imported, which is done by dragging the name of the external field from the left pane of the window to its corresponding field on the right. (Note that the Category column from the spreadsheet does not have an equivalent in the Actinic database.) After you have associated each field, as shown in the following list, the Product Links window should look similar to Figure 16-9.
   - ProdID = Product Reference
   - Product Name = Short Description
   - Description = Full Description
   - Price = Price
   - Image = Image filename

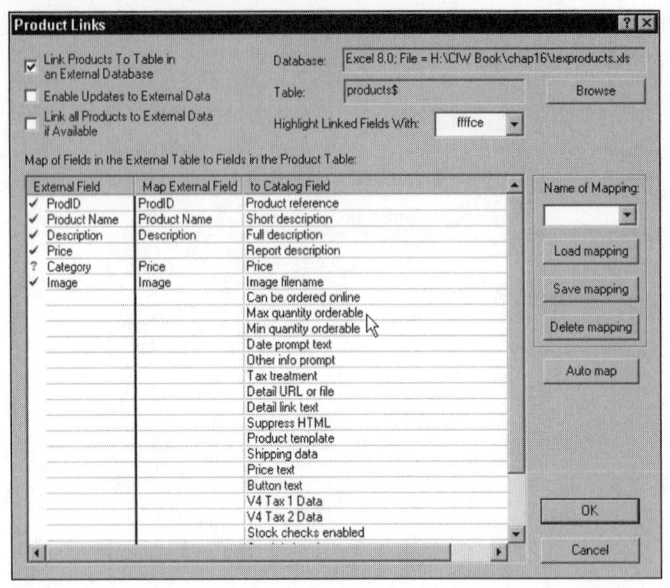

Figure 16-9: Associating external columns with Actinic fields

6. Click OK to import the products.
7. The new products are imported into a folder called Unallocated External Products. From this folder, you can drag each product into the appropriate category or sub-category. When you're finished, your Actinic Business interface should look similar to Figure 16-10.

Editing imported products

Note that the newly imported products have different icons next to them than the products you entered directly. The icons next to the imported products indicate that they are stored in an external data source (and must be edited using that database). The icon on the Gift Basket product now indicates that it was updated from an external data source.

Upon opening an imported product for editing, notice that its fields are highlighted and can't be edited. If you wish to edit an imported product in Actinic Business, you can uncheck the Use External Data checkbox in the Edit window.

Now would be a good time to preview your store or even to post it to your server to see how it looks. To publish your site, click the Publish icon in the navigator.

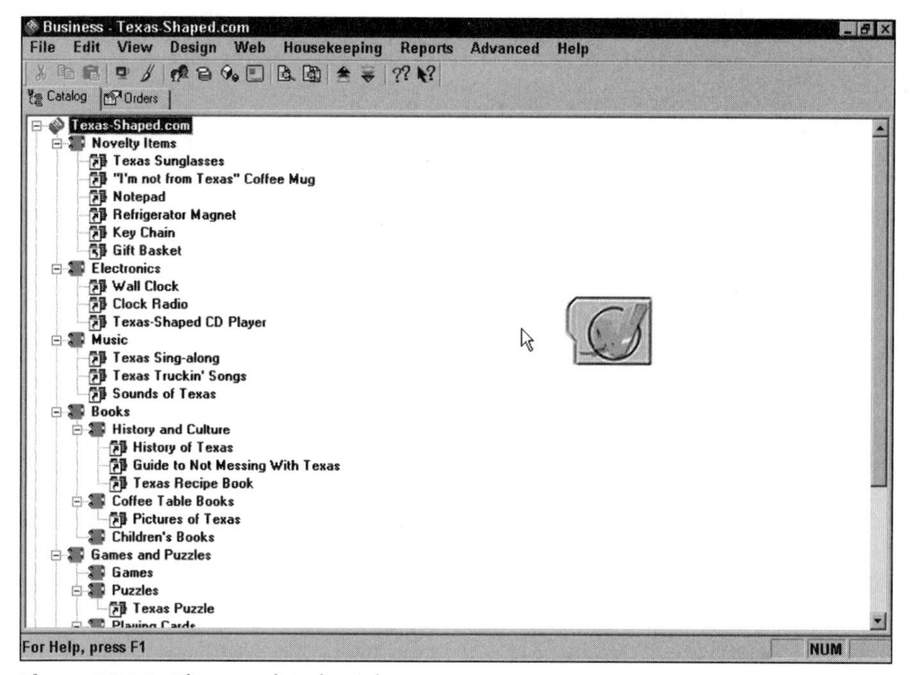

Figure 16-10: The populated catalog

Add-ons and upgrades

Sometimes you may want to enhance basic product offerings in ways that may add to their prices. For example, you may want to offer batteries with a radio, or offer a limited number of signed copies of a book that you also offer unsigned. You can accomplish these things using a concept Actinic Business refers to as *components*.

To give customers the option of purchasing batteries with the clock radio, follow these steps:

1. Right-click on the Clock Radio product, and select New Component from the pop-up menu that appears.
2. Name the new component **AA Batteries** and click OK.
3. Right-click on the new component and choose Edit from the pop-up menu to bring up the Component Edit window, as shown in Figure 16-11.

You can also simply double-click on a product or category to bring up its Component Edit window.

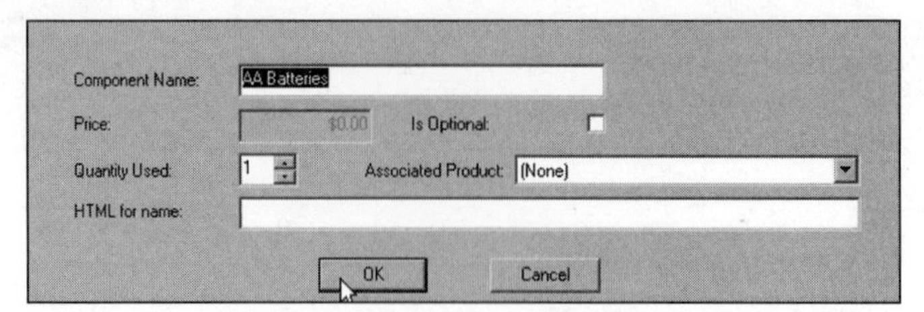

Figure 16-11: The Component Edit window

4. Make the batteries optional by checking the box to the right of Is Optional.
5. To associate the batteries with the Clock Radio, select the Clock Radio from the Associated Product drop down list.
6. Note that you can't edit the price of the batteries. To be able to give the components a price, you need to change the pricing model for the Clock Radio. Double-click on the Clock Radio and select Sum of Product and Component Prices from the Pricing Model drop-down list.
7. Close the Clock Radio product listing and open the Component Edit window. Enter **$5.99** into the price field for the batteries.
8. To inform the customer of the additional charge for the batteries, enter **AA Batteries (adds $5.99 to price)** into the field called HTML for name.

Adding attributes and options to products

Attributes and options are choices for products that don't affect their prices. The following steps show you how to add size options to the Texas Sunglasses product:

1. Right-click on the Texas Sunglasses and select New Attribute from the pop-up menu.
2. Give the attribute the name **Size**.
3. Right-click Size and select New Choice from the pop-up menu.
4. Give your new choice the name **Small**.
5. Repeat Steps 3 and 4 to add the following additional choices:
   - Medium
   - Large
   - Huge
   - Texas-sized
6. Preview the catalog to see how the choices appear. The choices appear as radio buttons by default, as shown in Figure 16-12.

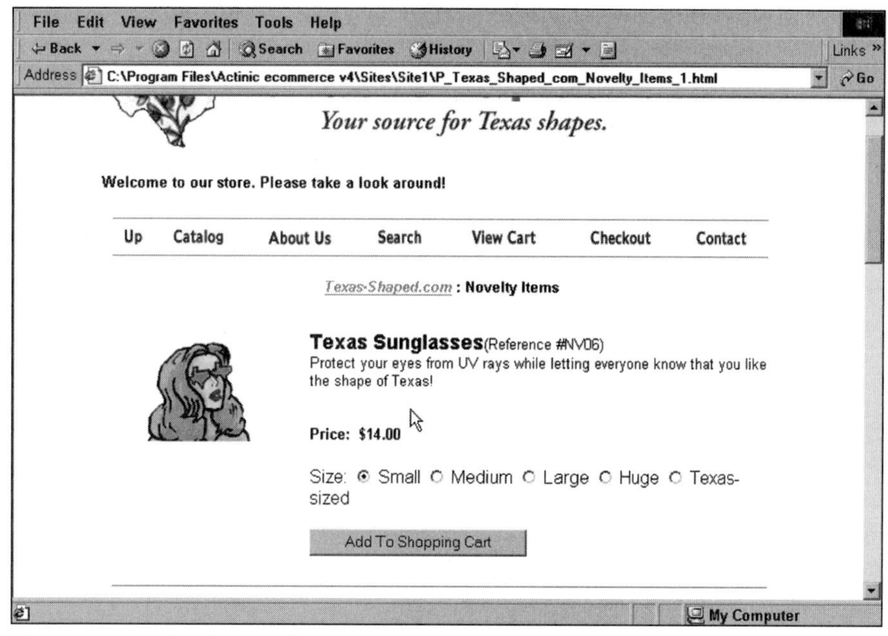

Figure 16-12: Product attributes

As you can see in Figure 16-12, having the attributes display as radio buttons doesn't work very well in this instance. There are two possible solutions that would make this display more attractive: The first is to put each option on its own line. The second is to use a different type of form, such as a drop-down list, for the Size attribute. You can try out both of these solutions using the Attribute Edit window.

1. Double-click the Size attribute to view its Attribute Edit window.
2. Change the value of the UI Widget field to Drop down list. Or, select <BR> from the Separator drop-down list.
3. Use the Offline Preview feature to view the results.

Key Point Summary

Carefully organizing your catalog is one of the most important things you can do to make your e-commerce site more usable. This chapter covered the concepts of catalog organization and then gave you hands-on experience with an e-commerce catalog. The key concepts covered in this chapter are:

✦ A catalog is a group of products or services that can be browsed by customers.

✦ Online catalogs can be either searched or browsed.

- XHTML is a cross between HTML and XML. It allows you to create HTML pages that can take advantage of the data structuring capabilities of XML.
- The three major components of an online catalog are categories, products, and attributes.
- Options and attributes are choices that the user needs to make after he or she has chosen a particular product.
- The first step in categorizing your products is to establish or analyze your business objectives for the site.
- The second step in creating a catalog is to gather data about the products.
- The third step in creating a catalog is to place the products into categories and sub-categories.

✦ ✦ ✦

STUDY GUIDE

You started this chapter with a general discussion of online catalogs, and finished with a detailed look at adding categories, products, and attributes to a storefront created with Actinic Business. In the following sections, you take a step back and test your knowledge of the concepts covered in this chapter.

Assessment Questions

1. What are the two methods for navigating an online catalog?

A. Hunting and pecking

B. Searching and browsing

C. Searching and querying

D. Hiding and seeking

2. How does XML improve the ability of a Web page to be searched?

A. XML creates a database, or index, of Web pages.

B. XML locates the text a user searches for.

C. XML is the future of the Web.

D. XML can be used to describe the data in a Web page.

3. What is the difference between an attribute and a component in Actinic Business?

A. Attributes use custom images.

B. Attributes are variations to a single product, whereas components are used for add-on products or options.

C. Components are variations to a single product, whereas attributes are used for add-on products or options.

D. Components can use custom images and code.

Scenario

You're in charge of creating an online catalog for an office supply store. A debate has arisen within the company about the best way to organize the wide variety of products currently stocked in aisle 4 of the store on the Web site. Some of the products in question are shown in the following list. To keep the Web design simple, the number of top-level categories must be kept to a minimum. How would you organize these products into a minimal number of top-level categories and any number of sub-categories?

- Rubber erasers
- Number 2 pencils
- Fountain pens
- Crayons
- Color pencils
- Staplers
- Staples
- Markers
- Pencil sharpeners
- Paper clips
- Large paper clips
- Binder clips

Lab Exercise

Lab 16-1 Adding custom properties to a product

This exercise shows you how to add custom properties to products in Actinic Business. An example of a situation in which you may want to use custom properties would be in the case of a book. You'd probably want to list the Author's name, the publisher, and additional information about the product. Follow these steps to add information to one of the book listings in the Texas-Shaped.com catalog:

1. In the main window of Actinic business, choose Define Custom Properties from the Advanced menu.
2. In the properties grid that appears, click on the + in the upper left corner to add a new row to the window.

3. Type **Author** under the Property header. The Custom Property Name field is filled in as you type.
4. Click the + in the upper left corner of the grid to add another new row to the window.
5. Type **Release Date** in the Property column, as shown in Figure 16-13.

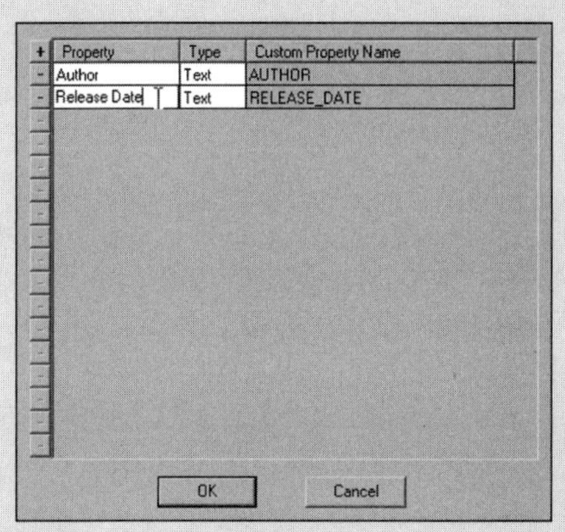

Figure 16-13: Creating custom properties

6. Click OK to exit the window.
7. Double-click the History of Texas product in the main Actinic catalog window, click the Advanced button to open the Advanced window, and then choose the Properties tab.
8. Click the + in the upper left corner of the properties grid to add a new row.
9. Select Author from the drop-down list of properties, and then enter a value (such as the author's name) into the Values row.
10. Repeat this process to add a Release Date property.
11. Check Use as CUSTOMVAR for both properties.
12. Open the Template Manager from the Advanced menu.
13. Click the Product Line button in the Section tab.
14. Find the line in the source code that reads:

```
<BR>NETQUOTEVAR:PRODUCTDESCRIPTION
```

    and type the following text after it:

```
<BR>CUSTOMVAR:AUTHOR
<BR>CUSTOMVAR:RELEASE_DATE
```

Note that NETQUOTEVAR:PRODUCTDESCRIPTION may appear twice in your template. Use your text editor's search feature to make sure you've located every instance of this text and added the CUSTOMVAR text after each.

15. Save and close the template, and then preview your catalog to see the new properties listed underneath the product description.

Answers to Chapter Questions

Chapter pre-test

1. Dividing products in your catalog into categories makes it easier for customers to locate items by navigating through your site.
2. Product attributes are characteristics, or properties, of products. Examples of product attributes include color and size.
3. The role of a shopping cart is to keep track of the items a customer wants to purchase.

Assessment questions

1. **B.** The two methods for navigating an online catalog are Searching and Browsing (see "Understanding Online Catalog Functions and Components").
2. **D.** XML is a flexible language for data description (see "XML to the Rescue").
3. **B.** Attributes are generally displayed as drop-down lists or radio buttons, and are used for options such as size and color. Components are used for extras, such as batteries or protective coatings (see "Structuring a hierarchical catalog").

Scenario

There are countless ways to organize these products into categories, but not all of them make sense. Here's one way to do it:

```
A. Writing and Erasing
   1. Pencils
      a. Number 2 pencils
   2. Color pencils
   3. Markers
      a. Markers
   4. Pens
      a. Fountain pens
```

```
    5. Erasers
       a. Rubber erasers
    6. Crayons
    7. Pencil sharpeners
 B. Connecting and Joining
    1. Staplers
    2. Staples
    3. Paper clips
       a. Large paper clips
       b. Binder clips
```

For More Information . . .

- **Argus Center for Information Architecture.** http://argus-acia.com
- **Web Content Accessibility Guidelines 1.0.** www.w3.org/TR/WAI-WEBCONTENT
- **Information Architecture Guide.** www.argus-inc.com/iaguide/index.shtml

17

CHAPTER

Processing Online Transactions

EXAM OBJECTIVES

- Credit card processing
- Digital cash
- Online check processing
- Transaction services

CHAPTER PRE-TEST

1. What is a payment gateway?
2. What payment methods are used in e-commerce?
3. What advantages does immediate credit card processing provide?
4. Is it possible to accept personal checks for online purchases?
5. Who is ultimately responsible for a fraudulent credit card charge — the merchant or the bank that approves the transaction?

✦ Answers to these questions can be found at the end of the chapter. ✦

In this chapter, you find out about payment processing for Internet transactions. You examine the methods and issues associated with accepting credit cards, checks, and digital cash for online transactions. In addition, you discover what business policies need to be established before transactions can be processed.

Understanding Online Transactions

Arguably, the most important part of conducting e-commerce is gathering payment for your products and services. This is also one of the most complex aspects of e-commerce. Not only does an e-commerce site need a means of processing payments, but it also needs to determine how customers are charged for shipping and other expenses.

Forms of payment

Online shopping gives users access to more products than ever before, but there must be a simple way to purchase these products. In the real world, a shopper at a store can present cash, check, or a credit card; therefore, a merchant can prevent check or credit card fraud by requesting photo identification. Shopping over a distance — such as online shopping — removes the ability to conduct this security check. Indeed, e-commerce is prone to the same problems that have plagued telephone and mail order merchants for decades: how to receive payment and verify its authenticity over a distance.

Until the introduction of the credit card in the 1950s, checks and money orders were the most common methods of payment in such transactions. Both are much less susceptible to fraud than credit card transactions. However, one of the most appealing aspects of online shopping — as opposed to mail order and catalog shopping — is the immediacy of purchase. Although it can take several days for the product to arrive, the transaction is completed immediately and without a sales representative. As a result, the convenience and immediacy of credit cards have made them the most popular form of payment for e-commerce transactions.

Additional charges

In e-commerce businesses, just as in traditional businesses, there are additional charges — beyond the total of the costs of the products — that need to be made for each transaction. These include:

- Tax
- Shipping
- Handling
- Service charges

Let's take a look at each of these charges in more detail.

Tax

To comply with local taxing authorities, you need to collect the proper taxes from your customers. Internet purchases are not taxable if the company selling the product does not have a presence in the state in which the purchaser resides. If your company has only one physical location, you only need to charge tax to customers in your state.

Many states have a base sales tax, and then local municipalities charge additional sales taxes on top of the state sales tax. In most cases, the best way to handle this situation is to charge a uniform tax rate for in-state sales that is an average of the total sales taxes charged in the various regions of the state.

As a very simplified example of such a situation, consider a state with six counties. Each county charges an additional sales tax ranging from 1 percent to 2.5 percent on top of the statewide 4 percent sales tax. The county sales taxes break down as shown in Table 17-1.

Table 17-1
Hypothetical State with Six County Sales Taxes

County name	*County sales tax*	*Total sales tax charged (county tax + 4% state sales tax)*
Bullock County	1%	5%
Hughes County	2%	6%
McCurdy County	1.25%	5.25%
McDaniel County	2.5%	6.5%
Strain County	1.75%	5.75%
Treadwell County	2%	6%

If you average the total sales taxes charged in each county, you end up with 5.75 percent. By charging all of your in-state customers 5.75 percent regardless of the county in which they live, you save your company a lot of paperwork and tricky programming. In addition, when the time comes to pay your sales taxes, you're likely to have collected just about the right amount.

Shipping

Shipping charges are usually based on the type of shipping service used and the weight of the package. Every package your e-commerce company ships could conceivably be weighed, and the purchaser could be charged accordingly. However, in the interest of expediency, most — if not all — e-commerce companies develop simpler shipping charge formulas, as follows:

- **Base charge.** If your company offers multiple shipping carriers and services (for example, Priority Mail, FedEx 2-Day, and FedEx Overnight), you may want to start with a base charge to cover the difference of price in these services. For instance, you could charge a base price of $2.00 for Priority Mail, $4.00 for FedEx 2-Day, and $6.00 for FedEx Overnight.
- **Weight parameter.** Next, you need to add a parameter based on the weight of the products purchased. Models for this parameter could include an average weight for several classes of products, plus a multiplier to account for quantities of more than one. For example, a customer who purchased five CDs and one stereo might be charged $.75 per CD (5 x $.75 = $3.75) and $10.00 for the stereo for a total of $13.75 in shipping plus the base cost of the service selected. If this hypothetical purchase were being sent via Priority Mail, the total cost would be $15.75 ($13.75 for weight and $2.00 for Priority Mail).
- **Flat rate.** For companies that sell only one type of product, shipping formulas can be simpler than this. It may even make sense to charge a flat rate for shipping in some circumstances.

Handling

Some companies are accustomed to charging a handling fee on top of the shipping fee. This fee covers the cost of an employee assembling and packaging a customer's products for shipping, and any other activities related to getting the order out the door and to the customer. Other companies prefer to roll these costs into the cost of shipping.

If your company sells some very heavy or cumbersome products, you may want to add a special handling charge to these items. This charge also needs to be set up as a part of your checkout process.

Service charges

Service charges are almost always tied to a particular product or class of products. Products requiring extra service charges may include easily broken items, such as glass, collectible or rare items, or even large and cumbersome products, as mentioned in the previous section.

Transaction participants

Online transactions involve many participants. The following list covers the major players and describes their roles in detail:

- **Customer.** The customer is the Web user who initiates a transaction at an online store and specifies the form of payment he or she prefers.

- **Merchant.** The merchant can also be referred to as the online store, the e-commerce company, or the seller. The merchant offers products and/or services for sale via an e-commerce Web site.
- **Processing network.** The processing network is the means by which payment is processed. It encompasses banks, payment gateways, fraud checking services, and credit card processors, as well as the infrastructures for communicating with one another and with the merchant.
- **Card/check/digital cash issuing bank or company.** The issuer of a credit card, check, or digital cash can authorize or deny use of a payment method.

Be sure to familiarize yourself with these online transaction participants and their roles.

- **Merchant's bank.** This is the bank that provides the online store's merchant account.
- **Trusted third party.** A trusted third party is used to verify the merchant's identity to the customer and the customer's identity to the merchant. This is usually a certifying authority (CA).

See Chapter 19 for more information on certifying authorities.

Selecting Payment Methods

The de facto method of payment in e-commerce is the credit card. There are other methods available, however. It can be worth it to offer some alternative forms of payment on your Web site. After all, the more options you give a customer, the more likely he or she is to purchase from your site.

Online payment terms and concepts

When discussing online payment options, it's useful to be familiar with the following terms and concepts:

- **Merchant account.** An account that a merchant opens at a bank to process credit card transactions.
- **Credit card processor.** A bank that provides credit card processing services to merchants. This can also be a company whose sole business is credit card processing.
- **Payment gateway.** A service that provides an automated link to the credit card processor in order to authorize or deny transactions in real time. The payment gateway removes the human element from online credit card purchases.
- **Private digital network (PDN).** A secure computer network through which credit card transaction information is exchanged with a credit card processor.

- **Automated clearing house (ACH) network.** A network used by the Federal Reserve and all financial institutions in the U.S. for inter-bank transfer of funds.
- **Independent sales organization (ISO).** A credit card processing service that caters to small online businesses, which often have difficulty opening their own merchant accounts with banks.

Assessing the options

When deciding which payment options your site will offer to your customers, it's important to weigh the following primary questions:

- How convenient is this form of payment to our customers?
- How difficult is this form of payment to implement within our company?

Every company assigns a different weight to each question and determines a balance between the two, as follows:

- If your company is small and strapped for cash and personnel, the second question is more important.
- If getting the maximum number of site visitors to buy is your primary concern, the first question rises to the top.
- Offering credit card processing only is generally accepted and should not cost you too many customers. After all, those who do not have credit cards are probably not accustomed to buying online anyway.
- Many potential buyers, however, may be wary of submitting their credit card information to a merchant from whom they've never made a purchase.

Payment alternatives that can be offered for credit-card wary customers include:

- **Telephone ordering.** The customer places an order over the phone after using the Web site to select products.
- **Sending checks by mail.** The customer places an order and then sends a check for payment. Fulfillment of the order is delayed until the check has been received and cleared.
- **Online check processing.** The customer enters check information to make a payment from his or her checking account.
- **Digital cash.** The customer pays one vendor for digital cash and uses the digital cash as payment at participating e-commerce sites.

Credit card processing, online check processing, and digital cash are discussed in the following sections of this chapter. The telephone ordering and check mailing options are not discussed in detail because they do not require any specialized e-commerce knowledge and are in the realm of traditional business practices.

Processing credit cards

Credit card processing

Using credit cards is by far the most common way to make purchases via the Web. Credit cards have been processed electronically for decades via private digital networks to which merchants and processors are connected. Because credit card transactions are already handled electronically, they have been easily integrated into e-commerce.

Credit card information is gathered from customers by the check-out process, also commonly referred to as a *shopping cart*. The information associated with each transaction is housed in a database. Payment processing can take place immediately or be done manually.

See Chapter 19 for information on how to secure transaction information that is saved in a database.

Manual credit card processing

Manual processing is not as old fashioned as it sounds — it simply means delaying the credit card processing until an actual employee of the e-commerce company initiates the processing. This processing can be done using a terminal (as in a real-world store), but it is usually faster to use payment-processing software, such as POS Charge or PC Authorize. These programs can be installed on a desktop computer and used to process transactions by sending batches to a processing center using a private digital network.

Real-time credit card processing

Payment gateways are services that provide an e-commerce site with real-time credit card processing over the Internet. These services bypass the step that requires a human to send the payment information to the processing center. The payment information is automatically sent and the transaction completed within moments. The customer is then informed whether his or her purchase has been authorized or declined by the processing center.

The payment gateway provides an automatic link between the merchant and the credit card processor. The credit card processor then deposits funds in the merchant's account when the products are shipped.

There are several advantages to using payment gateways:

✦ **No delay.** The customer knows immediately whether his or her transaction has been approved. There's no need to follow up with the customer in the event that the credit card is declined.

✦ **Less overhead.** The process does not require intervention or supervision by a person — for the majority of the time, at any rate. This frees up company employees who would otherwise be needed to complete the transactions manually.

✦ **All-in-one services.** Many online credit card processing services offer a merchant account, credit card processor, and payment gateway in a package deal. This means you only need to set up your site to work with the payment gateway. Everything else is handled for you by the payment gateway service.

✦ **Fraud protection.** Many payment gateways have fraud protection services included or as an optional add-on.

Preparing for online credit card transactions

To implement online credit card transactions, the following steps must be completed:

Be sure you're familiar with these three requirements for online credit card transactions.

1. **Prepare the site and server.** Your Web server (or hosting company) must be set up to accept credit cards. If you're hosting the site internally, you need to set up the server software to collect credit card information. Many Web hosting companies offer this service as an add-on feature to their hosting package.
2. **Set up an online merchant account.** An online merchant account is needed to process credit card transactions. A merchant ID and terminal ID are typically included.
3. **Install payment software.** A manual-payment software package or an automated-payment gateway service is necessary to exchange information with your credit card processor.

Many companies offer online credit card processing packages, which include a merchant account, credit card processor, fraud check, and payment gateway. Such packages eliminate the need to complete each of these steps. In many cases, a Web hosting company is able to take care of everything listed here.

Credit card fraud

Online sales are classified as *card not present* transactions, which means merchants are ultimately responsible for determining whether a charge is fraudulent. In the e-commerce world, it can be difficult to determine whether or not a transaction is fraudulent.

One reliable way of counteracting this risk is by investing in an Address Verification System (AVS). An AVS is usually available from your merchant account provider as an add-on feature. It works by comparing the billing address entered for a transaction with the billing address for the credit card used in the transaction. Most payment gateway vendors support AVS as well.

AVS is not foolproof, but can help curtail fraud. If fraud becomes a big issue on your site, you can require AVS approval for all transactions.

The credit card authorization process

Credit card authorization is a complicated process involving many entities, but it can be completed almost instantaneously. Figure 17-1 provides an overview of the process. The following sections look at each step in closer detail.

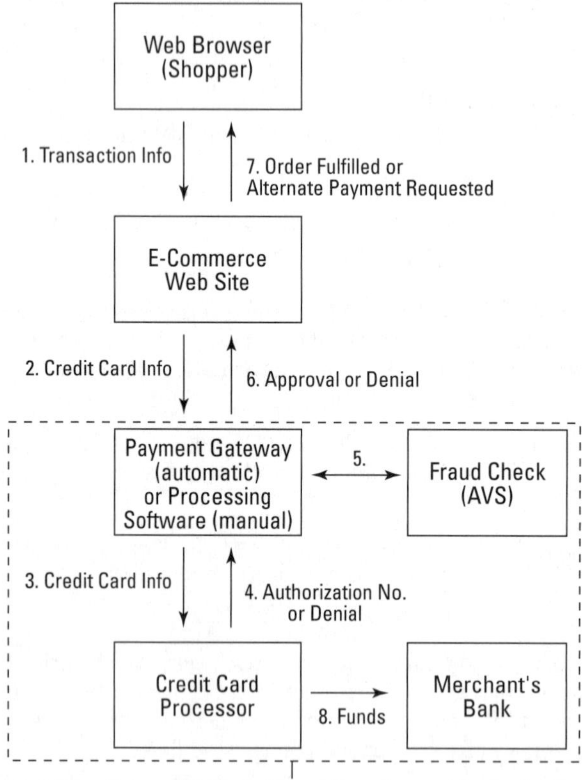

Figure 17-1: Overview of the credit card authorization process

1. **Transaction initiated by customer.** The customer selects products for purchase from the online store and completes the checkout process. All transaction information — products, quantities, name and address, credit card information, and total cost — is sent to the e-commerce Web site server.

2. **Credit card information sent to payment gateway or processing software.** The pertinent credit card information — total cost, card number, expiration date, cardholder name, and billing address — is sent to the payment gateway service or the desktop credit card processing software.

In the case of a site using processing software, the credit card information is stored in a database and accessed when an actual human is ready to process the transaction. If a site uses a payment gateway, the information is instantaneously transmitted to the payment gateway service, which then proceeds with the following step.

3. **Credit card information is sent to processor.** The payment gateway or processing software sends the credit card information to a credit card processor. The processor checks with the credit card company or an automated clearinghouse to determine whether the credit card can be used. If the credit card has, for instance, been reported stolen, the account has been closed, or the credit limit has been reached, use of the credit card is denied.
4. **Processor approves or denies use of card.** The credit card processor replies to the payment gateway or processing software with either an authorization number or a denial of the credit card.
5. **Fraud check.** If the credit card is approved by the processor, most companies conduct a fraud check using an AVS and/or an automated fraud check service. This is often rolled into the services provided by a payment gateway.
6. **Approval or denial sent to Web site.** After the fraud check is complete, the payment gateway or processing software informs the Web site server of whether the transaction can continue with the current credit card information.
7. **Inform customer.** In the case of Web sites using a payment gateway, the customer is informed if his or her credit card has been denied before the transaction is complete. If the credit card is denied, the customer can be prompted for alternate payment — another credit card or a check or digital cash if the Web site offers such alternatives. In the case of an approved transaction, the customer is informed of the success of his or her transaction, and the order information is then routed through the company for fulfillment.
8. **Transfer funds.** The credit card processor authorizes the transfer of funds to the merchant's bank after the order is fulfilled — i.e., shipped to the customer.

Handling digital cash

Digital cash

The strict definition of *digital cash* is a system that allows a person to pay for goods or services by transmitting a number from one computer to another. Digital cash numbers are unique (like serial numbers on dollar bills) and are issued by a bank or via a vendor company. There are other services, such as *stored value services*, that are also commonly referred to as digital cash.

Digital cash—also called e-money, e-cash, and many other combinations of terms for currency and high-techiness—is an ongoing experiment. Some e-commerce pundits have pronounced it dead, but many companies are still embarking on digital cash projects.

The need for digital cash

In order to truly bring e-commerce to every stratum of society and every country in the world, a viable alternative to credit cards, as well as checks, needs to be introduced for completing online transactions. Many people in the U.S., as well as other countries, do not use credit cards—either as a matter of principle or because they cannot be approved for credit.

In many countries, banks operate in substantially different ways than the ways we're accustomed to in the U.S. For instance, many European countries do not use checks. Instead, funds are transferred by sending a request to your bank along with the account number and bank information of the company or person to whom you would like to pay money. Credit cards are also less common in Europe than in the U.S.

The U.S. currently dominates the e-commerce market, but as this dominance wanes, it's possible that other countries may adopt credit cards out of necessity. More likely, however, a more universal alternative will emerge.

Experiments in digital cash currently underway

Today, many companies are taking the lead in making digital cash a reality. Their approaches are varied, but the common goal is to provide online consumers with an alternative to credit cards. The following sections take a quick look at some of these companies and their services.

InternetCash

InternetCash is a pre-paid stored value card that can be purchased at participating real-world retailers and then used to pay for purchases at participating online retailers. It's similar to a pre-paid phone card, and caters to those who don't have credit cards or are uncomfortable giving credit card information over the Internet.

Flooz

Flooz is another stored value service, but it involves no actual card, as InternetCash does. The currency purchased is referred to as *flooz*. Flooz is paid for online at the Flooz Web site and can then be used at any retailer that accepts Flooz payments. Flooz must be purchased using a credit card, so its main advantage for customers is they only have to give their credit card information to one online company (Flooz) rather than to every online retailer from which a product is bought.

Flooz does not remove the need for a credit card entirely, which may be why the company markets its service as a means of online gift-giving. The primary focus of the service is to give a gift certificate that can be used at multiple online stores, although an individual can also open an account, add money to it, and then use the account to pay for online purchases.

Securelynx

Securelynx is a digital wallet software program that users can download and install on their desktop computers. The software stores payment information (primarily credit card information) and works with participating online retailers to exchange digital certificates. The information is also encrypted by the software before it's transferred over the Internet. This way, both the customer and the merchant are certain of one another's identities, and the customer knows his or her credit card information is secure.

Securelynx is currently available only to holders of MasterCards from participating Canadian credit unions.

PayPal

PayPal is a secure network for making payments directly. It's currently used primarily as a way for individuals to exchange money, especially for online auctions. It can also be used by Web retailers to accept payment for goods and services.

Money can be paid using either a credit card or a bank account, and PayPal provides a secure network for exchanging the money. It can also be used by businesses to pay customers or employees (such as rebates or incentives).

Evaluating the digital cash option

Digital cash can provide a level of security and anonymity for customers that can make them more comfortable when purchasing products from your online store. Many digital cash services also open the world of Web shopping to those without credit cards. By offering a digital cash alternative, your online store becomes open to more potential customers.

Most digital cash programs require merchants to become members of their network. This can help drive traffic to your site, but can also place a burden on your programmers, because they need to set up the necessary components to work with the digital cash service. Time will tell whether digital cash catches on, and which services are most popular with consumers. It's important for those in the e-commerce industry to keep up with the latest digital cash trends and technologies.

Online check processing

Online check processing

Accepting checks over the Web seems like a contradiction in terms — after all, checks must be filled out and signed by the customer in the presence of the cashier, right? Well, where there's a will there's a way, and the fact is that some consumers just prefer to pay by check, or they just don't have credit cards. Why should such consumers be denied the ability to shop online?

Several services currently offer online check processing, including:

✦ Authorize.Net

✦ CyberSource

✦ Electracash

✦ eDebit

The technological challenge of accepting checks online is not quite as daunting as one might initially assume. After all, ATM cards have been used for making purchases for some time now. Merchants that accept ATM cards are a part of a secure network that transfers checking account information electronically with a member of the automated clearing-house network. Transactions are approved and funds are transferred immediately.

To take advantage of this technology on the Web, an online store simply needs to:

✦ Become a member of a clearing-house network and set up its Web site to process checking account information.

✦ Allow customers to enter the bank routing (ABA) numbers and account numbers into a form on the e-commerce site — not unlike entering a credit card number.

✦ After the information has been entered, initiate an authorization procedure very similar to credit card processing, with fraud controls such as AVS used to verify the authenticity of the purchase.

Online check processing is a great way to accept payment – unless you're selling soft goods that are delivered electronically. Once a check is processed, there's still a chance the check may be returned for insufficient funds (commonly referred to as a *bounced check*). Delivery should be delayed until the check has cleared. If your products are downloadable over the Web, this might not be possible.

Setting Up Transactions with Actinic

In this section, you take a look at the way transactions are set up in Actinic Business. Follow these steps:

1. Start Actinic.
2. In the Actinic window, choose Business Settings from the View menu.
3. Click on the Payment tab to bring it to the front (see Figure 17-2). The section in the top left area of the screen is the Payment Options area. This is where you select the payment options for your customers. The following list examines the options one by one:

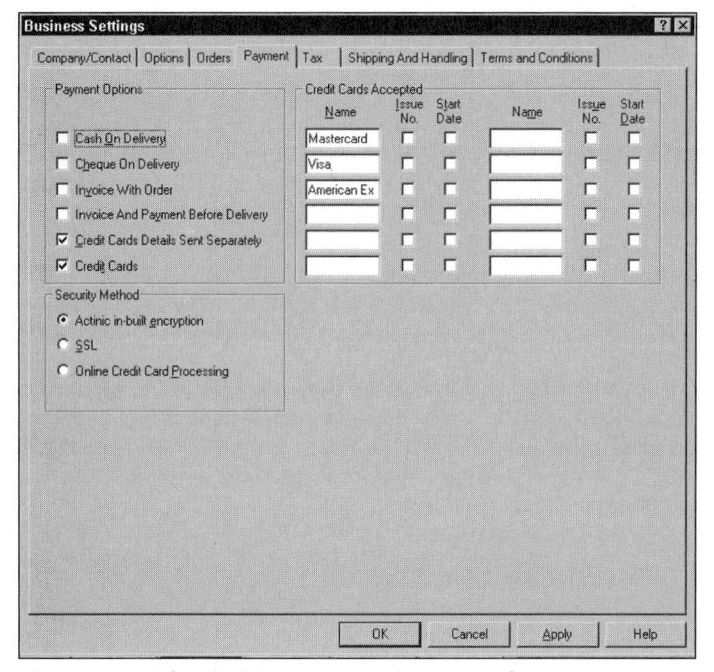

Figure 17-2: The Business Settings Payment tab

- **Cash On Delivery.** Commonly referred to as *C.O.D.*, this method of payment is not very common in the U.S. anymore. The postal carrier collects payment from the customer upon delivery of the package.
- **Cheque On Delivery.** Very similar to C.O.D. except a check is accepted instead of cash.
- **Invoice With Order.** This option allows the product to be shipped before payment is processed. An invoice is enclosed in the package and the customer is expected to remit payment upon receiving the package.
- **Invoice And Payment Before Delivery.** This option means the company sends an invoice to the customer and then awaits payment before shipping the products ordered. This is less risky than the previous three options while still eliminating the need for a credit card.
- **Credit Cards Details Sent Separately.** This option lets the customer print an order form that lists the products ordered and the total cost. The customer can then fill in his or her credit card information on the form and fax or mail it to the company.
- **Credit Cards.** This is the traditional credit card method — the customer enters his or her credit card information, which is either sent to the company or to the credit card processing service.

4. Select the checkboxes in front of Invoice And Payment Before Delivery, Credit Cards Details Sent Separately, and Credit Cards. These are the most common methods of completing online transactions.
5. In the top right is an area labeled Credit Cards Accepted. This is where you list the credit cards your company accepts for payment. MasterCard, Visa, and American Express are already listed. Now, add the Discover card to that list. In the field immediately below the field with American Express in it, enter **Discover**.
6. The checkboxes after the Name field for each credit card enable you to specify whether your company requires an issue number or start date for any of the credit cards. Leave these unchecked.
7. In the bottom left of the window is the Security Method area. By default, Actinic in-built encryption is selected. Leave this selected. This means that the credit card information is sent to your computer (encrypted) and is accessible via Actinic. You can then use computer-based, manual credit card processing to finish the transactions.
8. Now that you've set up the payment methods, move on to the tax set-up by clicking the Tax tab (see Figure 17-3).

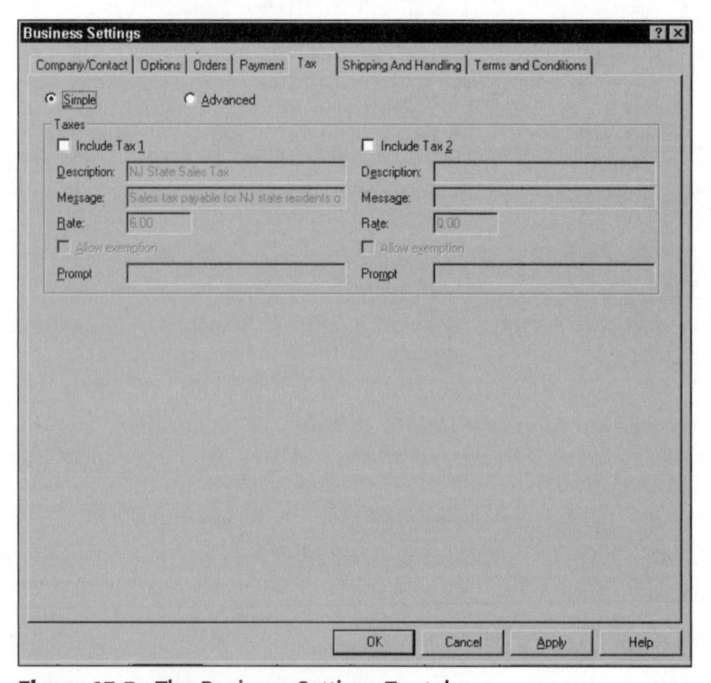

Figure 17-3: The Business Settings Tax tab

9. There are two options: Simple and Advanced. Leave Simple selected for now.
10. Check the checkbox labeled Include Tax 1.
11. In the field labeled Description, enter **TX State Sales Tax**.
12. In the field labeled Message, enter **Sales tax payable by Texas residents only**.
13. In the field labeled Rate, enter **8.25**. This is the percentage tax to be charged.
14. Check the box labeled Allow exemption.
15. In the field labeled Prompt, enter **Tax-exempt agency (proof required)**.
16. Now that you've entered your tax information, move on to shipping and handling information by clicking the Shipping And Handling tab (see Figure 17-4).

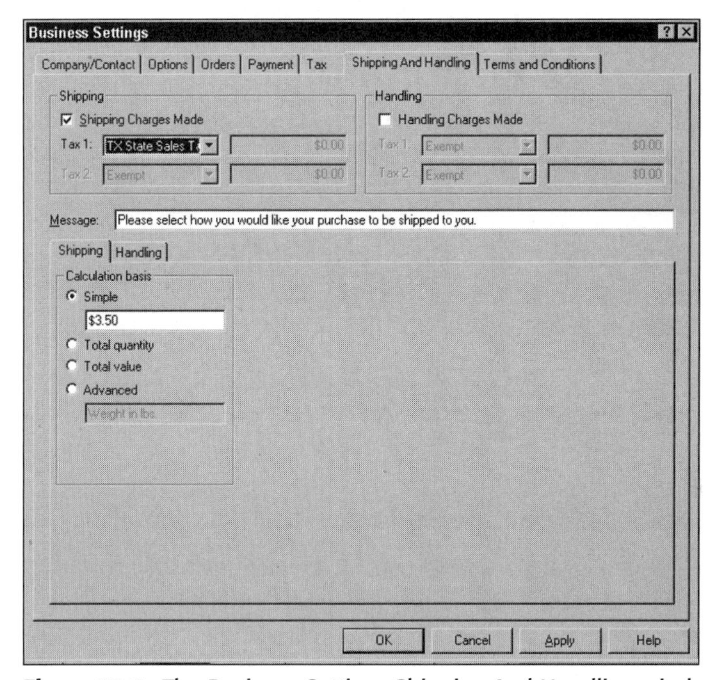

Figure 17-4: The Business Settings Shipping And Handling window

17. First, specify whether shipping charges and handling charges are made and whether those charges are subject to sales tax by activating the Shipping Charges Made checkbox and selecting TX State Sales Tax from the drop-down menu beneath it. Activate the Handling Charges Made box and select Exempt from the drop-down menu to leave handling charges untaxed.

18. Next, set a shipping rate based on the total price of the order. Select the Shipping tab (on the lower half of the Shipping And Handling tab of the Business Settings window) and click the Total value radio button. Many new fields should appear, as shown in Figure 17-5.

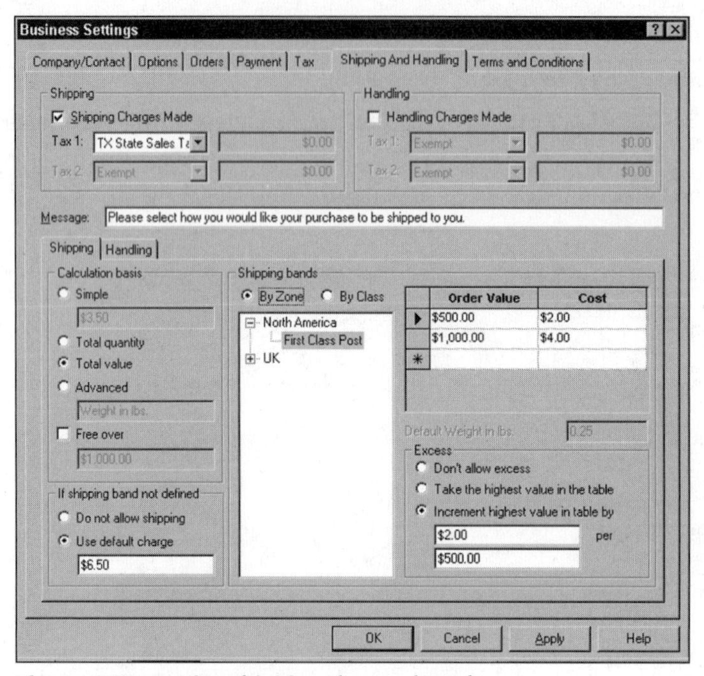

Figure 17-5: Setting shipping charges by value

19. In the area labeled Shipping bands, select the By Class radio button.

20. The field immediately below the radio buttons shows a hierarchy of shipping classes. Highlight North America by clicking it once.

21. The table to the right specifies shipping charges for North America based on total value. Enter the information shown in Table 17-2. If there's information already in the table, replace it with the information in Table 17-2.

Table 17-2
Data for Shipping Charges

Order Value	*Cost*
15.00	2.00
30.00	2.50
45.00	3.00

22. In the area labeled Excess, specify how values in excess of $45.00 should be handled. Select Increment highest value in table by and enter **$0.50** per **$15.00** in the fields provided. For every $15 increment beyond $45.00, the shipping charge will increase by 50 cents.

23. Staying in the Shipping and Handling window, click the Handling tab to bring forward the handling settings (see Figure 17-6).

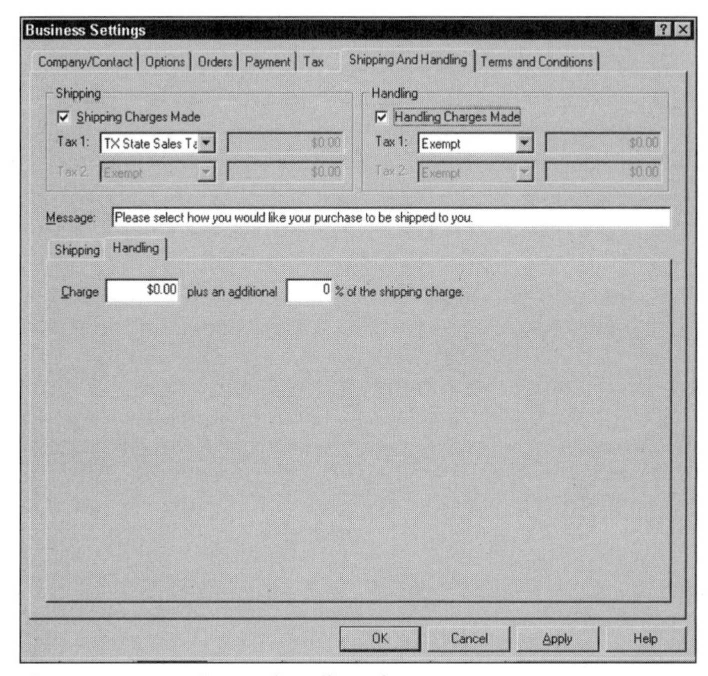

Figure 17-6: Setting up handling charges

24. Enter data in the proper fields to charge **$1.00** plus an additional **10%** of the shipping charge.

25. Click OK to close the Business Settings window.

26. You're done! Now, publish your site and make a test purchase to see how your new settings look.

Working with Payment Gateways

Transaction services

There are many companies that offer payment gateway services these days. The following list names just a few:

- **Authorize.Net.** www.authorizenet.com
- **ClearCommerce.** www.clearcommerce.com
- **CyberCash.** www.cybercash.com
- **BCE Emergis.** www.emergis.com
- **OrderTrust.** www.ordertrust.com
- **Trintech.** www.trintech.com
- **VeriFone (a division of Hewlett-Packard).** www.hp.com/solutions1/verifone/

To better understand the services provided, let's take a look at three representative examples of payment gateway services.

Authorize.Net

Authorize.Net's WebLink service enables e-commerce Web sites to accept credit cards as payment and processes the transactions immediately. Members of the service can copy and paste special HTML code into their checkout page in order to send customers' credit card information to the WebLink system. The information is encrypted using 40 or 128 bit Secure Sockets Layer (SSL) technology and is then sent to a secure transaction server. The service forwards the information to the appropriate financial institution using a secure private network. After the authorization process is complete, the customer receives notification of approval or denial. The whole process usually takes about five seconds.

See Chapter 19 for more information on Secure Sockets Layer (SSL) technology.

The system is fairly simple to integrate into the Web site—after all, just a few lines of HTML code need to be added. WebLink is compatible with most shopping cart systems in use today.

Authorize.Net also offers a manual credit card processing alternative called Virtual Terminal. Virtual Terminal is very similar to using the credit card terminals currently found in retail stores—except it's Web-based and accessible through any browser on any computer. The merchant simply fills out a form with the pertinent transaction information, and then the information is sent and processed in much the same way as the WebLink system. This can be a good alternative for low-volume stores.

ClearCommerce

ClearCommerce Merchant Engine software is a system that is installed and run on the same Web server that houses the e-commerce Web site. It's configured to exchange information with credit card processors directly, using encryption for security.

Merchant Engine requires a larger commitment of resources in terms of set up, because it is hosted and run on the Web server. By contrast, Authorize.Net's WebLink is hosted on Authorize.Net's servers; the e-commerce site's Web server simply sends information to it.

The advantage of using Merchant Engine is that it can be configured to a specific e-commerce company's needs. For instance, the fraud-check component, Fraud Shield, can be configured to your company's specifications. The system comes with a library of built-in rules that can be turned on or off according to your wishes. It also includes a Fraud Rule-Builder tool with which custom rules can be created.

The ClearCommerce service can also be accessed by hosting your site with a ClearCommerce Service Provider. These Web site hosting companies offer ClearCommerce processing and fraud protection as add-on services. By using a ClearCommerce Service Provider, you can relieve your staff of the need to install and maintain the Merchant Engine software, while still being able to take advantage of its functionality.

CyberCash

CyberCash Cash Register processes credit cards online by sending credit card information to a CyberCash transaction server, which then handles the processing and returns an approval or decline to the Web site. To communicate with the transaction server, a merchant using Cash Register must install a software application called the Merchant Connection Kit (MCK) on the Web server computer. The MCK encrypts the information and establishes a secure connection between the Web server and the CyberCash server to enable a real-time credit card transaction.

CyberCash offers Fraud Patrol as an add-on to the Cash Register service or as a standalone service. Fraud Patrol is a sophisticated fraud-detection program powered by a neural network that learns from each transaction. The credit card information is submitted to Fraud Patrol over the Internet, and the program evaluates factors such as billing and shipping addresses, e-mail address activity, and past fraud on the card, to determine a fraud risk level for the transaction. This level is then compared to the acceptable fraud risk level selected by the client company, and the transaction is rejected if the risk exceeds the acceptable level set by the company.

CyberCash also makes credit card processing software called WebAuthorize. WebAuthorize is a full software solution used by companies that host their own Web sites. The software is configured by the merchant to work with the merchant's credit card processor, financial institution, and merchant account.

Key Point Summary

In this chapter, you learned about online transactions, participants in the transaction process, the credit card authorization process, and alternative forms of payment. Key points to remember are:

- Forms of online payment include credit cards, checks, and digital cash.
- Credit cards can be processed manually or via a payment gateway.
- A payment gateway is a service for processing credit cards in real time over the Internet.
- To process online credit card transactions, an e-commerce company needs a merchant account, a credit card processing service, and processing software or a payment gateway.
- Digital cash is a system for online payment that protects the customer from having to give his or her credit card information to the merchant.
- Checks can be accepted as payment online by having customers enter their bank routing numbers and account numbers from one of their checks.
- Online retailers are ultimately liable for fraudulent credit card purchases made at their sites.
- Many online credit card processing services include fraud protection.

✦ ✦ ✦

STUDY GUIDE

The following sections give you a chance to test your knowledge on the vital topic of payment processing for Internet transactions. The "Lab Exercises" section provides you with first-hand experience in registering a CyberCash test account and in setting up Actinic to work with CyberCash.

Assessment Questions

1. Which of the following is *not* a step required when preparing your Web site for online credit card transactions?

A. Install payment software or service

B. Set up fraud check service

C. Set up merchant account

D. Prepare site and server

2. When does the transfer of funds to a merchant account take place in the credit card transaction process?

A. As soon as the card is authorized

B. When the customer receives the product

C. When the product is shipped

D. When the customer authorizes it

3. What is digital cash?

A. A system that allows a person to pay for goods or services by transmitting a number from one computer to another

B. A system for converting money to electronic information

C. Money that only exists in cyberspace

D. An online gift certificate

4. Why is online check processing risky for sellers of soft goods that can be downloaded over the Web?

A. It is too slow.

B. Risk of unreliable information.

C. Risk of bounced checks.

D. People who don't have credit cards shouldn't buy soft goods.

5. What is a disadvantage of digital cash payments for the merchant?

A. Difficulty of knowing whether digital cash is legitimate.

B. They are slow to be paid.

C. Not many customers use them.

D. You need to install software on the server or join a network.

6. Which of the following is a tool for fighting fraudulent credit card transactions?

A. Private Digital Network (PDN)

B. Address Verification System (AVS)

C. Independent Sales Organization (ISO)

D. Virtual Private Network (VPN)

7. Which of the following products is used to automate online credit card transactions?

A. Actinic Business

B. Flooz

C. CyberCash Cash Register

D. PayPal

8. The online check processing procedure most closely resembles which of the following processes?

A. Online credit card processing

B. Digital cash processing

C. Transaction processing

D. Inventory processing

Scenario

You're the owner of a small online store. The site does not currently accept payments online. Customers must print an order form after selecting products and then send the form along with a check or credit card information to your company via mail or fax.

For the last six months, traffic at your site has been brisk, but only some of the visitors have actually purchased products. Many abandon the checkout process part way through. You suspect that some customers are put off by the fact that they cannot order from your company without having to print the form.

You decide to try online transactions. Which of the following forms of payment is likely to be the most successful for your situation and why?

✦ Online check processing

✦ Digital cash

✦ Online credit card payments

Lab Exercises

Lab 17-1 Register for a CyberCash test account

In this exercise, you open a test account with CyberCash. Once completed, you're ready to set up your site to use CyberCash on a test basis. This test account is free of charge and cannot be converted into a real CyberCash account.

1. In your browser, go to `http://register.cybercash.com`.
2. When the CyberCash registration page loads, in the left column is brief information for new users. Click New Merchants to start the registration process (see Figure 17-7).

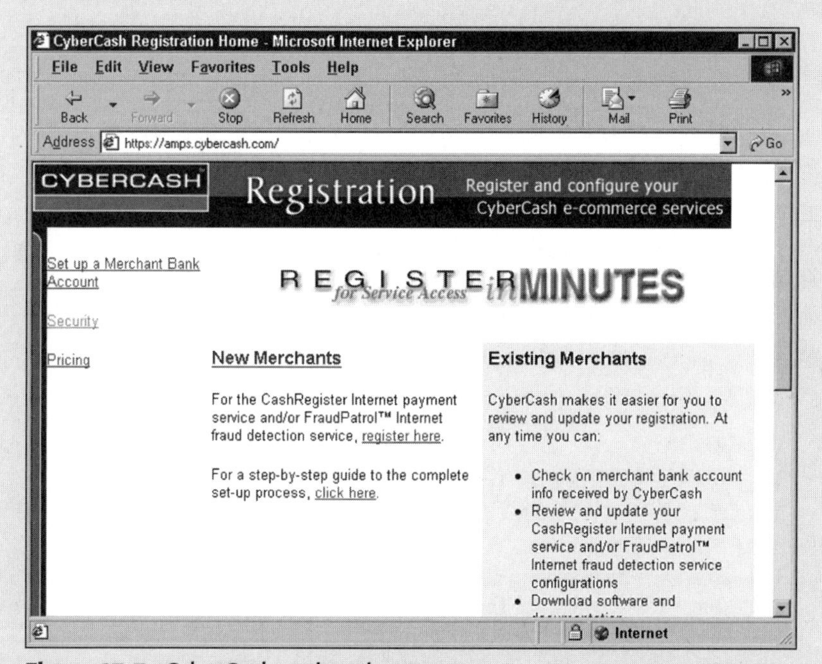

Figure 17-7: CyberCash registration page

3. To begin the registration process, you need to enter an e-mail address and password in the form on the next page (see Figure 17-8). Enter your e-mail address, make up a password, and be certain to make a note of these.

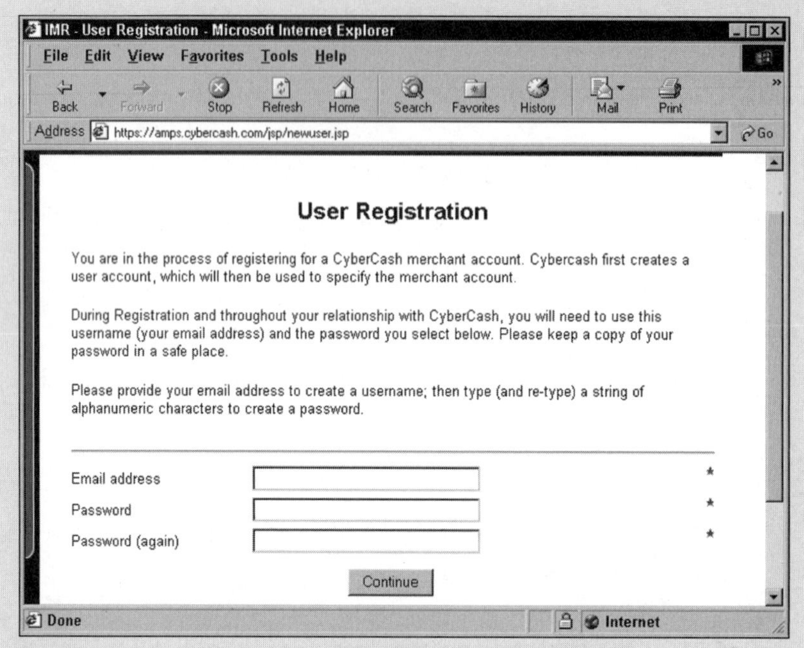

Figure 17-8: Entering your e-mail address and password

4. Click Continue to submit your information.
5. The next screen confirms that your account has been created. Click Continue.
6. On the next screen, you create a new CyberCash ID. To make a test account, you need to enter the URL `https://amps.cybercash.com/jsp/newmerchant.jsp?cpc=TEST` in your browser to convert to test mode.
7. After the new page has loaded, it should be very similar to the one you just left — but it's a test page (see Figure 17-9). You must enter a Doing Business As (DBA) name. If you were creating an account for use with an actual business, this DBA name would need to be same as the one you use with your financial institution. In this case, enter **Texas-Shaped.com** or anything else you'd like to use for test purposes.

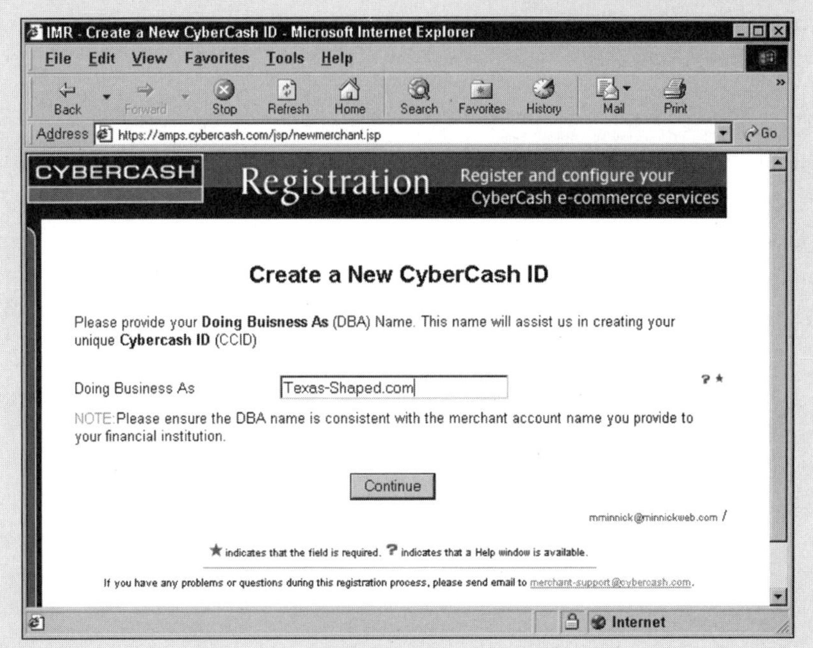

Figure 17-9: Creating a new CyberCash ID

8. Click Continue to submit this information.
9. The next screen confirms your CyberCash ID (CCID). Your CCID is in the middle of the screen, in bold. Write this down before continuing.
10. Click Continue.
11. The next screen is the General Merchant Information page (see Figure 17-10). Enter the following information for each field (you can enter alternate information if you'd like):

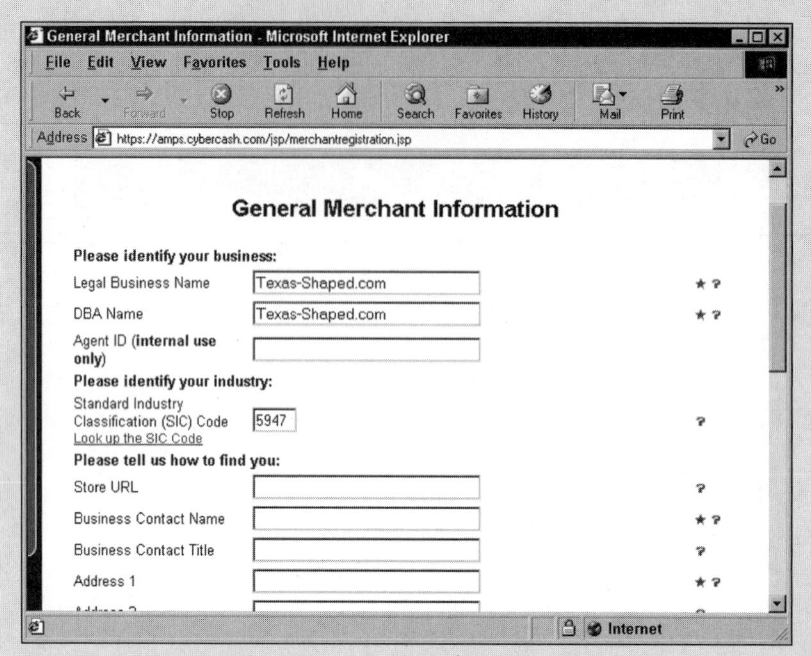

Figure 17-10: General Merchant Information page

- Legal Business Name: **Texas-Shaped.com**
- DBA Name: **Texas-Shaped.com**
- Agent ID: *leave blank*
- Standard Industry Classification (SIC) Code: **5947** (This is the code for Card, Gift, Novelty, and Souvenir Shops. To find a different code, click Look up the SIC Code.)
- Store URL: `www.texas-shaped.com`
- Business Contact Name: *enter your name*
- Business Contact Title: **Owner**
- Address 1: *enter your address*
- City: *enter your city*
- State: *select your state*
- Zip: *enter your zip code*
- Country: *select your country*

- Time Zone: *select your time zone*
- Business E-mail Address: *enter your e-mail address*
- Business Phone: *enter your phone number*

12. At the end of the form, read the statement, click the Yes radio button, and click Continue to submit your information.
13. The Storefront Software & ASP Information page should appear (see Figure 17-11). In the Storefront Software scrollbox, select Custom Other.

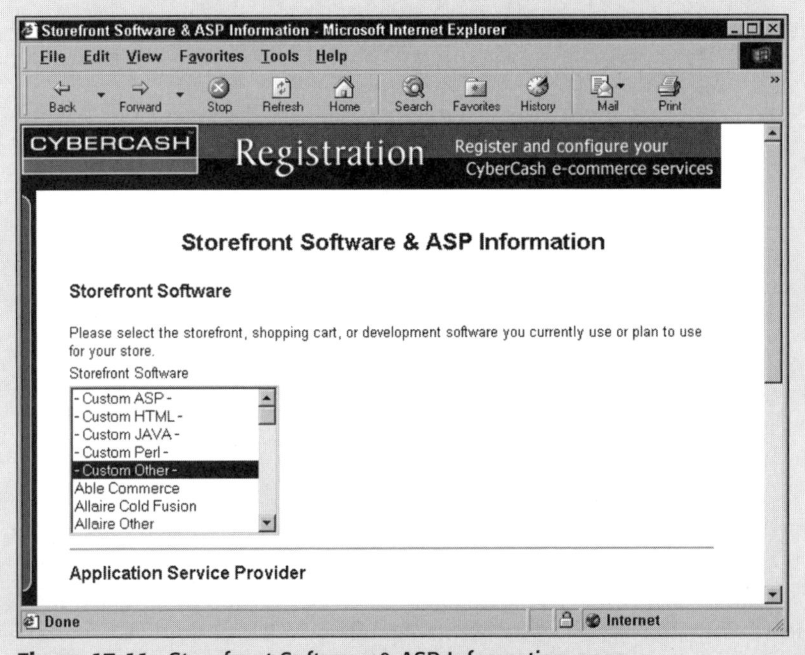

Figure 17-11: Storefront Software & ASP Information page

14. In the Application Service Provider scrollbox, select NONE.
15. Click Continue.
16. In the next screen, choose your CyberCash service. Select CashRegister Internet Payments System by clicking the radio button in front of it.
17. Click Continue to make your selection.
18. The next screen presents you with the CyberCash Service Agreement. Read the Service Agreement. When you reach the bottom of the page, click the I Accept radio button, and then click Continue to accept the terms of the Service Agreement.

19. On the next screen, create a password for accessing the CyberCash E-Commerce Services Manager. See Figure 17-12 for a look at this screen. Make up a password and enter it into the appropriate fields. Make a note of the password and the user name created by CyberCash.

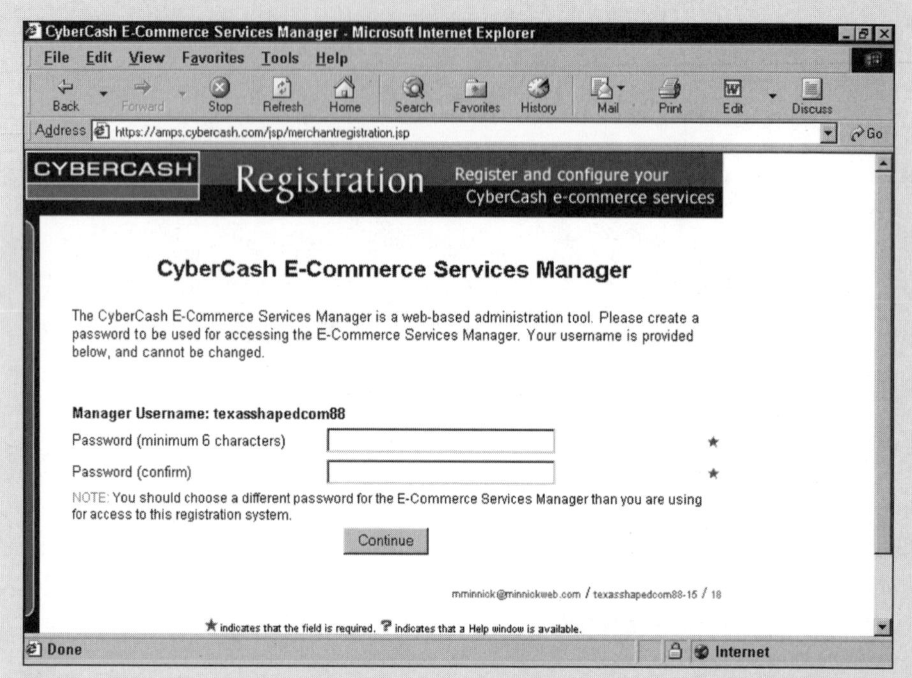

Figure 17-12: Creating a password for CyberCash E-Commerce Services Manager

20. Click Continue.

21. The next page is the Software Download and Integration page. Because you're using Actinic, you don't need to download anything. Scroll to the bottom of the page and click Continue.

Depending on your set up, you may need to download software components from the Software Download and Integration page. If you were hosting a site on your own computer, you'd need to download the Merchant Connection Kit (MCK).

22. The next page confirms that your registration is complete. It also gives you two important pieces of information: your CyberCash ID and Merchant Key. Write these down.

23. Click Finish.

24. You're automatically taken to the CyberCash Merchant Control Panel (see Figure 17-13). Click Logout to close the Merchant Control Panel.

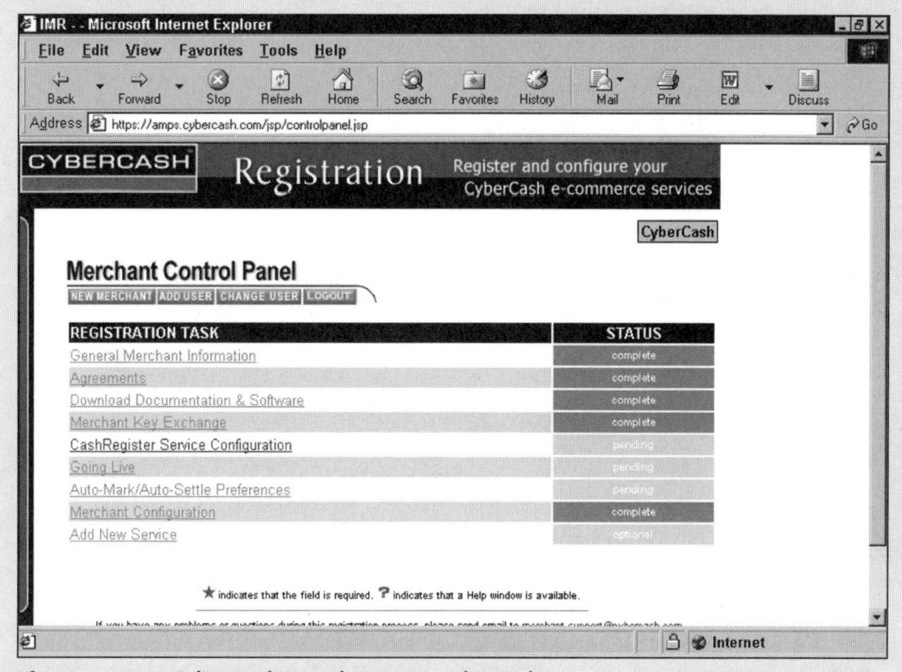

Figure 17-13: CyberCash Merchant Control Panel

Lab 17-2 Setting up Actinic to work with CyberCash

Now that you've registered for a test account with CyberCash CashRegister, you need to prepare your Web site to work with CyberCash. In this example, you use Actinic to set up your Texas-Shaped.com case study site, so it can use CyberCash to process credit cards.

1. Open Actinic on your computer.

2. Select Business Settings from the View menu.

3. In the Business Settings window, click the Payment tab to bring the payment options information form to the front. Your screen should look like Figure 17-14.

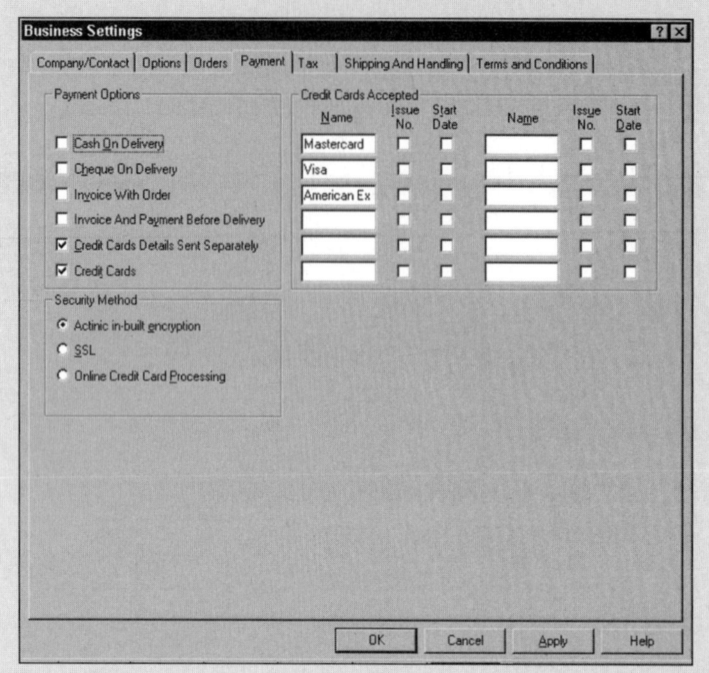

Figure 17-14: The Business Settings window with the Payment tab selected

4. In the Security Method area, click the radio button labeled Online Credit Card Processing. A new area should appear to the right of the Security Method area. This area is labeled Online Credit Card Provider (see Figure 17-15).
5. From the drop-down menu in the Online Credit Card Provider area, select CyberCash.
6. Click Configure.
7. A new window labeled Online Credit Card Provider Configuration should appear (see Figure 17-16). In the fields provided, enter your Merchant ID (CyberCash ID from Step 22 in the previous section) and Secret Key (Merchant Key from Step 22 in the previous section) in the fields provided. Confirm the Secret Key by entering it again in the field labeled Confirm Key.
8. In the Operation area, leave the default, Run in test mode, selected.
9. In the SSL URL area, leave the Live URL field blank, and enter the URL of your CyberCash test site in the Test URL field.
10. Click OK to make these changes and close the window.
11. Use your Actinic site to test CyberCash.

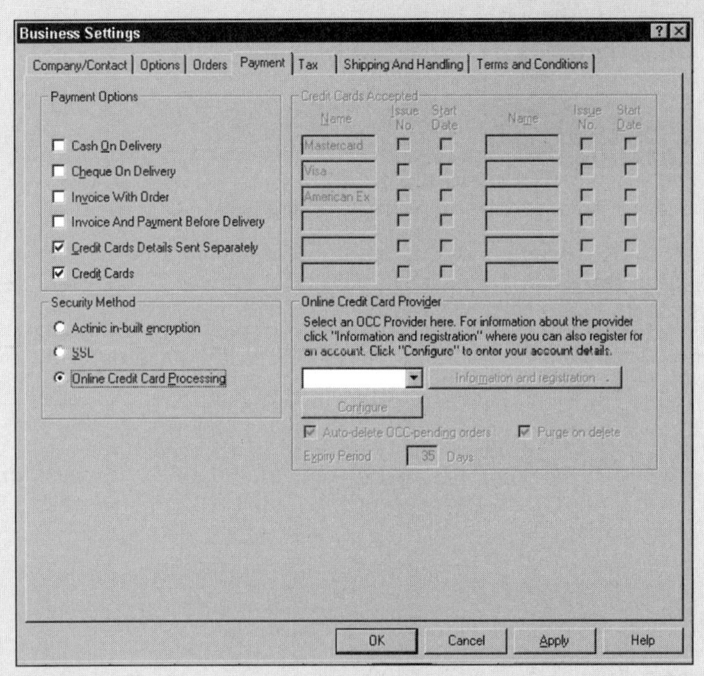

Figure 17-15: The Online Credit Card Provider area appears when Online Credit Card Processing is selected.

Figure 17-16: Online Credit Card Provider Configuration window

Answers to Chapter Questions

Chapter pre-test

1. A payment gateway is a service that provides an automated link with a credit card processor to authorize or deny a transaction in real time.

2. Credit cards are the most common method of payment in e-commerce transactions. Alternatives are online check processing and digital cash services.

3. Immediate online credit card processing requires no regular human involvement, which reduces company overhead costs, and is faster than manual methods.

4. Yes, it is possible to accept personal checks for online purchases.

5. The merchant is ultimately responsible for fraudulent credit card purchases, not the bank or credit card processor that approves the transaction.

Assessment questions

1. **B.** A fraud check service is not required for credit card processing, although it is advisable (see "Processing credit cards").

2. **C.** In most cases, funds are transferred after the order is fulfilled — which is, by definition, when the product is shipped (see "The credit card authorization process").

3. **A.** The correct definition of digital cash is: *A system that allows a person to pay for goods or services by transmitting a number from one computer to another* (see "Handling digital cash").

4. **C.** The risk of bounced checks is the reason that sellers of downloadable soft goods should be wary of online check processing. If the product has already been downloaded and the check is returned for insufficient funds, the merchant may have difficulty collecting payment from the customer (see "Online check processing").

5. **D.** To accept any form of digital cash as payment, a merchant needs to either install special software on the server or join a network of merchants who accept a certain kind of payment (depending upon the service). This can add a burden to your programming department (see "Handling digital cash").

6. **B.** An Address Verification System (AVS) compares the billing address entered for a transaction and the billing address on file with the financial institution that issued the credit card (see "Credit card fraud").

7. **C.** CyberCash Cash Register is a service for automatically processing credit cards online (see "Working with Payment Gateways").

8. **A.** The online check processing procedure most closely resembles the processing of credit cards online (see "Online check processing").

Scenario

Credit card processing is the first payment method that should be implemented, for two reasons:

- It's the most common and expected form of payment for online transactions.
- It's relatively easy to implement.

After your online credit card processing system is in place and working smoothly, you can begin to assess your customers' demand for alternatives such as digital cash and check processing. Of course, you should still allow customers to print out the form and send it in — some established customers are used to doing that and may be resistant to change.

For More Information . . .

- **PC Authorize.** www.authorizeit.com/pcauth.htm. Credit card processing software
- **POS Charge.** www.webmall.net/poscharge/. Credit card processing software
- **InternetCash.** www.internetcash.com. Pre-paid card for shopping on the Web without a credit card
- **Flooz.** www.flooz.com. Online gift-giving service also used as a stored value service
- **Securelynx.** www.securelynx.com. Digital wallet software
- **PayPal.** www.paypal.com. Secure network for exchanging money
- **Electracash.** www.electracash.com. Online check processing service
- **eDebit.** www.edebit.net. Online check processing service
- **eCheck Secure.** www.micrmart.com/echeck.htm. Online check acceptance service
- **Authorize.Net.** www.authorizenet.com. Offers products for online credit card processing and check processing
- **ClearCommerce.** www.clearcommerce.com. Makes software for online credit card processing
- **CyberCash.** www.cybercash.com. Software and services for online credit card processing and fraud detection

CHAPTER 18

Supporting E-Services

✦ ✦ ✦ ✦

EXAM OBJECTIVES

- Supporting asynchronous service
- Supporting synchronous service
- Supporting self-service
- Knowledge bases

CHAPTER PRE-TEST

1. What tools are available for supporting asynchronous e-service?
2. What kinds of skills do e-service customer support representatives need to have?
3. What is an e-mail management system?
4. What is another term for co-browsing?
5. Where does FAQ data usually come from?

✦ Answers to these questions can be found at the end of the chapter. ✦

In Chapter 6, you learned about the wide variety of types of online customer service, or e-service. In this chapter, you learn about the tools available for creating and supporting these e-services, and how to integrate such tools and services into your company's structure and processes.

Understanding E-Services Support

E-commerce has drastically changed the role of customer service representatives. Although the dream of e-commerce may often conjure up images of a store that tends itself without need of human intervention, the reality is quite different. Support for e-commerce is different from support for traditional commerce, but customer service can't be non-existent if your store is to succeed. Many argue that the virtual shopping world demands a higher level of customer service than traditional commerce does. Here's why:

- The lack of a physical store presence can elicit doubts from many potential customers as to the reality of their purchases. A strong and clear customer service presence can help allay fears that a product ordered may never show up, or that a defective product can't be returned and replaced by an online store.
- Because the confidence of customers in the online store sits squarely on the shoulders of your customer service representatives, it's vitally important that you have the right people supporting your customer service effort. This means hiring experts, retraining existing support personnel, or outsourcing the effort to another company.

In the following sections, you'll take a look at some of the specific challenges of e-service to your customer service staff.

New expertise needed

In traditional commerce, telephone customer service representatives typically handle just a few responsibilities, such as taking new customer orders, checking order status, and perhaps telling the customer about specially discounted items. In a case such as this, customer service representatives must understand and know how to use the company's order processing software to enter and check the status of orders. In addition, they should have common sense, good telephone manners, and some troubleshooting skills.

However, these skills do not immediately transfer to customer service for an online store. Customer service representatives for an e-commerce company are not often called upon to place an order or check the status of an order, because these functions are typically performed by the customer on the Web site. The customer service representatives on an e-commerce site may be called upon to perform more complex tasks. The skills necessary can include:

- **Web expertise.** E-service customer support representatives assist customers of varying technical competencies with using the Web site. This can be a lot more challenging than initially assumed. For instance, the customer service representative needs to be an expert at using the company's site, which means being able to recall how all of the main functions of the site work at a moment's notice. He or she also needs to be able to describe these functions in such a way that the customer understands them.
- **High-level customer inquiry skills.** The customer support representative needs to be able to handle complex situations. By the time a customer calls about an online order, the nature of the problem is most likely complex. After all, straightforward inquiries and problems can be handled on the Web site automatically.
- **E-mail skills.** E-commerce customer service representatives need to be skilled users of the company's e-mail system and also be capable of composing polite, coherent, and brief e-mails to customers about their problems. The tone of customer support e-mail is important and customer service representatives need to be trained to compose e-mails that do not sound brusque or insensitive, as e-mails often do.

Challenges of staffing

Another key challenge of e-commerce customer service is determining how many employees to have staffing your customer service department. Naturally, you'll need representatives available 24 hours a day; however, how many are needed for any given chunk of time is dependent upon your site's traffic patterns.

If, for instance, your site is most popular with customers in the United States and Canada, you need many representatives during waking hours for those countries. The overnight hours, however, can be more leanly staffed.

Even during the waking hours for the majority of your customers, the ebb and flow of customer traffic may evolve into a predictable pattern. Perhaps from 7 p.m. on the east coast to 11 p.m. on the west coast are your busiest times. These are the times your customers get home from work and check on the status of an order or encounter difficulties while attempting to purchase a product on your site.

Support options

The tools you need to provide for your online store are highly dependent upon the kind of service you provide for your Web site. For instance:

- **Synchronous support.** This type of support is very demanding in terms of staffing because you need to have enough representatives to support every customer who requests one.
- **Asynchronous support.** This type can usually be taken care of hours after the customer has submitted the request.

See Chapter 6 for more detailed definitions and explanations of synchronous and asynchronous support.

- **Self-service support.** This simply requires regular maintenance.

A clear understanding of asynchronous service, synchronous service, and self-service will help you on the exam.

There are many tools available for supporting your customer service effort. The leading companies offering these tools are:

- **eGain.** Offers customer service software geared toward the online support efforts of large companies.
- **Kana.** Provides products to integrate the sales, marketing, and support efforts of online companies.
- **E.piphany.** Offers customer service applications (called *modules*) that can be used together or as standalone software.
- **Siebel.** Makes software used to manage and integrate the variety of support technologies used in e-service, from live assistance to e-mail.
- **netCustomer.** An Application Service Provider (ASP) that hosts customer support applications for online companies and also provides customer support representatives as necessary.
- **Talisma.** Offers a full range of e-service software. Also provides professional services (setting up the software at your site) and outsourcing.

For Web addresses of the customer service support sites mentioned in this section, see the "For More Information . . ." section at the end of this chapter.

In the following sections, we take a look at the specific challenges of synchronous, asynchronous, and self-service e-services and the tools available to help your company meet the challenges.

Supporting Asynchronous E-Services

Supporting asynchronous service

Asynchronous e-services are customer support models in which the customer submits an inquiry that is responded to hours or days after it's submitted. The two main asynchronous service models are:

- E-mail
- Web forms

In both models, the customer submits information for response via e-mail. By using Web forms, you steer the customer into providing certain information he or she may not have remembered to include in the inquiry, such as the kind of computer and browser being used at the time of a technical problem.

E-mail management systems

The results of the Web form or e-mail inquiry are then routed to the e-commerce company's e-mail server, which, in most cases, routes the information into an e-mail management system. The e-mail management system then routes the information to a customer support representative.

Why you need one

An e-mail management system is necessary for just about any online customer support department with more than a few representatives. To understand why, imagine that your Web site listed the following contacts for customer support via e-mail:

- **Order inquiries:** Joanne, `joanne@companyname.com`
- **Technical difficulties:** Sylvia, `sylvia@companyname.com` or Roderick, `roderick@companyname.com`
- **Inventory questions:** Marcus, `marcus@companyname.com`
- **Returns:** Marianne, `marianne@companyname.com`
- **Order cancellation:** Hazel, `hazel@companyname.com`
- **Address changes:** Ian, `ian@companyname.com`
- **Credit card problems:** Kathy, `kathy@companyname.com` or Beth, `beth@companyname.com`

Then suppose Hazel, who handles incoming e-mails regarding order cancellation requests, goes on vacation to Tahiti for two weeks. Kathy, the department manager, plans to handle order cancellations while Hazel is on vacation. Before she leaves, Kathy asks Hazel to set up her e-mail software so all her e-mails are forwarded to Kathy while she's gone. But Hazel forgets to do it and all of the order cancellation requests collect in her e-mail inbox while she's in Tahiti. By the time she returns, most of the orders have already been shipped, so the customers have to return the merchandise to receive their refunds.

This kind of problem can be avoided by using an e-mail management system. These systems funnel e-mails into one or several queues depending upon the kind of inquiry being made. A team of customer support representatives can then pick up the e-mails from the queue one by one, in the order in which they were received, depending upon which representatives are in the office at any given time. Such systems are configurable to your customer service department's specific needs and circumstances.

How it works

In the case of the previous example, one e-mail address could be set up: `support@companyname.com`. Then, all of the e-mails could be put into a queue. Any one of the customer support representatives could then open the inquiry and help the customer. In most cases, customer service representatives can perform all of the basic support functions. It's likely that all of the representatives listed in the previous example can check the status of an order, answer questions about inventory, and enter an address change. It may require manager authorization to change credit card information or process a return, but these contingencies could also be built into the system.

E-mail management systems can also be programmed to:

- Send automatic replies to customers notifying them that their e-mails have been received and to expect responses within a given length of time.
- Route e-mails to specific queues based on key words and phrases in the subject line and body.
- Allow customer service representatives to redirect messages to different queues based on information in the messages.
- Track the state of an e-mail. (See the following section on case management systems for a full explanation of *states*.)
- Automatically suggest responses for an e-mail based on keywords and phrases.
- Provide response templates so customer service representatives do not need to type commonly used text (such as greetings, closings, and standard product information) for each e-mail response.

Leading vendors of e-mail management systems include:

- Talisma
- Siebel
- eGain

For Web addresses of the e-mail management sites mentioned in this section, see the "For More Information . . ." section at the end of this chapter.

Case management systems

Case management systems are very similar to the customer support databases used in traditional commerce. Each new customer inquiry, or *case*, is given a case number, and the customer information and the problem or inquiry is saved into the database. Each case is assigned a *state*, which is changed by customer service representatives as the case is handled.

The state of a case is simply the status of the case — for example, the case has not been looked at, the case has been forwarded to another customer service representative or to another department, or the problem has been solved and the case closed. The state of a case can be changed while the case is being worked on. However, once a case is closed, it generally stays that way.

Cases can also be put into queues for a team of customer service representatives to handle, much like in e-mail management systems. For instance, an inquiry about the state of an order may be sent to a customer service representative, Mary, via e-mail. Upon receipt of the e-mail, Mary enters the following pertinent information into the case management system:

- **Case Number:** 2133 (automatically generated by the software)
- **Date of Inquiry:** 01/19/01
- **Customer Name:** John Doe
- **Type of Problem:** Order Delivery
- **Customer Service Rep:** Mary Q.
- **Details:** Mr. Doe e-mailed on 1/19/01 to report that a product he ordered on 1/05/01 had not yet been received. Will forward inquiry to fulfillment customer support.
- **State:** Sent to fulfillment queue

The next morning, the case is picked up by Horatio in the fulfillment department. He checks on the status of the order, sees that it was delayed at the warehouse for three days and was shipped via UPS Ground on 1/10/01. He e-mails the customer to let him know to expect the package to arrive by 1/24/01 and adds the following information to the case:

- **Customer Service Rep:** Horatio A.
- **Date of Action:** 01/20/01
- **Details:** Checked order information. Product was delayed at warehouse for 3 days. Shipped by UPS Ground on 1/10/01. Allowing 2 weeks for delivery; should arrive by 1/24/01. E-mailed customer to let him know cause of delay and when to expect the package.
- **State:** Closed

Most cases are more complex this one, with more than two steps before they are closed. This simple example, however, illustrates how a case management system helps define a workflow for asynchronous customer service and ensures that customer inquiries are not lost in the shuffle.

Furthermore, the entire history of a case can be viewed, cases can be searched and reported on, and, if necessary, reopened, if it turns out the case was not actually resolved. In our example, if John Doe didn't receive his package by 1/24/01 and sent another e-mail, the case could be reopened, updated with this information, and a new course of action could be taken (such as contacting UPS to find out the location of the package).

Many e-mail management systems for online customer service also provide the functionality of a case management system. In a real world situation, an e-mail management system alone may do the job. If you decide to go with an e-mail management system, make sure it can be used to track phone calls and other methods of inquiry, or that it can coordinate with the systems your company uses to track those inquiries.

Leading vendors of case management systems include:

✦ Nortel Networks (formerly Clarify)

✦ Kana

✦ Siebel

For Web addresses of the case management sites mentioned in this section, see the "For More Information . . ." section at the end of this chapter.

Supporting Synchronous E-Services

Supporting synchronous service

Synchronous service — online customer service offered in real time — is the closest thing online stores have to customer interaction as it is conducted in traditional commerce. It fulfills the need every customer is bound to have from time to time — to talk to a person who can help them immediately. Synchronous services currently used in e-commerce are:

✦ Live chat

✦ Remote browser control or co-browsing

Synchronous e-services present a greater challenge for customer support representatives than asynchronous e-services do. The reason for this lies in the very nature of synchronous service — because it's provided in real time, it is vital to have an adequately staffed customer service department to handle the traffic, *at all times*. For this reason, these *live* services are more often outsourced than asynchronous services.

In the following sections, the challenges and solutions specific to each type of synchronous e-service are covered.

Be sure that you understand the basics of chat service and remote control, and the scenarios in which they work best.

Chat services

Chat services are very similar to the well-known chat rooms of the Web. Web surfers can converse with each other in real time, with the messages printed on screen. The difference is that a chat service used for customer service is a connection between one customer service representative and one customer. Customer support chats are usually fairly short. If a customer needs help finding something on the site, the customer support representative can either describe how to get there or use remote control to *push* the browser to the correct location. The customer support representative can also help guide a user through the checkout process.

Live chat services can be the best way to communicate with customers who are hard of hearing or deaf. It's faster than using Telecommunications Device for Deaf (TDD) phones and can be done while the user is online. It's a great way to make your site more accessible and provide a valuable service to all of your customers at the same time.

Live chat challenges

Challenges for an online company implementing a chat support service include:

- ✦ The software supporting the chat service needs to be installed on the Web server and also on the desktops of the customer service representatives. (In some cases, the service is available to customer service representatives via a secure Web site.)
- ✦ Customer service representatives need to be trained on how to use the software and the proper etiquette to use when chatting.
- ✦ For maximum efficiency, each customer service representative may need to handle multiple chats at one time. Maintaining these multiple conversations requires the ultimate in multi-tasking skills!
- ✦ Each request for chat support needs to be responded to quickly. It's no good to keep customers waiting for a service that is supposed to speed up response times.
- ✦ It's not always possible to offer immediate support for a particular issue, although the user may expect it. More complex inquiries may take longer. If so, they should be routed to the asynchronous support system for a response via e-mail.
- ✦ Staffing must be adequate enough to handle the load; however, having too many customer service representatives assigned to chat is not cost-effective. Limiting chat support to specific hours of the day can help alleviate this problem.

Outsourcing live chat services

Because of these challenges, chat support is often outsourced. Companies that provide such outsourcing have a large number of customer support representatives servicing a number of Web sites. When a request for chat comes from your Web site, the customer service representative knows the user is at your site and provides information specific to your site.

Such services often charge on a per-chat or per-minute basis, which helps you keep costs in line with the actual service you're providing to your customers. After all, you could easily over-estimate the number of people who want to chat, leaving your customer service representatives under-employed, while you're paying them! Outsourcing can help prevent this problem.

Leading vendors of chat support software and outsourcing include:

- Kana
- Talisma
- Live Person
- Live Assistant
- Brightware

For Web addresses of the chat support software and outsourcing sites mentioned in this section, see the "For More Information . . ." section at the end of this chapter.

Remote control or co-browsing

Remote control is also commonly called *co-browsing* or *co-navigating*. It's essentially a software program that allows a customer service representative to help customers by pushing URLs to the customer's browser. The customer's browser is automatically taken to the URL that the customer support representative pushed, without the user having to do anything.

How it works

Remote control is usually used in concert with a live chat support session. For example, consider the following chat transcript:

Customer Support Representative (CSR): Welcome to Live Chat! How can I help you?

Customer: Hi. I am trying to find out how your sizes work — like is a large a size 12 or a size 14?

CSR: It sounds like you are looking for the women's sizing chart. Is that right?

Customer: Yes! That's what I need.

CSR: Shall I push your browser to the page with that information?

Customer: Yes, please.

The customer support representative then sends an order to the customer's browser, which is then automatically forwarded to the Web page where the women's clothes sizing chart can be found.

Benefits and challenges of remote control

Remote control can help customer service representatives assist customers more efficiently. Instead of describing how to get to a page on the site, customer service representatives can just send (push) the customer's browser to the correct page.

The software company HipBone is pioneering a new, more advanced kind of remote control that enables customer service representatives to manipulate Web page components on the user's browser. For example, a form can be filled in for a customer remotely. See `www.hipbone.com` for more information.

Some of the challenges for a customer support department using remote control are:

- As with the chat support feature, the customer support staff has to learn how to use new software.
- The co-browsing software also needs to be installed and configured on the Web server.
- Customer support representatives should try not to become too dependent on remote control — it's not the solution to every problem.

Leading vendors of remote control browsing software include:

- Kana
- net2gether
- NetDive

For Web addresses of the customer service support sites mentioned in this section, see the "For More Information . . ." section at the end of this chapter.

Supporting Self-Service Options

Supporting self-service

Some of the most effective forms of e-service are the self-service options. Although it may sound like such modes of e-service would just take care of themselves, they actually need frequent attention to maintain their usefulness. They are called self-service, because they do not require interaction between customers and customer support representatives.

Some forms of self-service e-service commonly used today are:

✦ Account maintenance areas

✦ Frequently asked questions (FAQ) lists

✦ Knowledge bases

✦ Web-based HTML help systems

✦ Bulletin boards and newsgroups

In the following sections, we take a look at the unique challenges of supporting each type of self-service, and the tools available to support them.

Account maintenance areas

An account maintenance area is a password-protected area of an e-commerce site where a customer can access and change information about his or her account, such as:

✦ Default shipping address

✦ Default credit card information (if any is saved)

✦ Order details and status

✦ Order history

✦ Shipment tracking

Account maintenance areas require access to the customer information and order information database(s). This data is then plugged into the HTML pages dynamically, depending upon which customer is signed on. Such applications are built using database integration tools such as Active Server Pages (ASP), Cold Fusion, and Common Gateway Interface (CGI) scripts.

Many mid-level and high-level e-commerce packages include account maintenance area functionality. The most important aspect of programming an account maintenance area is security. After all, if an unauthorized person is allowed to access sensitive customer information, your customer's privacy and credit card information could be used fraudulently, and your company's reputation may be in jeopardy.

See Chapter 19 for comprehensive information on security for e-commerce sites.

FAQ

An FAQ list is a collection of the most common questions asked by your customers. Such lists are usually hosted on one Web page or on several pages divided by category, if the list is rather long.

Assembling an FAQ list

Often, the most difficult part of assembling a FAQ list is getting your customer service representatives to contribute to the list. They are the ones who have the most contact with customers, after all, so they know which questions are asked most often. Because customer service representatives are quite busy, however, you may need to set aside time for each team member to contribute to the FAQ list.

Another way to make it easier for your employees to contribute to the list is to automate the process. An internal Web site could be set up in which authorized users could enter their contributions to the list. Make sure an answer is included for each question that is submitted.

Alternatively, if your company has implemented a system for tracking customer inquiries (such as the case management systems previously described), reports can be run on the system database. The results of these reports can be used to develop your FAQ list.

Tips for an effective FAQ

FAQ lists are most effective when they include the following items:

- ✦ **Links.** Whenever possible, link the answers to the appropriate area of the Web site. For example, if the question is, "How can I change my shipping address?" link the answer to the account maintenance area.
- ✦ **Categories.** If your FAQ list is more than 7-10 questions long, divide it into categories, whether on one page or several pages. This can help your customers find their questions faster.
- ✦ **An alternative.** Be sure to include an alternative for customers who can't find what they're looking for on the FAQ list. This alternative can be a link to another kind of support, such as e-mail or live chat.

Knowledge bases

Knowledge bases

A knowledge base is a database of customer support issues and inquiries that is searchable by customers via a Web page. It's essentially an FAQ list constructed as a database. Because it's a database, however, it can house much more information than an FAQ list, without becoming unwieldy. As a database, it's more complicated to set up than an FAQ list. For complex Web sites, however, long-term advantages can outweigh any difficulties initially encountered with set up.

Many companies also use knowledge bases to provide online support for their products — especially computer hardware and software. This is often the only way to handle the large number of customer support requests such a company receives.

Many issues are solved through the self-service knowledge base, and many more are referred to customer service representatives. Still, the load on actual humans is reduced.

How a knowledge base works

In most cases, the entry point to a knowledge base is a Web form. Some are more complex than others, but in most cases, the user is asked to enter one or more keywords and to select a type of inquiry—such as technical or non-technical—or to choose from products or product lines.

Once the user has entered information and clicked the form's submit button, he or she is presented with either a list of successful matches or a notification that the query returned no matches. If there are no matches, the user can try again. Otherwise, the user searches the list of matches for the information he or she requires.

Many knowledge bases also allow users to enter new queries if their searches don't return any results. This is often how knowledge bases are improved and expanded.

How to populate a knowledge base

A knowledge base consists of database records. Each record typically has a title, description, a lengthy text area for the information or answer to the query, a date, an identification number, and any other information a company may deem necessary.

For a company with an established customer support software system, such as a case management system, populating a knowledge base can be as easy as exporting data from the customer support system and importing it into the knowledge base. However, in most cases, the time should be taken to edit the database records after they have been imported. Many of the records from the case management system may be virtual duplicates in terms of the questions asked. In a knowledge base, every single customer inquiry does not need to be represented—when more than one customer has asked the same question, the records can be consolidated into one question.

Tips for a successful knowledge base

The following guidelines can be helpful when developing a knowledge base:

- **Avoid duplicate questions.** Consolidate identical questions into one record, so users of the knowledge base are not confused by a large number of successful matches.
- **Maintain the knowledge base regularly.** Frequent maintenance of the knowledge base is necessary for it to remain useful to customers.
- **Be pro-active, anticipating customers' needs.** When a new product or site feature is released, anticipate user questions and enter them into the knowledge base.

✦ **Update existing entries.** If a new release of a software product fixes a problem in a previous release, add that information (along with a link to the new version) to the knowledge base entry about the problem.

Knowledge base software vendors

Knowledge bases are becoming more frequently included in comprehensive e-service support packages. Some of the leading vendors are:

✦ **Talisma.** Offers a knowledge base product called Self Help. Searches can be conducted using keywords and questions.

✦ **Kana.** The Kana Service package includes a knowledge base, personalization technology, and a case management tool.

✦ **RightNow Technologies.** The RightNow Web tool integrates several modes of customer service to produce a dynamic knowledge base.

For Web addresses of the knowledge base vendor sites mentioned in this section, see the "For More Information . . ." section at the end of this chapter.

Web-based help systems

Web-based help systems are custom-coded sets of Web pages that contain customer support information. They are usually developed using Dynamic HTML (DHTML) or Java.

Web-based help systems are becoming common ways to offer customers support for software and other products. In the newest versions of many software programs, it's not uncommon to be taken to a Web site after choosing Help from the menu bar.

Web-based help systems are not only for software. They can also be used to provide customer support for e-commerce. For an excellent example of a Web-based help system, see the Microsoft Developer Network site at `http://msdn.microsoft.com`.

Bulletin boards and newsgroups

As described in Chapter 6, bulletin boards and newsgroups fall into the category of self-service when customers answer each other's questions. However, when a customer service representative answers questions, they are asynchronous services.

Typically, a combination of the two modes is what happens in practice. Some questions are answered by fellow customers, and, occasionally, a customer service representative steps in to answer questions that go unanswered for more than a few hours or days (depending upon the company's service standards).

Tips for success

To maintain a successful bulletin board or newsgroup, keep the following guidelines in mind:

- **Monitor posts.** Even if your bulletin board or newsgroup is entirely self-service, be sure to monitor user posts to make sure they are on-topic, and to remove those that aren't. Your site can quickly become the host of unwanted conversations if this step is not taken.
- **Update information.** If a response to a past question becomes outdated or irrelevant, be sure to update the original post with the new information. That way, users can follow a thread to its accurate, up-to-date conclusion instead of getting an outdated answer.
- **Answer promptly.** If your customers' postings are answered by customer support representatives, make sure they're answered promptly.
- **Post guidelines and instructions.** Be sure to inform your customers of how the bulletin board or newsgroup works, how soon to expect an answer, and the approved topics of conversation.

Bulletin board and newsgroup vendors

There are many bulletin board and newsgroup software programs available for free or for insignificant amounts of money that are downloadable over the Internet. Vendors that provide more robust packages include:

- **Pushpin.** A CGI-based forum software program features full set of bulletin board capabilities and an administration area for the board moderator.
- **vBulletin.** Developed using PHP Hypertext Preprocessor (PHP) and mySQL, vBulletin allows for multiple boards and features a user-friendly Web-based administration area.
- **Encore Web Forum.** Offered by Aborior, this bulletin board software is highly customizable and can be used on almost any Web server platform.

For Web addresses of the bulletin board and newsgroup software sites mentioned in this section, see the "For More Information . . ." section at the end of this chapter.

Key Point Summary

This chapter covered the challenges of supporting e-services and the tools available to meet these challenges. The key points are:

- Customer support representatives working in e-services need a more technical tool set than those in traditional customer service.
- The tools needed to support your site's e-services depend on the kind of e-service you're providing.
- An e-mail management system is a software application that routes e-mails into queues for response by customer support representatives.
- A case management system is a software application that tracks customer problems and inquiries as they are worked on by the customer support team.
- E-mail management and case management systems are used in asynchronous support models.
- Chat services and remote control are used to provide synchronous service.
- Complex requests and questions submitted by customers using synchronous service often are re-routed to an asynchronous service system, if they cannot be answered relatively quickly.
- Self-service options — such as account maintenance areas, FAQ lists, knowledge bases, Web-based help systems, bulletin boards, and newsgroups — are often the most effective, and most frequently used, forms of e-service.

✦ ✦ ✦

STUDY GUIDE

In this chapter, you read in-depth information on the tools available for supporting e-service. Test and expand your knowledge with the questions and exercises in this study guide.

Assessment Questions

1. Which of the following is the most accurate definition of a knowledge base?
   - **A.** A static list of helpful information on how to use a Web site or product
   - **B.** A database of information on how to use a Web site or product that is searchable through a Web form
   - **C.** A forum for exchanging information on the use of a product or Web site
   - **D.** A core set of knowledge in a particular subject
2. Which of the following is *not* a typical means for populating a knowledge base?
   - **A.** Gathering information from customer support representatives
   - **B.** Exporting data from the company's case management system
   - **C.** Selecting customer inquiries for inclusion
   - **D.** Allowing customers to answer each other's questions
3. Which of the following is a form of asynchronous service?
   - **A.** Live chat
   - **B.** Account management area
   - **C.** E-mail
   - **D.** Web-based help
4. Why is staffing for asynchronous service easier than for synchronous service?
   - **A.** Asynchronous service can take place after the user has stopped browsing; synchronous service must be responded to immediately.
   - **B.** Synchronous service can take place after the user has stopped browsing; asynchronous service must be responded to immediately.
   - **C.** Asynchronous service requires more employees.
   - **D.** Asynchronous service cannot be outsourced.

5. What kind of customer inquiries are best suited to live chat support?

A. Simple questions about how to find a part of the Web site

B. Change of address requests

C. Shipment tracking requests

D. Questions about the status of a previously placed order

6. Which of the following is the best definition of remote control, or co-browsing?

A. Two users browsing a Web site at the same time

B. A system that allows a customer service representative to send a Web page to a user

C. A system that allows a customer service representative to direct a user's browser to a particular Web page

D. A device for controlling a browser from a distance

7. Which of the following is *not* an example of a kind of Web self-service?

A. Account maintenance area

B. Bulletin board

C. Knowledge base

D. E-mail

8. Which of the following is *not* a possible result of leaving a bulletin board unmoderated?

A. Unwelcome, off-topic conversations are carried out on the bulletin board.

B. Questions go unanswered.

C. Users give each other incorrect answers to problems.

D. No one uses the bulletin board.

Scenario

Suppose your customer support department handles the following types of inquiries via e-mail:

- When a package was shipped
- When a shipment will arrive
- Whether an order has been fulfilled

- Order cancellations
- Changes to existing orders (quantity changes, shipping address changes, etc.)
- Billing address changes
- Default shipping address changes
- Gift certificate redemption
- Account balance inquiries
- Refund requests

Your department is buying an e-mail management system and you need to decide how these types of inquiries will be sorted into queues. On your customer support form, you have decided to include a menu of topics from which customers can choose, and a text box where customers can describe their specific situations and send the information in the form. Based on this, answer the following questions:

- What choices would you put in the topic drop-down list?
- What queues would you set up based on these choices?

Lab Exercise

Lab 18-1 Experiencing live chat

In this lab exercise, you experience live chat from the user's point of view by visiting a live chat at the Web site of Talisma, a company that sells chatting software.

1. Point your browser to `http://www.talisma.com`.
2. You'll see the Talisma home page. Click Go Straight to Site to skip the Flash intro page.
3. The next page is the main information page for Talisma. In the top right hand corner is an icon labeled Chat Now. Click this icon.
4. The top half of the window becomes an area for chatting. Wait a few moments for a representative to pick up the chat.
5. A customer service representative should open the chat and introduce him or herself. See Figure 18-1. On the right is a box for you to respond. Click inside the box and type the following: **Thank you for helping me out today. I am looking for information on Talisma's Chat program.**

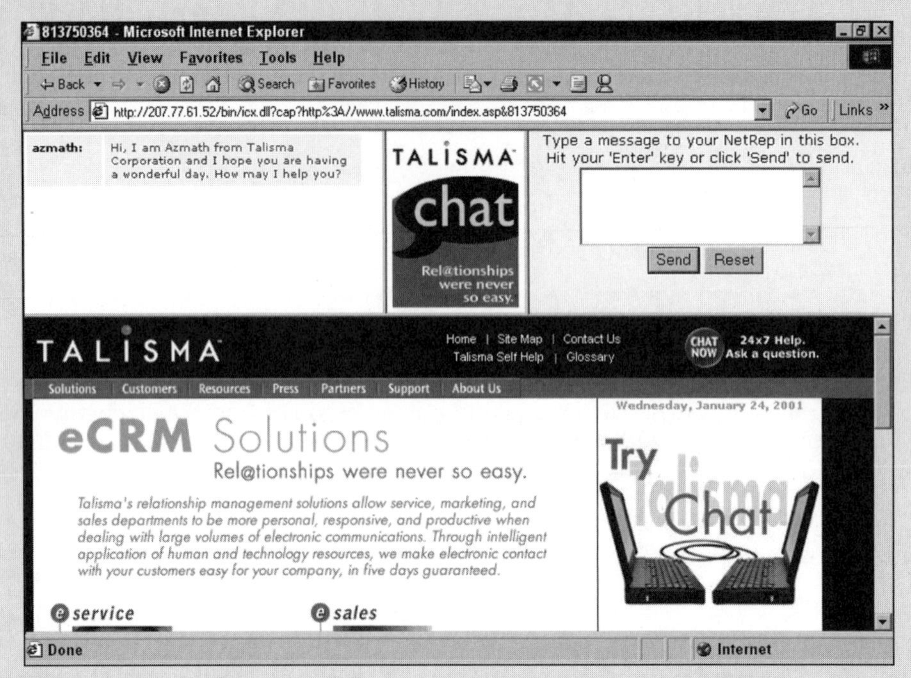

Figure 18-1: Chatting with a Talisma customer support representative

6. Click the Send key to send your message. You should see it appear in the transcript on the left.
7. The customer service representative may offer to push you to a page with this information. If they don't, ask them to.
8. After you're pushed to a page, the page to which your browser has been pushed should appear in the lower frame of the browser screen.
9. Continue chatting as long as you like. When you're ready to stop, tell the customer service representative and they should close the chat window for you.

Answers to Chapter Questions

Chapter pre-test

1. E-mail management systems and case management systems are tools for supporting asynchronous e-services.
2. E-service customer support representatives need to have technical skills such as Web expertise and e-mails skills as well as high-level problem solving skills.

3. An e-mail management system is a software program that routes e-mails into queues, which are monitored by multiple customer service representatives.
4. Alternative terms for co-browsing are remote control and co-navigation.
5. FAQ data usually comes from a company's case management system and the customer support representatives themselves.

Assessment questions

1. **B.** A knowledge base is a database of information and questions and answers about a product or Web site. It's accessible through a Web form or a Web page (see "Knowledge bases").
2. **D.** Customers are able to answer each other's questions in a bulletin board or newsgroup, not a knowledge base. The other answers are all common ways of populating a knowledge base (see "How to populate a knowledge base").
3. **C.** E-mail is the only form of asynchronous service listed. Live chat is synchronous service; Web-based help and an account management area are examples of self-service (see "Supporting Asynchronous E-Services").
4. **A.** Asynchronous service doesn't demand an immediate answer, and therefore does not require a critical mass of customer service representatives at any given time. Answers C and D are incorrect because synchronous service usually demands more employees, and asynchronous service can be outsourced (see "Supporting Asynchronous E-Services").
5. **A.** Simple requests are most well suited to live chat support, because they do not require extensive research or access to another software application, and can therefore be answered almost immediately (see "Chat services").
6. **C.** Remote control is a system that allows a customer service representative to direct a user's browser to a particular Web page. It is not sending a Web page, but rather sending a URL to the browser, which the browser is then directed to open (see "Remote control or co-browsing").
7. **D.** E-mail is a form of asynchronous service (see "Supporting Self-Service Options").
8. **D.** Leaving a board unmoderated would not necessarily lead to disuse. The other answers are likely to occur in a bulletin board situation, however (see "Bulletin boards and newsgroups").

Scenario

There are many possible answers to this scenario. The answer you come up with is largely dependent upon your opinions and experiences. One possible answer is described here:

✦ Too many options in the topic drop-down can cause more misdirected e-mails, because customers may not be exactly sure where their inquiries fit in. Offer the following broad topics in the drop-down menu:

  • Shipment status (when a package was shipped, when a shipment may arrive)

  • Orders (whether an order has been fulfilled, canceled, or changed)

  • Account maintenance (billing address changes, gift certificate redemption, account balance inquiries)

  • Other (refund requests and other infrequent inquiries)

✦ Your e-mail queues could correspond exactly to these topics. A team of customer support representatives would take messages from the queues either based on specific duties (i.e., individuals assigned to one queue) or as a catch-all (all staff members answer messages from all queues in the order they're received). A manager, for instance, could review the Other queue before it's passed to a customer service representative, because it might contain unusual requests that need managerial approval.

✦ These decisions depend largely on the size of your customer support staff. In small departments, the queues may serve as guidelines rather than a division of labor. In larger departments, they can be used to assign duties.

For More Information . . .

✦ **eGain.** www.egain.com. E-services support software for large companies.

✦ **Kana.** www.kana.com. E-services support integrated with sales and marketing products.

✦ **E.piphany.** www.epiphany.com. E-services support applications that can be used together in a suite.

✦ **Siebel.** www.siebel.com. E-services applications that manage and coordinate a variety of e-service technologies.

✦ **netCustomer.** www.netcustomer.com. E-services application and personnel ASP geared toward companies looking for an outsourced solution.

✦ **Talisma.** www.talisma.com. Full suite of e-services applications and services, including outsourcing.

✦ **Nortel Networks.** www.nortelnetworks.com. Provides Clarify customer support products.

✦ **Live Person.** www.liveperson.com. Online customer support chat software.

✦ **Live Assistant.** www.liveassistant.com. Chat software for e-service.

- **Brightware.** www.brightware.com. Customer support software for online businesses, including chat and remote control products.
- **net2gether.** www.net2gether.com. Remote control browsing software.
- **NetDive.** www.netdive.com. Vendor of live customer service software.
- **Pushpin.** www.pushpin.com. Forum software.
- **RightNow Technologies.** www.rightnow.com. Vendor of a knowledge base Web tool and more.
- **vBulletin.** www.vbulletin.com. Bulletin board software for medium and large sites.
- **Encore Web Forum.** www.aborior.com/products/encore/index.shtml. Customizable Web forum software. A free demo is available for download.

CHAPTER 19

E-Commerce Transaction Security

✦ ✦ ✦ ✦

EXAM OBJECTIVES

- Authentication and identification
- Encryption and decryption
- Certificates
- X.509v3
- Electronic commerce security myths

CHAPTER PRE-TEST

1. What are the five purposes security serves in electronic commerce?
2. What is non-repudiation?
3. What is the difference between symmetric and asymmetric encryption?
4. What is a message digest?
5. What is the purpose of a Certifying Authority (CA)?
6. What are the four types of digital certificates?
7. What is SSL?
8. What is X.509?

✦ Answers to these questions can be found at the end of the chapter. ✦

Security is vital to commerce of any kind, and systems designed to prevent fraud and theft are parts of every traditional and electronic commerce system. In this chapter, you get a broad overview of e-commerce security, learn why it's important, and discover how the different parts of e-commerce systems can be secured.

Understanding E-Commerce Security

The Internet is probably one of the most complex entities ever created by humans. As a result, it's full of bugs, security holes, and vulnerabilities. The great thing about the Internet is that it is designed to keep running in spite of problems.

Individual sites on the Internet, however, are much less resilient. Web sites need to be protected from malicious attacks as well as from people who are just snooping around. As in the world outside of the Internet, where there's money, there are thieves. Where there are thieves, however, there are good locks and security systems.

Security on the Internet serves five purposes:

- Authentication and identification
- Access control
- Data confidentiality
- Data integrity
- Non-repudiation

In the following sections, we define and explain each of these purposes of security.

Establishing identification and authentication

Authentication and identification

Identification and authentication ensure that someone is who he or she claims to be. As the following sections illustrate, these concepts, although similar, can have very different implications when dealing with a traditional versus an Internet application.

By traditional means

When you write a check to your local grocery store, the cashier typically asks for your driver's license or another form of identification. This practice serves the following purposes:

- To verify that you are the person whose name is on the check
- To allow the cashier to record your driver's license number, which helps the merchant locate you if the check bounces

Similarly, when you go to a doctor's office, you go through a process of identification and authentication to make sure that your doctor is actually a doctor and not someone merely pretending to be one. Some of the steps involved in this process might include examining the degrees on the wall, comparing the office to other doctors' offices you've been in, and so forth. You may also have done some research in advance, such as asking a trusted family member or friend for a recommendation, or verifying the doctor's identity with an organization such as the American Medical Association.

On the Internet

On the Internet, many of the methods we use for verifying identity and authenticity in the real world are meaningless. Anyone can display a picture of a supermodel on his or her free home page and claim to be that person. Although it's unlikely that a super model would create a *free* Web site, you would have a hard time proving or disproving this claim.

One form of proof would be to personally ask the super model. You could also ask someone you trust and who is a mutual friend of both you and the super model. If the owner of the site actually is who she claims to be, she may become tired of constantly affirming her identity to every visitor to the site.

To speed the process of verifying identification, the owner of a Web site can obtain a certificate from a third party that has done the research and verified the authenticity of the site. As long as the third party can be trusted, visitors to the site only need to check the certificate to confirm that the site belongs to the person claiming ownership. This, in fact, is how digital certificates work. You'll learn more about this in the "Understanding Digital Certificates" section later in this chapter.

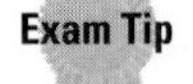

It's important to know that digital certificates provide authentication.

Managing access control

Access control is the process of limiting access to resources. In the physical world, access control is most often provided using locks and keys. Newer and more advanced access control systems may use unique identifying characteristics such as thumb prints or voice prints instead of keys. Either way, the concept is the same: Let in some people and keep others out.

In computer systems, and on the Internet, access control is provided by a variety of mechanisms, as follows:

✦ User names and passwords are the most common way of securing computing resources.

✦ You can also limit the times during which resources can be used (only during business hours, for example).

✦ You can further limit users by host name.

Ensuring data confidentiality

Data confidentiality deals with the ability of parties to exchange information without it being read by anyone else. This is where cryptography comes in. *Cryptography* is the use of complicated mathematics to render data unreadable to prying eyes. The basic concepts behind cryptography are simple to understand. You'll explore these concepts in more detail in the "Understanding Cryptography" section later in this chapter.

Ensuring data integrity

Data integrity deals with the validity of data. Examples of data integrity questions include:

✦ Is this e-mail the same as when it was sent?

✦ Are these the actual stock prices?

✦ Has the image on the television been modified?

Integrity is different from authentication. Authentication deals with who sent a message or who authorized a purchase, whereas integrity deals with whether the data in that message or the details of the purchase were modified after they were sent.

Integrity also does not deal with the accuracy of data. Accuracy tells how data relates to the world. Integrity deals with the data's relation to itself over time.

Ensuring non-repudiation

Non-repudiation is defined as the method used to prevent the parties involved in a transaction from denying that they agreed to a sale or purchase. In the physical world, a signed credit card receipt from a store provides non-repudiation for both the merchant and the customer. The customer uses the receipt to prove that an item he or she is returning was actually purchased at that store. The merchant, on the other hand, can use its copy of the receipt in the event that the customer denies he or she purchased the item and demands a refund from the credit card company.

Non-repudiation is provided using authentication and auditing. We've already talked about authentication in the "Establishing identification and authentication" section. Auditing is generally done by monitoring a server's logs. Without auditing your secure system, you may have hackers running wild on your system and not even know it.

Understanding Cryptography

Encryption and decryption

Cryptography is the study of the development of methods of secret writing. Cryptography has been used for thousands of years to protect secrets. Hundreds of methods of secret writing have been designed, and hundreds of ways have been found to defeat the different methods of secret writing, which keeps the inventors of cryptographic systems busy coming up with new methods of secret writing.

Cryptography terms

Today, cryptography is more widely used than ever, and an understanding of cryptographic techniques and technologies is vital to understanding e-commerce security. Before you continue, you need to understand the following terms:

- **Plaintext.** A message that can be read by humans.
- **Ciphertext.** Text that has been disguised to make it unreadable by humans.
- **Encryption.** The process of creating ciphertext from plaintext.
- **Decryption.** The process of restoring the plaintext from ciphertext.
- **Cipher.** A cryptographic algorithm used to encrypt and decrypt messages.
- **Key.** A value used by a cryptographic algorithm to encrypt and decrypt messages. Keys are the element of a cryptosystem that are unique to particular users of the system. As a result of the use of keys, the best encryption methods available today are open source. Anyone can find out how they work, but this doesn't aid in decryption, because keys are still kept secret. The same is true of real world keys and locks. Anyone can find out how a door lock works (they have pins that can be set to various positions), but to open the lock, you need the correct key.

Evaluating encryption strength

The strength of encryption depends on the following three factors:

- **The strength of the algorithm.** Over the years, many algorithms that were thought to be unbreakable have proven to have flaws that could be exploited to crack the code.

The encryption standards we discuss in this chapter have all been thoroughly tested over time and have proven to be reliable. This is not to say that they're unbreakable, but the effort required to break them is so great that it outweighs the potential benefits of doing so.

✦ **The secrecy of the key.** Naturally, if a third party intercepts the key, no message encrypted with that key is safe. This is actually the biggest problem with secret key encryption — it requires that all of the parties involved must securely exchange a key to exchange secure messages.

In a later section of this chapter, you'll look at public key encryption, or asymmetric encryption, which does not require the parties who wish to exchange secure messages to share a key.

✦ **The length of the key.** The longer the key, the more possible keys there are. The more possible keys that exist, the more difficult it is for someone to discover the key using a *brute force attack*. In a brute force attack, each possible key is tried until the correct one is found. This approach is not the most brilliant way to crack a code, but it works.

Calculating security in key lengths

The length of a key is specified in bits. Because bits can have one of two possible values, the number of possible combinations of a key doubles for each additional bit in the key length and can be expressed as 2^n, where n is the number of bits.

For example, a 2-bit key has 2^2, or 4 possible combinations. A 10-bit key has 2^{10}, or 1024 possible combinations. This is still extremely weak encryption. A 40-bit key has 1,099,511,627,776 possible values. Now we're getting somewhere. Still, a 40-bit key could be cracked in 1998 in 18 minutes. With the increasing speed of computers, 40-bit keys just don't cut it today.

Today, it's common for keys to be at least 128 bits. Using this key length, it would take today's fastest computers millions of years to try out every possible key combination. Because we cannot predict future computing advances, many experts today recommend key lengths of 1024 bits.

Key length is not the only factor that determines the security of a cryptosystem. It would also take a long time to try every possible combination on a padlock, or every possible key to a door lock, but this is not the most efficient way to defeat these security methods. It's much easier to cut the lock or break a window.

Types of Cryptography

There are three types of encryption that are commonly used today:

✦ Symmetric encryption

✦ Asymmetric encryption

✦ One-way encryption

The next sections look at each of these encryption types in detail.

Knowing these three types of encryption, the difference between them, and how each uses keys is important and heavily emphasized on the exam.

Symmetric encryption

Symmetric encryption is also known as private key encryption, session key encryption, shared key encryption, and secret-key encryption. In private key encryption, the parties sharing information must all have an identical, secret key. Symmetric key encryption is one of the oldest forms of secret writing.

Block ciphers

One type of symmetric encryption algorithm is the *block cipher*, which uses a key to transform a block of plaintext into a block of ciphertext of the same length. Reversing the transformation that encrypted the plaintext decrypts the ciphertext.

A very simple example of symmetric encryption using a block cipher is as follows: Mr. Smith and Mr. Jones wish to exchange secret messages. During their daily meetings, Mr. Smith hands Mr. Jones a piece of paper containing a key. Today's key is the following:

```
TODAYSKEY
```

In addition to the key, both Mr. Smith and Mr. Jones must know the algorithm they are using. In this case, it's the one known as the modern Vigenère cipher. (This is referred to as the modern Vigenère cipher because it's a watered-down version of the cipher originally created by Blaise de Vigenère in the 16th century.)

This cipher works by encrypting plaintext using a key and a table, such as the one shown in Table 19-1.

Table 19-1
The Modern Vigenère Table

a	*b*	*c*	*d*	*e*	*f*	*g*	*h*	*i*	*j*	*k*	*l*	*m*	*n*	*o*	*p*	*q*	*r*	*s*	*t*	*u*	*v*	*w*	*x*	*y*	*z*	
A	A	B	C	D	E	F	G	H	I	J	K	L	M	N	O	P	Q	R	S	T	U	V	W	X	Y	Z
B	B	C	D	E	F	G	H	I	J	K	L	M	N	O	P	Q	R	S	T	U	V	W	X	Y	Z	A
C	C	D	E	F	G	H	I	J	K	L	M	N	O	P	Q	R	S	T	U	V	W	X	Y	Z	A	B
D	D	E	F	G	H	I	J	K	L	M	N	O	P	Q	R	S	T	U	V	W	X	Y	Z	A	B	C
E	E	F	G	H	I	J	K	L	M	N	O	P	Q	R	S	T	U	V	W	X	Y	Z	A	B	C	D
F	F	G	H	I	J	K	L	M	N	O	P	Q	R	S	T	U	V	W	X	Y	Z	A	B	C	D	E
G	G	H	I	J	K	L	M	N	O	P	Q	R	S	T	U	V	W	X	Y	Z	A	B	C	D	E	F
H	H	I	J	K	L	M	N	O	P	Q	R	S	T	U	V	W	X	Y	Z	A	B	C	D	E	F	G
I	I	J	K	L	M	N	O	P	Q	R	S	T	U	V	W	X	Y	Z	A	B	C	D	E	F	G	H
J	J	K	L	M	N	O	P	Q	R	S	T	U	V	W	X	Y	Z	A	B	C	D	E	F	G	H	I
K	K	L	M	N	O	P	Q	R	S	T	U	V	W	X	Y	Z	A	B	C	D	E	F	G	H	I	J
L	L	M	N	O	P	Q	R	S	T	U	V	W	X	Y	Z	A	B	C	D	E	F	G	H	I	J	K
M	M	N	O	P	Q	R	S	T	U	V	W	X	Y	Z	A	B	C	D	E	F	G	H	I	J	K	L
N	N	O	P	Q	R	S	T	U	V	W	X	Y	Z	A	B	C	D	E	F	G	H	I	J	K	L	M
O	O	P	Q	R	S	T	U	V	W	X	Y	Z	A	B	C	D	E	F	G	H	I	J	K	L	M	N
P	P	Q	R	S	T	U	V	W	X	Y	Z	A	B	C	D	E	F	G	H	I	J	K	L	M	N	O
Q	Q	R	S	T	U	V	W	X	Y	Z	A	B	C	D	E	F	G	H	I	J	K	L	M	N	O	P
R	R	S	T	U	V	W	X	Y	Z	A	B	C	D	E	F	G	H	I	J	K	L	M	N	O	P	Q
S	S	T	U	V	W	X	Y	Z	A	B	C	D	E	F	G	H	I	J	K	L	M	N	O	P	Q	R
T	T	U	V	W	X	Y	Z	A	B	C	D	E	F	G	H	I	J	K	L	M	N	O	P	Q	R	S
U	U	V	W	X	Y	Z	A	B	C	D	E	F	G	H	I	J	K	L	M	N	O	P	Q	R	S	T
V	V	W	X	Y	Z	A	B	C	D	E	F	G	H	I	J	K	L	M	N	O	P	Q	R	S	T	U
W	W	X	Y	Z	A	B	C	D	E	F	G	H	I	J	K	L	M	N	O	P	Q	R	S	T	U	V
X	X	Y	Z	A	B	C	D	E	F	G	H	I	J	K	L	M	N	O	P	Q	R	S	T	U	V	W
Y	Y	Z	A	B	C	D	E	F	G	H	I	J	K	L	M	N	O	P	Q	R	S	T	U	V	W	X
Z	Z	A	B	C	D	E	F	G	H	I	J	K	L	M	N	O	P	Q	R	S	T	U	V	W	X	Y

The alphabet across the top of the table is the plaintext alphabet. The one along the left site is the key alphabet. To begin encrypting a message using this key, you find the first plaintext letter in the top alphabet, and then trace down that column until it intersects with the row containing the first key letter. Repeat this process for each letter of the plaintext, repeating the key as necessary. For example, Listing 19-1 shows the plaintext, key, and ciphertext for a message encrypted using this method.

Listing 19-1: The key, plaintext, and ciphertext for a message encrypted with the modern Vigenère cipher

```
key     TODAYSKEYTODAYSK
plain   hereisthemessage
cipher  ASUEGKDLCFSVSYYO
```

Any one who intercepts the ciphertext will see only gibberish (ASUEGKDLCFSVSYYO). A person who knows how to decode the message and who has the key is able to decrypt this message easily. For example, given the first letter in the ciphertext (A), and the first letter in the key (T), you simply locate the T in the key letter column (to the left), and then follow that row until you find the A. Follow that column up to the top to locate the first plaintext letter, which happens to be h.

Although this is a simple example of symmetric encryption, it illustrates the basic principles involved and the use of a key to make it possible for a publicly known algorithm to provide security. This particular cipher is fairly easy to crack (especially when a large amount of ciphertext is provided or when the key is short), and does not provide much security.

The following encryption algorithms use symmetric key encryption:

✦ **Data Encryption Standard (DES).** DES is the most widely used symmetric encryption algorithm. It was designed by IBM for the U.S. government in the 1970s and uses a 56-bit key. Today, it is widely considered to be obsolete and vulnerable to cracking.

✦ **Triple-DES.** Triple-DES encrypts data by running it through DES encryption three times — forwards, backwards, and then forwards again. During the backwards run, it uses a second 56-bit key. It is considered to be a good successor to DES, because it doesn't require new algorithms.

✦ **RC4.** Created by Ron Rivest, RC4 is a very fast encryption algorithm that is frequently used by the Secure Sockets Layer (SSL) protocol. It uses a variable key length.

RC4 was originally a trade secret of RSA Data Security, Inc, but the algorithm was anonymously posted to the Internet in September of 1994. RC4 has been cracked using brute force attacks and is beginning to show signs of age.

- **RC5.** RC5 uses a variable key length as well as variable block sizes and a variable number of rounds.

RC5 with a 32-bit key (RC5-32) was cracked in 1997 by an organization called distributed.net, which uses computers connected through the Internet to try possible keys. Since 1997, distributed.net has been trying to crack a message encoded in RC5-64. As of early 2001, the rate at which distributed.net is testing possible keys is 127,000,000,000 keys per second.

- **Skipjack.** Created by the National Security Agency (NSA), Skipjack uses an 80-bit key and a 64-bit 32-round block cipher.
- **International Data Encryption Algorithm (IDEA).** IDEA uses a 128-bit key to operate on 64-bit plaintext blocks in eight iterations.
- **Blowfish.** An encryption algorithm developed by Bruce Schneier in 1993 that has a variable key length from 32 to 448-bits.
- **Twofish.** Also designed by Bruce Schneier, Twofish was a finalist to become the new standard encryption of the U.S. government.
- **Advanced Encryption Standard (AES).** AES is the name for the new standard that will replace DES as the U.S. government's standard cipher.

One-time pads

One-time pads are the simplest, and the most secure type of cryptographic algorithm. Unfortunately, they are very impractical for most purposes. The idea behind a one-time pad is that you have a pad containing key letters. To encrypt a message using this pad, you add each letter in the pad to a letter in the plaintext, and never use a key letter more than once. The result is a key that is the same length as the original message.

For example, assume that the key is:

```
TUSCKR
```

and the plaintext is:

```
monkey
```

To encrypt the plaintext, you would add the numerical values of the letters and subtract 26 if the result is greater than 26. In the previous example, the plaintext would be encrypted as:

```
20+13 = 33 - 26 = 7 = g
21+15 = 36 - 26 = 10 = j
19+14 = 33 - 26 = 7 = g
3+11 = 14 = n
11+5 = 16 = p
18+25 = 43 - 26 = 17 = q
```

or

```
ciphertext = gjgnpq
```

Starting with this ciphertext, it's impossible to figure out the plaintext without the key. Unfortunately, things aren't always so neat in the real world. Here's why:

- It's often impractical to exchange one-time pads.
- People make mistakes, which often compromise one-time pad systems.
- It's not realistic to encrypt large items using one-time pads, because the key must be just as large as the item being encrypted.

Because of these limitations, one-time pads are not used in Internet security.

Asymmetric encryption

Asymmetric encryption does not require two parties who want to exchange encrypted data to share a key. In fact, using asymmetric encryption, two complete strangers can send each other encrypted messages that can only be read by the intended recipient.

Whereas the idea behind symmetric encryption is centuries old, asymmetric encryption is a very new technology. Whitfield Diffie and Martin Hellman first proposed it in 1976.

Asymmetric, or public key, encryption relies on algorithms that are easy to calculate in one direction but very difficult to calculate in the opposite direction. For example, it's easy to multiply two large prime numbers together to get a product, but it's very difficult to factor the large product to arrive at the two factors that were originally multiplied together.

Although you don't need to understand the mathematical details of public key encryption systems to use them, you can find out these details easily on the Web. A place to begin is `www.rsasecurity.com`. Remember that keys make it possible for the actual algorithms to be public knowledge.

The public key concept

Here's how public key encryption works: Mr. Smith uses software to create two keys: a public key and a private key. He keeps the private key in a safe place and doesn't share it with anyone. He does share the public key, however. There are vast databases of public keys on the Internet where he can post his public key. He can also post his public key on his Web site, and even rent a billboard to display it to the world if he likes.

Mrs. Jones also has a public key and a private key. Mrs. Jones wants to send a secret message to Mr. Smith (who she has never met). While driving home from work one day, she stops to copy Mr. Smith's public key from the billboard she passes every day. (She could also just look at his Web site, or look him up in a directory.) Using Mr. Smith's public key, Mrs. Jones is able to encrypt a message to him. This message is only readable by Mr. Smith, because only his private key can decrypt it. Figure 19-1 illustrates this process.

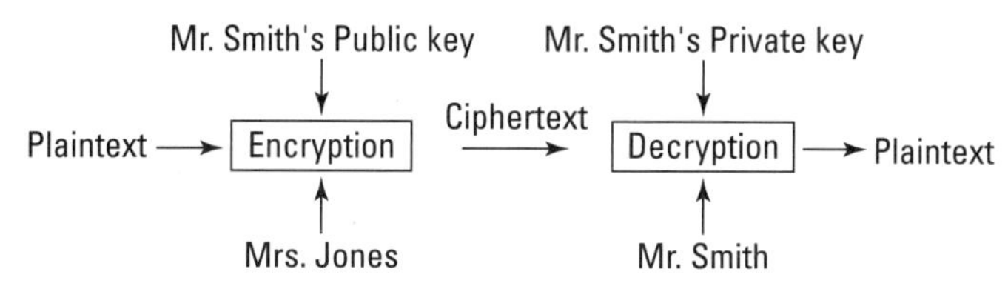

Figure 19-1: Public-key (asymmetric) encryption

How it works

Public key encryption has the following characteristics:

✦ The ciphertext is calculated by applying the algorithm with a public key on the plaintext. The ciphertext is decrypted by applying the algorithm with the private key.

✦ It's very difficult to calculate the private key from the public key.

✦ The public and private keys are easy to calculate, but not easy to guess.

In 1991, Phil Zimmerman released his public key encryption software, Pretty Good Privacy (PGP), as freeware. As a result, PGP quickly became the most widely used method for sending encrypted e-mail, and Zimmerman was the target of a three-year criminal investigation. The government held that strong cryptography was illegally exported to foreign countries as a result of PGP's publication. The case was eventually dropped and Network Associates, Inc. now owns and publishes PGP. PGP is still freely available for non-commercial uses at `http://web.mit.edu/network/pgp.html`.

The standard that is used by most public key encryption products, including PGP, is RSA. RSA was created by and named after Ron Rivest, Avi Shamir, and Rick Adleman in 1978 at the Massachusetts Institute of Technology (MIT). The key length used in RSA encryption is variable. Common key lengths in RSA security are 528-bit, 1024-bit, and 2048-bit.

One-way encryption

One-way encryption is just what it sounds like: A way to encrypt data so it's not feasible to decrypt it. One-way encryption uses *hash functions*, which calculate a kind of digital fingerprint for a piece of digital data. The result of a hash function is much smaller than the data that was input into the function, but it's very difficult to create two different inputs into a hash function that would produce the same result or to derive the input from the result of the hash function. One-way hash functions are commonly used to store passwords, personal identification numbers, and so forth.

How hash functions work

For example, assume that Laura's password is Cucumber23. When she first sets her password on a Web site or computer, the computer performs a one-way hash of this password and stores the result. For example, the result is t78dnkdur. The next time Laura returns to the site, she must enter the password. She's granted access if the password she enters, when run through the same hash function, matches the value stored on the computer.

Because it's nearly impossible to calculate the password from the one-way hash, anyone who manages to access the database where the passwords are stored would not be able to do anything with them.

One-way encryption also provides authentication and integrity. For example, if you send a letter to someone with a one-way hash of that letter, the recipient can hash the letter and compare the results to the hash you sent. If the two hashes match, you can be sure the letter has not been modified in transit. Applications of one-way encryption for providing authentication and integrity are sometimes known as *message digests*.

Current sources

One-way encryption is a part of nearly every Internet protocol. Some of the hash functions in use today are:

- **Secure Hash Algorithm (SHA-1).** The U.S. government's standard hash function.
- **RIPEMD-160.** The European one-way hash algorithm standard.
- **MD4.** An old, and obsolete (but still widely used), hash function developed by Ron Rivest.
- **MD5.** The latest in the series of hash functions developed by Ron Rivest. It involves several steps and results in a 128-bit message digest.

Understanding Digital Certificates

Certificates

The biggest advantage to public key encryption is that it allows strangers to communicate with each other. This capability, however, also results in one of public key encryption's biggest weakness: people claiming to be people who they aren't.

In face-to-face transactions, we have safeguards to protect against identity theft or people who lie about their identities. We check drivers' licenses at liquor stores and we verify signatures at the bank. If you happen to be Little Red Riding Hood, you've learned to look at grandmother's teeth.

With public key encryption, however, anyone can create a public key, associate someone's (or some organization's) name with it, and claim to be that person or organization. Another person might then be fooled into giving confidential information or a basket of goodies to the wrong party. Public key encryption only works when users have a way to associate a public key with an identity.

As we mentioned earlier, one way to verify the identity of someone using a public key is to have a third party who is trusted by both parties certify that a user really is who he or she claims to be.

The trusted authority does this by creating a message, called a *certificate*, that contains the public key and the identity of its owner. The trusted authority then signs the certificate using its private key. As long as the trusted authority has done its job and verified the identity of the key owner, you can be sure that the owner of the certificate is who he or she claims to be.

The X.509v3 standard

X.509v3

X.509v3 is the name of the standard that established the format and contents of the certificates that are most widely used on the Internet. The full name of the X.509v3 standard is the International Telecommunication Union Telecommunication Standardization Sector (ITU-T) Recommendation X.509v3. Table 19-2 shows the elements of certificates that are defined in the X.509v3 standard.

Table 19-2
X.509v3 Certificate Elements

Field	*Description*
Version	The version number of the certificate. This is currently 1, 2, or 3.
Serial number	A unique serial number for the certificate file.
Signature algorithm ID	Indicates which message digest algorithm was used to sign the certificate file so it can be verified using the same message digest.
Issuer name	The name of the company that issued the certificate. For public certificates on the Internet, this is most often VeriSign or Thawte.
Validity period	The time during which the certificate is valid. The start date is the date the certificate was issued, and the end date is usually one year from the start date. Certificates cannot be used past their expiration dates.
Subject name	Contains the holder of the certificate's ID. For server certificates, the subject name might contain the name of the company and department that owns the Web site, the domain name of the company, the business city, state, and country.
Subject public key information	Contains the holder of the certificate's public key.
Issuer's unique identifier	Contains a unique number that identifies the issuer of the certificate.
Subject's unique identifier	Contains a unique number that identifies the holder of the certificate.
Extensions	Extensions were added to X.509 in version 3. Extensions can contain any type of information that the CA wants. This can include further information about the holder of the certificate, such as date of birth.
Signature	A cryptographic signature created using the contents of all of the previous fields. This is also known as the fingerprint or thumbprint.

Types of certificates

There are four types of certificates:

✦ **Certificate authority certificates.** This can be thought of as the master certificate. This is owned by a trusted certificate provider, such as VeriSign or Thawte, and is used to sign other certificates.

✦ **Server certificates.** Server certificates are the certificates used to identify Web servers and their owners. Server certificates are necessary to use SSL.

✦ **Personal certificates.** Personal certificates are used to identify individuals.

✦ **Software publisher certificate.** Software authors use these certificates to sign software they distribute. A consumer of the software can then check the certificate to ensure that the software is from whom it claims to be from.

Certifying Authorities

Third parties that issue digital certificates are called *Certifying Authorities* (CAs). Anyone can be a CA and issue certificates. Certificates are often used within company networks to authenticate users. A network administrator, or anyone else for that matter, can issue these certificates. For certificates to be useful, however, the CA must be trusted by all of the parties involved in a transaction, and it must be possible for the signature on the certificate to be checked.

CAs can also issue certificates to other CAs. These CAs can then issue certificates to users. The end user only needs to include all of the CAs between himself or herself and the root in order to prove the legitimacy of the certificate.

How CAs work

For example, assume that a CA, called BigCA, gives a certificate authority certificate to LittleCA. LittleCA may then give a certificate to TinyCA. TinyCA may then give a certificate to Debbie. BigCA may have also given a certificate to PetitCA, which may have then given a certificate to John. This relationship is shown in Figure 19-2.

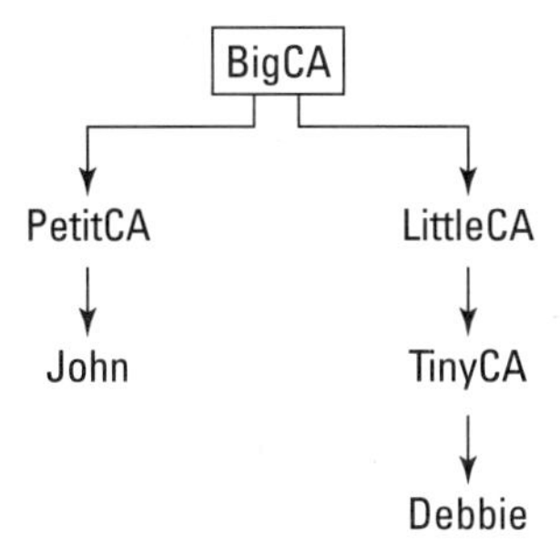

Figure 19-2: A chain of certificates

Both Debbie and John share a common CA, BigCA. When Debbie gets a message from John, she can use BigCA's public key to verify PetitCA's identity, and then use PetitCA's identity to verify John's identity. This is called traversing the trust chain.

Certificates on the Internet

On the Internet, the vast majority of the server certificates are issued by VeriSign or Thawte Consulting. In December 1999, VeriSign acquired Thawte, but Thawte continues to issue certificates separately. The major Web browsers come with the public keys for both of these CAs. When you go to a secure Web site, your Web browser check's the site's certificate against the public keys it knows for the CA that issued the Web site's server certificate.

If everything checks out, you're shown a message or simply an icon, indicating that the connection is secure. If the public keys don't match or if the browser doesn't recognize the CA that issued the server certificate, you will get a different message that will indicate that something is not right about the certificate.

Viewing certificate information

To view information about the certificate being used by a server, follow these steps:

1. Enter a secure area of an e-commerce site. You can usually get to a secure area by beginning the checkout process.
2. If you're using Internet Explorer, you see a lock icon in the lower right corner of your browser window. If you're using Netscape Navigator, the lock icon in the lower-left or lower-right corner of the screen is locked. In Internet Explorer, double-click the lock icon to open the certificate information window, as shown in Figure 19-3.

Figure 19-3: Internet Explorer's Certificate Information window

3. Use the tabs in the certificate information window to view the certificate details, and the certification path for a particular certificate, as shown in Figure 19-4.

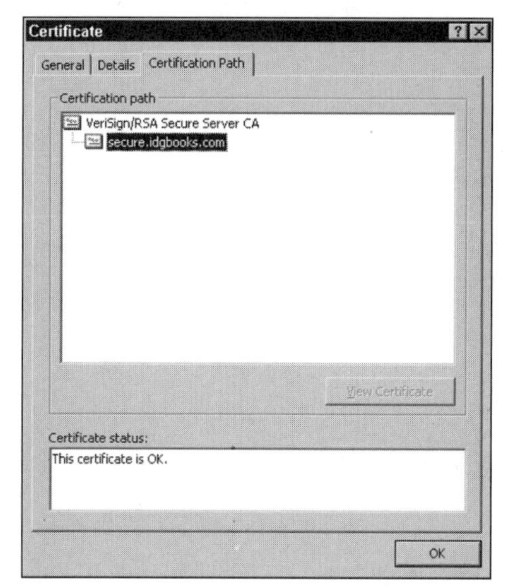

Figure 19-4: Viewing the certification path

4. In Netscape Navigator, click the lock icon to view the security information window, as shown in Figure 19-5.

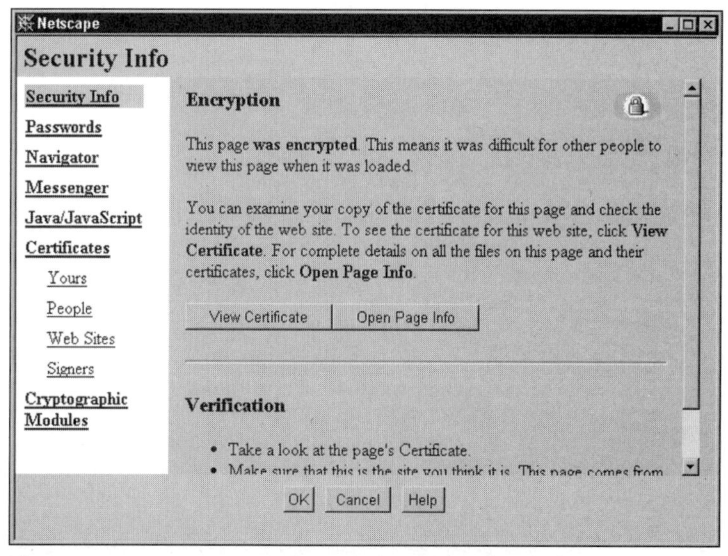

Figure 19-5: Netscape Navigator's Security Info window

5. View the certificate in Netscape Navigator by clicking the View Certificate button. The certificate information is shown in a separate window (see Figure 19-6).

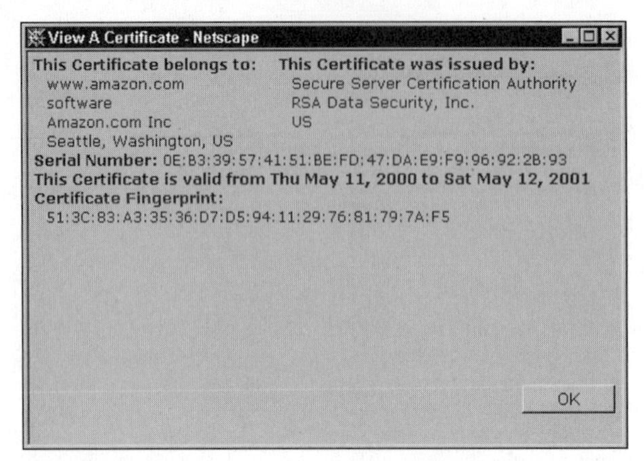

Figure 19-6: Viewing certificate details with Netscape Navigator

Certificate revocation lists

Certificates may be revoked for a variety of reasons. These reasons range from certificates being expired and never renewed, to issues such as compromised private keys. No matter why a certificate is revoked, users and protocols that depend on certificates for authentication must be notified if a certificate is no longer valid.

For this reason, CAs maintain revocation lists. Protocols that use certificates (including SSL) have the capability to verify certificates against the CAs revocation list when the certificate is downloaded to a user.

Working with Certificates

A digital certificate is required to enable SSL (Secure Sockets Layer) on a Web server. In this section, you take a look at what SSL is, and then you find out how to request a certificate and install it on Internet Information Server (IIS).

SSL

The Secure Sockets Layer (SSL) protocol was created by Netscape communications. Today, SSL is built into most Web servers and Web browsers. To enable SSL, you simply need to install a digital certificate. SSL was submitted to the Internet Engineering Task Force (IETF) for standardization, and the new standard based on SSL is called Transport Layer Security (TLS).

The SSL security protocol provides the following types of security for TCP/IP connections:

✦ Data encryption

✦ Server authentication

✦ Message integrity

✦ Optional client authentication

How Internet data is transported

To understand SSL, it's important to understand how data is transmitted across the Internet. How data is transported and routed over the Internet is governed by the Transmission Control Protocol/Internet Protocol (TCP/IP). Other protocols, such as the Hypertext Transfer Protocol (HTTP), the Lightweight Directory Access Protocol (LDAP), the Internet Message Access Protocol (IMAP), and the File Transfer Protocol (FTP) run on top of TCP/IP. Protocols that operate on top of TCP/IP are said to be high-level protocols. The layer at which they operate is called the *Application layer.*

SSL operates below the Application layer, but above TCP/IP. What this means is SSL secures all of the traffic that operates at the Application layer. The relationship between TCP/IP, SSL, and the Application layer is shown in Figure 19-7.

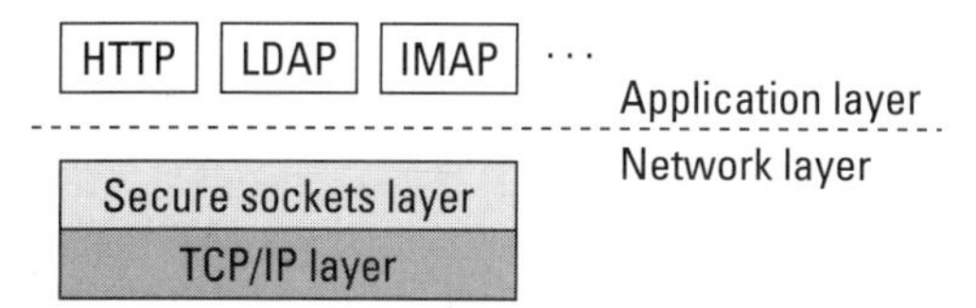

Figure 19-7: SSL runs above TCP/IP, but underneath high-level protocols.

Establishing an SSL connection

The steps involved in establishing an SSL connection are as follows:

1. The client (Web browser) sends a request to the secure server.
2. The server sends its certificate to the client. These first two steps are known as the *handshake.*
3. The client checks the certificate to make sure that it was issued by a trusted CA. If it was, the connection continues. If there's a problem with the certificate, the connection may be terminated. Alternatively, the browser may ask the user if he or she would like to proceed without authenticating the server.
4. The CA validates the server to the client.

5. The client tells the server what types of encryption it supports.
6. The server checks the list of ciphers that the browser sent and chooses the strongest form they have in common. The server then informs the client of this choice.
7. The client uses this cipher to generate a session key. A *session key* is a symmetric encryption key that is used only for this transaction. The client encrypts the symmetric key using the server's public key and sends it to the server.
8. The server decrypts the session key. The client and the server now share a symmetric key that they can use to exchange data securely.

SSL uses both symmetric and asymmetric encryption.

The previous steps illustrate the basic process that is followed every time you visit a secure Web site. An optional step in the SSL protocol, which isn't used very often with public sites, is that the server may authenticate the client. This step requires the client, or visitor to the site, to have a personal certificate that identifies him or her. Because most people do not have personal digital certificates, requiring this step hampers the ability of a site to conduct e-commerce (although this step increases the level of security somewhat).

See the lab exercise in this chapter to learn how to get a personal certificate.

Requesting a digital certificate

Certificates can currently be requested from VeriSign or Thawte, and must be renewed (for a fee) every year. The price for a certificate depends on the type of certificate and from whom you purchase it, as follows:

- Server certificates from VeriSign currently range from $1000 to $1300 for a commerce site. (VeriSign also allows you to request a trial certificate, which is valid for 14 days.)
- Thawte currently charges $125 for a regular certificate and $300 for a *SuperCert*, which enables strong encryption for international transactions.
- Discount certificates can also be obtained from Entrust (`www.entrust.com`). Entrust's certificate authority certificate is signed by Thawte.

To request a digital certificate, you first need to use your Web server to generate a certificate service request (CSR). To generate a CSR using Microsoft IIS on Windows 2000, follow these steps:

1. Launch the Internet Services Manager.

See Chapter 13 for more information on the Internet Services Manager and IIS.

2. Right-click on your default Web site in the Internet Services Manager and select Properties from the pop-up menu to open the Default Web Site Properties window.
3. Click the Directory Security tab to bring the Directory Security properties sheet to the front, as shown in Figure 19-8.

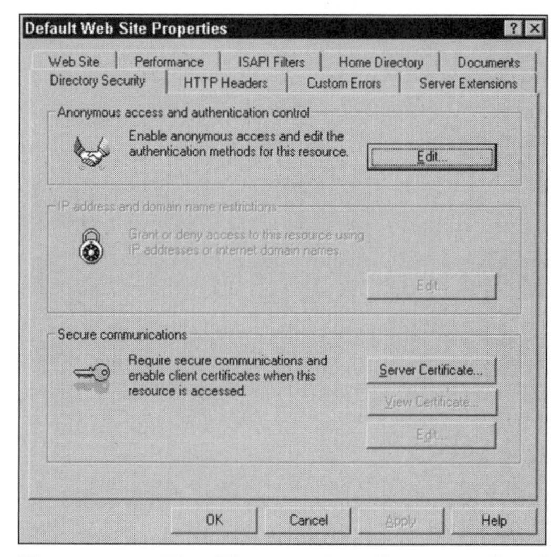

Figure 19-8: The Directory Security properties sheet

4. Click the Server Certificate button to start the IIS Certificate Wizard.
5. Read the first screen of this wizard, which contains basic information about the IIS Certificate Wizard, and then click Next.
6. The next screen asks you if you want to create a new certificate, assign a certificate to the server, or import a certificate from a backup. Choose to create a new certificate and click Next.
7. The next screen may give you the option of only preparing a certificate request, or both preparing a certificate request and sending it to a CA. This screen is shown in Figure 19-9. Choose to only prepare the request.

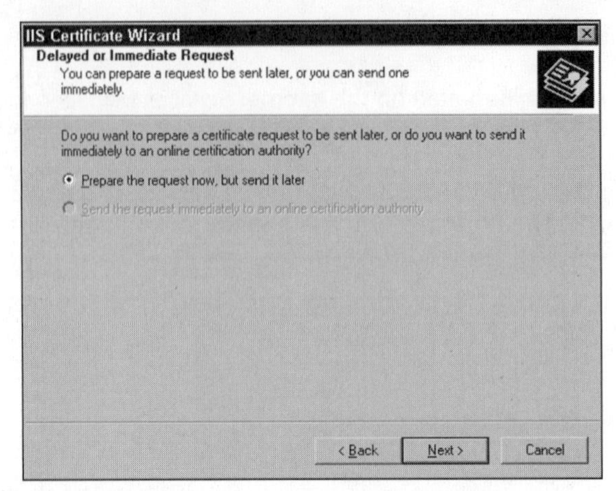

Figure 19-9: Screen asking whether to only prepare a request or prepare and submit a request

8. The next screen asks you for a name for your certificate and the length of the key you want the certificate to have. Enter a name for the certificate and select a bit length (these values don't matter much for this exercise). Click Next.
9. The wizard then asks for information about your organization. This is where you enter the name of the business or organization that owns the server. The information here must uniquely identify your organization. After you've completed this step, click Next.
10. Enter the name of the site. This is the domain name of your site, if it's connected to the Internet, or the name of your site on your local intranet. Click Next.
11. Enter the requested geographical information: city (or locality), state (or province), and country. The name of your state must not be abbreviated. For example, type **California**, not **CA** or **Calif**. Click Next.
12. Choose where to save the certificate request on your computer and click Next.
13. You're shown a summary of the information in your certificate request. At this point, you can either go back and make changes to this information or click Next to generate the request. If you're happy with the information you entered, click Next to generate the request.
14. The next screen informs you that the request has been generated, as shown in Figure 19-10. You may click the link in this window to view a security site at Microsoft.

Figure 19-10: The end of the IIS Certificate Wizard

15. To view your certificate request, locate it and open it using a text editor. It should look something like the certificate request shown in Figure 19-11.

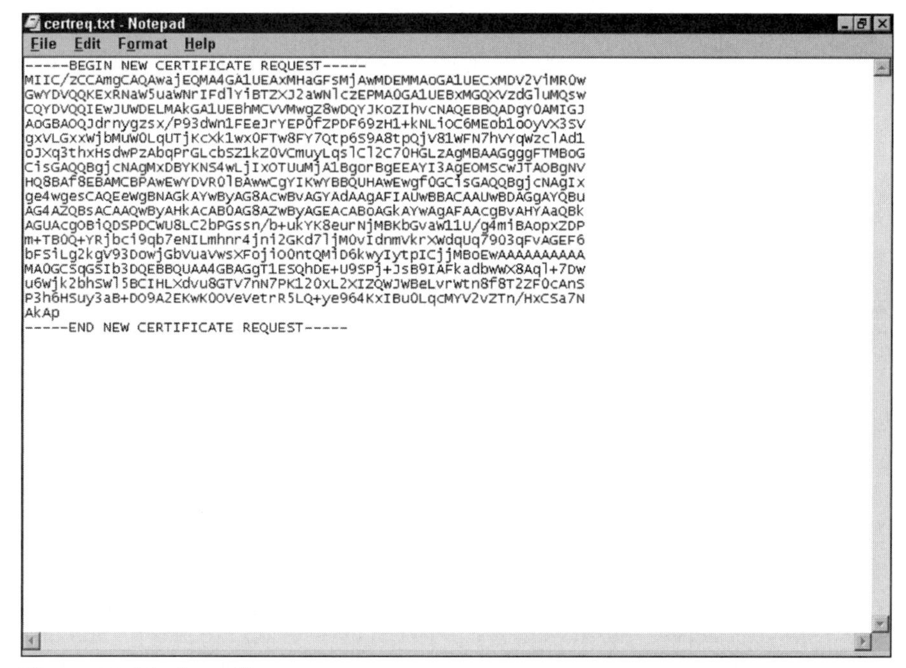

Figure 19-11: A certificate request

Submitting a Certificate Server Request file

To submit your CSR to VeriSign for a free trial certificate, follow these steps:

1. Go to `http://www.verisign.com`.
2. Select Get a server certificate from the drop-down menu or from the home page navigation. You should see a page called Web Site Trust Services.
3. Click the link to the free trial. This is currently labeled Try under the various available certificate packages. A form will appear.
4. After filling out this form, submit it.
5. When the Enrollment page is displayed, scroll to the bottom and click the green Continue button.
6. The next screen tells you to generate a CSR. You've already done this so click Next.
7. In the next screen, you're asked to paste your CSR into a form. To do this, open the file containing your CSR using a text editor and paste it into the form. After you've done this, click Continue.
8. If you generated a CSR with a key length of 512 bits, you see a warning message. You may ignore this warning or create a new CSR with a longer key length. When you are finished, click Continue.
9. You're then asked to verify the information from your CSR and to enter further information to complete the application. This screen also asks you to read the server agreement. Do this and then click Accept.
10. The next screen notifies you that you will be getting an e-mail containing the trial certificate.

Your trial certificate should arrive within an hour. When it does, you can use the instructions in the following section to install it on your server.

Installing a digital certificate

When the e-mail from VeriSign containing your trial certificate arrives, follow these steps to install it on your server:

1. Open the Web Site properties window and choose the Directory Security tab. Open the IIS Certificate Wizard.
2. Click Next. Because you already created a CSR and a key has been created on your server, you should see different choices on the second screen. These choices are Process the pending request and install the certificate, and Delete the pending request, as shown in Figure 19-12. Choose to install the certificate.

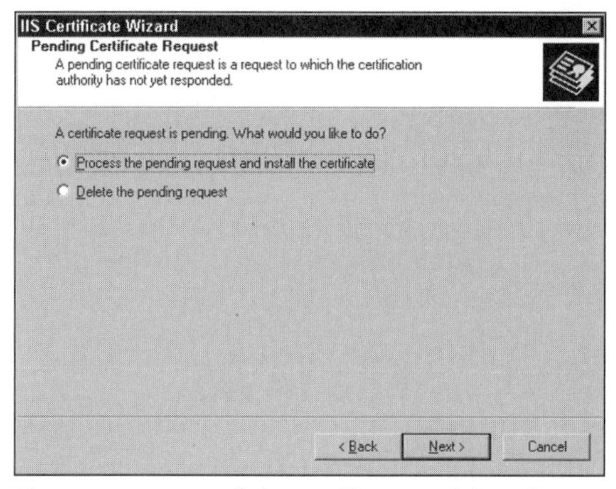

Figure 19-12: Install the certificate or delete the pending request.

3. Open the e-mail you received from VeriSign. Copy the certificate information from the e-mail and paste it into a text document. The certificate should start with a line that says START CERTIFICATE and end with a line that says END CERTIFICATE. Make sure that these lines are in the new text document you create. Save this document somewhere on your computer with the extension `.cer`.

4. In the IIS Certificate Wizard, locate the certificate file you just saved and select it, as shown in Figure 19-13.

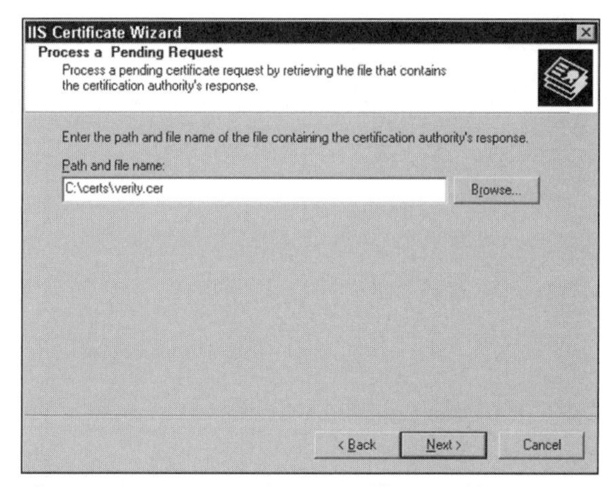

Figure 19-13: Processing a pending certificate request

5. Click Next. You're shown the certificate information.
6. Click Next again to install the certificate and click Finish.

Your trial server certificate is now installed. To use this certificate, however, you need to install the Test CA Root on each browser you intend to use with the server on which you just installed the certificate. This is not required with regular certificates. To download and find out how to install the Test CA Root, go to `http://digitalid.verisign.com/server/trial/trialStep4.htm`.

Securing a Directory or File in IIS

To secure a directory or file in IIS, follow these steps:

1. In the Internet Services Manager, open your Web site and highlight a directory or file you wish to secure or for which you want to create a new virtual directory.
2. Right-click on the directory or file, and select Properties. In the Properties window, bring the Directory Security Properties sheet to the front (or the File Security tab if you're securing a file).
3. Click the Edit button in the Secure Communications section of the window.
4. In the Secure Communications window, check the box next to Require secure channel (SSL), as shown in Figure 19-14.

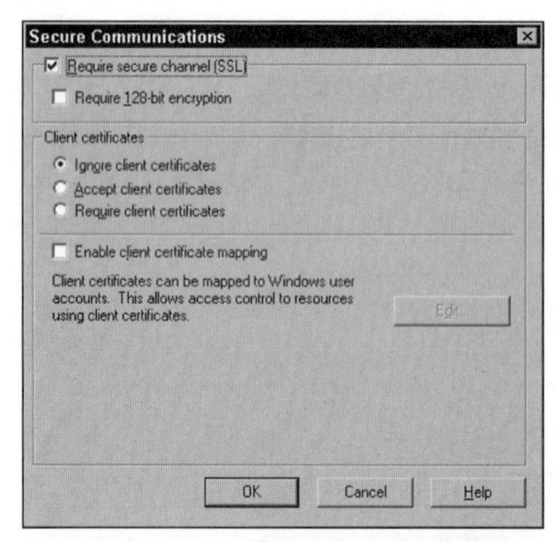

Figure 19-14: Enabling SSL for a directory

5. Close the Secure Communications and Properties windows by clicking OK twice, and then close the Internet Services Manager to save the changes.

6. Attempt to access the directory or file you just created using `https://`*`yourservername/directoryorfilename`*. Note that you must use `https://` to access a directory secured with SSL.
7. If everything is correctly installed, you'll see an indication in your browser that the page you're viewing is secure.

Using Secure Electronic Transactions

In 1995, an alliance of MasterCard, Netscape Communications, IBM, and others introduced the Secure Electronic Payment Protocol (SEPP). Several days later, Visa and Microsoft introduced the Secure Transaction Technology (STT). For a while, the two major credit card companies were each supporting different protocols for electronic payment.

In 1996, however, the two protocols were merged and became Secure Electronic Transactions (SET). The steps involved in an SET transaction are:

1. The card holder indicates that he or she wants to make a credit card purchase.
2. The merchant sends the buyer an invoice, the merchant certificate, and the merchant bank's certificate.
3. The card holder checks the certificates.
4. The card holder sends order information to the merchant, encrypted with the merchant's public key.
5. The merchant generates an authorization request and sends it to the merchant bank.
6. The merchant bank sends a request for payment authorization through an acquirer or other bank card channels.
7. The acquirer gets a response from the card holder's bank and sends a settlement response to the merchant's bank.
8. The card holder's bank authorizes (or denies) the payment and sends a response to the merchant.

It was thought that SET would eventually become the single payment standard on the Internet. However, SET never really caught on and, today, it's becoming apparent that it's not really needed.

Although SET is not widely used, and it appears it won't ever be, there may still be a question or two about it on the exam.

E-Commerce Security Issues

Electronic commerce security myths

To understand why security is so important to e-commerce, you need to understand the risks of doing business electronically. As an e-commerce merchant, you must protect your customers' personal and payment information from theft, and your site from attack. The survival of your company depends upon this.

Besides simply providing the best security you can, you also need to assure your customers that their information is safe on your site. Unfortunately, many Web users are extremely reluctant to reveal personal information on the Web. These fears, whether justified or not, can prevent visitors to your site from becoming customers.

To convince potential customers, you need an awareness of several commonly held beliefs about e-commerce security and the truths behind them. The following beliefs are discussed in detail in the following sections:

- ✦ Hackers can copy any credit card information transmitted across the Internet.
- ✦ The encryption used on the Internet can be easily broken.
- ✦ All you need to do to protect a Web site is install a digital certificate.
- ✦ It's impossible to secure a Web site.

Prosoft's exam materials refer to the following statements as "Myths of Electronic Commerce."

Hackers can copy any credit card information transmitted across the Internet

It's possible for a third-party to intercept and copy information transmitted between two computers on the Internet. This is done using programs called *packet sniffers*. Packet sniffers simply allow users to view all of the network traffic coming and going through their subnets. Essentially, packet sniffers allow you to see what everyone around you is viewing on the Internet. By filtering this information, hackers can locate particular pieces of information, such as credit card numbers or passwords.

However, a packet sniffer cannot specifically target any one person's credit card information for interception. A packet sniffer must be on the same wire as the target and must be listening at the right time. Because of the volume of data transmitted over the Internet, and because so much of it is not credit card information, this is not the best or most common way to steal information. In fact, the risk that a hacker will intercept your credit card information while it's in transit across the Internet is extremely small. Use of encryption for transmitting sensitive data easily defeats packet sniffers.

The biggest risk to users' personal information and payment information on the Internet is improperly protected databases residing on Web servers. Rather than wasting time filtering network packets looking for a few unencrypted passwords or credit card numbers, it's much easier for hackers to locate sites that don't properly secure their databases. Thousands of credit card numbers can be obtained from a single unsecured database.

The encryption used on the Internet can be easily broken

The most common security protocol used on the Internet is Secure Sockets Layer (SSL). SSL 3.0 supports a variety of standard ciphers, including RC4, DES, and Triple DES, with key-lengths of between 40- and 168-bits. Given enough time, and enough computing power, any cipher (except a one-time pad) can be broken through a brute-force attack. However, the resources and time required to break any of the ciphers used by SSL are so great, it's not worth a criminal's time to try.

All you need to do to protect a Web site is install a digital certificate

Digital certificates enable Web servers to use SSL. SSL provides authentication and encryption to data in transit over the Internet. It does not, however, protect data stored on the Web server.

As mentioned earlier, user data is in more danger once it arrives at an e-commerce site than it is when it's traveling across the Internet. How data is stored and used by an e-commerce merchant is at least as important as how it's transmitted. Unfortunately, typical users see a lock or key icon on their browsers (the indication that a site is using SSL) and assume it's safe to share personal data with the vendor. This is not always the case, as demonstrated by the many high-profile sites that have had their databases breached.

It's impossible to secure a Web site

Absolute security cannot be achieved. You can, however, achieve a level of security high enough to make the effort required to penetrate it far outweigh the potential benefits of doing so.

Security can be expensive, but it's important to remember how much you stand to lose if your security is breached. The right security measures can be more than adequate against the types of attacks to which a site is likely to be subjected.

Some attacks, however, are harder to guard against. Most Web servers would not survive a direct attack from a terrorist wielding a hand grenade, although an attack from a dreaded insider or disgruntled former employee is more likely. This risk of physical damage to equipment and insider attack can be reduced with good policies and careful monitoring and auditing.

Key Point Summary

In this chapter, you examined the important topic of e-commerce security. Security involves much more than just encryption and passwords. Making sure your e-commerce site is secure must be an on-going process involving authentication, integrity, cryptography, access control, auditing, and regular monitoring. Here's a review of the major points covered in this chapter:

- Security on the Internet serves five purposes: authentication and identification, access control, data confidentiality, data integrity, and non-repudiation.
- Authentication and identification are provided by digital certificates.
- Access control is most commonly provided using passwords.
- Data confidentiality is provided using cryptography.
- Data integrity is provided using message digests.
- Non-repudiation is provided using authentication with auditing.
- Encryption is the process of creating ciphertext from plaintext.
- Decryption is the process of creating plaintext from ciphertext.
- A cipher is a cryptographic algorithm used to encrypt and decrypt messages.
- Encryption strength depends on three factors: the strength of the algorithm, the secrecy of the key, and the length of the key.
- Symmetric encryption, or private key encryption, uses a single, shared key for both encryption and decryption.
- Examples of encryption algorithms that use symmetric encryption include: DES, RC4, RC5, Twofish, and AES.
- Asymmetric Encryption, or public key encryption, uses a public key for encryption and a private key for decryption. This allows strangers to exchange encrypted messages.
- One-way encryption is used to create digital fingerprints. One-way hash functions are a type of one-way encryption that is used to create message digests.
- MD4 and MD5 are examples of hash functions.
- Data can be intercepted on the Internet using packet sniffers. This is not the easiest or most common way to steal payment information, however.
- The goal of encryption is to make the resources and time required to break a code not worth the potential rewards for doing so.
- Web site security requires more than just installing a digital certificate.
- It's not impossible to achieve a high level of security.
- Certifying Authorities (CAs) act as trusted third parties.

- The standard that defines the format and contents of a digital certificate is X.509v3.
- The four types of digital certificates are certificate authority certificates, server certificates, personal certificates, and software publisher certificates.
- Certificates may be revoked. Certifying Authorities (CAs) maintain lists of revoked certificates.
- Secure Sockets Layer (SSL) is a protocol that provides data encryption, server authentication, message integrity, and optional client authentication for TCP/IP connections.
- To enable SSL on most Web servers, you just need to install a digital certificate.
- SSL uses symmetric and asymmetric encryption.
- Secure Electronic Transactions (SET), a protocol for conducting secure payments, was created as a joint effort between VISA and MasterCard.
- SET uses both Symmetric and Asymmetric encryption.

✦ ✦ ✦

STUDY GUIDE

E-commerce security is a large and complex subject. It's also heavily emphasized on the CIW E-Commerce exam. Make sure you know the answers to all of the assessment questions in the chapter and that you study the key points carefully.

Assessment Questions

1. How is authentication provided in SSL?

   A. Using digital certificates

   B. Using symmetric encryption

   C. Using access control

   D. Using passwords

2. What is symmetric encryption?

   A. A digital fingerprint

   B. A type of encryption requiring both participants to share a secret key

   C. A type of encryption requiring both participants to have a public key and a private key

   D. A way to ensure a message is the same when it arrives as it was when it was sent

3. What is asymmetric encryption?

   A. A digital fingerprint

   B. A type of encryption requiring both participants to share a secret key

   C. A type of encryption requiring both participants to have a public key and a private key

   D. A way to ensure a message is the same when it arrives as it was when it was sent

4. What is a message digest?

   A. A single message containing shortened versions of multiple other messages

   B. An application of symmetric encryption

   C. A type of encryption impossible to crack

   D. An application of one-way encryption used to check data integrity

5. What type of digital certificate can be used to identify a person?

   A. A certificate authority certificate

   B. A server certificate

   C. A personal certificate

   D. A software publisher certificate

6. Which type of certificate can be used to sign other certificates?

   A. A certificate authority certificate

   B. A server certificate

   C. A personal certificate

   D. A software publisher certificate

7. Which security services are provided by Secure Sockets Layer (SSL)?

   A. Encryption and credit card authorization

   B. Encryption and access control

   C. Auditing and authentication

   D. Encryption and authentication

8. Which of the following best describes the steps involved in establishing an SSL connection?

   A. Handshake, client checks the server's certificate, client and server agree on a symmetric encryption algorithm, client sends session key encrypted using server's public key, data is exchanged using the session key

   B. Handshake, client and server agree on a symmetric encryption algorithm, client checks the server's certificate, the client sends a session key encrypted using the server's public key, data is exchanged using the session key

   C. The client checks the server's certificate, handshake, the client sends a session key encrypted using the server's public key, client and server agree on a symmetric encryption algorithm, data is exchanged using the session key

   D. The client sends a session key encrypted using the server's public key, client and server agree on a symmetric encryption algorithm, client checks the server's certificate, handshake, data is exchanged using the session key

9. Which of the following statements is not true?

A. It's possible to achieve a good level of security for an e-commerce site.

B. Hackers can intercept and use passwords and credit card numbers that aren't encrypted.

C. Installing a digital certificate and using SSL guarantees that your e-commerce site is secure.

D. Most of the types of encryption used on the Internet cannot be easily broken by most people or organizations.

Scenarios

1. Security of cryptography is partially based on the length of the key. As you learned in this chapter, the number of possible keys can be calculated using 2^n, where n is the length of the key, in bits. This same formula works for any other type of key. For example, if a lock has 5 pins, and each pin has 10 possible settings, the lock has 5^{10}, or 100,000 possible combinations. In this scenario, do the following:

- Calculate the number of possible combinations for several cryptographic algorithms. In the first column of Table 19-3, you find the name of an algorithm; in the second column, you find the key length (in bits).
- Write the number of possible keys in the third column.

Table 19-3
Numbers of Possible Key Combinations

Algorithm	*Key length (bits)*	*Number of combinations*
DES	56	
RC5-32	32	
RC5-64	64	
RSA	528	

2. It's usually much more likely someone will guess a password, and thus gain access to a private key, than they will guess a key. Given this assumption, perform the following:

- Assume (for simplicity) that a password only uses lowercase letters, isn't necessarily a word, and is six characters long. Calculate the number of possible passwords.

- Even though this number shows that passwords are generally much less secure than the keys they protect, why is this number essentially meaningless?

Lab Exercise

Lab 19-1 Obtaining a personal digital certificate

1. Go to `http://www.thawte.com/certs/personal/contents.html`.
2. Click the Enroll button.
3. Read the terms of use carefully. If you agree with these terms, click the Next button at the bottom of the screen.
4. Enter the information about your identity that is requested on the next few screens.
5. On the screen that asks for your password, read the information carefully and choose a good password you won't forget.
6. When you finish the first step of the enrollment process, an e-mail will be sent to you. Wait for this e-mail.
7. When you get the e-mail from Thawte, go to the address it contains and enter the Probe and Ping values that were sent to you. You're now registered with Thawte and can obtain a personal digital certificate.
8. To obtain a certificate, log-in by clicking the Next button and entering your ID and password.
9. Select the software you want to use the certificate with from the list, and then click Get X.509 Certificate.
10. Click Next on the screen that asks about the Common name and Employment.
11. Select the e-mail addresses you wish to include on your certificate and then click Next.
12. Click Next until you get to the screen that asks if you'd like to configure the optional certificate extensions. Choose Accept Default Extensions.
13. Read the instructions for generating a private key.
14. Review the final information. If you're happy with it, click Finish. A certificate request is generated, and you're notified via e-mail when the certificate is ready. After you have the certificate, you can install it in your e-mail program or Web browser.

Answers to Chapter Questions

Chapter pre-test

1. The five purposes served by security in electronic commerce are:
   - Authentication and identification
   - Access control
   - Data confidentiality
   - Data integrity
   - Non-repudiation
2. Non-repudiation assures that every action is provable. It's provided using authentication and auditing.
3. Symmetric encryption requires participants to share a key. Asymmetric encryption doesn't require a shared key.
4. A message digest is the result of using a hash function on a plaintext message. It can be used to provide authentication and integrity.
5. Certifying Authorities (CAs) act as trusted third parties for digital certificates.
6. The four types of digital certificates are: certificate authority certificates, server certificates, personal certificates, and software publisher certificates.
7. SSL, or Secure Sockets Layer, is a protocol used to secure TCP/IP connections on the Internet.
8. X.509 is the standard that specifies the format and content of digital certificates.

Assessment questions

1. **A.** SSL uses digital certificates. Digital certificates provide authentication and identification through the use of a trusted third party (see "Establishing identification and authentication").
2. **B.** Symmetric encryption is also called shared key encryption or secret key encryption (see "Symmetric encryption").
3. **C.** Asymmetric encryption does not require the use of a shared key. It requires a public and a private key (see "Asymmetric encryption").
4. **D.** Message digests are created using hash functions, which are used in one way encryption (see "One-way encryption").
5. **C.** Personal digital certificates identify individuals (see "Understanding Digital Certificates").

6. **A.** In order to issue certificates, you must have a certificate authority certificate (see "Understanding Digital Certificates").

7. **D.** SSL provides encryption using symmetric and asymmetric encryption, and authentication using digital certificates (see "SSL").

8. **A.** The first step in establishing an SSL connection between a server and a client is the handshake. During the handshake, the client sends a request to the browser (using https) and the server sends its certificate to the client (see "SSL"). The other steps are as follows:

   - The client then checks the certificate.
   - The client then informs the server of the types of symmetric encryption it supports. The server chooses the strongest type of encryption it has in common with the client and informs the client of this choice.
   - The client generates a session key using this type of encryption. The session key is sent to the server using the server's public key.
   - The server decrypts the session key, and begins communicating with the client using this key.

9. **C.** There are no guarantees of security. Using SSL and digital certificates is only part of the solution. To be fairly sure your site is secure, you need to make sure the operating system is secure, passwords are secure, and the database is secure. You also need to regularly monitor your site and keep abreast of current security issues and new server vulnerabilities as they are discovered (see "E-Commerce Security Issues").

Scenarios

1. To give you an idea of just how large the numbers in Table 19-3 are, consider the number of possible keys for RC5-64 (see the completed table shown here). If you were able to try a billion keys per year, it would take you 50 million years to try all of them. Distributed.net (`http://distributed.net/`) is currently punching away at the possible keys at a rate much faster than that — at over 100 billion keys per second. At that rate, it will still take nearly six years for distributed.net to try all of the possible combinations.

Algorithm	*Key length (bits)*	*Number of combinations*
DES	56	7.2×10^{16}
RC5-32	32	4,294,967,296
RC5-64	64	1.8×10^{19}
RSA	528	8.8×10^{158}

2. The number of possible combinations of 6 letters (where case doesn't matter) is 26^6, or 308,915,776. This is much smaller than any of the numbers in Table 19-3 from the first scenario. Now, consider the following:
   - The reason this number is irrelevant, however, is that people don't simply choose random letters for passwords. Most often, people choose passwords that mean something to them, such as their dog's name, a word, a date, a favorite place, or a favorite food. The easiest way to crack a password is simply to find out something about the person who created the password.
   - In addition, people often store their passwords close to, or on, their computers. Rather than writing a program to try each possible password to a system, it's often possible to simply look in a desk drawer or under the keyboard.

For More Information . . .

- **Crypto-Gram Newsletter.** http://www.counterpane.com/crypto-gram.html. A free monthly e-mail newsletter from Bruce Schneier
- **SSL 3.0 Specification.** http://home.netscape.com/eng/ssl3/index.html
- **Generating a CSR and key pair with Windows 2000 / Internet Information Services 5.0.** www.entrust.net/tech/miis50/csr.htm
- **W3C Security Resources.** www.w3.org/Security/
- **Computer Security Resource Center (CSRC).** http://csrc.nist.gov
- **Microsoft Security.** www.microsoft.com/security
- **CERT Coordination Center.** www.cert.org
- **Rootshell.** www.rootshell.org

CHAPTER 20

Managing E-Business Information

✦ ✦ ✦ ✦

EXAM OBJECTIVES

- Integrating information systems
- Oracle and SQL Server relational databases
- Order tracking

CHAPTER PRE-TEST

1. What is the most efficient means of storage for e-business information?
2. Why does an e-commerce Web site need to access the e-business information database?
3. Why do staff members in various departments of an e-commerce company need to access the e-business information database?
4. How is customer access to sensitive information in the e-business information database protected from use by unauthorized individuals?
5. What is the significance of a unique identifier field in a relational database?

✦ Answers to these questions can be found at the end of the chapter. ✦

After your site is set up to accept orders, you need to store the information for each order and transaction. Storing data in a way that makes the appropriate information easily accessible to employees is vital. Your company's information systems need to be highly integrated, if not one in the same. In this chapter, you learn about data storage and retrieval, how to track inventory, and how to provide order information to customers.

Understanding E-Business Information Needs and Requirements

Integrating information systems

For traditional commerce companies, moving from manual information storage to computer-based information storage has been a challenge in recent decades. For e-commerce companies, information storage has been computerized from the start, and it's relatively simple to integrate the various aspects of information storage within the company.

Storing e-business information

In an e-commerce business, the following needs to be stored:

- ✦ Customer information
- ✦ Product catalog information
- ✦ Order information (including payment information)
- ✦ Inventory information

Import/export model

In many cases, customer, product, order, and inventory information are housed in separate databases. It's possible to integrate the databases at various levels, simply by exporting and importing data from one database into another on a regular basis.

For example, the quantities of products ordered during a particular time frame could be exported from the order-processing database to the product catalog database once a day (or once an hour) to update stock levels. Or, the net income from orders could be exported from the order-processing database to the accounting database at set intervals to record the company's income.

Using a relational database

Many online storefront packages (and custom-developed systems) put product catalog data and order-processing data in separate tables in the same relational database. All other data relating to the Web site, such as inventory and customer information, is often included in the same database. This way, the data can interact in a more fluid manner than with the export/import model. For example, as soon as an item is ordered, the stock number in the product catalog table is reduced by one. This reduces the chance of a customer getting outdated information on the availability of a particular item (see the following section for an elaboration of this concept).

Internal business data, such as accounting systems, personnel information, and so on, should be kept in separate systems that are not connected to the Web site.

Online access for customers

For many customers, time is of the essence. They need to know whether your company has the product they need and if it's available for immediate shipment.

Product availability

In the online shopping world, customers are unable to determine the inventory of products unless this information is posted on the Web site. It is, therefore, vitally important that your information system is integrated into the Web site, so availability information is displayed for the user.

Several popular e-commerce sites, such as Amazon.com and Egghead.com, display availability information on the detail page for each product. The actual quantity of the product in stock is not displayed, but information on when the item can be shipped is shown (based on the quantity in stock). Using internal business rules, the availability can be Usually ships within 24 hours, Usually ships in 2-3 business days, or any number of other possibilities.

See Chapter 18 for more information on account maintenance areas.

Order status

To reduce the number of phone calls to your customer support staff, it's also rather important to provide accessible information on previously placed orders to established customers. This is usually done by creating an account maintenance area. These password-protected areas give customers access to information on past orders, such as their status and any tracking numbers used in shipping.

To display order status information in a Web page, order-processing information must be accessible via your Web site. Integrating all of the data into one relational database facilitates this.

Company-wide access for staff

Product catalog and order-processing information should also be accessible throughout the company so employees in various departments can access the information they need. Many systems allow administrators to create different views of the company information database for different users. Here's how it works:

✦ **Order fulfillment.** This view could be created for use by the employees in the order-processing center. It would contain information such as products and quantities ordered, chosen shipping method, and shipping address, but it would not contain credit card information.

✦ **Customer support.** This view could give customer support representatives access to the same information as in the order fulfillment view, but with additional information, such as all orders for a particular customer, order status, and any inquiries from the customer that have come in via telephone or e-mail.

✦ **Employee input.** Administrators can also set up a system whereby employees can change information based on the functions available to them in their view. For instance, order fulfillment staff should be able to change the status of a given order after it has been shipped (or this can be done automatically). In addition, a customer support representative should be able to cancel a pending order or change the shipping address.

These functions and views are built in to many e-commerce software packages. Some also offer customizable views.

Managing Inventory

Inventory management is extremely important in any business. Making sure you have the products that your customers want — or can get them quickly — is essential to your business's success. In e-business, the rate at which products are sold can make inventory management much more fast-paced than it is in traditional business. Rapidly fluctuating demand for particular products can also take e-businesses by surprise. This section explores the issues and challenges of managing inventory for an e-commerce company.

Make sure that you're familiar with the terms in this section.

Determining inventory levels

The term *inventory* refers to the quantity of a specific product that is kept by the seller, from when it's acquired or produced to when a buyer purchases it. Determining the quantity of a particular item that should be kept in inventory is an inexact science. The amount of inventory that a company keeps on hand of any particular product depends upon three factors:

✦ Time needed to acquire or produce the product

✦ Cost of the product

✦ Demand for the product

Make sure you know the three factors that affect inventory levels.

The following sections look at each of these factors in greater detail.

Time

The time needed to acquire or produce the product refers to any delays between when the product is ordered from the supplier (or when an order to manufacture a product is submitted) and when it is delivered to the seller. In the case of a product that is purchased from a supplier, this is the time it takes the supplier to deliver the product — assuming the supplier has stock on hand. If the product is being manufactured by the same company that sells it, the pertinent time frame is the time it takes the manufacturing department to produce the item.

It's important to factor in this variable when determining the optimum stock levels for a particular product. You need to be sure to submit a new order for a given quantity of the product with enough time allowed for the new order to arrive at your warehouse before the current stock of the product is sold out.

Cost

The cost of a product is either the cost paid to the supplier or the investment your company makes to produce the item — in terms of expenses for labor and parts. Expensive items require more capital outlay in order to be kept in large quantities in stock. As long as the products are in your inventory, the products have been paid for by your company, but not sold yet for a profit. This means that your company has that much less cash on hand.

This factor has a large impact on the stock levels of products. It's important to invest only the minimum amount necessary in product acquisition to meet your customers' demand. Any more than that and your company is taking an unnecessary loss in operating cash.

Demand

On the most basic level, *demand* means that the more popular a particular item is, the higher the quantity of that item your company should have in inventory. The concept of demand, however, can become more complex in the following ways:

✦ **Unexpected surges in popularity.** If your stock levels are altered to reflect a popularity spike, they need to be re-set after it has dropped off. Other products may be consistently steady sellers; therefore, a large supply of these products should always be kept on hand.

✦ **Time and cost factors.** Expensive items and those that take a while to produce need to be available in sufficient quantities to meet customer demand. After all, if your site has a delay in shipping a product, but one of your competitors does not, you may lose business. For example, if your company's inventory methods cause a three-day delay in shipping computers, potential customers may find they can buy new computers from one of your competitors and have them shipped within 24 hours.

✦ **The level of online demand.** Many online businesses have found traditional methods of inventory control inadequate for the huge demand of online shoppers. After all, by being online, your products are made available to more people than ever before. A traditional company transitioning to online commerce may find it needs to stock more products than was necessary before.

✦ **The rate of orders.** Also, the rate at which orders come in to an online business can be overwhelming, and can deplete the inventory of a given product within a day. Companies that experience such changes need to rethink their inventory procedure.

Managing inventory data

Oracle and SQL Server relational databases

Inventory data — and, in fact, all data relating to an e-business — is typically kept in a database of some sort. The most commonly used databases are Oracle and Microsoft SQL Server, which are both relational databases.

For more specific information on the features and capabilities of Oracle and Microsoft SQL Server, see Chapter 12.

Relational databases

Relational databases consist of multiple tables of information. Each table is made up of fields (which correspond to columns when the database is presented graphically) and records (which correspond to rows). Each record contains a value for each field. Relational databases function as follows:

✦ Data stored in separate tables can be *related* through the use of key fields, usually ID numbers, in each table. For example, each customer in a customer information table is given an ID number. Each order in an order information table contains a field for a customer ID, which relates the order to the customer who placed the order.

✦ In such databases, inventory data is commonly kept in the same database as the product catalog information, but in a separate table. The inventory levels are then associated with individual products, usually by a product identification number.

For more information on relational databases, see Chapter 12.

To better visualize this relationship, consider Table 20-1. It represents a few records in a database table for a hypothetical product catalog.

Table 20-1
A Few Records of a Product Catalog Table

Product ID	*Product name*	*Description*	*Price*
BK0012	Complete Works of Shakespeare	This lovely hardbound volume contains all of Shakespeare's plays and poems . . .	$125.00
CD0892	Greatest Composers, vol. 2	The second volume in the Greatest Composers series . . .	$16.99
CD0991	Greatest Composers, vol. 3	The third volume in the Greatest Composers series . . .	$16.99

Now, consider Table 20-2, which shows the information for each of these products that is housed in the inventory table.

Table 20-2
A Few Records from an Inventory Table

Product ID	*Current inventory*	*Reorder at*
BK0012	10	2
CD0892	50	20
CD0991	200	120

As you can see, the product catalog table houses the information displayed to customers browsing the e-commerce Web site. The inventory table holds only information pertaining to the stock levels of the products and when the item should be reordered. This separation of data into two tables makes data access more efficient for both customers and internal staff.

In Table 20-2, not only is the current inventory tracked, but also the quantity at which the product should be reordered. Popular items, such as the *Greatest Composers, vol. 3* CD (CD0991) are kept in higher quantities than the expensive, less popular *Complete Works of Shakespeare* in hardback (BK0012).

Most real-world e-commerce databases would be more complex than this example. For instance, a field specifying a quantity to be ordered might be included. Another possibility is to have a field specifying how many products are currently on order.

Database access from the Web site

The information in databases can be accessed by e-commerce Web sites using a database-accessing technology such as Active Server Pages (ASP). The database is queried as the HTML page is loaded, and the information returned is displayed in designated locations on the Web page.

See Chapter 12 for more information on Active Server Pages (ASP) and similar technologies.

Displaying inventory data to the customer

A rule can be specified for how the inventory levels are presented to the customer. For instance, the actual quantity of a product in inventory could be displayed, or the quantity in inventory plus the quantity on order. A rule could also be set up to specify inventory levels below which each particular product displays "Ships in 2-3 days" on the Web site rather than "Ships within 24 hours."

Tracking Orders

Order tracking

Order information is kept in a database table in much the same way as product catalog information and inventory information. Once an order is placed on the e-commerce Web site, a new record is created in the database.

Table 20-3 is a view of a few records in a hypothetical database table of order information.

Table 20-3
A Few Records in a Table of Order Information

Order ID	*Date*	*Customer ID*	*Product ID*	*Quantity*	*Status*
MM0872556	01/28/2001	0045199	CD0991	1	01
MM0872557	01/28/2001	1028895	CD0991	3	01
MM0872558	01/28/2001	0388841	CD0892	1	01
MM0872530	01/22/2001	0006772	BK0012	1	03
MM0872533	01/22/2001	0008156	CD0991	5	10

A real order information database table would allow for more than one product per order, and would be related to payment method and transaction information.

Let's take a look at the fields in the order information table (Table 20-3) one by one.

✦ **Order ID.** The order identification number is the unique number by which an order is identified. Everything else about two orders could be identical, but a unique ID number keeps them distinguishable.

✦ **Date.** The date on which the order was placed.

✦ **Customer ID.** The unique customer identification number relates a customer from the customer information table with this order. The customer's name and billing address don't need to be saved in the order information table, because they are already in the customer information table.

✦ **Product ID.** The identification number of the product being purchased relates the order with a product from the product catalog table.

✦ **Quantity.** This is the number of units of the product that were ordered.

✦ **Status.** All orders come into the database with the same status. In this case, a numerical naming convention is used to designate status, as follows:

- 01 = Awaiting payment
- 02 = Payment received, not yet shipped
- 03 = Shipped
- 10 = Canceled

If online credit card processing were used in this example, all orders would enter the database with a status of 02.

Storing customer information

As you learned in the previous section, an order information table references both the customer information table (via the Customer ID field) and the product catalog table (via the Product ID field). The product catalog table (Table 20-1) provides the product ID, product name, description, and price of the products ordered. The customer information table (Table 20-4) provides address information for the customers.

Table 20-4
A Few Records from a Customer Information Table

Customer ID	*First name*	*Last name*	*Address*	*Zip code*
0006772	Mabel	Buckley	222 Main St.	78000
0008156	Jorge	Alvarez	1822 Bach Way	00212
0045199	Alice	Jones	555 E. 55th St	94100
0388841	Ellen	Nguyen	56 W. Regal Cove	75000
1028895	Krishnamurthy	Muhkerjee	5788 Turtledove Rd	78700

Tracking order status

In the examples presented thus far, a numerical convention for designating a status for each order has been used. A numerical standard is useful for maintaining data integrity. As an order is processed, many employees may change the status of the order. If employees were able to enter words and letters into the status field, there would be a great risk for misspellings and other errors that might delay the processing of the order. By giving employees access to only a few numerical codes, this potential risk is greatly diminished.

As the order is processed, the status changes. For example, an employee in the payment-processing department makes sure that payment has been received. After it has, this employee must have access to the database (at least to the Status field) so he or she can change the status to 02 (Payment received, not yet shipped).

The order information is then routed to the fulfillment department. After the product has been shipped, an employee in that department changes the status to 03 (Shipped). In addition, customer support representatives need access to the database to change the status to 10 (Canceled) if necessary.

There would be more potential status codes in a real-world situation, such as codes for backordered items, partially shipped orders, and other contingencies.

Customer access to order information

In Chapter 18, you learned about the self-service option of account maintenance areas. These are password-protected areas of an e-commerce Web site in which established customers can review their account information and past orders.

Granting access and securing data

In order to allow customers to access information on their past orders, the order information database table must be accessible via the Web site. As long as a customer ID is associated with each order, this should not be difficult.

Customer access to sensitive information in the database, such as address and payment information, should be controlled using a unique identifier (ID) for each customer, and through authentication tied to a user name and password for each customer. The unique identifier can also be tied into the computer using the Web site — that is, by using a *cookie*.

A cookie is a mechanism that allows a server-side program, such as a Common Gateway Interface (CGI) script, to store and retrieve information on the client-side of a Hypertext Transfer Protocol (HTTP) connection. Of course, the identity of the user should be verified using the user name and password before access to sensitive information is given.

See Chapter 19 for more information on security.

Viewing order information

All records from the order information table that have a customer ID equal to the customer ID of the person who is logged in to the account information area can be listed. The customer can then select one of these orders and view details about it, such as the products ordered and the status of the order.

See Chapters 6 and 18 for more information on account maintenance areas.

Key Point Summary

This chapter covered the uses of e-business information — how to store it, and how to access it. You also learned about inventory management — how to determine the stock levels of particular products based on their popularity and other factors. The key points in this chapter are:

- ✦ In an e-commerce business, the following information needs to be stored:
  - Customer information
  - Product catalog information

- Order information (including payment information)
- Inventory information

✦ E-business information is most commonly stored in relational databases, because they reduce duplication of data and are less time-consuming to maintain than other types of databases.

✦ It's important to provide shoppers with inventory and/or availability information on your Web site, so they know how quickly a product can be shipped before they purchase it.

✦ Employees throughout the company need access to information in the database that is pertinent to their jobs. In some cases, they also need to be able to change information in the database. Specialized views and access permissions can be set up on a job-specific basis to provide and limit access.

✦ Inventory is the quantity of a specific product that is kept by the seller between when it is acquired or produced and when a customer purchases it.

✦ The actual quantity that is in stock at any one time is called the inventory level or the stock level for a particular product.

✦ The optimum stock level for a given product is determined by weighing the following factors:

- Time
- Cost
- Demand

✦ Inventory data can be managed in a separate database table of the e-business's relational database.

✦ The data in the inventory data table is related to the product information data using a unique identifier for each product.

✦ Product and quantities in the order information table should be used to automatically reduce the inventory levels of the ordered products when an order is placed (or, alternatively, when an order is shipped).

✦ Orders are kept in a database table and tracked until they are fulfilled.

✦ Using a numerical naming convention to specify the status of an order can reduce data input errors.

✦ Giving customers access to order information requires security, unlike inventory information, because it contains sensitive information.

✦ Security for account maintenance areas can be provided by cookies, unique identifiers, and user name/password combinations.

✦ ✦ ✦

STUDY GUIDE

This chapter covered the ways e-business information is managed and explored the challenges related to information management. Check what you've learned with the assessment questions and scenarios contained in the following sections. Then, put that knowledge to work in the lab exercises. Good luck!

Assessment Questions

1. What are the four main types of information that need to be stored by an e-commerce company?

A. Customer information, product catalog information, order information, and inventory information

B. Inventory information, stock level information, payment information, and customer information

C. Product information, order information, payment information, and stock level information

D. Product catalog information, cost information, demand information, and inventory information.

2. What are the three factors that effect inventory levels?

A. Database integration, demand, and sales

B. Data, manufacturing, and cost

C. Time, demand, and cost

D. Cost, demand, and cash reserves

3. Which of the following is the best definition of inventory?

A. The quantity of a product kept by the supplier

B. The quantity of a product ordered by the seller

C. The quantity of a product kept by the seller

D. The quantity of a product kept by the manufacturer

4. How is information organized in a relational database?

A. In a single table consisting of records (rows) and fields (columns)

B. In multiple tables consisting of records (rows) and fields (columns)

C. On individual Web pages corresponding to a product category

D. In tables consisting of rows

5. How has e-commerce affected traditional inventory control methods?
   - A. It has not changed them significantly.
   - B. It has led to frequent overstocks because of oversupply.
   - C. It has confirmed that most business' inventories are adequate.
   - D. It has led to frequent shortages because of demand.
6. Which piece of information uniquely identifies an order in an order information database table?
   - A. The credit card number
   - B. The product ID number
   - C. The date and time of the order
   - D. The order ID number

Scenario

In this scenario, you test your understanding of how tables in a relational database are interrelated. To start, take a look at Table 20-5, which contains a few rows from a table of order information for an e-commerce site.

Table 20-5
Order Information Table

Order ID	*Date*	*Customer ID*	*Product 1*	*Product quantity*	*Product 2*	*Product 2 quantity*
000081	1/30/01	002886	AU-041	1	AU-501	1
000652	2/15/01	010068	AU-055	1	BK-228	2
001005	2/28/01	002067	BK-228	2	EL-052	1

Table 20-6 contains information relating to the information in Table 20-5.

Table 20-6
Customer Information Table

Customer ID	*First name*	*Last name*	*Address*	*Zip code*	*Phone #*
002067	Greg	Montes	622 E. 12th St	98222	808-555-5555
002886	Erin	Chong	3215 Grant Wy	97155	503-555-4776
010068	Myra	Taylor	1588 Lilypad Rd	78700	512-555-8155

Table 20-7 also contains information relating to the information in Table 20-5.

Table 20-7
Product Information Table

Product ID	*Title*	*Author/artist*	*Description*	*Price*	*Format*
AU-041	Meet the PopStarGirlz!	PopStarGirlz	Debut effort from Dutch singing sensation.	$14.99	CD
AU-055	Doo Wop Classics	Various	Compilation of 15 doo wop classics!	$9.99	CD
AU-501	Ooh Baby	PopStarGirlz	Follow-up to smash-hit debut.	$17.99	CD
BK-228	Everything I Need to Know I Learned from a Talking Spoon	Dr. Ian Bingsley	The title says it all.	$11.50	BK-Paper
EL-052	Super Deluxe CD player		Great budget CD Player	$127.00	Electronics

Keeping in mind what you learned in this chapter about relational databases, answer the following questions:

1. Who ordered two copies of *Everything I Need to Know I Learned from a Talking Spoon* and one copy of *Doo Wop Classics*?
2. What products did Greg Montes buy?
3. To which address were two PopStarGirlz albums shipped?
4. How many copies of *Everything I Need to Know I Learned from a Talking Spoon* were sold in the orders listed in Table 20-5?

Lab Exercises

The following labs assume you've done the exercises in the previous chapters relating to the building of the sample Web site (Texas-Shaped.com) with Actinic Business.

For more information on building Texas-Shaped.com with Actinic Business, see Chapters 14, 15, and 16.

Lab 20-1 Monitoring inventory using Actinic Business, part 1

Actinic Business features stock monitoring tools to help you keep an accurate count of on-hand products and that let you know when to re-order. In this exercise, you learn how to use this functionality via the Stock tab in the advanced Product Details window and an alternative method using the Stock Levels window.

The first step is to enable stock monitoring for each of the products in your catalog. To use the advanced Product Details Stock tab procedure, follow these steps:

1. Open Actinic Business.
2. In the Catalog Tree, highlight the product Texas Sunglasses by clicking on it. Choose Edit from the Edit menu, or right-click on the highlighted words and select Edit from the pop-up menu. The Product Details window shown in Figure 20-1 appears.

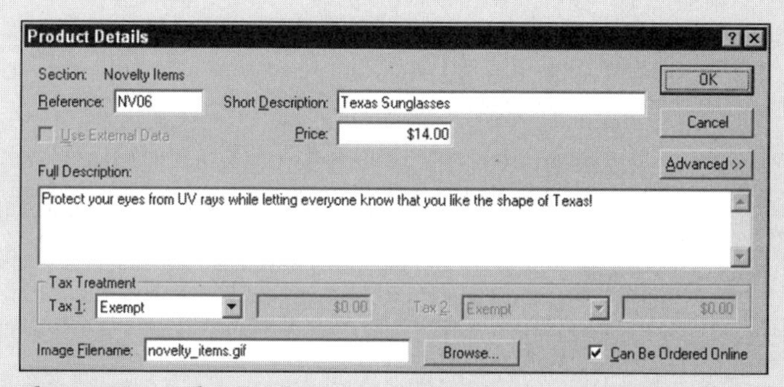

Figure 20-1: The Product Details for the Texas Sunglasses window

3. Click the Advanced button to open up the advanced product details area. The window is extended to accommodate the advanced options.
4. The advanced area consists of five tabs. Click the Stock tab to bring it to the front. Your window should now look like Figure 20-2.

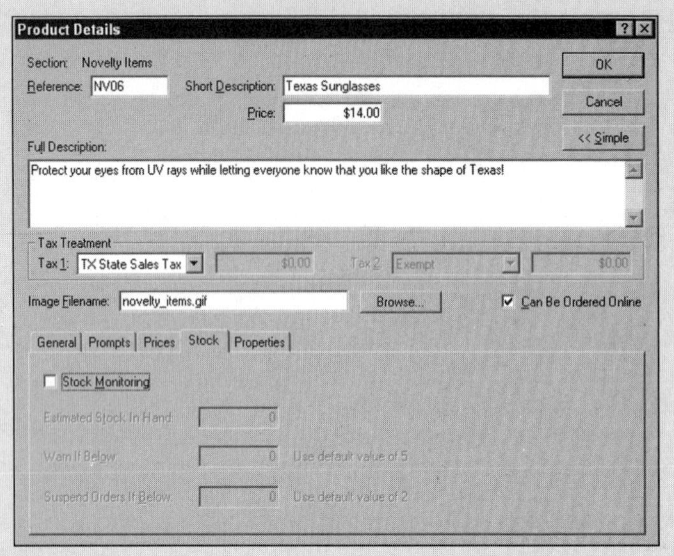

Figure 20-2: Advanced Product Details window with the Stock tab in front

5. Click the checkbox labeled Stock Monitoring to activate stock monitoring for this item.
6. In the field labeled Estimated Stock In Hand, enter **50**. This is the total quantity of the product that you currently have in inventory.
7. In the field labeled Warn If Below, enter **10**. If the orders processed bring the total amount in inventory below 10, Actinic will issue a warning to you, so you can re-stock the product in time to accommodate demand.
8. In the field labeled Suspend Orders If Below, enter **5**. If the total inventory gets to be below 5, orders for this product will be temporarily suspended at the Web site.
9. Click OK to close the window.
10. To make the changes active on your test site, update the Web site by choosing Update Website from the Web menu.

Setting stock levels and other stock monitoring variables can also be done through the Stock Levels window, as follows:

1. Select Stock Monitoring from the View menu in Actinic. The Stock Levels window should look like Figure 20-3.

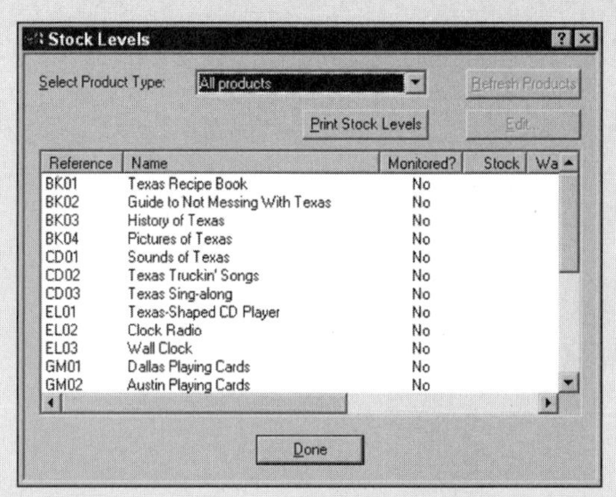

Figure 20-3: The Stock Levels window

2. The window needs to be expanded to view all of the information displayed in the table. To expand the window, move your cursor to the bottom right corner of the window until it turns into an arrow with two arrowheads at a diagonal angle. Click and hold, drag the mouse to expand the window until it looks like Figure 20-4, and then release the mouse button.

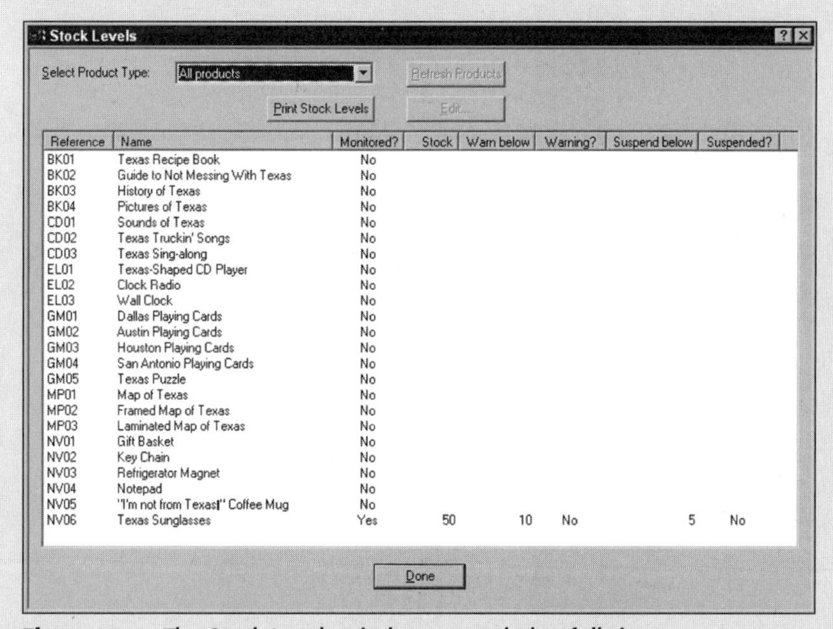

Figure 20-4: The Stock Levels window expanded to full size

3. Each product is listed in the main field of this window, with the stock monitoring information to the right. To edit the first product, highlight it by clicking on it, then click the Edit button. The Edit Stock Levels window shown in Figure 20-5 appears.

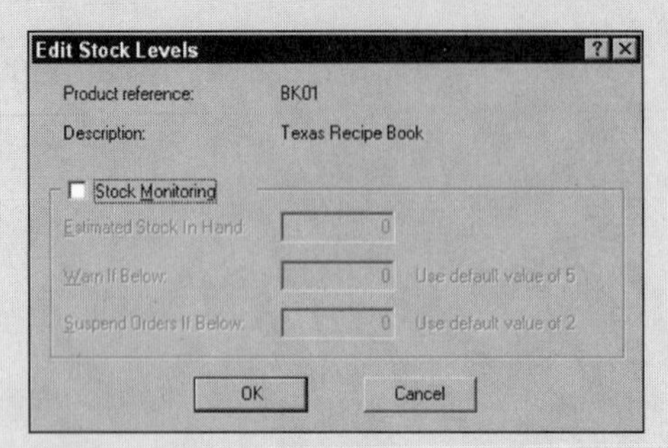

Figure 20-5: The Edit Stock Levels window

4. Click the Stock Monitoring checkbox to activate stock monitoring for this item.
5. In the field labeled Estimated Stock In Hand, enter **15**.
6. Leave the Warn If Below and Suspend Orders If Below fields set to **0**. The default values of 5 and 2 (respectively) will automatically be used.
7. Click OK to close the window. In the Stock Levels window, the new values for the first product should now be visible, as in Figure 20-6.

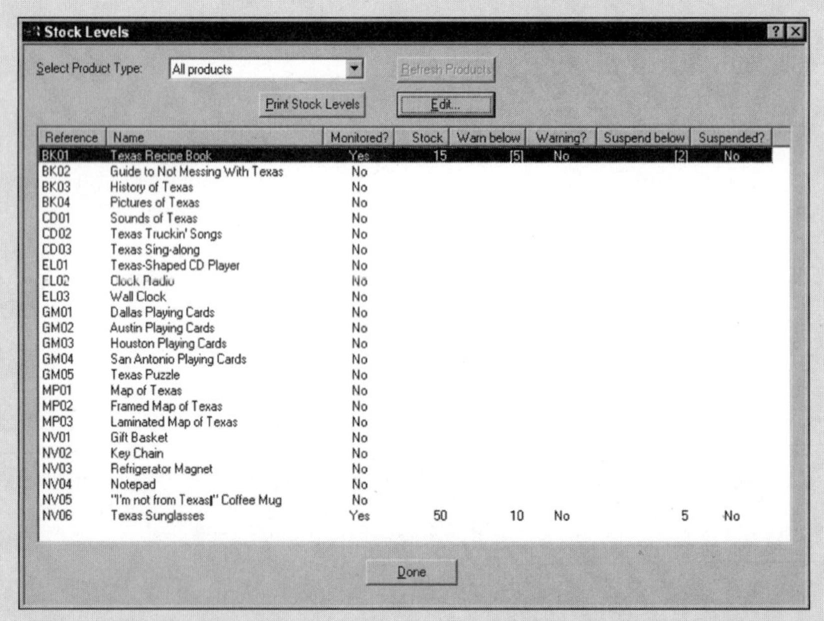

Figure 20-6: The Stock Levels window with new information for the first product listed

8. Repeat the previous steps for each product in the catalog. Enter a quantity between **10** and **50** for each product, and leave the Warn If Below and Suspend Orders If Below fields set to **0**.
9. When you're done, click the Done button at the bottom of the Stock Levels window. You've set up stock monitoring for your entire catalog!
10. To make the changes active on your test site, update the Web site by choosing Update Website from the Web menu.

Lab 20-2 Order processing in Actinic Business

In this exercise, you place several orders on your test site, download them to your desktop, and use Actinic to process the orders. You'll also see how the Stock Monitoring functionality you set up in Lab 20-1 is affected by the orders.

1. The first step is to place several test orders on your test site. To do this, go to your test site in your browser and place the following orders:
   - Order one refrigerator magnet, one notepad, one "I'm not from Texas..." mug, and one pair of Texas sunglasses, size small. Use the following address and credit card information: Mabel Buckley, 222 Main Street, Smallville, TX 78000. Visa card #4111-1111-1111-1111. Use an expiration date that is in the future.
   - Order one copy of the *Texas Truckin' Songs* CD and one deck of Austin Playing Cards. Select the Invoice and Payment Before Delivery payment option, and use the address: Alice Jones, 555 E. 55th Street, Big Town, CA 94100.
2. Now return to the Actinic main window (or start Actinic if it's not open).
3. Download the new orders from your Web site by choosing Retrieve Orders from the Web menu.
4. A dialog box appears while your orders are being downloaded. Click OK when the process is complete.
5. To view the newly downloaded orders, click the Orders tab (next to the Catalog tab above the main Actinic work area). Your screen should look like Figure 20-7.

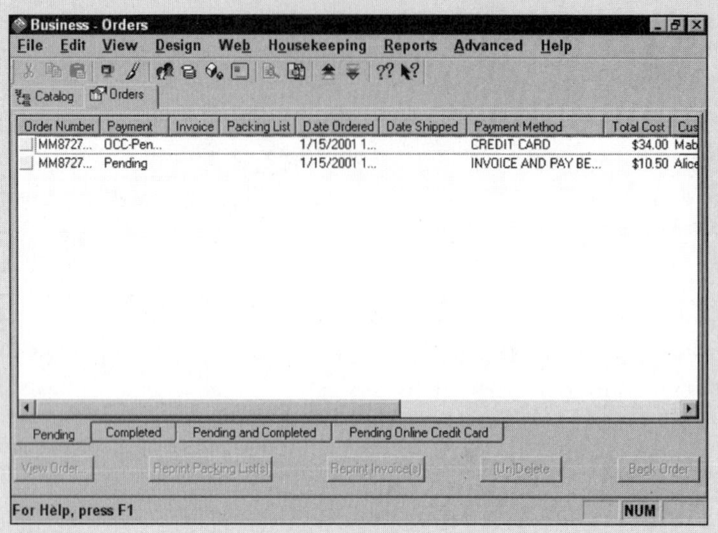

Figure 20-7: Viewing orders in Actinic

6. To view the details of the first order on the list, highlight that order by clicking once on it, and then click the View Order button at the bottom of the window. The Order details window should open.
7. If the Customer tab is not selected, click it to bring it to the front (see Figure 20-8).

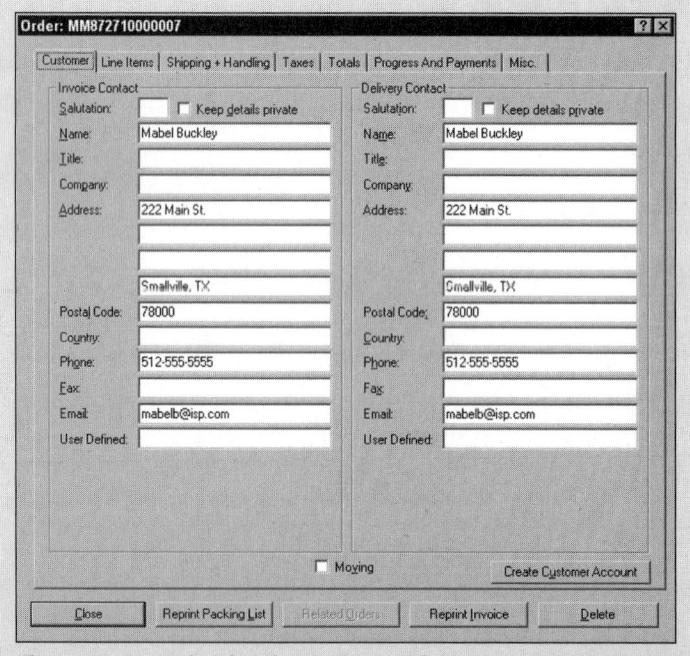

Figure 20-8: Order details window, with Customer tab selected

8. The first thing to do is process payment. In the case of this order, the fictitious customer Mabel Buckley submitted her credit card information online and it was transmitted to you via the Internet. You used a manual credit card processing method to process the payment. Next, you record the payment in Actinic. Click the Progress And Payments tab to bring it to the front as shown in Figure 20-9.

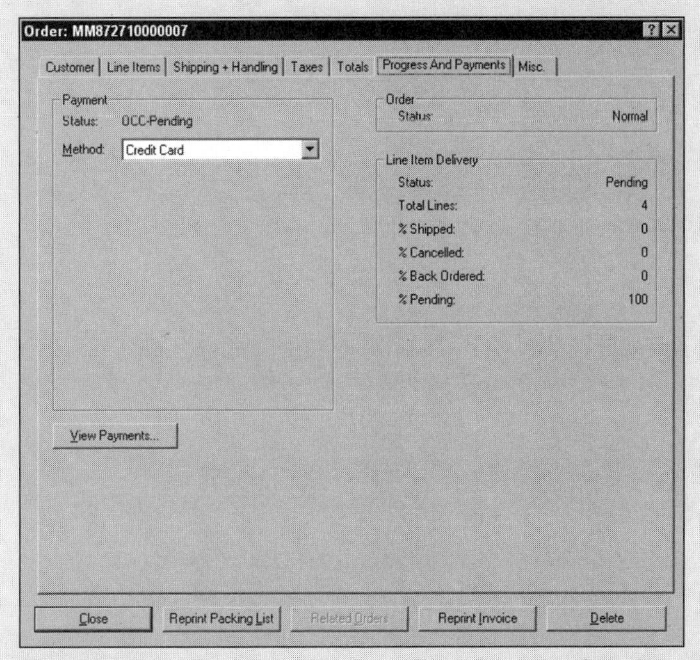

Figure 20-9: Order details window, with Progress And Payments tab selected

9. Click the View Payments button. The payment history window should open.
10. To record a payment, click the New Entry button.
11. The form is automatically populated with information indicating a successful transaction (see Figure 20-10). This is efficient for the user because in most cases, transactions are successful. If the transaction returned an error or was otherwise incomplete, the appropriate option can be selected from the Status drop-down menu. In this case, leave the status as Received.

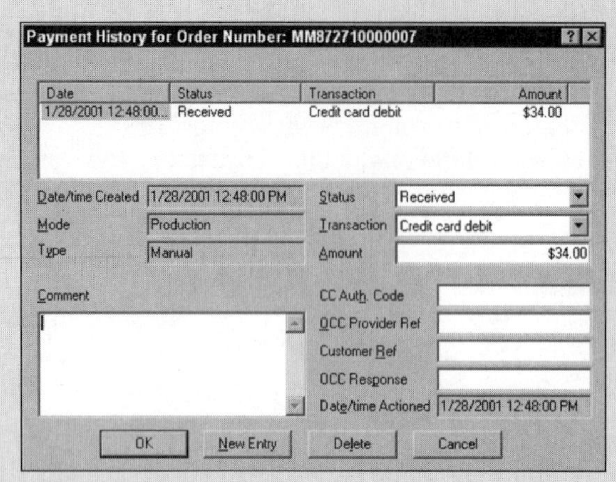

Figure 20-10: Recording a successful transaction

12. Click OK to close the window.
13. Now, you'll need to record the items as shipped and print an invoice or packing list. Click the Line Items tab to bring it to the front (see Figure 20-11).

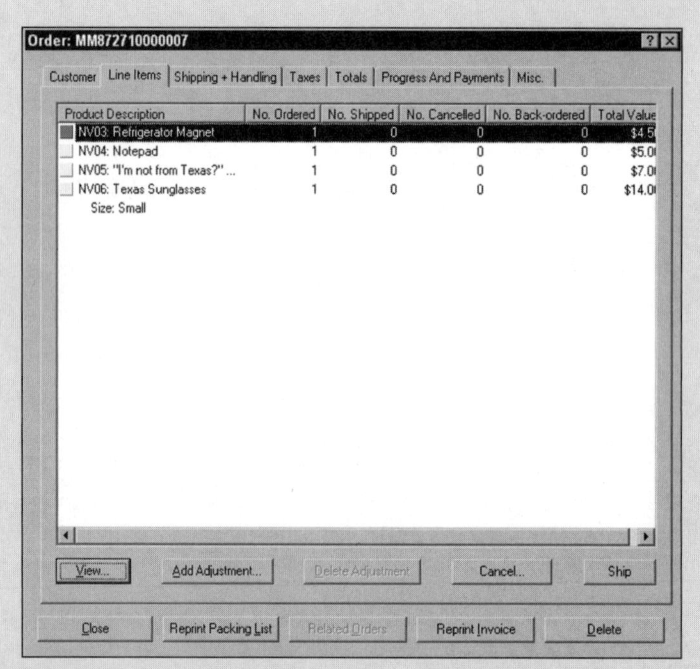

Figure 20-11: Order details window, with Line Items tab selected

14. Highlight the first line and click the View button. The Order Line window shown in Figure 20-12 opens.

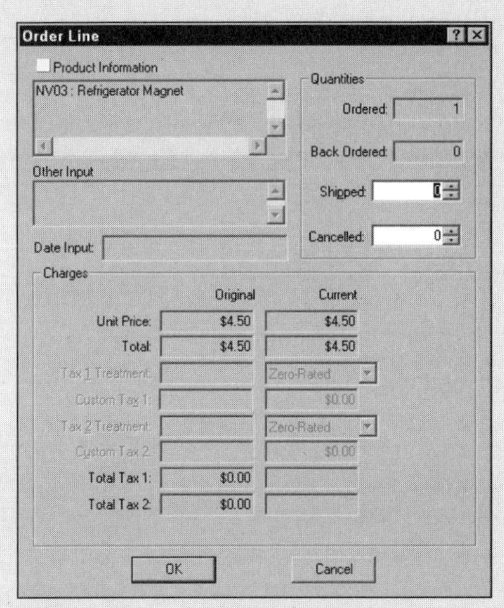

Figure 20-12: The Order Line window

15. In the Shipped field, enter the number **1**.
16. Click OK to close the window. In the Line Items window, the first line should have a check mark in front of it, indicating the item has been shipped.

Tip

There is a faster way to mark items as shipped. In the Order details window, Line Items tab shown in Figure 20-11, select the line item you want to ship to highlight it. Click the Ship button at the bottom of the window. The program automatically records that the number of items ordered was shipped.

17. Repeat the previous two steps (or use the method shown in the Tip) for the remaining items.
18. At the bottom of the Order details window (Figure 20-11), click the Print Invoice button.
19. From the pop-up menu that appears, select Standard Report.
20. Click OK to print. Figure 20-13 shows you a view of the invoice.

Reprint **Order No.:** MM8727-1000-0007

Texas-Shaped.com
PO Box 270266
Austin, TX
USA 78727
Phone:
Email: tex@texas-shaped.com

Fax:
Web site: www.texas-shaped.com

INVOICE

Customer:

Mabel Buckley
222 Main St.
Smallville, TX
78000
Phone: 512-555-5555
Email: mabelb@isp.com

Date ordered: 15 Jan 2001
Payment method: Online credit card
Payment status: Full Payment Received

Shipping Method: Default

Product code	description	Tax code(s)	Qty ship.	Qty back.	Unit price	Total cost
NV03	Refrigerator Magnet		1		$4.50	$4.50
NV04	Notepad		1		$5.00	$5.00
NV05	"I'm not from Texas?" Coffee Mug		1		$7.00	$7.00
NV06	Texas Sunglasses (Size: Small)		1		$14.00	$14.00
					Subtotal	$30.50
					Shipping	$3.50
					Total	$34.00

Payments:

Date	Payment type	Amount	Comment
28 Jan 2001	Credit card debit	$34.00	

Figure 20-13: The order invoice

21. Now that you've printed the invoice, the order is automatically marked as completed, and can be made visible by clicking the Completed tab at the bottom of the Order view in Actinic (see Figure 20-14).

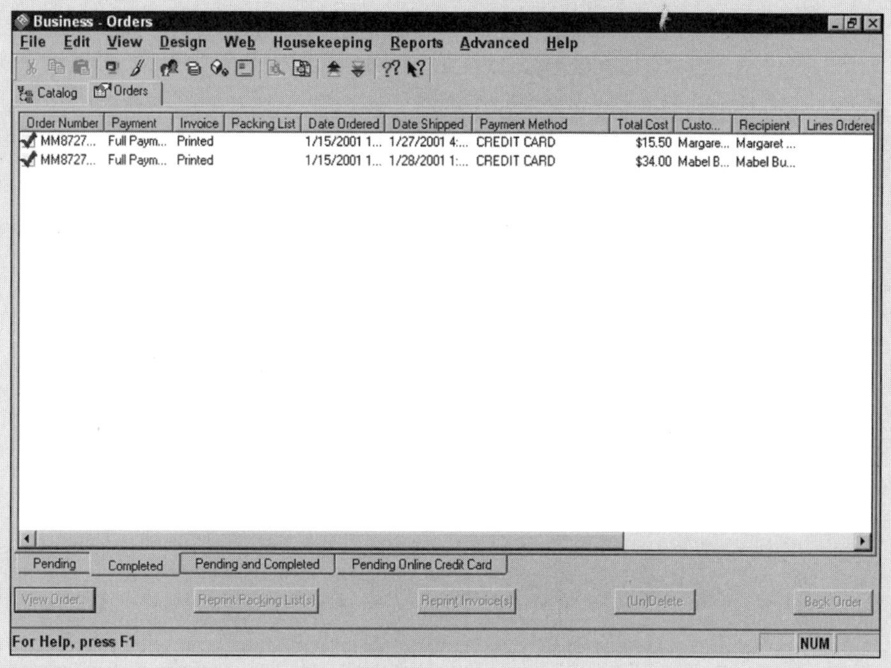

Figure 20-14: Viewing completed orders

22. Repeat this Lab Exercise using the second test order you placed.

Lab 20-3 Monitoring inventory using Actinic Business, part 2

Now that you've completed several test orders, you can check on your stock levels to see how they were affected.

1. In Actinic Business, select Stock Monitoring from the View menu.
2. In the Stock Levels window, select All Products from the drop down menu labeled Select Product Type. Note the other options available:
   - **Ordering suspended.** Lists all products for which ordering has been suspended because of insufficient stock. This automatically kicks in once stock levels are below the number specified in the Suspend Below field.
   - **Stock warning given.** Lists all products for which a low stock warning has been given. Low stock warnings are automatically issued when the stock level for a given product dips below the number in the Warn Below field.
   - **Stock monitoring enabled.** If the stock levels of only some of the products in your catalog are monitored by Actinic, only these show up in this view.
3. Your new stock levels are displayed, as shown in Figure 20-15.

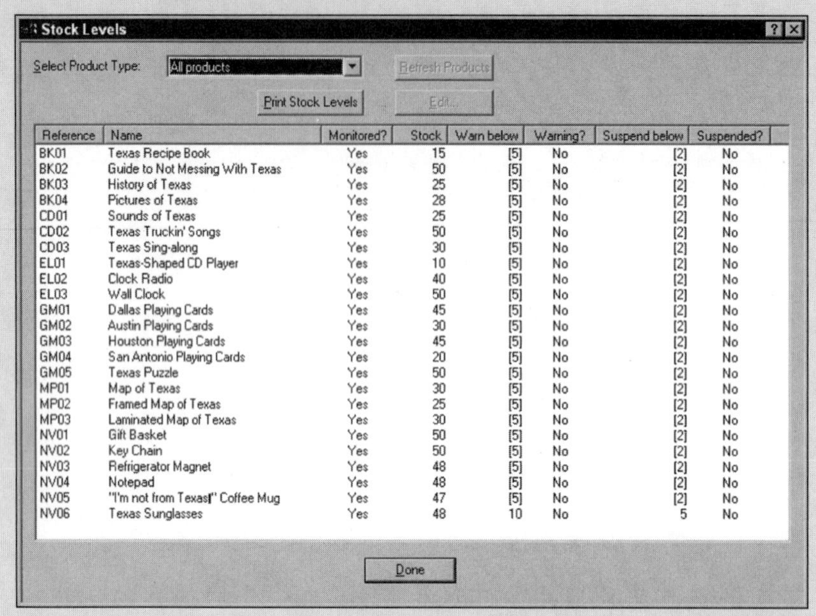

Reference	Name	Monitored?	Stock	Warn below	Warning?	Suspend below	Suspended?
BK01	Texas Recipe Book	Yes	15	[5]	No	[2]	No
BK02	Guide to Not Messing With Texas	Yes	50	[5]	No	[2]	No
BK03	History of Texas	Yes	25	[5]	No	[2]	No
BK04	Pictures of Texas	Yes	28	[5]	No	[2]	No
CD01	Sounds of Texas	Yes	25	[5]	No	[2]	No
CD02	Texas Truckin' Songs	Yes	50	[5]	No	[2]	No
CD03	Texas Sing-along	Yes	30	[5]	No	[2]	No
EL01	Texas-Shaped CD Player	Yes	10	[5]	No	[2]	No
EL02	Clock Radio	Yes	40	[5]	No	[2]	No
EL03	Wall Clock	Yes	50	[5]	No	[2]	No
GM01	Dallas Playing Cards	Yes	45	[5]	No	[2]	No
GM02	Austin Playing Cards	Yes	30	[5]	No	[2]	No
GM03	Houston Playing Cards	Yes	45	[5]	No	[2]	No
GM04	San Antonio Playing Cards	Yes	20	[5]	No	[2]	No
GM05	Texas Puzzle	Yes	50	[5]	No	[2]	No
MP01	Map of Texas	Yes	30	[5]	No	[2]	No
MP02	Framed Map of Texas	Yes	25	[5]	No	[2]	No
MP03	Laminated Map of Texas	Yes	30	[5]	No	[2]	No
NV01	Gift Basket	Yes	50	[5]	No	[2]	No
NV02	Key Chain	Yes	50	[5]	No	[2]	No
NV03	Refrigerator Magnet	Yes	48	[5]	No	[2]	No
NV04	Notepad	Yes	48	[5]	No	[2]	No
NV05	"I'm not from Texas!" Coffee Mug	Yes	47	[5]	No	[2]	No
NV06	Texas Sunglasses	Yes	48	10	No	5	No

Figure 20-15: The Stock Levels window

4. If you placed the orders specified in Lab 20-2, your stock levels should have been reduced in the following manner:
   - Refrigerator magnets reduced by one
   - Notepads reduced by one
   - "I'm not from Texas..." mugs reduced by one
   - Texas sunglasses reduced by one
   - Texas Truckin' Songs CDs reduced by one
   - Austin Playing Cards reduced by one

Answers to Chapter Questions

Chapter pre-test

1. The most efficient means of storage for e-business information is a relational database. Relational databases allow different kinds of data to be housed in different tables in the same database. This means that:

   a. Data does not need to be imported and exported between various databases.

   b. Duplicate data does not need to be kept for the information to be complete.

2. An e-commerce Web site needs to access the e-business information database to provide customers with inventory (or availability) information, account information, and information on previously placed orders. Access is provided by technologies such as Active Server Pages (ASP) and Cold Fusion.
3. Staff members in various departments of an e-commerce company need to be able to access the e-business information database to have access to the information they need to do their jobs. Job-specific views and editing controls can be set up to control who has access to what information.
4. Customer access to sensitive information in the database (such as address and payment information) is controlled by the use of a unique identifier for each customer, and through authentication tied to a user name and password for each customer.
5. The unique identifier field in a relational database is the key to creating relationships between the tables in the database. For instance, a record in an order information table can reference a customer using the customer's ID number, or unique key. Detailed information on the customer is kept in the customer information table in a record identified by its unique ID number.

Assessment questions

1. **A.** The four main types of information that need to be stored by an e-commerce company are customer information, product catalog information, order information, and inventory information. Payment information is a part of order information (see "Understanding E-Business Information Needs and Requirements").
2. **C.** The three factors effecting inventory levels are time, demand, and cost (see "Determining inventory levels").
3. **C.** Inventory is the quantity of a product that is kept by the seller between when it's acquired or produced and when a buyer purchases it (see "Managing Inventory").
4. **B.** The information in a relational database is stored in multiple tables consisting of records (rows) and fields (columns). For more information, see "Managing inventory data."
5. **D.** E-commerce has led to frequent shortages because of demand, causing e-commerce companies to rethink traditional inventory control methods (see "Managing Inventory").
6. **D.** The order ID number is the only piece of order information guaranteed to be unique. Therefore, it's used to identify each order in an order information database table (see "Tracking Orders").

Scenario

This scenario tested whether you were able to follow the relationships between the tables in the relational database to answer the questions posed. The correct answers are:

1. Myra Taylor ordered two copies of *Everything I Need to Know I Learned from a Talking Spoon* and one copy of *Doo Wop Classics.* Order 000652 was placed by customer 010068, who is Myra Taylor.
2. Greg Montes bought two copies of *Everything I Need to Know I Learned from a Talking Spoon* and a Super Deluxe CD Player. Greg, customer 002067, placed order 001005, which contained product BK-228 (*Everything I Need to Know I Learned from a Talking Spoon*) with a quantity of two and product EL-052 (Super Deluxe CD Player) with a quantity of one.
3. Two PopStarGirlz albums were shipped to 3215 Grant Wy. In order 000081, one copy each of products AU-041 (*Meet the PopStarGirlz!*) and AU-501 (*Ooh Baby* by the PopStarGirlz) were shipped to customer 002886, who is Erin Chong. Her address is 3215 Grant Wy.
4. Four copies of *Everything I Need to Know I Learned from a Talking Spoon* (Product BK-228) were sold in the orders listed in Table 20-5 — two in order 000652 and two in order 001005.

For More Information . . .

- ✦ **The Center for Inventory Management.** `www.centerforinventorymanagement.org`. Information on inventory management theory and systems, plus a newsletter.
- ✦ **Actinic Software.** `www.actinic.com`. Full product information, downloads, and registration of the software.

Managing an E-Commerce Web Site

✦ ✦ ✦ ✦

EXAM OBJECTIVES

- Log file analysis
- Traffic tracking
- Performance testing

CHAPTER PRE-TEST

1. What are the three tasks involved in site administration and management?
2. What tasks should be included in maintaining site content?
3. What are the clues to a user that a site is dead?
4. What is a bottleneck?
5. What is the difference between a hit and a page view?
6. What is the purpose of load testing?

✦ Answers to these questions can be found at the end of the chapter. ✦

After your e-commerce site is up and running, you can maximize its effectiveness with regular log file analysis, traffic tracking, and performance testing. This chapter explains the types of maintenance and monitoring every e-commerce site needs. It also demonstrates the tools and techniques of site management, which not only help you understand how your site is doing, but also help you make continuous improvements.

Understanding E-Commerce Site Management

So, you have a detailed business plan, you've created a killer site, and your entire staff has been has been working overtime to ensure success. You're finally ready to open the doors and let in the world. Congratulations!

Perhaps you sent out a mailing or bought advertisements in magazines and newspapers to coincide with the launch of your site. Maybe you're introducing your new site at an industry trade show or with a press release. Maybe your launch strategy involves a combination of all of these, plus some things that have never been done before. However you choose to let the world know that your site is open, the goal is to start getting visitors and possibly customers.

Online Promotion is covered in Chapter 4.

No matter how much testing you've done, and no matter how ready you think your staff is, opening a site to the public always introduces problems and challenges that you didn't think of during development. Even if you've done your stress testing and think your site is bullet-proof, it's just not the same as flinging open the doors of your site to browsers, buyers, spiders, and potential hackers.

Your site needs regular monitoring and maintenance to keep running at peek performance.

Site Administration Basics

In practice, Web site administration is different for every possible combination of operating systems, Web servers, supporting software, databases, payment gateways, and so forth. To effectively maintain your site, you must be intimately familiar with the hardware and software running it. Having this knowledge and knowing what to do with it is typically the job of the Information Technology (IT) department or of the Webmaster.

The three primary tasks of regular site administration and management include:

✦ Monitoring and maintaining site content

✦ Monitoring and maintaining security

✦ Monitoring and improving performance

Each of these tasks is comprised of specific jobs, which must be done regularly to ensure that your site continues to operate as well as it can. In the following sections, you'll explore each of the jobs of site management, as well as the vital topic of site responsiveness.

Monitoring and maintaining site content

Visitors to Web sites expect the content of the site to be updated regularly. We have all had the experience of visiting a site, becoming interested in the content of the site, and then being disappointed when the date at the bottom of the page is 1996. If the date on the site hasn't been updated in years, it's unlikely that the content of the site has been updated. If the site in question is an e-commerce site, it's highly unlikely it's still in business — and you probably wouldn't want to do business with a site that hasn't been updated since 1996 — even if it is still active.

The Web is somewhat like low earth orbit. Web sites stick around for a long time after they've been abandoned, just like satellites. Web users are getting used to distinguishing between junk and active sites, and have become very good at it — maybe even too good. What this means for you, as the site owner, is that you better have a very active and very aggressive site updating policy.

Recognizing the signs of a dead site

There are numerous visual clues, obvious to sophisticated users, that your site is old and/or your business has joined the ranks of the once high-flying dot-coms, whose orbits are deteriorating in anticipation of their eventual burn-up in the atmosphere. The signs of a dead site include:

✦ **Copyright dates and/or last updated dates are not current.** Seeing an old copyright date or a list of copyright dates prior to the current year may indicate the site just didn't make it. In addition, a last updated date that's more than a few months old may indicate a dead site.

✦ **Old-looking Web design.** Everyone knows what the hot elements in Web site design from before 1997 look like. Most Web fanatics can pick out a site designed in 1998, and there are often telltale signs of a site designed in 1999 that hasn't been updated since then.

✦ **Broken links.** Even if your site is kept up-to-date, the sites you link to might not be. It's important to check external and internal links regularly to make sure they're still relevant.

✦ **Obsolete technology.** Many technologies have come and gone over the years. Consider *push technology* or some of the multimedia formats all the rage two or three years ago. If your site relies on a plug-in that is no longer available, this is a big tip-off your site's not being updated.

✦ **Language or phrases from past Web eras.** If your site says something like, "You must be using Netscape 3.0 to view this site" or "This site is optimized for (insert anything here)," you need to get out of the Stone Age.

There still are browser incompatibilities today, but they are vastly different from the incompatibilities of 1997. Today, over 95 percent of Web users use a graphical browser that supports JavaScript, Java, frames, Cascading Style Sheets (CSS), and Secure Sockets Layer (SSL). In addition, the vast majority of people are using computers with at least a 15-inch color monitor set to at least 800x600 pixel resolution and 16-bit color. The general consensus among most Web designers today is that it's important to design for maximum compatibility and accessibility, but if someone is using an obsolete browser or computer, they're aware of this and they know Web sites are going to look strange.

Getting users to bookmark your site

After you get someone to visit your site, you have a unique opportunity to gain loyal customers. It's much easier for someone to return to a site where they've already been than to look for new sites. Despite the millions of available sites, most people return to the same ones day after day.

Your goal in maintaining the content of your site is for people to bookmark it so they can return again easily. *Bookmarking* is the Web equivalent of adding a phone number to the speed dial. Even though bookmarking a site is simple to do and doesn't require any sort of commitment to returning to the bookmarked site, people don't seem to take the act of bookmarking lightly. If someone visits your site for the first time and perceives that it isn't regularly maintained, they are very unlikely to bookmark it and are also unlikely to visit again.

Later in this chapter, you find out how to measure how successful you are in getting visitors to return to your site and even how many people are bookmarking it.

Breaking out the tasks of effective maintenance

The people responsible for maintaining site content, such as an editorial department, an IT department, or a combination of technical and non-technical people, have the following jobs:

✦ Updating Web pages

✦ Updating and maintaining the site database

✦ Checking for broken links

✦ Creating and maintaining backups

Each of these functions is vital to the management of an e-commerce site's content. The following sections explore each of these in more detail.

Updating Web pages

Updating the non-product content of a site is just as important as updating product information. Every Web site has a large variety of pages that need to be kept up to date, as follows:

- **The home page.** This page, especially, needs to be altered in some way on a regular basis. Many e-commerce sites display featured products or special offers on the home page. Some have regularly updated areas on the home page for news or product update information. Many sites use personalization databases and information about a customer's past purchases and stated preferences to create custom-tailored home pages. Personalized home pages range in the amount of personalization they feature. Some merely display a personalized "Welcome" message. Other sites, such as Amazon.com, go as far as to customize the navigation of the site based on individual users.
- **Other pages.** Additional pages that need to be updated regularly include company information, help pages, policy information pages, press releases, shipping information, and more.

Done well, an e-commerce site can become more than just a place for people to buy things. Your site has the potential to become the first place people go when they need more information about an existing purchase or when they need information about a product they are considering purchasing (hopefully from you). Your site may also have the potential to become a central location for people to come together to discuss shared interests. The possibilities for building a community and marketing your products are enormous. However, you must be willing to make a commitment to regular updating and maintenance of your site's content.

Chapter 3 covers e-commerce marketing in detail.

Not only do you need to be aggressive in posting new information, but you also need to make sure that old, out-of-date information is removed from your site. Press releases five years old may no longer fit with the company line or your current strategy. Rather than having people get the wrong idea about your company from reading old information, just remove it.

Updating and maintaining the site database

Most e-commerce sites rely heavily on databases. Some of the types of e-commerce data that are stored in databases include product information, customer information, order information, shipping rates, and tax tables. All of this data requires updating.

For paper catalogs, people have come to expect that a product listed in the catalog might not actually still be available. Paper catalogs take time to assemble, print, and mail. If a color or size that's listed in a paper catalog is no longer correct, people generally understand that paper catalogs (and other such items) go out of date.

Web users are not as understanding. The Web makes it possible for you to quickly make changes to a product's description, price, and availability. Visitors to your site expect that everything that is listed is actually available and that description and options are accurate.

The best way to keep Web databases up-to-date with the physical realities of your business, such as inventory and available options, is to create an online store that is integrated into your whole business. Therefore, each piece of information (such as product descriptions or inventory data) only needs to be updated in one place for it to be instantly updated across the organization. For businesses where the Web site is the entire business, this is typically not a problem. In this case, the storefront software generally updates inventory as products are ordered and every part of the business process can be controlled using software that is tied in to the Web site. For other businesses, integrating offline systems with online systems can be expensive and problematic.

Chapter 11 discusses the issues involved in integrating legacy systems with online storefronts.

Checking for broken links

Nearly every large site has some broken links somewhere. Having broken links is inevitable and is a result of the HTML-style of one-way hyperlinking. Broken links occur for a variety of reasons, including:

✦ Simple typos by the person writing the HTML

✦ Internal pages that have moved

✦ External pages you don't have control over that have moved

✦ Sites that were once linked to, but have since moved or been shut down

Finding broken links and fixing them can be time-consuming and tedious work. Although there are software products available for locating broken links, correcting these errors once they are found must still be done manually, in most cases.

Although there are tools that are specifically designed for testing links on a site, you can also use a log file analysis tool, such as the one discussed later in this chapter in the "Analyzing Log Files" section, to locate broken links.

Creating and maintaining backups

Creating and maintaining backups is such an important part of running an e-commerce business that we hate to put it in the last chapter of this book. If you don't create backup copies of your site content and databases, you're taking an even bigger risk than if you don't secure your site from possible attack by hackers. Let's say this as clearly as possible:

Make backups of all of your data on a daily basis (if not more often) and keep a copy of the backups in a secure, OFF-SITE location!

Most hosting companies offer backup services for the Web sites they host. Be sure to ask for the details of any backup system before you sign a contract.

Here are a few important things to remember when creating and implementing your backup strategy:

- ✦ **Invest in a high-quality and reliable system.** For your internal data, such as contracts, invoices, accounting information, and customer information, you need to invest in some sort of reliable and safe backup system. Simply creating copies of important files is not enough.
- ✦ **Limit access.** To protect you from accidental deletion of backups, your files need to be stored somewhere where only a select few people have access to them.
- ✦ **Store backups off-site.** To protect you in case something awful happens to your office or your server (like a fire), you need to store backups off-site. Safe deposit boxes work well for storing off-site backups, and there are company's that provide backup storage services for electronic data.
- ✦ **Anticipate natural disasters.** Company's located in regions prone to earthquakes or other natural disasters should keep their backups somewhere less likely to experience natural disasters.
- ✦ **Prepare for hardware failures.** E-commerce businesses depend upon an array of very flaky hardware components. Unfortunately, the single component most prone to failure is the one you least want to fail: the hard drive. Every hard drive has an estimated life span. You may be surprised to learn that hard drives are only supposed to last 2 to 6 years. If you haven't had to deal with a hard drive failure, you're very lucky. The hard fact is that your e-commerce site will grind to a halt and you will lose everything if you don't back up your data on every computer that has anything to do with your business.
- ✦ **Use removable media.** To fully protect and preserve your business data, you need to back it up onto removable media, not onto an internal hard drive. Backups are usually stored on slower, cheaper, but also more reliable types of media than hard drives. Tape drives are the traditional choice. Table 21-1 shows a comparison of the expected life spans of different storage media.

Table 21-1
Expected Life Spans of Storage Media

Type of media	*Expected life span*
Floppy disk	1 year
Magnetic hard drive	2 to 5 years
Magnetic tape	3 to 30 years
Optical CD-RW	75 to 100 years
CD-ROM	200 years

✦ **Consider an Internet backup service.** Internet backup services are becoming more popular as they become more reliable and trustworthy. With an Internet backup service, you install software on your computer or network that indexes your data files. These files are then encrypted and sent over the Internet to the backup company according to a schedule that you set. When you need to recover files, you simply log into your account with the backup company and download them. Some of these companies also send you CD-ROMs containing your data, if you request them. Figure 21-1 shows the software for one such service, Connected TLM.

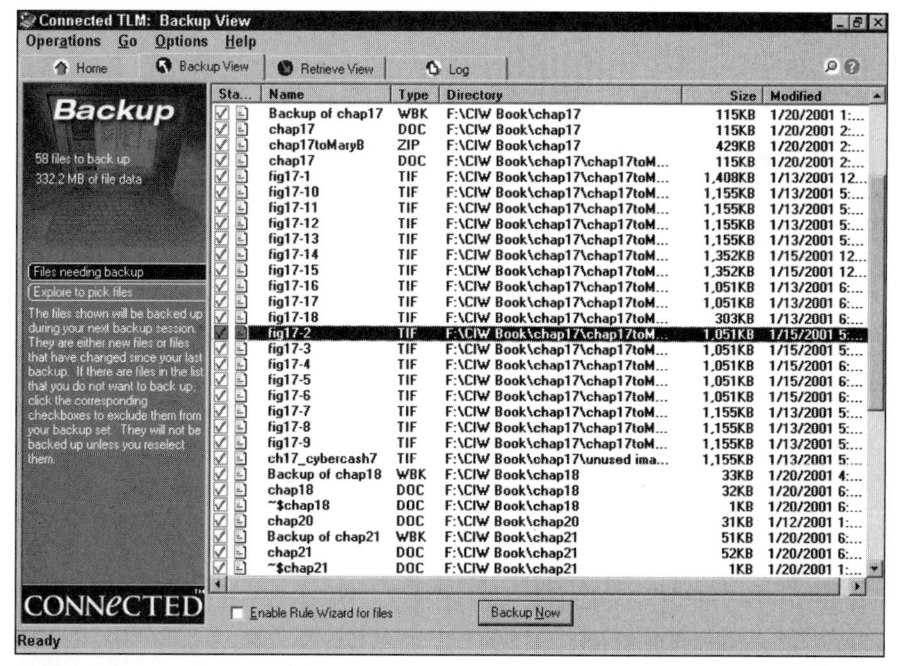

Figure 21-1: Connected TLM

You never know when disaster will strike. Just before beginning this chapter, we were reminded just how important backups are. The fan in the server that holds all of our business's data (as well as the content of this book) chose to stop working late one night. This caused the power supply, the processor, the motherboard, and the hard drive to all overheat and die. If we didn't have backups, this book might have never been finished.

Monitoring and maintaining security

Simply planning and creating a secure site is not enough. The security of your site must be continually tested and analyzed. New ways to break, or break into, different servers and software are found all the time. As new vulnerabilities are discovered, software vendors create security patches to block the holes. System administrators need to be aware of security patches, as well as vulnerabilities that might require part of the site to be reprogrammed.

Software vendors, as well as organizations such as Carnegie Mellon Software Engineering Institute CERT (Computer Emergency Response Team) Coordination Center (`www.cert.org`), regularly provide security updates on their Web sites and via e-mail.

By being informed about security risks, and by monitoring your site regularly, it's possible to operate an e-commerce site that is relatively secure from hacking.

Chapter 19 talks more about securing your site and auditing it to make sure it stays secure.

Monitoring and maintaining performance

A big part of Web site usability not discussed in detail yet is server performance. One way to measure performance is by throughput. *Throughput* is the amount of data that can be served to users over a given period of time. Another way to measure performance is by the number of connections from clients that the server can accept during a period of time.

Throughput and performance are important concepts to understand.

Enhancing request and response speed

Ideally, a server should be able to handle every HTTP request it gets as soon as the request arrives. In this case, the only delays between when a user clicks a link and when the user sees the requested page are caused by the time it takes for the request to travel to the server and for the server to retrieve the page and send it back to the user. This ideal HTTP request and response is shown in Figure 21-2.

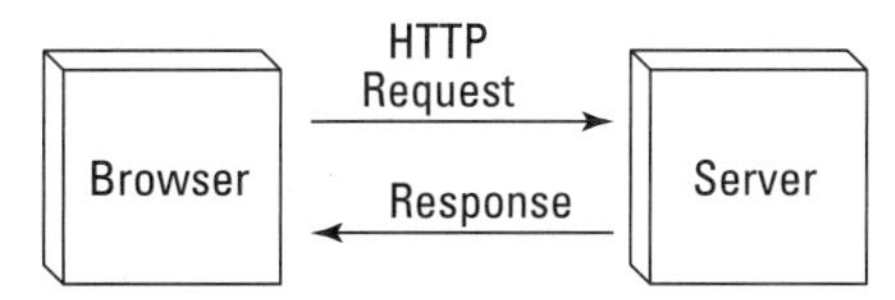

Figure 21-2: An ideal HTTP request and response

The scenario that most closely resembles the ideal HTTP request and response is a Web server that only serves one site, has a relatively low amount of traffic, and is only serving static HTML pages. This scenario is relatively rare today, however.

Web sites are most often served from a computer hosting many other sites and running programs that must work together with the Web server to generate HTML pages before they are returned to the client. Some of the tasks performed by server programs include:

- ✦ Reading and writing to databases
- ✦ Performing security checks
- ✦ Creating files on the server
- ✦ Authenticating credit cards

A single click of a link by a user may require the server to do any or all of these things and more. Multiply this single click by the thousands of requests a busy site must serve each minute, and you have the potential for significant performance degradation.

Using queuing

You should understand queuing, and how it relates to Web server performance.

To help deal with this performance problem, Web servers use queuing, which works as follows:

- ✦ A Web server's primary input queue is where all of the requests to a Web server arrive and wait to be processed.
- ✦ How quickly the Web server processes requests in its queue depends on factors such as network drivers, how well the operating system manages CPU and memory resources, and the amount of CPU and memory resources available.
- ✦ If the number of requests exceeds the ability of the server to process them, the size of the queue increases until there's no more space in the queue. At this point, the server has to start rejecting requests.

Dealing with bottlenecks

Even today's high-speed processors and Web servers can become overwhelmed by heavy traffic. Because a server must go through a series of steps in order to return a requested page to a client, every component in this series of steps has the potential to slow down the process. The result is a bottleneck.

A *bottleneck* is the delay in transmission of data over the Internet or within a computer system. If your site is designed well, and your Web server is configured to handle the amount of traffic your site regularly receives with ease, bottlenecks are rare. However, if your site is suddenly written about in the newspaper, or suddenly becomes very popular, a spike in the number of users can result in users having to suffer through long delays to use your site, or, worse, users could simply not be allowed in. Your chance for the 15 minutes of fame that could substantially increase your sales can suddenly turn into an event in which thousands of people who want to buy things from you get a very bad first impression of your site.

Several actions can be taken to correct bottlenecks, including:

- ✦ Speeding up the part of your server that is causing the bottleneck.
- ✦ Using multiple copies of the component where the bottleneck is occurring. For example, most large Web sites use replication and load balancing to divide the HTTP requests in the queue between multiple servers.

Chapter 12 discusses servers and load balancing.

- ✦ Increasing the capacity of the queues in the system so they can accept more requests before rejecting visitors.

In order to know when bottlenecks occur or when there's a risk of bottlenecks, you need to monitor your site's traffic. Besides simply telling you how many people have visited your site, tracking site traffic can also provide you valuable information about how people get to your site, when people visit your site, and much more. These topics are dealt with in greater detail later in this chapter.

Site responsiveness

The speed of a Web site (rather than just the server) is measured by how long a page takes to load in a user's browser. This statistic, which is often much more telling than raw server performance, is called *responsiveness*. Responsiveness can be thought of as performance from the user's perspective. It takes into account factors such as the size of requested files as well as delays caused by the Internet.

Responsiveness and performance are linked together, but performance is not the most important factor in determining responsiveness. For example, a typical Web page may contain five graphics as well as the HTML page that contains the graphics. Load time, in such a case, is affected as follows:

✦ **Connection speed.** The load time of this page depends, first of all, on the speed of the user's Internet connection.

✦ **File size.** The second factor is the size of the files that need to be sent to the user.

✦ **Server performance.** The third factor is how quickly the server can send these files (i.e., its performance).

The following sections of this chapter explore specific tools for monitoring your site's performance, responsiveness, security, traffic, and content.

Analyzing Log Files

Log file analysis

Most Web servers have the capability to keep log files that provide details about each processed HTTP request. Each file requested by a client causes a single line to be written to a log file. A typical log file entry might look like this:

```
123.austin.rr.com - - [21/Jan/2001:01:41:51 -0500]
"GET /index.html HTTP/1.1" 200 2443
"http://www.google.com/search?q=sandwich&hl=de&lr="
"Mozilla/4.0 (compatible; MSIE 5.01; Windows 95)"
```

This entry breaks down as follows:

✦ The first part of this log entry is the IP address or name of the computer from which the visitor is requesting a file. In this case, the requester is a computer named 123 in the austin.rr.com domain.

✦ This part of the log entry is followed by a delimiter, the double dashes (- -) and the time and date of the request.

✦ Following the time and date is the HTTP request that was sent by the browser. This part, which is in quotation marks, tells you the requested file (`index.html`), the HTTP method used to request the file (GET), and the protocol used (HTTP 1.1).

✦ Following the request is the HTTP status code. In this case, the status code is 200, which indicates the request was successful.

✦ The next number is the size, in bytes, of the requested file (2443).

For more information about HTTP and HTTP status codes, see Chapter 12.

✦ The next URL, in quotes, is called the *referer*. Note that this is actually how it's spelled (with a missing *r*). This is just the way someone decided this would be spelled and it stuck. The referer tells where this visitor to this page came from. In this case, the visitor came from `http://www.google.com`. If the referer address is a search engine, as it is here, it can also tell you what the user searched for to find your site. In this case, they searched for the word "sandwich."

✦ The next part of the log entry indicates the browser and version number, as well as the operating system the visitor used. In this case, the visitor was using Microsoft Internet Explorer, version 5.01 on Windows 95.

A line similar to this one is created for each HTML file, each image, each script, and anything else anyone or any Web spider requests from your site. Log files can quickly grow to enormous sizes. In fact, it's not uncommon for improperly managed log files to fill up the entire hard drive of a Web server and cause the system to crash or slow to a crawl.

Data that can be collected or calculated using log files

Log files can provide a great deal of information. Some of the information includes:

✦ Number of requests made. This number is also known as the number of hits. Remember that a *hit* is any HTTP request. Therefore, a single person viewing a Web page that contains five graphics would generate six hits — one for the HTML file, and one for each of the graphics.

✦ Total number of files and kilobytes served.

✦ Number of requests by the type of file. For example, you can find out how many HTML pages were viewed. This statistic is also known as *page views*.

✦ How many distinct visitors (by IP address) came to your site.

✦ How many computers from each domain visited your site. For example, you can tell how many people from austin.rr.com or aol.com visited your site.

✦ Number of requests for specific files or directories. A particularly useful statistic might be how many people viewed your site's home page, the contact information page, or the employment information page.

✦ How much time people spent on certain pages or on the site as a whole.

✦ Which browsers and types of computers are used to visit your site.

✦ How people linked to your site or found your site.

All of this information can be useful in improving your site and your site's usability for its actual audience. There is, however, legitimate concern among Web users that log files can be used to watch them.

Tracking individual users using log files is generally not as easy as gathering aggregate data about users. However, there are ways to track individual users and connect their movements through your site to their actual identities. This is usually done by writing a file containing information about the user, called a cookie, to the user's browser. If you track users' movements through your site using cookies, you should reveal that you do so, as well as reveal what the information gathered is used for, in your privacy statement.

For more information on cookies, see Chapter 20. For more on privacy statements, please see Chapter 2.

Data not collected by log files

Some types of information cannot be accurately deduced from log files, including:

✦ **Individuals' identity.** Unless a user provides identifying information by logging into your site, it's not possible to link log file entries to individuals.

✦ **Number of human users.** Log files record users as IP addresses. Any entry in a log file may be a search engine spider or some other automated visitor. Although it's possible to look for and screen many well-known Web spiders, there's no foolproof way to only count actual human visitors.

✦ **Qualitative data.** Log files cannot record information such as why people come to your site, what they think of your site, and what they do with the information from your site.

Internet Explorer actually does provide one way to at least partially judge how many people really like your site. When a person bookmarks a page using Internet Explorer 5 or newer, his or her browser looks for a small graphic on your server with the name `favicon.ico`. This file, if it's present, can contain a small graphic that will be displayed in the user's Favorites menu next to the name of the site. Searching your log files for requests for this file (whether you have one or not) will tell you how many Internet Explorer 5 (or newer) users bookmarked your site.

✦ **Files that weren't viewed at all.** Unless a file is requested, it won't be contained in the log files.

✦ **Where the user went after leaving your site.** Your log files cannot record a user's movements outside of your server.

Because of the size and the amount of data server log files contain, numerous software applications are available to help you extract meaningful reports from all this raw data.

Using WebTrends Log Analyzer

Traffic tracking

Perhaps the best known, and most widely used, of the report generation tools is WebTrends Log Analyzer from WebTrends Software. Installation and use instructions are the topic of the following sections.

Installing and starting WebTrends Log Analyzer

To install and start up WebTrends Log Analyzer for the first time, follow these steps:

1. Locate the WebTrends Log Analyzer trial version installer on the CD that came with this book, or download it from `www.webtrends.com/products/log`.
2. Double-click the `wtltrail.exe` file to begin the installation. The first window that appears is the license agreement. After reading this agreement, click Accept to proceed. You should see a screen similar to the one shown in Figure 21-3.

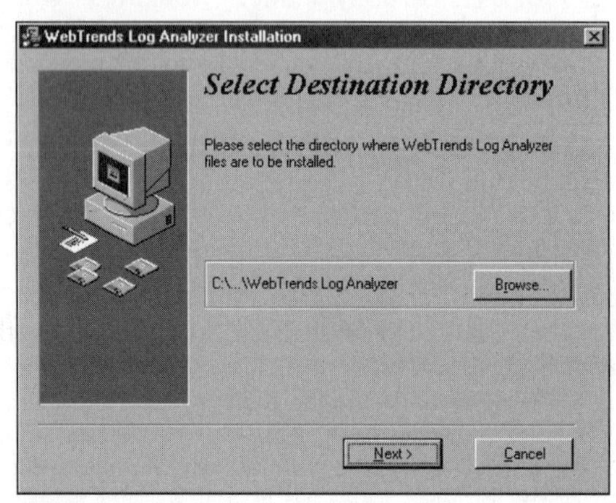

Figure 21-3: Beginning the WebTrends Log Analyzer Trial installation

3. Select the directory in which you want to install the software or just choose the default directory. Click Next.
4. The following screen asks you to choose what to install. Make sure that everything in this window is checked, and then click Next.
5. When you get to the screen that says you're now ready to install the software, click Next.
6. If you have Internet Information Services (IIS) installed, you'll see a message asking you if you would like to install a filter to enable extended logging. You won't need this filter for this chapter, but if you want to learn about it on your own, installing it won't do any harm.
7. When installation is complete, click Finish to quit the installation program.
8. Locate the WebTrends trial program and start the software. A registration window appears in which you must enter some information about yourself before you can proceed.

9. After registering your trial version of the software, you're asked if you would like WebTrends to scan for log files. Click No. You should see a screen similar to the one shown in Figure 21-4.

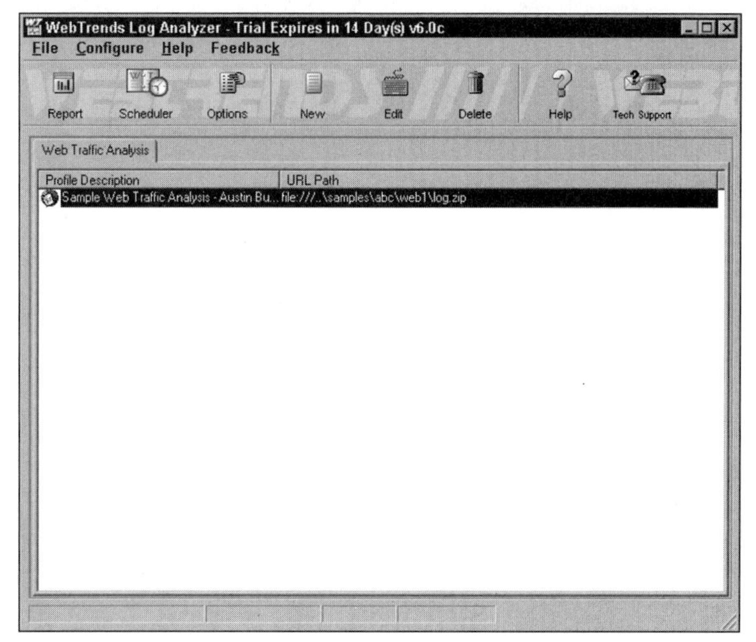

Figure 21-4: The main WebTrends Log Analyzer window

Viewing and editing a sample profile

WebTrends Logfile Analyzer creates attractive, detailed reports from raw server log files. WebTrends also allows you to create a profile for each site you manage. This profile tells you the name of the site, the URL of the site, and the location of the site log files, among other things. When you first install the software, a profile is preconfigured for the sample log files. To view and edit this sample profile, follow these steps:

1. Highlight the sample profile by clicking it in the main WebTrends Log Analyzer window.
2. Click the Edit button to view the window shown in Figure 21-5.

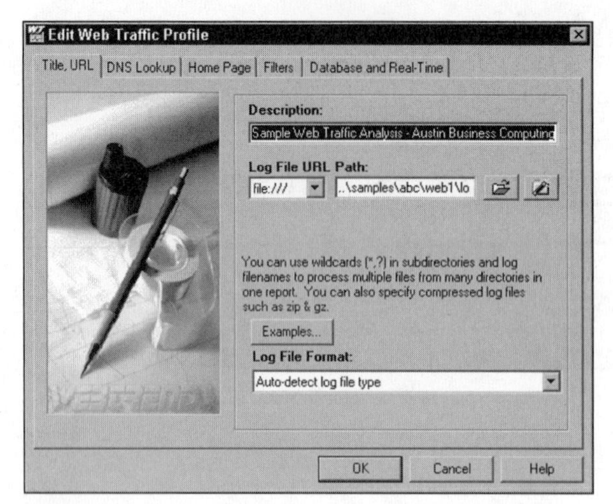

Figure 21-5: The Edit Web Traffic Profile window

3. The first sheet in this tabbed window is the Title, URL sheet. Set the name of your site and the location of the log file you want to analyze.
4. The second tab is called DNS Lookup. The drop-down list in this sheet determines whether WebTrends will attempt to look up IP addresses to get domain names. If you select Resolve Mode, report generation takes longer, but it may result in a report with more domain names (such as aol.com), rather than IP addresses (192.168.1.1, for example).
5. In the third tab (Home Page), specify the location of the site and the name of the default documents used by your site.
6. In the next tab, Filters, decide what types of content to include or exclude from the report based on factors such as file types, referers, browser type, data and time, and so forth.
7. The last tab (Database and Real Time) allows you to specify whether you want to store analysis data in a database. By choosing this option, additional options are made available to you. When you're finished looking at the profile information, close this window by clicking OK or Cancel.

Generating a report

The following steps show how to generate a report using the sample log file:

1. Double click the sample profile, or highlight it and click the Report button. You should see the window shown in Figure 21-6.

Figure 21-6: The Create Report window

2. Leave the information in the Range and Format tabs as they are. Click on the Save As/Mail To tab to bring it to the front.
3. Specify a location where you'd like to save the report.
4. In the Style tab, browse through the different choices and make any changes you want.
5. Bring the Content tab to the front and click the plus sign next to Technical Statistics. View the available statistics. Notice that if you highlight a line, you can change the type of graph used to display that statistic.
6. Scroll to the bottom of the list in this window and check the box next to Glossary. This includes a glossary of terms in the report that is generated.
7. When you're happy with the settings for this report, click the Start button to begin the report generation.
8. After a while (depending on the speed of your computer) the report is completed and opened in your Web browser (see Figure 21-7).

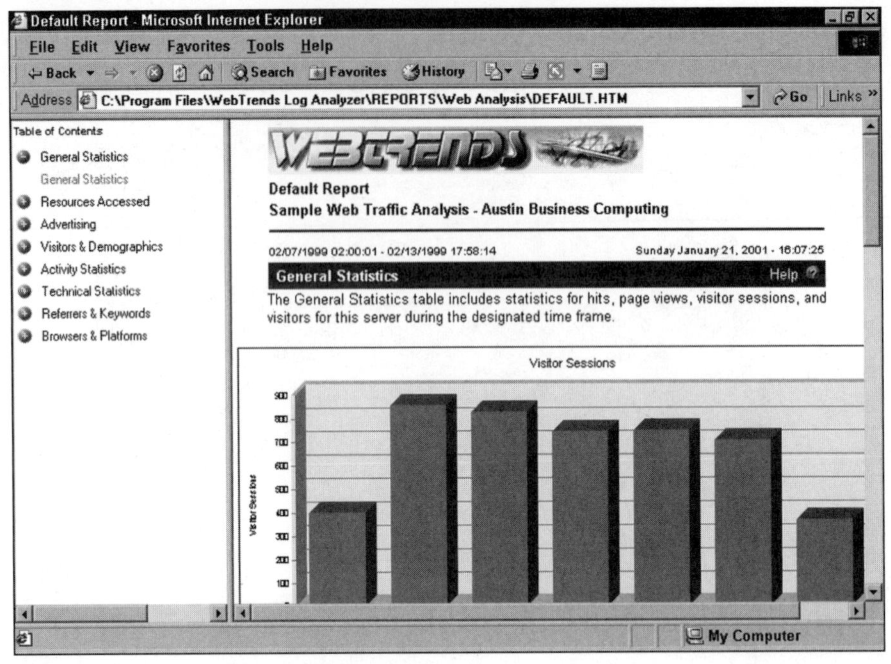

Figure 21-7: A sample WebTrends report

9. Click the links in the left frame to view the different parts of this report.

Assessing Web Performance

Performance testing

Tools for measuring how well your Web site performs are abundant. Make sure to do ample research before choosing one, however. There are free tools that are better than many of the commercial tools, and there are commercial tools that cost thousands of dollars and, for the right sites, are well worth the investment. Two specific types of Web performance monitoring tools are:

✦ Load-testing tools

✦ Web page diagnostic tools

Load testing

To assess the amount of traffic your server can handle, you should use a load-testing tool. Generally, load-testing software simulates many different types of users accessing your site simultaneously in order to give you an idea of where the bottlenecks on your site might occur.

Load testing should be done during testing of a site, before you take the site public.

Different tools measure a site's performance differently. To get the most accurate results from performance testing, use several different tools, as well as human testing.

Web page diagnostics

Another type of performance testing checks various factors in the actual Web pages being served. These factors include browser compatibility, HTML style, spelling, and load time. Of these, perhaps the most important is load time testing.

Load time testing measures how quickly a site loads into a user's browser at different connection speeds. One popular tool for testing load time and other aspects of Web site design is Netscape's Web Site Garage. To try Web Site Garage, follow these steps:

1. Go to `http://www.websitegarage.com`.
2. Enter the URL for any site into the text box. You may optionally enter your e-mail address.
3. Press the Go button. After a few moments, you should see a diagnostic report.

The results of any Web site diagnostic or testing tool, especially free ones designed for mass-market appeal, should be taken with a grain of salt. Although tools such as Web Site Garage can be very useful in helping to diagnose potential problems, they judge your site using very narrow criteria, which may or may not be meaningful for specific sites.

Key Point Summary

This chapter introduced the key components of e-commerce site management. Here's a review of the information covered in this chapter:

✦ E-commerce sites require regular monitoring and maintenance.

✦ The three primary tasks that should be done as part of regular site administration are:

- Monitoring and maintaining site content
- Monitoring and maintaining security
- Monitoring and improving performance

- The tasks involved in maintaining site content are:
  - Updating Web pages
  - Updating and maintaining the site database
  - Checking for and repairing broken links
  - Creating and maintaining backups
- Available disk space, memory, and processing power are factors that influence queue performance.
- Bottlenecks occur when the Web server cannot handle all of the requests coming into it.
- A bottleneck is a delay in transmission of data over the Internet or within a computer system.
- Ways to eliminate or reduce bottlenecks include:
  - Speeding up the part of your server that is causing the bottleneck
  - Using multiple copies (replicating) of the component causing the bottleneck
  - Increasing the capacity of the queues in the system
- Server log files record information about each request made to the server.
- Load testing is the simulation of heavy traffic on your Web site to measure the site's performance.
- Web page diagnostic tools can be used to locate problems with HTML pages.

✦ ✦ ✦

STUDY GUIDE

Site management is an ongoing, constantly evolving process. Use the following assessment questions to review what you learned in this chapter, and then use the lab exercises, scenarios, and links to more information to continue learning about this very important part of operating an e-commerce site.

Assessment Questions

1. How is site performance measured?

   A. By the amount of data served in a certain period of time

   B. By counting the number of visitors to the site

   C. By calculating the average length of a visit to the site

   D. By the number of bottlenecks

2. Which one of the following cannot by revealed through log file analysis?

   A. Number of hits

   B. Number of requests for specific pages

   C. A user's reasons for visiting your site

   D. A user's click path

3. If your server experiences bottlenecks, how can replication and load balancing help?

   A. Replication and load balancing increase the speed of the queue.

   B. Replication and load balancing divide the requests between multiple servers, thus reducing the amount of work any one server needs to do.

   C. Replication and load balancing are techniques for increasing the speed of a server.

   D. Replication and load balancing can be used to reduce the number of people who visit your site.

4. How can you measure the responsiveness of a site?

   A. By counting the number of visitors to the site

   B. By calculating the average length of a visit to the site

   C. By the number of pages served in a certain period of time

   D. By calculating the delay between a file request and when the user sees the file

5. Which of the following is not a way to reduce or eliminate bottlenecks?

   A. Speed up the component causing the bottleneck

   B. Replicate the component causing the bottleneck

   C. Repair broken links

   D. Increase the capacity of the system queues

6. Which of the following is the best server backup solution? (Choose the best answer.)

   A. The site is backed up to another hard drive in the same machine every hour.

   B. The site is copied to a tape drive daily, and a copy of the backup is stored off-site.

   C. The Webmaster makes a copy of the site before he or she makes any changes to the site.

   D. The server has a CD-R drive and files are backed up to CD every day.

Scenario

Begin this scenario by clearing your browser's cache (in Internet Explorer, open the Internet Options from the Tools menu and delete the Temporary Internet Files), and then perform the following:

1. Visit the home pages of several well-known, large e-commerce Web sites. Use a watch (or the clock on your computer screen) to keep track of the time between when you request the site (when you first click a link to the site or press the Enter key after entering the address into your browser) and when the site is done loading. Make sure you visit the sites at about the same time of day.
2. Look at the number and size of graphics on the home page, the amount of customized content, and the general complexity of the page. If there are any sites that stand out as either very slow to load or very quick to load, make guesses as to why. For the purposes of the scenario, assume the particular site is not experiencing an extraordinarily high or low amount of traffic when you visit.

Lab Exercise

Lab 21-1 Testing for broken links

1. Go to `http://www.netmechanic.com/toolbox/power_user.htm`.
2. Enter a Web site address into the form and leave all of the checkboxes checked in Question #2.

3. Question #3 gives you the option of checking one page and getting instant results or checking five pages and having the results e-mailed to you. For now, just choose to test one page.
4. Scroll to the bottom of the page (and feel free to choose other options before you get there). Click the Test Now button, and then observe the following:
   - A progress bar should appear while all the links on the page you submitted are tested.
   - After all the links have been checked, you should see a report containing the results, and additional information, such as HTML errors and page weight.
5. Click on the link titled View a Detailed Report to view more information about each of the areas NetMechanic checked on the page you submitted.

Answers to Chapter Questions

Chapter pre-test

1. The three tasks involved in site administration and management are:
   - Monitoring and maintaining site content
   - Monitoring and maintaining security
   - Monitoring and improving performance
2. The tasks that should be a part of maintaining site content are:
   - Updating Web pages
   - Updating and maintaining the site database
   - Checking for broken links
   - Creating and maintaining backups
3. Some of the clues that a site is dead or out of date include: old dates, old design, broken links, obsolete technology, old language and phrases, and old information.
4. A bottleneck is a slowdown in the system.
5. A hit is any request for any single file. A page view is a request for an HTML page.
6. Load testing is used to assess how much traffic your server can handle.

Assessment questions

1. **A.** One way to measure performance is by how much data the server can serve during a certain period of time. This is also called *throughput.* For example, a Web server might be able to serve 100 Mbits per second (see "Monitoring and maintaining performance").
2. **C.** Qualitative data cannot be determined from log files (see "Data not collected by log files").
3. **B.** Replication and load balancing decrease bottlenecks by increasing the number of servers, thus reducing the amount of processing any one server has to handle (see "Monitoring and maintaining performance").
4. **D.** Responsiveness is performance from the end user's point of view. In the scenario for this chapter, you measured the responsiveness of several sites (see "Monitoring and maintaining performance").
5. **C.** Although checking and repairing links is important to maintaining a site, it does not reduce or eliminate bottlenecks (see "Monitoring and maintaining performance").
6. **B.** Daily tape backups stored off-site are the best solution in this list, because they're stored off-site and are done on a regular schedule (see "Creating and maintaining backups").

Scenario

It's not possible to give one answer to this scenario, of course, but the results of our tests, using a cable modem at about 5:00 central time are shown as follows:

1. The load times for the sites we tested (as evidenced by Table 21-2) were all extremely good, which is due in large part to our Internet connection. (Note that these times are very rough and unscientific, but they may provide some interesting information nonetheless. Your times may vary.)

Table 21-2
Load Times for Sites Tested by the Authors

Site URL	*Time to load*
`www.amazon.com`	4 seconds
`www.cdnow.com`	3 seconds
`www.sharperimage.com`	5 seconds
`www.dell.com`	3.5 seconds
`www.bn.com`	4.5 seconds

Generally, you'll find very large stores do an excellent job at keeping load times low. Smaller stores, without the resources or experience of the big Web merchants, often do a much worse job.

2. The factors that affect load time are:
   - The size of the HTML page
   - The number and size of graphics
   - The size and number of other included files, such as Java applets and scripts
   - The amount of processing that must be done on the server

For More Information . . .

- **Mindcraft's Web Server Performance Reports.** www.mindcraft.com/perfreports/web/index.html
- **CERT Coordination Center.** www.cert.org
- **webperformance testing tools.** www.webperfcenter.com
- **Demystify your log files.** www.builder.com/Servers/LogFile/ss01.html

✦ ✦ ✦

What's on the CD-ROM

This appendix provides you with information on the contents of the CD-ROM attached to the inside, rear cover of this book; as well as sections on system requirements and use instructions for Windows, Linux, and the Mac OS. A brief troubleshooting guide is included at the end of this appendix. In addition, a variety of storefront and e-commerce enabling software; source code, graphics, and resources from the examples presented in the preceding chapters; and an electronic, searchable version of the book — viewable with Adobe Acrobat Reader (also on the CD) — are included on the CD.

What's on the CD

Following sections are a summary of the contents of the CD-ROM arranged by category.

Applications

The following programs are included on this CD:

- ✦ Actinic Business for Windows (trial version)
- ✦ AbleCommerce for Windows (evaluation)
- ✦ Apache HTTP Server for Windows
- ✦ MySQL for Windows
- ✦ Adobe Acrobat Reader

Server software

The programs in Table A-1 are programs you install on the Web server to perform actions in response to user requests.

Table A-1
Server Software

Name	*Type of program*	*Version*	*URL*
ColdFusion Server Professional	Application server	Trial version	www.allaire.com
ActivePerl	Perl interpreter	GNU software	www.activeperl.com
Apache HTTP Server HTTP server		Open source	www.apache.org
Microsoft Windows NT 4.0 Option Pack	Operating system upgrade	Free upgrade	http://microsoft.com/ntserver/nts/downloads/recommended/NT4OptPk/default.asp
MySQL	Relational database management system	GNU software	www.mysql.com

Allaire has been acquired by Macromedia. This doesn't pose any immediate changes, but it may in the near future.

E-commerce store-building software

The programs in Table A-2 assist in the development of an e-commerce Web site.

Table A-2
E-Commerce Store-Building Software

Name	*Type of software*	*Version*	*URL*
Actinic Business 1.0	E-commerce site development software	Trial version	www.actinic.com
AbleCommerce 3.0	E-commerce site development software	Trial version	www.ablecommerce.com

Site management software

WebTrends Log Analyzer software is a server log file analysis tool. It comes in a trial version and you can find out more information at `www.webtrends.com`.

An important note on the software

The types of programs are on the CD-ROM may be governed by certain rules and restrictions. Please observe the following:

- **GNU and open source software.** These types are governed by their own licenses, which are included with the software. Such software is free and there are generally no restrictions on its distribution or use. See the software license for more details.
- **Trial, demo, or evaluation versions.** These are usually limited either by time or functionality (such as being unable to save projects).

Source code, graphics, and resources

The CD contains source code and examples from several chapters in addition to the graphics and other resources needed to build the example e-commerce Web site, Texas-Shaped.com. To find these elements on the CD, look inside the CODE folder. You can also use the index.html file located there to browse the following contents:

- **Chapter xx.** These folders contain chapter source code and examples.
- **Companies mentioned.** This folder has an html file that will link you to all the companies mentioned in this book.
- **Resources.** This folder has an html file that will link you to useful e-commerce sites on the web.
- **Texas-Shaped.com.** The resources for building the sample Web site can be found in this folder.

Electronic version of *CIW E-Commerce Certification Bible*

The complete (and searchable) text of this book is on the CD-ROM in Adobe's Portable Document Format (PDF), readable with the Adobe Acrobat Reader (also included on the CD). For more information on Adobe Acrobat Reader, go to `www.adobe.com`.

Using the CD

Before installing the CD, make sure your computer meets the minimum system requirements listed in the following sections. If your computer doesn't match most of these requirements, you may have a problem using the contents of the CD. You need at least 300MB of hard drive space to install all the software from this CD.

System requirements vary depending on the software you install. The minimum system requirements listed here are intended as a guideline.

With Microsoft Windows

The system requirements for Microsoft Windows 9*x*, Windows NT 4.0, or Windows 2000 are:

✦ PC with a Pentium processor or equivalent

✦ 64MB RAM (128MB recommended)

✦ Internet connection

✦ A CD-ROM drive

To install the items from the CD on your hard drive, follow these steps:

1. Insert the CD into your computer's CD-ROM drive.
2. View the contents of the CD-ROM using Windows Explorer or by clicking the My Computer icon on your desktop.
3. Locate the software you wish to install.
4. Either double-click on the program's installation program to install it, or follow the directions contained in the `readme` file in the CD directory for the program.

With Linux

Although we've included Windows versions of the software on the CD, many of these products are also available for Linux. Refer to Table A-3 for a product-by-product breakdown of your options. The system requirements for Linux are:

✦ PC with a Pentium processor or equivalent

✦ 64MB RAM (128MB recommended)

✦ Internet connection

✦ A CD-ROM drive

Table A-3
Options for Linux users

Software	*Linux equivalent*	*Download URL*
Actinic Business 1.0	The Actinic Business development environment currently only runs on Windows. Sites developed using Actinic Business can be hosted on Linux servers, however.	n/a
ColdFusion Server Professional 4.5.1	ColdFusion Server 4.5.1 Professional for Linux	`www.allaire.com/download`
AbleCommerce 3.0	AbleCommerce is not currently available for Linux.	n/a
ActivePerl	Perl	`www.perl.com`
WebTrends Log Analyzer	WebTrends Log Analyzer is currently only available for Windows. There are, however, many similar products that run on Linux.	`www.linux.org/apps/all/Administration/Log_Analyzers.html`
Apache HTTP Server	Apache HTTP Server	`www.apache.org`
MySQL	MySQL	`www.mysql.com`
Adobe Acrobat Reader	Adobe Acrobat Reader	`www.adobe.com/products/acrobat/readstep.html`

To open the items from the CD, follow these steps:

1. Log in as root.
2. Insert the CD into your computer's CD-ROM drive.
3. Mount the CD-ROM.
4. Launch a graphical file manager to view the items on the CD.

With Mac OS

Although we've included Windows versions of the software on the CD, many of these products (or similar products) are also available for Macintosh. Refer to Table A-4 for a product-by-product breakdown of your options.

Mac OSX is based on Unix, so many products available for Unix operating systems run on Macintosh computers with OSX installed.

The recommended system requirements for Macintosh users are:

- ✦ Macintosh with PowerPC processor
- ✦ 64MB RAM (128MB recommended)
- ✦ Internet connection
- ✦ A CD-ROM drive

Table A-4
Options for Macintosh Users

Software	***Macintosh equivalent***	***Download URL***
Actinic Business 1.0	No Macintosh version is available. However, sites created using Actinic Business can run on MacOS servers.	n/a
ColdFusion Server Professional 4.5.1	ColdFusion Server is currently not available for Macintosh.	n/a
AbleCommerce 3.0	AbleCommerce is not available for Macintosh.	n/a
ActivePerl	MacPerl	`www.macperl.com`
WebTrends Log Analyzer	WebTrends Log Analyzer is currently only available for Windows. There are, however, many similar products that run on Macintosh.	`www.macupdate.com/internet.php?sub=6`
Apache HTTP Server	Apache HTTP Server (for OSX)	`http://httpd.apache.org/dist/httpd/binaries/`
MySQL	MySQL is currently not available for Macintosh. The most popular database system for Macintosh is Filemaker Pro.	`www.filemaker.com`
Adobe Acrobat Reader	Adobe Acrobat Reader	`www.adobe.com/products/acrobat/readstep.html`

To open the items from the CD, follow these steps:

1. Insert the CD into your computer's CD-ROM drive.
2. Double click the CD icon on your desktop.
3. Locate the item you wish to view.
4. Double-click the file you want to open, or use the Open command from the appropriate program.

Troubleshooting

If you have difficulty installing or using the CD-ROM programs, try the following solutions:

✦ **Turn off any anti-virus software.** Installers sometimes mimic virus activity and can make your computer incorrectly believe it's being infected by a virus. (Be sure to turn the anti-virus software back on later.)

✦ **Close all running programs.** The more programs you're running, the less memory is available to other programs. Installers also typically update files and programs; if you keep other programs running, installation may not work properly.

If you still have trouble with the CD, please call the Hungry Minds Books Worldwide Customer Service phone number: (800) 762-2974. Outside the United States, call (317) 572-3993. Hungry Minds Books provides technical support only for installation and other general quality control items; for technical support on the applications themselves, consult the program's vendor.

✦ ✦ ✦

Sample Exam

The CIW E-Commerce Designer exam consists of 60 questions. You must answer 45 (75%) of these questions correctly to pass. The following 60 questions are representative of the questions asked on the exam. Answers to the questions can be found at the end of this appendix.

Sample Questions

1. Which of the following is the best definition of e-commerce?

A. Commerce conducted using the Internet.

B. The selling of electronics online.

C. An integration of communications, data management, and security capabilities that facilitates the exchange of information about the sale of goods and services.

D. The sale of products or services using credit cards.

2. What are the characteristics of B2B e-commerce?

A. Low volume, low margin

B. High volume, low margin

C. Low volume, high margin

D. High volume, high margin

3. Which of the following is not an advantage of e-commerce?

A. Reduced overhead

B. Easier access to new markets

C. Reduced paperwork

D. Fewer security problems than traditional commerce

4. What is a VPN?

    A. Virtual Private Network

    B. Virtual Privacy Node

    C. Virtual Peer Network

    D. Virtual Protection Net

5. What are the two main branches of intellectual property law?

    A. Trademark law and copyright law

    B. Copyright and industrial property law

    C. Patent law and trademark law

    D. Copyright law and patent law

6. Which three pieces of information need to be included in an e-commerce site's privacy statement?

    A. Partner Web sites, data types gathered, and encryption techniques

    B. Encryption method, how data is used, and marketing messages

    C. Type of encryption, digital certificate ID, and backup information

    D. Transfer of information, information gathering, and use of information

7. Which three areas are covered by industrial property law?

    A. Inventions, industrial designs, and trademarks and service marks

    B. Inventions, music, and reports

    C. Electronic publishing, package designs, and trademarks and service marks

    D. Inventions, electronic publishing, and trademarks and service marks

8. Which law puts limits on the liability of an Internet Service Provider (ISP) in an intellectual property lawsuit involving the content of a hosted site?

    A. Internet Tax Freedom Act

    B. Copyright law

    C. Digital Millennium Copyright Act

    D. Electronic Commerce Act

9. What is the main purpose of a Terms of Use agreement for areas of Web sites where customers can post messages?

    A. To explain pricing to customers

    B. To tell customers how to use the site

    C. To protect Web sites from lawsuits

    D. To protect the Web site's trademarks

10. What is the DNDRS?

    A. Data Network Distribution and Recovery System

    B. Do Nothing Day Reorganizing Service

    C. Distributed Name Discovery and Retention System

    D. Domain Name Dispute Resolution Service

11. Which of the follow pieces of information is least likely to be in a site's list of frequently asked questions (FAQ)?

    A. How to redeem a gift certificate

    B. Return policy

    C. Product information

    D. How to change or cancel an order

12. What is the best, and most responsible, type of e-mail marketing?

    A. Opt-out

    B. Opt-in

    C. Rented lists

    D. Bought lists

13. Which of the following terms is used to describe goods that can take advantage of instant fulfillment?

    A. Hard goods

    B. Soft goods

    C. Tangible goods

    D. Interactive goods

14. Which of the following is not a growth driver? (Choose the best answer.)

    A. Constant availability

    B. Global market

    C. Lack of physical contact

    D. Increasing bandwidth

15. Which of the following is the least appropriate type of user information for a Web site to collect about individual users?

    A. Types of products ordered

    B. Credit card information

    C. Address information

    D. Responses to instant poll questions

16. What does it mean for a product to have a global market niche? (Choose the best answer.)

A. The product has been adapted for many different languages and cultures.

B. The product is available worldwide.

C. The product appeals to a very large group of people, and is not limited geographically in its appeal.

D. The product can be exported easily.

17. What is the difference between a publisher site and a marketer site?

A. Publisher sites have unique content, whereas marketer sites purchase content from third parties.

B. Publisher sites are Web sites for paper publications and marketer sites are Web-only.

C. Publisher sites sell advertising and marketer sites sell products (and therefore usually buy advertising).

D. Publisher sites promote their own products, and marketer sites promote other business's products.

18. What are Web portals?

A. Portals are Web sites intended to be a central starting point for Web browsing.

B. Portals are services that make it easy to browse the Web.

C. Portals provide Internet users with access to the entire Internet.

D. Portals make it possible for Web browsers to locate other Web sites.

19. How is a banner ad click rate calculated?

A. Number of clicks per visitor

B. Number of clicks per hit

C. Number of clicks per impression

D. Number of clicks per page view

20. What is the difference between a *hit* and a *page view*? (Choose the best answer.)

A. A *hit* is any request for a file, and a *page view* is a request for an HTML file.

B. A *page view* is any request for a file, and a *hit* is a request for an HTML file.

C. A *hit* is only registered if the request comes from a user, and not if the request comes from a Web spider or search engine. *Page views* count all requests.

D. A *page view* may be a request for a GIF image, and a *hit* may not.

21. What is the purpose of the `meta` element (tag) in HTML documents?

A. The `meta` element improves the load time of a Web page.

B. The `meta` element increases traffic to your site.

C. The `meta` element improves browser compatibility by specifying information about how a Web page should look.

D. The `meta` element provides information about the document that can be used by programs, such as search engines.

22. What is spam? (Choose the best answer.)

A. Large amounts of e-mail

B. Unsolicited e-mail

C. Offensive e-mail

D. E-mail that is sent to many people

23. How should e-mail mailing lists be acquired?

A. Subscribers should opt-in.

B. Subscribers can opt-out.

C. You should rent lists of e-mail addresses.

D. You should purchase lists of e-mail addresses.

24. What is the most basic principle of Web site usability? (Choose the best answer.)

A. Don't use frames.

B. The less a user has to think about how to use the site, the more usable the site is.

C. Navigation should be kept to a minimum.

D. A usable site is a site that has a large number of links to other sites.

25. What is a click pattern?

A. A design created on an electronic canvas using mouse clicks

B. A rhythm tapped out using a computer mouse

C. A pattern of clicks used to discover where users are most likely to click in a monitor

D. A route, or path, taken by visitors to a Web site to reach specific information

26. Which of the following tasks is not part of information architecture?

A. Understanding who the user will be

B. Monitoring security systems

C. Determining what content should be included on a Web site

D. Organizing a Web site's content

27. What are the components of a content inventory?

A. Functionality and usability

B. Functionality and structure

C. Functionality and information

D. Information and structure

28. What is the goal of e-service? (Choose the best answer.)

A. To upsell customers, or convince them to buy more expensive products or upgrades

B. To create loyal customers for your product or service

C. To encourage customers to read the manual

D. To get customers to use online customer service options, thereby reducing your costs

29. Which of the following is not an example of synchronous e-service?

A. Voice connections

B. Online chat

C. Co-browsing

D. E-mail

30. Which of the following is not an example of an asynchronous e-service option? (Choose the best answer.)

A. E-mail

B. Web forms

C. Remote control

D. Message boards

31. Which of the following is not an advantage of using Web forms over e-mail? (Choose the best answer.)

A. Web forms can ask the customer specific questions that can help a customer service representative address the issue easier.

B. Web forms enable synchronous e-service.

C. Web forms help the customer express their problem more clearly.

D. Web forms can be submitted to scripts for processing, sorting, and routing.

32. Which of the following is an example of self-service e-service? (Choose the best answer.)

A. E-mail

B. FAQ

C. Co-browsing

D. Telephony

33. Which of the following is not true of self-service e-service? (Choose the best answer.)

A. It's more expensive and requires more staff than synchronous e-service.

B. It can be the fastest and most efficient way to provide customer service.

C. After it's established, it's less expensive to maintain than other forms of e-service.

D. It should not be the only customer service option that you provide.

34. Which of the following is an advantage to using synchronous support options? (Choose the best answer.)

A. Low cost

B. Highly personalized service

C. Creates community

D. Synchronous service options are searchable

35. What type of commerce most often uses Electronic Data Interchange (EDI)?

A. Business-to-consumer

B. Consumer-to-consumer

C. Business-to-business

D. Consumer-to-business

36. Which of the following is not a reason for a company to use EDI?

A. The company is required to use EDI to do business with another company.

B. The company operates on a very tight margin.

C. The company handles a large volume of repetitive transactions.

D. The company wishes to break into the small business market.

37. What is Internet EDI?

A. EDI conducted over the Internet.

B. A form of EDI purchased over the Internet.

C. A standard type of EDI messaging developed on the Internet.

D. Internet EDI is just another name for traditional EDI.

38. For which types of transactions is Open Buying on the Internet (OBI) designed?

A. High dollar, low volume

B. High margin, low volume

C. High volume, low dollar

D. High dollar, high volume

39. What is the standard for EDI messaging in North America?

A. S/MIME

B. X.509

C. ANSI X12

D. OTP

40. What is the correct order of the four steps involved in an OBI transaction?

A. Order placement, money transfer, approval by buying organization, and transfer to the selling organization for fulfillment

B. Approval by buying organization, order placement, money transfer, and transfer to the selling organization for fulfillment

C. Order placement, approval by the requisitioner, transfer to the selling organization for fulfillment, and money transfer

D. Order placement, approval by the buying organization, transfer to the selling organization for fulfillment, and money transfer

41. Which of the following is not an advantage of using an entry-level e-commerce outsourcing solution? (Choose the best answer.)

A. Low-cost

B. Ease of set-up

C. High level of customization ability

D. Doesn't require many (if any) employees to set up and maintain

42. Which of the following types of e-commerce is best suited to entry-level e-commerce outsourcing? (Choose the best answer.)

A. Selling of specialty or niche products

B. High volume, low margin e-commerce

C. Highly customizable products

D. High volume, high margin e-commerce

43. Which of the following statements is not true of mid-level storefront solutions?

A. Mid-level storefronts provide more customization capabilities than entry-level storefronts.

B. Mid-level storefronts generally cost more to set up and maintain than entry-level storefronts.

C. Mid-level storefronts support a greater variety of e-commerce functions than entry-level storefronts.

D. Mid-level storefronts require you to have an in-house Web server.

44. Which of the following technologies does not help increase the performance and reliability of a Web site? (Choose the best answer.)

A. Clustering

B. Load balancing

C. Bottlenecking

D. Failover

45. Which of the following businesses would most likely benefit from using high-level storefront software?

A. A bakery

B. A large, multinational reseller of office supplies

C. A home-based business

D. A hot-air balloon manufacturer

46. What is the correct order of phases in the phased approach to e-commerce implementation?

A. Information-only Web site, limited transactions, full transactions, integrating legacy systems

B. Integrating legacy systems, information-only Web site, limited transactions, full transactions

C. Limited transactions, information-only Web site, full transactions, integrating legacy systems

D. Full transactions, limited transactions, information-only Web site, integrating legacy systems

47. What is Common Gateway Interface (CGI)?

  A. A protocol that allows browsers to understand Web servers

  B. A method of encrypting data on the Internet

  C. A way for Web servers to communicate with other programs

  D. A language for creating dynamic Web pages

48. What is a payment gateway?

  A. It allows vendors to accept digital cash.

  B. It provides secure order forms for e-commerce storefronts.

  C. It ensures the security of payments made over the Internet.

  D. It's a service that provides an automated link with a credit card processor to authorize or deny a transaction in real time.

49. Which of the following statements is true? (Choose the best answer.)

  A. It's possible for a hacker to intercept any data on the Internet by using a packet sniffer.

  B. To secure a Web site, all you need to do is install a digital certificate.

  C. It's possible to secure a Web site.

  D. It's easy to crack the types of encryption used on the Internet.

50. What services are provided by digital certificates?

  A. Encryption and data integrity

  B. Authentication and identification

  C. Identification and data confidentiality

  D. Data integrity and authentication

51. What is the function of message digests?

  A. To provide data integrity

  B. To provide access control

  C. To provide summaries of multiple messages

  D. To process messages

52. Which of the following is an example of a Certifying Authority (CA)?

  A. Verifone

  B. VeriSign

  C. SSL

  D. SET

53. What is the role of a Certifying Authority (CA)?

A. To certify the security of an e-commerce Web site

B. To provide a secure connection for transaction processing

C. To encrypt data for transport over the Internet

D. To act as a trusted third party in a secure transaction

54. Which standard defines the format and contents of a digital certificate?

A. EDI

B. SET

C. X.509v3

D. SSL

55. A message digest is an example of which kind of encryption?

A. Asymmetric encryption

B. Symmetric encryption

C. One-way encryption

D. Mutual encryption

56. Which of the following is the best description of *asymmetric* encryption?

A. Uses a public key for both encryption and decryption

B. Uses a public key for encryption and a private key for decryption

C. Uses a single, shared key for both encryption and decryption

D. Uses hash functions to calculate a digital fingerprint for a piece of digital data

57. Which of the following is the best description of *symmetric* encryption?

A. Uses a public key for both encryption and decryption

B. Uses a public key for encryption and a private key for decryption

C. Uses a single, shared key for both encryption and decryption

D. Uses hash functions to calculate a digital fingerprint for a piece of digital data

58. Which type of digital certificate is used to enable communications using SSL?

A. Certificate authority certificate

B. Server certificate

C. Personal certificate

D. Software publisher certificate

59. Which types of encryption are used by SSL?

A. Symmetric and asymmetric encryption

B. One-time pads and symmetric encryption

C. Block ciphers and one-time pads

D. Asymmetric encryption and one-way encryption

60. What are the steps involved in establishing secure communications between a browser and a server using SSL?

A. 1. Handshake; 2. client tells server what type of encryption it supports; 3. server picks the strongest form of encryption that it shares with the client; 4. client generates a session key; 5. server decrypts the session key; 6. session key can then be used for secure communications.

B. 1. Handshake; 2. server tells the client what type of encryption to use; 3. server generates session key; 4. session key can then be used for secure communications.

C. 1. Handshake; 2. client sends a session key to the server; 3. server decrypts the session key; 4. session key can then be used for secure communications.

D. 1. Handshake; 2. server tells the client what type of encryption it supports; 3. client picks the strongest form of encryption that it shares with the server; 4. server generates a session key; 5. client decrypts the session key; 6. session key can then be used for secure communication.

Answers to Sample Questions

1. C. One of the definitions of e-commerce used in this book is: E-commerce is an integration of communications, data management, and security capabilities that facilitates the exchange of information about the sale of goods and services.

2. B. Business-to-Business e-commerce is characterized by high volume, low margin transactions.

3. D. E-commerce has just as many security problems, if not more, than traditional commerce.

4. A. Virtual Private Networks (VPNs) are secure networks that use the Internet.

5. B. The two main branches of intellectual property law are: copyright and industrial property law.

6. D. A privacy statement should include information about transfer of information, information gathering, and use of information.

7. A. The three areas covered by industrial property law are inventions, industrial designs, and trademarks and service marks.

8. C. The Digital Millennium Copyright Act of 1998 limits an ISP's liability in intellectual property lawsuits involving their hosted sites.

9. C. A Terms of Use agreement for a message board can be used to require the author to relinquish rights to messages they post, or to give permission for the message to be circulated. Terms of Use agreements can also require users to accept responsibility for posting copyrighted materials to which they have no rights.

10. D. DNDRS is the acronym for the World Intellectual Property Organization's Domain Name Dispute Resolution Service.

11. C. FAQ lists generally contain information about using the site, or about the company, rather than about specific products.

12. B. Opt-in lists, in which people on the list specifically ask to receive the e-mails, are the only responsible way to use bulk e-mail for marketing. Other methods are considered spam.

13. B. Soft, or intangible goods are products that can be delivered electronically, including software, information, and music.

14. C. Lack of personal interaction with customers is a barrier to growth, because customers often equate personal interaction with good customer service. E-commerce companies must work hard to overcome this belief.

15. D. Most Web sites that have instant polls, such as portal sites, should store poll question answers only in aggregate. Unless there's a good reason, of which users are aware, associating instant poll question answers with individual users should not be done.

16. C. Products with a global market niche are products that appeal to people regardless of geographic boundaries.

17. C. Publisher sites depend on advertising revenue. Marketer sites sell products.

18. A. Portals typically aggregate information such as news, weather, and search capabilities in order to serve as a starting point for Web browsing.

19. C. A banner ad click rate is the number of clicks per impression. Remember that a banner impression is equal to one display of a banner ad.

20. A. A hit is any HTTP request. A page view is any request for an HTML file.

21. D. The `meta` element is a mechanism for including information about the document or the site in HTML pages.

22. B. Spam, as used on the Internet, refers to unsolicited, usually marketing-related, e-mail.

23. A. You should only send bulk e-mail to opt-in lists of subscribers.

24. B. Usability means making your Web site easy to use.

25. D. Click patterns are routes that users take through your site that can be discovered by analyzing log files. They can be used to increase the usability of a Web site.

26. **B.** Monitoring security systems, although very important, is not a part of information architecture.
27. **C.** The content of a Web site includes functionality and information. The information architect must organize the content to create a usable Web site.
28. **B.** The ultimate goal of customer service, and therefore e-service, is to create loyal customers.
29. **D.** E-mail is not considered synchronous e-service.
30. **C.** Remote control is not asynchronous service, because it involves real-time interaction between the company and a customer.
31. **B.** Web forms, like e-mail, are an asynchronous e-service option.
32. **B.** FAQ lists are a very popular self-service option.
33. **A.** Self-service is generally much less expensive than synchronous service.
34. **B.** Although synchronous service options are generally more expensive, they allow you to provide highly personalized service.
35. **C.** Because of its high cost of entry, and because it's designed for high volume transactions, EDI is mostly used in business-to-business e-commerce.
36. **D.** Most small businesses do not use EDI. Wanting to reach this market is therefore not a good reason to use EDI.
37. **A.** Internet EDI, or EDI that uses the public Internet rather than private networks, is making EDI accessible to more companies by lowering the cost and entry barriers.
38. **C.** It's estimated that high-volume, low-dollar transactions make up 80 percent of a typical organization's purchases.
39. **C.** Commonly called the X12 standard, the full name of the North American standard for EDI is ANSI X12 850 EDI.
40. **D.** Order placement, approval by the buying organization, transfer to the selling organization for fulfillment, and money transfer. The steps in an OBI transaction are designed to provide safeguards against fraud and unauthorized purchases.
41. **C.** Although entry-level outsourced storefronts are a great way to get started in e-commerce, they provide minimal customization options.
42. **A.** Entry-level e-commerce outsourcing solutions are best suited for low-volume, high-margin e-commerce. The sale of specialty items generally fits this description.
43. **D.** Although you may have the option of hosting a mid-level storefront in-house, it's rarely a requirement.

44. C. Bottlenecking is a server problem. The other options help to eliminate bottlenecks and other server problems.

45. B. A large, multinational reseller of office supplies would benefit from a high-level storefront, which is well suited to high-volume businesses.

46. A. The first step in taking your business online using the phased approach is an information-only site. The final step is to integrate your legacy systems with your full transaction Web site.

47. C. CGI is a way for Web servers to communicate with other programs.

48. D. Payment gateways enable real-time credit card processing.

49. C. Securing a Web site means insuring the level of effort required to hack the site is much greater than the potential benefits that could be gained from doing so.

50. B. Digital certificates provide authentication and identification.

51. A. Message digests provide data integrity.

52. B. VeriSign is a CA.

53. D. A CA acts as a trusted third party.

54. C. The X.509v3 standard defines the format and contents of a digital certificate.

55. C. A message digest is an example of one-way encryption.

56. B. Asymmetric encryption uses a public key for encryption and a private key for decryption.

57. C. Symmetric encryption uses a single, shared key for both encryption and decryption.

58. B. Server certificates are used to enable SSL.

59. A. SSL uses asymmetric encryption to exchange a private key so a server and a client can communicate securely using symmetric encryption.

60. A. The correct steps involved in establishing secure communications using SSL are: 1. Handshake; 2. client tells server what type of encryption it supports; 3. server picks the strongest form of encryption that it shares with the client; 4. client generates a session key; 5. server decrypts the session key; 6. session key can then be used for secure communications.

✦ ✦ ✦

Exam Objectives Matrix

This appendix lists each of the topics covered in Prosoft's instructor-led class, E-Commerce Strategies and Practices (5ECSP), and the skills measured by the 1D0-425 CIW E-Commerce Designer exam. For each topic, we've referenced the chapters and sections in which the subject matter is covered in this book.

Note that the information is presented by topic in table format to give you a quick overview and reference. It breaks down as follows:

- **Table C-1:** Electronic Commerce Foundations
- **Table C-2:** Law and the Internet
- **Table C-3:** Web Marketing Goals
- **Table C-4:** Online Product Promotion
- **Table C-5:** Site Usability
- **Table C-6:** Consumer Service Methods
- **Table C-7:** Business-to-Business Frameworks
- **Table C-8:** Site Creation Packages: Outsourcing
- **Table C-9:** Implementation and Case Studies
- **Table C-10:** Site Creation Software
- **Table C-11:** Site Development Implementation
- **Table C-12:** Customizing an E-Commerce Site
- **Table C-13:** Online Catalog
- **Table C-14:** Payment Gateways
- **Table C-15:** E-Services Support
- **Table C-16:** Transaction Security
- **Table C-17:** Web Site Management
- **Table C-18:** Order Tracking

Table C-1
Electronic Commerce Foundations

Exam topic	*Chapter*	*Section*
Types of electronic commerce	Chapter 1	Models for E-Commerce
	Chapter 1	Types of E-Commerce Implementations
E-commerce trends and practices	Chapter 1	E-Commerce Trends and Forecasts
E-commerce solutions	Chapter 1	Types of E-Commerce Implementations
Hardware and software	Chapter 1	Hardware requirements
	Chapter 1	Software requirements
Ingredients of a Web storefront	Chapter 1	Key Concepts for E-Commerce
Seven ingredients to success	Chapter 1	The Seven Keys to E-Commerce Success
The virtual enterprise	Chapter 1	Moving Toward the Virtual Enterprise

Table C-2
Law and the Internet

Exam topic	*Chapter*	*Section*
Legal concerns with	Chapter 2 e-commerce sites	Understanding the Legal Side of Online Business
Electronic publishing	Chapter 2	Electronic publishing
Intellectual property issues	Chapter 1	Open Issues for E-Commerce
	Chapter 2	Intellectual property
	Chapter 2	Intellectual Property Law and the Internet
Areas of liability	Chapter 2	Liability exposures
Privacy and confidentiality	Chapter 1	Open Issues for E-Commerce
	Chapter 2	Confidentiality and Privacy Matters
	Chapter 3	Responsible Web Marketing
Jurisdiction	Chapter 2	Understanding Legal Jurisdiction

Exam topic	*Chapter*	*Section*
Internet taxation	Chapter 1	Open Issues for E-Commerce
	Chapter 2	Taxing the Internet
International tax	Chapter 2	International Business Issues
Customs and tariffs	Chapter 2	International Business Issues

Table C-3
Web Marketing Goals

Exam topic	*Chapter*	*Section*
Online marketing strategies	Chapter 3	Understanding Web Marketing
E-commerce drivers and barriers to growth	Chapter 3	Growth drivers
	Chapter 3	Growth barriers
Product pricing	Chapter 3	Pricing Products
Product distribution and availability	Chapter 3	Managing Product Delivery
Demographics, psychographics, and audience data	Chapter 3	Understanding Audiences

Table C-4
Online Product Promotion

Exam topic	*Chapter*	*Section*
Promotions	Chapter 4	Understanding Online Promotion
Site categories	Chapter 4	Categorizing Web Sites
Banner ads	Chapter 4	All About Banner Ads
Tracking	Chapter 4	Tracking ad effectiveness
Banner exchange	Chapter 4	Bartering for banners
Referral programs	Chapter 4	Banner referrals
Affiliate programs	Chapter 8	Affiliate programs

Table C-5
Site Usability

Exam topic	***Chapter***	***Section***
Importance of audience usability	Chapter 5	Understanding Web Usability
Click patterns	Chapter 5	Click patterns
Screen flow	Chapter 5	Web Site Structure and Screen Flow
Usability analysis	Chapter 5	Analyzing Web Site Usability

Table C-6
Consumer Service Methods

Exam topic	***Chapter***	***Section***
E-service	Chapter 6	Defining E-Service
Synchronous and asynchronous service	Chapter 6	Synchronous e-service
	Chapter 6	Asynchronous e-service
	Chapter 18	Supporting Asynchronous E-Services
	Chapter 18	Supporting Synchronous E-Services
Self service	Chapter 6	Self-service
	Chapter 18	Supporting Self-Service Options

Table C-7
Business-to-Business Frameworks

Exam topic	***Chapter***	***Section***
Business-to-Consumer (B2C)	Chapter 1	Models for E-Commerce
	Chapter 7	Understanding Online Business Models
Business-to-Business (B2B)	Chapter 1	Models for E-Commerce
	Chapter 7	Understanding Online Business Models
	Chapter 7	Business-to-Business Networks

Exam topic	Chapter	Section
Electronic Data Interchange (EDI)	Chapter 7	All About Electronic Data Interchange
Open Buying on the Internet (OBI)	Chapter 7	Open Buying on the Internet
Open Trading Protocol (OTP)	Chapter 7	Open Trading Protocol

Table C-8 Site Creation Packages: Outsourcing

Exam topic	Chapter	Section
The online instant storefront	Chapter 1	Types of E-Commerce Implementations
	Chapter 8	Understanding Entry-Level E-Commerce Outsourcing
The mid-level instant storefront	Chapter 1	Types of E-Commerce Implementations
	Chapter 9	Understanding Mid-Level Online Storefront Packages
The high-level storefront	Chapter 1	Types of E-Commerce Implementations
	Chapter 10	Understanding High-Level Online Storefront Packages

Table C-9 Implementation and Case Studies

Exam topic	Chapter	Section
Creating a company	Chapter 11	Creating a Company Presence Online
Phased approach implementation	Chapter 11	Establishing a Presence in Phases
Case studies and lessons learned	Chapter 11	E-Commerce Case Studies
Implementation of an e-commerce site	Chapter 14	(Entire chapter)
	Chapter 15	(Entire chapter)
	Chapter 16	(Entire chapter)
	Chapter 17	(Entire chapter)

Table C-10
Site Creation Software

Exam topic	*Chapter*	*Section*
Web server overview	Chapter 12	Understanding the Web server's role
	Chapter 13	Understanding Microsoft's IIS
Internet Information Server (IIS)	Chapter 12	Web server options
Preparation and examining IIS	Chapter 12	Microsoft IIS
	Chapter 13	IIS Features and Functions
	Chapter 13	IIS Installation
	Chapter 13	Managing IIS

Table C-11
Site Development Implementation

Exam topic	*Chapter*	*Section*
ORACLE8 and SQL Server	Chapter 12	Database options
The role of the database	Chapter 12	Database options
Available options for developing an online storefront	Chapter 8	Understanding Entry-Level E-Commerce Outsourcing
	Chapter 9	Mid-Level Storefront Options
	Chapter 9	More mid-level options
	Chapter 10	High-Level Storefront Options
	Chapter 12	Choosing an E-Commerce Site Development Environment
	Chapter 14	(Entire chapter)

Table C-12
Customizing an E-Commerce Site

Exam topic	*Chapter*	*Section*
Customizing the look and feel	Chapter 15	Understanding Web Site Customization
	Chapter 15	Customizing Look and Feel
	Chapter 15	Customizing the User Interface

Table C-13
Online Catalog

Exam topic	*Chapter*	*Section*
Products and Components	Chapter 16	Understanding Online Catalog Functions
Attributes	Chapter 16	Adding attributes and options to products

Table C-14
Payment Gateways

Exam topic	*Chapter*	*Section*
Credit card processing	Chapter 17	Processing credit cards
Digital cash	Chapter 17	Handling digital cash
Electronic commerce security myths	Chapter 19	E-Commerce Security Issues
CyberCash	Chapter 17	Working with Payment Gateways
Online check processing	Chapter 17	Online check processing

Table C-15
E-Services Support

Exam topic	*Chapter*	*Section*
E-service software	Chapter 6	Providing E-Service
	Chapter 18	Understanding E-Services Support
Knowledge bases	Chapter 18	Knowledge bases

Table C-16
Transaction Security

Exam topic	*Chapter*	*Section*
Security concerns with e-commerce sites	Chapter 19	Understanding E-Commerce Security
Encryption and decryption	Chapter 19	Understanding Cryptography
Authentication and identification	Chapter 19	Establishing identification and authentication
Certificates	Chapter 19	Understanding Digital Certificates
X.509v3	Chapter 19	The X.509v3 standard
Payment and security requirements	Chapter 17	Preparing for online credit card transactions
	Chapter 19	E-Commerce Security Issues
Payment and purchase order process	Chapter 17	Processing credit cards

Table C-17
Web Site Management

Exam topic	*Chapter*	*Section*
Log file analysis	Chapter 5	Page Usage and Access Behavior
	Chapter 21	Analyzing Log Files
Traffic tracking	Chapter 5	Page Usage and Access Behavior
Performance testing	Chapter 21	Assessing Web Performance

Table C-18 **Order Tracking**		
Exam topic	***Chapter***	***Section***
Order tracking	Chapter 20	Tracking Orders

✦ ✦ ✦

APPENDIX D

Exam Tips

✦ ✦ ✦ ✦

This appendix consists of many of the questions you may have concerning the CIW E-Commerce Designer exam. The questions and their answers, in addition to useful tips, are each dealt with in a separate section. Everything from prerequisites for the text, where to take it, and how much it costs, to what to do after you've gotten the results is covered.

What Are the Prerequisites?

The CIW Foundation exam (1D0-410) is the prerequisite to the E-commerce Designer exam. To achieve CIW certification, you must at least take the Foundations exam along with the E-commerce Designer exam. Passing the E-commerce Designer exam alone does not result in certification.

Where Can I Take the Test?

Like all CIW exams, the E-commerce Designer exam is available worldwide through VUE and Prometric. Exam candidates must register with either VUE or Prometric, schedule an exam appointment, and pay the *candidate fee* — which is the price of the test.

Information on VUE and Prometric locations can be found at their Web sites. VUE's URL is `www.vue.com` and their CIW registration page is `www.vue.com/ciw/`. For information on Prometric, visit their registration site at `www.2test.com`.

For the latest information from CIW on taking the test, visit `www.ciwcertified.com` and click on Exams and then on Taking the Exam.

How Do I Register?

As mentioned in the previous section, you can register through VUE or Prometric as follows:

- **VUE.** To register with VUE, visit www.vue.com/contact/obtainCIWLogin.html to obtain a CIW VUE Login. After you complete this process, you can register for the exam by visiting www.vue.com/ciw/ciwexam.html and clicking on Register for an exam.
- **Prometric.** To obtain a Prometric Web User Login, visit www.2test.com/GetAptcCustomerData.jsp. When you have your login information (user name and password), return to the home page at www.2test.com, and choose Information Technology Certifications from the drop-down menu. Click the Go button to register for the exam.

How Do I Cancel My Exam Appointment?

After you've registered for the exam, you'll receive a confirmation along with instructions on how to cancel the exam appointment. General cancellation your exam appointment confirmation materials in case of any discrepancies.

VUE

After you've registered for the exam, you can cancel it on the VUE Web site *if the appointment is more than 24 hours away.* Visit www.vue.com/testing/index.html and click on Cancel an exam.

If your exam appointment is less than 24 hours away, you need to contact the testing center or a VUE agent directly. To locate the VUE agent closest to you, check out the VUE Telephone Directory at www.vue.com/student-services/vuephone.html.

Prometric

Exams can be canceled one business day prior to your scheduled exam appointment, before 7:00 p.m. CST. That's all the information currently available regarding Prometric cancellations.

How Much Does It Cost?

The fee for a CIW exam in the United States and Canada is U.S. $125. The exam fee outside the United States and Canada is approximately U.S. $125, depending upon local currency exchange rates. Contact your testing center to determine the exact rate in your local currency.

How Long Is the Test?

The test consists of 60 questions. You're given 75 minutes to complete the exam.

Can I Bring Anything with Me into the Testing Center?

You're not allowed to bring any materials into the testing center. A pencil and scratch paper are available upon request.

How Do I Get My Results?

After you complete the exam, the results are displayed on your testing station computer screen. A printed copy of your exam score is also available from the testing center staff. Be sure to save this copy for your records.

What Happens if I Pass?

If you've already passed the Foundations exam (1D0-410), you're awarded Certified Internet Webmaster Professional (CIWP) status. You'll receive your certificate four to eight weeks after passing the exam.

What Do I Do if I Fail?

If you fail the exam, we recommend that you immediately take some notes on the exam topics you found especially difficult. Study these topics closely until you feel prepared to take the exam again.

If you fail the exam, you may retake it as many times as you like. But, you have to pay the candidate fee ($125) each time you take it, so be sure to be prepared before you schedule another appointment.

What if I Have a Problem with the Test, or a Question on the Test?

Thorough information on all CIW exams can be found at the CIW Web site, `www.ciwcertified.com`.

If you can't find the answer to your question there, contact the CIW Exam and Certification Department at `exam@CIWcertified.com`, or choose the appropriate contact from the CIW Contacts page (select Contacts from the CIW home page: `www.ciwcertified.com`).

What's the Next Step (the Next Exam to Take)?

After you've passed the Foundations exam (1D0-410) and the E-commerce Designer exam, you can take the Site Designer exam (1D0-420) to achieve Master CIW Designer certification.

✦ ✦ ✦

APPENDIX E

E-Commerce Resources Online

✦ ✦ ✦ ✦

All Internet-based topics have a plethora of information available online, and e-commerce is no exception. This appendix contains a list of Web sites, separated by topic, that you can visit to learn more about the technologies, concepts, and products we discussed in this book. You can also find this list in an HTML file on the CD-ROM. You can even import these links into your Internet Explorer favorites if you like.

It's no secret: The Web is a rapidly changing environment. Therefore, by the time you get to this appendix (or this book for that matter), some of the URLs listed may not work anymore. If you come across a nonfunctioning URL, try going to its root to verify that the information you seek is still on the site. For example, if you're looking for the Books section of the LANWrights Web site at `www.lanw.com/books` and it's not there, try going to `www.lanw.com` and checking if there's still a Books link listed, or something similar.

B2B E-commerce resources

- **B2BExplorer.** `www.b2bexplorer.com`
- **The 2000 NetMarketing 200 Best B-To-B Web Sites by Category.** `www.netb2b.com/netMarketing200/2000/index.html`
- **20,000 Products on B2B Forward Auction Creator Great Shop.** `www.greatshop.com/ecstat.html`

Case studies

- **ZDNet's E-Commerce Case Studies.** `www.zdnet.com/ecommerce/`
- **CIO Magazine's E-Commerce Case Studies.** `www.cio.com/forums/ec/ec_case.html`
- **Microsoft's E-Commerce Case Studies by Implementation Goals.** `www.microsoft.com/business/ecommerce/casestudies/`

Customer service

- **RoboHELP Product Demonstrations.** www.ehelp.com/RoboHELP/demos/
- **Internet.com's CRM Library.** http://ecommerce.internet.com/resources/library/crm
- **eHelp Corporation.** www.ehelp.com
- **Customer Service Resources at the Open Directory Project.** www.dmoz.org/Business/Customer_Service/Resources
- **Customer Service Review.** www.csr.co.za
- **Aborior: Advanced Web Software.** www.aborior.com
- **E.piphany.** www.epiphany.com
- **eGain Communications Corp.** www.egain.com
- **HipBone.** www.hipbone.com
- **Kana.** www.kana.com
- **n2g Guided Web Tours.** www.net2gether.com
- **netCustomer.** www.netcustomer.com
- **PushPin.** www.pushpin.com
- **Siebel Systems.** www.siebel.com
- **Talisma.** www.talisma.com
- **vBulletin.** www.vbulletin.com

Database information

- **Choosing a Relational Database.** http://philip.greenspun.com/wtr/dead-trees/53011.htm
- **Database Comparison.** www.isu.edu/~jacoelai/database%20comparison.htm
- **Microsoft SQL Server: An Overview of Transaction Processing Concepts and the MS DTC.** http://msdn.microsoft.com/library/backgrnd/html/msdn_dtcwp.htm
- **Oracle Underground Frequently Asked Questions.** www.orafaq.org/faq.htm

Internet demographics

- **CommerceNet Research Center.** www.commerce.net/research/stats/stats.html
- **Internet and E-Commerce Statistics: What They Mean and Where to Find Them on the Web.** www.cnie.org/nle/st-36.html
- **Yahoo! Web Statistics and Demographics.** http://dir.yahoo.com/Computers_and_Internet/Internet/World_Wide_Web/Statistics_and_Demographics/
- **Jupiter Research.** www.jup.com

Design and architecture

- **lynda.com.** www.lynda.com

Usability

- **Alertbox: Jakob Nielsen's Column on Web Usability.** www.useit.com/alertbox/
- **Interview: Web Usability Past, Present, and Future.** http://webword.com/interviews/nielsen.html
- **Usable Web.** www.usableweb.com
- **goodexperience.com.** www.goodexperience.com
- **WebWord.com Usability and Human Factors for the Internet.** http://webword.com

Information architecture

- **Information Architecture.** http://uncle-netword.com/articles/writeweb3.html
- **O'Reilly's Information Architecture for the World Wide Web, Chapter 2: Introduction to Information Architecture.** www.oreilly.com/catalog/infotecture/chapter/ch02.html

Color

- **WebVoodoo's Web Design Clinic – Color Theory 101.** www.webdesignclinic.com/ezine/v1i1/color/

E-commerce standards and technologies

- **World Wide Web Consortium.** www.w3.org
- **eXtropia Home Page.** www.extropia.com
- **The Data Interchange Standards Association (DISA).** www.disa.org
- **Advanced Data Exchange (ADX).** www.adx.com/

OBI

- **Netscape Commerce Applications Products.** http://home.netscape.com/commapps/products/index.html
- **OBI Glossary.** www.openbuy.org/obi/library/glossary.html
- **The OBI Consortium.** www.openbuy.org

Open market

- **CNET.com – Open Market Transact (V.5.0).** www.cnet.com/enterprise/0-9562-707-2896744.html

EDI

- **The PERWILL Electronic Data Interchange (EDI) Product Demonstration.** www.perwill.com/Product/productdemo/html/demo-01.htm
- **IBM Web-EDI demonstration.** www.edidemo.ihost.com/edidemo/edidemo.html
- **XML-EDI Demonstration.** www.sgml.u-net.com/xml-edi/demo.htm
- **XML.com – XML and EDI Lessons Learned and Baggage to Leave Behind.** www.xml.com/pub/1999/08/edi/
- **E-commerce and EDI (Electronic Data Exchange) – a CompInfo Directory.** www.compinfo-center.com/tpedi-t.htm

E-commerce software

- **A comprehensive list of E-Commerce Software.** www.owlnet.rice.edu/~mgmt632/storefro.htm

Entry-level e-commerce outsourcing

- **MerchandiZer.** www.merchandizer.com
- **Complete Merchant.** www.completemerchant.com
- **Bigstep.** www.bigstep.com

- **Amazon.** www.amazon.com
- **Yahoo! Stores.** http://store.yahoo.com
- **eBay's How to Sell Page.** http://pages.ebay.com/help/basics/n-selling.html

Mid-level storefront solutions

- **Actinic.** www.actinic.com
- **iHTML Merchant.** www.ihtmlmerchant.com
- **Mercantec – Providers of SoftCart E-Commerce Software and Services.** www.mercantec.com
- **O'Reilly Software WebSite.** http://website.oreilly.com
- **Smith Micro.** www.smithmicro.com
- **AbleCommerce.** www.ablecommerce.com
- **iCommerce.** www.icommerce.com
- **Maestro Software.** www.maestrocommerce.com
- **Smith Micro Software.** www.smithmicro.com
- **Maestro Commerce.** www.maestrocommerce.com

High-level storefront solutions

- **DevX Enterprise Zone.** www.enterprise-zone.com
- **Open Market: The Future of Business.** www.openmarket.com
- **E-Commerce Times Store Software Guide.** www.ecommercetimes.com/product_guide/store_software
- **Internet.com's E-Commerce Product Guide.** http://products.ecommerce-guide.com

HTTP

- **HTTP Pocket Reference Excerpt.** www.oreilly.com/catalog/httppr/chapter/http_pkt.html
- **HTTP Header Viewer.** www.delorie.com/web/headers.html
- **HTAccess Authentication Tutorial.** www.maestrocommerce.com

Internet business info

- **Electronic Commerce Resource Center.** www.ecrc.ctc.com
- **Internet.com's Electronic Commerce Guide.** http://ecommerce.internet.com
- **TheStandard.com Home page.** www.thestandard.com
- **ZDNet Business & Tech E-Commerce Home.** www.zdnet.com/enterprise/e-business/
- **E-Commerce 101.** www.merchant-account-4u.com/ecom101.htm
- **Best B-to-B Web Sites by Category.** www.netb2b.com/netMarketing200/2000/

Legal info

- **Tax on Internet Sales – Nolo's Legal Encyclopedia.** www.nolo.com/encyclopedia/articles/ilaw/internet_tax.html
- **The Electronic Frontier Foundation.** www.eff.org
- **The Internet Law and Policy Forum.** www.ilpf.org
- **The Internet Law Journal.** www.tilj.com
- **Bitlaw.** www.bitlaw.com
- **The World Intellectual Property Organization's Domain Name Dispute Resolution Service.** http://arbiter.wipo.int/domains/
- **TRUSTe.** www.truste.org
- **Electronic Commerce and Law Report.** http://web.bna.com/eplr.htm
- **UCLA Online Institute for Cyberspace Law and Policy.** www.gseis.ucla.edu/iclp/hp.html
- **WIPO Arbitration and Mediation Center.** http://arbiter.wipo.int/domains/

Marketing and promotion

- **eMarketer.** www.emarketer.com
- **Promotion 101 – Web Marketing Info Center.** www.promotion101.com
- **Coalition for Advertising Supported Information and Entertainment (CASIE).** www.casie.org
- **Millward Brown IntelliQuest.** www.intelliquest.com

- **Banner Ad Placement Effectiveness Study from Webreference.com.** www.webreference.com/dev/banners/
- **Search Engine World.** www.searchengineworld.com
- **EmailAbuse.org.** http://emailabuse.org
- **Search Engine Watch.** www.searchenginewatch.com

Operating systems

- **BSD Today – Your Daily Source for BSD News and Information.** www.bsdtoday.com
- **The Linux Home Page at Linux Online.** www.linux.org
- **Windows 2000 Server Overview.** www.microsoft.com/windows2000/guide/server/overview/default.asp
- **ZDNet Interactive Week Chris Coleman Explains BSD Unix.** www.zdnet.com/intweek/stories/news/0,4164,2631373,00.html

Payment processing

- **History of Credit Cards.** www.didyouknow.com/creditcards.htm
- **E-Commerce 101 – Learn All About Merchant Accounts and Credit Card Processing.** www.merchant-account-4u.com/ecom101.htm
- **Authorize.Net.** www.authorizenet.com
- **BCE Emergis.** www.emergis.com
- **Clear Commerce.** www.clearcommerce.com
- **CyberCash, Inc.** www.cybercash.com
- **CyberSource.** www.cybersource.com
- **Electracash.** www.electracash.com
- **Didyouknow.com's History of Credit Cards.** www.didyouknow.com/creditcards.htm
- **SecureLynx.** www.securelynx.com
- **PayPal.** www.paypal.com
- **Trintech.** www.trintech.com
- **eDebit.** www.edebit.com
- **Verifone.** www.hp.com/solutions1/verifone

Security

- **Counterpane Internet Security.** www.counterpane.com
- **Entrust Technologies.** www.entrust.com
- **Security and Encryption Links.** www.cs.auckland.ac.nz/~pgut001/links.html
- **Rootshell.** http://rootshell.com/beta/news.html
- **RSA Security.** www.rsasecurity.com

Secure Sockets Layer (SSL)

- **Secure Sockets Layer.** http://home.netscape.com/security/techbriefs/ssl.html
- **Netscape's Introduction to SSL.** http://developer.netscape.com/docs/manuals/security/sslin/index.htm
- **SSL 3.0 Specification.** http://home.netscape.com/eng/ssl3/index.html

Secure Electronic Transactions (SET)

- **Webmaster's Domain SET – Who Needs It (Web Techniques, Aug 1998).** www.webtechniques.com/archives/1998/08/webm/

Digital certificates

- **Thawte Digital Certificate Services.** www.thawte.com
- **VeriSign Inc.** www.verisign.com
- **Entrust.** www.entrust.com

Site management

- **Connected.** www.connected.com
- **NetMechanic.** www.netmechanic.com
- **Web Site Garage.** http://websitegarage.netscape.com/

Test resources

- **Exam Guide for 1DO-425.** http://www.ciwcertified.com/exams/1d0425.asp

Web server info

- **Netcraft Web Site Finder and Survey.** www.netcraft.com
- **Netscape Server Products.** http://home.netscape.com/servers/index.html
- **Apache.org.** www.apache.org
- **Remote Administration.** www.support.nedcomp.nl/iishelp/iis/htm/core/iiahttp.htm

✦ ✦ ✦

Checklist: Planning E-Commerce

✦ ✦ ✦ ✦

Preparation is the key to any e-commerce success story. The following checklists take the major topics of this book and condense them into handy lists of to-do items. This is no substitute for reading the entire book, but it can help you recall the key elements of e-commerce site development, maintenance, and management without having to refer to the original material.

Planning

✦ Evaluate whether your existing business is suitable to online commerce.

✦ Determine the advantages to your company of opening an online store.

✦ Evaluate the potential disadvantages of an online store for your company.

✦ Establish methods to overcome these potential disadvantages.

✦ Consider the type of e-commerce implementation your company requires. Your options are:

- Entry-level outsourcing
- Mid-level storefront software
- High-level storefront software
- Custom development

✦ Decide whether your site will be hosted in-house or with an ISP.

✦ Determine what software will be used to serve the site.

✦ Determine what software will be used to develop the site.

✦ Develop a timeline and budget for the project. *Beware of overly aggressive, underfunded plans.*

Marketing

- Determine your e-commerce site's target market.
- Determine which business model, business-to-consumer (B2C) or business-to-business (B2B), is best suited for your company's e-commerce site.
- Evaluate the differences between your traditional business model and your e-commerce business model.
- Decide whether to include online community-building components on your site. Your options include:
  - Customer reviews
  - Message boards
  - Chat areas
  - Personal pages

Set-up

- Register a domain name for your e-commerce site.
- Open an account with an ISP, or, if hosting in-house, install the proper hardware at your site and establish a high-speed connection to the Internet.
- Hire employees or contractors to program the site.
- Hire a Web designer to create your site's graphics and user interface.
- Purchase the necessary equipment (computers and software) for developing the site.

Advertising and promotion

- Develop a plan for generating demand for your products and/or services.
- Decide whether to offer banner ad space on your site to advertisers.
- Develop an affiliate program, if appropriate.
- Plan some promotions for your site, such as contests and newsletters.
- Begin advertising on other Web sites.
- Begin advertising in traditional media.
- Take appropriate measures to have your site be one of the top 10 or 15 results for appropriate queries at major search engine sites.
- Provide incentives for repeat customers, such as free shipping or quantity discounts.

Transaction processing

- ✦ Decide which of the following payment options to offer:
  - Credit cards (automatic or manual electronic processing)
  - Checks (via mail or electronic processing)
  - Electronic funds
  - Stored value programs
- ✦ Determine business methods for processing payment.
- ✦ Select a payment processing service or software component that supports your needs and business methods.
- ✦ Open a merchant account that works in conjunction with the payment processing service or software component you've chosen.
- ✦ Implement the payment processing solution on your site and test it thoroughly.

Order fulfillment

- ✦ Determine a workflow for processing orders.
- ✦ Purchase (or develop) and implement order-tracking software.
- ✦ Generate automatic e-mails to customers to confirm order placement and provide expected ship date and customer service contact information.
- ✦ After an order has been shipped, e-mail the customer to let him or her know when the items were shipped and any tracking number associated with the package.
- ✦ Continuously evaluate your stock levels versus demand for products, and adjust your orders from distributors accordingly.
- ✦ For intangible goods, such as software and other electronic files, offer the products for immediate secure download over the Internet.
- ✦ Try to establish volume-based discounts with one or more shipping companies to help reduce your shipping costs.

Customer service

- ✦ Establish business methods for supporting your customers.
- ✦ Decide whether to offer customers a toll-free number, or to just take inquiries via e-mail.
- ✦ Set up an e-mail management system or a customer support case management system.

- ✦ Hire employees for a customer service center, or outsource this role to an appropriate company.
- ✦ Develop an FAQ list and post it on your site.
- ✦ Include a self-service customer support area on your site.
- ✦ Develop a password-protected account maintenance area of your site for established customers.
- ✦ Decide whether to use personalization software to provide users with information based on their past purchases.
- ✦ Decide whether to offer advanced customer service functionality, such as:
  - Remote control (co-browsing)
  - Voice connections (telephony)
  - Knowledge databases (knowledge base)

Security

- ✦ Determine the type(s) of security your site will use. Consider the following technologies and standards:
  - Secure Sockets Layer (SSL)
  - Secure Electronic Transactions (SET)
  - S/MIME
- ✦ Use strong encryption to secure sensitive data.
- ✦ Obtain a digital certificate for your site.
- ✦ Be sure to establish security measures and procedures for the information housed on the server.
- ✦ Consider having your site's security audited by a professional security consultant.
- ✦ After you've adequately secured your site, consider how you will convince customers and potential customers that your site is secure.
- ✦ Implement procedures to make sure your site stays secure. These procedures should include:
  - Be informed of any security patches to your server software, and install them as soon as they are released.
  - Conduct regular audits of your site's security.
  - Monitor server log files for suspicious activity.
  - Control internal access to sensitive data.

Legal issues

- Determine the potential legal problems of your online business. Consider potential for intellectual property issues, privacy issues, as well as taxation and jurisdictional issues.
- Establish privacy and confidentiality standards and methods to protect your customers' information.
- Determine whether your products may be illegal in any part of the world.

Globalization

- Develop alternate versions of your Web site in languages appropriate to your clientele.
- Decide whether your site will accept payment in multiple currencies.
- Become familiar with customs duties affecting your products.
- If your site is geared toward an international audience, eliminate American lingo and colloquialisms.

Web site maintenance

- Determine the tasks required to maintain your site. Set up a proposed schedule for maintenance.
- Hire employees or contractors to provide site maintenance.
- Conduct regular tests of site performance and upgrade software or hardware as necessary.
- Continuously monitor your site for possible security breaches.

Site management

- Continuously monitor your site for outdated content.
- Perform regular backups of your site.
- Conduct regular log file analysis by running frequent reports in a log analysis software program. Use this information to improve your site.

✦ ✦ ✦

Companies and Products Mentioned

This appendix provides you with an alphabetical listing of all the companies and products mentioned in this book, including the URL for the company or product as well as the chapter in which it was discussed.

Remember that the Web is a rapidly changing environment, and some of the URLs listed may no longer work. If you come across a URL that doesn't work, try going to the root of the URL (the main company address) to verify that the information you seek is still on the site.

- **7-Eleven.** *Convenience store information-only site.* `www.7eleven.com`: mentioned in Chapter 11
- **24/7 Media.** *Web advertising.* `www.247media.com`: mentioned in Chapter 4

A

- **Able Solutions Corporation.** *Auction Builder.* `www.ablecommerce.com`: mentioned in Chapter 10
- **Able Solutions Corporation.** *AbleCommerce.* `www.ablecommerce.com`: mentioned in Chapter 9
- **Actinic Software.** *Actinic Catalog.* `www.actinic.com`: mentioned in Chapters 9, 12, 14, 15, 16, 17, 20
- **Amazon.** *Online retailer.* `www.amazon.com`: mentioned in Chapters 1, 3
- **Amazon.** *Amazon Auctions.* `www.amazon.com`: mentioned in Chapter 8
- **Amazon.** *zShops.* `www.amazon.com`: mentioned in Chapters 3, 8
- **America Online.** *AOLServer.* `www.aol.com`: mentioned in Chapter 12

- **American Express.** *Credit card service.* `www.americanexpress.com`: mentioned in Chapter 17
- **Apache.** *Apache Web Server.* `www.apache.org`: mentioned in Chapter 12
- **Apple Computer.** *Macintosh OS.* `www.apple.com`: mentioned in Chapter 12
- **Arborior.** *Encore Web Forum.* `www.aborior.com`: mentioned in Chapter 18
- **Auction Broker Software.** *The Auction Broker.* `www.auctionbroker.com`: mentioned in Chapter 10
- **Auction Works.** *Auction Works.* `www.auctionworks.com`: mentioned in Chapter 10
- **Authorize.Net.** *Payment authorization service.* `www.authorizenet.com`: mentioned in Chapter 17

B

- **Barnes & Noble.** *Book retailer.* `www.bn.com`: mentioned in Chapters 1, 3, 11
- **Barnes & Noble.** *Affiliate Network.* `www.barnesandnoble.com/affiliate`: mentioned in Chapter 8
- **BCE Emergis.** *E-commerce infrastructure provider.* `www.emergis.com`: mentioned in Chapter 17
- **Best Buy.** *Online retailer.* `www.bestbuy.com`: mentioned in Chapter 3
- **Beyond Solutions.** *Visual Auction.* `www.beyondsolutions.com`: mentioned in Chapter 10
- **BigFoot.** *Web directory.* `www.bigfoot.com`: mentioned in Chapter 2
- **BigStep.** *Bigstep.com* `www.bigstep.com`: mentioned in Chapter 8
- **BMW.** *Automotive dealer.* `www.bmw.com`: mentioned in Chapter 3
- **BrightWare.** *Converse.* `www.brightware.com`: mentioned in Chapter 6
- **Broadvision.** *Business Commerce.* `www.broadvision.com`: mentioned in Chapter 10

C

- **Caldera Systems.** *Caldera Linux.* `www.calderasystems.com`: mentioned in Chapter 12
- **Carfax.** *Vehicle History Reports.* `www.carfax.com`: mentioned in Chapter 11
- **CD Now.** *C2 Program.* `www.cdnow.com`: mentioned in Chapter 8

- **Center for Inventory Management.** *Business management and consulting.* www.centerforinventorymanagement.org/: mentioned in Chapter 20
- **CERT Coordination Center.** *Security Advisories.* www.cert.org: mentioned in Chapters 19, 21
- **Cisco Systems.** *Intelligent Contact Management Solutions.* www.cisco.com/warp/public/180/prod_plat/cust_cont/icm: mentioned in Chapters 1, 6
- **CityAuction.** *Online auctions.* www.cityauction.com: mentioned in Chapter 8
- **ClearCommerce.** *Payment and credit card processing software.* www.clearcommerce.com: mentioned in Chapter 17
- **CNET.** *CNET Auctions.* http://auctions.cnet.com: mentioned in Chapter 8
- **Commerce One.** *Auction Solutions.* www.commerceone.com: mentioned in Chapter 10
- **CommerceNet.** *Web user statistical information.* www.commerce.net: mentioned in Chapters 1, 3
- **Compaq.** *Tru64.* www.tru64unix.compaq.com: mentioned in Chapter 12
- **Complete Merchant.** *CompleteMerchant.* www.completemerchant.com: mentioned in Chapter 8
- **Connected.** *Connected TLM.* www.connected.com: mentioned in Chapter 21
- **Corel.** *Corel Linux.* http://linux.corel.com: mentioned in Chapter 12
- **Counterpane Internet Security, Inc.** *Crypto-Gram Newsletter.* www.counterpane.com: mentioned in Chapter 19
- **CyberAtlas.** *Web population information.* http://cyberatlas.internet.com: mentioned in Chapter 3
- **CyberCash.** *Online payment service.* www.cybercash.com: mentioned in Chapter 17
- **CyberSource.** *E-commerce transaction suite.* www.cybersource.com: mentioned in Chapter 17
- **CyberSpace HQ.** *AddWeb.* www.cyberspacehq.com: mentioned in Chapter 4

D

- **Debian.** *Debian GNU/Linux.* www.debian.org: mentioned in Chapter 12
- **Dell Computer.** *Computer manufacturer.* www.dell.com: mentioned in Chapters 3, 11
- **Discover Bank.** *Credit card service.* www.discovercard.com: mentioned in Chapter 17

- **DomainGuideBook.com.** *International domain name information.* www.domainguidebook.com/international: mentioned in Chapter 3
- **Doubleclick.** *Web advertising.* www.doubleclick.com: mentioned in Chapter 4

E

- **E.piphany.** *CRM software.* www.epiphany.com: mentioned in Chapter 18
- **eBay.** *Online auction site.* www.ebay.com: mentioned in Chapter 8
- **eDebit.** *Online check processing.* www.edebit.com: mentioned in Chapter 17
- **eGain.** *Customer service software.* www.egain.com: mentioned in Chapter 18
- **eMarketer.** *Internet marketing information and services.* www.emarketer.com: mentioned in Chapter 3
- **Entrust.** *Digital Certificates.* www.entrust.com: mentioned in Chapter 19
- **Epic Systems.** *B2B Toolkit.* www.epic-systems.com: mentioned in Chapter 7
- **Excite.** *Search engine.* www.excite.com: mentioned in Chapters 3, 4
- **Excite.** *Excite Auctions.* http://auctions.excite.com: mentioned in Chapter 8
- **eXTReMe Tracking.** *Web site traffic tracking service.* www.extreme-dm.com: mentioned in Chapter 4

F

- **FairMarket.** *AuctionPlace.* www.fairmarket.com: mentioned in Chapter 10
- **Federal Express.** *Shipping service.* www.fedex.com: mentioned in Chapters 1, 17
- **FileMaker Software.** *FileMaker Pro.* www.filemaker.com: mentioned in Chapter 12
- **FishNet, Inc.** *FishCart SQL.* www.fishcart.org: mentioned in Chapter 12
- **Flooz.** *Digital cash service.* www.flooz.com: mentioned in Chapters 1, 17
- **Forstle, Inc.** *Pushpin.* www.pushpin.com: mentioned in Chapter 18

G

- **Great Circle Associates.** *Majordomo.* www.greatcircle.com/majordomo: mentioned in Chapter 4

H

- **Hewlett-Packard.** *HP-UX.* www.hp.com/products1/unix/operating/index.html: mentioned in Chapter 12
- **Hipbone.** *Co-browsing software.* www.hipbone.com: mentioned in Chapter 18
- **HipHip Software.** *MerchandiZer.* www.merchandizer.com: mentioned in Chapter 8
- **Homegrocer.** *Online grocer.* www.homegrocer.com: mentioned in Chapter 1

I

- **IBM.** *AIX.* www.ibm.com/servers/aix: mentioned in Chapter 12
- **IBM.** *Ariba.* www.ariba.com: mentioned in Chapter 10
- **IBM.** *DB2.* www.ibm.com: mentioned in Chapter 12
- **IBM.** *WebSphere Commerce Suite.* www.ibm.com/websphere: mentioned in Chapters 7, 10
- **iCommerce.** *ShopZone.* www.icommerce.com: mentioned in Chapters 1, 9
- **Ifilm.** *Video on demand.* www.ifilm.com: mentioned in Chapter 3
- **Imex Exchange.** *International business exchange.* www.imex.com: mentioned in Chapter 2
- **Informix Software.** *UniVerse.* www.informix.com: mentioned in Chapter 12
- **Inline Internet Systems.** *iHTML Merchant.* www.ihtmlmerchant.com: mentioned in Chapter 9
- **International Business Systems.** *LiveAssistance.* www.liveassistance.com: mentioned in Chapter 6
- **Internet Cash Corporation.** *Internet cash.* www.internetcash.com: mentioned in Chapter 17
- **Internet World.** *Print and online magazine.* www.internetworld.com: mentioned in Chapter 4
- **Intershop.** *Efinity.* www.intershop.com: mentioned in Chapter 10
- **Interworld.** *Commerce Exchange.* www.interworld.com: mentioned in Chapter 10

J

- **Jelsoft Enterprises Limited.** *vBulletin.* www.vbulletin.com: mentioned in Chapter 18
- **Jupiter Research.** *Research reports.* www.jup.com: mentioned in Chapter 3

K

- **Kana.** *Kana E-business Platform.* www.kana.com: mentioned in Chapter 18
- **Kentucky Fried Chicken.** *Fast food site.* www.kfc.com: mentioned in Chapter 3

L

- **Lands' End.** *Lands' End Live Support.* www.landsend.com: mentioned in Chapters 1, 6, 18
- **Liquidation.com.** *Surplus goods exchange.* www.liquidation.com: mentioned in Chapter 7
- **ListMate.** *Bulk e-mail management software.* www.listmate.com: mentioned in Chapter 4
- **LivePerson.** *LivePerson.* www.liveperson.com: mentioned in Chapter 6
- **Looksmart.** *Web directory.* www.looksmart.com: mentioned in Chapter 4

M

- **MasterCard.** *Credit card service.* www.mastercard.com: mentioned in Chapter 19
- **Mercantec.** *SoftCart.* www.mercantec.com: mentioned in Chapter 9
- **Microsoft.** *Access.* www.microsoft.com: mentioned in Chapter 12
- **Microsoft.** *BizTalk Server.* www.microsoft.com: mentioned in Chapter 10
- **Microsoft.** *Internet Explorer.* www.microsoft.com: mentioned in Chapter 5
- **Microsoft.** *Internet Information Service (IIS).* www.microsoft.com: mentioned in Chapters 12, 13
- **Microsoft.** *Microsoft Developer Network.* http://msdn.microsoft.com: mentioned in Chapter 18
- **Microsoft.** *SQLServer.* www.microsoft.com: mentioned in Chapter 12
- **Microsoft.** *Windows 2000.* www.microsoft.com: mentioned in Chapter 12
- **Microsoft bCentral.** *LinkExchange.* www.bcentral.com: mentioned in Chapter 4
- **MOAI.** *LiveExchange.* www.moai.com: mentioned in Chapter 10
- **Monster.com.** *Job Board.* www.monster.com: mentioned in Chapter 1
- **MovieFlix.** *Video on demand.* www.movieflix.com: mentioned in Chapter 3
- **MySQL.** *MySQL.* www.mysql.com: mentioned in Chapter 12

N

- **Netscape.** *CommerceXpert.* `http://home.netscape.com/commapps/products`: mentioned in Chapter 7
- **Netscape.** *Netscape Navigator.* `http://home.netscape.com/products`: mentioned in Chapter 1
- **Netscape.** *Web Site Garage.* `www.websitegarage.com`: mentioned in Chapter 21
- **Network Solutions.** *Domain name information.* `www.networksolutions.com`: mentioned in Chapter 11
- **Nua.** *Internet Surveys.* `www.nua.ie/surveys`: mentioned in Chapter 3

O

- **Open Market.** *Open Market E-Business Suite.* `www.openmarket.com`: mentioned in Chapter 10
- **Oracle.** *Oracle8/8i.* `www.oracle.com`: mentioned in Chapter 12
- **O'Reilly Software.** *WebSite Professional.* `http://website.oreilly.com`: mentioned in Chapter 12

P

- **PayPal.** *Online payment service.* `www.paypal.com`: mentioned in Chapter 17
- **Peapod.** *Online grocer.* `www.peapod.com`: mentioned in Chapter 1
- **PETsMART.** *Pet supply store.* `www.petsmart.com`: mentioned in Chapter 11
- **PowerMailBox.** *Outsourced bulk e-mail management.* `www.powermailbox.com`: mentioned in Chapter 4
- **Priceline.** *Custom pricing online.* `www.priceline.com`: mentioned in Chapter 1

R

- **Red Hat.** *Red Hat Linux.* `www.redhat.com`: mentioned in Chapter 12
- **RegisterIt.** *Web site registration.* `http://register-it.netscape.com/`: mentioned in Chapter 4

S

- **Salon.** *Online magazine.* `www.salon.com`: mentioned in Chapter 4
- **Securelynx.** *Digital wallet.* `www.securelynx.com`: mentioned in Chapter 17
- **SGI.** *IRIX.* `www.sgi.com/software`: mentioned in Chapter 12
- **Slackware.** *Slackware Linux.* `www.slackware.com`: mentioned in Chapter 12
- **SmartAge.** *SmartClicks.* `www.smartage.com`: mentioned in Chapter 4
- **Smith Micro Software.** *WebCatalog.* `www.smithmicro.com`: mentioned in Chapter 9
- **Strictly Exchange.** *Strictly Exchange.* `www.expressbid.com`: mentioned in Chapter 10
- **Stronghold.** *Secure Web Server.* `www.c2.net`: mentioned in Chapter 12
- **SubmitIt.** *Web site registration.* `www.submitit.com`: mentioned in Chapter 4
- **Sun Microsystems.** *iPlanet Web server.* `www.iplanet.com`: mentioned in Chapter 12
- **Sun Microsystems.** *Solaris.* `www.sun.com/solaris`: mentioned in Chapter 12
- **SupplyWorks.** *Manufacturing procurement site.* `www.supplyworks.com`: mentioned in Chapter 7
- **SuSE.** *SuSE Linux.* `www.suse.de`: mentioned in Chapter 12
- **Switchboard.** *Directory.* `www.switchboard.com`: mentioned in Chapter 2
- **Sybase.** *Adaptive Server.* `www.sybase.com`: mentioned in Chapter 12

T

- **Talisma.** *eSource.* `www.talisma.com`: mentioned in Chapter 18
- **Target.** *Retailer.* `www.target.com`: mentioned in Chapter 5
- **Thawte.** *Digital certificates.* `www.thawte.com`: mentioned in Chapter 19
- **TradeOut.** *B2B exchange.* `www.tradeout.com`: mentioned in Chapter 7
- **Trintech.** *PayWare.* `www.trintech.com`: mentioned in Chapter 17
- **TRUSTe.** *Privacy statement generator.* `www.truste.org/wizard`: mentioned in Chapter 2

U

- **United Parcel Service (UPS).** *Shipping service.* `www.ups.com`: mentioned in Chapter 3

V

- ✦ **Verifone.** *SoftPay.* `www.verifone.com`: mentioned in Chapter 17
- ✦ **VeriSign.** *Digital certificates.* `www.verisign.com`: mentioned in Chapter 19

W

- ✦ **WalMart.** *Retailer.* `www.walmart.com`: mentioned in Chapter 5
- ✦ **Webmonkey.** *Online magazine.* `http://hotwired.lycos.com/webmonkey`: mentioned in Chapter 4
- ✦ **WebPositionGold.** *WebPositionGold.* `www.webpositiongold.com`: mentioned in Chapter 4
- ✦ **WebSTAR.** *Server Suite.* `www.starnine.com`: mentioned in Chapter 12
- ✦ **WebSTAT.** *Web site traffic tracking service.* `www.webstat.com`: mentioned in Chapter 4
- ✦ **WebTrends.** *WebTrends Log File Analyzer.* `www.webtrends.com`: mentioned in Chapters 5, 21
- ✦ **Webvan.** *Online grocer.* `www.webvan.com`: mentioned in Chapter 1
- ✦ **WhitePages.com.** *Directory.* `www.whitepages.com`: mentioned in Chapter 2
- ✦ **Works.com.** *Online purchasing management application.* `www.works.com`: mentioned in Chapter 7
- ✦ **World Wide Web Consortium.** *Jigsaw Java Server.* `www.w3.org/Jigsaw`: mentioned in Chapter 12
- ✦ **WorldTariff.** *Duty and tax information.* `www.worldtariff.com`: mentioned in Chapter 2

Y

- ✦ **Yahoo!** *Search engine.* `www.yahoo.com`: mentioned in Chapters 3, 4, 5
- ✦ **Yahoo!** *Yahoo! People Search.* `http://people.yahoo.com`: mentioned in Chapter 2
- ✦ **Yahoo!** *Yahoo! Shopping.* `http://shopping.yahoo.com`: mentioned in Chapter 1
- ✦ **Yahoo!** *Yahoo! Stores.* `http://store.yahoo.com`: mentioned in Chapter 8

Z

- **Zelerate, Inc.** *AllCommerce*. `http://allcommerce.sourceforge.net/`: mentioned in Chapter 12
- **Zeus.** *Zeus Web Server*. `www.zeus.co.uk/products/ws`: mentioned in Chapter 12
- **Zip2.** *Directory*. `www.zip2.com`: mentioned in Chapter 2

✦ ✦ ✦

E-Commerce Bibliography

✦ ✦ ✦ ✦

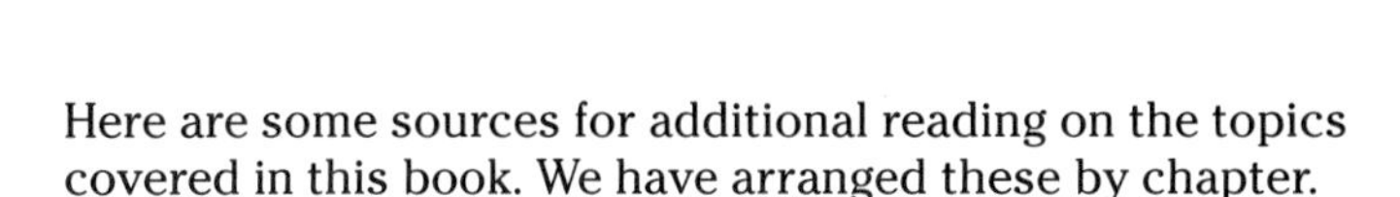

Here are some sources for additional reading on the topics covered in this book. We have arranged these by chapter.

Chapter 1: E-Commerce Overview

- Amor, Daniel. *The E-business (R)evolution.* Upper Saddle River, NJ: Prentice Hall, 1999.
- Cashin, Jerry. *E-Commerce Success: Building a Global Business Architecture.* Charleston, SC: Computer Technology Research Corporation, 1999.
- Deise, Martin V., Conrad Nowikow, Patrick King, and Amy Wright. *Executive's Guide to E-Business: From Tactics to Strategy.* New York, NY: John Wiley and Sons, 2000.
- Fellenstein, Craig, and Ron Wood. *Exploring E-commerce, Global E-business and E-solutions.* Upper Saddle River, NJ: Prentice Hall, 2000.
- Hakman, Kevin. "E-Commerce Tutorial." Webmonkey, January 1999. `http://hotwired.lycos.com/webmonkey/e-business/building/tutorials/tutorial3.html`.
- Hartman, Amir, John G. Sifonis and John Kador. *Net Ready: Strategies for Success in the E-conomy.* New York, NY: McGraw-Hill Professional Publishing, 2000.
- Korper, Steffano, Juanita Ellis, and Jerry D. Gibson. *The E-Commerce Book: Building the E-Empire.* San Diego, CA: Academic Press, 1999.
- Kosiur, David. *Understanding Electronic Commerce.* Redmond, WA: Microsoft Press, 1997.
- Microsoft Mastering. *eCommerce Development: Business to Consumer.* Redmond, WA: Microsoft Press, 1999
- Minoli, Daniel, and Emma Minoli. *Web Commerce Technology Handbook.* New York: McGraw-Hill Publishing Company, 1998.

- Reynolds, Janice. *The Complete E-Commerce Book: Design, Build & Maintain a Successful Web-based Business.* Gilroy, CA: CMP Books, 2000.
- Schwartz, Evan I. *Digital Darwinism: 7 Breakthrough Business Strategies for Surviving in the Cutthroat Web Economy.* New York, NY: Broadway Books, 1999.
- Schwartz, Evan I. *Webonomics: Nine Essential Principles for Growing Your Business on the World Wide Web.* New York, NY: Bantam Doubleday Dell, 1998.

Chapter 2: Legal Issues and the Internet

- Bick, Jonathan. *101 Things You Need to Know About Internet Law.* New York, NY: Three Rivers Press, 2000.
- Brinson, J. Dianne, and Mark F. Radcliffe. *Internet Law and Business Handbook : A Practical Guide.* Menlo Park, CA: Ladera Press, 2000.
- Butler, Susan P. *eBusiness Legal Kit For Dummies®.* Hungry Minds, 2000.
- Edwards, Lillian, and Charlotte Waelde, editors. *Law and the Internet : Regulating Cyberspace.* Oxford, UK: Hart Publishing, 1997.
- Lessig, Lawrence. *Code and Other Laws of Cyberspace.* New York, NY: Basic Books, 2000.
- Rosenoer, Jonathan. *Cyberlaw: the Law of the Internet.* New York, NY: Springer Verlag, 1997.
- Stim, Richard. *Getting Permission: How to License and Clear Copyrighted Materials Online and Off.* Berkeley, CA: Nolo Press, 1999.

Chapter 3: Marketing to the Web

- Brondmo, Hans Peter, and Geoffrey Moore. *The Engaged Customer: The New Rules of Internet Direct Marketing.* New York, NY: HarperBusiness, 2000.
- Carpenter, Phil. *eBrands: Building an Internet Business at Breakneck Speed.* Cambridge, MA: Harvard Business School Press, 2000.
- Godin, Seth, and Don Peppers. *Permission Marketing: Turning Strangers Into Friends, and Friends into Customers.* New York, NY: Simon & Schuster, 1999.
- Hagel, John, and Arthur G. Armstrong. *Net Gain: Expanding Markets Through Virtual Communities.* Cambridge, MA: Harvard Business School Press, 1997.
- Hanson, Ward. *Principles of Internet Marketing.* Cincinnati, OH: Southwestern College Publishing, 1999.
- Janal, Daniel S. *Dan Janal's Guide to Marketing on the Internet: Getting People to Visit, Buy and Become Customers for Life.* New York, NY: John Wiley and Sons, 2000.

- Modahl, Mary. *Now or Never: How Companies Must Change Today to Win the Battle for Internet Consumers.* New York, NY: HarperBusiness, 1999.
- Mougayar, Walid. *Opening Digital Markets : Battle Plans and Business Strategies for Internet Commerce.* New York, NY: McGraw-Hill, 1997.
- Ries, Al, and Laura Ries. *The 11 Immutable Laws of Internet Branding.* New York, NY: HarperBusiness, 2000.
- Schmitt, Bernd H., and Alex Simonson. *Marketing Aesthetics: The Strategic Management of Brands, Identity and Image.* Free Press, 1997.
- Smith, Bud, and Frank Catalano. *Internet Marketing For Dummies®.* New York, NY: Hungry Minds, 2000.
- Zimmerman, Jan. *Marketing on the Internet.* Gulf Breeze, FL: Maximum Press, 2000.

Chapter 4: Online Promotion Techniques

- Kinnard, Shannon. *Marketing With Email : A Spam-Free Guide to Increasing Awareness, Building Loyalty, and Increasing Sales by Using the Internet's Most Powerful Tool.* Gulf Breeze, FL: Maximum Press, 1999.
- Roberts, Stevan, Michelle Feit, and Robert W. Bly. *Internet Direct Mail : The Complete Guide to Successful E-Mail Marketing Campaigns.* Lincolnwood, IL: NTC Business Books, 2000.
- Schwartz, Alan. "Spread the Word with Mailing Lists." Web Techniques Magazine, June 2000. `www.webtechniques.com/archives/2000/06/schwartz/`.
- Sweeney, Susan. *101 Ways to Promote Your Web Site.* Gulf Breeze, FL: Maximum Press, 2000.
- Wong, Thomas. *101 Ways to Boost Your Web Traffic: Internet Promotion Made Easier.* Union City, CA: Intesync, 2000.
- Zeff, Robbin Lee, and Brad Aronson. *Advertising on the Internet, 2nd Edition.* New York, NY: John Wiley and Sons, 1999.

Chapter 5: Building Usable Web Sites

- Gardner, Elizabeth. "Special Report: Design Usability." Internet World Magazine, December 15, 2000. `www.internetworld.com/121500/12.15.00feature1long.jsp`.
- Krug, Steve. *Don't Make Me Think! A Common Sense Approach to Web Usability.* Indianapolis, IN: Que, 2000.

- Maran, Ruth. *HTML: Your visual blueprint for designing effective Web sites.* New York, NY: Hungry Minds, 1999.
- Nielsen, Jakob. *Designing Web Usability: The Practice of Simplicity.* Indianapolis, IN: New Riders, 1999.
- Pearrow, Mark. *Web Site Usability Handbook.* Hingham, MA: Charles River Media, 2000.
- Raskin, Jef. *The Humane Interface: New Directions in Designing Interactive Systems.* Reading, MA: Addison Wesley Longman, 2000.
- Weinman, Lynda. *Designing Web Graphics.3.* Indianapolis, IN: New Riders, 1999.

Chapter 6: E-Service for E-Customers

- Cox, Beth. "Poor Customer Service Cost E-Tailers $6 Billion in '99." Internet News, July 2000. `www.internetnews.com/ec-news/article/0,,4_410081,00.html`.
- Lang, Paul. "Online Customer Service: Best (and Worst) Practices." Sell It!, January 2001. `http://sellitontheweb.com/ezine/opinion074.shtml`.
- LeClaire, Jennifer, and Liza Picozzi. "Oversee Customer Service Processes." Workz.com, August 2000. `www.workz.com/content/1015.asp`.
- Newell, Frederick. *Loyalty.com: Customer Relationship Management in the New Era of Internet Marketing.* New York, NY: McGraw-Hill Professional Publishing, 2000.
- Sham, Laurie. "Outsourcing Online Customer Service: Providing Web Consumers With Human Interaction Is Key To Online Success." Planet IT, June 2000. `www.planetit.com/techcenters/docs/e_business-e_commerce/product_review/PIT20000622S0030`.
- Zemke, Ron, and Thomas K. Connellan. *E-Service: 24 Ways to Keep Your Customers-When the Competition Is Just a Click Away.* AMACOM, 2000.

Chapter 7: Supporting Business-to-Business Activities Online

- Carr, David F. "B2B Exchanges that Work: Integrators Build Browser-Based Bridges to Legacy Systems." Internet World Magazine, December 1, 2000. `www.internetworld.com/120100/12.01.00internettech1.jsp`.
- Cunningham, Michael J. *B2B: How to Build a Profitable E-Commerce Strategy.* Cambridge, MA: Perseus Press, 2000.
- Fingar, Peter, Harsha Kumar, and Tarun Sharma. *Enterprise E-commerce.* Tampa, FL: Meghan Kiffer Press, 2000.
- Memishi, Ruhan. "B2B Exchanges Survival Guide." Internet World Magazine, January 1, 2001. `www.internetworld.com/010101/01.01.01feature1.jsp`.

✦ Norris, Grant, John Dunleavy, James R. Hurley, John D. Balls, and Kenneth M. Hartley. *E-Business and ERP: Transforming the Enterprise.* New York, NY: John Wiley and Sons, 2000.

✦ Silverstein, Barry. *Business-to-Business Internet Marketing.* Gulf Breeze, FL: Maximum Press, 2000.

✦ Sloane, Tim, Seema Phull and Ketan Patel. "Efficient Business-to-Business Relationships: How Analytics and XML Can Help." Web Techniques Magazine, November 2000. www.webtechniques.com/archives/2000/11/sloane/.

Chapter 8: Entry-Level E-Commerce Outsourcing

✦ Gray, Daniel. *The Complete Guide to Associate & Affiliate Programs on the Net: Turning Clicks Into Cash.* New York, NY: McGraw-Hill Professional Publishing, 1999.

✦ Helmstetter, Greg, and Pamela Metivier. *Affiliate Selling: Building Revenue on the Web.* New York, NY: John Wiley and Sons, 2000.

✦ Holden, Greg. *Internet Auctions for Dummies.* New York, NY: Hungry Minds, 1999.

✦ Prince, Dennis L. *Starting Your Online Auction Business.* Roseville, CA: Prima Publishing, 2000.

✦ Sinclair, Joseph T. *eBay the Smart Way: Selling, Buying, and Profiting on the Web's #1 Auction Site.* AMACOM, 1999.

✦ Woerner, Roland, Stephanie Becker, and Marsha Collier. *eBay for Dummies.* New York, NY: Hungry Minds, 1999.

Chapter 9: Mid-Level Online Storefront Packages

✦ Ginsburg, Lynn and Josef Pusedu. "Setting Up eShop." WebTools.com, November 2000. www.webtools.com/story/ecommerce/TLS20001122S0001.

✦ Tapper, Sandy. "Web Sites Off the Rack." Web Techniques Magazine, October 2000. www.webtechniques.com/archives/2000/10/tapper/.

✦ Thomas, Evany. "E-Storefront Options for Small Businesses." Webmonkey, July 1999. http://hotwired.lycos.com/webmonkey/99/29/index3a.html.

Chapter 10: High-level Online Storefront Packages

✦ Carr, David F. "Mix and Match: Custom Sites from Common Components." Internet World Magazine, January 1, 2001. www.internetworld.com/010101/01.01.01internettech1.jsp.

✦ Forta, Ben. *Allaire Spectra E-Business Construction Kit.* Chicago, IL: Wrox Press, 2000.

✦ Howard, Robert. *Site Server 3.0 Personalization and Membership.* Chicago, IL: Wrox Press, 1998.

✦ Microsoft Corporation. *Microsoft Commerce Server 2000 Resource Kit.* Redmond, WA: Microsoft Press, 2001.

Chapter 11: Case Studies: Creating an E-Commerce Company

✦ Friedlein, Ashley. *Web Project Management: Delivering Successful Commercial Web Sites.* San Francisco, CA: Morgan Kaufmann Publishers, 2000.

✦ Harmon, Paul, Michael Rosen and Michael Guttman. *Developing E-Business Systems and Architectures: A Manager's Guide.* San Francisco, CA: Morgan Kaufmann Publishers, 2000.

✦ Haylock, Christina Ford, editor, Len Muscarella, and Steve Case. *Net Success: 24 Leaders in Web Commerce Show You How to Put the Web to Work for Your Business.* Holbrook, MA: Adams Media Corporation, 1999.

✦ Holden, Greg. *Starting an Online Business For Dummies.* New York, NY: Hungry Minds, 2000.

✦ May, Paul Richard. *The Business of E-Commerce: From Corporate Strategy to Technology.* Cambridge, UK: Cambridge University Press, 2000.

✦ Plant, Robert T. *eCommerce: Formulation of Strategy.* Upper Saddle River, NJ: Prentice Hall, 2000.

✦ Rony, Ellen, and Peter R. Rony. *The Domain Name Handbook: High Stakes and Strategies in Cyberspace.* Gilroy, CA: CMP Books, 1998.

Chapter 12: Going Behind the Scenes

✦ Bellomo, Michael. *Linux©: Your visual blueprint to the Linux© platform.* New York, NY: Hungry Minds, 2000.

✦ Bellomo, Michael. *Master Red Hat© Linux© VISUALLY™.* New York, NY: Hungry Minds, 2000.

✦ Bellomo, Michael. *Unix™: Your visual blueprint to the universe of Unix™.* New York, NY: Hungry Minds, 2000.

✦ Ben-Natan, Ron, and Ori Sasson. *IBM Websphere Starter Kit.* Berkeley,CA: Osborne McGraw-Hill, 2000.

✦ Forta, Ben. *The ColdFusion 4.0 Web Application Development Kit.* Indianapolis, IN: Macmillan Publishing Company, 1998.

- Hanna, Philip. *Instant Java Servlets.* Berkeley, CA: Osborne McGraw-Hill, 2000.
- Harms, David. *JSP, Servlets, and MySQL.* New York, NY: Hungry Minds, 2001.
- Laurie, Ben, and Peter Laurie. *Apache: The Definitive Guide, 2nd Edition.* Sebastopol, CA: O'Reilly and Associates, 1999.
- Maran, Ruth. *Active Server™ Pages 3.0: Your visual blueprint for developing interactive Web sites.* New York, NY: Hungry Minds, 2000.
- Murdock, Kelly L. *JavaScript™: Your visual blueprint for building dynamic Web pages.* New York, NY: Hungry Minds, 2000.
- Negus, Christopher. *Red Hat® Linux® Bible.* New York, NY: Hungry Minds, 2000.
- Sery, Paul G., and Eric Harper. *Red Hat® Linux® 6 in Small Business.* New York, NY: Hungry Minds, 1999.
- Spainhour, Stephen, and Robert Eckstein. *Webmaster in a Nutshell, 2nd Edition.* Sebastopol, CA: O'Reilly and Associates, 1999.
- Whitehead, Paul and Eric Kramer. *Perl: Your visual blueprint for building Perl scripts.* New York, NY: Hungry Minds, 2000.
- Wing, Kelleigh, Paul Whitehead and Ruth Maran. *Internet and World Wide Web Simplified® 3rd Edition.* New York, NY: Hungry Minds, 1999.

Chapter 13: Working with Internet Information Server

- Buczek, Greg. *Instant ASP Scripts.* Berkeley, CA: Osborne McGraw-Hill, 1999.
- Butow, Eric. *Master Windows® 2000 Server VISUALLY™.* New York, NY: Hungry Minds, 2000.
- Hatfield, Bill. *Active Server Pages for Dummies.* Hungry Minds, 1999.
- Homer, Alex, David Sussman, Brian Francis, George Reilly, Dino Esposito, Andrea Chiarelli, Bill Kropog, Craig McQueen, Godfrey Nolan, Simon Robinson, John Schenken, and Kent Tegel. *Professional Active Server Pages 3.0.*Chicago, IL: Wrox Press, 1999.
- Powers, Shelley. *Developing ASP Components.* Sebastopol, CA: O'Reilly and Associates, 1999.

Chapter 14: Working with E-Commerce Software: Actinic Business

- Actinic Software LLC. *Getting Started With Actinic Business.* East Brunswick, NJ: Actinic Software LLC, 2000.

Chapter 15: Customizing an E-Commerce Site

- Johnson, Jeff. *GUI Bloopers: Don'ts and Do's for Software Developers and Web Designers.* San Francisco, CA: Morgan Kaufmann, 2000.
- Maran, Ruth. *Creating Web Pages with HTML Simplified® 2nd Edition.* New York, NY: Hungry Minds, 1999.
- Maran, Ruth. *Teach Yourself HTML VISUALLY™.* New York, NY: Hungry Minds, 1999.
- Meyer, Eric A. *Cascading Style Sheets: The Definitive Guide.* Sebastopol, CA: O'Reilly and Associates, 2000.
- Musciano, Chuck, and Bill Kennedy. *HTML & XHTML: The Definitive Guide.* Sebastopol, CA: O'Reilly and Associates, 2000.
- Valentine, Chelsea, and Chris Minnick. *XHTML.* Indianapolis, IN: New Riders, 2001.
- Weinman, Lynda. *<Creative HTML Design.2>.* Indianapolis, IN: New Riders, 2001.

Chapter 16: Creating Online Catalogs

- Brogden, Bill, and Chris Minnick. *Java Developer's Guide to E-Commerce with XML and JSP.* Alameda, CA: Sybex, 2000.
- Donnelly, Vanessa. *Designing Easy-to-Use Web Sites.* Reading, MA: Addison-Wesley, 2000.
- Limeback, Rudy. "Web Site Architecture 101." evolt.org, December 17, 1999. `http://evolt.org/article/web_site_architecture_101/4090/635/`.
- Rashty, David and Isaac Waisburg. "Introduction to Information Architecture." Educorner, March 2000. `http://educorner.com/courses/ia/`.
- Reiss, Eric L. *Practical Information Architecture: A Hands-On Approach to Structuring Succesful Web Sites.* Reading, MA: Addison-Wesley, 2000.
- Rosenfeld, Louis, and Peter Morville. *Information Architecture for the World Wide Web.* Sebastopol, CA: O'Reilly and Associates, 1998.
- Shiple, John. *Information Architecture Tutorial.* Webmonkey, 1998. `http://hotwired.lycos.com/webmonkey/design/site_building/tutorials/tutorial1.html`
- Vander Veer, Emily A. *XML: Your Visual Blueprint for Building Expert Web Pages.* New York, NY: Hungry Minds, 2001.
- Veen, Jeffrey. *The Art and Science of Web Design.* Indianapolis, IN: Que, 2000.
- West, Aaron. "The Art of Information Architecture." iBoost Journal. `www.iboost.com/build/backend/arch/644.htm`.

Chapter 17: Processing Online Transactions

- Bannan, Karen J. "A Hundred Ways to Pay." Internet World Magazine, February 15, 2001. www.internetworld.com/021501/02.15.01internettech1.jsp.
- Collett, Stacy. "New Online Payment Options Emerging." Computerworld, January 2000. www.computerworld.com/cwi/story/0,1199,NAV47_ST040981,00.html.
- Obie, Delilah. "Alternative Online Payment Options." Workz.com, August 2000. www.workz.com/content/644.asp.
- Obie, Delilah. "Understand Merchant Accounts and their Fees." Workz.com, August 2000. www.workz.com/content/403.asp.
- Toussaint, Alex. "Processing Credit Cards for Online Payment." MSDN Online Web Workshop, April 1999. http://msdn.microsoft.com/workshop/server/commerce/creditcard.asp.

Chapter 18: Supporting E-Services

- Brown, Stanley A., editor. *Customer Relationship Management: A Strategic Imperative in the World of E-Business.* New York, NY: John Wiley and Sons, 2000.
- Cusack, Michael. *Online Customer Care: Strategies for Call Center Excellence.* Milwaukee, WI: American Society for Quality, 1998.
- Rosenheim, Mimi. "Keeping Customers on the Line." Web Techniques Magazine, February 2001. www.webtechniques.com/archives/2001/02/corp/.
- Seybold, Patricia. *Customers.com: How to Create A Profitable Business Strategy for the Internet & Beyond.* New York, NY: Times Books, 1998.
- Seybold, Patricia. *The Customer Revolution.* New York, NY: Crown, 2001.
- Siegel, David. *Futurize Your Enterprise: Business Strategy in the Age of the E-customer.* New York, NY: John Wiley and Sons, 1999.
- Sims, Dave. "You Asked for It! Solving the Customer Support Dilemma." Web Techniques Magazine, November 1999. www.webtechniques.com/archives/1999/11/sims/.

Chapter 19: E-Commerce Transaction Security

- Adams, Carlisle, and Steve Lloyd. *Understanding the Public Key Infrastructure.* Indianapolis, IN: New Riders, 1999.
- Curtin, Matt. "On Guard: Fortifying Your Site Against Attack." Web Techniques Magazine, April 2000. www.webtechniques.com/archives/2000/04/curtin/.

- Fenghhi, Jalal, and Peter Williams. *Digital Certificates: Applied Internet Security.* Reading, MA: Addison-Wesley, 1998.
- Ford, Warwick, and Michael S. Baum. *Secure Electronic Commerce: Building the Infrastructure for Digital Signatures and Encryption.* Upper Saddle River, NJ: Prentice Hall, 2000.
- Garfinkel, Simson, with Gene Spafford. *Web Security & Commerce.* Sebastopol, CA: O'Reilly and Associates, 1997.
- Ghosh, Anup K. *E-Commerce Security: Weak Links, Best Defenses.* New york, NY: John Wiley and Sons, 1998.
- Jepson, Brian. "Safety in Numbers." Web Techniques Magazine, November 2000. www.webtechniques.com/archives/2000/11/jepson/.
- Merkow, Mark S., James Breithaupt and Ken Wheeler. *Building SET Applications for Secure Transactions.* New York, NY: John Wiley and Sons, 1998.
- Smith, Richard E. *Internet Cryptography.* Reading, MA: Addison-Wesley, 1997.
- Stallings, William. *Cryptography and Network Security: Principles and Practice.* Upper Saddle River, NJ: Prentice Hall, 1998.
- Stein, Lincoln D. *Web Security: A Step-by-Step Reference Guide.* Reading, MA: Addison-Wesley, 1998.
- Zwicky, Elizabeth D., Simon Cooper, and D. Brent Chapman. *Building Internet Firewalls, Second Edition.* Sebastopol, CA: O'Reilly and Associates, 2000.

Chapter 20: Managing E-Business Information

- Imhoff, Claudia, Lisa Loftis and Jonathan G. Geiger. *Building the Customer-Centric Enterprise: Data Warehousing Techniques for Supporting Customer Relationship Management.* New York, NY: John Wiley and Sons, 2001.
- Mesrobian, Edmond, and Brian Ringer. "Toward Successful E-fulfillment: It's All in the SKU." Web Techniques Magazine, January 2000. www.webtechniques.com/archives/2000/01/mesrobian/.
- Poirier, Charles C., and Michael J. Bauer. *E-Supply Chain: Using the Internet to Revolutionize Your Business.* San Francisco, CA: Berrett-Koehler, 2000.

Chapter 21: Managing an E-Commerce Web Site

- Annunzio, Susan, and Julie Liesse. *eLeadership: Proven Techniques for Creating an Environment of Speed and Flexibility in the Digital Economy.* Free Press, 2001.
- Berry, Margaret. "Building Your Web Team." Web Techniques Magazine, January 2001. www.webtechniques.com/archives/2001/01/berry/.

- Greening, Dan R. "Data Mining on the Web: There's Gold in that Mountain of Data." Web Techniques Magazine, January 2000. `www.webtechniques.com/archives/2000/01/greening/`.
- Killelea, Patrick. *Web Performance Tuning.* Sebastopol, CA: O'Reilly and Associates, 1998.
- Menasce, Daniel A., and Virgilio A. F. Almeida. *Scaling for E-Business: Technologies, Models, Performance, and Capacity Planning.* Upper Saddle River, NJ: Prentice Hall, 2000.
- Reynolds, Matthew. *Beginning E-Commerce with Visual Basic, ASP, SQL Server 7.0 and MTS.* Chicago, IL: Wrox Press, 2000.
- Schwartz, Evan I. *Digital Darwinism: 7 Breakthrough Business Strategies for Surviving in the Cutthroat Web Economy.* New York, NY: Broadway Books, 1999.

✦ ✦ ✦

Glossary

access control The process of limiting access to resources.

ACEC See *Advisory Commission on Electronic Commerce (ACEC).*

ACH network See *Automated Clearing House (ACH) network.*

Active Server Pages (ASP) A collection of Microsoft technologies that allows developers to create Web applications using client-side and server-side code.

ad click A recorded click on a Web advertisement by a user.

Address Verification System (AVS) A method of reducing credit card fraud by comparing the billing address entered for a transaction to the billing address for the credit card used in the transaction.

Advanced Encryption Standard (AES) The name for the new standard that will replace DES as the U.S. government's standard cipher.

Advisory Commission on Electronic Commerce (ACEC) Created by the Internet Tax Freedom Act of 1998, the ACEC explored the issues related to Internet taxation, and submitted a report to the U.S. Congress in April 2000.

AES See *Advanced Encryption Standard (AES).*

affiliate program A relationship between two Web sites in which the affiliated site links to the affiliate site in exchange for commissions on products purchased through the links.

ASP See *Active Server Pages (ASP).*

asymmetric encryption Also known as public-key encryption, asymmetric encryption relies on algorithms that are easy to calculate in one direction, but very difficult to calculate in the opposite direction. The result is that two people who have never met and who do not share a secret key can exchange encrypted messages.

asynchronous service Customer service that involves a customer and a representative of the company interacting, but not in real-time.

Automated Clearing House (ACH) network A network used by the Federal Reserve and all financial institutions in the U.S. for inter-bank transfer of funds.

AVS See *Address Verification System (AVS).*

B2B See *business-to-business e-commerce (B2B).*

B2C See *business-to-consumer e-commerce (B2C).*

banner ad networks Companies that collect a large pool of Web sites that offer advertising, and then divide these sites into categories. Impressions and click-throughs are then sold to advertisers for placement on a group of Web sites, not an individual Web site.

banner advertisements An image advertisement on a Web page that links to a page on the advertiser's Web site.

banner trading network A network of sites in which each member site agrees to display the banner ads of the other members.

block cipher A symmetric encryption algorithm that uses a key to transform a block of plaintext into a block of ciphertext of the same length. Reversing the transformation that encrypted the plaintext decrypts the ciphertext.

blowfish An encryption algorithm developed by Bruce Schneier in 1993 that has a variable key length from 32 to 448-bits.

bottleneck The delay in transmission of data over the Internet or within a computer system.

brute force attack A method of discovering a cyptographic key by trying each possible key until the correct one is found.

business-to-business e-commerce (B2B) Commerce between businesses. Characterized by high volume, low margin transactions.

business-to-consumer e-commerce (B2C) Commerce conducted between a business and an individual. Characterized by low-volume, high margin transactions.

buying organization In Open Buying on the Internet (OBI), the organization to which the requisitioner belongs, and to whom the OBI server being used by the requisitioner belongs.

CAs See *Certifying Authorities (CAs).*

CASIE See *Coalition for Advertising Supported Information and Entertainment (CASIE).*

Certifying Authorities (CAs) Third parties that issue digital certificates.

certificate authority certificate The type of certificate that is owned by a trusted certificate provider, such as VeriSign or Thawte. It's used to sign other certificates.

certificate revocation lists Lists of revoked certificates that are kept by Certifying Authorities (CAs).

CGI See *Common Gateway Interface (CGI).*

cipher A cryptographic algorithm that is used to encrypt and decrypt messages.

ciphertext Text that has been disguised to make it unreadable by humans.

click path The route that a visitor takes through a Web site.

click patterns Click patterns, or click paths, are routes that users take through a Web site. By studying click patterns, you can discover usability problems on your site.

click rate A measurement of the number of clicks on a banner ad per number of impressions. This number is typically given as a percentage.

clickthrough See *ad click.*

clustering A way to group multiple Web servers to be able to serve higher traffic volume than any one server could serve individually.

Coalition for Advertising Supported Information and Entertainment (CASIE) Founded in 1994 by the Association of National Advertisers (ANA) and the American Association of Advertising Agencies (AAAA) with the stated purpose of guiding "the development of interactive advertising and marketing."

co-browsing A technology that allows a customer support representative to control the customer's browser.

commerce The exchange of goods and services for money.

Commerce Service Provider (CSP) A company that handles the day-to-day operation of e-commerce sites, including setting up payment processing, backing up the sites, providing a secure environment, and hosting the storefront software.

Common Gateway Interface (CGI) A protocol that is used to extend the capabilities of Web servers by allowing them to communicate with other programs.

communication services Method of transferring information from buyer to seller.

community building The process of developing a loyal group of customers with something in common.

component-based development The method of creating software by assembling modules from a variety of vendors.

component-based Web site development A method of developing a Web site by assembling independent parts that can each be customized separately and can be arranged in multiple different ways.

confidentiality The principle of maintaining the privacy of information.

cookie A mechanism that allows a server-side program (such as a CGI script) to store and retrieve information on the client-side of an HTTP connection.

copyright law Protects original works that have traditionally been the product of an individual's effort — such as literary, musical, artistic, photographic, and audio-visual works.

cost-per-click (CPC) An Internet marketing formula used to price ad banners.

cost-per-thousand (CPM) A formula used by Internet marketers to price ad banners.

CPC See *cost-per-click (CPC).*

CPM See *cost-per-thousand (CPM).*

credit card fraud Illegal use of a credit card.

credit card processor A bank that provides credit card processing services to merchants.

cross-selling The marketing practice of showing customers similar products to the ones they select or are currently viewing.

cryptography The art of protecting information by encrypting it.

CSP See *Commerce Service Provider (CSP).*

custom pricing The method of pricing products or services based partially on direct customer request.

customer service Providing assistance to customers and potential customers.

customs Taxes (commonly called duties, tolls, or imposts) or restrictions placed on items when crossing international borders.

data confidentiality Deals with the ability of parties to exchange information without it being read by anyone else.

data element A single piece of information. The most basic part of an EDI message.

Data Encryption Standard (DES) The most widely used symmetric encryption algorithm. It was designed by IBM for the U.S. government in the 1970s and uses a 56-bit key.

data integrity Deals with the validity of data.

data management services Define the exchange format of information.

database A collection of data designed for search and retrieval.

decryption The process of restoring plaintext from ciphertext.

DES See *Data Encryption Standard (DES).*

digest authentication The World Wide Web Consortium's authentication standard.

digital cash A method of online payment in which a customer pays one vendor for digital cash and then uses the digital cash as payment at participating e-commerce sites.

directory server A server that manages user account information.

e-commerce 1) Commerce conducted via any electronic medium. 2) The integration of communication, data management, and security capabilities that allows organizations to exchange information about the sale of goods and services.

EDI See *Electronic Data Interchange (EDI).*

EDI messages The containers in which EDI transaction sets are exchanged.

Electronic Data Interchange (EDI) A standard format for sharing business data.

electronic publishing The use of computers to distribute information and data.

encryption The process of creating ciphertext from plaintext.

e-service Online customer service.

Extensible Hypertext Markup Language (XHTML) A cross between HTML and XML. It allows you to use familiar HTML elements, but it also allows you to take advantage of the data structuring capabilities of XML.

Extensible Markup Language (XML) A meta markup language derived from SGML that was designed for use on the Web.

failover Allows a server in a cluster to take over for another server in the event that there is a failure.

File Transfer Protocol (FTP) A protocol used to send and receive files.

Fortezza The U.S. Government security standard.

FTP See *File Transfer Protocol (FTP).*

fulfillment Process of delivering a purchased product to a customer.

GIF See *Graphic Interchange Format (GIF).*

global market niche A market niche that is not limited by geographic boundaries.

Graphic Interchange Format (GIF) A very common bit-mapped graphic file format used on the Web.

growth barriers The e-commerce factors that limit the growth of e-commerce businesses.

growth drivers The e-commerce factors that encourage growth of e-commerce businesses.

hard goods See *tangible goods.*

hit A single request for a file from a Web site. Every image, object, and Web page is recorded as a hit.

HTTP server See *Web server.*

IDEA See *International Data Encryption Algorithm (IDEA).*

identification The process of ensuring that someone is who he or she claims to be.

impression An instance in which a particular advertisement is downloaded to a user's computer, and displayed in the user's browser.

independent entry-level storefront An online storefront that is built using a service that provides businesses with a pre-defined structure in which to put their online store. The service provider hosts the database, or catalog, of products for each store, processes transactions, and usually hosts the Web site.

Independent Sales Organization (ISO) Credit card processing service that caters to small online businesses that often have difficulty opening their own merchant accounts with banks.

industrial design The shape or ornamentation given to a manufactured article to make it appealing or unique.

industrial property The part of intellectual property law that protects inventions, trademarks, and industrial designs.

information architecture The practice of designing organization, labeling, navigation, and searching systems to help people find and manage information more successfully.

in-house hosting Hosting of a Web site on a computer that exists in the same location as the business that owns it.

instant fulfillment The practice of allowing immediate download of a product over the Internet.

intangible goods Also called soft goods, intangible goods are products that can be delivered electronically over the Web, such as music, multimedia, and software.

intellectual property The concept by which the creator of an idea or work of art has control over its expression or use.

intelligent agent Software that works autonomously on behalf of a user.

International Data Encryption Algorithm (IDEA) An encryption algorithm that uses a 128-bit key to operate on 64-bit plaintext blocks in eight iterations.

internationalization The trend towards making the Web less English language-centric.

Internet EDI EDI that is conducted using the Internet.

Internet Server Application Programming Interface (ISAPI) A high-performance replacement for CGI that was developed by Microsoft.

Internet Tax Freedom Act (ITFA) The 1998 U.S. federal law that imposed a three-year moratorium on new Internet taxes and established the Advisory Commission on Electronic Commerce (ACEC).

invention A new process or practice that solves a specific problem, or represents a new way of doing business.

ISAPI See *Internet Server Application Programming Interface (ISAPI).*

ISO See *Independent Sales Organization (ISO).*

ITFA See *Internet Tax Freedom Act (ITFA).*

key A value used by a cryptographic algorithm to encrypt and decrypt messages.

knowledge base A database of customer support issues and inquiries that is searchable by customers via a Web page.

leased line A direct wire between a telecommunications carrier and the customer.

load balancing The technology that routes traffic between the different servers in a cluster so they share an equal amount of the work.

load testing A way to measure the amount of traffic that a server can handle.

log file analysis The process of using Web server log files to determine information such as how long users typically spend at your site; which pages are most frequently visited; how many visitors are using overseas domains; and what the most typical paths through the site are.

manual credit card processing Delaying the credit card processing until an actual employee of the e-commerce company initiates the processing.

marketer sites Web sites that are not dependent upon advertising. Instead, these sites market and sell their own products or services.

MD4 A widely used hash function that was developed by Ron Rivest.

MD5 A hash function developed by Ron Rivest. It involves several steps and results in a 128-bit message digest.

merchant account An account that a merchant opens at a bank in order to process credit card transactions.

message digest An application of one-way encryption that is used to provide authentication and data-integrity.

META tags HTML elements (also called tags) that contain information about the document or Web page.

MIME See *Multipurpose Internet Mail Extensions (MIME).*

Mosaic The first graphical Web browser.

Multipurpose Internet Mail Extensions (MIME) A standard protocol that provides a general structure to the content of Internet mail and allows files to be associated with different applications.

OBI See *Open Buying on the Internet (OBI).*

one-time pad A system of symmetric encryption that uses a key length that is the same as the message length.

one-way encryption A way to encrypt data using a hash function so that it is infeasible to decrypt it. One-way encryption is used to create message digests and digital fingerprints.

Open Buying on the Internet (OBI) A freely available Internet e-commerce standard for business-to-business transactions.

Open Trading Protocol (OTP) A protocol for the development of software products that will permit product interoperability for the electronic purchase that is independent of the chosen payment mechanism.

opt-in A method of creating an e-mail list in which subscribers voluntarily ask to be added to the list.

opt-out A method of creating an e-mail list in which people are added to the list without their permission. The members can then ask to be removed.

OTP See *Open Trading Protocol (OTP).*

outsourced hosting Hosting of a Web site at a location separate from the location of the business that owns it.

outsourcing The contracting of work to another company.

packet sniffer Software that allows the user to view all of the network traffic that is coming and going through their subnet.

page view A single request for a Web page. It's similar to a hit, except that images and objects are not counted — just Web pages. Page views are a more accurate gauge of site traffic than hits.

patent Gives an inventor the exclusive right to use a process or make and sell a specific product for a given length of time.

payment authority An organization that acts as a neutral third party to settle the financial component of the transaction.

payment gateway A service that provides an automated link with the credit card processor to authorize or deny a transaction in real time.

payment infrastructure The method used by a merchant to receive payment for products or services.

payment processing The process of transferring funds from the buyer to the seller.

PDN See *private digital network (PDN).*

personal certificate The type of certificate that is used to identify individuals.

personalization The practice of customizing a Web site for an individual user, or allowing users to customize how they view the site.

plaintext A message that can be read by humans.

portals Web sites that function as a central location for Web browsing by providing services such as current news, weather information, and, most importantly, a Web site directory or search engine.

privacy statement A Web site's disclosure of what types of information are captured by the site and how user information gathered through the site is used by the owner of the site.

private digital network (PDN) A secure computer network through which credit card transaction information is exchanged with a credit card processor.

processing network The means by which payment is processed. It encompasses banks, payment gateways, fraud checks, and credit card processors, and their infrastructures for communicating with one another and with the merchant.

publisher sites A Web site that sells advertising. Examples of publisher sites include portals and content-oriented sites, such as magazines.

RC4 A very fast encryption algorithm that is frequently used by the Secure Sockets Layer (SSL) protocol. It uses a variable key length.

RC5 An encryption algorithm that uses a variable key length as well as variable block sizes and variable number of rounds.

RDBMS See *Relational Database Management System (RDBMS).*

real-time credit card processing Credit card processing that takes place when an order is placed, using a payment gateway.

Relational Database Management System (RDBMS) Software that manages records that are related to each other using multiple tables.

requisitioner The person or software that initiates a purchase transaction in Open Buying on the Internet (OBI).

responsiveness How long a page takes to load in a user's browser. Responsiveness can be thought of as performance from the user's perspective.

revision tracking The practice of tracking changes that are made to software or a Web site.

rich media A term used to describe banner ads that use Shockwave, Flash, Java, or other technologies to provide a level of interactivity that is not possible with GIF images.

RIPEMD-160 The European one-way hash algorithm standard.

roles-based security A system of security that allows different users or groups of users to be assigned levels of access to a system.

RSA The most frequently used standard for public-key encryption. It was created by and named after Ron Rivest, Avi Shamir and Rick Adleman in 1978 at the Massachusetts Institute of Technology (MIT).

search engine A Web site that indexes the contents of other Web sites and allow visitors to search this index.

Secure Electronic Transactions (SET) A protocol for processing payments securely over the Internet.

Secure Hash Algorithm (SHA-1) The U.S. government's standard hash function.

Secure Multipurpose Internet Mail Extensions (S/MIME) A standard for allowing encrypted e-mail messages to be exchanged among different e-mail programs.

Secure Sockets Layer (SSL) The protocol that enables secure communications between the Web server and the browser.

security certificate A mechanism used for authenticating people, businesses, or servers over the Internet.

security mechanisms Mechanisms used to provide security services such as authentication, data integrity, and data confidentiality.

segment A collection of related data elements in an EDI message.

self-serve e-service E-service options that do not require interaction with a customer service representative.

selling organization In Open Buying on the Internet (OBI), this is company that has an OBI server and is offering the product or service for sale.

server certificate The type of certificate that is used to identify Web servers and their owners. A server certificate is necessary to use SSL.

Server-Gated Cryptography (SGC) A protocol used by financial institutions for transmitting documents across the Internet.

SET See *Secure Electronic Transactions (SET).*

SGC See *Server-Gated Cryptography (SGC).*

SGML See *Standard Generalized Markup Language (SGML).*

SHA-1 See *Secure Hash Algorithm (SHA-1).*

skipjack An encryption algorithm that was created by the National Security Agency (NSA). It uses an 80-bit key and a 64-bit 32-round block cipher.

S/MIME See *Secure Multipurpose Internet Mail Extensions (S/MIME).*

soft goods See *intangible goods.*

software publisher certificate The type of certificate that is used by software publishers to sign software they distribute.

spam Unsolicited e-mail.

SQL See *Structured Query Language (SQL).*

SSL See *Secure Sockets Layer (SSL).*

Standard Generalized Markup Language (SGML) A system for describing the structure of documents that was standardized by the International Organization for Standardization (ISO) in 1986.

standardization The trend towards adoption of standards.

Structured Query Language (SQL) A language that is usually used by programs to access databases.

symmetric encryption Also known as private-key encryption, session-key encryption, shared-key encryption, or secret-key encryption. In private-key encryption, the parties that are sharing information must all have an identical, secret key.

synchronous service Service that is delivered personally and in real time.

tangible goods Also called hard goods, tangible goods are physical objects.

targeted marketing The practice of determining where and by whom your promotions will be seen.

tariffs The taxes that states and countries charge for goods brought across their borders.

telephony Live voice connections over the Internet.

telnet A protocol for connecting to remote computers.

three-tier computing A model of computing that separates the software into three tiers (or layers): the client tier (also known as the user interface), the application tier (also known as the business logic), and the data storage tier.

tile Banner ads that are not as wide, and are smaller, than traditional banner ads. Tiles are generally 120 pixels by 60 pixels, or 125 pixels by 125 pixels.

TLS See *Transport Layer Security (TLS).*

trademarks and service marks Something that a company uses to distinguish its products or services from those of competitors.

trading partners Organizations that exchange EDI messages.

transaction set The EDI equivalent of a paper form. It describes the order and format of the data to be exchanged.

Transport Layer Security (TLS) The new Internet Engineering Task Force (IETF) standard for securing Internet data during transport. It's based on Secure Sockets Layer (SSL).

Triple-DES Triple-DES encrypts data by running it through DES encryption three times — forwards, backwards, and then forwards again. During the backwards run, it uses a second 56-bit key.

trusted third party A means of verifying the merchant's identity to the customer, and the customer's identity to the merchant. This is usually a Certifying Authority (CA).

twofish An encryption algorithm that was created by Bruce Schneier and was one of the finalists to become the Advanced Encryption Standard (AES).

Uninterruptible Power Supply (UPS) A backup power unit that provides electricity in case of a power outage.

unique user Each individual computer (and, by association, each person) that accesses a Web site.

UPS See *Uninterruptible Power Supply (UPS).*

up-selling The marketing practice of showing customers upgrades to the products they select.

usability Capable of being used. A usable Web site is one that keeps the amount that the user needs to think about how the site works to a minimum.

usability testing The practice of allowing people who are unfamiliar with a Web site to attempt to use it. Usability tests can reveal ways that a site can be made more usable.

Value Added Network (VAN) A network used to facilitate EDI messaging.

VAN See *Value Added Network (VAN).*

VBScript A scripting language that is based on Microsoft's Visual Basic programming language. It's frequently used with Active Server Pages (ASP).

virtual directories A way to map computer directories to Web server directories.

virtual enterprise A decentralized, and typically short-lived, group of people working together through the Internet on a per-project basis.

Virtual Private Network (VPN) Secure network that uses the public Internet.

virtual server A technology that allows one physical server to host multiple Web sites.

visit A series of requests made by a unique user, usually during a 30-minute time frame. Visits are also recorded in the log file, and can be used to analyze how users move through your site.

VPN See *Virtual Private Network (VPN).*

WAP See *Wireless Application Protocol (WAP).*

Web directory An organized, and generally searchable, collection of information about Web sites. Directories are different from search engines in that they are not as automated.

Web server 1) The computer that is used to serve Web pages. 2) HTTP server software.

Wireless Application Protocol (WAP) A standard for providing Web information to wireless devices, such as mobile phones.

World Wide Web A global hypertext information system that uses the Internet as its transport mechanism.

X.509v3 The name of the standard that established the format and contents of the certificates that are most widely used on the Internet.

XHTML See *Extensible Hypertext Markup Language (XHTML).*

XML See *Extensible Markup Language (XML).*

Index

A

D

E

F

G

N

O

P

Q

R

S

T

U

X

Y

Z

Hungry Minds, Inc.
End-User License Agreement

READ THIS. You should carefully read these terms and conditions before opening the software packet(s) included with this book ("Book"). This is a license agreement ("Agreement") between you and Hungry Minds, Inc. ("HMI"). By opening the accompanying software packet(s), you acknowledge that you have read and accept the following terms and conditions. If you do not agree and do not want to be bound by such terms and conditions, promptly return the Book and the unopened software packet(s) to the place you obtained them for a full refund.

1. **License Grant.** HMI grants to you (either an individual or entity) a nonexclusive license to use one copy of the enclosed software program(s) (collectively, the "Software") solely for your own personal or business purposes on a single computer (whether a standard computer or a workstation component of a multi-user network). The Software is in use on a computer when it is loaded into temporary memory (RAM) or installed into permanent memory (hard disk, CD-ROM, or other storage device). HMI reserves all rights not expressly granted herein.
2. **Ownership.** HMI is the owner of all right, title, and interest, including copyright, in and to the compilation of the Software recorded on the disk(s) or CD-ROM ("Software Media"). Copyright to the individual programs recorded on the Software Media is owned by the author or other authorized copyright owner of each program. Ownership of the Software and all proprietary rights relating thereto remain with HMI and its licensers.
3. **Restrictions On Use and Transfer.**
   (a) You may only (i) make one copy of the Software for backup or archival purposes, or (ii) transfer the Software to a single hard disk, provided that you keep the original for backup or archival purposes. You may not (i) rent or lease the Software, (ii) copy or reproduce the Software through a LAN or other network system or through any computer subscriber system or bulletin-board system, or (iii) modify, adapt, or create derivative works based on the Software.
   (b) You may not reverse engineer, decompile, or disassemble the Software. You may transfer the Software and user documentation on a permanent basis, provided that the transferee agrees to accept the terms and conditions of this Agreement and you retain no copies. If the Software is an update or has been updated, any transfer must include the most recent update and all prior versions.
4. **Restrictions on Use of Individual Programs.** You must follow the individual requirements and restrictions detailed for each individual program in What's on the CD-ROM appendix of this Book. These limitations are also contained in the individual license agreements recorded on the Software Media. These limitations may include a requirement that after using the program for a specified

period of time, the user must pay a registration fee or discontinue use. By opening the Software packet(s), you will be agreeing to abide by the licenses and restrictions for these individual programs that are detailed in What's on the CD-ROM appendix and on the Software Media. None of the material on this Software Media or listed in this Book may ever be redistributed, in original or modified form, for commercial purposes.

5. Limited Warranty.

(a) HMI warrants that the Software and Software Media are free from defects in materials and workmanship under normal use for a period of sixty (60) days from the date of purchase of this Book. If HMI receives notification within the warranty period of defects in materials or workmanship, HMI will replace the defective Software Media.

(b) **HMI AND THE AUTHOR OF THE BOOK DISCLAIM ALL OTHER WARRANTIES, EXPRESS OR IMPLIED, INCLUDING WITHOUT LIMITATION IMPLIED WARRANTIES OF MERCHANTABILITY AND FITNESS FOR A PARTICULAR PURPOSE, WITH RESPECT TO THE SOFTWARE, THE PROGRAMS, THE SOURCE CODE CONTAINED THEREIN, AND/OR THE TECHNIQUES DESCRIBED IN THIS BOOK. HMI DOES NOT WARRANT THAT THE FUNCTIONS CONTAINED IN THE SOFTWARE WILL MEET YOUR REQUIREMENTS OR THAT THE OPERATION OF THE SOFTWARE WILL BE ERROR FREE.**

(c) This limited warranty gives you specific legal rights, and you may have other rights that vary from jurisdiction to jurisdiction.

6. Remedies.

(a) HMI's entire liability and your exclusive remedy for defects in materials and workmanship shall be limited to replacement of the Software Media, which may be returned to HMI with a copy of your receipt at the following address: Software Media Fulfillment Department, Attn.: *CIW E-Commerce Designer Certification Bible*, Hungry Minds, Inc., 10475 Crosspoint Blvd., Indianapolis, IN 46256, or call 1-800-762-2974. Please allow four to six weeks for delivery. This Limited Warranty is void if failure of the Software Media has resulted from accident, abuse, or misapplication. Any replacement Software Media will be warranted for the remainder of the original warranty period or thirty (30) days, whichever is longer.

(b) In no event shall HMI or the author be liable for any damages whatsoever (including without limitation damages for loss of business profits, business interruption, loss of business information, or any other pecuniary loss) arising from the use of or inability to use the Book or the Software, even if HMI has been advised of the possibility of such damages.

(c) Because some jurisdictions do not allow the exclusion or limitation of liability for consequential or incidental damages, the above limitation or exclusion may not apply to you.

7. **U.S. Government Restricted Rights.** Use, duplication, or disclosure of the Software for or on behalf of the United States of America, its agencies and/or instrumentalities (the "U.S. Government") is subject to restrictions as stated in paragraph (c)(1)(ii) of the Rights in Technical Data and Computer Software clause of DFARS 252.227-7013, or subparagraphs (c) (1) and (2) of the Commercial Computer Software-Restricted Rights clause at FAR 52.227-19, and in similar clauses in the NASA FAR supplement, as applicable.

8. **General.** This Agreement constitutes the entire understanding of the parties and revokes and supersedes all prior agreements, oral or written, between them and may not be modified or amended except in a writing signed by both parties hereto that specifically refers to this Agreement. This Agreement shall take precedence over any other documents that may be in conflict herewith. If any one or more provisions contained in this Agreement are held by any court or tribunal to be invalid, illegal, or otherwise unenforceable, each and every other provision shall remain in full force and effect.

CD-ROM Installation Instructions

The contents of this page will give you a quick start in installing the CD-ROM included with this book. The CD contains a variety of storefront and e-commerce enabling software; source code, graphics, and resources from the examples presented in the preceding chapters; and an electronic, searchable version of the book.

For detailed information on the contents of the CD-ROM — as well as specific options for users of Windows, Linux, and the Mac OS — see Appendix A. Troubleshooting guidelines, notes on software restrictions, and system requirements are also included in this appendix.

Before installing the CD, make sure your computer meets the minimum system requirements listed in Appendix A. Although we've included Windows versions of the software on the CD, many of these products are also available for Linux and the Mac OS. Refer to Tables A-3 and A-4 in Appendix A for a product-by-product breakdown of your options. You will need at least 300MB of hard drive space to install all the software from this CD.

- ✦ **Microsoft Windows.** To install the items from the CD on your hard drive, follow these steps:
  1. Insert the CD into your computer's CD-ROM drive.
  2. View the contents of the CD-ROM using Windows Explorer or by clicking the My Computer icon on your desktop.
  3. Locate the software you wish to install.
  4. Either double-click on the program's installation program to install it, or follow the directions contained in the readme file in the CD directory for the program.
- ✦ **Linux.** To open the items from the CD, follow these steps:
  1. Log in as root.
  2. Insert the CD into your computer's CD-ROM drive.
  3. Mount the CD-ROM.
  4. Launch a graphical file manager to view the items on the CD.
- ✦ **Mac OS.** To open the items from the CD, follow these steps:
  1. Insert the CD into your computer's CD-ROM drive.
  2. Double-click the CD icon on your desktop.
  3. Locate the item you wish to view.
  4. Double-click the file you want to open, or use the Open command from the appropriate program.